CONTENT KNOWLEDGE: A COMPENDIUM OF STANDARDS AND BENCHMARKS FOR K–12 EDUCATION

2ND EDITION

JOHN S. KENDALL AND ROBERT J. MARZANO

McREL
Mid-continent Regional Educational Laboratory
Aurora, Colorado USA

ASCD
Association for Supervision and Curriculum Development
Alexandria, Virgina USA

McREL

Mid-continent Regional Educational Laboratory, Inc.

2550 S. Parker Rd., Suite 500 • Aurora, CO 80014 USA

Telephone: 303-337-0990 • Fax: 303-337-3005

Web site: http://www.mcrel.org/ • E-mail: info@mcrel.org

Tim Waters, *Executive Director*

Lou Cicchinelli, *Deputy Director*

ASCD

Association for Supervision and Curriculum Development

1250 N. Pitt Street • Alexandria, Virginia 22314-1453 USA

Telephone: 1-800-933-2723 or 703-549-9110 • Fax: 703-299-8631

Web site: http://www.ascd.org • E-mail: member@ascd.org

Gene R. Carter, *Executive Director*

Michelle Terry, *Assistant Executive Director, Program Development*

Nancy Modrak, *Director, Publishing*

This publication is based on work sponsored wholly, or in part, by the Office of Educational Research and Improvement, Department of Education, under Contract Number RP91002005. The content of this publication does not necessarily reflect the views of OERI or any other agency of the U.S. Government.

ASCD Stock no. 197254   ASCD member price: $39.95 nonmember price: $47.95   s9/97

This report is available on the Internet via McREL's Web site at http://www.mcrel.org/. The standards and benchmarks are linked by hypertext and can be searched.

Library of Congress Cataloging-in-Publication Data

Kendall, John S.

    Content knowledge : a compendium of standards and benchmarks for k-12 education / John S. Kendall and Robert J. Marzano. — 2nd ed.

      p. cm.

    Rev. ed. of: The systematic identification and articulation of content standards and benchmarks. c1995.

    Includes bibliographical references (p.).

    ISBN 0-87120-301-4 (pbk.)

    1. Education—Standards—United States. 2. Education—United States—Curricula—Evaluation. 3. School improvement programs—United States.

I. Marzano, Robert J. II. Kendall, John S. Systematic identification and articulation of content standards and benchmarks. III. Title.

LB3060.83.K46 1997   97-37866

379.1'58—dc21   CIP

Table of Contents

Acknowledgments

This volume is the second edition of a work that first began as a series entitled *The Systematic Identification and Articulation of Content Standards and Benchmarks*, first published in April 1993 and last updated in November 1995. The first issue provided a treatment of mathematics; with this edition, all nine subject areas identified in the national goals are addressed, as well as health, physical education, behavioral studies, and technology, in addition to those areas identified as important by the Secretary's Commission on Achieving Necessary Skills.

A study as ambitious as this one is always the product of the hard work and creative insight of a number of individuals. The following individuals had major responsibilities for identifying various standards and benchmarks in this report:

Shelly Wasson shared major responsibility for the identification of standards and benchmarks in science, health, the arts, and foreign language, for additions to the section on life skills, for the verification of standards and benchmarks in geography, and for document preparation.

Jennifer Norford shared major responsibility for the identification of standards and benchmarks in economics and behavioral studies, and for the revision of standards and benchmarks in mathematics.

Lisa Schoch-Roberts shared major responsibility for the identification of standards and benchmarks in physical education and for the revision of standards and benchmarks in United States and world history for an earlier report.

Michael Shea shared major responsibility for the identification of standards and benchmarks in civics.

Nathalie Bleuzé shared major responsibility for the revision of standards and benchmarks in mathematics and economics, and for citations in civics.

Jessica Logan shared major responsibility for the identification of standards and benchmarks in technology and for the revision of standards and benchmarks in foreign language and life skills.

Chris Snyder shared major responsibility for revision of standards and benchmarks in U.S. and world history, and for the revision of standards and benchmarks in the language arts.

Therese Sarah shared major responsibility for the initial identification of standards and benchmarks in U.S. history and K–4 history, for draft standards in economics, and assisted in the identification of the geography benchmarks.

Bradley Kennedy shared major responsibility for the initial identification of standards and benchmarks in world history, for draft standards in foreign language, and for the verification of standards in the arts.

Laura Lloyd shared major responsibility for citation updates of standards and benchmarks in physical education, health education, behavioral studies, and the arts.

Mary Lee Barton shared major responsibility for an earlier revision of standards and benchmarks in the language arts.

Audrey Peralez contributed to the original identification of geography standards in an earlier report. The contributions that these individuals have made to this study cannot be overstated.

The authors would also like to thank the following individuals for their initial reviews of various national reports and documents: Tom Barlow, Sandy Berger, Jan Birmingham, Linda Brannan, Susan Everson, Joan Grady, Toni Haas, Bob Keller, Fran Mayeski, Barbara McCombs, Joann Sebastian-Morris, Diane Paynter, Sylvia Parker, Jerome Stiller, Jo Sue Whisler, and Terry Young. Barb Gaddy provided editorial support. Carol Loredo assisted with word processing. Thanks also to David Frost, Shae Isaacs, Linda Brannan, Brad Wherry, and Peter Lund who assisted in the production, design, and distribution of this and previous updates in print and electronic media.

Others have also supported this effort through their thoughtful discussions of issues raised in this report. The authors would like to thank C. L. Hutchins, Alice Krueger, Debra Pickering, and Janie Pollock especially, among many other colleagues.

JSK
RJM

June 1997

Foreword

The information contained in this book represents seven years worth of work on the part of numerous individuals at the Mid-continent Regional Educational Laboratory (McREL) in Aurora, Colorado. The purpose of the project that generated this book was to survey and consolidate the many national- and state-level efforts to identify what K-12 students should know and be able to do in a variety of subject areas. To accomplish this goal, McREL researchers consulted 116 national- and state-level documents that address standards and benchmarks in various subject domains. This effort produced the 255 standards with their accompanying 3,968 benchmarks that are detailed in this text.

At a practical level, the standards and benchmarks in this document are intended as a resource or a reference for schools or entire districts that are attempting to generate their own standards and benchmarks or, more commonly, to revise and augment the standards and benchmarks provided by their local state department of education. To illustrate, assume that a school or district was attempting to augment the standards and benchmarks provided by its state department. Using this compendium, the school or district could add to or alter details in its state document with the assurance that its alterations and additions were implicitly or explicitly validated in 116 different documents. In short, this document can be a valuable tool in the design of a standards-based system. It is important to note, however, that this document does not address the implementation of standards (although we do briefly discuss a few implementation issues in Section 4). The lack or brevity of our discussion should not be interpreted as an indication that implementation issues are of little importance. Indeed, once a comprehensive and high-quality set of standards and benchmarks has been created for a school or district, the most treacherous part of creating a standards-based approach to schooling is yet to come.

Implementation issues are so important that we have written a separate book to deal with them entitled *A Comprehensive Guide to Designing Standards-Based Districts, Schools, and Classrooms* (Marzano & Kendall, 1996). That book describes in detail the various alternative ways a school or district might approach the following issues:

- the format in which standards and benchmarks should be written

- how to set performance standards

- who should be involved in writing standards and benchmarks

- how standards and benchmarks should be assessed

- how progress on standards and benchmarks should be reported to students and parents

- how to teach effectively to standards and benchmarks

- who should be held accountable for successful performance on standards and benchmarks

- what to do with students who do not meet standards

The *Comprehensive Guide* also discusses in depth conceptual and historical issues such as the relationship between standards-based education, outcome-based education, and mastery learning; the linkages between standards-based education and the behavioral objectives movement; the relationship between current advances in performance assessment and standards-based education; the distinctions between a standards-based system and a standards-referenced system.

These and other issues discussed in the *Comprehensive Guide* must be thoroughly understood and addressed if a school or district is to successfully design and implement a standards-based approach to schooling. Consequently, we recommend that readers become thoroughly familiar with this text and with *A Comprehensive Guide to Designing Standards-Based Districts, Schools, and Classrooms*. In fact, this text and the *Comprehensive Guide* are meant to be used in tandem: One provides the resources with which powerful standards and benchmarks can be designed; the other provides guidance in implementing standards and benchmarks once they are constructed.

We sincerely hope that our work and that of the many staff members at McREL who have helped create these books will be a valuable tool for schools and districts as they embark on the sometimes difficult journey of organizing schools around standards.

1. The Call for Standards

Many educators see the publication of the now-famous report *A Nation at Risk* (National Commission on Excellence in Education, 1983) as the initiating event of the modern standards movement. Few calls to action have been so often quoted as the dire pronouncements from that report: "The educational foundations of our society are presently being eroded by a rising tide of mediocrity that threatens our very future as a nation and a people. . . . We have, in effect been committing an act of unthinking, unilateral educational disarmament" (National Commission on Excellence in Education, 1983, p. 5).

Amid growing concerns about the educational preparation of the nation's youth, President Bush and the nation's governors called an Education Summit in Charlottesville in September 1989. That summit concluded with the establishment of six broad goals for education that were to be reached by the year 2000. The goals and their rationale are published under the title *The National Education Goals Report: Building a Nation of Learners* (National Education Goals Panel [NEGP], 1991). Two of the goals (3 and 4) related specifically to academic achievement:

> Goal 3: By the year 2000, American students will leave grades 4, 8, and 12 having demonstrated competency in challenging subject matter including English, mathematics, science, history, and geography; and every school in America will ensure that all students learn to use their minds well, so they may be prepared for responsible citizenship, further learning, and productive employment in our modern economy.

> Goal 4: By the year 2000, U.S. students will be first in the world in science and mathematics achievement.

The goals were outlined in the State of the Union of 1990, a year which also saw congress establish the National Education Goals Panel (NEGP); the following year, congress established the National Council on Education Standards and Testing (NCEST). Collectively, these two groups were charged with addressing unprecedented questions regarding American education such as, What is the subject matter to be addressed? What types of assessments should be used? What standards of performance should be set?

These efforts had an impact on national subject-matter organizations, who sought to establish standards in their respective areas. Many of these groups looked for guidance from the National Council of Teachers of Mathematics (NCTM), which preempted the public mandate for standards by publishing the *Curriculum and Evaluation Standards for School Mathematics* in 1989. The National Academy of Sciences used the apparent success of the NCTM standards as the impetus for urging Secretary of Education Lamar Alexander to underwrite national standards-setting efforts in other content areas. According to Diane Ravitch, then an assistant secretary of education, "Alexander bankrolled the projects out of his office's discretionary budget" (in Diegmueller, 1995, p. 5). The National Science Teachers Association (NSTA) and the American Association for the Advancement of Science (AAAS) quickly launched independent attempts to identify standards in science. Efforts soon followed in the fields of civics, dance, theater, music, art, language arts, history, and social studies, to name a few. (An overview of the movement to establish standards in the core subject areas is reported in Table 1.1) Since 1990 the movement has acquired considerable momentum at the state level as well. As of 1996, 48 states were developing common academic standards (Gandal, 1996).

Table 1.1

1983	*A Nation at Risk* is published, calling for reform of the U.S. education system.
1983	Bill Honig, elected state superintendent of California public schools, begins a decade-long revision of the state public school system, developing content standards and curriculum frameworks.
1987	The National Council of Teachers of Mathematics (NCTM) writing teams begin to review curriculum documents and draft standards for curriculum and evaluation.
1989	Charlottesville, VA: The nation's fifty governors and President Bush adopt National Education Goals for the year 2000. One goal names five school subjects—English, mathematics, science, history, and geography—for which challenging national achievement standards should be established.
1989	NCTM publishes *Curriculum and Evaluation Standards for School Mathematics*.
1989	Project 2061 of the American Association for the Advancement of Science (AAAS) publishes *Science for all Americans*, describing what "understandings and habits of mind are essential for all citizens in a scientifically literate society."
1990	In his State of the Union address, President Bush announces the National Education Goals for the year 2000; shortly thereafter, he and Congress establish a National Education Goals Panel (NEGP).
1990	The Secretary's Commission on Achieving Necessary Skills (SCANS) is appointed by the Secretary of Labor to determine the skills young people need to succeed in the world of work.
1990	The New Standards Project, a joint project of the National Center on Education and the Economy and the Learning Research and Development Center, is formed to create a system of standards for student performance in a number of areas.
1990, fall:	The Mid-continent Regional Educational Laboratory (McREL) begins the systematic collection, review, and analysis of noteworthy national and state curriculum documents in all subject areas.
1991	SCANS produces *What Work Requires of Schools*, which describes the knowledge and skills necessary for success in the workplace.
1991, June:	Secretary of Education Lamar Alexander asks Congress to establish the National Council on Education Standards and Testing (NCEST). The purpose of NCEST is to provide a vehicle for reaching bipartisan consensus on national standards and testing.
1992, Jan:	NCEST releases its report, *Raising Standards for American Education*, to Congress, proposing an oversight board, the National Education Standards and Assessment Council (NESAC), to certify

content and performance standards as well as "criteria" for assessments.

1992, Jan: The National Council for the Social Studies names a task force to develop curriculum standards.

1992, spring: The National History Standards Project receives funding from the National Endowment for the Humanities and the U.S. Department of Education.

1992, spring: The National Association for Sport and Physical Education begins work on Outcomes for Quality Physical Education Programs, which will form the basis of standards in Physical Education.

1992, June: The Consortium of National Arts Education receives funding from the U.S. Department of Education, the National Endowment for the Arts, and the National Endowment for the Humanities to write standards in the arts.

1992, July: The Center for Civic Education receives funds from the U.S. Department of Education and the Pew Charitable Trusts for standards development in civics and government.

1992, July: The Geography Standards Education Project creates the first draft of geography standards.

1992, Oct: The Committee for National Health Education Standards is funded by the American Cancer Society.

1992, Nov: The Bush administration awards funds to create English standards to a consortium of three organizations: the National Council of Teachers of English, the International Reading Association, and the Center for the Study of Reading at the University of Illinois.

1993, Jan: The National Standards in Foreign Language Project becomes the seventh and final group to receive federal funds for standards development.

1993, April: McREL publishes its first technical report on standards, *The Systematic Identification and Articulation of Content Standards and Benchmarks: An Illustration Using Mathematics*.

1993 AAAS's Project 2061 publishes *Benchmarks for Science Literacy*.

1993, Nov: NEGP's Technical Planning Group issues "Promises to Keep: Creating High Standards for American Students," referred to as the "Malcolm Report." The report calls for the development of a National Education Standards and Improvement Council (NESIC), which would give voluntary national standards a stamp of approval.

1993, Nov: The National Research Council, with major funding from the U.S. Department of Education and the National Science Foundation, establishes the National Committee on Science Education Standards and Assessment (NCSESA) to oversee standards development in content, teaching, and assessment.

1994, Jan: McREL publishes *The Systematic Identification and Articulation of Content Standards and Benchmarks: Update, January 1994*, which provides a synthesis of standards for science, mathematics, history, geography, communication and information processing, and life skills.

1994, Feb: The Standards Project for English Language Arts, a collaborative effort of the Center for the Study of Reading, the International Reading Association, and the National Council of Teachers of English, publishes the draft *Incomplete Work of the Task Forces of the Standards Project for English Language Arts.*

1994, March: President Clinton signs into law Goals 2000: Educate America Act. This legislation creates the National Education Standards and Improvement Council (NESIC) to certify national and state content and performance standards, opportunity-to-learn standards, and state assessments; adds two new goals to the national education goals; brings to nine the number of areas for which students should demonstrate "competency over challenging subject matters." The subject areas now covered include foreign languages, the arts, economics, and civics and government.

1994, March: The U.S. Department of Education notifies the Standards Project for the English Language Arts that it will not continue funding for the project, citing a lack of progress.

1994, March: The Consortium of National Arts Education Associations, funded by the U.S. Department of Education, the National Endowment for the Arts, and the National Endowment for the Humanities, publishes the arts standards (dance, music, theatre, and the visual arts).

1994, fall: The National Council on Social Studies publishes *Curriculum Standards for the Social Studies: Expectations for Excellence.*

1994, Oct: Lynne Cheney, past chair of the National Endowment for the Humanities (NEH), criticizes the U.S. history standards in the *Wall Street Journal* two weeks before their release. (NEH, with the U.S. Department of Education, funded development of the U.S. history standards.)

1994, Oct: U.S. history standards are released; world history and K-4 history are released shortly thereafter.

1994, Oct: The Geography Education Standards Project publishes *Geography for life: National Geography Standards.*

1994, Nov: The Center for Civic Education, funded by the U.S. Department of Education and the Pew Charitable Trusts, publishes standards for civics and government education.

1995, Jan: Gary Nash, National History Standards Project codirector, agrees to revise the history standards; the U.S. Senate denounces the history standards in a 99-1 vote.

1995, April: The U.S. Department of Education withdraws assurance of a $500,000 grant to the National Council on Economic Education for the development of standards in economics.

1995, May: The Joint Committee on National Health Education Standards releases *National Health Education Standards: Achieving Health Literacy.*

1995, summer: The National Association for Sport and Physical Education publishes *Moving Into the Future: National Standards for Physical Education.*

1995, Oct: The National Council on Economic Education, using funds from private sources, convenes a drafting committee to develop standards; projected publication is winter 1996.

1995, Nov: The New Standards Project releases a three-volume "consultation draft" entitled *Performance*

	Standards for English language arts, mathematics, science, and "applied learning."
1995, Dec:	McREL publishes *Content Knowledge: A Compendium of Standards and Benchmarks for K-12 Education*, a synthesis of standards in all subject areas, including behavioral studies and life skills.
1995	The National Business Education Association publishes *National Standards for Business Education: What America's Students Should Know and be Able to Do in Business*.
1996, Jan:	The National Standards in Foreign Language Education Project publishes *Foreign Language Learning: Preparing for the 21st Century*.
1996, Jan:	The National Research Council publishes *National Science Education Standards*.
1996, March:	The National Education Summit is held. Forty state governors and more than 45 business leaders convene. They support efforts to set clear academic standards in the core subject areas at the state and local levels. Business leaders pledge to consider the existence of state standards when locating facilities.
1996, March:	The National Council of Teachers of English and the International Reading Association publish *Standards for the English Language Arts*.
1996, April:	Revised history standards are published. A review in the *Wall Street Journal* by Diane Ravitch and Arthur Schlesinger, professor emeritus at City University of New York, endorses the standards. Lynn Cheney renews her criticism of the history standards, determining that the revision does not go far enough.
1996	The International Technology Education Association, supported by a grant from the National Science Foundation and the National Aeronautics and Space Administration, releases a guiding document for the development of standards in technology.
1997, Feb:	President Clinton, in his State of the Union Address, calls for every state to adopt high national standards, and declares that "by 1999, every state should test every 4th grader in reading and every 8th grader in math to make sure these standards are met."
1997	EconomicsAmerica releases *Voluntary National Content Standards in Economics* in paper copy and on CD-ROM.

The Case for Standards

Why are standards important? There appear to be three principle reasons advanced for the development of standards: standards serve to clarify and raise expectations, and standards provide a common set of expectations.

Former Assistant Secretary of Education Diane Ravitch is commonly recognized as one of the chief architects of the modern standards movement. In her book *National Standards in American Education: A Citizens Guide* (1995), Ravitch provides a common-sense rationale for standards:

> Americans . . . expect strict standards to govern construction of buildings, bridges,

highways, and tunnels; shoddy work would put lives at risk. They expect stringent standards to protect their drinking water, the food they eat, and the air they breathe. . . . Standards are created because they improve the activity of life. (pp. 8-9)

Ravitch (1995) asserts that just as standards improve the daily lives of Americans, so, too, will they improve the effectiveness of American education: "Standards can improve achievement by clearly defining what is to be taught and what kind of performance is expected" (p. 25).

Such a view is apparently shared by many. The polling firm Public Agenda conducted a number of surveys on the issue of standards over the last several years. They found that most Americans strongly support higher standards that are clear and specific (Farkas, Friedman, Boese & Shaw, 1994), believing that higher expectations produce better performance. Teachers, as well, support proposals to raise standards, which they expect to improve their students' academic performance (Johnson & Farkas, 1996). A recent finding indicates that students also see value in standards, saying that higher standards will make them work harder, and they expect to learn more as a result (Friedman & Duffet, 1997).

The Standards Project
Although much effort has been devoted to the development and implementation of standards, no consensus has emerged as to what form "standards" should take or how they should be used. The result is that the character, scope, and level of detail provided in standards often vary significantly from one subject area to another. Some subject-area groups have argued that the disciplines are so inherently different that a common approach to standards is not possible (Viadero, 1993). However, our analysis of standards from a wide range of subject areas confirms that a number of basic techniques can be successfully applied to describe content knowledge regardless of the domain. The application of this process provides content knowledge expressed in a roughly equivalent format across subject areas, which should facilitate communication of and about standards. Clear standards provide clearer expectations for students and the possibility of better communication among teachers, administrators, parents, and the larger community. Without such a common format, even the basics of a school system can break down. Reporting student progress on standards, for example, becomes quickly problematic if one subject area describes standards in terms of a performance vignette, as is the case with work done by the Standards Project for the Language Arts, while another subject area describes standards in terms of specific components of information and skills, as is the case with the National Council of Teachers of Mathematics. When demands on schooling become more complex, as for example when teachers seek to design lesson plans that incorporate standards from more than one discipline, a lack of common language can overburden innovative work.

The purpose of our project is to address the major issues surrounding content standards, provide a model for their identification, and apply this model in order to identify standards and benchmarks in the subject areas. This project has been documented in a series of reports and updates (Marzano & Kendall, 1993; Kendall & Marzano, 1994, 1995, 1996). For this edition, all subjects have been revised to incorporate newly released materials or to add supporting citations. More substantive revisions have been made to standards in mathematics, science, history, language arts, and economics. Standards in technology appear for the first time. The introductory sections remain unchanged, except for those sections in which the standards have been modified significantly, or to note additional citation material; these sections describe the issues surrounding standards identification and the method adopted to produce the standards and benchmarks provided in this report.

The next section of this report, Section 2, provides an overview of the current state of development across subject areas. Section 3 describes in greater detail the types of technical and conceptual differences that have become apparent since the beginning of the standards movement and describes the model of standards and benchmarks adopted for this study. Section 4 addresses the broader issues about the organization and selection of standards. Section 5 describes the overall process used in this project to identify standards and benchmarks, and Section 6 lays out the format and citation strategy used in the standards sections. Sections 7 through 20 provide standards and benchmarks for 14 separate areas, each section prefaced by a discussion of the process involved in generating those standards.

2. Work Completed and Work in Progress

Before describing the model of standards and benchmarks that is the basis for this project, it is useful to briefly consider the major efforts that are completed or underway to identify standards and benchmarks. These efforts, of course, form the database from which this project draws.

Mathematics

It is certainly no exaggeration to say that the publication of *Curriculum and Evaluation Standards for School Mathematics* in 1989 by the National Council of Teachers of Mathematics (NCTM) ushered in a new era relative to the role of national organizations in the practice of schooling. Through the *Standards* document, NCTM helped to form a new perspective on how national subject-area groups can contribute to the improvement of education when it delineated, for three levels (K–4, 5–8, and 9–12), a consensus on what students should know and be able to do and how that might best be demonstrated in the classroom. Other organizations soon followed NCTM's lead. The influence of the NCTM *Standards* is reflected in another useful resource for the identification of mathematics content: an assessment framework for mathematics developed for the National Assessment of Educational Progress (NAEP)[1]. This document, *Mathematics Framework for the 1996 National Assessment of Educational Progress* (n.d.), organizes the subject area into five sections, each providing up to a dozen statements presented as benchmark indicators; benchmark material is identified by the grade at which it should be introduced and when it should be assessed at both informal and formal levels.

In addition, NCTM has published *Assessment Standards for School Mathematics* (May 1995), which is organized around six standards: important mathematics content, enhanced learning, equity, openness, valid inferences, and coherence. The publication also provides guidelines on the use of assessments for different purposes such as to make instructional decisions, monitor student progress, evaluate student achievement, and evaluate programs.

Science

In science, three efforts have contributed significantly to the development of standards. The National Research Council (NRC) published the *National Science Education Standards* in December 1996. Material related directly to content standards fills over one-third of the work's 262 pages, while additional chapters address standards for science teaching and professional development, as well as assessment, program, and system standards. The science content standards are written for three grade levels: K-4, 5-8, and 9-12. At each grade level, seven general science topics are addressed. Standards related to these topics become increasingly comprehensive at each grade level.

The second effort within the field of science comes from the American Association for the

---

[1]NAEP ("the nation's report card"), a nationally representative assessment of student knowledge in various subject areas, is a congressionally mandated project of the National Center for Education Statistics, the U.S. Department of Education; NAEP's policy guidelines are formulated by the National Assessment Governing Board (NAGB).

Advancement of Science (AAAS). Working from the foundation they helped build in *Science for All Americans* (1992), AAAS's Project 2061 provides over 60 "literacy goals" in science as well as mathematics, technology, and the social sciences. These goals are well articulated across levels K–2, 3–5, 6–8, and 9–12. This effort, published as *Benchmarks for Science Literacy* (1993), includes a useful discussion and presentation of the research base available to those who worked on the project.

In addition to these efforts, the National Science Teachers Association (NSTA) has published the *Scope, Sequence and Coordination of National Science Education Content Standards* (Aldridge, 1995) as an addendum to *The Content Core: A Guide for Curriculum Designers* (Pearsall, 1993). This supplement is designed to make the *Core* more consistent with the recently published NRC standards. NSTA has also released *A High School Framework for National Science Education Standards* (Aldridge, 1995), developed under a grant from the National Science Foundation. Like the addendum to the *Core*, this framework builds directly from the November 1994 draft of the NRC science standards. Essential generalizations in physics, chemistry, biology, Earth and space sciences, and other areas organize the framework. Each generalization is described in some detail with a list of the relevant concepts, empirical laws, and theories or models that students will need in order to acquire a solid grounding in the topic. These subsections are presented in grade sequence (9, 10–12) and include a recommended learning sequence.

The *California Science Framework* (1990) reflects indebtedness to the work done in *Science for All Americans*. Additionally, the *Framework* shows its influence in the standards work from NRC. However, since it is a curriculum framework rather than a standards document, it provides considerably more detail than found in the *Benchmarks* or in the NRC standards and seems to complement them both. The *Framework* presents the content of the physical, earth, and life sciences at four levels (K–3, 3–6, 6–9, and 9–12) through what it calls the "major themes of science": energy, evolution, patterns of change, scale and structure, stability, and systems and interactions.

Finally, material on science in the schools is available from *Science Objectives: 1990 Assessment, Science Assessment and Exercise Specifications for the 1994 NAEP* and *Science Framework for the 1996 National Assessment of Educational Progress*.

History

The History Standards Project, directed by the National Center for History in the Schools (NCHS), first published three sets of standards: *National Standards for History for Grades K–4, National Standards for United States History,* and *National Standards for World History* (NCHS, 1995). Publication of the standards drew immediate criticism, launched by Lynn Cheney who, as former head of the National Endowment for the Humanities, had approved funding for the project ("History Standards," *Education Daily*, January 1995). Others joined the debate, either condemning the history standards outright or making recommendations for their improvement. A group of historians, practitioners, and public figures, convened by the Council of Basic Education (CBE), reviewed the documents and concluded that the "overwhelming majority of criticisms was targeted at the teaching examples in the documents, rather than at the actual standards for student achievement" ("Review panels," CBE, October 1995). The teaching examples are absent from a new, basic edition of the standards, *National Standards for History* (NCHS, 1996). This edition also takes into account recommendations from the group convened by CBE, as well as recommendations from other interested individuals. In addition to addressing the traditional content of history studies, the standards documents from NCHS share a treatment on Historical Thinking, which includes such standards as Chronological Thinking and Historical Comprehension.

There are a number of other useful resources available for the articulation of standards in a history curriculum. One document is *Lessons From History: Essential Understandings and Historical Perspectives Students Should Acquire* (Crabtree, Nash, Gagnon, & Waugh, 1992), a comprehensive description of K–12 history education. It was on the basis of this noteworthy work that NCHS was funded to develop national standards. Another well-received guide is *Building a History Curriculum: Guidelines for Teaching History in the Schools* (Bradley Commission on History in the Schools, 1988). Although this document is general in scope, it does offer a useful focus on the historical perspective that students should acquire in their study of history. Recently the National Council for History Education published the first in a planned series of standards documents, *Building a U.S. History Curriculum: A Guide to Using Themes and Selecting Content*. Companion booklets in western civilization and world history will be published in the next two years, as well as a guide for history in the early grades. Three companion documents will be published in the next two years: booklets in western civilization and in world history and a guide for history in the early grades.

Other useful documents include two works from NAEP: *Framework for the 1994 National Assessment of Educational Progress U.S. History Assessment* (n.d.) and *Provisional Item Specifications for U.S. History* (1992). As in other recent work from NAEP, the framework organizes its subject matter into themes such as Change and Continuity in American Democracy, The Gathering and Interactions of Peoples, Cultures and Ideas, and The Changing Role of America in the World. The framework recommends some preliminary achievement levels (basic, proficient, and advanced) at 4th, 8th, and 12th grades. The descriptions of subject matter are fairly general. For example, an 8th-grade student at the basic level should, among other things, "have a beginning understanding of the fundamental political ideas and institutions of American life, and their historical origins" (p. 38). The *Item Specifications*, however, provide a greater level of detail in "defining questions," organized by theme, for students at the 4th, 8th, and 12th grades.

Language Arts

In the language arts, the Standards Project for the English Language Arts (SPELA) was initially supported by the Fund for Improvement and Reform of Schools and Teaching (FIRST) of the Office of Educational Research and Improvement. Initiated in September of 1992, SPELA was designed to be a three-year collaborative effort of the Center for the Study of Reading (CSR), the International Reading Association (IRA), and the National Council of Teachers of English (NCTE). SPELA produced one complete draft of its standards entitled *Incomplete Work of the Task Forces of the Standards Project for the English Language Arts* (1994). That draft contained five strands (Reading/Literature, Writing, Language, Real World Literacy, and Interconnections), each listing two or three standards described at a general level. This draft was to go through a number of iterations until a final document was produced. However, on March 18, 1994, the U.S. Department of Education notified SPELA that it would not continue funding for the project. According to NCTE, funding for the project was halted because of a number of "philosophical differences" between SPELA and the Department of Education. These differences included a disagreement over the inclusion of delivery standards, which was supported by SPELA, and the lack of attention to a specific canon of children's literature, which was not supported by SPELA. However, the primary reason for cessation of funding appears to be the federal government's assertion that SPELA was not attending to the basic task of identifying what students should know and be able to do in the English language arts. As noted by Janice Anderson, interim director of FIRST at the time funding was halted, SPELA had not made "substantial progress toward meeting the objectives" of the project. The proposed standards, she stated, "are vague and often read as opinions and platitudes," focus too much on process rather than content, and lack "a coherent conceptual framework" ("NCTE/ IRA Say Standards Effort Will Continue," *The Council Chronicle*, June 1994).

NCTE and IRA vowed to complete the project even without federal support and produced an incomplete draft entitled *Standards for the English Language Arts* (NCTE, October 1995). That draft articulated 11 very general standards but did not address benchmarks at different developmental levels. As in the case with the SPELA document, this later effort met with criticism due to its lack of specificity. According to an article in *Education Daily*, the eleven standards that the IRA and NCTE drafted "deliberately say little more than that students should be able to read a wide range of texts and write effectively using various strategies. . . .The document elaborates on each standard, but doesn't break down specific competencies students should show at various grade levels, as do standards in other disciplines." (*Education Daily*, October 25, 1995, p. 1). The final version of their work, *Standards for the English Language Arts,* published in 1996, contains 12, rather than 11, standards and includes other modifications. Companion works, such as the *Standards in Practice* series, provide information from which benchmarks for each standard can be inferred.

Although its efforts were not designed to produce standards per se, the National Assessment of Educational Progress has produced a number of documents that provide guidance as to the nature and format of English language arts standards. For example, the *Description of Writing Achievement Levels—Setting Process and Proposed Achievement Level Definitions* (1992) provides explicit descriptions of basic, proficient, and advanced performance in writing. These level descriptions can quite easily be translated into expectations about what students should know and be able to do in the area of composition. In the area of reading, the *Assessment and Exercise Specifications: NAEP Reading Consensus Project: 1992 NAEP Reading Assessment* (1990) not only provides a detailed description of what students should know and be able to do at various grade levels but also details the types of materials students should be able to read.

The Arts
Standards for the arts, prepared under a grant from the U.S. Department of Education, the National Endowment for the Arts, and the National Endowment for the Humanities, were published in 1994

by the Consortium of National Arts Education Associations. The design of the final document, *What Every Young American Should Know and Be Able to Do in the Arts*, has been greatly simplified over earlier drafts. Standards for dance, music, theatre, and the visual arts are organized into K–4, 5–8, and 9–12 grade clusters. Each field contains from six to nine content standards, articulated across all grade clusters. Within each grade cluster for a given content standard, several achievement standards are provided. For example, in the visual arts section, a content standard found within each grade range, "Understanding the visual arts in relation to history and cultures," has three achievement standards associated with it for the 5–8 level. One such achievement standard states, "Students know and compare the characteristics of art works in various eras and cultures."

In addition, NAEP, working closely with the authors of the national standards for the arts, has developed an *Arts Education Assessment Framework* (1994). For dance, music, theatre, and the visual arts, the framework describes the learning expected of students in (1) knowledge and understanding about the arts and (2) perceptual, technical, expressive, and intellectual/reflective skills. The assessment framework is a matrix in which the knowledge and skills for each discipline form one axis and the application of this knowledge and skill forms the other. Application in the arts is defined as students creating, performing, or responding to the arts.

Civics

The Center for Civic Education (CCE) has published *National Standards for Civics and Government* (1994). The standards are presented for K–4, 5–8 and 9–12; major areas organize some 70-plus content standards. Each content standard has associated with it a set of key concepts that students should know in order to meet the standard. The standards are organized into five areas: civic life, politics, and government; the foundations of the U.S. political system; the values and principles of U.S. constitutional democracy; the relationship of U.S. politics to world affairs; and the role of the citizen. Each area is presented as a question, and each of the five outermost questions (e.g., What is government and what should it do?) has more specific questions that organize the content standards beneath them (e.g., What are major ideas about the purposes of government and the role of law in society?). The CCE has also produced a source book of impressive scope and detail, *Civitas: A Framework for Civic Education* (Quigley & Bahmmeller, 1991), which contains more than 600 pages of information about civics.

In addition, the NAEP Civic Consensus Project, drawing heavily on the *National Standards for Civics and Government*, has produced the *Civics Framework for the 1998 National Assessment of Educational Progress* (n.d.). The framework outlines preliminary descriptions of three levels of achievement—basic, proficient, and advanced—for civic knowledge and skills that students should possess at grades 4, 8, and 12.

Economics

Economics was included as a core subject in the Goals 2000 Educate America Act. In April 1995, however, the Department of Education decided not to provide grant money to assist the National Council on Economic Education (NCEE). Nevertheless, NCEE continued work with funding from private sources and has recently published *Voluntary National Content Standards in Economics* (1997). As anticipated, the work closely follows *A Framework for Teaching Basic Economic Concepts with Scope and Sequence Guidelines, K–12* (Saunders & Gilliard, 1995). Twenty standards are identified, each supplied with a rationale. Organized beneath the standards at 4th, 8th, and 12th grades are benchmarks; these are paired with descriptions of what students can do to demonstrate their understanding of the benchmarks. The standards are available in *Virtual Economics: An Interactive Center for Economic Education /Version 2.0,* a CD-ROM that includes an extensive library of activities, lessons, and other resources that are hypertext linked to the content standards.

Foreign Language

The development of standards for foreign language was undertaken by the American Council on the Teaching of Foreign Languages (ACTFL) in partnership with a number of foreign language associations. Funded by a grant from the Department of Education and the National Endowment for the Humanities, the National Standards in Foreign Language Education Project published *National Standards for Foreign Language Education* (1996). The standards are organized under five goal areas for students: communicate in languages other than English (Communication), gain knowledge and understanding of other cultures (Culture), connect with other disciplines and acquire information (Connections), develop insight into own language and culture (Comparisons), and participate in multilingual communities (Communities). The communication area contains three standards; other goals contain two standards each—for a total of eleven standards, which are articulated at three levels: K–4, 5–8, and 9–12. A rationale statement follows each goal and standard. Sample progress indicators are provided for each goal by level.

Geography

The Geography Education Standards Project has published *Geography for Life: National Geography Standards* (1994). The document provides 18 standards articulated for grades K–4, 5–8, and 9–12. The standards are organized under six areas: The World in Spatial Terms, Places and Regions, Physical Systems, Human Systems, Environment and Society, and The Uses of Geography. At each grade level, a standard is defined by three to six activities, each of which is exemplified by three "learning opportunities," that is, activities described at a greater level of detail than the standard. Certainly the most visually interesting of the standards documents, with numerous high-quality photographs and illustrations on glossy paper, it reflects indebtedness to one of the codevelopers on the project, the National Geographic Society.

The writing committee of the Geography Standards Project, in addition to the consensus process, relied chiefly upon two sources for their material. The first, *Guidelines for Geographic Education* (Joint Committee on Geographic Education, 1984), provides an instructional framework for teaching and learning geography by structuring content around five themes: Location, Place, Human-Environmental Interaction, Movement, and Regions. The second, NAEP's *Geography Assessment Framework for the 1994 National Assessment of Educational Progress* (1992), uses material from the five themes to develop three content areas for assessment: Space and Place, Environment and Society, and Spatial Dynamics and Connections. The assessment framework recommends the development of questions that measure students' cognitive abilities "at a basic Knowing level, a more complex Understanding level, and an Applying level that covers a broad range of thinking skills" (p. 3). This three-tiered approach, together with three content areas, forms a matrix within which essential assessment questions are developed.

Another source for detailed information on geography comes from NAEP's *Item Specifications* (1992) for the 1994 Assessment. This document provides some detailed descriptions as to the basic, proficient, and advanced levels of achievement in geography. For example, "Eighth grade basic" means that students should be able to, among other things, "solve fundamental locational questions using latitude and longitude; interpret simple map scales; identify continents, oceans, and selected countries and cities. . . ."(p. 54). The *Item Specifications* provide greater levels of detail in terms of how cells in the NAEP matrix might be developed.

Health

The Joint Committee on National Health Education Standards, funded by the American Cancer Society, has published *National Health Education Standards: Achieving Health Literacy* (1995). The committee developed seven standards, each with rationale statements and "performance indicators" for students at grades K–4, 5–8, and 9–11. The material is organized both by standards and by grade levels. The work includes a set of "opportunity to learn" standards designed to provide direction for the policies, resources, and activities that should facilitate the implementation of the health education standards. In addition, a table is provided that maps the topics covered in the health standards to related adolescent risk behaviors.

Physical Education

The National Association for Sport and Physical Education (NASPE) has published *Moving into the Future: National Standards for Physical Education: A Guide to Content and Assessment* (1995). The report lists seven standards with benchmarks at grades K, 2, 4, 6, 8, 10, and 12. These grade-level descriptions of the standards include rationale statements, sample benchmarks, and assessment examples. The assessment examples are quite extensive, providing numerous ideas for student and group projects and for student portfolios, all with suggested criteria for assessment. Standards from the self-funded group were based on NASPE's 1992 publication, *Outcomes of Quality Physical Education Programs*.

Social Studies

The National Council for the Social Studies (NCSS) has published *Expectations of Excellence: Curriculum Standards for Social Studies* (1994). As the title indicates, NCSS recognizes a distinction between content and curriculum. It describes this distinction by noting that the role of the social studies is to provide "overall curriculum design and comprehensive student performance expectations, while the individual discipline standards (civics and government, economics, geography, and history) provide focused and enhanced content detail" (p. viii). The document underscores this organizing role of curriculum standards through the elaboration of 10 "thematic strands" such as Culture, Time, Continuity and Change, and Individual Development and Identity.

Each theme is provided with a list of student performance expectations and classroom activities appropriate for the early grades, middle grades, and high school. Across all 10 strands, 241 performance expectations are described. A useful appendix provides "essential skills for social studies," organized under the categories of Acquiring Information, Organizing and Using Information, and Interpersonal Relationships and Social Participation. Each area is defined by goal statements and a "suggested strength of instructional effort" (i.e., minimum or none, some, major, and intense) toward reaching those goals at levels K–3, 4–6, 7–9, and 10–12.

Technology

The Technology for All Americans Project, undertaken by International Technology Education Association (ITEA), has received funding from the National Science Foundation and the National Aeronautics and Space Administration. The goal of Phase II of the project is to develop kindergarten through 12th grade content standards with benchmarks at 2nd, 5th, 8th, and 12th grade. A recent report from ITEA, *Technology for All Americans: A Rationale and Structure for the Study of Technology* (1996), describes the "universals" and structure upon which the development of standards and technology should be based; universals are characterized as knowledge, processes, and contextual systems. Knowledge, for example, includes categories related to the nature and evolution of technology, contextual relationships or linkages with other subject areas, and technological concepts and principles. No draft standards have yet been made available. Completion of content standards is targeted for the year 1999.

The World of Work

Progress is also being made in delineating the knowledge and skills students should have to be successful and productive in the world of work. The Secretary's Commission on Achieving Necessary Skills (SCANS) and the report the commission produced, *What Work Requires of Schools* (1991), has helped to focus attention on standards that address higher-order thinking and reasoning skills, as well as personal traits and interpersonal skills that students should acquire. This document adds a strong voice to the call from other standards groups for greater attention to the development of students' critical thinking skills, their ability to communicate, and their ability to work in groups.

A complementary effort was undertaken by the American Society for Training and Development (ASTD), representing "50,000 practitioners, managers, administrators, educators and researchers in the field of human development" (Carnevale, Gainer, & Meltzer, 1990, p. xiii). An ASTD research team, funded through a grant from the U.S. Department of Labor, reviewed the literature and polled its members to determine what skills were most desired by employers. The team identified 16 skill areas, including traditional academic areas such as reading, writing, and computation, as well as nontraditional areas such as interpersonal skills, self-esteem, and negotiation. Their findings were published in *Workplace Basics: The Essential Skills Employers Want* (Carnevale, Gainer, & Meltzer, 1990).

Finally, the National Business Education Association has published *National Standards for Business Education: What America's Students Should Know and Be Able To Do in Business* (1995). The standards cover a wide range of subjects, including marketing, management, accounting, production, and finance as well as basic skills in computation, communication, decision-making, and problem solving.

International Efforts

Organizations outside the United States have also contributed to the definition of content for the curriculum. Material from two of these organizations has been cited in this report.

The International Baccalaureate Organization, headquartered in Geneva, Switzerland, has 469 member schools in 66 countries throughout the world; 187 are public or private high schools in the United States or Canada. Examinations for the International Baccalaureate (IB) are based upon a rigorous and comprehensive syllabus. The IB diploma is recognized and accepted by universities worldwide.

The Australian Education Council has produced a number of documents as part of an effort it describes as the most significant collaborative curriculum development project in the history of Australian education. Two documents were found to be of particular use, *English: A Curriculum Profile for Australian Schools* and *Technology A Curriculum Profile for Australian Schools.*

State-Level Efforts

Work on the development of academic standards, undertaken by just a few states in the early 1990s, has increased dramatically. According to a recent review from the American Federation of Teachers (Gandal, 1996), 48 states are now in the process of developing academic standards. Most of these states are also developing assessments to determine whether their students are meeting their standards. The review, *Making Standards Matter, 1996: An Annual Fifty-State Report on Efforts to Raise Academic Standards,* found that the quality and specificity of the standards vary by state and within states, by subject. However, there are a number of exemplary efforts that contribute to the establishment of quality standards and benchmarks.

In Summary

Efforts continue in the development and implementation of standards. For most subject areas, there is one or more set of standards published by a nationally recognized group of subject-area experts. In addition, states are publishing standards in the subject areas. One can infer that if a school, district, or state is to design a schooling system based on standards, these many and varied efforts must be reconciled to some degree.

3. Standards: A Common Language

Section 1 alluded to the difficulties created by the variety of perspectives taken by various groups on the scope, purpose, and nature of standards. In order to develop an internally consistent model of standards and benchmarks, we address the significant problems that have resulted and describe our approach to their resolution. Here we consider four problems: (1) multiple documents, (2) varying definitions of standards, (3) differing types of content description, (4) differing grade ranges, and (5) varying levels of generality.

Multiple Documents

A number of subject areas have multiple documents that address the standards in that domain. For example, *Curriculum and Evaluation Standards for School Mathematics*, published by NCTM (1989), is certainly considered the "official" description of what students should know and be able to do in the field of mathematics. However, mathematics standards and benchmarks also are explicitly and implicitly articulated in each of the following documents:

- *Benchmarks for Science Literacy* (1993), by Project 2061 of the American Association for the Advancement of Science (AAAS)

- *Framework for the 1994 National Assessment of Educational Progress Mathematics Assessment* (1992), by the National Assessment of Educational Progress (NAEP)

- *Performance Standards: English Language Arts, Mathematics, Science, Applied Learning, Volume 1, Elementary School* (1997a) by the National Center on Education and the Economy

- *Performance Standards: English Language Arts, Mathematics, Science, Applied Learning, Volume 2, Middle School* (1997b) by the National Center on Education and the Economy

- *Performance Standards: English Language Arts, Mathematics, Science, Applied Learning, Volume 3, High School* (1997c) by the National Center on Education and the Economy

- *Group 5 Mathematics Guide* (1993) by the International Baccalaureate Organization

- *Middle Years Programme: Mathematics* (1995e) by the International Baccalaureate Organization

Science provides another example of multiple source documents. Three documents provide descriptions of essential student knowledge and skill in science as determined by three national organizations: the National Research Council, the American Association for the Advancement of Science, and the National Science Teacher's Association (see Section 2, Science, for a discussion).

Additionally, a description of important science content also can be found in documents from NAEP, the International Baccalaureate Organization, and the New Standards Project.

In most subject areas there exist different, and sometimes competing, views of what content is important; certainly no single document represents a comprehensive view of the content for a particular subject. Yet a comprehensive review is important for anyone who intends to identify important information and skills at the level of a school, district, or state. To address this need, we determined to identify the significant documents for each subject area and synthesize the content they address in a useful, comprehensive set of statements concerning what students should know and be able to do. At the end of the process, we had consulted 116 documents (listed in Appendix A), across 14 areas of study.

Varying Definitions of Standards

Different documents among, and even within, subject areas define standards in various ways. To illustrate, consider the following elements taken from the NCTM document *Curriculum and Evaluation Standards for School Mathematics* (1989):

a. *Students use estimation to check the reasonableness of results.*
b. *Students recognize and appreciate geometry in their world.*
c. *Students use mathematics in other curriculum areas.*

These elements are presented as standards in the NCTM document but are very different in nature. Element *a* describes a skill or an ability a person might use to solve a real-life problem. For example, one might use estimation to determine whether the gas pump total generally squares with the price of a gallon of gas multiplied by the number of gallons that were required to fill the tank in the car. Conversely, element *b* does not describe a commonly used skill. It is difficult to imagine many day-to-day situations that would demand an ability to recognize and appreciate geometry in the world. This element rather describes a goal of the curriculum, that is, a perspective or disposition that students might acquire as a result of the successful completion of studies in mathematics. Thus, it should not be identified as knowledge or skill. Similarly, element *c* does not describe student knowledge or skill but might be interpreted as a recommendation as to how to design other areas of the curriculum to work in concert with mathematics instruction. Evidence for this comes from the fact that element *c* appears in NCTM's Standard 4, Mathematical Connections. The first four standards in the NCTM guide (the other three being Mathematics as Problem Solving, Mathematics as Communication, Mathematics as Reasoning) were first designated as principles, not standards. For reasons of accommodation, since regretted by the chair of the NCTM Commission on Standards, the first four principles were also given the name *standards*, and confusion has resulted ever since (T.A. Romberg, personal communication, June 24, 1997).

It is our belief that curriculum goals and principles should not be part of a description of content standards. Content standards describe the knowledge and skills that students should attain. Curriculum standards, on the other hand, can describe overarching goals, or ways in which the curriculum should be orchestrated to achieve a desired result. In either case, curriculum standards do not explicitly describe student knowledge and skills as do content standards. Mixing both types of standards as if there were no significant difference creates unnecessary confusion.

Differing Types of Content Description

Closely related to the problem of differing definitions for a standard is the problem of differing formats for the description of the content of a standard. One method, alluded to above, is simply to describe the content as information and skills. For example, the National Research Council (NRC) describes the following as a fundamental concept for a life science standard in grades 5-8:

> *All organisms are composed of cells — the fundamental unit of life. Most organisms are single cells; other organisms, including humans, are multicellular.* (p. 156)

This is a fairly straightforward description of what a student should know.

A contrasting approach is to present the content in the form of an activity or performance indicator. For example, the following, identified as a performance indicator, is provided by the Joint Committee on National Health Education Standards (NCHES):

> *As a result of health instruction in Grades 5-8, students will explain how health is influenced by the interaction of body systems* (p. 17)

In this case, information that the student should know is not directly described as in the previous example. Presumably, the student who successfully completes this activity has acquired the requisite information and/or skills for this topic within the specified grade range.

Finally, another common format for communicating the content of a standard is the performance task. A performance task, in comparison with an activity, can be thought of as providing a greater level of detail and specificity, both in terms of the context of the task and the information or skill that might be required to complete the task successfully. For example, the following task appears in the National History Standards (National Center for History in the Schools, 1994c):

> *Analyze pictures of hunter-gatherer sites in places such as Danube fishing villages, the Lascaux caves in France, and hunter sites in northern regions. Contrast these with agricultural sites such as those found in Jericho, Çatal Hüyük, Banpo village in North China, and the TehuacánValley in Mexico. How do hunter-gatherer sites differ from agricultural sites?* (p. 48)

This task specifies a specific focus for study—the differences between hunter-gatherer sites and agricultural sites—and the context within which the student acquires and demonstrates this knowledge, that is, through the comparison and contrast of pictures or drawings of the sites. Thus, it differs from the simpler activity approach to content description.

There are a number of different ways in which content has been described in the national reports. Our goal, to provide a synthesis of content from differing documents within each of the subject areas, requires a consistent description of content. We have chosen to describe content in the information and skills format. There are several reasons for this. First, the information and skills description, as opposed to the activity or task description, does not require the reader to make inferences from the activity or task to the information and skills that would be required for successful demonstration of that task; rather, student information and skills are described in a straightforward manner. Second, the activity or task description tends to be narrowly prescriptive in that it characterizes not only what the student should know and be able to do, but how the student should demonstrate this knowledge. Thus, the content described is likewise narrowed; users may erroneously believe that the skill or information required by the activity or task is a complete description of the information or skill the student should acquire. Finally, although the information provided in a task or activity may be useful for teachers as a guide for instruction or classroom assessment, when the primary purpose of description is to delineate the information and skills that are essential for students, such activity descriptions confound the issue of how students are to demonstrate competence with the content of the curriculum. Once the content has been determined, of course, delineating various ways knowledge might be presented and demonstrated is appropriate. Until the content is identified, however, we believe it is best to keep the two kinds of description separate.

The documents consulted for this project differ considerably in the ways in which content is described; some presented unique challenges of interpretation. The introductory pages for each subject-area section in this report provide a brief summary of the type of analysis that was required given the documents that were used.

As a consequence of the method of standards description adopted for this project, the material identified in this report has some noteworthy characteristics. Specifically, the information that comprises standards identified within this report generally falls into one of three broad categories representing three general types of knowledge. Such distinctions have proved useful in descriptions of learning (Anderson, 1990). At a basic level, knowledge within any domain can be organized into the categories exemplified in Table 3.1.

The first column contains examples of knowledge that involves processes. These processes may or may not be performed in a linear fashion. For example, performing long division is a process: you perform one step, then another, and so on. Reading a map also involves certain steps, but these steps, unlike those in long division, do not have to be performed in any set order. You might read the name of the map first, then look at the legend, or you might just as effectively perform these steps in reverse order. Knowledge of this sort is usually called *procedural knowledge*. One might think of such knowledge as composed of the *skills and processes* important to a given content area.

Table 3.1

Procedural *The learner is able to...*	Declarative *The learner understands...*	Contextual *The learner...*
read a map	the concept of a geographic region	knows when to use a map instead of a globe
perform long division	the concept of a numerator	models numbers using number line
set up an experiment	the characteristics of an amoeba	classifies organisms
shoot a free throw	the rules of basketball	knows when to use man-to-man vs. zone coverage
edit an essay	the conventions of punctuation	uses appropriate tone and style for a selected audience

The examples in the second column do not involve a process or a set of steps. Acquiring this type of knowledge involves understanding the component parts. For example, knowledge of the concept of "a geographic region" includes understanding the characteristics of a variety of regions, knowing criteria that give a region identity and how regional boundaries can change, and so on. This type of knowledge is commonly called *declarative knowledge*. One might think of such knowledge as composed of the *information* important to a given content area.

The last column contains items that are not simply declarative or procedural but that specify knowledge acquired in a unique context. One might think of contextual knowledge as *information* acquired only during the execution of some *process*, or a kind of *process* that gains special meaning only when applied to certain kinds of *information*. Column three contains examples of information and/or skills that are in part defined by the conditions under which they are learned. For example, "to classify" is a skill or procedure; to understand the characteristics of organisms is declarative knowledge, or information; but knowledge constructed while classifying organisms is a special type of knowledge, also known as taxonomy. Students learn how structure, function, biochemistry, and behavior can be used to classify organisms; they also know how a taxonomy can describe the degree of relatedness between organisms. Another example of contextual knowledge can be found in the following example from Language Arts:

Represents key ideas and supporting details in outline or graph form

This describes not simply a skill the student must acquire—using an outline or a graph—but a knowledge of key ideas and supporting details and how they can be represented in such formats.

This report, then, identifies all content as belonging to one of the three categories described above. The reader is referred to Section 6, "How the Subject Area Sections Are Structured," for a description of how the category of each item can be identified. Generally speaking, however, content that is declarative in nature usually begins with the stem "understands that . . ." or "knows that . . .". Content that is procedural in nature begins with verbs, such as "uses", "solves," and "predicts." Content that is contextual in nature also begins with verbs or verb phrases but tends to look more like activities in that a particular skill is described in terms of the information or knowledge about or upon which the skill is applied.

It is of interest to note that some subject areas are more heavily declarative or procedural in nature. Contextual knowledge, which is a special case, is not common. Table 3.2 displays the distribution of the types of knowledge across the subject areas in this report:

Table 3.2

	Declarative	Procedural	Contextual
Mathematics	142	63	21
Science	257	8	-
History	1241	23	18
Language Arts	15	248	11
Geography	230	4	4
Arts	147	96	26
Civics	426	-	1
Economics	159	-	-
Foreign Language	39	35	10
Health	121	13	2
Physical Education	47	42	16
Behavioral Studies	100	-	-
Technology	56	36	2
Life Skills	67	231	21
Total	3047	789	132

Differing grade ranges

Regardless of their position on standards, most groups acknowledge the need to identify expected or anticipated skill or understanding at various developmental levels. These statements of expected knowledge are referred to as *benchmarks*. To illustrate, consider the following content standard within science:

Understands basic concepts about the structure and properties of matter

At the 12th-grade level, the benchmark, or expected level of understanding, might be described in the following way:

- *Knows that the physical properties of a compound are determined by its molecular structure (e.g., constituent atoms, distances and angles between them) and the interactions among these molecules*

At the 8th-grade level, the benchmark or expected level of understanding might be

- *Knows that atoms often combine to form a molecule (or crystal), the smallest particle of a substance that retains its properties*

Theoretically, these benchmarks, or subcomponents of a standard, could be identified at all grade levels. However, the trend seems to be to develop benchmarks at a few key levels. For example, the National Assessment of Educational Progress (NAEP) identifies benchmarks at grades 4, 8, and 12. The American Association for the Advancement of Science (Project 2061) identifies benchmarks at grades 2, 5, 8, and 12.

In this model, benchmarks identify expected understanding or skill at various grade levels, with a preference for articulating benchmarks at primary, upper elementary, middle, and high school within each standard. However, these levels of identification may be different in some content areas, depending on the availability of source materials. The reader is referred to the introductory sections of each content area to determine what levels have been identified for that area.

Differing Levels of Generality

The benchmark is the smallest unit of analysis for this study. As described above, it can be characterized as being declarative, procedural, or contextual in the type of knowledge it describes. The "size" of a benchmark is more problematic and seems best described in practical rather than theoretical terms. A practical description begins from what appears to be common among the benchmarks that we have identified within the subject areas.

From our observations, a benchmark seems to have a lower and an upper limit. As to the lower limit, in no case does it appear to describe specifics of information or specific skills that an average student could master quickly, assuming that the benchmark has been placed at the appropriate grade level.

25

This lower limit means that a declarative benchmark would never be equivalent to a short list of facts, for example; nor would a two-step algorithm be identified as a procedural benchmark at the 4th-grade level. This provides a rough starting point for the lower level of a benchmark.

A useful reference point for a benchmark, particularly at the lower end of the interval, is the behavioral objective. A benchmark is "larger" than a behavioral objective. Measurement expert Robert Mager (1962), described what came to be called a *behavioral objective* as consisting of three key elements: a target behavior, a description of conditions under which the behavior is demonstrated, and criteria for acceptable performance. By limiting the description of information and skill to a behavior and to the conditions under which that behavior is demonstrated, this approach necessarily required many, many thousands of behavioral objectives to describe the knowledge within a given content domain. Benchmarks, by contrast, do not describe the behavior of students who meet an objective, nor do they narrow the description of information and skills to a particular set of conditions. (A contextual benchmark, discussed above, is a special case. It describes a general context for knowledge use rather than the specific conditions under which that knowledge could or should be demonstrated).

Thus, a single behavioral objective could not address all of the content described within a benchmark, but a single benchmark could be the source of a number of instructional objectives. This characteristic of benchmarks, at least as they appear in this report, is in part explained by the fact that the articulation of standards and benchmarks is not an attempt to organize learning or learning activities within a model for instruction. Rather, this approach uses a cognitive theory of knowledge types to assist in the analysis and identification of information and skills.[1] At the lower limit, then, a benchmark does not prescribe instructional objectives. That is, as said of the NCTM standards in a report from the National Academy of Education Panel (Shepard, 1993), they "do not delineate specific instructional activities, [but] they do set the direction for what should be taught" (p. 3).

In summary, a benchmark can be described as an "interval" of levels of generality in the description of information and skills. In this section, we have attempted to describe some of the characteristics of the lower end of that interval. Benchmarks do not describe trivial or "easy" information and skills for the developmental level at which they are found. They are not descriptions of information and skill that have been narrowed through behavioral objectives or by being translated into an instructional activity.

Where the lower bounds of a benchmark have some identifiable characteristics, the characteristics

---

[1]This process has been applied to documents, however, that have been developed by educators with understanding or belief about knowledge structures within their subject areas as well as what research says about the proper sequencing for the development of particular knowledge and skills. Clearly, then, the documents we have analyzed could well reflect the influence of certain theories of learning or theories of instruction. When this information (e.g., the sequence for learning about computation across K–12) is preserved in this study, it is better understood as a useful "side-effect" of our method, not a result of it.

of the upper bound are much more vague. That is, within this study it became difficult to determine the point at which the component of a standard seemed too broad in scope or too generally stated to be characterized as a benchmark. In fact, at the next broader level of generality, we found that depending upon the document we analyzed, this level was either treated as a topic organizer or identified as a complete standard. The national history standards documents from NCHS were found to have at least four tiers of organization. In the design for the world history standards, for example, historical eras provided the most general structure. The level just beneath eras was identified as the standard level. Beneath the standard level there was no detailed information, but three or four more specific statements were given, under which benchmark-level information was provided.

The subject area of science offers a convenient example of the variance in approaches to levels of generality, inasmuch as two organizations have recently put considerable effort into the development of science standards, each using a different organizational scheme. Project 2061's *Benchmarks for Science Literacy* (1993) articulates most standards (termed *literacy goals*) across K–12. In practice, this means that a standard is described at a level that is broad enough to be articulated with benchmarks at each of four developmental levels: K–2, 3–5, 6–8, and 9–12. For example, one standard, or literacy goal, is on "the structure of matter." This idea is expressed at the earliest developmental level in terms such as the following:

By the end of the 2nd grade, students should know that

- *Objects can be described in terms of the materials they are made of (clay, cloth, paper, etc.) and their physical properties (color, size, shape, weight, texture, flexibility, etc.). (p. 76)*

At the upper level, 9–12, a sample benchmark under the same overarching idea is

By the end of the 12th grade, students should know that

- *The configuration of atoms in a molecule determines the molecule's properties. Shapes are particularly important in how large molecules interact with others. (p. 80)*

Contrasting material comes from the National Research Council (NRC), which was funded by the Department of Education to develop standards for science. If we search for an idea similar to the one found at the early grades in the *Benchmarks*, we find it in the following, which is identified as a content standard:

As a result of the activities in grades K–4, all students should develop an understanding of

- *Properties of objects and materials*
- *Position and motion of objects*

- *Light, heat, electricity, and magnetism* (p. 123)

Concepts related to these topics, or subcomponents, are elaborated under the heading "fundamental ideas that underlie this standard." At that level, the following description is found for "properties of objects and materials":

- *Objects have many observable properties, including size, weight, shape, color, temperature, and the ability to react with other substances.* (p. 127)

This demonstrates a dramatically different way of organizing very similar information. In this document, the standard has several organizing topics, each of which is defined at a greater level of detail. These details describe information and skills at about the same level as found in the benchmarks from Project 2061's *Benchmarks*. The benchmark information differs essentially in two ways: In the NRC document, benchmarks appear in a standard that is complete at grade level, rather than articulated across grades; and these benchmarks also appear arranged under topic headings.

Although the categories in these two documents differ, the same or very similar material is covered. For example, the corollary to the 12th-grade benchmark from Project 2061 on the structure of molecules (see example above) can be found in the NRC document as part of a different standard, which has six organizing subcomponents (p. 176), under one of which ("structure and properties of matter") the following information can be found:

- *The physical properties of compounds reflect the nature of the interactions among its molecules. These interactions are determined by the structure of the molecule, including the constituent atoms and the distances and angles between them.* (p. 179)

In short, NRC has determined that standards should be categories of information not so broad as to encompass a common set of information across K–12. This articulation does appear, however, at the next larger level of organization. That is, all the benchmark information presented in the examples above from the NRC document is organized under the category Physical Science.

In this study, wherever possible, we describe standards at a level of generality that is broad enough to allow the articulation of benchmarks across K–12. Sometimes this approach required the reorganization of material from the subject-area documents. However, this organization was considered advantageous in that it organized information and skills systematically across subject areas without any apparent loss of critical information. In addition, as mentioned at the outset (see Section 1 — The Call for Standards) this consistency of format provides a clearer system-wide picture for those who wish to integrate benchmarks from different subject areas but who also need to keep track of how and what curriculum they have addressed.

Standards, as found in the documents analyzed for this study, appeared at different levels of organization and structure. Standards provide a way of organizing information, that is, the benchmarks that identify important declarative, procedural, and contextual knowledge. This organization itself may provide information on how "pieces" of knowledge can be logically sequenced for students' ease of learning. For example, a study of research findings by the authors of *Benchmarks for Science Literacy* (1993) led them to the following kinds of adjustments for writing benchmarks:

> 1) Stating less-sophisticated precursors of an idea. For example, research suggests that the notion of a "fair comparison" can be understood in lower grades as a preliminary form of the later concept of a controlled experiment.

> 2) Adding prerequisite components for learning outcomes. For example, research draws attention to the need for understanding how people see things by reflected light as a prerequisite to a benchmark for understanding the phases of the moon.

> 3) Changing benchmarks to different grade levels. For example, research shows that natural selection is still a difficult idea for many college students—even after special instruction. So the benchmark for natural selection was moved form 8th grade (where some teachers thought it could be taught) to 12th grade.   (p. 328)

It should be noted that the approach to benchmark writing discussed here—that is, the sequencing of information based upon the idea that learning occurs in a step-by-step fashion, leading to the understanding of more complex concepts or principles—may not be an approach that works well for all types of knowledge. Science is a nomothetic discipline, that is, it has as its focus universal laws or principles. Thus, it may be possible to arrange benchmarks to serve overarching ideas, for example, benchmarks that build toward the understanding of a general principle. The discipline of history provides a counter-example. History is an idiographic discipline, that is, one that has as its primary interest the nonabstract (e.g., specific individuals and concrete events). The discipline of history does not seek to extract universal ideas or laws from the stream of people and occurrences that it studies. Thus, with respect to this discipline, benchmark writing may not involve a step-by-step approach to larger generalizations but, rather, may simply entail the description of important facts, events, and episodes. Therefore, one would expect to find benchmarks organized by historical eras, rather than by ideas or principles.

In this report, the standards we have developed reflect both the character of the draft materials available to us and the model we have developed for identifying knowledge. There are other ways that benchmarks can be grouped, however, and except for the caution that developmentally sequenced information, when available, should not be lost, there appears to be no compelling reason that districts or schools should not feel free to organize benchmarks in whatever way they find most useful.

4. Other Issues

In Section 3, we considered the problems presented to anyone wishing a comprehensive description of subject-area content, given the diverse nature of the many relevant documents. We also described the approach we have taken in this report in an effort to address those problems. In this section we consider the broader issues that have arisen around the standards movement, particularly those that relate to the type of standards that are identified. In this section we consider three issues regarding types of standards: (1) world-class versus literacy standards, (2) thinking and reasoning standards, and (3) lifelong learning standards.

World-Class Versus Literacy Standards

Almost from the inception of the standards movement the call has been made for standards that are "world class." Goal 4 of the 1989 Education Summit, convened by President Bush and attended by President Clinton, then governor of Arkansas, declared that "by the year 2000, U.S. students will be first in the world of achievement in science and mathematics achievement." (NEGP, 1991, p. 4). The Education Summit of 1996 saw a recommitment to this goal, "As Governors, we commit to the development and establishment of internationally competitive academic standards" (National Governors Association, 1996, p. 4).

"World-class," however, remains a somewhat elusive concept; implicitly, as measurement expert Robert Linn has noted, such a term suggests a desire to compare student performance rather than that students should attain some absolute standard (1995, p. 15). There appears to be an increasing disparity between the performance of American students and the performance of students from other countries on international tests; however, the implications for optimum student performance can be significant, in terms of their impact on teaching and learning (for a discussion of world-class performance see Marzano & Kendall, 1996, pp. 32-34).

Although some of the national standards documents aspire to world-class standards, most have adopted what might be called a "literacy" approach. In a literacy approach, standards are written to help the student become a functioning adult in American society. For example, AAAS's Project 2061 describes the standards in its *Benchmarks for Science Literacy* (1993) as "levels of understanding and ability that *all* students are expected to reach on the way to becoming science-literate" (p. xiii). This accords with another view of science literacy that "...*doing* science is clearly different from *using* science; scientific literacy concerns only the latter" (Hazen & Trefil, 1993) [italics, the authors']. In other words, a distinction can be drawn between science education that serves to prepare students to become adult science professionals as opposed to science education that serves to help students become adults who have a useful understanding of science as it affects their everyday lives.

Another view of the issue is provided by NCTM. In its *Curriculum and Evaluation Standards for School Mathematics* (1989), NCTM identifies literacy standards for all students. However, it additionally identifies standards, such as those listed below, for those who wish to pursue mathematics study at an advanced level:

- construct proofs for mathematical assertions, including indirect proofs and proofs by mathematical induction;
- use circular functions to model periodic real-world phenomena; and
- analyze the graphs of polynomial, rational, radical, and transcendental functions. (pp. 143, 163, 180)

We have chosen to describe standards for student literacy. There are two reasons for this. First, to describe standards beyond what is expected of each and every student puts no practical bound on the areas covered; for example, this compendium of standards would otherwise include any elective course that might be currently available, from agriculture to advanced mathematics to zoology. Second, it is beyond the scope of this study to address the complex issue of student performance, much less how student performance compares internationally. We can thus state the boundaries of this project as they relate to the description of standards: the material identified for analysis was the content that subject-area organizations propose as essential for all students to learn, whether those students plan to enter the world of work directly from high school or go on to higher education.

Thinking and Reasoning Standards
In our study of the national and state standards documents used to construct this report, we found that virtually all of them either implicitly or explicitly acknowledge the importance of thinking and reasoning. This is not surprising given the historical emphasis educators have placed on thinking and reasoning. Over 80 years ago, education philosopher John Dewey (1916) wrote, "The sole direct path to enduring improvement in the methods of instruction and learning consists in centering upon the conditions which exact, promote, and test thinking" (p. 6). Similarly, in 1961, the National Education Association identified the improvement of thinking and reasoning as central to American education:

> In the general area of the development of the ability to think, there is a field for new research of the greatest importance. It is essential that those who have responsibility for management and policy determination in education commit themselves to expansion of such research and to the application of the fruits of this research. This is the context in which the significant answers to such issues as educational technology, length of the school year, and content of teacher education must be sought and given. (Educational Policies Commission, 1961, pp. 14-15)

More recently, calls for the enhancement of thinking and reasoning in American education have come from the National Science Board Commission on Pre-college Education in Mathematics, Science and Technology (1983), the College Board (1983), the National Education Association (Futrell, 1987), and the American Federation of Teachers (1985). Additionally, the need to enhance students' abilities to think and reason is explicitly stated in Goal 3 of six national education goals established at the first Education Summit in Charlottesville, Virginia. (See chapter 1 for a discussion of the summit.) As mentioned previously, Goal 3 explicitly targeted the subjects of English, mathematics, science, history, and geography. In addition, it noted that "every school in America will ensure that all students learn to use their minds well so they may be prepared for responsible citizenship, further learning, and productive employment in our modern economy" (NEGP, 1991, p. ix).

Although there is agreement as to the importance of enhancing thinking and reasoning, there is not much agreement on the manner in which thinking and reasoning should be articulated in standards. One approach is to establish a set of standards on generic reasoning. For example, the document *Workplace Basics: The Essential Skills Employers Want* (Carnevale, Gainer, & Meltzer, 1990), identifies Creative Thinking as one of the 16 skills that are important to the workplace. Similarly, the New Standards Project (New Standards, 1997) includes a category of standards called Applied Learning, which involves a variety of forms of problem solving. Thinking skills identified in this manner are stated as generic mental processes that cut across all content areas. A second approach is reflected in the NCTM's *Curriculum and Evaluation Standards* (1989), which articulates a standard entitled Mathematical Reasoning. Within this category, those reasoning processes presumed to be specific to mathematics, but useful within the various subdisciplines of mathematics, are identified. Similarly, *National Standards for United States History* (NCHS, 1994)b includes a category called Historical Thinking. This involves such abilities as chronological thinking, historical research, and historical comprehension. Finally, the third perspective is exemplified by the Geography Education Standards Project in *Geography for Life: National Geography Standards* (1994). Here no set of standards nor any one specific standard addresses thinking and reasoning. Rather, the benchmarks are stated in terms of performance tasks. (This format for articulating standards and benchmarks was discussed in Section 3.) These performance tasks require the use of thinking and reasoning abilities. To illustrate, consider the following benchmark, which makes explicit the need to make inferences—an important reasoning process:

- [Students] make inferences about differences in the personal geographies of men and women.

A cursory review of the literature in cognitive psychology would seem to favor the latter two positions concerning an approach to thinking and reasoning skills. Specifically, strong arguments have been made against the isolation of thinking and reasoning skills (Glaser, 1984; Resnick, 1987). However, it is important to note that these arguments focus upon instruction, not upon the identification of standards. The case has been well articulated that thinking and reasoning should not be taught in isolation of specific content. Quite obviously, one cannot think about nothing. Thinking and reasoning processes and strategies must be used with content, and to use any content other than that important to specific disciplines makes little sense.

However, articulating thinking and reasoning standards is quite another matter. Under the assumption that the primary purpose of standards is to give educators direction about the skills and abilities that should be the focus of instruction and assessment, one can infer that it is critical to identify explicit thinking and reasoning standards. If important thinking and reasoning approaches are only found embedded in content, there can be no way to ensure that students have explored content in as many thoughtful ways as possible. To illustrate, consider the following performance task, again taken from *Geography for Life* (Geography Education Standards Project, 1994):

> Compare the economic opportunities for women in selected regions of the world using culture to explain the differences. (p. 203)

This performance task describes one way in which a student might demonstrate knowledge of a content standard in geography. The important knowledge within the performance task, however, could be demonstrated in a variety of different ways. For example, the student could be asked to predict where women will have the most freedom and opportunity in the next decade. But what of the ability to make comparisons? If the ability is considered important enough that a student should be able to apply this skill in geography, then making comparisons should be identified and addressed as systematically as the content, rather than as an incidental part of a performance task embedded in a geography standard. Otherwise, whether a student uses comparison or not will be determined by the luck of the draw, that is, only if he or she is asked to perform this particular performance task. Clearly, such a hit-or-miss approach will characterize any effort that does not fully articulate and address the thinking and reasoning skills that should be brought to the study of content. Thus, the third approach to thinking and reasoning skills—embedding them in performance tasks—has severe limitations.

The second approach found in the various national reports—identifying thinking and reasoning skills within specific subject areas—also proves problematic. Many of the thinking and reasoning skills and abilities identified within specific subject areas are, in fact, quite general. For example, the NCTM standard of Mathematical Reasoning primarily specifies such general thinking and reasoning abilities as making conjectures, making inferences, and making corrections. These processes are as important in science and history (and so on) as they are in mathematics.

Given the inherent problems with two of the three approaches, we determined to identify those explicit thinking and reasoning standards that cut across all content areas. In our report, these standards are found under Section 20, Life Skills.

Lifelong Learning Standards

As their name indicates, lifelong learning standards deal with information and skills that are used throughout life in a variety of contexts. Such information and skills are commonly associated with the world of work. Lifelong learning standards gained national prominence when the Secretary's Commission on Achieving Necessary Skills (SCANS) published the report *What Work Requires of Schools: A SCANS Report for America 2000* (1991). The commission spent 12 months "talking to business owners, to public employees, to the people who manage employees daily, to union officials, and to workers on the line and at their desks. We have talked to them in their stores, shops, government offices, and manufacturing facilities" (p. v). The strong message from all quarters was that American students must be taught a variety of skills and abilities to be productive members of the work force. Many of these skills and abilities went beyond the traditional academic subjects commonly found in the curriculum. For example, the SCANS report identified a "three-part foundation of skills and personal qualities" (p. vii). The first part of the foundation involved traditional academic content, such as reading, writing, arithmetic and mathematics, speaking, and listening. The second part of the foundation involved the thinking skills of "thinking creatively, making decisions, solving problems, seeing things in the mind's eye, knowing how to learn, and reasoning" (p. vii). The third part of the foundation involved lifelong learning skills, such as individual responsibility, self-esteem, sociability, self-management, and integrity.

A complimentary work to the SCANS report, entitled *Workplace Basics: The Essential Skills Employers Want* (Carnevale, Gainer, & Meltzer, 1990), was published by the American Society for Training and Development (ASTD), which represents "approximately 50,000 practitioners, managers, administrators, educators, and researchers in the field of human resource development" (p. xiii). The set of skills identified in this work was almost identical to that articulated in the SCANS report. From these two reports, one can infer that the American work force is giving America's educators a strong message: Teach and reinforce lifelong learning skills.

This same message has also been heard from parents. The polling firm Public Agenda surveyed a representative sample of parents regarding what should be taught in the schools. Their report is entitled *First Things First: What Americans Expect From Public Schools* (Farkas, Friedman, Boese, & Shaw, 1994). It noted that 88% of those surveyed said, among other things, that schools should teach and reinforce work-related competencies, such as punctuality, dependability, and self-discipline.

Finally, it appears that educators have reached the same opinion about lifelong learning skills. Specifically, the American Association of School Administrators polled 55 noted educators, referred to as the "Council of 55," regarding what schools should teach to prepare students for the 21st century. The council identified interpersonal skills, including being part of a team, as critical to success in the next century (Uchida, Cetron, & McKenzie, 1996).

In summary, there is a great deal of agreement regarding the importance of teaching generic skills that are useful within the workplace. For this reason, we have identified these skills separately. They are listed under Section 20, Life Skills.

5. The Process Used in This Report

Although some variations exist in the manner in which standards from different domains were addressed, a general process was followed to identify the standards in this report.

Identify Significant Reports

In February of 1990, President Bush announced the national educational goals that he and state governors had established. One of those was that by the year 2000, American students would demonstrate mastery over challenging subject matter in core subject areas. Congress has since defined and expanded the goal areas to include the domains of English, mathematics, science, foreign languages, civics and government, economics, arts, history, and geography. Additionally, the educational goals state that all students should have access to physical education and health education to ensure they are healthy and fit. Given this national mandate for improved student performance in these areas, the most significant documents in the fields were identified and examined. For this report, 116 documents were consulted to construct standards and benchmarks.

In addition to these areas, documents were also reviewed for the domain of the workplace. Workplace standards, were developed to meet the growing demand for a smoother transition from school to the workplace, as made evident from recent Skills Standards efforts funded by the Departments of Education and Labor.

It is important to note that a number of documents used were in draft form. All relevant documents are discussed in the appropriate subject sections.

Select Reference Documents

Since there was more than one document within many of the domains considered, a reference report was selected for each domain. Reference documents were selected based on their completeness, perceived acceptance by the subject discipline community, and compatibility with the perspective of standards and benchmarks taken in this report.

Identify Standards and Benchmarks

Once a reference document was selected, standards and their benchmarks were identified. This was done from both "top-down" and "bottom-up" perspectives. A top-down perspective was taken when a reference document contained explicit standards that were at a level of generality consistent with the position on standards taken in this study. In such cases, the standard found in the reference document was accepted with minor modifications, or if rewritten, kept close to the original meaning. Benchmarks were then identified for each standard. Depending upon the character of the document, this process could entail the straightforward identification of explicitly stated benchmarks or an analysis of the material to find information about knowledge and skills that was implicit. This would be the case, for example, if essential knowledge and skills were presented in the form of an instructional activity rather than as a description of the important knowledge and skills. In some cases, however, a reference document articulated standards at a different level of generality (too general or too specific) or in a different format (performance or curriculum standards as opposed to content standards). In such situations, implicit and explicit benchmark components (declarative, procedural, and contextual elements) were identified first. These were then organized into standards. In effect, such standards were designed from the bottom up.

Integrate Information from the Other Documents

When the analysis of the reference document was complete, information from the other documents was then integrated into the standards and benchmarks identified from the reference document. On some occasions, the analysis of secondary documents within a domain illustrated a need to create new standards that were not explicit or implicit in the reference document.

Organize Standards into Categories

In all, this report describes 3,968 benchmarks distributed among 255 standards. These standards have been organized into 14 major categories. In a number of cases, the organization was straightforward; for example, standards generated from and referenced to science documents were placed under the category of science. Such an approach was followed for the areas of mathematics, geography, and history. For other categories, the bottom-up approach, which characterized the formation of standards from benchmarks, also was used to organize similar standards into larger areas. The standards and benchmarks and their categories are listed in figure 5.1.

Figure 5.1 The standards and benchmarks identified in this document

	Standards	Benchmarks
Mathematics	9	226
Science	16	265
History Historical Understanding	2	48
K–4 History (As Implemented[1])	8 (±4)	108 (±54)
U.S. History (As Implemented[1])	31 (±10)	404 (±135)

World History
  (Core Material[2])
    (As Implemented[1])
  (Related Material[2])
    (As Implemented[1])
	46
	
	(±15)
	
	(±15)
		510
		(±170)
		212
		(±71)

Language Arts	8	274
Geography	18	238
Connections Dance Music Theatre Visual Arts Arts (total)	1 6 7 6 5 25	13 62 80 72 42 269
Civics	29	427
Economics	10	159
Foreign Language	5	84
Health	10	136
Physical Education	5	105
Behavioral Studies	4	100
Technology	5	94
Thinking & Reasoning Working with Others Self-regulation Life Work Life Skills (total)	6 5 6 7 24	121 51 59 78 309

[1]The numbers shown for history standards are not equivalent to numbers in other subject areas, inasmuch as a history standard can be achieved in any one of the three years of study recommended by NCHS. Thus, the number of applicable standards for any one year is less than the total number listed here. For a discussion, see History, Section 9.

[2]The national standards project for world history (expanded ed.) identified material that is essential (core) as well as supplementary material that may be used at discretion (related).

6. How the Subject-Area Sections Are Structured

As described previously, standards may be procedural or declarative statements or may be statements that describe broader categories; they may be taken directly from draft documents or may have been constructed inductively or extrapolated from an analysis of the documents in the subject area. The benchmarks in this document, however, are all statements of declarative, procedural, and contextual knowledge taken from a wide range of national reports. In most cases, these benchmarks are organized under the standards at four levels:

Level I	=	K–2, or primary
Level II	=	3–5, or upper elementary
Level III	=	6–8, or middle school
Level IV	=	9–12, or high school

However, in some areas, either because of the nature of the content or source materials, the levels are identified somewhat differently. Because of this, the level identifications are best understood as indicators of relative difficulty, rather than strictly equivalent to a range of grades. Attention should be paid to the parentheses following the levels to identify the grade range. For example, in the case of U.S. History, there are three levels identified:

Level II (Grades 5–6)
Level III (Grades 7–8)
Level IV (Grades 9–12)

Whereas in the standards for history at K–4, there are two levels:

Level I (Grades K–2)
Level II (Grades 3–4)

In this example it should be clear that Level II is a relative description, defining grades 3–4 for history in the early grades and grades 5–6 in the U.S. history standards.

The standards are organized and reported in the 13 categories described in the previous section. Each standard within a category is numbered consecutively (the numbering sequence has no significance and was done for ease of reference). The benchmarks are listed immediately under each standard and presented by level (I-IV). A set of codes, called a citation log, appears flush right and just above each benchmark and standard. A key for the log appears at the bottom of each page, so that readers are provided with the following information: the cognitive character of the benchmark (whether it describes declarative, procedural, or contextual knowledge); a page number citation for each instance in which the information was found in reference and supporting documents; the nature of that citation (whether the information was found explicitly stated or could be implied from other statements); and finally, in the case of duplicates, where very similar benchmarks can be found within the same subject area.

To illustrate:

(GE,115)

5. Understands the concept of regions

Level I (Grades K-2)

BD (GE,115;EI,13;NI,35;TI,10;DI,4.1.2)
- Knows areas that can be classified as regions according to physical criteria (e.g., landform regions, soil regions, vegetation regions, climate regions, water basins) and human criteria (e.g., political regions, population regions, economic regions, language regions)

"Understands the concept of regions" appears as the fifth standard in the geography section, and the benchmark shown is from Level I. Just above the benchmark, and flush right, is the abbreviation "BD," followed by the "citation log": (GE,115;EI,13;NI,35;TI,10;DI,4.1.2). A key like the following is provided for each subject area:

Codes (right side of page):	BD = Benchmark, Declarative; BP = Benchmark, Procedural; BC = Benchmark, Contextual	
1st letter of each code in parentheses	*2nd letter of code*	*Number*
G = GESP: National Geography Standards	E = Explicitly stated in document	Page number of cited document
E = JCGE: Guidelines for Geographic Education	I = Implied in document	*or, for duplicates,*
IE, IG = Int'l Bacc.:Environmental Systems, Geography		Standard number & level of duplicate
N = NAEP: Item Specifications in Geography		
T = GENIP: K-6 Geography: Themes, Key Ideas		
D = Duplicated in another standard		

The key identifies "BD" as a benchmark that describes declarative knowledge. Within the parentheses that follow "BD," there a number of documents cited, separated by semicolons. The first code, GE,115, indicates that the information described in the benchmark can be found explicitly stated (E) in the National Geography Standards (G) on page 115; the second citation, EI,13, indicates that the same information, although not explicitly stated, is implied in (or, can be inferred from) material on page 13 of the Guidelines for Geographic Education. Similarly, the same information can be inferred from two additional documents, the NAEP item specifications and *K–6 Geography* (full citations for all reports are found in the bibliography). The last piece of information "DI,4.1.2" indicates that another benchmark contains very closely related information. In this case, that particular benchmark is under the standard number 4, at level 1, and is the second bulleted item.

Additionally, when the idea expressed at the standard level has been identified in supporting documents, that information is provided in parentheses, flush right, just above the standard statement. In the example above, the idea that students should have a general understanding of the concept of regions is found (GE,115) in the Geography Standards document on page 115.

MATHEMATICS

7. Mathematics

The following process was used to identify standards and benchmarks for mathematics:

Identification of Significant Reports
Two basic reports were identified as the primary documents representing the current thinking on standards in mathematics: *Curriculum and Evaluation Standards for School Mathematics* (NCTM, 1989) and the *Mathematics Framework for the 1996 National Assessment of Educational Progress* (NAEP, n.d.). The NCTM document was a major contributor to the national awareness of the benefits of identifying standards in content domains, and it is probably the most successful standards document published to date in terms of the breadth of its acceptance. Additionally, even though it is not as widely known, the NAEP framework has provided strong conceptual guidance to the development of mathematics education. To prepare for the 1994 NAEP mathematics assessment, the National Assessment Governing Board awarded a contract in the fall of 1991 to the College Board to develop item specifications for the 1994 assessments. Explicit in this project was an alignment with the NCTM standards, inasmuch as they were believed to reflect the most current thinking on what students should know and be able to do in mathematics. The process of developing the recommendations for the planned 1994 mathematics assessment occurred between September, 1991 and March, 1992 and resulted in the publication of the report *Framework for the 1994 National Assessment of Educational Progress Mathematics Assessment* (NAEP, 1992b). Due to a budget shortfall, however, the mathematics assessments were rescheduled from 1994 to 1996 and a new framework was issued entitled *Mathematics Framework for the 1996 National Assessment of Educational Progress* (NAEP, n.d.). Although the two documents were similar in many respects, there were some differences. Given that it was the more current work, and encompassed all the material found in the 1994 framework, the 1996 framework was used in this report.

In addition to these documents which focus solely on mathematics, *Benchmarks for Science Literacy* (Project 2061, 1993) contains a section entitled The Mathematical World. This section parallels and details many of the standards found in *Curriculum and Evaluation Standards* (NCTM, 1989). Also, the *New Standards Project* has published three documents that report mathematics standards and benchmarks at elementary, middle, and high school levels. Those documents are *Performance standards: English Language Arts, Mathematics, Science, Applied Learning, Volume 1, Elementary School* (1997a); *Performance Standards: English Language Arts, Mathematics, Science, Applied Learning, Volume 2, Middle School* (1997b); and *Performance Standards: English Language Arts, Mathematics, Science, Applied Learning, Volume 3, High School* (1997c).

Finally, two documents from the International Baccalaureate Organization were also consulted: *Group 5 Mathematics Guide* (1993) and *Middle Years Programme: Mathematics* (1995e).

Selection of the Reference Document
Because of its wide recognition, the NCTM document was selected as the reference report. Additionally, the report had characteristics amenable to the standards/benchmarks model used in this study. Specifically, the report explicitly identifies standards at three developmental levels—grades

43

K–4, 5–8, and 9–12. The latter two levels corresponded well with levels 3 and 4 used in this study. However, the elements identified in the K–4 level of the NCTM document were necessarily reclassified into Level 1 (primary) or Level 2 (upper elementary) for the purposes of this study.

Identification of Standards and Benchmarks and Integration of Information from Other Documents

Close examination of the NCTM levels indicated that in some cases there appeared to be little designed relationship between the content in one developmental level and that in the next. In addition, new types of knowledge and skill were sometimes introduced at a superordinate level within a standard that seemed to have no developmental relationship to the knowledge and skill identified in the subordinate level. Consequently, many elements within the various NCTM standards and levels were reclassified as more appropriately fitting within another standard. This reclassification process was highly influenced by the NAEP document. Where the NCTM document identifies 13 standards at Levels 1 and 2, and 14 standards at Level 3, the NAEP document identifies five general categories articulated at three levels roughly equivalent to the three NCTM levels. Our reclassification tended to collapse some of the NCTM standards such that the final set of nine standards (see below) resembled the NAEP classification as much as it did the NCTM classification. In effect, our reclassification tended to erode the original structure of the NCTM document.

Another factor contributing to the erosion of the structure of the NCTM organizational structure was its inclusion of explicit standards regarding mathematics as reasoning and mathematics as communication. For reasons discussed in Section 3 of this report, many of the elements identified within the NCTM standard on mathematics as reasoning were judged to be more appropriately classified under one of the standards within our thinking and reasoning category, and some of the elements within the NCTM standard on mathematics as communication were judged to be more appropriately classified under one of the standards within our language arts category.

Finally, a number of the elements in the NCTM document were identified either as "expert" in nature or curriculum standards, as opposed to content standards, and were not included in the analysis.

For the most part, the information in the Project 2061, New Standards, and International Baccalaureate documents was integrated into the standards generated from the NCTM and NAEP reports. The one exception to this general rule was Standard 9, Understands the General Nature and Uses of Mathematics. As the title indicates, this standard deals with general awarenesses about mathematics and its relationship to other disciplines, particularly science. This standard was generated solely from the Project 2061 document *Benchmarks for Science Literacy*.

Summary of Standards for Mathematics

1. Uses a variety of strategies in the problem-solving process
2. Understands and applies basic and advanced properties of the concepts of numbers
3. Uses basic and advanced procedures while performing the processes of computation
4. Understands and applies basic and advanced properties of the concepts of measurement
5. Understands and applies basic and advanced properties of the concepts of geometry
6. Understands and applies basic and advanced concepts of statistics and data analysis
7. Understands and applies basic and advanced concepts of probability
8. Understands and applies basic and advanced properties of functions and algebra
9. Understands the general nature and uses of mathematics

(ME,23,75,137;PE,41-42;S1E,63;S2E,57;S3E,54)

1. Uses a variety of strategies in the problem-solving process

Level I (Grades K-2)

BP (ME,24;PE,22;S1E,63)
- Draws pictures to represent problems

BC (ME,26;PI,41-42;S1E,64)
- Uses discussions with teachers and other students to understand problems

BC (ME,23;PI,41-42;S1E,63)
- Explains to others how she or he went about solving a numerical problem

BP (ME,24;PI,41-42;S1I,63)
- Makes organized lists or tables of information necessary for solving a problem

BP (ME,24;PE,21;S1E,63)
- Uses whole number models (e.g., pattern blocks, tiles, or other manipulative materials) to represent problems

Level II (Grades 3-5)

BP (ME,24,26-27;PE,41-42;S1E,63)
- Uses a variety of strategies to understand problem situations (e.g., discussing with peers, stating problems in own words, modeling problem with diagrams or physical objects, identifying a pattern)

BP (ME,26,27;PE,22;S1E,63)
- Represents problems situations in a variety of forms (e.g., translates from a diagram to a number or symbolic expression)

BD (ME,26;PI,41-42;S1I,63)
- Understands that some ways of representing a problem are more helpful than others

BP (ME,24,30;PI,41-42;S1I,63)
- Uses trial and error and the process of elimination to solve problems

BD (ME,30;PI,41-42;S1I,63)
- Knows the difference between pertinent and irrelevant information when solving problems

BD (ME,30;PI,41-42;S1E,64)
- Understands the basic language of logic in mathematical situations (e.g., "and," "or," "not")

BC (ME,23,29;PE,23,29;S1E,63,64)
- Uses explanations of the methods and reasoning behind the problem solution to determine reasonableness of and to verify results with respect to the original problem

BD (ME,30-31;PE,29,35;S1I,64)
- Understands basic valid and invalid arguments (e.g., counter examples, irrelevant approaches)

Codes (right side of page):   BD = Benchmark, Declarative; BP = Benchmark, Procedural; BC = Benchmark, Contextual
1st letter of each code in parentheses   *2nd letter of code*   *Number*
M = NCTM: Curric. & Eval. Standards for Math   E = Explicitly stated in document   Page number of cited document
2 = Project 2061: Benchmarks for Science Literacy   I = Implied in document
B1,B2 = International Baccalaureate Math: Middle, High
P = NAEP: Mathematics Assessment Framework
S1,S2,S3 = New Standards: Elementary, Middle, High

Level III (Grades 6-8)

- BC (MI,75;B1I,7;PI,41-42;S2E,57)
  Understands how to break a complex problem into simpler parts or use a similar problem type to solve a problem

- BP (ME,76-77;B1E,7;PE,41-42;S2E,57)
  Uses a variety of strategies to understand problem-solving situations and processes (e.g., considers different strategies and approaches to a problem, restates problem from various perspectives)

- BD (ME,77;B1I,7;PI,41-42;S2I,57)
  Understands that there is no one right way to solve mathematical problems but that different methods (e.g., working backward from a solution, using a similar problem type, identifying a pattern) have different advantages and disadvantages

- BP (ME,75,76;B1I,7;PE,41-42;S2E,57)
  Formulates a problem, determines information required to solve the problem, chooses methods for obtaining this information, and sets limits for acceptable solutions

- BP (ME,78;B1E,7;PI,41-42;S2E,58)
  Represents problem situations in and translates among oral, written, concrete, pictorial, and graphical forms

- BP (ME,77,82;B1E,7;PE,35;S2E,57)
  Generalizes from a pattern of observations made in particular cases, makes conjectures, and provides supporting arguments for these conjectures (i.e., uses inductive reasoning)

- BP (ME,81-82;B1E,7;PE,35;S2E,57,58)
  Constructs informal logical arguments to justify reasoning processes and methods of solutions to problems (i.e., uses informal deductive methods)

- BD (ME,78-79;B1E,9;PI,41-42;S2E,58)
  Understands the role of written symbols in representing mathematical ideas and the use of precise language in conjunction with the special symbols of mathematics

- BD (ME,81;B1E,7;PE,23,35;S2E,57)
  Uses a variety of reasoning processes (e.g., reasoning from a counter example, using proportionality) to model and to solve problems

Level IV (Grades 9-12)

- BP (ME,137;B2E,7;PE,41-42;S3E,54)
  Uses a variety of strategies (e.g., identify a pattern, use equivalent representations) to understand new mathematical content and to develop more efficient solution methods or problem extensions

- BP (ME,176,178;2E,291;B2E,14;PI,22;S3E,54)
  Constructs algorithms for multi-step and non-routine problems

---

Codes (right side of page):   BD = Benchmark, Declarative; BP = Benchmark, Procedural; BC = Benchmark, Contextual
1st letter of each code in parentheses   *2nd letter of code*   *Number*
M = NCTM: Curric. & Eval. Standards for Math   E = Explicitly stated in document   Page number of cited document
2 = Project 2061: Benchmarks for Science Literacy   I = Implied in document
B1,B2 = International Baccalaureate Math: Middle, High
P = NAEP: Mathematics Assessment Framework
S1,S2,S3 = New Standards: Elementary, Middle, High

- Understands the concept of a mathematical proof

  BD (ME,143,144-145;PI,29,35;S3E,54)

- Constructs logical verifications or counter examples to test conjectures and to justify algorithms and solutions to problems (i.e., uses deductive reasoning)

  BP (ME,143,144,159,160-161;B2E,7;PE,29,35;S3E,54)

- Uses formal mathematical language and notation to represent ideas, to demonstrate relationships within and among representation systems, and to formulate generalizations

  BP (ME,140;B2E,7;PI,41-42;S3E,56)

- Understands the difference between a statement that is verified by mathematical proof (i.e., a theorem) and one that is verified empirically using examples or data

  BD (ME,145;PI,29,35;S3I,54)

- Understands connections between equivalent representations and corresponding procedures of the same problem situation or mathematical concept (e.g., a zero of a function corresponds to an *x*-intercept of the graph of the function)

  BD (ME,146,148;B2E,7;PI,41-42;S3E,54)

- Understands the components of mathematical modeling (i.e., problem formulation, mathematical model, solution within the model, interpretation of solution within the model, validation in original real-world problem situation)

  BD (ME,138,139;2E,38;B2I,7;PI,41-42;S3E,54)

2. Understands and applies basic and advanced properties of the concepts of numbers

(ME,38,87,91,184;PE,20;S1E,60;S2E,54;S3E,50)

Level I (Grades K-2)

- Understands that numbers are symbols used to represent quantities or attributes of real-world objects

  BD (MI,38;2I,36,211;PI,21;S1E,60)

- Counts whole numbers (i.e., both cardinal and ordinal numbers)

  BP (ME,39;2E,211;PE,21;S1E,60)

- Understands symbolic, concrete, and pictorial representations of numbers (e.g., written numerals, objects in sets, number lines)

  BD (MI,38,39;PE,21-22,34;S1E,60)

- Understands basic whole number relationships (e.g., 4 is less than 10, 30 is 3 tens)

  BD (ME,38,39;2E,211;PE,22;S1E,60)

- Understands the concept of a unit and its subdivision into equal parts (e.g., one object, such as a candy bar, and its division into equal parts to be shared among four people)

  BD (ME,57;2E,211;PI,22;S1E,60)

Codes (right side of page): BD = Benchmark, Declarative; BP = Benchmark, Procedural; BC = Benchmark, Contextual
1st letter of each code in parentheses *2nd letter of code* *Number*
M = NCTM: Curric. & Eval. Standards for Math E = Explicitly stated in document Page number of cited document
2 = Project 2061: Benchmarks for Science Literacy I = Implied in document
B1,B2 = International Baccalaureate Math: Middle, High
P = NAEP: Mathematics Assessment Framework
S1,S2,S3 = New Standards: Elementary, Middle, High

Level II (Grades 3-5)

- Understands the relationships among fractions, decimals, mixed numbers, and whole numbers

  BD (ME,57,87;PE,21,22;S1E,60)

- Understands equivalent forms of basic percents, fractions, and decimals (e.g., ½ is equivalent to 50% is equivalent to .5) and when one form of a number might be more useful than another

  BD (ME,57,87;PI,22;S1E,60)

- Understands the basic difference between odd and even numbers

  BD (MI,38;PE,23;S1E,60)

- Understands the basic meaning of place value

  BD (ME,39;PE,21;S1E,60)

- Understands the relative magnitude of whole numbers, fractions, decimals, and mixed numbers

  BD (ME,40;PE,22;S1E,60)

- Uses models (e.g., number lines, two-dimensional and three-dimensional regions) to identify, order, and compare numbers

  BC (ME,88;PE,22;S1E,60)

Level III (Grades 6-8)

- Understands the relationships among equivalent number representations (e.g., whole numbers, positive and negative integers, fractions, ratios, decimals, percents, scientific notation, exponentials) and the advantages and disadvantages of each type of representation

  BD (ME,87;B1E,9;PE,21;S2E,54)

- Understands the characteristics and properties (e.g., order relations, relative magnitude, base-ten place value) of the set of rational numbers and its subsets (e.g., whole numbers, fractions, decimals, integers)

  BD (ME,87,91;B1E,9,11;PI,21,22;S2E,54)

- Understands the role of positive and negative integers in the number system

  BD (ME,91,93;B1E,9,11;PE,23;S2E,54)

- Understands basic number theory concepts (e.g., prime and composite numbers, factors, multiples, odd and even numbers, square numbers, roots, divisibility)

  BD (ME,91,93;B1E,9;PE,23;S2E,54)

- Understands the characteristics and uses of exponents and scientific notation

  BD (ME,87,88;B1E,11,13;PE,21;S2I,54)

Codes (right side of page):   BD = Benchmark, Declarative; BP = Benchmark, Procedural; BC = Benchmark, Contextual

1st letter of each code in parentheses   *2nd letter of code*   *Number*

M = NCTM: Curric. & Eval. Standards for Math   E = Explicitly stated in document   Page number of cited document

2 = Project 2061: Benchmarks for Science Literacy   I = Implied in document

B1,B2 = International Baccalaureate Math: Middle, High

P = NAEP: Mathematics Assessment Framework

S1,S2,S3 = New Standards: Elementary, Middle, High

MREL

- Understands the structure of numeration systems that are based on numbers other than 10 (e.g., base 60 for telling time and measuring angles, Roman numerals for dates and clock faces) _{BD (2E,213;B1E,27)}

- Understands the concepts of ratio, proportion, and percent and the relationships among them _{BD (ME,87,89;B1E,9;PE,23;S2E,54)}

Level IV (Grades 9-12)

- Understands the properties (e.g., relative magnitude, density, absolute value) of the real number system and its subsystems (e.g., irrational numbers, natural numbers, integers, rational numbers) _{BD (ME,184;B1E,11;B2E,10;PI,21,23;S3E,50)}

- Understands the properties and basic theorems of roots, exponents (e.g., $[b^m][b^n] = b^{m+n}$), and logarithms _{BD (ME,144,185-186;B1E,11,13;B2E,14,46;PI,21;S3I,50)}

- Understands that mathematical systems that appear to be very different may have the same structural underpinnings (e.g., binary multiplication, a series electrical circuit, and the logical operation "and" have the equivalent roles of "0," "off," and "false," as well as of "1," "on," and "true," respectively) _{BD (ME,184,185;2E,214;PI,21,22;S3I,54)}

- Uses number theory concepts (e.g., divisibility and remainders, factors, multiples, prime, relatively prime) to solve problems _{BP (MI,184;PE,23;S3E,50)}

- Uses discrete structures (e.g., finite graphs, matrices, sequences) to represent and to solve problems _{BP (ME,178;B1E,9;B2E,17,46;PE,35)}

3. **Uses basic and advanced procedures while performing the processes of computation** _(ME,36,41,44,94,176;PE,20;S1E,60;S2E,54;S3E,50)

Level I (Grades K-2)

- Adds and subtracts whole numbers _{BP (ME,41;2E,290;PE,22;S1E,60)}

- Solves real-world problems involving addition and subtraction of whole numbers _{BP (ME,41;2E,290;PE,22;S1I,60)}

- Understands common terms used with estimation (e.g., "about," "near," "closer to," "between," "a little less than") _{BD (ME,36;PE,22-23;S1E,60)}

Codes (right side of page):   BD = Benchmark, Declarative; BP = Benchmark, Procedural; BC = Benchmark, Contextual
1st letter of each code in parentheses   *2nd letter of code*   *Number*
M = NCTM: Curric. & Eval. Standards for Math   E = Explicitly stated in document   Page number of cited document
2 = Project 2061: Benchmarks for Science Literacy   I = Implied in document
B1,B2 = International Baccalaureate Math: Middle, High
P = NAEP: Mathematics Assessment Framework
S1,S2,S3 = New Standards: Elementary, Middle, High

50

MREL

- Understands the inverse relationship between addition and subtraction
  BD (ME,43;PI,22;S1E,60)

Level II (Grades 3-5)

- Adds, subtracts, multiplies, and divides whole numbers and decimals
  BP (ME,41,94;2E,290;PE,22;S1E,60)

- Adds and subtracts simple fractions
  BP (ME,59;2I,290;PI,22)

- Uses specific strategies (e.g., front-end estimation, rounding) to estimate computations and to check the reasonableness of computational results
  BP (ME,37;PE,22,23;S1E,60)

- Performs basic mental computations (e.g., addition and subtraction of whole numbers)
  BP (ME,44;2E,290;PI,22;S1E,60)

- Determines the effects of addition, subtraction, multiplication, and division on size and order of numbers
  BP (ME,43;PE,22:S1I,60)

- Understands the properties of and the relationships among addition, subtraction, multiplication, and division (e.g., reversing the order of two addends does not change the sum; division is the inverse of multiplication)
  BD (ME,43;PI,22;S1E,60,62)

- Solves real-world problems involving number operations (e.g., computations with dollars and cents)
  BP (ME,41;PE,22,23;S1E,60)

- Knows the language of basic operations (e.g., "factors," "products," "multiplication")
  BD (ME,42;S1I,64)

Level III (Grades 6-8)

- Adds, subtracts, multiplies, and divides whole numbers, fractions, decimals, integers, and rational numbers
  BP (ME,94;2I,291;B1E,9;PE,22;S2E,54,58)

- Understands exponentiation of rational numbers and root-extraction (e.g., squares and square roots, cubes and cube roots)
  BD (MI,87,91;B1E,9,13;PE,35;S2E,54)

- Selects and uses appropriate computational methods (e.g., mental, paper and pencil, calculator, computer) for a given situation
  BC (ME,94;B1I,9;PE,22;S2E,58)

- Understands the correct order of operations for performing arithmetic computations
  BD (MI,94;B1E,9;PE,35;S2E,58)

Codes (right side of page):   BD = Benchmark, Declarative; BP = Benchmark, Procedural; BC = Benchmark, Contextual
1st letter of each code in parentheses   *2nd letter of code*   *Number*
M = NCTM: Curric. & Eval. Standards for Math   E = Explicitly stated in document   Page number of cited document
2 = Project 2061: Benchmarks for Science Literacy   I = Implied in document
B1,B2 = International Baccalaureate Math: Middle, High
P = NAEP: Mathematics Assessment Framework
S1,S2,S3 = New Standards: Elementary, Middle, High

- BP (ME,81,82-83,94,96;B1I,9;PE,23;S2E,54)
  Uses proportional reasoning to solve mathematical and real-world problems (e.g., involving equivalent fractions, equal ratios, constant rate of change, proportions, percents)

- BD (MI,91,92;B1E,9,11;PE,22;S2E,54)
  Understands the properties of operations with rational numbers (e.g., distributive property, commutative and associative properties of addition and multiplication, inverse properties, identity properties)

- BD (ME,95;B1I,9;PE,22;S2I,58)
  Knows when an estimate is more appropriate than an exact answer for a variety of problem situations

- BD (ME,95;PE,22;S2I,57)
  Understands how different algorithms work for arithmetic computations and operations

Level IV (Grades 9-12)

- BP (ME,150;B2E,10,44;PE,35;S3I,50)
  Adds, subtracts, multiplies, divides, and simplifies rational expressions

- BP (ME,150;B2E,10,44;PE,35;S3I,50)
  Adds, subtracts, multiplies, divides, and simplifies radical expressions containing positive rational numbers

- BD (2E,291;B2I,14,46;PI,23)
  Understands various sources of discrepancy between an estimate and a calculated answer

- BP (ME,150;B2E,46;PE,35;S3E,50)
  Uses a variety of operations (e.g., finding a reciprocal, raising to a power, taking a root, taking a logarithm) on expressions containing real numbers

- BD (ME,150,177;B1E,13;B2E,17,52;PE,35)
  Understands basic applications of and operations on matrices

- BP (ME,178;B1E,13;B2E,17,46;PE,36;S3I,50)
  Uses recurrence relations (i.e., formulas expressing each term as a function of one or more of the previous terms, such as the Fibonacci sequence or the compound interest equation) to model and to solve real-world problems (e.g., home mortgages, annuities)

- BD (ME,176,178-179;PE,32;S3E,50)
  Understands counting procedures and reasoning (e.g., use of the Addition Counting Principle to find the number of ways of arranging objects in a set, the use of permutations and combinations to solve counting problems)

Codes (right side of page):   BD = Benchmark, Declarative; BP = Benchmark, Procedural; BC = Benchmark, Contextual
1st letter of each code in parentheses   *2nd letter of code*   *Number*
M = NCTM: Curric. & Eval. Standards for Math E = Explicitly stated in document Page number of cited document
2 = Project 2061: Benchmarks for Science Literacy I = Implied in document
B1,B2 = International Baccalaureate Math: Middle, High
P = NAEP: Mathematics Assessment Framework
S1,S2,S3 = New Standards: Elementary, Middle, High

52

MREL

(ME,36,51,116;PE,24;S1E,61;S2E,55;S3E,51)

4. Understands and applies basic and advanced properties of the concepts of measurement

Level I (Grades K-2)

BD (ME,51;2E,290;PE,24;S1E,61)

- Understands the basic measures length, width, height, weight, and temperature

BD (ME,51;2E,290;PE,24;S1E,61)

- Understands the concept of time and how it is measured

BD (ME,52;2E,290;PI,25;S1E,61,64)

- Knows processes for telling time, counting money, and measuring length, weight, and temperature, using basic standard and non-standard units

BP (ME,51;2E,290;PE,25;S1I,61,64)

- Makes quantitative estimates of familiar linear dimensions, weights, and time intervals and checks them against measurements

Level II (Grades 3 5)

BD (ME,51;2E,290;PE,25;S1E,61)

- Understands the basic measures perimeter, area, volume, capacity, mass, angle, and circumference

BC (MI,51;2I,290;PE,25;S1E,64)

- Selects and uses appropriate tools for given measurement situations (e.g., rulers for length, measuring cups for capacity, protractors for angle)

BD (ME,52;2E,290;PI,26;S1I,61)

- Knows approximate size of basic standard units (e.g., centimeters, feet, grams) and relationships between them (e.g., between inches and feet)

BD (MI,51;PE,25;S1E,61)

- Understands relationships between measures (e.g., between length, perimeter, and area)

BD (ME,52;2E,212)

- Understands that measurement is not exact (i.e., measurements may give slightly different numbers when measured multiple times)

BP (ME,37,51,53;2E,290;PE,25;S1E,61,64)

- Uses specific strategies to estimate quantities and measurements (e.g., estimating the whole by estimating the parts)

BC (ME,52;PE,25;S1E,61)

- Selects and uses appropriate units of measurement, according to type and size of unit

---

Codes (right side of page):　　　　BD = Benchmark, Declarative; BP = Benchmark, Procedural; BC = Benchmark, Contextual
1st letter of each code in parentheses　　　　*2nd letter of code*　　　　*Number*
M = NCTM: Curric. & Eval. Standards for Math　　　E = Explicitly stated in document　　　Page number of cited document
2 = Project 2061: Benchmarks for Science Literacy　　I = Implied in document
B1,B2 = International Baccalaureate Math: Middle, High
P = NAEP: Mathematics Assessment Framework
S1,S2,S3 = New Standards: Elementary, Middle, High

Level III (Grades 6-8)

- Understands the basic concept of rate as a measure (e.g., miles per gallon)

  BD (ME,116;B1E,9;PE,26)

- Solves problems involving perimeter (circumference) and area of various shapes (e.g., parallelograms, triangles, circles)

  BP (MI,116,118;B1I,10;PE,25;S2I,55)

- Understands the relationships among linear dimensions, area, and volume and the corresponding uses of units, square units, and cubic units of measure

  BD (ME,114-115;B1I,10,11;PI,25;S2E,55)

- Solves problems involving units of measurement and converts answers to a larger or smaller unit within the same system (i.e., standard or metric)

  BC (MI,116;2E,291;PE,26;S2E,55)

- Understands the concepts of precision and significant digits as they relate to measurement (e.g., how units indicate precision)

  BD (MI,117;2E,291;B1E,9;PE,26)

- Selects and uses appropriate units and tools, depending on degree of accuracy required, to find measurements for real-world problems

  BC (ME,116,117;PE,25;S2I,55,58)

- Understands formulas for finding measures (e.g., area, volume, surface area)

  BD (ME,116,118;B1E,11;PE,25-26;S2I,58)

- Selects and uses appropriate estimation techniques (e.g., overestimate, underestimate, range of estimates) to solve real-world problems

  BP (ME,116,117;PE,22;S2I,58)

- Understands procedures for basic indirect measurements (e.g., using grids to estimate area of irregular figures)

  BD (ME,116,118-119;PE,26)

Level IV (Grades 9-12)

- Solves problems involving rate as a measure (e.g., velocity, acceleration)

  BP (MI,151;2E,291;PE,26;S3E,51)

- Understands the concepts of absolute and relative errors in measurement

  BD (2I,291;PE,26)

- Selects and uses an appropriate direct or indirect method of measurement in a given situation (e.g., uses properties of similar triangles to measure indirectly the height of an inaccessible object)

  BC (MI,157-158;B2E,18;PE,26)

Codes (right side of page):   BD = Benchmark, Declarative; BP = Benchmark, Procedural; BC = Benchmark, Contextual
1st letter of each code in parentheses   *2nd letter of code*   *Number*
M = NCTM: Curric. & Eval. Standards for Math   E = Explicitly stated in document   Page number of cited document
2 = Project 2061: Benchmarks for Science Literacy   I = Implied in document
B1,B2 = International Baccalaureate Math: Middle, High
P = NAEP: Mathematics Assessment Framework
S1,S2,S3 = New Standards: Elementary, Middle, High

- Solves real-world problems involving three-dimensional measures (e.g., volume, surface area)

  BP (MI,157,158;B2E,48;PE,25;S3E,51)

5.   **Understands and applies basic and advanced properties of the concepts of geometry**

(ME,48,112,157,161,163;PE,26;S1E,61;S2E,55;S3E,51)

Level I (Grades K-2)

- Understands basic properties of (e.g., number of sides, corners, square corners) and similarities and differences between simple geometric shapes

  BD (ME,49;PE,29;S1E,61)

- Understands the common language of spatial sense (e.g., "inside," "between," "above," "below," "behind")

  BD (ME,49;PE,28;S1E,61)

- Understands that geometric shapes are useful for representing and describing real world situations

  BD (MI,48;2E,26,27,223;PE,29;S1I,61)

- Understands that patterns can be made by putting different shapes together or taking them apart

  BD (MI,60;2E,26;PE,28;S1E,61)

Level II (Grades 3-5)

- Knows basic geometric language for describing and naming shapes (e.g., trapezoid, parallelogram, cube, sphere)

  BD (ME,48,49,113;PI,27;S1E,61)

- Understands basic properties of figures (e.g., two- or three-dimensionality, symmetry, number of faces, type of angle)

  BD (MI,49;PE,29;S1E,61)

- Predicts and verifies the effects of combining, subdividing, and changing basic shapes

  BC (ME,48;PE,28;S1I,61)

- Understands that shapes can be congruent or similar

  BD (ME,114;PE,28;S1E,61)

- Uses motion geometry (e.g., turns, flips, slides) to understand geometric relationships

  BC (ME,49,114;2E,223;PE,28;S1E,61)

- Understands characteristics of lines (e.g., parallel, perpendicular, intersecting) and angles (e.g., right, acute)

  BD (ME,113;MI,49;PI,29;S1I,61)

Codes (right side of page):   BD = Benchmark, Declarative; BP = Benchmark, Procedural; BC = Benchmark, Contextual
1st letter of each code in parentheses   *2nd letter of code*   *Number*
M = NCTM: Curric. & Eval. Standards for Math   E = Explicitly stated in document   Page number of cited document
2 = Project 2061: Benchmarks for Science Literacy   I = Implied in document
B1,B2 = International Baccalaureate Math: Middle, High
P = NAEP: Mathematics Assessment Framework
S1,S2,S3 = New Standards: Elementary, Middle, High

BD (ME,83;2E,223;PE,26;S1E,61)

- Understands how scale in maps and drawings shows relative size and distance

Level III (Grades 6-8)

BP (ME,112-113;B1E,10,11;PI,27,29)

- Uses geometric methods (i.e., an unmarked straightedge and a compass using an algorithm) to complete basic geometric constructions (e.g., perpendicular bisector of a line segment, angle bisector)

BD (ME,112,113;B1E,10,11;PI,29;S2E,55)

- Understands the defining properties of three-dimensional figures (e.g., a cube has edges with equal lengths, faces with equal areas and congruent shapes, right angle corners)

BD (ME,112,113;2E,224;PI,29;S2E,55)

- Understands the defining properties of triangles (e.g., the sum of the measures of two sides of a triangle must be greater than the measure of the third side)

BD (ME,112,114;B1E,10,11;PE,28;S2E,55)

- Understands geometric transformations of figures (e.g., rotations, translations, dilations)

BD (MI,113,115;B1E,10;PE,28;S2E,55)

- Understands the relationships between two- and three-dimensional representations of a figure (e.g., scale drawings, blueprints, planar cross sections)

BD (ME,114-115;B1E,14;PE,28;S2E,55)

- Understands the mathematical concepts of similarity (e.g., scale, proportion, growth rates) and congruency

BD (ME,115;B1I,11;PI,28;S2E,55)

- Understands the concept of tessellation (i.e., a repetitive pattern of polygons that fit together with no gaps or holes)

BD (ME,113-114;B1E,11;PE,28)

- Understands the basic concept of the Pythagorean Theorem

Level IV (Grades 9-12)

BD (ME,161;PE,29;S3I,54)

- Understands that objects and relations in geometry correspond directly to objects and relations in algebra (e.g., a line in geometry corresponds to a set of ordered pairs satisfying an equation of the form $ax + by = c$)

BP (ME,163,164;B2E,18;PE,28;S3E,51)

- Uses the Pythagorean Theorem and its converse and properties of special right triangles (e.g., 30°-60°-90° triangle) to solve mathematical and real-world problems

BC (ME,162;B1E,10,11;PE,28;S3I,51)

- Uses synthetic (i.e., pictorial) representations and analytic (i.e., coordinate) methods to solve

---

Codes (right side of page):   BD = Benchmark, Declarative; BP = Benchmark, Procedural; BC = Benchmark, Contextual
1st letter of each code in parentheses   *2nd letter of code*   *Number*
M = NCTM: Curric. & Eval. Standards for Math   E = Explicitly stated in document   Page number of cited document
2 = Project 2061: Benchmarks for Science Literacy   I = Implied in document
B1,B2 = International Baccalaureate Math: Middle, High
P = NAEP: Mathematics Assessment Framework
S1,S2,S3 = New Standards: Elementary, Middle, High

problems involving symmetry and transformations of figures (e.g., problems involving distance, midpoint, and slope; determination of symmetry with respect to a point or line)

- Understands the characteristics and uses of vectors (e.g., representations of velocity and force)

  BD (ME,161,162;B2E,17;PE,29)

- Uses geometric constructions (e.g., the parallel to a line through a given point not on the line, line segment congruent to a given line segment) to complete simple proofs, to model, and to solve mathematical and real-world problems

  BP (MI,161;B1E,10,11;PI,27;S3I,55)

- Uses basic operations on vectors (e.g., vector addition, scalar multiplication)

  BP (ME,161,162;B2E,17;PE,29)

- Understands the basic concepts of right triangle trigonometry (e.g., basic trigonometric ratios such as sine, cosine, and tangent)

  BD (ME,163,164;B1E,14;B2E,18,48;PE,28,36;S3E,51)

- Uses trigonometric ratio methods to solve mathematical and real-world problems (e.g., determination of the angle of depression between two markers on a contour map with different elevations)

  BD (ME,163,164;PE,28,36;S3E,51)

- Understands the basic properties and uses of polar coordinates

  BD (ME,163;B2I,18;PE,34)

- Uses inductive and deductive reasoning to make observations about and to verify properties of and relationships among figures (e.g., the relationship among interior angles of parallel lines cut by a transversal)

  BC (ME,158,159;PE,29;S3E,54)

- Uses properties of and relationships among figures to solve mathematical and real-world problems (e.g., uses the property that the sum of the angles in a quadrilateral is equal to 360 degrees to square up the frame for a building; uses understanding of arc, chord, tangents, and properties of circles to determine the radius given a circular edge of a circle without the center)

  BC (ME,157-158;B2E,45;PE,28;S3E,51)

6. Understands and applies basic and advanced concepts of statistics and data analysis

(ME,54,105,167;PE,29;S1E,62;S2E,56;S3E,53)

Level I (Grades K-2)

- Understands that observations about objects or events can be organized and displayed in simple graphs

  BD (ME,54-55;2E,211;PE,31;S1E,62)

Codes (right side of page):   BD = Benchmark, Declarative; BP = Benchmark, Procedural; BC = Benchmark, Contextual
1st letter of each code in parentheses   *2nd letter of code*   *Number*
M = NCTM: Curric. & Eval. Standards for Math   E = Explicitly stated in document   Page number of cited document
2 = Project 2061: Benchmarks for Science Literacy   I = Implied in document
B1,B2 = International Baccalaureate Math: Middle, High
P = NAEP: Mathematics Assessment Framework
S1,S2,S3 = New Standards: Elementary, Middle, High

57   MREL

BD (MI,54,55;2E,227)
- Understands that one can find out about a group of things by studying just a few of them

Level II (Grades 3-5)

BD (ME,54;PI,31;S1E,62)
- Understands that data represent specific pieces of information about real-world objects or activities

BD (MI,54,55;2E,228;PI,31;S1I,62)
- Understands that spreading data out on a number line helps to see what the extremes are, where the data points pile up, and where the gaps are

BD (ME,107;2E,228;PI,31;S1I,62)
- Understands that a summary of data should include where the middle is and how much spread there is around it

BP (ME,54-55;PE,31;S1E,62)
- Organizes and displays data in simple bar graphs, pie charts, and line graphs

BP (ME,54,55;PE,31;S1E,62)
- Reads and interprets simple bar graphs, pie charts, and line graphs

BD (ME,55;PI,31;S1E,62)
- Understands that data come in many different forms and that collecting, organizing, and displaying data can be done in many ways

BD (MI,54;2E,228;PE,31;S1E,62)
- Understands the basic concept of a sample (e.g., a large sample leads to more reliable information; a small part of something may have unique characteristics but not be an accurate representation of the whole)

Level III (Grades 6-8)

BD (ME,107;2E,229,291;B1E,14;PE,31;S2E,56)
- Understands basic characteristics of measures of central tendency (i.e., mean, mode, median)

BD (MI,107;2E,224;B1E,14;PE,31;S2E,56)
- Understands basic characteristics of frequency and distribution (e.g., range, varying rates of change, gaps, clusters)

BD (ME,106-107;2E,229;B1E,14;PE,31)
- Understands the basic concepts of center and dispersion of data

BP (ME,105-106;B1E,10;PE,31;S2E,56)
- Reads and interprets data in charts, tables, plots (e.g., stem-and-leaf, box-and-whiskers, scatter), and graphs (e.g., bar, circle, line)

Codes (right side of page):   BD = Benchmark, Declarative; BP = Benchmark, Procedural; BC = Benchmark, Contextual
1st letter of each code in parentheses   *2nd letter of code*   *Number*
M = NCTM: Curric. & Eval. Standards for Math   E = Explicitly stated in document   Page number of cited document
2 = Project 2061: Benchmarks for Science Literacy   I = Implied in document
B1,B2 = International Baccalaureate Math: Middle, High
P = NAEP: Mathematics Assessment Framework
S1,S2,S3 = New Standards: Elementary, Middle, High

- Uses data and statistical measures for a variety of purposes (e.g., formulating hypotheses, making predictions, testing conjectures)

  BP (ME,106;B1I,14;PE,31;S2E,56)

- Organizes and displays data using tables, graphs (e.g., line, circle, bar), frequency distributions, and plots (e.g., stem-and-leaf, box-and-whiskers, scatter)

  BP (ME,105-106;B1I,10;PE,31,S2E,56)

- Understands faulty arguments, common errors, and misleading presentations of data

  BC (MI,105;PE,32;S2E,56)

- Understands that the same set of data can be represented using a variety of tables, graphs, and symbols and that different modes of representation often convey different messages (e.g., variation in scale can alter a visual message)

  BD (ME,106;2E,230;PI,31;S2I,56)

- Understands the basic concept of outliers

  BD (ME,108;PE,31)

- Understands basic concepts about how samples are chosen (e.g., random samples, bias in sampling procedures, limited samples, sampling error)

  BD (ME,106;2E,229;B1I,10;PE,31;S2I,56)

Level IV (Grades 9-12)

- Selects and uses the best method of representing and describing a set of data (e.g., scatter plot, line graph, two-way table)

  BP (ME,167,169;B2E,14,54;PE,31;S3E,53)

- Understands measures of central tendency and variability (e.g., standard deviation, range, quartile deviation) and their applications to specific situations

  BD (ME,167-168;2E,230;B2E,15,54;PE,31;S3I,53)

- Understands the concept of correlation (e.g., the difference between a "true" correlation and a "believable" correlation; when two variables are correlated)

  BD (ME,167,168-169;2E,230;PE,31;S3I,53)

- Understands different methods of curve-fitting (e.g., median-fit line, regression line) and various applications (e.g., making predictions) of these methods

  BD (ME,167,168;B2E,15;PE,32;S3E,53)

- Understands how outliers may affect various representations of data (e.g., a regression line might be strongly influenced by a few aberrant points, whereas the scatter plot for the same data might suggest that the aberrant points represent mistakes)

  BD (ME,169;PE,31;S3I,53)

- Understands how the reader's bias, measurement error, and display distortion can affect the interpretation of data

  BC (ME,169;2E,230;PE,31;S3I,53)

Codes (right side of page):   BD = Benchmark, Declarative; BP = Benchmark, Procedural; BC = Benchmark, Contextual
1st letter of each code in parentheses   *2nd letter of code*   *Number*
M = NCTM: Curric. & Eval. Standards for Math   E = Explicitly stated in document   Page number of cited document
2 = Project 2061: Benchmarks for Science Literacy   I = Implied in document
B1,B2 = International Baccalaureate Math: Middle, High
P = NAEP: Mathematics Assessment Framework
S1,S2,S3 = New Standards: Elementary, Middle, High

McREL

BD (ME,167,169;B2E,15,54,56;PE,31)
- Understands sampling distributions, the central limit theorem, and confidence intervals

BD (ME,167,169;2E,230;B2E,14,15;PE,31;S3I,53)
- Understands how concepts of representativeness, randomness, and bias in sampling can affect experimental outcomes and statistical interpretations

BD (MI,105;2E,230;PI,32;S3E,53)
- Understands that making an inference about a population from a sample always involves uncertainty and the role of statistics is to estimate the size of that uncertainty

(ME,54,109,171;PE,29;S1E,62;S2E,56;S3E,53)
7. Understands and applies basic and advanced concepts of probability

Level I (Grades K-2)

BD (MI,54;2E,227;PI,32;S1E,62)
- Understands that some events are more likely to happen than others

BD (MI,54;2E,227;PI,32;S1I,62)
- Understands that some events can be predicted fairly well but others cannot because we do not always know everything that may affect an event

Level II (Grades 3-5)

BD (ME,54;2I,227;PI,32;S1I,62)
- Understands that the word "chance" refers to the likelihood of an event

BP (ME,56;2E,229;PI,32;S1E,62)
- Recognizes events that are sure to happen, events that are sure not to happen, and events that may or may not happen (e.g., in terms of "certain," "uncertain," "likely," "unlikely")

BD (MI,110;2E,227;PI,32;S1I,62)
- Understands that when predictions are based on what is known about the past, one must assume that conditions stay the same from the past event to the predicted future event

BD (MI,110;2E,227;PI,32;S1I,62)
- Understands that statistical predictions are better for describing what proportion of a group will experience something (e.g., what proportion of automobiles will be involved in accidents) rather than which individuals within the group will experience something, and how often events will occur (e.g., how many sunny days will occur over a year) rather than exactly when they will occur

BP (ME,109;PE,32;S1E,62)
- Uses basic sample spaces (i.e., the set of all possible outcomes) to describe events

---

Codes (right side of page):   BD = Benchmark, Declarative; BP = Benchmark, Procedural; BC = Benchmark, Contextual
1st letter of each code in parentheses   *2nd letter of code*   *Number*
M = NCTM: Curric. & Eval. Standards for Math   E = Explicitly stated in document   Page number of cited document
2 = Project 2061: Benchmarks for Science Literacy   I = Implied in document
B1,B2 = International Baccalaureate Math: Middle, High
P = NAEP: Mathematics Assessment Framework
S1,S2,S3 = New Standards: Elementary, Middle, High

McREL

Level III (Grades 6-8)

- BP (ME,109,110;2I,229;B1E,14;PE,32;S2E,56)

  Determines probability using mathematical/theoretical models (e.g., table or tree diagram, area model, list, counting procedures, sample space)

- BP (ME,109;2I,229;B1E,12;PE,32;S2I,56)

  Determines probability using simulations or experiments

- BD (ME,109;2I,229;PE,32;S2E,56)

  Understands how predictions are based on data and probabilities (e.g., the difference between predictions based on theoretical probability and experimental probability)

- BD (ME,109;2E,229;PI,32;S2I,56)

  Understands that the measure of certainty in a given situation depends on a number of factors (e.g., amount of data collected, what is known about the situation, how current data are)

- BD (ME,109;2E,229;PI,32;S2I,56)

  Understands the relationship between the numerical expression of a probability (e.g., fraction, percentage, odds) and the events that produce these numbers

Level IV (Grades 9-12)

- BD (ME,171,173;PI,32;S3I,53)

  Understands the concept of a random variable

- BD (ME,171;B2E,15,53;PE,32)

  Understands the concepts of independent and dependent events and how they are related to compound events and conditional probability

- BP (ME,171;2I,230;B2I,53;PE,32;S3E,53)

  Uses a variety of experimental, simulation, and theoretical methods (e.g., counting procedures, trees, formulas for permutations and combinations, Monte Carlo simulations, statistical experiments) to determine probabilities

- BD (ME,171;B2I,53;PI,32;S3I,53)

  Understands the differences among experimental, simulation, and theoretical probability techniques and the advantages and disadvantages of each

- BC (ME,171,174;B2E,15,54;PE,31;S3E,53)

  Understands the properties of the normal curve (i.e., the graph used to approximate the distribution of data for many real-world phenomena) and how the normal curve can be used to answer questions about sets of data

- BD (ME,171;B2E,15;PE,32;S3E,53)

  Understands the concept of discrete probability distribution

---

Codes (right side of page):   BD = Benchmark, Declarative; BP = Benchmark, Procedural; BC = Benchmark, Contextual
1st letter of each code in parentheses   *2nd letter of code*   *Number*
M = NCTM: Curric. & Eval. Standards for Math   E = Explicitly stated in document   Page number of cited document
2 = Project 2061: Benchmarks for Science Literacy   I = Implied in document
B1,B2 = International Baccalaureate Math: Middle, High
P = NAEP: Mathematics Assessment Framework
S1,S2,S3 = New Standards: Elementary, Middle, High

MREL

(ME,60,98,102,150,154;PE,33;S1E,62;S2E,56;S3E,52)

8.   Understands and applies basic and advanced properties of functions and algebra

Level I (Grades K-2)

BC (ME,60;2I,26;PE,34;S1E,62)
- Recognizes regularities in a variety of contexts (e.g., events, designs, shapes, sets of numbers)

BP (ME,30,61;PE,34;S1E,62)
- Extends simple patterns (e.g., of numbers, physical objects, geometric shapes)

Level II (Grades 3-5)

BC (ME,60,61;2E,27;PE,34;S1E,62)
- Recognizes a wide variety of patterns (e.g., basic linear patterns such as [2, 4, 6, 8 . . .] ; simple repeating and growing patterns) and the rules that explain them

BD (ME,61-62;PE,34;S1I,62)
- Understands that the same pattern can be represented in different ways (e.g., geometrically or numerically; the pattern of numbers [7, 14, 21, 28 . . .] is equivalent to the mathematical relationship $7 \times n$)

BD (ME,62;PE,34;S1E,62)
- Knows that a variable is a letter or symbol that stands for one or more numbers

BD (ME,102;PI,35;S1E,62)
- Understands the basic concept of an equality relationship (i.e., an equation is a number sentence that shows two quantities that are equal)

BP (ME,43;2I,217-218;PI,35;S1I,60,62)
- Solves simple open sentences involving operations on whole numbers (e.g., $\Box + 17 = 23$)

BD (MI,98,102;PE,34;S1E,61)
- Knows basic characteristics and features of the rectangular coordinate system (e.g., the horizontal axis is the X axis and the vertical axis is the Y axis)

Level III (Grades 6-8)

BD (ME,102;B1I,9;PI,35;S2I,56)
- Knows that an expression is a mathematical statement using numbers and symbols to represent relationships and real-world situations (e.g., equations and inequalities with or without variables)

BD (ME,102-103;2E,219;B1I,9;PE,34;S2E,56)
- Understands that a variable can be used in many ways (e.g., as a placeholder for a specific unknown, such as $x + 8 = 13$; as a representative of a range of values, such as $4t + 7$)

Codes (right side of page):   BD = Benchmark, Declarative; BP = Benchmark, Procedural; BC = Benchmark, Contextual
1st letter of each code in parentheses   *2nd letter of code*   *Number*
M = NCTM: Curric. & Eval. Standards for Math   E = Explicitly stated in document   Page number of cited document
2 = Project 2061: Benchmarks for Science Literacy   I = Implied in document
B1,B2 = International Baccalaureate Math: Middle, High
P = NAEP: Mathematics Assessment Framework
S1,S2,S3 = New Standards: Elementary, Middle, High

- BD (ME,102;B1I,11,13;PE,34;S2E,56)

  Understands various representations (e.g., tables, graphs, verbal descriptions, algebraic expressions, Venn diagram) of patterns and functions and the relationships among these representations

- BD (ME,98;B1E,11;PE,36;S2E,56)

  Understands the basic concept of a function (i.e., functions describe how changes in one quantity or variable result in changes in another)

- BP (ME,102,104;B1E,9;PE,35;S2E,56)

  Solves linear equations using concrete, informal, and formal methods (e.g., using properties, graphing ordered pairs, using slope-intercept form)

- BP (ME,102,104;B1E,9,13;PE,35;S2E,56)

  Solves simple inequalities and non-linear equations with rational number solutions, using concrete and informal methods

- BD (ME,98;2E,219,PI,34)

  Understands special values (e.g., minimum and maximum values, x- and y-intercepts, slope, constant ratio or difference) of patterns, relationships, and functions

- BD (MI,102,B1E,9,11;PE,35;S2I,58)

  Understands basic operations (e.g., combining like terms, expanding, substituting for unknowns) on algebraic expressions

- BP (MI,102;B1E,10;PE,34;S2I,56)

  Uses the rectangular coordinate system to model and to solve problems

- BP (MI,102;B1I,11,13;PE,35;S2I,56)

  Solves simple systems of equations graphically

- BD (MI,81,82,98,100;B1I,13;PE,34;S2E,56)

  Understands the properties of arithmetic and geometric sequences (i.e., linear and exponential patterns)

Level IV (Grades 9-12)

- BD (ME,154;B1E,11;B2E,19,58;PE,36;S3E,52)

  Understands appropriate terminology and notation used to define functions and their properties (e.g., domain, range, function composition, inverses)

- BP (ME,150;B2I,12,13;PE,34;S3E,52)

  Uses expressions, equations, inequalities, and matrices to represent situations that involve variable quantities and translates among these representations

- BD (ME,163;B2E,18,49;PE,36)

  Understands characteristics and uses of basic trigonometric functions (e.g., the sine and cosine functions as models of periodic real-world phenomena)

Codes (right side of page):   BD = Benchmark, Declarative; BP = Benchmark, Procedural; BC = Benchmark, Contextual

1st letter of each code in parentheses   *2nd letter of code*   *Number*

M = NCTM: Curric. & Eval. Standards for Math   E = Explicitly stated in document   Page number of cited document

2 = Project 2061: Benchmarks for Science Literacy   I = Implied in document

B1,B2 = International Baccalaureate Math: Middle, High

P = NAEP: Mathematics Assessment Framework

S1,S2,S3 = New Standards: Elementary, Middle, High

- BD (ME,151,180;B1E,13;B2E,12,13,47;PI,34;S3E,51,52)

  Understands properties of graphs and the relationship between a graph and its corresponding expression (e.g., maximum and minimum points)

- BD (ME,151-152;B2E,12,47;PE,36;S3I,52)

  Understands basic concepts (e.g., roots) and applications (e.g., determining cost, revenue, and profit situations) of polynomial equations

- BD (ME,154;B2E,12;PI,36;S3E,52)

  Understands the concept of a function as the correspondences between the elements of two sets (e.g., in algebra, functions are relationships between variables that represent numbers; in geometry, functions relate sets of points to their images under motions such as flips, slides, and turns; in the "real-world," functions are mathematical representations of many input-output situations)

- BP (ME,154;PE,36;S3E,52)

  Uses a variety of models (e.g., written statement, algebraic formula, table of input-output values, graph) to represent functions, patterns, and relationships

- BD (ME,155;B1E,13;B2I,12,13;PE,36;S3E,52)

  Understands the general properties and characteristics of many types of functions (e.g., direct and inverse variation, general polynomial, radical, step, exponential, logarithmic, sinusoidal)

- BD (ME,154;PE,36;S3I,52)

  Understands the effects of parameter changes on functions and their graphs

- BD (ME,156;B1E,13;B2E,13;PI,36;S3E,52)

  Understands the basic concept of inverse function and the corresponding graph

- BP (ME,178;MI,150,154;B1E,13;B2E,12,47,53;PE,35;S3E,52)

  Uses a variety of methods (e.g., with graphs, algebraic methods, and matrices) to solve systems of equations and inequalities

- BD (ME,142,176,177,181;B2E,17,46;PE,35;S3E,52)

  Understands formal notation (e.g., sigma notation, factorial representation) and various applications (e.g., compound interest) of sequences and series

- BP (ME,152-153;B2E,12,47,51;PE,36)

  Uses a variety of methods (e.g., approximate solutions, such as bisection, sign changes, and successive approximation) to solve complex equations (e.g., polynomial equations with real roots)

Codes (right side of page):   BD = Benchmark, Declarative; BP = Benchmark, Procedural; BC = Benchmark, Contextual

1st letter of each code in parentheses   *2nd letter of code*   *Number*

M = NCTM: Curric. & Eval. Standards for Math   E = Explicitly stated in document   Page number of cited document

2 = Project 2061: Benchmarks for Science Literacy   I = Implied in document

B1,B2 = International Baccalaureate Math: Middle, High

P = NAEP: Mathematics Assessment Framework

S1,S2,S3 = New Standards: Elementary, Middle, High

9.   Understands the general nature and uses of mathematics

(2E,23)

Level I (Grades K-2)

BD (2E,27,32,36)

- Not appropriate for this level

Level II (Grades 3-5)

BD (2E,36)

- Understands that numbers and the operations performed on them can be used to describe things in the real world and predict what might occur

BD (2E,27)

- Understands that mathematical ideas and concepts can be represented concretely, graphically, and symbolically

Level III (Grades 6-8)

BD (2E,32)

- Understands that mathematics has been helpful in practical ways for many centuries

BD (2E,37)

- Understands that mathematicians often represent real things using abstract ideas like numbers or lines; they then work with these abstractions to learn about the things they represent

Level IV (Grades 9-12)

BD (2E,29)

- Understands that mathematics is the study of any pattern or relationship, but natural science is the study of those patterns that are relevant to the observable world

BD (2E,29)

- Understands that mathematics began long ago to help solve practical problems; however, it soon focused on abstractions drawn from the world and then on abstract relationships among those abstractions

BD (2E,29)

- Understands that in mathematics, as in other sciences, simplicity is one of the highest values; some mathematicians try to identify the smallest set of rules from which many other propositions can be logically derived

---

Codes (right side of page):   BD = Benchmark, Declarative; BP = Benchmark, Procedural; BC = Benchmark, Contextual
1st letter of each code in parentheses   *2nd letter of code*   *Number*
M = NCTM: Curric. & Eval. Standards for Math   E = Explicitly stated in document   Page number of cited document
2 = Project 2061: Benchmarks for Science Literacy   I = Implied in document
B1,B2 = International Baccalaureate Math: Middle, High
P = NAEP: Mathematics Assessment Framework
S1,S2,S3 = New Standards: Elementary, Middle, High

- Understands that theories in mathematics are greatly influenced by practical issues; real-world problems sometimes result in new mathematical theories and pure mathematical theories sometimes have highly practical applications
  BD (2E,29)

- Understands that new mathematics continues to be invented even today, along with new connections between various components of mathematics
  BD (2E,29)

- Understands that science and mathematics operate under common principles: belief in order, ideals of honesty and openness, the importance of review by colleagues, and the importance of imagination
  BD (2E,33)

- Understands that mathematics provides a precise system to describe objects, events, and relationships and to construct logical arguments
  BD (2E,33)

- Understands that the development of computers has opened many new doors to mathematics just as other advances in technology can open up new areas to mathematics
  BD (2E,33)

- Understands that mathematics often stimulates innovations in science and technology
  BD (2E,33)

- Understands that mathematicians commonly operate by choosing an interesting set of rules and then playing according to those rules; the only limit to those rules is that they should not contradict each other
  BD (2E,38)

Codes (right side of page):   BD = Benchmark, Declarative; BP = Benchmark, Procedural; BC = Benchmark, Contextual
1st letter of each code in parentheses   *2nd letter of code*   *Number*
M = NCTM: Curric. & Eval. Standards for Math   E = Explicitly stated in document   Page number of cited document
2 = Project 2061: Benchmarks for Science Literacy   I = Implied in document
B1,B2 = International Baccalaureate Math: Middle, High
P = NAEP: Mathematics Assessment Framework
S1,S2,S3 = New Standards: Elementary, Middle, High

SCIENCE

8. Science

The following process was used to identify standards and benchmarks for science:

Identification of Significant Reports
Three reports were identified as significant for representing current thinking on content standards in science: the *National Science Education Standards* (National Research Council, 1994), Project 2061's *Benchmarks for Science Literacy* (1993), and the National Science Teachers Association's (NSTA) *Scope, Sequence, and Coordination of Secondary School Science: The Content Core* (Pearsall, 1993). A total of twelve additional documents were found useful for citation support of the benchmarks. These documents include California Department of Education's *Science Framework for California Public Schools* (1991) and three reports from the National Assessment of Educational Progress, *Science Objectives for 1990, Exercise Specifications for 1994 NAEP,* and *Science Framework for the 1996 National Assessment of Educational Progress.* The *New Standards Project* has published three documents that report science standards and benchmarks at elementary, middle, and high school levels. Those documents are *Performance Standards: English Language Arts, Mathematics, Science, Applied Learning, Volume 1, Elementary School* (1997a); *Performance Standards: English Language Arts, Mathematics, Science, Applied Learning, Volume 2, Middle School* (1997b); and *Performance Standards: English Language Arts, Mathematics, Science, Applied Learning, Volume 3, High School* (1997c). Finally, the International Baccalaureate Organization has published curriculum material that identifies significant content in science. Those documents are International Baccalaureate *Middle Years Programme: Sciences* (1995f), *Biology* (1996b), *Chemistry* (1996c), *Environmental Systems* (1996f), and *Physics* (1996i).

Selection of the Reference Document
The National Research Council's *National Science Education Standards* was selected as the reference document. The effort was supported by the National Science Foundation, the U.S. Department of Education, the National Aeronautics and Space Administration, among others. It represents the efforts of teachers, scientists, and science educators across the country.

Identification of Standards and Benchmarks
The content standards from NRC which "outline what students should know, understand, and be able to do in natural science" (p. 103), are grouped into categories at three grade levels (K-4, 5-8, and 9-12). The number of standards varies by grade level within each of seven categories:

> Science as inquiry
> Physical science
> Life science
> Earth and space science
> Science and technology
> Science in personal and social perspectives
> History and nature of science

A final area, "unifying concepts and processes," is not articulated for grade levels, but is intended for development across K-12 science education.

Science information in NRC's document is articulated for K-12 at the category level, but not at the standard level. That is, each standard and its associated content appears only once, and at one level (K-4, 5-8, or 9-12). For example, in the physical sciences under the heading "Earth and space science," a standard with the topic "Objects in the sky" appears with two related standards at grades K-4 only; at grades 5-8, three standards are under that category, and a closely related topic is "Earth in the solar system." At grades 9-12, four standards cover the area, and the one nearest in content to "Earth in the solar system" or "Objects in the sky" is the "Origin and evolution of the universe." Thus, the 66 standards are closely related within six categories, but are not articulated across the grade ranges by standard. Since our model calls for the articulation of standards across grade levels wherever possible, some reorganization of content was necessary. Although in part the benchmarks were constructed into standards from "the ground up," there was strong guidance provided by the structure of standards available from Project 2061's *Benchmarks for Science Literacy*.

At the benchmark level, Project 2061's *Benchmarks* proved very useful for distinguishing content at the grade ranges selected for this study: K-2, 3-5, 6-8, and 9-12. Material from the NRC reference document was added to or revised in four cases: 1) when minor modification of a benchmark statement allowed for additional citation support, 2) when the original statement carried more than one basic idea and was divided into components, 3) when stylistic changes helped the sense of the statement, and 4) when benchmark statements not in the science standards document were added because the information was found to appear consistently in the other major documents identified for science.

Additionally, there were a few instances of content duplication across standards. In each case that the subject material appeared to be redundant across standards, it was also clear that the same benchmarks within a standard served the purpose of preparing students for more complex, related ideas at later benchmark levels. For this reason, the duplicates were not deleted as would otherwise be done, but cross-referenced in the citation log. (For more detail, see Section 6, How the Subject-Area Sections are Structured.)

Finally, it should be noted that with the addition of a separate section on technology in this report, content material directly related to that subject has been moved from the science standards. Such topics as the interaction of technology with science and with society will now be found in the technology section.

Integration of Information from Other Documents

The documents used to integrate information were NSTA's *Content Core* and the *California Science Framework*. Each was referenced to provide science teachers with ready access to sources via page number citations keyed to the benchmarks. In addition, *Content Core* and Project 2061's *Benchmarks* provided a means for evaluating whether additional benchmarks should be added to the reference document. If information found at the appropriate level in either document could not be found in the NRC document then it was identified for possible inclusion as an additional benchmark. A compiled list of this information was then compared against information in the *California Science Framework* and the three documents from NAEP. If the information was found to be present in at least two documents (*Content Core* and/or *Benchmarks,* and one of the four documents just cited), the information was synthesized as a new benchmark. Evidence for this process can be found by an examination of the "citation log" associated with each benchmark: if the benchmark does not show a reference to the NRC document, then it was added to the document using the process just described.

Additional documents were cited to provide users with links from the benchmarks to supporting materials. Such documents were the *Performance Standards* series from New Standards and the series of science curriculum materials from the International Baccalaureate Organization.

Summary of Standards for Science

Earth and Space
1. Understands basic features of the Earth
2. Understands basic Earth processes
3. Understands essential ideas about the composition and structure of the universe and the Earth's place in it

Life Sciences
4. Knows about the diversity and unity that characterize life
5. Understands the genetic basis for the transfer of biological characteristics from one generation to the next
6. Knows the general structure and functions of cells in organisms
7. Understands how species depend on one another and on the environment for survival
8. Understands the cycling of matter and flow of energy through the living environment
9. Understands the basic concepts of the evolution of species

Physical Sciences
10. Understands basic concepts about the structure and properties of matter
11. Understands energy types, sources, and conversions, and their relationship to heat and temperature
12. Understands motion and the principles that explain it
13. Knows the kinds of forces that exist between objects and within atoms

Nature of Science
14. Understands the nature of scientific knowledge
15. Understands the nature of scientific inquiry
16. Understands the scientific enterprise

(2E,66)

1.   Understands basic features of the Earth

Level I (Grades K-2)

BD (SE,134;CE,93,99,106;N1I,133;PI,57,58,60)
- Knows that Earth materials consist of solid rocks, soils, liquid water, and the gases of the atmosphere

BD (2E,67;N1I,133;PI,59)
- Knows that water can be a liquid or a solid and can be made to change from one form to the other, but the amount of water stays the same

BD (SI,134;2E,67;CE,111;FE,53;N1I,133;PE,61)
- Knows that short-term weather conditions (e.g., temperature, rain, snow) can change daily, and weather patterns change over the seasons

Level II (Grades 3-5)

BD (2E,68;CE,99;FI,54;IMI,29;N1I,133;PE,59;DI,10.2.4)
- Knows that water can change from one state to another (solid, liquid, gas) through various processes (e.g., freezing, condensation, precipitation, evaporation)

BD (CE,101;PE,59)
- Knows the major differences between fresh and ocean waters

BD (2E,68;CE,99;PI,59)
- Knows that clouds and fog are made of tiny droplets of water

BD (2E,68;CE,106;FI,53)
- Knows that air is a substance that surrounds us, takes up space, and moves around us as wind

BD (2E,68;CI,79;FE,55;N1I,133;PE,63)
- Knows that night and day are caused by the Earth's rotation on its axis

BD (SE,134;CI,84;N1E,133;PE,62)
- Knows that the Sun provides the light and heat necessary to maintain the temperature of the Earth

Level III (Grades 6-8)

BD (2E,69;CE,86;PE,74;TE,95)
- Knows that the Earth is the only body in our solar system that appears able to support life

BD (SE,159;2E,68-69;CE,90;IME,29;PE,65,68,70;TI,79-80;N2I,93)
- Knows that the Earth is comprised of layers including a core, mantle, lithosphere, hydrosphere, and atmosphere

---

Codes (right side of page):   BD = Benchmark, Declarative; BP = Benchmark, Procedural; BC = Benchmark, Contextual
1st letter(s) of each code in parentheses   *2nd letter of code*   *Number*
S = NRC: National Science Education Standards   E = Explicitly stated in document   Page number of cited document
2 = Project 2061: Benchmarks for Science Literacy   I = Implied in document   *or, for duplicates:*
C = CDE: Science Framework for CA Public Schools   Standard number & level of duplicate
F = NAEP: 1996 Science Framework
IB,IC,IE,IM,IP: Int'l Bacc.: Biology, Chemistry,   P = NAEP: Science Assess./Exercise Specifications
    Environ. Systems, Middle Yrs Science, Physics   T = Pearsall: NSTA: The Content Core
N1,N2,N3: New Standards: Elementary, Middle, High   D = Duplicated in another standard
O = NAEP: 1990 Science Objectives

MCREL

BD (SE,160;CE,108;IEE,23;IME,29,30;PE,70-71;TE,80)

- Knows the composition and structure of the Earth's atmosphere (e.g., temperature and pressure in different layers of the atmosphere, circulation of air masses)

BD (SE,160;CI,108;PI,72;TI,80)

- Knows ways in which clouds affect weather and climate (e.g., precipitation, reflection of light from the Sun, retention of heat energy emitted from the Earth's surface)

BD (SE,161;2E,69;IME,126;N2I,93;PE,76;TE,89)

- Knows how the tilt of the Earth's axis and the Earth's revolution around the Sun affect seasons and weather patterns (i.e., heat falls more intensely on one part or another of the Earth's surface during its revolution around the Sun)

BD (SE,160;2E,69;FI,53,55;IEE,27;N2I,93;PE,68,69,73)

- Knows factors that can impact the Earth's climate (e.g., changes in the composition of the atmosphere; changes in ocean temperature; geological shifts such as meteor impacts, the advance or retreat of glaciers, or a series of volcanic eruptions)

BD (SE,160;2E,69;CE,99;FE,55;IBE,125;IME,30;N2I,93;PI,68;TE,82)

- Knows the processes involved in the water cycle (e.g., evaporation, condensation, precipitation, surface run-off, percolation) and their effects on climatic patterns

BD (SI,160;CE,99;FE,54;IBE,34;N2I,93;PE,70)

- Knows the properties that make water an essential component of the Earth system (e.g., its ability to act as a solvent, its ability to remain a liquid at most Earth temperatures)

BD (SE,161;CI,108-109;FI,56,61;IEI,23;N2I,93;PE,71;TE,84;DI,11.3.3)

- Knows that the Sun is the principle energy source for phenomena on the Earth's surface (e.g., winds, ocean currents, the water cycle, plant growth)

Level IV (Grades 9-12)

BD (SE,189;N3I,83;PE,80,85-86)

- Knows the major external and internal sources of energy on Earth (e.g., the Sun is the major external source of energy; the decay of radioactive isotopes and gravitational energy from the Earth's original formation are primary sources of internal energy)

BD (SI,189;2E,70;FI,54;IEI,24;IMI,125;N3I,83;PE,84)

- Knows that weather and climate involve the transfer of energy in and out of the atmosphere

BD (SE,189;2E,70;FI,54;IEE,23,24;IMI,125;N3I,83;PI,83-85;TI,86)

- Knows how winds and ocean currents are produced on the Earth's surface (e.g., effects of unequal heating of the Earth's land masses, oceans, and air by the Sun; effects of gravitational forces acting on layers of different temperatures and densities in the oceans and air; effects of the rotation of the Earth)

Codes (right side of page):   BD = Benchmark, Declarative; BP = Benchmark, Procedural; BC = Benchmark, Contextual

1st letter(s) of each code in parentheses   *2nd letter of code*   *Number*

S = NRC: National Science Education Standards   E = Explicitly stated in document   Page number of cited document

2 = Project 2061: Benchmarks for Science Literacy   I = Implied in document   *or, for duplicates:*

C = CDE: Science Framework for CA Public Schools   Standard number & level of duplicate

F = NAEP: 1996 Science Framework

IB,IC,IE,IM,IP: Int'l Bacc.: Biology, Chemistry,   P = NAEP: Science Assess./Exercise Specifications

    Environ. Systems, Middle Yrs Science, Physics   T = Pearsall: NSTA: The Content Core

N1,N2,N3: New Standards: Elementary, Middle, High   D = Duplicated in another standard

O = NAEP: 1990 Science Objectives

- Knows how life is adapted to conditions on the Earth (e.g., force of gravity that enables the planet to retain an adequate atmosphere, intensity of radiation from the Sun that allows water to cycle between liquid and vapor)

BD (2E,70;TI,95)

(2E,71)

2. Understands basic Earth processes

Level I (Grades K-2)

BD (2E,72;CI,93;PI,57-58)

- Knows that rocks come in many different shapes and sizes (e.g., boulders, pebbles, sand)

Level II (Grades 3-5)

BD (2E,72;CI,93,94;FI,55)

- Knows that smaller rocks come from the breakage and weathering of bedrock and larger rocks

BD (2E,72;CI,93-94;FI,55;N1I,133;PI,57-58)

- Knows that rock is composed of different combinations of minerals

BD (2E,72;N1I,133;PE,58)

- Knows the composition and properties of soils (e.g., components of soil such as weathered rock, living organisms, products of plants and animals; properties of soil such as color, texture, capacity to retain water, ability to support plant growth)

BD (SE,134;2E,72;FI,55;N1I,133;PE,57)

- Knows how features on the Earth's surface are constantly changed by a combination of slow and rapid processes (e.g., weathering, erosion, and deposition of sediment caused by waves, wind, water, and ice; sudden changes in the landscape caused by landslides, volcanic eruptions, and earthquakes)

BD (SE,134;CE,95;N1I,132;PI,64)

- Knows that fossils provide evidence about the plants and animals that lived long ago and the nature of the environment at that time

Level III (Grades 6-8)

BD (SI,160;2E,73;IMI,31;PE,66-67;TE,85)

- Knows components of soil and other factors that influence soil texture, fertility, and resistance to erosion (e.g., plant roots and debris, bacteria, fungi, worms, rodents)

Codes (right side of page):	BD = Benchmark, Declarative; BP = Benchmark, Procedural; BC = Benchmark, Contextual

1st letter(s) of each code in parentheses	2nd letter of code	Number
S = NRC: National Science Education Standards	E = Explicitly stated in document	Page number of cited document
2 = Project 2061: Benchmarks for Science Literacy	I = Implied in document	or, for duplicates:
C = CDE: Science Framework for CA Public Schools		Standard number & level of duplicate
F = NAEP: 1996 Science Framework		
IB,IC,IE,IM,IP: Int'l Bacc.: Biology, Chemistry,	P = NAEP: Science Assess./Exercise Specifications	
Environ. Systems, Middle Yrs Science, Physics	T = Pearsall: NSTA: The Content Core	
N1,N2,N3: New Standards: Elementary, Middle, High	D = Duplicated in another standard	
O = NAEP: 1990 Science Objectives		

- BD (2I,73;CE,94;PE,66;TE,79)
  Knows that sedimentary, igneous, and metamorphic rocks contain evidence of the minerals, temperatures, and forces that created them

- BD (SE,160;2E,73;N2I,93;PI,66;TE,81)
  Knows processes involved in the rock cycle (e.g., old rocks at the surface gradually weather and form sediments that are buried, then compacted, heated, and often recrystallized into new rock; this new rock is eventually brought to the surface by the forces that drive plate motions, and the rock cycle continues)

- BD (SE,160;CE,91;IEE,28;IMI,29;N2I,93;TI,80)
  Knows that the Earth's crust is divided into plates that move at extremely slow rates in response to movements in the mantle

- BD (SE,160;2I,73;CE,91;IEE,28;N2I,93;PI,65-66;TI,86-87)
  Knows how land forms are created through a combination of constructive and destructive forces (e.g., constructive forces such as crustal deformation, volcanic eruptions, and deposition of sediment; destructive forces such as weathering and erosion)

- BD (2E,73,246;FI,55;N2I,93;PE,66,77;TE,80)
  Knows how successive layers of sedimentary rock and the fossils contained within them can be used to confirm the age, history, and changing life forms of the Earth, and how this evidence is affected by the folding, breaking, and uplifting of layers

- BD (SE,160;CE,96;N2I,93;PE,77;TE,80)
  Knows that fossils provide important evidence of how life and environmental conditions have changed on the Earth over time (e.g., changes in atmospheric composition, movement of lithospheric plates, impact of an asteroid or comet)

Level IV (Grades 9-12)

- BD (SE,189;CI,97;FE,55;IBE,126;IMI,30,60;N3I,83;PI,79,83;DI,8.4.1)
  Knows that elements exist in fixed amounts and move through the solid Earth, oceans, atmosphere, and living things as part of geochemical cycles (e.g., carbon cycle, nitrogen cycle)

- BD (2E,74;N3I,83;PI,79;TI,94)
  Knows that throughout the rock cycle (e.g., formation, weathering, sedimentation, reformation), the total amount of material stays the same as its form changes

- BD (SE,189;2E,74,248;FE,56;IEE,28;IME,29;N3I,83;PE,80-81;TE,93-94)
  Understands the concept of plate tectonics (e.g., the outward transfer of the Earth's internal heat and the action of gravitational forces on regions of different density drive convection circulation in the mantle; these convection currents propel the Earth's crustal plates, which

---

Codes (right side of page):   BD = Benchmark, Declarative; BP = Benchmark, Procedural; BC = Benchmark, Contextual

1st letter(s) of each code in parentheses   *2nd letter of code*   *Number*

S = NRC: National Science Education Standards   E = Explicitly stated in document   Page number of cited document

2 = Project 2061: Benchmarks for Science Literacy   I = Implied in document   *or, for duplicates:*

C = CDE: Science Framework for CA Public Schools   Standard number & level of duplicate

F = NAEP: 1996 Science Framework

IB,IC,IE,IM,IP: Int'l Bacc.: Biology, Chemistry,   P = NAEP: Science Assess./Exercise Specifications

   Environ. Systems, Middle Yrs Science, Physics   T = Pearsall: NSTA: The Content Core

N1,N2,N3: New Standards: Elementary, Middle, High   D = Duplicated in another standard

O = NAEP: 1990 Science Objectives

move very slowly, pressing against one another in some places and pulling apart in other places)

- BD(SI,189-190;2E,74;FE,56;PE,80-81;TE,86-87,93-94)
  Knows effects of the movement of crustal plates (e.g., earthquakes occur along the boundaries between colliding plates; sea floor spreading occurs where plates are moving apart; mountain building occurs where plates are moving together; volcanic eruptions release pressure created by molten rock beneath the Earth's surface)

- BD (SE,189;CE,96;IBI,107-108;IPI,42-43;N3I,83;PE,89;TE,87,92-93;DI,10.4.8)
  Knows methods used to estimate geologic time (e.g., observing rock sequences and using fossils to correlate the sequences at various locations; using the known decay rates of radioactive isotopes present in rock to measure the time since the rock was formed)

- BD (SE,190;2I,74;CE,109;N3I,83;PI,89)
  Knows how the evolution of life on Earth has changed the composition of the Earth's atmosphere through time (e.g., one-celled forms of life emerged more than 3.5 billion years ago; evolution of photosynthesizing organisms produced most of the oxygen in the modern atmosphere)

(2E,61)
3. Understands essential ideas about the composition and structure of the universe and the Earth's place in it

Level I (Grades K-2)

- BD (SI,134;2E,62;CI,84)
  Knows that the stars are innumerable, unevenly dispersed, and of unequal brightness

- BD (SE,134;2E,62;CE,79;FI,52,55;N1E,133;PI,62,63)
  Knows basic patterns of the Sun and Moon (e.g., the Sun appears every day, and the Moon appears sometimes at night and sometimes during the day; the Sun and Moon appear to move from east to west across the sky; the Moon appears to change shape over the course of a month)

Level II (Grades 3-5)

- BD (2E,63;CE,80;FI,55;N1I,133;PI,62)
  Knows that the Earth is one of several planets that orbit the Sun, and the Moon orbits around the Earth

---

Codes (right side of page):	BD = Benchmark, Declarative; BP = Benchmark, Procedural; BC = Benchmark, Contextual
1st letter(s) of each code in parentheses	*2nd letter of code* *Number*
S = NRC: National Science Education Standards	E = Explicitly stated in document Page number of cited document
2 = Project 2061: Benchmarks for Science Literacy	I = Implied in document *or, for duplicates:*
C = CDE: Science Framework for CA Public Schools	Standard number & level of duplicate
F = NAEP: 1996 Science Framework	

IB,IC,IE,IM,IP: Int'l Bacc.: Biology, Chemistry,   P = NAEP: Science Assess./Exercise Specifications
    Environ. Systems, Middle Yrs Science, Physics   T = Pearsall: NSTA: The Content Core
N1,N2,N3: New Standards: Elementary, Middle, High   D = Duplicated in another standard
O = NAEP: 1990 Science Objectives

MREL

- BD (SI,134;2E,63;CI,80;N1I,133)
  Knows that the patterns of stars in the sky stay the same, although they appear to slowly move from east to west across the sky nightly, and different stars can be seen in different seasons

- BD (SI,134;2E,63;CE;80;N1I,133)
  Knows that planets look like stars, but over time they appear to wander among the constellations

- BD (2E,63;CI,84;PE,62-63)
  Knows that telescopes magnify distant objects in the sky (e.g., the Moon, planets) and dramatically increase the number of stars we can see

- BD (2E,63;CE,80)
  Knows that astronomical objects in space are massive in size and are separated from one another by vast distances (e.g., many stars are more massive than our Sun but so distant they look like points of light)

Level III (Grades 6-8)

- BD (SI,160;2E,64;CI,81;IMI,29;PI,75)
  Knows characteristics of our Sun and its position in the universe (e.g., the Sun is a medium-sized star; it is the closest star to Earth; it is the central and largest body in the Solar System; it is located at the edge of a disk-shaped galaxy)

- BD (SI,160;2E,64;CE,81-82;IME,29;IPI,78;N2E,93;PE,73-74;TE,90-91)
  Knows characteristics and movement patterns of the nine planets in our Solar System (e.g., planets differ in size, composition, and surface features; planets move around the Sun in elliptical orbits; some planets have moons, rings of particles, and other satellites orbiting them)

- BD (2E,68;PI,74;TI,95)
  Knows that the planet Earth and our Solar System appear to be somewhat unique, although similar systems might yet be discovered in the universe

- BD (SE,161;2E,95;CE,55;IPE,79;N2I,93;PI,76)
  Knows that gravitational force keeps planets in orbit around the Sun and moons in orbit around the planets

- BD (SI,160;CE,82;2E,64;IMI,29;N2I,93;PE,74;TE,90)
  Knows characteristics and movement patterns of asteroids, comets, and meteors

- BD (SE,160;2I,69;CE,81;FI,52;N2E,93;PI,73-74;TE,83,84)
  Knows how the regular and predictable motions of the Sun and Moon explain phenomena on Earth (e.g., the day, the year, phases of the Moon, eclipses, tides, shadows)

Codes (right side of page):   BD = Benchmark, Declarative; BP = Benchmark, Procedural; BC = Benchmark, Contextual
1st letter(s) of each code in parentheses   *2nd letter of code*   *Number*
S = NRC: National Science Education Standards   E = Explicitly stated in document   Page number of cited document
2 = Project 2061: Benchmarks for Science Literacy   I = Implied in document   *or, for duplicates:*
C = CDE: Science Framework for CA Public Schools   Standard number & level of duplicate
F = NAEP: 1996 Science Framework
IB,IC,IE,IM,IP: Int'l Bacc.: Biology, Chemistry,   P = NAEP: Science Assess./Exercise Specifications
    Environ. Systems, Middle Yrs Science, Physics   T = Pearsall: NSTA: The Content Core
N1,N2,N3: New Standards: Elementary, Middle, High   D = Duplicated in another standard
O = NAEP: 1990 Science Objectives

- BD (2E,64;CE,81-82;PE,75)

  Knows that many billions of galaxies exist in the universe (each containing many billions of stars), and that incomprehensible distances separate these galaxies and stars from one another and from the Earth

Level IV (Grades 9-12)

- BD (SE,190;2E,65;CE,85;IPE,86-87;N3I,83;PE,87;TE,98)

  Knows that although the origin of the universe remains one of the greatest questions in science, current scientific evidence supports the "big bang" theory, which states that between 10 and 20 billion years ago, the entire contents of the universe expanded explosively into existence from a single, hot, dense chaotic mass; our solar system formed from a nebular cloud of dust and gas about 4.6 billion years ago

- BD (SI,190;2E,65;CE,86;IPE,88;N3E,83;PE,86-87;TE,97)

  Knows the ongoing processes involved in star formation and destruction (e.g., stars condense by gravity out of clouds of molecules of the lightest elements; nuclear fusion of light elements into heavier ones occurs in the stars' extremely hot, dense cores, releasing great amounts of energy; some stars eventually explode, producing clouds of material from which new stars and planets condense)

- BD (2E,65;CE,82-83;IPE,85;PE,87;TE,97)

  Knows common characteristics of stars in the universe (e.g., types of stars include red and blue giants, white dwarfs, neutron stars, and black holes; stars differ in size, temperature, and age, but they all appear to be made up of the same elements and to behave according to the same principles; most stars exist in systems of two or more stars orbiting around a common point)

- BD (2E,65;CE,89;IPI,82,86;PE,88)

  Knows ways in which technology has increased our understanding of the universe (e.g., visual, radio, and x-ray telescopes collect information about the universe from electromagnetic waves; computers interpret vast amounts of data from space; space probes gather information from distant parts of the Solar System; accelerators allow us to simulate conditions in the stars and in the early history of the universe)

- BD (2E,92;CE,86-87;IPE,86-87;PE,87;TE,97-98;DI,12.4.3)

  Knows that evidence suggests that our universe is expanding (e.g., the Doppler shift of light from distant galaxies reaching telescopes on Earth suggests that galaxies are moving away from the Earth; the relationship of the red shift to the "big bang" theory of the origin of the universe)

Codes (right side of page):	BD = Benchmark, Declarative; BP = Benchmark, Procedural; BC = Benchmark, Contextual

1st letter(s) of each code in parentheses   *2nd letter of code*   *Number*

S = NRC: National Science Education Standards   E = Explicitly stated in document   Page number of cited document

2 = Project 2061: Benchmarks for Science Literacy   I = Implied in document   *or, for duplicates:*

C = CDE: Science Framework for CA Public Schools   Standard number & level of duplicate

F = NAEP: 1996 Science Framework

IB,IC,IE,IM,IP: Int'l Bacc.: Biology, Chemistry,   P = NAEP: Science Assess./Exercise Specifications

     Environ. Systems, Middle Yrs Science, Physics   T = Pearsall: NSTA: The Content Core

N1,N2,N3: New Standards: Elementary, Middle, High   D = Duplicated in another standard

O = NAEP: 1990 Science Objectives

(2E,101)

4. Knows about the diversity and unity that characterize life

Level I (Grades K-2)

BD (2E,102,123;CE,118;N1I,132;PI,115)
- Knows that plants and animals have features that help them live in different environments

Level II (Grades 3-5)

BD (2E,103;CI,122;PI,115)
- Knows different ways in which living things can be grouped (e.g., plants/animals; pets/nonpets; edible plants/nonedible plants) and purposes of different groupings

BD (SE,129;CE,119;FE,67;IMI,42;N1I,132;PE,118)
- Knows that plants and animals progress through life cycles of birth, growth and development, reproduction, and death; the details of these life cycles are different for different organisms

Level III (Grades 6-8)

BD (SI,157-158;2E,104;CE,122-123;IME,36;N2I,92;PE,121;TE,47)
- Knows ways in which living things can be classified (e.g., taxonomic groups of plants, animals, and fungi; groups based on the details of organisms' internal and external features; groups based on functions served within an ecosystem such as producers, consumers, and decomposers)

BD (SI,158;2E,104;CE,119-120;FE,68;IMI,38-39;N2I,92;TI,47)
- Knows that animals and plants have a great variety of body plans and internal structures that serve specific functions for survival (e.g., digestive structures in vertebrates, invertebrates, unicellular organisms, and plants)

BD (2E,104;CE,137;IBE,56,110;IMI,43,80;N2I,92)
- Knows that for sexually reproducing organisms, a species comprises all organisms that can mate with one another to produce fertile offspring

BD (SE,158;CE,118;IBE,108;N2I,92)
- Knows evidence that supports the idea that there is unity among organisms despite the fact that some species look very different (e.g., similarity of internal structures in different organisms, similarity of chemical processes in different organisms, evidence of common ancestry)

Codes (right side of page):   BD = Benchmark, Declarative; BP = Benchmark, Procedural; BC = Benchmark, Contextual

1st letter(s) of each code in parentheses   *2nd letter of code*   *Number*

S = NRC: National Science Education Standards   E = Explicitly stated in document   Page number of cited document

2 = Project 2061: Benchmarks for Science Literacy   I = Implied in document   *or, for duplicates:*

C = CDE: Science Framework for CA Public Schools   Standard number & level of duplicate

F = NAEP: 1996 Science Framework

IB,IC,IE,IM,IP: Int'l Bacc.: Biology, Chemistry,   P = NAEP: Science Assess./Exercise Specifications

    Environ. Systems, Middle Yrs Science, Physics   T = Pearsall: NSTA: The Content Core

N1,N2,N3: New Standards: Elementary, Middle, High   D = Duplicated in another standard

O = NAEP: 1990 Science Objectives

Level IV (Grades 9-12)

BD (SE,185;2E,105;CE,123;IBE,81-82;IMI,43;N3I,82)
- Knows how organisms are classified into a hierarchy of groups and subgroups based on similarities that reflect their evolutionary relationships (e.g., shared derived characteristics inherited from a common ancestor; degree of kinship estimated from the similarity of DNA sequences)

BD (2E,105;CI,123;N3I,82;TI,53)
- Knows how variation of organisms within a species increases the chance of survival of the species, and how the great diversity of species on Earth increases the chance of survival of life in the event of major global changes

(2E,106)
5. Understands the genetic basis for the transfer of biological characteristics from one generation to the next

Level I (Grades K-2)

BD (SE,129;2E,107;CE,128;FE,67;PI,115-116)
- Knows that plants and animals closely resemble their parents

BD (2E,107;CI,128;FE,67;PE,115)
- Knows that differences exist among individuals of the same kind of plant or animal

Level II (Grades 3-5)

BD (SE,129;2E,107;CI,128;N1I,132)
- Knows that many characteristics of an organism are inherited from the parents of the organism (e.g., eye color in human beings, fruit or flower color in plants), and other characteristics result from an individual's interactions with the environment (e.g., people's table manners, ability to ride a bicycle)

Level III (Grades 6-8)

BD (SE,157;CE,118;IMI,38;N2I,92;TE,48)
- Knows that reproduction is a characteristic of all living things and is essential to the continuation of a species

BD (SE,157;2E,108;CE,120,128;IBE,57;IME,38-40,77-78;96-97;N2E,92;PI,124;TE,48)
- Understands asexual and sexual reproduction (e.g., in asexual reproduction, all the genes come from a single parent; in sexual reproduction, an egg and sperm unite and half of the genes come from each parent, so the offspring is never identical to either of its parents;

Codes (right side of page): BD = Benchmark, Declarative; BP = Benchmark, Procedural; BC = Benchmark, Contextual
1st letter(s) of each code in parentheses | 2nd letter of code | Number
S = NRC: National Science Education Standards | E = Explicitly stated in document | Page number of cited document
2 = Project 2061: Benchmarks for Science Literacy | I = Implied in document | or, for duplicates:
C = CDE: Science Framework for CA Public Schools | | Standard number & level of duplicate
F = NAEP: 1996 Science Framework
IB,IC,IE,IM,IP: Int'l Bacc.: Biology, Chemistry, | P = NAEP: Science Assess./Exercise Specifications
   Environ. Systems, Middle Yrs Science, Physics | T = Pearsall: NSTA: The Content Core
N1,N2,N3: New Standards: Elementary, Middle, High | D = Duplicated in another standard
O = NAEP: 1990 Science Objectives

sexual reproduction allows for greater genetic diversity; asexual reproduction limits the spread of disadvantageous characteristics through a species)

BD (SE,157;CE,128;N2I,92)
- Knows that the characteristics of an organism can be described in terms of a combination of traits; some traits are inherited and others result from interactions with the environment

BD (SE,157;2I,108;CE,129;IBE,41;IME,78;N2I,92;PE,122)
- Knows that hereditary information is contained in genes (located in the chromosomes of each cell), each of which carries a single unit of information; an inherited trait of an individual can be determined by either one or many genes, and a single gene can influence more than one trait

BD (SI,157;2I,108;CE,129;IBI,41,74;N2I,92;IMI,78;PE,122)
- Knows how dominant and recessive traits contribute to genetic variation within a species

Level IV (Grades 9-12)

BD (SE,185;2I,108;CE,129;FI,69;IBE,36-37,65;IMI,78;N3E,82;TI,55)
- Knows the chemical and structural properties of DNA and its role in specifying the characteristics of an organism (e.g., DNA is a large polymer formed from subunits of four kinds [A, G, C, and T]; genetic information is encoded in genes as a string of these subunits, and replicated by a templating mechanism; each DNA molecule in a cell forms a single chromosome)

BD (SE,185;CE,129;FE,70;IBI,40,75;IMI,78;N3I,82;PE,128-129;TE,55)
- Knows ways in which genes (segments of DNA molecules) may be altered and combined to create genetic variation within a species (e.g., recombination of genetic material; mutations; errors in copying genetic material during cell division)

BD (SE,185;2E,125;CI,135;IBI,40,74;N3I,82;PI,129-130)
- Knows that new heritable characteristics can only result from new combinations of existing genes or from mutations of genes in an organism's sex cells; other changes in an organism cannot be passed on

BD (SE,185;2E,108;CE,129;FI,70;PE,130;TI,55)
- Knows that mutations and new gene combinations may have positive, negative, or no effects on the organism

BD (SE,185;FI,69;IBE,42;IMI,78-79;TI,52)
- Knows features of human genetics (e.g., most of the cells in a human contain two copies of each of 22 chromosomes; in addition, one pair of chromosomes determines sex [XX or XY]; transmission of genetic information to offspring occurs through egg and sperm cells that

---

Codes (right side of page): BD = Benchmark, Declarative; BP = Benchmark, Procedural; BC = Benchmark, Contextual

1st letter(s) of each code in parentheses 2nd letter of code Number

S = NRC: National Science Education Standards E = Explicitly stated in document Page number of cited document

2 = Project 2061: Benchmarks for Science Literacy I = Implied in document *or, for duplicates:*

C = CDE: Science Framework for CA Public Schools Standard number & level of duplicate

F = NAEP: 1996 Science Framework

IB,IC,IE,IM,IP: Int'l Bacc.: Biology, Chemistry, P = NAEP: Science Assess./Exercise Specifications

Environ. Systems, Middle Yrs Science, Physics T = Pearsall: NSTA: The Content Core

N1,N2,N3: New Standards: Elementary, Middle, High D = Duplicated in another standard

O = NAEP: 1990 Science Objectives

contain only one representative from each chromosome pair; dominant and recessive traits explain how variations that are hidden in one generation can be expressed in the next)

(2E,110)

6. Knows the general structure and functions of cells in organisms

Level I (Grades K-2)

BD (SE,129;2I,111;CE,116;N1I,132;PE,119;DI,8.1.1)
- Knows that animals require air, water, food, and shelter; plants require air, water, nutrients, and light

Level II (Grades 3-5)

BD (SE,129;CE,116;IMI,40;N1E,132;PI,116)
- Knows that each plant or animal has different structures which serve different functions in growth, survival, and reproduction (e.g., humans have distinct structures of the body for walking, holding, seeing, and talking)

Level III (Grades 6-8)

BD (SE,156;2E,112;CE,116;IMI,75;PI,123-124;TE,47)
- Knows that all organisms are composed of cells, which are the fundamental units of life; most organisms are single cells, but other organisms (including humans) are multicellular

BD (SE,156;2E,112;CE,127;IBI,33;IMI,44,76;N2I,92;PI,123-124)
- Knows that cells convert energy obtained from food to carry on the many functions needed to sustain life (e.g., cell growth and division, production of materials that the cell or organism needs)

BD (SE,156;CE,120,127;IBE,64;N2E,92;PI,125)
- Knows the levels of organization in living systems, including cells, tissues, organs, organ systems, whole organisms, and ecosystems, and the complementary nature of structure and function at each level

BD (SE,156;2I,112;CE,118;FI,68;IBE,52-58,82,85,95,96;IMI,38,75;N2I,92;PE,125;TE,47,49)
- Knows that multicellular organisms have a variety of specialized cells, tissues, organs, and organ systems that perform specialized functions (e.g., digestion, respiration, reproduction, circulation, excretion, movement, control and coordination, protection from disease)

BD (SE,157;FI,68;IBI,54,79-80;IMI,83-86;N2I,92;PI,126)
- Knows that disease in organisms can be caused by intrinsic failures of the system or infection

---

Codes (right side of page):	BD = Benchmark, Declarative; BP = Benchmark, Procedural; BC = Benchmark, Contextual

1st letter(s) of each code in parentheses — *2nd letter of code* — *Number*

S = NRC: National Science Education Standards — E = Explicitly stated in document — Page number of cited document

2 = Project 2061: Benchmarks for Science Literacy — I = Implied in document — *or, for duplicates:*

C = CDE: Science Framework for CA Public Schools — Standard number & level of duplicate

F = NAEP: 1996 Science Framework

IB,IC,IE,IM,IP: Int'l Bacc.: Biology, Chemistry, — P = NAEP: Science Assess./Exercise Specifications
   Environ. Systems, Middle Yrs Science, Physics — T = Pearsall: NSTA: The Content Core

N1,N2,N3: New Standards: Elementary, Middle, High — D = Duplicated in another standard

O = NAEP: 1990 Science Objectives

MREL

by other organisms

Level IV (Grades 9-12)

- BD (SE,184;2E,113;CE,127;IBE,31-32,63;IME,75;N3E,82;PE,131;TE,51)
Knows the structures of different types of cell parts (e.g., cell wall; cell membrane; cytoplasm; cell organelles such as the nucleus, chloroplast, mitochondrion, Golgi apparatus, vacuole) and the functions they perform (e.g., transport of materials, storage of genetic information, photosynthesis and respiration, synthesis of new molecules, waste disposal)

- BD (SE,184,186;CE,128;FI,69;IBI,33-39;IME,45,75;N3I,82;PE,131;TI,51)
Understands the chemical reactions involved in cell functions (e.g., food molecules taken into cells are broken down to provide the chemical constituents needed to synthesize other molecules; enzymes facilitate the breakdown and synthesis of molecules)

- BD (SE,184;2I,109;CE,128;IBE,64;TE,56)
Understands cell differentiation (e.g., the progeny from a single cell form an embryo in which the cells multiply and differentiate to form the many specialized cells, tissues, and organs that comprise the final organism; each cell retains the basic information needed to reproduce itself)

- BD (SE,184;2I,114;CE,128;FE,69;IBI,33-39;N3I,82;PI,131)
Knows how cell functions are regulated through changes in the activity of the functions performed by proteins and through the selective expression of individual genes, and how this regulation allows cells to respond to their environment and to control and coordinate cell growth and division

- BD (SE,184;2E,114;CE,129;FE,69;IBE,67;N3I,82;PE,131;TE,55)
Knows that the genetic information stored in DNA provides instructions for protein synthesis in cells

- BD (2E,114;CE,129;IBE,67-68,99-100;TI,53)
Knows the structures of proteins (e.g., long, usually folded chain molecules made from 20 different types of smaller amino acid molecules that are arranged in different sequences) and the role of proteins in cell function

- BD (SE,187;CI,121;FI,69;IBE,116-117;IME,65;N3I,82;PI,133)
Understands the structure and functions of nervous systems in multicellular animals (e.g., nervous systems are formed from specialized cells that conduct signals rapidly through the long cell extensions that make up nerves; nerve cells communicate with each other by secreting specific excitatory and inhibitory molecules)

Codes (right side of page):   BD = Benchmark, Declarative; BP = Benchmark, Procedural; BC = Benchmark, Contextual
1st letter(s) of each code in parentheses   *2nd letter of code*   *Number*
S = NRC: National Science Education Standards   E = Explicitly stated in document   Page number of cited document
2 = Project 2061: Benchmarks for Science Literacy   I = Implied in document   *or, for duplicates:*
C = CDE: Science Framework for CA Public Schools   Standard number & level of duplicate
F = NAEP: 1996 Science Framework
IB,IC,IE,IM,IP: Int'l Bacc.: Biology, Chemistry,   P = NAEP: Science Assess./Exercise Specifications
   Environ. Systems, Middle Yrs Science, Physics   T = Pearsall: NSTA: The Content Core
N1,N2,N3: New Standards: Elementary, Middle, High   D = Duplicated in another standard
O = NAEP: 1990 Science Objectives

7. **Understands how species depend on one another and on the environment for survival** (2E,115)

Level I (Grades K-2)

- Knows that living things are found almost everywhere in the world and that distinct environments support the life of different types of plants and animals BD (SE,129;2E,116;CE,136)

Level II (Grades 3-5)

- Knows that the behavior of individual organisms is influenced by internal cues (e.g., hunger) and external cues (e.g., changes in the environment), and that humans and other organisms have senses that help them to detect these cues BD (SE,129;CE,119;IMI,62;N1I,132)

- Knows that an organism's patterns of behavior are related to the nature of that organism's environment (e.g., kinds and numbers of other organisms present, availability of food and resources, physical characteristics of the environment) BD (SE,129;2I,116;CE,137;N1I,132)

- Knows that changes in the environment can have different effects on different organisms (e.g., some organisms move in, others move out; some organisms survive and reproduce, others die) BD (SE,129;2E,116;CE,140;N1I,132)

- Knows that all organisms (including humans) cause changes in their environments, and these changes can be beneficial or detrimental BD (SE,129;CE,137;N1E,132)

Level III (Grades 6-8)

- Knows how an organism's ability to regulate its internal environment enables the organism to obtain and use resources, grow, reproduce, and maintain stable internal conditions while living in a constantly changing external environment BD (SE,157;CI,119;IBI,55-56,129;N2I,92;PE,126;TE,48)

- Knows that organisms can react to internal and environmental stimuli through behavioral response (e.g., plants have tissues and organs that react to light, water, and other stimuli; animals have nervous systems that process and store information from the environment), which may be determined by heredity or from past experience BD (SE,157;CE,119;IBE,112-117;IMI,62,63;N2I,92;TI,48)

Codes (right side of page): BD = Benchmark, Declarative; BP = Benchmark, Procedural; BC = Benchmark, Contextual
1st letter(s) of each code in parentheses   *2nd letter of code*   *Number*
S = NRC: National Science Education Standards   E = Explicitly stated in document   Page number of cited document
2 = Project 2061: Benchmarks for Science Literacy   I = Implied in document   *or, for duplicates:*
C = CDE: Science Framework for CA Public Schools   Standard number & level of duplicate
F = NAEP: 1996 Science Framework
IB,IC,IE,IM,IP: Int'l Bacc.: Biology, Chemistry,   P = NAEP: Science Assess./Exercise Specifications
   Environ. Systems, Middle Yrs Science, Physics   T = Pearsall: NSTA: The Content Core
N1,N2,N3: New Standards: Elementary, Middle, High   D = Duplicated in another standard
O = NAEP: 1990 Science Objectives

BD (SI,157-158;2E,117;CE,139;IBE,124;IEE,20;PI,126;TE,54)
- Knows ways in which species interact and depend on one another in an ecosystem (e.g., producer/consumer, predator/prey, parasite/host, relationships that are mutually beneficial or competitive)

BD (SE,157;2I,117;CE,137;IBE,44;IEI,19;IMI,37,60;N2I,92;TE,49)
- Knows that all individuals of a species that occur together at a given place and time make up a population, and all populations living together and the physical factors with which they interact compose an ecosystem

BD (SE,158;2E,117;CE,137;IBE,123;IEE,21,22;IMI,37;N2I,92;TE,50)
- Knows factors that affect the number and types of organisms an ecosystem can support (e.g., available resources; abiotic factors such as quantity of light and water, range of temperatures, and soil composition; disease; competition from other organisms within the ecosystem; predation)

BD (SE,158;2E,104;CE,139;IBI,124;IEE,19;IME,36,59;N2E,92)
- Knows relationships that exist among organisms in food chains and food webs

Level IV (Grades 9-12)

BD (SE,186;2E,117;CE,141;FE,69,70;IBE,48;N3I,82;PE,134-135;TI,54)
- Knows how the interrelationships and interdependencies among organisms generate stable ecosystems that fluctuate around a state of rough equilibrium for hundreds or thousands of years (e.g., growth of a population is held in check by environmental factors such as depletion of food or nesting sites, increased loss due to larger numbers of predators or parasites)

BD (SE,186;2E,117;CE,142;FI,70;IBE,49,127-128;IEI,25,26,28,39-41,44-46;IMI,37,70-74;N3I,82)
- Knows ways in which humans can modify ecosystems and cause irreversible effects (e.g., human population growth, technology, and consumption; human destruction of habitats through direct harvesting, pollution, and atmospheric changes)

(2E,118)
8. Understands the cycling of matter and flow of energy through the living environment

Level I (Grades K-2)

BD (2E,119;CE,116,136,138;PE,119;DI,6.1.1)
- Knows that plants and animals need certain resources for energy and growth (e.g., food, water, light, air)

Codes (right side of page):   BD = Benchmark, Declarative; BP = Benchmark, Procedural; BC = Benchmark, Contextual
1st letter(s) of each code in parentheses   *2nd letter of code*   *Number*
S = NRC: National Science Education Standards   E = Explicitly stated in document   Page number of cited document
2 = Project 2061: Benchmarks for Science Literacy   I = Implied in document   *or, for duplicates:*
C = CDE: Science Framework for CA Public Schools   Standard number & level of duplicate
F = NAEP: 1996 Science Framework
IB,IC,IE,IM,IP: Int'l Bacc.: Biology, Chemistry,   P = NAEP: Science Assess./Exercise Specifications
   Environ. Systems, Middle Yrs Science, Physics   T = Pearsall: NSTA: The Content Core
N1,N2,N3: New Standards: Elementary, Middle, High   D = Duplicated in another standard
O = NAEP: 1990 Science Objectives

Level II (Grades 3-5)

- Knows that the transfer of energy (e.g., through the consumption of food) is essential to all living organisms

  BD (2E,119;CI,139;FI,67;PE,95)

- Knows the organization of simple food chains and food webs (e.g., green plants make their own food with sunlight, water, and air; some animals eat the plants; some animals eat the animals that eat the plants)

  BD (SE,129;2E,119;CE,139;FI,67;PE,119-120)

Level III (Grades 6-8)

- Knows how energy is transferred through food webs in an ecosystem (e.g., energy enters ecosystems as sunlight, and green plants transfer this energy into chemical energy through photosynthesis; this chemical energy is passed from organism to organism; animals get energy from oxidizing their food, releasing some of this energy as heat)

  BD (SE,158;2E,120;CE,139;FI,61,68;IBE,47;IEI,19;IME,59;N2I,92;PE,126)

- Knows how matter is recycled within ecosystems (e.g., matter is transferred from one organism to another repeatedly, and between organisms and their physical environment; the total amount of matter remains constant, even though its form and location change)

  BD (2E,120;CE,139;IBI,45;IEI,19,20;IME,60;N2I,92;PI,126;TI,50)

Level IV (Grades 9-12)

- Knows that as matter and energy flow through different levels of organization in living systems and between living systems and the physical environment, chemical elements (e.g., carbon, nitrogen) are recombined in different ways

  BD (SE,186-187;CE,139;IBE,47-48,126;IEE,20;N3I,82;PI,135;DI,2.4.1)

- Knows that because all matter tends toward more disorganized states, living systems require a continuous input of energy to maintain their chemical and physical organizations

  BD (SE,186;2E,121;CI,139;FI,60;IEI,20;N3I,82)

- Understands how the processes of photosynthesis and respiration in plants transfer energy from the Sun to living systems (e.g., chloroplasts in plant cells use energy from sunlight to combine molecules of carbon dioxide and water into complex, energy-rich organic compounds, and release oxygen to the environment)

  BD (SE,184,186;CE,128;FI,69;IBE,45-48,69-73,101-105;ICE,77-78;IEE,20;IME,46-47;N3E,82;PE,131;TE,51)

- Knows that the complexity and organization of organisms accommodates the need for

  BD (SE,186;CE120;IBI,129-133;IMI,44-58;N3I,82;PI,133)

obtaining, transforming, transporting, releasing, and eliminating the matter and energy used to sustain the organism

- BD (SE,186;2E,121;CE,137;IBE,123;N3I,82;TI,54)
  Knows how the amount of life an environment can support is limited by the availability of matter and energy and the ability of the ecosystem to recycle materials

(2E,122)

9.   Understands the basic concepts of the evolution of species

Level I (Grades K-2)

- BD (2E,123;CE,121;N1I,132)
  Knows that some kinds of organisms that once lived on Earth have completely disappeared (e.g., dinosaurs, trilobites, mammoths, giant tree ferns, horsetail trees)

Level II (Grades 3-5)

- BD (2E,123;CE,130;N1E,132)
  Knows that fossils of past life can be compared to one another and to living organisms to observe their similarities and differences

Level III (Grades 6-8)

- BD (SI,158;2E,124;CE,133;IMI,81;N2I,92)
  Knows that the fossil record, through geologic evidence, documents the appearance, diversification, and extinction of many life forms

- BD (SE,158;2I,124;CE,132-133;FI,68;IBE,48-49;IME,80-82;N2I,92)
  Knows basic ideas related to biological evolution (e.g., diversity of species is developed through gradual processes over many generations; biological adaptations, such as changes in structure, behavior, or physiology, allow some species to enhance their reproductive success and survival in a particular environment)

- BD (SE,158;CE,132,133;IEI,42-43;N2I,92)
  Understands the concept of extinction and its importance in biological evolution (e.g., when the environment changes, the adaptive characteristics of some species are insufficient to allow their survival; extinction is common; most of the species that have lived on the Earth no longer exist)

Codes (right side of page):   BD = Benchmark, Declarative; BP = Benchmark, Procedural; BC = Benchmark, Contextual
1st letter(s) of each code in parentheses   *2nd letter of code*   *Number*
S = NRC: National Science Education Standards   E = Explicitly stated in document   Page number of cited document
2 = Project 2061: Benchmarks for Science Literacy   I = Implied in document   *or, for duplicates:*
C = CDE: Science Framework for CA Public Schools   Standard number & level of duplicate
F = NAEP: 1996 Science Framework   _____
IB,IC,IE,IM,IP: Int'l Bacc.: Biology, Chemistry,   P = NAEP: Science Assess./Exercise Specifications
     Environ. Systems, Middle Yrs Science, Physics   T = Pearsall: NSTA: The Content Core
N1,N2,N3: New Standards: Elementary, Middle, High   D = Duplicated in another standard
O = NAEP: 1990 Science Objectives

Level IV (Grades 9-12)

- BD (2E,125;CI,132;FI,70;PI,129-130)
Knows that heritable characteristics, which can be biochemical and anatomical, largely determine what capabilities an organism will have, how it will behave, and how likely it is to survive and reproduce

- BD (SI,185,187;2E,125;CE,135;FI,70;IBE,48-49;IEI,42;N3I,82;PI,129;TE,56)
Knows that natural selection leads to organisms that are well suited for survival in particular environments, so that when an environment changes, some inherited characteristics become more or less advantageous or neutral, and chance alone can result in characteristics having no survival or reproductive value

- BD (SE,185;2E,125;CE,134;IBI,37,106-109;IEI,42;IMI,81;N3I,82;PI,130;TI,56-57)
Knows how natural selection and its evolutionary consequences provide a scientific explanation for the diversity and unity of past and present life forms on Earth (e.g., recurring patterns of relationship exist throughout the fossil record; molecular similarities exist among the diverse species of living organisms; the millions of different species living today appear to be related by descent from common ancestors)

- BD (SE,185;2I,125;CE,134-135;N3I,82;PI,130;TI,56)
Knows that the basic idea of evolution is that the Earth's present-day life forms have evolved from earlier, distinctly different species as a consequence of the interactions of (1) the potential for a species to increase its numbers, (2) the genetic variability of offspring due to mutation and recombination of genes, (3) a finite supply of the resources required for life, and (4) the ensuing selection by the environment of those offspring better able to survive and leave offspring

- BD (SI,185;2E,125;CI,132;IBE,106-107;IMI,82;PI,89)
Knows the history of the origin and evolution of life on Earth (e.g., life on Earth is thought to have begun 3.5 – 4 billion years ago as simple, one-celled organisms; during the first two billion years, only microorganisms existed; after cells with nuclei developed about a billion years ago, increasingly complex multicellular organisms evolved)

(2E,75)
10. Understands basic concepts about the structure and properties of matter

Level I (Grades K-2)

- BD (SE,127;2E,76;CE,41;FE,57;N1I,132;PE,91)
Knows that different objects are made up of many different types of materials (e.g., cloth, paper, wood, metal) and have many different observable properties (e.g., color, size, shape,

---

Codes (right side of page):	BD = Benchmark, Declarative; BP = Benchmark, Procedural; BC = Benchmark, Contextual

1st letter(s) of each code in parentheses — *2nd letter of code* — *Number*

S = NRC: National Science Education Standards   E = Explicitly stated in document   Page number of cited document
2 = Project 2061: Benchmarks for Science Literacy   I = Implied in document   *or, for duplicates:*
C = CDE: Science Framework for CA Public Schools   Standard number & level of duplicate
F = NAEP: 1996 Science Framework
IB,IC,IE,IM,IP: Int'l Bacc.: Biology, Chemistry,   P = NAEP: Science Assess./Exercise Specifications
   Environ. Systems, Middle Yrs Science, Physics   T = Pearsall: NSTA: The Content Core
N1,N2,N3: New Standards: Elementary, Middle, High   D = Duplicated in another standard
O = NAEP: 1990 Science Objectives

McREL

weight)

BD (2E,76;CI,42-43;FI,57;N1I,132)
- Knows that things can be done to materials to change some of their properties (e.g., heating, freezing, mixing, cutting, dissolving, bending), but not all materials respond the same way to what is done to them

Level II (Grades 3-5)

BD (SE,127;PE,93)
- Knows that objects can be classified according to their properties (e.g., magnetism, conductivity, density, solubility)

BD (2E,77;CE,42)
- Knows that materials may be composed of parts that are too small to be seen without magnification

BD (SE,127;CI,43;PE,91)
- Knows that properties such as length, weight, temperature, and volume can be measured using appropriate tools (e.g., rulers, balances, thermometers, graduated cylinders)

BD (SE,127;2I,77;CE,42;FI,57;IMI,34,35,102;N1I,132;PI,92,93;DI,1.2.1)
- Knows that materials have different states (solid, liquid, gas), and some common materials such as water can be changed from one state to another by heating or cooling

BD (2E,77;CE,43;IME,103;PE,92)
- Knows that the mass of a material remains constant whether it is together, in parts, or in a different state

Level III (Grades 6-8)

BD (2E,78;CE,42;FE,57;PE,98;TE,64)
- Knows that matter is made up of tiny particles called atoms, and different arrangements of atoms into groups compose all substances

BD (2I,78;CE,43;PE,98;TE,64,66)
- Knows that atoms often combine to form a molecule (or crystal), the smallest particle of a substance that retains its properties

BD (2E,78;CE,43;ICE,28;IME,35;IPI,30,33;PE,99;TE,66)
- Knows that atoms are in constant, random motion (atoms in solids are close together and don't move about easily; atoms in liquids are close together and stick to each other, but move about easily; atoms in gas are quite far apart and move about freely)

Codes (right side of page):	BD = Benchmark, Declarative; BP = Benchmark, Procedural; BC = Benchmark, Contextual
1st letter(s) of each code in parentheses	*2nd letter of code* — *Number*
S = NRC: National Science Education Standards	E = Explicitly stated in document — Page number of cited document
2 = Project 2061: Benchmarks for Science Literacy	I = Implied in document — *or, for duplicates:*
C = CDE: Science Framework for CA Public Schools	— Standard number & level of duplicate
F = NAEP: 1996 Science Framework	
IB,IC,IE,IM,IP: Int'l Bacc.: Biology, Chemistry,	P = NAEP: Science Assess./Exercise Specifications
Environ. Systems, Middle Yrs Science, Physics	T = Pearsall: NSTA: The Content Core
N1,N2,N3: New Standards: Elementary, Middle, High	D = Duplicated in another standard
O = NAEP: 1990 Science Objectives	

- BD (SE,154;2E,78;CE,45;FE,57;IMI,104;PE,98)
  Knows that substances that contain only one kind of atom are pure elements, and over 100 different kinds of elements exist; elements do not break down by normal laboratory reactions (e.g., heating, exposure to electric current, reaction with acids)

- BD (SI,154;2E,78-79;CI,45;ICE,25;PE,98)
  Knows that many elements can be grouped according to similar properties (e.g., highly reactive metals, less-reactive metals, highly reactive nonmetals, almost completely nonreactive gases)

- BD (SE,154;CE,45;FE,57;IMI,35,103;N2I,92;PI,98)
  Knows that substances react chemically in characteristic ways with other substances to form new substances (compounds) with different characteristic properties

- BD (2E,79;CE,50;ICE,22;IME,106;N2I,92;PE,98;TE,61-62)
  Understands the conservation of matter in physical and chemical change (e.g., no matter how substances within a closed system interact with one another, or how they combine or break apart, the total weight of the system remains the same; the same number of atoms weighs the same, no matter how the atoms are arranged)

- BD (SE,154;CE,43;ICI,82-83;IME,35,103;PE,98;TE,61)
  Knows methods used to separate mixtures into their component parts (e.g., boiling, filtering, chromatography, screening)

- BD (2E,78;CE,47;FI,58;ICE,46;IME,111;TE,63)
  Knows factors that influence reaction rates (e.g., types of substances involved, temperature, concentration, surface area)

- BD (2E,78-79;TE,63)
  Knows that oxidation involves the combining of oxygen with another substance (e.g., burning, rusting)

Level IV (Grades 9-12)

- BD (SE,178-179;2E,80;CI,44;FE,57;ICE,24-25;IME,105;N3I,82;TE,70)
  Understands how elements are arranged in the periodic table, and how this arrangement shows repeating patterns among elements with similar properties (e.g., numbers of protons, neutrons, and electrons; relation between atomic number and atomic mass)

- BD (SE,178;2E,80;CE,44;ICI,24,26-28;IMI,109-110;N3I,82;TE,71)
  Knows how the electron configuration of atoms governs the chemical properties of an element as atoms interact with one another by transferring or sharing electrons that are furthest from the nucleus

---

Codes (right side of page):   BD = Benchmark, Declarative; BP = Benchmark, Procedural; BC = Benchmark, Contextual

1st letter(s) of each code in parentheses	*2nd letter of code*	*Number*
S = NRC: National Science Education Standards	E = Explicitly stated in document	Page number of cited document
2 = Project 2061: Benchmarks for Science Literacy	I = Implied in document	*or, for duplicates:*
C = CDE: Science Framework for CA Public Schools		Standard number & level of duplicate
F = NAEP: 1996 Science Framework		
IB,IC,IE,IM,IP: Int'l Bacc.: Biology, Chemistry,	P = NAEP: Science Assess./Exercise Specifications	
Environ. Systems, Middle Yrs Science, Physics	T = Pearsall: NSTA: The Content Core	
N1,N2,N3: New Standards: Elementary, Middle, High	D = Duplicated in another standard	
O = NAEP: 1990 Science Objectives		

- BD (SE,179;2I,80;CE,45-46;ICI,26-27;IMI,109-110;N3I,82;TI,71)

  Knows that atoms may be bonded together into molecules or crystalline solids, and compounds are formed from chemical bonds between two or more different kinds of atoms

- BD (SE,179;2I,80;ICI,42-43;IME,110-111;N3I,82;TE,71)

  Knows that the physical properties of a compound are determined by its molecular structure (e.g., constituent atoms, distances and angles between them) and the interactions among these molecules

- BD (SE,178;2E,80,253;CE,43;ICE,23;IME,108;IPE,42-43;N3I,82;TI,70,119)

  Knows the structure of an atom (e.g., negative electrons occupy most of the space in the atom; neutrons and positive protons make up the nucleus of the atom; protons and neutrons are almost two thousand times heavier than an electron; the electric force between the nucleus and electrons holds the atom together)

- BD (2E,80;CE,48;IBE,34;ICI,26,42;N3I,82;TI,70-71;DI,13.4.2)

  Knows that the number of electrons in an atom determines whether the atom is electrically neutral or an ion (i.e., electrically neutral atoms contain equal numbers of protons and electrons; a positively charged atom has lost one or more electrons; a negatively charged atom has gained one or more electrons)

- BD (SE,178;2E,80;CE,46;ICE,23;IME,108,137;N3I,82;TE,70)

  Knows that most elements have two or more isotopes (i.e., atoms that differ in the number of neutrons in the nucleus); although the number of neutrons has little effect on how the atom interacts with others, it does affect the mass and stability of the nucleus

- BD (SE,178;2E,80;CE,46;IBI,107-108;ICI,77;IPE,42-43;N3E,82;TE,119;DI,2.4.5)

  Knows how radioactive isotopes can be used to estimate the age of materials that contain them because radioactive isotopes undergo spontaneous nuclear reactions and emit particles and/or wavelike radiation; the decay of any one nucleus cannot be predicted, but a large group of identical nuclei decay at a predictable rate, which can be used to estimate the material's age

- BD (2E,80;CE,44;IPI,84)

  Knows that electrons, neutrons, and protons are made up of even smaller constituents

- BD (SE,179;2E,80;CI,53;ICE,31,45,58-59;N3I,82;TE,69)

  Knows that chemical reactions can take place at vastly different rates (e.g., from the few femtoseconds required for an atom to move a fraction of a chemical bond distance to geologic time scales of billions of years), and reaction rates depend on a variety of factors (e.g., how often the reacting atoms and molecules encounter one another; temperature; properties, including shape, of the reacting species)

Codes (right side of page):   BD = Benchmark, Declarative; BP = Benchmark, Procedural; BC = Benchmark, Contextual

1st letter(s) of each code in parentheses   *2nd letter of code*   *Number*

S = NRC: National Science Education Standards   E = Explicitly stated in document   Page number of cited document

2 = Project 2061: Benchmarks for Science Literacy   I = Implied in document   *or, for duplicates:*

C = CDE: Science Framework for CA Public Schools   Standard number & level of duplicate

F = NAEP: 1996 Science Framework

IB,IC,IE,IM,IP: Int'l Bacc.: Biology, Chemistry,   P = NAEP: Science Assess./Exercise Specifications

   Environ. Systems, Middle Yrs Science, Physics   T = Pearsall: NSTA: The Content Core

N1,N2,N3: New Standards: Elementary, Middle, High   D = Duplicated in another standard

O = NAEP: 1990 Science Objectives

- BD (CE,51;IMI,109;TE,73)
  Understands the complete mole concept and ways in which it can be used (e.g., actual mass vs. relative mass; relationship between the mole and the volume of a mole of molecules; relevance of molar volume and Avogadro's hypothesis)

- BD (SE,179;CE,53;IBE,68,100;N3I,82;TI,75-76)
  Knows that chemical reactions can be accelerated by catalysts (e.g., some chemical reactions may be catalyzed by metal surfaces; chemical reactions in living systems are often catalyzed by protein molecules called enzymes)

- BD (SE,179;IBE,34-35;ICE,36-39,52-57,61-15;IMI,112,116-118;TI,75)
  Knows the variety of structures that may be formed from the bonding of carbon atoms (e.g., synthetic polymers, oils, the large molecules essential to life) and their roles in various chemical reactions, including those required for life processes

- BD (SE,179;ICE,33-35,49-52,60-61,87;N3I,82;TE,69,73-74)
  Knows that a large number of important reactions involve the transfer of either electrons (oxidation/reduction reactions) or hydrogen ions (acid/base reactions) between reacting ions, molecules, or atoms

- BD (SE,179;CI,48;ICE,85;IMI,119 120;N3I,82;PI,110)
  Understands radical reactions and their role in natural and human processes (e.g., ozone and green house gases in the atmosphere; burning and processing of fossil fuels; formation of polymers; explosions)

(2I,81)
11. Understands energy types, sources, and conversions, and their relationship to heat and temperature

Level I (Grades K-2)

- BD (2E,83;CI,61;PE,95)
  Knows that the Sun supplies heat and light to Earth

- BD (SE,127;CE,64;N1E,132)
  Knows that heat can be produced in many ways (e.g., burning, rubbing, mixing substances together)

- BD (SE,127;CE,68;FI,60;N1I,132;PI,95)
  Knows that electricity in circuits can produce light, heat, sound, and magnetic effects

---

Codes (right side of page):	BD = Benchmark, Declarative; BP = Benchmark, Procedural; BC = Benchmark, Contextual

1st letter(s) of each code in parentheses   *2nd letter of code*   *Number*

S = NRC: National Science Education Standards   E = Explicitly stated in document   Page number of cited document

2 = Project 2061: Benchmarks for Science Literacy   I = Implied in document   *or, for duplicates:*

C = CDE: Science Framework for CA Public Schools   Standard number & level of duplicate

F = NAEP: 1996 Science Framework

IB,IC,IE,IM,IP: Int'l Bacc.: Biology, Chemistry,   P = NAEP: Science Assess./Exercise Specifications

    Environ. Systems, Middle Yrs Science, Physics   T = Pearsall: NSTA: The Content Core

N1,N2,N3: New Standards: Elementary, Middle, High   D = Duplicated in another standard

O = NAEP: 1990 Science Objectives

Level II (Grades 3-5)

- BD (2I,84;CE,63;FE,60;PE,94)

  Knows that heat is often produced as a byproduct when one form of energy is converted to another form (e.g., heat is produced by mechanical and electrical machines)

- BD (SE,127;2E,84;CE,67)

  Knows that heat can move from one object to another by conduction and that some materials conduct heat better than others

- BD (SE,127;CE,68;N1I,132;PI,93)

  Knows the organization of a simple electrical circuit (e.g., battery or generator, wire, a complete loop through which the electrical current can pass)

Level III (Grades 6-8)

- BD (SE,155;2E,85;CE,62;FI,59;IMI,33;N2I,92;PI,100;TI,105-106)

  Knows that energy is a property of many substances (e.g., heat energy is in the disorderly motion of molecules and in radiation; chemical energy is in the arrangement of atoms; mechanical energy is in moving bodies or in elastically distorted shapes; electrical energy is in the attraction or repulsion between charges)

- BD (SI,155;2E,85;CE,61;FE,59;IME,33;IPE,29-30;N2I,92;PE,101;TI,65)

  Understands that energy cannot be created or destroyed but only changed from one form to another

- BD (SE,155;CI,62;FE,61;TE,65;DI,1.3.9)

  Knows how the Sun acts as a major source of energy for changes on the Earth's surface (i.e., the Sun loses energy by emitting light; some of this light is transferred to the Earth in a range of wavelengths including visible light, infrared radiation, and ultraviolet radiation)

- BD (SI,155;2E,85;CE,65,67;IME,124-125;IPE,32;N2I,92;TE,107)

  Knows that heat can be transferred through conduction, convection, and radiation; heat flows from warmer objects to cooler ones until both objects reach the same temperature

- BD (SE,155;IMI,34,126-129;IPI,38-39;PE,101)

  Knows that electrical circuits provide a means of transferring electrical energy to produce heat, light, sound, and chemical changes

- BD (SE,155;2I,85;CI,62;FI,60;ICI,29;N2I,92;TE,64)

  Knows that most chemical and nuclear reactions involve a transfer of energy (e.g., heat, light, mechanical motion, electricity)

Level IV (Grades 9-12)

BD (SE,180;2E,86;CE,66;FE,60;IPI,51,70;N3I,82;PE,110;TI,114)
- Knows that although the total energy of the universe remains constant, matter tends to become steadily less ordered as various energy transfers occur (e.g., by collisions in chemical and nuclear reactions, by light waves and other radiations), and the energy tends to spread out uniformly

BD (SE,180;CE,62;IMI,33,136-137;IPI,29;TI,114)
- Knows that all energy can be considered to be either kinetic energy (energy of motion), potential energy (depends on relative position), or energy contained by a field (electromagnetic waves)

BD (SE,180;2I,86;CE,65;IPE,31;N3I,82;TI,121)
- Understands the relationship between heat and temperature (heat energy consists of the random motion and vibrations of atoms, molecules, and ions; the higher the temperature, the greater the atomic or molecular motion)

BD (SE,179;2I,86;CE,47;ICI,29-30,44-45;IMI,119;IPI,32;N3I,82)
- Understands that chemical reactions either release or consume energy (i.e., some changes of atomic or molecular configuration require an input of energy; others release energy)

BD (SE,180-181;2E,86;CI,75;ICI,81;IMI,137;IPE,58,65;N3I,82;TE,124)
- Knows how the energy associated with individual atoms and molecules can be used to identify the substances they comprise; each kind of atom or molecule can gain or lose energy only in particular discrete amounts, and thus can absorb and emit light only at wavelengths corresponding to these amounts

BD (SE,178;2E,86;FE,61;ICE,76-77;IMI,137-138;IPE,58-59,66;N3I,82;TE,121)
- Knows that nuclear reactions convert a fraction of the mass of interacting particles into energy (fission involves the splitting of a large nucleus into smaller pieces; fusion is the joining of two nuclei at extremely high temperature and pressure) and release much greater amounts of energy than atomic interactions

(2E,87)

12.   Understands motion and the principles that explain it

Level I (Grades K-2)

BD (SE,127;2E,89;CE,75-76;N1E,132)
- Knows that vibrating objects produce sound

BD (SE,127;CE,73;N1E,132;PI,97)
- Knows that light travels in a straight line until it strikes an object

---

Codes (right side of page):   BD = Benchmark, Declarative; BP = Benchmark, Procedural; BC = Benchmark, Contextual
1st letter(s) of each code in parentheses   *2nd letter of code*   *Number*
S = NRC: National Science Education Standards   E = Explicitly stated in document   Page number of cited document
2 = Project 2061: Benchmarks for Science Literacy   I = Implied in document   *or, for duplicates:*
C = CDE: Science Framework for CA Public Schools   Standard number & level of duplicate
F = NAEP: 1996 Science Framework
IB,IC,IE,IM,IP: Int'l Bacc.: Biology, Chemistry,   P = NAEP: Science Assess./Exercise Specifications
    Environ. Systems, Middle Yrs Science, Physics   T = Pearsall: NSTA: The Content Core
N1,N2,N3: New Standards: Elementary, Middle, High   D = Duplicated in another standard
O = NAEP: 1990 Science Objectives

- BD (SE,127;CE,53;FE,63;N1I,132;PE,96)

  Knows that the position of an object can be described by locating it relative to another object or the background

- BD (2E,89;CE,54;FI,64;PI,97)

  Knows that things move in many different ways (e.g., straight line, zigzag, vibration, circular motion)

- BD (SE,127;2E,89;CE,55;FI,63,64)

  Knows that the position and motion of an object can be changed by pushing or pulling

Level II (Grades 3-5)

- BD (SE,127;CE,76;N1I,132)

  Knows that the pitch of a sound depends on the frequency of the vibration producing it

- BD (SE,127;CE,73-74;FI,65;N1I,132;PI,97)

  Knows that light can be reflected, refracted, or absorbed

- BD (SE,127;CE,54;FI,63;N1E,132;PE,96)

  Knows that an object's motion can be described by tracing and measuring its position over time

- BD (2I,89;CE,55;FI,62,64;IMI,33;PE,96)

  Knows that when a force is applied to an object, the object either speeds up, slows down, or goes in a different direction

- BD (SI,127;2E,89;CI,56;PI,96)

  Knows the relationship between the strength of a force and its effect on an object (e.g., the greater the force, the greater the change in motion; the more massive the object, the smaller the effect of a given force)

Level III (Grades 6-8)

- BD (2E,90;CE,76;FE,64;IPI,33-34;PE,104;TI,109)

  Knows that vibrations (e.g., sounds, earthquakes) move at different speeds in different materials, have different wavelengths, and set up wave-like disturbances that spread away from the source

- BD (SE,155;CI,74;FI,65;IMI,133-134;IPI,34-35;PE,105)

  Knows ways in which light interacts with matter (e.g., transmission, including refraction; absorption; scattering, including reflection)

- BD (2E,90;CE,73,74;IME,133;PI,105)

  Knows that only a narrow range of wavelengths of electromagnetic radiation can be seen by

---

Codes (right side of page):   BD = Benchmark, Declarative;   BP = Benchmark, Procedural;   BC = Benchmark, Contextual

1st letter(s) of each code in parentheses	*2nd letter of code*	*Number*
S = NRC: National Science Education Standards	E = Explicitly stated in document	Page number of cited document
2 = Project 2061: Benchmarks for Science Literacy	I = Implied in document	*or, for duplicates:*
C = CDE: Science Framework for CA Public Schools		Standard number & level of duplicate
F = NAEP: 1996 Science Framework		

IB,IC,IE,IM,IP: Int'l Bacc.: Biology, Chemistry,   P = NAEP: Science Assess./Exercise Specifications
    Environ. Systems, Middle Yrs Science, Physics   T = Pearsall: NSTA: The Content Core
N1,N2,N3: New Standards: Elementary, Middle, High   D = Duplicated in another standard
O = NAEP: 1990 Science Objectives

MREL

the human eye; differences of wavelength within that range of visible light are perceived as differences in color

BD (SE,154;IPE,25-26;PI,103;TI,104)

- Knows that an object's motion can be described and represented graphically according to its position, direction of motion, and speed

BD (SE,154;2I,90;CE,56,57;FE,64;IMI,33,136;IPI,26-27,45,61;N2E,92;PE,103-104;TI,104-105)

- Understands effects of balanced and unbalanced forces on an object's motion (e.g., if more than one force acts on an object along a straight line, then the forces will reinforce or cancel one another, depending on their direction and magnitude; unbalanced forces such as friction will cause changes in the speed or direction on an object's motion)

BD (SE,154;2E,90;CE,57;FE,64;IMI,32,33;N2I,92;TE,104-105)

- Knows that an object that is not being subjected to a force will continue to move at a constant speed and in a straight line

Level IV (Grades 9-12)

BD (SE,180;2I,92;CE,55;IPE,34;N3I,82;PI,113)

- Knows that waves (e.g., sound, seismic, water, light) have energy and can transfer energy when they interact with matter

BD (SE,180;2E,92;CE,62;FE,65;ICI,80-81;IMI,133;IPE,34,59-60;PI,113;TI,121,124)

- Knows the range of the electromagnetic spectrum (e.g., radio waves, microwaves, infrared radiation, visible light, ultraviolet radiation, x-rays, gamma rays); electromagnetic waves result when a charged object is accelerated or decelerated, and the energy of electromagnetic waves is carried in packets whose magnitude is inversely proportional to the wavelength

BD (2E,92;CE,78;FE,65;IME,135;IPE,53;PE,112;TE,124;DI,3.4.5)

- Knows that apparent changes in wavelength can provide information about changes in motion because the observed wavelength of a wave depends upon the relative motion of the source and the observer; if either the source or observer is moving toward the other, the observed wavelength is shorter; if either is moving away, the wavelength is longer

BD (2E,245;CE,74;IPE,89-91)

- Understands general concepts related to the theory of special relativity (e.g., in contrast to other moving things, the speed of light is the same for all observers, no matter how they or the light source happen to be moving; nothing can travel faster than the speed of light)

BD (SE,179-180;2E,91,92;CE,59;FE,64;IMI,135-136;IPE,27-29,45,61;N3I,82;PE,111,112;TE,112-113)

- Knows that laws of motion can be used to determine the effects of forces on the motion of objects (e.g., objects change their motion only when a net force is applied; whenever one

---

Codes (right side of page):   BD = Benchmark, Declarative; BP = Benchmark, Procedural; BC = Benchmark, Contextual

1st letter(s) of each code in parentheses	*2nd letter of code*	*Number*
S = NRC: National Science Education Standards	E = Explicitly stated in document	Page number of cited document
2 = Project 2061: Benchmarks for Science Literacy	I = Implied in document	*or, for duplicates:*
C = CDE: Science Framework for CA Public Schools		Standard number & level of duplicate
F = NAEP: 1996 Science Framework		
IB,IC,IE,IM,IP: Int'l Bacc.: Biology, Chemistry,	P = NAEP: Science Assess./Exercise Specifications	
Environ. Systems, Middle Yrs Science, Physics	T = Pearsall: NSTA: The Content Core	
N1,N2,N3: New Standards: Elementary, Middle, High	D = Duplicated in another standard	
O = NAEP: 1990 Science Objectives		

object exerts force on another, a force equal in magnitude and opposite in direction is exerted on the first object; the magnitude of the change in motion can be calculated using the relationship F=ma, which is independent of the nature of the force)

(2E,93)

13. Knows the kinds of forces that exist between objects and within atoms

Level I (Grades K-2)

- BD (2E,94;CE,68)
Knows that magnets can be used to make some things move without being touched

- BD (2E,94;CI,55)
Knows that things near the Earth fall to the ground unless something holds them up

Level II (Grades 3-5)

- BD (2E,94;CE,68)
Knows that electrically charged material pulls on all other materials and can attract or repel other charged materials

- BD (SE,127;2E,94;CE,68;N1E,132;PI,93-94)
Knows that magnets attract and repel each other and attract certain kinds of other materials (e.g., iron, steel)

- BD (2E,94;CE,55;PI,96)
Knows that the Earth's gravity pulls any object toward it without touching it

Level III (Grades 6-8)

- BD (2I,95;CE,69;IPE,39-40,55;PE,100;TE,108)
Knows that just as electric currents can produce magnetic forces, magnets can cause electric currents

- BD (SI,161;2E,95;CE,82;IMI,33;IPI,47-48,63;PI,76)
Understands general concepts related to gravitational force (e.g., every object exerts gravitational force on every other object; this force depends on the mass of the objects and their distance from one another; gravitational force is hard to detect unless at least one of the objects, such as the Earth, has a lot of mass)

Codes (right side of page):   BD = Benchmark, Declarative; BP = Benchmark, Procedural; BC = Benchmark, Contextual
1st letter(s) of each code in parentheses   *2nd letter of code*   *Number*
S = NRC: National Science Education Standards   E = Explicitly stated in document   Page number of cited document
2 = Project 2061: Benchmarks for Science Literacy   I = Implied in document   *or, for duplicates:*
C = CDE: Science Framework for CA Public Schools   Standard number & level of duplicate
F = NAEP: 1996 Science Framework
IB,IC,IE,IM,IP: Int'l Bacc.: Biology, Chemistry,   P = NAEP: Science Assess./Exercise Specifications
    Environ. Systems, Middle Yrs Science, Physics   T = Pearsall: NSTA: The Content Core
N1,N2,N3: New Standards: Elementary, Middle, High   D = Duplicated in another standard
O = NAEP: 1990 Science Objectives

Level IV (Grades 9-12)

- BD (SE,181;2E,97;CE,48;ICI,79;IPE,36;N3I,82;TI,68)

  Knows how different kinds of materials respond to electric forces (e.g., as insulators, semiconductors, conductors, superconductors)

- BD (2E,96;CE,69;N3I,82;TI,107;DI,10.4.6)

  Knows that materials that contain equal proportions of positive and negative charges are electrically neutral, but a very small excess or deficit of negative charges in a material produces noticeable electric forces

- BD (SE,180;2E,97;CE,70;IMI,131-132,139;IPI,39-40,55-56;N3I,82;PI,109;TE,115,121,123)

  Knows that magnetic forces are very closely related to electric forces and can be thought of as different aspects of a single electromagnetic force (moving electric charges produce magnetic forces and moving magnets produce electric forces); the interplay of these forces is the basis for electric motors, generators, radio, television, and many other modern technologies

- BD (2E,96;CE,48;ICI,27;IMI,104;N3I,82;TI,70-71,75)

  Knows that electromagnetic forces exist within and between atoms (e.g., electric forces between oppositely charged electrons and protons hold atoms and molecules together, and are involved in all chemical reactions; electric forces hold solid and liquid materials together and act between objects when they are in contact)

- BD (SE,178,180;2E,96,97;CI,58;ICI,76;IMI,110;IPI,57,65,83;TI,119)

  Knows that nuclear forces are much stronger than electromagnetic forces, which are vastly stronger than gravitational forces; the strength of nuclear forces explains why great amounts of energy are released from the nuclear reactions in atomic or hydrogen bombs, and in the Sun and other stars

- BD (SE,180;2E,96;CE,58;IPE,47-48,63;N3I,82)

  Knows that the strength of the gravitational force between two masses is proportional to the masses and inversely proportional to the square of the distance between them

- BD (SE,180;CI,58;IPE,36;N3I,82;TI,123)

  Knows that the strength of the electric force between two charged objects is proportional to the charges (opposite charges attract whereas like charges repel), and, as with gravitation, inversely proportional to the square of the distance between them

(2E,5)

14.   Understands the nature of scientific knowledge

Level I (Grades K-2)

BD (2E,6;OE,26)
- Knows that scientific investigations generally work the same way in different places and normally produce results that can be duplicated

Level II (Grades 3-5)

BD (2E,6;FI,26;OE,26)
- Knows that although the same scientific investigation may give slightly different results when it is carried out by different persons, or at different times or places, the general evidence collected from the investigation should be replicable by others

Level III (Grades 6-8)

BD (2E,7;OE,26)
- Knows that an experiment must be repeated many times and yield consistent results before the results are accepted as correct

BD (SE,171;2I,7)
- Knows that all scientific ideas are tentative and subject to change and improvement in principle, but for most core ideas in science, there is much experimental and observational confirmation

BD (SE,171;2I,7;OI,23-24)
- Understands that questioning, response to criticism, and open communication are integral to the process of science (e.g., scientists often differ with one another about the interpretation of evidence or theory in areas where there is not a great deal of understanding; scientists acknowledge conflicting interpretations and work towards finding evidence that will resolve the disagreement)

Level IV (Grades 9-12)

BD (SE,201)
- Knows ways in which science distinguishes itself from other ways of knowing and from other bodies of knowledge (e.g., use of empirical standards, logical arguments, skepticism)

BD (SE,176,201;FE,26;OI,24,26)
- Knows that scientific explanations must meet certain criteria to be considered valid (e.g.,

---

Codes (right side of page):   BD = Benchmark, Declarative; BP = Benchmark, Procedural; BC = Benchmark, Contextual
1st letter(s) of each code in parentheses   *2nd letter of code*   *Number*
S = NRC: National Science Education Standards   E = Explicitly stated in document   Page number of cited document
2 = Project 2061: Benchmarks for Science Literacy   I = Implied in document   *or, for duplicates:*
C = CDE: Science Framework for CA Public Schools   Standard number & level of duplicate
F = NAEP: 1996 Science Framework
IB,IC,IE,IM,IP: Int'l Bacc.: Biology, Chemistry,   P = NAEP: Science Assess./Exercise Specifications
    Environ. Systems, Middle Yrs Science, Physics   T = Pearsall: NSTA: The Content Core
N1,N2,N3: New Standards: Elementary, Middle, High   D = Duplicated in another standard
O = NAEP: 1990 Science Objectives

98

MREL

they must be consistent with experimental and observational evidence about nature, make accurate predictions about systems being studied, be logical, respect the rules of evidence, be open to criticism, report methods and procedures, make a commitment to making knowledge public)

BD (SE,201,204;2E,8;OE,26)

- Understands how scientific knowledge changes and accumulates over time (e.g., all scientific knowledge is subject to change as new evidence becomes available; some scientific ideas are incomplete and opportunity exists in these areas for new advances; theories are continually tested, revised, and occasionally discarded)

BD (SE,201,204;2E,8;IPI,77-78;OI,26)

- Knows that from time to time, major shifts occur in the scientific view of how the world works, but usually the changes that take place in the body of scientific knowledge are small modifications of prior knowledge

(2E,9)

15. Understands the nature of scientific inquiry

Level I (Grades K-2)

BD (2E,10;FE,26;N1I,134,135;OE,26)

- Knows that learning can come from careful observations and simple experiments

BD (SE,123;2E,10;FE,36;N1E,134;OI,20,21)

- Knows that tools (e.g., thermometers, magnifiers, rulers, balances) can be used to gather information and extend the senses

Level II (Grades 3-5)

BD (SE,122,123;2I,11;N1I,134;OE,21)

- Knows that scientific investigations involve asking and answering a question and comparing the answer to what scientists already know about the world

BD (SE,123;2E,11;N1I,135;OI,21)

- Knows that scientists use different kinds of investigations (e.g., naturalistic observation of things or events, data collection, controlled experiments), depending on the questions they are trying to answer

BP (SE,122;2I,11;N1E,135;OI,20,21)

- Plans and conducts simple investigations (e.g., makes systematic observations, conducts simple experiments to answer questions)

Codes (right side of page):	BD = Benchmark, Declarative; BP = Benchmark, Procedural; BC = Benchmark, Contextual

1st letter(s) of each code in parentheses   *2nd letter of code*   *Number*

S = NRC: National Science Education Standards   E = Explicitly stated in document   Page number of cited document

2 = Project 2061: Benchmarks for Science Literacy   I – Implied in document   *or, for duplicates:*

C = CDE: Science Framework for CA Public Schools   Standard number & level of duplicate

F = NAEP: 1996 Science Framework

IB,IC,IE,IM,IP: Int'l Bacc.: Biology, Chemistry,   P = NAEP: Science Assess./Exercise Specifications

     Environ. Systems, Middle Yrs Science, Physics   T = Pearsall: NSTA: The Content Core

N1,N2,N3: New Standards: Elementary, Middle, High   D = Duplicated in another standard

O = NAEP: 1990 Science Objectives

- BP (SE,122;FE,37;N1E,134;OE,21)
  Uses simple equipment and tools to gather scientific data and extend the senses (e.g., rulers, thermometers, magnifiers, microscopes, calculators)

- BD (SE,122,123;2E,11;FE,26;N1I,134;OE,21,23)
  Knows that good scientific explanations are based on evidence (observations) and scientific knowledge

- BD (SE,123;2I,11;N1I,135;OE,26)
  Knows that scientists make the results of their investigations public; they describe the investigations in ways that enable others to repeat the investigations

- BD (SE,123;N1I,135;OE,23)
  Knows that scientists review and ask questions about the results of other scientists' work

- BD (SI,122;2E,11;FE,26)
  Knows that different people may interpret the same set of observations differently

Level III (Grades 6-8)

- BD (SI,148;2E,12;FI,26;N2I,96;OE,21,24)
  Knows that there is no fixed procedure called "the scientific method," but that investigations involve systematic observations, carefully collected, relevant evidence, logical reasoning, and some imagination in developing hypotheses and explanations

- BP (SE,145;FI,26,38;N2E,96;OE,21)
  Designs and conducts a scientific investigation (e.g., formulates questions, designs and executes investigations, interprets data, synthesizes evidence into explanations, proposes alternative explanations for observations, critiques explanations and procedures)

- BD (2E,12;N2E,94;OI,21)
  Knows that observations can be affected by bias (e.g., strong beliefs about what should happen in particular circumstances can prevent the detection of other results)

- BP (SE,145;N2I,94)
  Uses appropriate tools (including computer hardware and software) and techniques to gather, analyze, and interpret scientific data

- BP (SE,145;FE,26,38;N2I,94;OE,24)
  Establishes relationships based on evidence and logical argument (e.g., provides causes for effects)

- BD (SE,145,148;2I,7;FE,26;OE,23,24)
  Understands the nature of scientific explanations (e.g., emphasis on evidence; use of logically consistent arguments; use of scientific principles, models, and theories; acceptance or displacement based on new scientific evidence)

Codes (right side of page):   BD = Benchmark, Declarative; BP = Benchmark, Procedural; BC = Benchmark, Contextual
1st letter(s) of each code in parentheses   *2nd letter of code*   *Number*
S = NRC: National Science Education Standards   E = Explicitly stated in document   Page number of cited document
2 = Project 2061: Benchmarks for Science Literacy   I = Implied in document   *or, for duplicates:*
C = CDE: Science Framework for CA Public Schools   Standard number & level of duplicate
F = NAEP: 1996 Science Framework
IB,IC,IE,IM,IP: Int'l Bacc.: Biology, Chemistry,   P = NAEP: Science Assess./Exercise Specifications
    Environ. Systems, Middle Yrs Science, Physics   T = Pearsall: NSTA: The Content Core
N1,N2,N3: New Standards: Elementary, Middle, High   D = Duplicated in another standard
O = NAEP: 1990 Science Objectives

McREL

- Knows that scientific inquiry includes evaluating results of scientific investigations, experiments, observations, theoretical and mathematical models, and explanations proposed by other scientists (e.g., reviewing experimental procedures, examining evidence, identifying faulty reasoning, identifying statements that go beyond the evidence, suggesting alternative explanations)

  BD (SE,148,171;2I,7;OI,23-24)

- Knows possible outcomes of scientific investigations (e.g., some may result in new ideas and phenomena for study; some may generate new methods or procedures for an investigation; some may result in the development of new technologies to improve the collection of data; some may lead to new investigations)

  BD (SE,148;2I,12;OI,21)

Level IV (Grades 9-12)

- Understands the use of hypotheses in science (e.g., selecting and narrowing the focus of data, determining additional data to be gathered; guiding the interpretation of data)

  BD (SE,175;2E,13)

- Designs and conducts scientific investigations by formulating testable hypotheses, identifying and clarifying the method, controls, and variables; organizing and displaying data; revising methods and explanations; presenting the results; and receiving critical response from others

  BP (SE,175;2I,13;N3I,85;OE,21)

- Knows that a wide range of natural occurrences may be observed to discern patterns when conditions of an investigation cannot be controlled

  BP (SI,176;2E,13;N3I,84;OE,20)

- Uses technology (e.g., hand tools, measuring instruments, calculators, computers) and mathematics (e.g., measurement, formulas, charts, graphs) to perform accurate scientific investigations and communications

  BP (SE,175,176;IPI,22-24;N3E,84)

- Knows that conceptual principles and knowledge guide scientific inquiries; historical and current scientific knowledge influence the design and interpretation of investigations and the evaluation of proposed explanations made by other scientists

  BD (SE,176;2I,13;FI,26-27,39;IPI,84;OI,26)

- Knows that scientists conduct investigations for a variety of reasons (e.g., to discover new aspects of the natural world, to explain recently observed phenomena, to test the conclusions of prior investigations, to test the predictions of current theories)

  BD (SE,176;2E,13;OE,21)

Codes (right side of page):	BD = Benchmark, Declarative; BP = Benchmark, Procedural; BC = Benchmark, Contextual	
1st letter(s) of each code in parentheses	*2nd letter of code*	*Number*
S = NRC: National Science Education Standards	E = Explicitly stated in document	Page number of cited document
2 = Project 2061: Benchmarks for Science Literacy	I = Implied in document	*or, for duplicates:*
C = CDE: Science Framework for CA Public Schools		Standard number & level of duplicate
F = NAEP: 1996 Science Framework		
IB,IC,IE,IM,IP: Int'l Bacc.: Biology, Chemistry,	P = NAEP: Science Assess./Exercise Specifications	
Environ. Systems, Middle Yrs Science, Physics	T = Pearsall: NSTA: The Content Core	
N1,N2,N3: New Standards: Elementary, Middle, High	D = Duplicated in another standard	
O = NAEP: 1990 Science Objectives		

101

BD (SE,175,176;2I,13;FI,26-27;N3I,85)
- Knows that investigations and public communication among scientists must meet certain criteria in order to result in new knowledge and methods (e.g., arguments must be logical and demonstrate connections between natural phenomena, investigations, and the historical body of scientific knowledge; the methods and procedures used to obtain evidence must be clearly reported to enhance opportunities for further investigation)

(2E,14)

16. Understands the scientific enterprise

Level I (Grades K-2)

BD (SI,138;2E,15;N1I,134)
- Knows that in science it is helpful to work with a team and share findings with others

Level II (Grades 3-5)

BD (SE,138,141;2E,16;N1I,133)
- Knows that people of all ages, backgrounds, and groups have made contributions to science and technology throughout history

BD (SE,141)
- Knows that although people using scientific inquiry have learned much about the objects, events, and phenomena in nature, science is an ongoing process and will never be finished

BD (SE,138;2I,54)
- Knows that scientists and engineers often work in teams to accomplish a task

Level III (Grades 6-8)

BD (SE,170,171;2I,17)
- Knows that people of all backgrounds and with diverse interests, talents, qualities, and motivations engage in fields of science and engineering; some of these people work in teams and others work alone, but all communicate extensively with others

BD (SE,170)
- Knows that the work of science requires a variety of human abilities, qualities, and habits of mind (e.g., reasoning, insight, energy, skill, creativity, intellectual honesty, tolerance of ambiguity, skepticism, openness to new ideas)

BD (SE,169;2E,17)
- Knows various settings in which scientists and engineers may work (e.g., colleges and

Codes (right side of page):   BD = Benchmark, Declarative;   BP = Benchmark, Procedural;   BC = Benchmark, Contextual
1st letter(s) of each code in parentheses   *2nd letter of code*   *Number*
S = NRC: National Science Education Standards   E = Explicitly stated in document   Page number of cited document
2 = Project 2061: Benchmarks for Science Literacy   I = Implied in document   *or, for duplicates:*
C = CDE: Science Framework for CA Public Schools   Standard number & level of duplicate
F = NAEP: 1996 Science Framework
IB,IC,IE,IM,IP: Int'l Bacc.: Biology, Chemistry,   P = NAEP: Science Assess./Exercise Specifications
   Environ. Systems, Middle Yrs Science, Physics   T = Pearsall: NSTA: The Content Core
N1,N2,N3: New Standards: Elementary, Middle, High   D = Duplicated in another standard
O = NAEP: 1990 Science Objectives

102

McREL

universities, businesses and industries, research institutes, government agencies)

- Understands ethics associated with scientific study (e.g., potential subjects must be fully informed of the risks and benefits associated with the research and their right to refuse to participate; potential subjects must be fully informed of possible risks to community and property) BD (SE,169;2E,17;N2I,96)

- Knows that throughout history, many scientific innovators have had difficulty breaking through accepted ideas of their time to reach conclusions that are now considered to be common knowledge BD (SE,171;2I,19;IPE,77-78)

- Knows ways in which science and society influence one another (e.g., scientific knowledge and the procedures used by scientists influence the way many individuals in society think about themselves, others, and the environment; societal challenges often inspire questions for scientific research; social priorities often influence research priorities through the availability of funding for research) BD (SE,169;N2I,93)

Level IV (Grades 9-12)

- Knows that throughout history, diverse cultures have developed scientific ideas and solved human problems through technology BD (SE,201;2E,19)

- Understands that individuals and teams contribute to science and engineering at different levels of complexity (e.g., an individual may conduct basic field studies; hundreds of people may work together on a major scientific question or technological problem) BD (SE,200;2I,19)

- Understands the ethical traditions associated with the scientific enterprise (e.g., commitment to peer review, truthful reporting about the methods and outcomes of investigations, publication of the results of work) and that scientists who violate these traditions are censored by their peers BD (SE,200-201;2E,20;N3I,85)

- Knows that science and technology are essential social enterprises, but alone they can only indicate what can happen, not what should happen BD (SE,199,201)

- Understands that science involves different types of work in many different disciplines (e.g., BD (SE,192;2E,19)

Codes (right side of page):	BD = Benchmark, Declarative; BP = Benchmark, Procedural; BC = Benchmark, Contextual

1st letter(s) of each code in parentheses · *2nd letter of code* · *Number*

S = NRC: National Science Education Standards	E = Explicitly stated in document	Page number of cited document
2 = Project 2061: Benchmarks for Science Literacy	I = Implied in document	*or, for duplicates:*
C = CDE: Science Framework for CA Public Schools		Standard number & level of duplicate
F = NAEP: 1996 Science Framework		
IB,IC,IE,IM,IP: Int'l Bacc.: Biology, Chemistry,	P = NAEP: Science Assess./Exercise Specifications	
Environ. Systems, Middle Yrs Science, Physics	T = Pearsall: NSTA: The Content Core	
N1,N2,N3: New Standards: Elementary, Middle, High	D = Duplicated in another standard	
O = NAEP: 1990 Science Objectives		

MREL

scientists in different disciplines ask different questions, use different methods of investigation, and accept different types of evidence to support their explanations; many scientific investigations require the contributions of individuals from different disciplines; new disciplines of science, such as geophysics and biochemistry, often emerge at the interface of older disciplines)

BD (SE,192;2I,47)

- Knows that creativity, imagination, and a good knowledge base are all required in the work of science and engineering

Codes (right side of page):   BD = Benchmark, Declarative; BP = Benchmark, Procedural; BC = Benchmark, Contextual
1st letter(s) of each code in parentheses   *2nd letter of code*   *Number*
S = NRC: National Science Education Standards   E = Explicitly stated in document   Page number of cited document
2 = Project 2061: Benchmarks for Science Literacy   I = Implied in document   *or, for duplicates:*
C = CDE: Science Framework for CA Public Schools   Standard number & level of duplicate
F = NAEP: 1996 Science Framework
IB,IC,IE,IM,IP: Int'l Bacc.: Biology, Chemistry,   P = NAEP: Science Assess./Exercise Specifications
   Environ. Systems, Middle Yrs Science, Physics   T = Pearsall: NSTA: The Content Core
N1,N2,N3: New Standards: Elementary, Middle, High   D = Duplicated in another standard
O = NAEP: 1990 Science Objectives

HISTORY

9. History

The following process was used to identify standards and benchmarks for history:

Identification of Significant Reports
Ten reports were determined to be appropriate for identifying significant history subject matter for K-12 schooling. Four reports originate from the National Center for History in the Schools (NCHS) History Standards Project: *National Standards for History for Grades K–4: Expanding Children's World in Time and Space* (1994a), *National Standards for United States History: Exploring the American Experience (1994b)*, *National Standards for World History: Exploring Paths to the Present* (1994c), and *National Standards for History* (1996). In addition, NCHS has also published a history survey, *Lessons From History: Essential Understandings and Historical Perspectives Students Should Acquire* (Crabtree, Nash, Gagnon, & Waugh, 1992). Two other significant documents are the *Provisional Item Specifications for the 1994 NAEP in U.S. History* (NAEP, n.d.) and *Historical Literacy: The Case for History in American Education* (Gagnon & Bradley Commission on History in the Schools, 1988). Also useful were documents from the National Council for the Social Studies (NCSS), *Expectations of Excellence: Curriculum Standards for Social Studies* (1994) and from the International Baccalaureate Organization, *History* (1996h) and the *Middle Years Programme: Humanities* (1995c).

Selection of the Reference Document
The NCHS national standards documents were selected as reference documents for world, United States, and K–4 history. The national standards documents were selected because they represent the efforts of a diverse group of historians from schools and universities. In addition, these documents provide a consistent level of detailed information for writing benchmarks by grade range (K–4 history supplies information for grades K–2 and K–4; United States and world history cover grades 5–6, 7–8, and 9–12). Such grade information is not within the scope of a work like *Lessons from History*, which deals primarily with what students should know by the end of their schooling, nor the material available from NAEP, which does not address world history. The NCHS documents were also used as the reference for standards in Historical Understanding, discussed below.

Identification of Standards and Benchmarks
Historical Understanding
In addition to the identification of the facts, events, and episodes of history, the history standards documents also address the following standards under the heading of Historical Thinking: (1) chronological thinking, (2) historical comprehension, (3) historical analysis and interpretation, (4) historical research capabilities and (5) historical issues-analyses and decision-making. These standards consist of 4 to 10 statements each. Our analysis showed that much of this material described general thinking and reasoning abilities or information processing abilities that could be applied to a variety of subject matter, and were not exclusive to history. In accord with our model, this material was integrated into the appropriate standards on thinking and reasoning (see Section 18. Life Skills). Two areas, however, appeared to be uniquely related to the study of history, and appear as standards under the category of Historical Understanding: the first treats chronological

relationships and patterns, and the second addresses the historical perspective. *Historical Literacy* provided supporting material for the historical perspective standard.

World and U.S. History

As noted in section 2, the basic edition of the national history standards, *National Standards for History*, has recently been published. Material from the basic edition has been incorporated into this report, which itself is based on the earlier NCHS expanded editions of *National Standards for U.S. History* and *National Standards for World History*. Thus, both the expanded and basic NCHS editions were used to construct standards and benchmarks. This approach was taken in order to meet the requirements of our model for standards, which seeks to conserve information regarding the appropriate grade level of material wherever that is possible. This grade level information was available in the expanded editions, but not conserved in the basic edition. That is, the expanded editions identified material suitable for grades 5-6, 7-8, and 9-12, while the basic edition identified only material at 5-12, 7-12, and 9-12. Although both editions are combined in this report, it is possible for the reader to discern what benchmark information was drawn from which edition, as well as what benchmark information was found to be common in both editions. For an explanation, see the section below, "How to identify edition sources. "

In order to understand the method used to render material from the expanded editions it is useful to provide a brief description of their structure. There are five levels of organization in the U.S. and world history documents from NCHS. The outermost level is a grouping by historical era. Each era, in turn, is comprised of two to four standards. Beneath the standard level are three other levels, the lowest of which is a description of student achievements that might exemplify attainment of the standard. It is only at this level, "examples of student achievement," that specific content is identified for grades 5–6, 7–8 and 9–12. The intervening levels, that is, the levels between the student achievement descriptions and the standard levels, can be conveniently viewed as topic organizers that serve to provide context.

In order to compose benchmarks, we analyzed the material at all organizational levels. These levels were then combined in such a way that grade level information was conserved as well as the context or topic within which this information was found. To take an example from the expanded edition, the following are tasks, or "examples of student achievement," at grades 9–12 of the *National Standards for World History*:

> Read selections from the philosopher Zhu Xi's conversations with his followers and from the *Schedule for Learning*, and discuss the basic ideas of Neo-Confucianism. Analyze how these ideas affected Chinese society, government, and education

> Read the instructions Zhu Xi gave on rites for honoring ancestors in his Family Rituals, and discuss the relationship between popular rites and Zhu Xi's Neo-Confucian philosophy

> Research how economic changes in China affected society. How mobile was the gentry

class? (p. 133)

These activities are related to the topic headings "...the major dynastic transition China experienced and the changes in Confucianism in the 10th and 13th centuries" and "...the growth of an economically powerful merchant class in China." The headings, in turn, are subsumed under a section beginning "Students should be able to demonstrate understanding of China's extensive urbanization and commercial expansion between the 10th and 13th century..." Taking this information into account, the following single benchmark was developed to cover the activities cited above at grades 9–12:

- Understands significant religious and economic aspects of Chinese society between the 10th and 13th centuries (e.g., the impact of economic growth on Chinese society and how it affected the gentry class; how Zhu Xi's basic ideas of Neo-Confucianism affected Chinese society, government, and education)

In one sense, the "stuff" of history — the defining facts, events, and episodes — is not amenable to such presentation by developmental levels; and aside from the advantages of introducing information in a chronological sequence, we have not discovered other arguments or research on how this kind of material might be benchmarked. As noted in *Lessons From History*, however, "Historical knowledge must go beyond the factual knowledge implicit in these lists — *important though that knowledge is* — to the explanations of the causes and consequences of these events and the interpretations which can be drawn concerning their enduring significance" (p. 48). What varies from grade level to grade level in the expanded editions of the standards documents from NCHS is the sophistication of the "examples of student achievement." These activities are somewhat problematic, in that they mix curriculum and performance with content standards. Additionally, these activities were criticized by a panel convened by the Council for Basic Education (see Section 2, "History") "for undermining principles of scholarship by asking leading questions or by inviting students to make easy moral judgments about historical questions that continue to be debated by scholars" ("Review panels," CBE, October 1995). Our analysis of these activities solely for content, however, did indicate some level of distinction between grades, for generally speaking, it was often possible to discern between grade levels a difference in the level of detail and depth of understanding demanded from students. Thus, when the activities of the expanded editions were examined solely for their content, and the specific and controversial task requirements were removed, they were found to provide useful information for the composition of benchmarks at a narrower range of grades than was available from the basic edition.

K-4 History

A similar, though somewhat simpler, content structure was found in the expanded edition of the *National Standards for History for Grades K–4*, as was found in the U.S. and world history documents, and the kind of analysis described above was applied to that document to generate the standards and benchmarks at the levels K–2 and 3–4.

Integration of Information from Other Documents
Historical Understanding
For material addressing the topics related to chronology and the historical perspective, a number of supporting documents were found to be useful. Primary among them was *Historical Literacy.* The *Curriculum Standards* document from NCSS also addresses these topics in the curriculum standard "Time, Continuity, & Change," and was used to provide supplementary citations. The International Baccalaureate Organization addresses closely related subjects in *History* (1996h) and the *Middle Years Programme: Humanities* (1995c) and these documents are cited in the benchmarks wherever appropriate.

World and U.S. History
The U.S. history standards include citations from NAEP's *Provisional Item Specifications for the 1994 NAEP in U.S. History.* The survey work from NCHS, *Lessons from History,* was also used to provide supplementary citations for both world and U.S. history.

A Note on the Number of History Standards
The number of standards identified for history in this document might at first appear formidable (see figure 5.1 in Section 5. The Process Used in this Report). However, when considered in terms of how these standards are designed for use, the number of standards in U.S. or world history is more closely comparable to the number of standards found in other subject areas. In history, unlike other areas, each set of benchmarks (at grades 5–6, 7–8, and 9–12) is designed to provide a full description of that standard; in other words, as is the case in most schooling now, material for one historical era is unlikely to be repeated at a different level of schooling. Once a standard is met at a particular grade level, the student is no longer required to meet it.

As an example, if a school or district should decide to teach the era on "Civil War and Reconstruction" at the 7–8 grade levels, the standards and benchmarks under that era would not be addressed again at 9–12. It is assumed, however, that the students would be familiar with benchmark material from the lower grade levels. For other subject-area standards in this report, by contrast, if a standard has benchmarks listed at more than one grade level, it indicates that the student is expected to meet benchmarks in the other grade levels listed.

Thus, as a hypothetical example, if the standards were implemented fairly evenly across grade levels, each student studying U.S. history would not be responsible for more than 10 standards (31 standards by the 3 years of study recommended by NCHS) at any one time. In world history, the design is only a little more complicated and results in greater flexibility. In addition to the design for implementation found in U.S. history, the authors of the expanded edition of world history have identified material as "core" or "related." Core material is deemed essential for a grounding in world history; "related" material is important, but not critical, and can be omitted if necessary. In this report, each benchmark in world history is designated as either "core" (C) or "related" (R). However, benchmarks that are found only in the NCHS basic edition do not have "core" or "related" designations.

How to identify edition sources

Benchmarks that appear prefixed with an arrow bullet (▸) represent material not found in the basic edition. Thus, all content in the following benchmark was found only in the expanded edition:

BD (AE,54)

▸ Understands how family and gender roles of different regions of colonial America changed across time (1600-1700)

Very frequently, the same topic was found in both editions, but more extensive information was available in the expanded edition. When both editions cover a similar topic, an arrow bullet within a benchmark indicates that the material following it is found only in the expanded edition, as in the following example:

BD (BE,79;AE,48;LI,55-57;NE,41,42)

● Understands aspects of the Spanish exploration, conquest, and immigration to the Americas in the centuries following Columbus (e.g., Spanish interactions with the Aztec, Inca, and Pueblo; ▸ the expeditions of Cabeza de Vaca and Francisco Vasquez de Coronado in the American Southwest; the conquest of Spanish America)

Finally, some new material is introduced that appears only in the basic edition. These benchmarks are prefixed with a square bullet (■).

Summary of Standards for Historical Understanding

1. Understands and knows how to analyze chronological relationships and patterns
2. Understands the historical perspective

(BE,60-61;AE,18;WE,18)

1. Understands and knows how to analyze chronological relationships and patterns

Level I (Grades K-2)

BP (BE,18;KE,19)
- Knows how to identify the beginning, middle, and end of historical stories, myths, and narratives

BP (BI,18;KE,19)
- Knows how to develop picture time lines ▶ of their own lives or their family's history

BC (BE,17;KE,19;SSI,34,51)
- Distinguishes among broad categories of historical time (e.g., long, long ago; long ago; yesterday; today; tomorrow)

BD (BE,18;KE,19)
- Understands calendar time in days, weeks, and months

BD (BI,18;KE,19;SSI,34,51)
- Knows how to identify change and continuity ▶ in his or her own life

Level II (Grades 3-5)

BD (BE,18 KE,19)
- Understands calendar time in years, decades, and centuries

BP (BE,18;KE,19;SSI,34,51)
- Knows how to construct time lines ▶ in significant historical developments that mark at evenly spaced intervals the years, decades, and centuries

BP (BE,18;KE,20;SSI,34,51)
- Knows how to interpret data presented in time lines (e.g., ▶ identify the time at which events occurred; the sequence in which events developed; what else was occurring at the time)

BP (BI,18;KE,20;SSI,34,51)
- Knows how to identify patterns of change and continuity ▶ in the history of the community, state, and nation, and in the lives of people of various cultures from times long ago until today

BC (BE,18;KE,19)
- Distinguishes between past, present, and future time

BD (KE,19)
▶ Understands the broadly defined eras of state and local historical events

---

Codes (right side of page):	BD = Benchmark, Declarative; BP = Benchmark, Procedural; BC = Benchmark, Contextual	
1st letter of each code in parentheses	*2nd letter of code*	*Number*
B = NCHS: basic edition	E = Explicitly stated in document	Page number of cited document
A = NCHS: U.S. History, expanded edition	I = Implied in document	
G = Gagnon: Historical Literacy		
IH,IU = Int'l. Bacc.: History, Humanities	*Symbol*	
K = NCHS: K-4 History, expanded edition	■ material appears only in NCHS basic edition	
L = Lessons from History	▶ material appears only in NCHS expanded edition	
SS = NCSS: Curric. Standards for Social Studies	● material appears in both NCHS editions	
W= NCHS: World History, expanded edition		

111

McREL

Level III (Grades 6-8)

- Knows how to diagram the temporal structure of events ▸ in autobiographies, biographies, literary narratives, and historical narratives, and understands the differences between them
  BP (BI,62;AE,21)

- Knows how to construct and interpret multiple tier time lines (e.g., ▸ a time line that contains important social, economic, and political developments in colonial history; a time line that compares developments in the English, French, and Spanish colonies in North America)
  BP (BI,63;AE,21)

- Knows how to calculate calendar time B.C. (before Christ) or B.C.E. (before the Common Era), and A.D. (Anno Domini) or C.E. (in the Common Era), determining the onset, duration, and ending dates of historical events or developments
  BP (BE,63;AE,21)

- Understands patterns of change and continuity in the historical succession of related events
  BD (BE,63;AE,21,22;SSE,34,82)

- Knows how to impose temporal structure on their historical narratives (e.g., working backward from some issue, problem, or event to explain its causes that arose from some beginning and developed through subsequent transformations over time)
  BP (BE,62;AE,21,22)

- ▸ Knows how to periodize events of the nation into broadly defined eras
  BP (AE,21)

Level IV (Grades 9-12)

- Knows how to identify the temporal structure and connections disclosed in historical narratives
  BP (BE,62;AE,22)

- Understands historical continuity and change ▸ related to a particular development or theme (e.g., the Industrial Revolution, the evolution of democracy in the U.S.)
  BD (BE,63;AE,22;SSE,34,113)

- Understands the organizing principles of alternative models of historical periodization
  BD (BE,63;AE,22)

- ▸ Understands alternative systems of recording time (e.g., Egyptian, Indian, Mayan, Muslim, Jewish), astronomical systems on which they are based (e.g., solar, lunar, semilunar), their fixed points for measuring time, and their strengths and weaknesses
  BD (AE,22)

Codes (right side of page):	BD = Benchmark, Declarative; BP = Benchmark, Procedural; BC = Benchmark, Contextual

1st letter of each code in parentheses   *2nd letter of code*   *Number*

B = NCHS: basic edition   E = Explicitly stated in document   Page number of cited document

A = NCHS: U.S. History, expanded edition   I = Implied in document

G = Gagnon: Historical Literacy

IH,IU = Int'l. Bacc.: History, Humanities   *Symbol*

K = NCHS: K-4 History, expanded edition   ■ material appears only in NCHS basic edition

L = Lessons from History   ▸ material appears only in NCHS expanded edition

SS = NCSS: Curric. Standards for Social Studies   ● material appears in both NCHS editions

W= NCHS: World History, expanded edition

MREL

(BI,60-61;AI,18-19;GE,25;WI,18-19)

2. Understands the historical perspective

Level II (Grades 5-6)

■ Knows how to view the past in terms of the norms and values of the time
BD (BE,19;GI,25)

● Understands that specific individuals had a great impact on history
BD (BE,21;KE,23;LI,41)

● Understands that specific ideas had an impact on history
BD (BE,21;KE,23;LI,41)

● Understands that "chance events" had an impact on history
BD (BE,21;KE,23;LI,41)

● Understands that specific decisions and events had an impact on history
BD (BI,21;KE,23;LI,41)

● Evaluates historical fiction according to the accuracy of its content and the author's interpretation
BD (BE,21;KE,23)

▶ Predicts how events might have turned out differently in one's local community if specific individuals or groups had chosen different courses of action
BP (KE,24;LI,41)

Level III (Grades 7-8)

● Understands that specific individuals and the values those individuals held had an impact on history
BD (GE,26;AI,27-28;BI,66;WE,24;LI,41)

● Analyzes the influence specific ideas and beliefs had on a period of history
BP (BE,66;AE,27;WI,25;LI,41)

● Analyzes the effect that specific "chance events" had on history
BP (BE,66;AE,27;GI,26;LI,41;WI,25)

● Analyzes the effects specific decisions had on history
BP (BI,66;AI,27;WI,25;LI,41)

● Understands that historical accounts are subject to change based on newly uncovered records and interpretations
BD (BE,66;AE,27;WE,28;LI,41;SSI,34,82)

● Knows different types of primary and secondary sources and the motives, interests, and bias
BD (BE,68;AE,28;GI,317;IUI,12;SI,34,82)

Codes (right side of page):	BD = Benchmark, Declarative; BP = Benchmark, Procedural; BC = Benchmark, Contextual

1st letter of each code in parentheses — *2nd letter of code* — *Number*

B = NCHS: basic edition — E = Explicitly stated in document — Page number of cited document
A = NCHS: U.S. History, expanded edition — I = Implied in document
G = Gagnon: Historical Literacy
IH,IU = Int'l. Bacc.: History, Humanities — *Symbol*
K = NCHS: K-4 History, expanded edition — ■ material appears only in NCHS basic edition
L = Lessons from History — ▶ material appears only in NCHS expanded edition
SS = NCSS: Curric. Standards for Social Studies — ● material appears in both NCHS editions
W= NCHS: World History, expanded edition

expressed in them (e.g., eyewittness accounts, letters, diaries, artifacts, photos; magazine articles, newspaper accounts, hearsay)

Level IV (Grades 9-12)

BP (BI,66;AI,27;GE,26;WI,25;LI,41)
- Analyzes the values held by specific people who influenced history and the role their values played in influencing history

BP (BI,66;AI,27;WI,25;LI,41)
- Analyzes the influences specific ideas and beliefs had on a period of history and specifies how events might have been different in the absence of those ideas and beliefs

BP (BI,66;AI,27;WI,25;LI,41)
- Analyzes the effects that specific "chance events" had on history and specifies how things might have been different in the absence of those events

BP (BI,66;AI,27;WI,28;LI,41)
- Analyzes the effects specific decisions had on history and studies how things might have been different in the absence of those decisions

BD (GE,25;LI,41)
- Understands that the consequences of human intentions are influenced by the means of carrying them out

BD (GE,25;LI,41)
- Understands that change and continuity are equally probable and natural

BP (GE,26;LI,41)
- Knows how to avoid seizing upon particular lessons of history as cures for present ills

BD (BE,66;AE,27;GE,26,314-315;LI,41)
- Understands how past events are affected by the irrational (e.g., the assassination of John F. Kennedy or Archduke Francis Ferdinand) and the accidental (e.g., the discovery of America by Christopher Columbus)

BC (BE,66;AI,28;LI,41;SSI,34,113;WI,28)
- Analyzes how specific historical events would be interpreted differently based on newly uncovered records and/or information

BD (GE,25;LI,41)
- Understands how the past affects our private lives and society in general

BP (GE,25;BI,64;IUI,12;LI,41)
- Knows how to perceive past events with historical empathy

BP (BE,64;AE,28;GI,317;IH,6;IUE,12;SSE,34,113)
- Knows how to evaluate the credibility and authenticity of historical sources

---

- Evaluates the validity and credibility of different historical interpretations

  BD (BE,64;AE,28;GI,316-317;IH,6)

- Uses historical maps to understand the relationship between historical events and geography

  BP (BE,64;AE,24)

Codes (right side of page):   BD = Benchmark, Declarative; BP = Benchmark, Procedural; BC = Benchmark, Contextual

1st letter of each code in parentheses	*2nd letter of code*	*Number*
B = NCHS: basic edition	E = Explicitly stated in document	Page number of cited document
A = NCHS: U.S. History, expanded edition	I = Implied in document	
G = Gagnon: Historical Literacy		
IH,IU = Int'l. Bacc.: History, Humanities		
K = NCHS: K-4 History, expanded edition	*Symbol*	
L = Lessons from History	■ material appears only in NCHS basic edition	
SS = NCSS: Curric. Standards for Social Studies	▸ material appears only in NCHS expanded edition	
W= NCHS: World History, expanded edition	● material appears in both NCHS editions	

McREL

Summary of Standards for Grades K-4 History

Topic 1 Living and Working Together in Families and Communities, Now and Long Ago
1. Understands family life now and in the past, and family life in various places long ago
2. Understands the history of the local community and how communities in North America varied long ago

Topic 2 The History of Students' Own State or Region
3. Understands the people, events, problems, and ideas that were significant in creating the history of their state

Topic 3 The History of the United States: Democratic Principles and Values and the People from Many Cultures who Contributed to its Cultural, Economic, and Political Heritage
4. Understands how democratic values came to be, and how they have been exemplified by people, events, and symbols
5. Understands the causes and nature of movements of large groups of people into and within the United States, now and long ago
6. Understands the folklore and other cultural contributions from various regions of the United States and how they helped to form a national heritage

Topic 4 The History of Peoples of Many Cultures Around the World
7. Understands selected attributes and historical developments of societies in Africa, the Americas, Asia, and Europe
8. Understands major discoveries in science and technology, some of their social and economic effects, and the major scientists and inventors responsible for them

(BE,26;KE,32)

1. Understands family life now and in the past, and family life in various places long ago

Level I (Grades K-2)

BD (BE,26;KE,32,33)
- Knows a family history through two generations (e.g., various family members and their connections)

BC (BE,26;KE,32,33)
- Understands family life today and how it compares with family life in the recent past and family life long ago (e.g., roles, jobs, schooling experiences)

BC (BE,26;KE,32,33)
- Knows the cultural similarities and differences in clothes, homes, food, communication, technology, and cultural traditions between families now and in the past

BC (BE,26;KE,32,33)
- Understands family life in a community of the past and life in a community of the present (e.g., roles, jobs, communication, technology, style of homes, transportation, schools, religious observances, cultural traditions)

BD (BE,27;KE,34)
- Understands personal family or cultural heritage through stories, songs, and celebrations

BD (BE,27;KE,34)
- Knows ways in which people share family beliefs and values (e.g., oral traditions, literature, songs, art, religion, community celebrations, mementos, food, language)

Level II (Grades 3-4)

BD (BE,27;KE,34)
- Knows the ways that families long ago expressed and transmitted their beliefs and values through oral tradition, literature, songs, art, religion, community celebrations, mementos, food, and language (e.g., ▸ celebration of national holidays, religious observances, and ethnic and national traditions; visual arts and crafts; hymns, proverbs, and songs)

BD (BE,27;KE,34,35)
- Understands the dreams and ideals that people from various groups have sought, some of the problems they encountered in realizing their dreams, and the sources of their strength and determination that families drew upon and shared (e.g., ▸ families arriving together in America and living together in rural or urban settings, traditions brought from their cultural past)

Codes (right side of page):   BD = Benchmark, Declarative; BP = Benchmark, Procedural; BC = Benchmark, Contextual
1st letter of each code in parentheses   *2nd letter of code*   *Number*
B = NCHS: basic edition   E = Explicitly stated in document   Page number of cited document
K = NCHS: K-4 History, expanded edition   I = Implied in document
N = NAEP: Provisional Item Specifications

Symbol
▸ material appears only in NCHS expanded edition
● material appears in both NCHS editions

McREL

BD (KE,32,33;NI,17)

► Understands daily life of a farm family from long ago (e.g., work, clothing, tools, food and food production in the early 1800's)

(BE,27;KE,36)

2. **Understands the history of a local community and how communities in North America varied long ago**

Level I (Grades K-2)

BD (BE,27;KE,36)

● Understands changes in community life over time (e.g., changes in goods and services; changes in architecture and landscape; change in jobs, schooling, transportation, communication, religion, recreation)

BD (BE,27;KE,36)

● Understands the contributions and significance of historical figures of the community

BD (BE,28;KE,38;NI,3)

● Understands the daily life and values of early Hawaiian or Native American cultures

BD (BE,28;KE,38;NI,7,8)

● Understands the daily life of a colonial community (e.g., Plymouth, Williamsburg, St. Augustine, San Antonio, Post Vincennes)

BD (BE,28;KE,38;NI,17)

● Understands life in a pioneer farming community (e.g., the Old Northwest, the prairies, the Southwest, eastern Canada, the Far West)

Level II (Grades 3-4)

BD (BE,27;KE,36,37)

● Knows of problems in the community's past, the different perspectives of those involved, the choices people had, and the solutions they chose

BD (BE,28;KE,38;NI,3)

● Knows geographical settings, economic activities, food, clothing, homes, crafts, and rituals of Native American societies long ago (e.g., Iroquois, Sioux, Hopi, Nez Perce, Inuit, Cherokee)

BD (BE,28;KE,38;NI,7)

● Understands the historical development and daily life of a colonial community (e.g., Plymouth, Williamsburg, St. Augustine, San Antonio, Post Vincennes)

Codes (right side of page):   BD = Benchmark, Declarative; BP = Benchmark, Procedural; BC = Benchmark, Contextual

1st letter of each code in parentheses	*2nd letter of code*	*Number*
B = NCHS: basic edition	E = Explicitly stated in document	Page number of cited document
K = NCHS: K-4 History, expanded edition	I = Implied in document	
N = NAEP: Provisional Item Specifications		

Symbol

► material appears only in NCHS expanded edition

● material appears in both NCHS editions

● Understands the challenges and difficulties encountered by people in pioneer farming communities (e.g., the Old Northwest, the prairies, the Southwest, eastern Canada, the Far West) BD (BE,28;KE,38,39;NI,17)

● Understands how geographical features contributed to the establishment and growth of communities such as mining towns (e.g., Sacramento) and trading settlements (e.g., New Orleans, Vincennes, Astoria) BD (BE,28;KE,38,39)

● Understands daily life in ethnically diverse urban communities long ago (e.g., a free African American community in Philadelphia, an Italian community in New York, a Chinese community in San Francisco) BD (BE,28;KE,38,39;NI,24)

▶ Knows the history of the local community since its founding, the people who came, the changes they brought, and significant events over time BD (KE,36,37)

▶ Understands changes in land use and economic activities in the local community since its founding (e.g., changes in technology, the work people did, transportation, local resources) BD (KE,36,37)

(BE,29;KE,36)

3. **Understands the people, events, problems, and ideas that were significant in creating the history of their state**

Level I (Grades K-2)

● Understands through legends, myths, and archaeological evidence the origins and culture of early Native Americans or Hawaiians who lived in the state or region BD (BE,29;KE,40,41;NI,3)

● Knows ways in which early explorers and settlers adapted to, used, and changed the environment of the state or region BD (BE,29;KE,41)

● Understands the reasons different groups came to the state or region BD (BE,30;KE,43)

● Understands the different lives, plans, and dreams of the various racial and ethnic groups who lived in the state 100-200 years ago BD (BE,30;KE,43)

Codes (right side of page): BD = Benchmark, Declarative; BP = Benchmark, Procedural; BC = Benchmark, Contextual
1st letter of each code in parentheses   *2nd letter of code*   *Number*
B = NCHS: basic edition   E = Explicitly stated in document   Page number of cited document
K = NCHS: K-4 History, expanded edition   I = Implied in document
N = NAEP: Provisional Item Specifications

Symbol
▶ material appears only in NCHS expanded edition
● material appears in both NCHS editions

119   MREL

- Understands how symbols, slogans, and mottoes represent the state $\quad$ BD (BE,31;KE,43,44)

- Knows important buildings, statues, and monuments in the state's history $\quad$ BD (BE,31;KE,46)

Level II (Grades 3-4)

- Understands differences between the lives of Native Americans or Hawaiians today and their lives 100 years ago $\quad$ BC (BE,29;KE,40,41)

- Understands geographic, economic, and religious reasons that brought the first explorers and settlers to the state or region, who they were, and where they settled $\quad$ BD (BE,29;KE,41)

- Understands the interactions that occurred between the Native Americans or Hawaiians and the first European, African, and Asian-Pacific explorers and settlers in the state or region $\quad$ BD (BE,29;KE,41;NI,6,7,15)

- Knows about the first inhabitants who lived in the state or region, each successive group of arrivals and their countries (or origin), and significant changes that developed as a result of each group's arrival $\quad$ BD (BE,30;KE,43,44)

- Understands the reasons recent immigrants came to the state or region, what their lives were like, and their experiences of adjustment (e.g., ► problems and opportunities experienced in housing, the workplace, and the community) $\quad$ BD (BE,30;KE,43,44)

- Understands patterns and changes in population over a period of time in a city or town in the state or region $\quad$ BD (BE,30;KE,43,44)

- Knows the chronological order of major historical events that are part of the states's history, their significance and the impact on people then and now, and their relationship to the history of the nation $\quad$ BD (BE,30;KE,45,46)

- Understands major historical events and developments in the state or region that involved interaction among various groups $\quad$ BD (BE,31;KE,45)

- Understands the influence of geography on the history of the state or region, and issues and approaches to problems (e.g., land use, environmental problems) $\quad$ BD (BE,31;KE,45)

Codes (right side of page):   BD = Benchmark, Declarative; BP = Benchmark, Procedural; BC = Benchmark, Contextual

1st letter of each code in parentheses	2nd letter of code	Number
B = NCHS: basic edition	E = Explicitly stated in document	Page number of cited document
K = NCHS: K-4 History, expanded edition	I = Implied in document	
N = NAEP: Provisional Item Specifications		

Symbol
► material appears only in NCHS expanded edition
● material appears in both NCHS editions

BD (BE,31;KE,46;NI,16)

- Understands how the ideas of significant people affected the history of the state

BD (BE,31;KE,46)

- Understands the unique historical conditions that influenced the formation of the state and how statehood was granted

BD (KE,46)

▸ Knows the origin of the names of places, rivers, cities, and counties, and knows the various cultural influences within a particular region

(BE,32;KE,38)

4. Understands how democratic values came to be, and how they have been exemplified by people, events, and symbols

Level I (Grades K-2)

BD (BE,32;KE,48,49;NE,10,11)

- Knows the English colonists who became revolutionary leaders and fought for independence from England (e.g., ▸ George Washington, Thomas Jefferson, Benjamin Franklin)

BD (BE,32;KE,48,49;NE,31,32)

- Understands how individuals have worked to achieve the liberties and equality promised in the principles of American democracy and to improve the lives of people from many groups (e.g., ▸ Rosa Parks, Martin Luther King, Jr.; Soujourner Truth; Cesar Chavez)

BD (BE,33;KE,50)

- Understands ways in which such fundamental values as fairness, protection of individual rights, and responsibility for the common good have been applied by different groups of people (e.g., ▸ students and personnel in the local school)

BD (BE,33;KE,50)

- Knows how different groups of people in the community have taken responsibility for the common good (e.g., ▸ the police department, the fire department, senior citizen home, soup kitchen)

BD (BE,33;KE,51)

- Understands how important figures reacted to their times and why they were significant to the history of our democracy (e.g., ▸ George Washington; Thomas Jefferson; Abraham Lincoln; Soujourner Truth; Susan B. Anthony; Mary McLeod Bethune; Eleanor Roosevelt; Martin Luther King, Jr.)

BD (BE,33;KE,51)

- Understands the ways in which people in a variety of fields have advanced the cause of

Codes (right side of page):   BD = Benchmark, Declarative; BP = Benchmark, Procedural; BC = Benchmark, Contextual
1st letter of each code in parentheses   *2nd letter of code*   *Number*
B = NCHS: basic edition   E = Explicitly stated in document   Page number of cited document
K = NCHS: K-4 History, expanded edition   I = Implied in document
N = NAEP: Provisional Item Specifications

Symbol
▸ material appears only in NCHS expanded edition
● material appears in both NCHS editions

121   MREL

human rights, equality, and the common good (e.g., ▸ Frederick Douglass, Clara Barton, Elizabeth Blackwell, Jackie Robinson, Rosa Parks, Jonas Salk, Cesar Chavez)

BD (BE,33;KE,52;NE,32)
- Understands the reasons that Americans celebrate certain national holidays (e.g., Martin Luther King, Jr. Day; the Fourth of July; Memorial Day)

BD (BE,33;KE,53)
- Knows the history of American symbols (e.g., the eagle, the Liberty Bell, George Washington as the "father of our country," the national flag)

BD (BE,33;KE,53;NI,24)
- Knows why important buildings, statues, and monuments (e.g., the White House, Lincoln Memorial, Statue of Liberty, Ellis Island, Angel Island, Mt. Rushmore, veterans' memorials) are associated with state and national history

BD (KE,50)
▸ Understands how people have helped newcomers get settled and learn the ways of the new country (e.g., family members, fraternal organizations, houses of worship)

Level II (Grades 3-4)

BD (BE,32;KE,49;NE,10,11)
- Understands the basic ideas set forth in the Declaration of Independence and the U.S. Constitution, and the figures responsible for these documents

BD (BE,32;KE,49;NI,10,11)
- Understands the basic principles of American democracy; right to life, liberty, and the pursuit of happiness; responsibility for the common good; equality of opportunity and equal protection of the law; freedom of speech and religion; majority rule with protection for minority rights; and limitations on government, with power held by the people and delegated by them to those officials whom they elected to office

BD (BE,32;KE,49;NE,21,31,32)
- Understands how people over the last 200 years have continued to struggle to bring to all groups in American society the liberties and equality promised in the basic principles of American democracy (e.g., ▸ Sojourner Truth; Harriet Tubman; Frederick Douglass; W.E.B. DuBois; Booker T. Washington; Susan B. Anthony; Martin Luther King, Jr.; Rosa Parks; Cesar Chavez)

BD (BE,33;KE,50)
- Understands the accomplishments of ordinary people in historical situations and how each struggled for individual rights or for the common good (e.g., ▸ James Armistead, Sybil Ludington, Nathan Beman, Lydia Darragh, Betty Zane)

Codes (right side of page):	BD = Benchmark, Declarative; BP = Benchmark, Procedural; BC = Benchmark, Contextual	
1st letter of each code in parentheses	*2nd letter of code*	*Number*
B = NCHS: basic edition	E = Explicitly stated in document	Page number of cited document
K = NCHS: K-4 History, expanded edition	I = Implied in document	
N = NAEP: Provisional Item Specifications		

Symbol
▸ material appears only in NCHS expanded edition
● material appears in both NCHS editions

- Understands how people in the local community have displayed courage in helping the common good (e.g., ▸ volunteering in unique situations including earthquakes, floods, and fires)
  BD (BE,33;KE,51)

- Understands historical figures who believed in the fundamental democratic values (e.g., justice, truth, equality, the rights of the individual, responsibility for the common good, voting rights) and the significance of these people both in their historical context and today
  BD (BE,33;KE,51,52)

- Understands how historical figures in the U.S. and in other parts of the world have advanced the rights of individuals and promoted the common good, and the character traits that made them successful (e.g., persistence, problem solving, moral responsibility, respect for others)
  BD (BE,33;KE,51,52)

- Understands the historical events and democratic values commemorated by major national holidays (e.g., Martin Luther King, Jr. Day; President's Day; Memorial Day; the Fourth of July; Labor Day; Veteran's Day; Thanksgiving)
  BD (BE,33;KE,52,53;NE,32)

- Knows the history of events and the historic figures responsible for such historical documents as the Mayflower Compact, the Declaration of Independence, the U.S. Constitution, the Bill of Rights, and the Emancipation Proclamation)
  BD (BE,33;KE,52,53)

- Knows the Pledge of Allegiance and patriotic songs, poems, and sayings that were written long ago, and understands their significance
  BD (BE,34;KE,53,54;NI,32)

- Understands how songs, symbols, and slogans demonstrate freedom of expression and the role of protest in a democracy (e.g., ▸ the Boston Tea Party, the abolition of slavery, women's suffrage, labor movements, the civil rights movement)
  BD (BE,34;KE,53,54)

▸ Understands why Americans and those who lead them (e.g., George Washington, Benjamin Franklin, and Thomas Jefferson) went to war to win independence from England
  BD (KE,48,49;NE,10)

▸ Understands how ordinary people have worked to contribute money and ideas to create or enhance our national symbols (e.g., French school children who raised money for the Statue of Liberty, Lee Iaccoca's work to restore Ellis Island)
  BD (KE,54)

▸ Understands how people have helped make the community a better place to live (e.g., working to preserve the environment, helping the homeless, restoring houses in low-income areas)
  BD (KE,51)

Codes (right side of page):   BD = Benchmark, Declarative; BP = Benchmark, Procedural; BC = Benchmark, Contextual

1st letter of each code in parentheses   *2nd letter of code*   *Number*

B = NCHS: basic edition   E = Explicitly stated in document   Page number of cited document

K = NCHS: K-4 History, expanded edition   I = Implied in document

N = NAEP: Provisional Item Specifications

Symbol

▸ material appears only in NCHS expanded edition

● material appears in both NCHS editions

MREL

(BE,34;KE,55)

5. Understands the causes and nature of movements of large groups of people into and within the United States, now and long ago

Level I (Grades K-2)

BD (KE,55)

▸   Understands what life was like for children and families "on the trail" when they moved from one part of the U.S. to another

Level II (Grades 3-4)

BD (BE,34;KE,55)

●   Knows the various movements (westward, northward, and eastward) of large groups of people in the history of the U.S.

BD (BE,34;KE,55;NI,15,16,18)

●   Knows about the forced relocation of Native Americans and how their lives, rights, and territories were affected by European colonization and expansion of the U.S. (e.g., Spanish colonization of the Southwest, Tecumseh's resistance to Indian removal, the Cherokee Trail of Tears, Black Hawk's War, the movement of the Nez Perce)

BD (BE,34;KE,55;NE,17)

●   Understands the experience of immigrants groups (e.g., where they came from, why they left, travel experiences, ports of entry and immigration screening, the opportunities and obstacles they encountered when they arrived; ▸ changes that occurred when they moved to the United States)

BD (BE,34;KE,55)

●   Knows the reasons why various groups (e.g., freed African Americans, Mexican and Puerto Rican migrant workers, Dust Bowl farm families) migrated to different parts of the U.S.

BD (BE,34;KE,55)

●   Understands the experiences of those who moved from farm to city during the periods when cities grew

---

Codes (right side of page):
1st letter of each code in parentheses
B = NCHS: basic edition
K = NCHS: K-4 History, expanded edition
N = NAEP: Provisional Item Specifications

BD = Benchmark, Declarative; BP = Benchmark, Procedural; BC = Benchmark, Contextual
2nd letter of code
E = Explicitly stated in document
I = Implied in document

Number
Page number of cited document

Symbol
▸ material appears only in NCHS expanded edition
● material appears in both NCHS editions

(BE,35;KE,57)

6. Understands the folklore and other cultural contributions from various regions of the United States and how they helped to form a national heritage

Level I (Grades K-2)

- Knows regional folk heroes, stories, or songs that have contributed to the development of the cultural history of the U.S. (e.g., ▸ Pecos Bill, Brer Rabbit, Paul Bunyan, Davey Crockett, John Henry, Joe Magarac) BD (BE,35;KE,57;NE,17)

▸ Knows the differences between toys and games children played long ago and the toys and games of today BD (KE,57)

Level II (Grades 3-4)

- Understands how regional folk heroes and other popular figures have contributed to the cultural history of the U.S. (e.g., ▸ frontiersmen such as Daniel Boone, cowboys, mountain men such as Jedediah Smith, American Indian Chiefs including Geronimo, and outlaws such as Billy the Kid) BD (BE,35,KE,57,58)

- Understands how stories, legends, songs, ballads, games, and tall tales describe the environment, lifestyles, beliefs, and struggles of people in various regions of the country BD (BE,35;KE,57,58)

- Understands how arts, crafts, music, and language of people from a variety of regions long ago influenced the nation BD (BE,35;KE,57,58)

(BE,36;KE,60)

7. Understands selected attributes and historical developments of societies in Africa, the Americas, Asia, and Europe

Level I (Grades K-2)

- Understands the main ideas found in folktales, stories of great heroism, fables, legends, and BD (BE,36;KE,61)

Codes (right side of page):	BD = Benchmark, Declarative; BP = Benchmark, Procedural; BC = Benchmark, Contextual	
1st letter of each code in parentheses	*2nd letter of code*	*Number*
B = NCHS: basic edition	E = Explicitly stated in document	Page number of cited document
K = NCHS: K 4 History, expanded edition	I = Implied in document	
N = NAEP: Provisional Item Specifications		
	Symbol	
	▸ material appears only in NCHS expanded edition	
	● material appears in both NCHS editions	

MREL

myths from around the world that reflect the beliefs and ways of living of various cultures in times past

- Knows the holidays and ceremonies of different societies (e.g., ▸ Christmas celebrations in Scandinavia, Germany, or England; Cinco de Mayo; the Chinese New Year; the Japanese tea ceremony; harvest and spring festivals) BD (BE,36;KE,61)

- Understands the daily life, history, and beliefs of a country as reflected in dance, music, or the other art forms (▸ such as paintings, sculptures, and masks) BD (BE,36;KE,61)

- Knows the journeys of Marco Polo and Christopher Columbus, the routes they took, and what happened as a result of their travels BD (BE,37;KE,62;NI,2,3,5)

Level II (Grades 3-4)

- Understands how historians learn about the past if there are no written records BD (BE,36;KE,60)

- Knows the effects geography has had on the different aspects of societies (e.g., the development of urban centers, food, clothing, industry, agriculture, shelter, trade) BD (BE,36;KE,60)

- Understands various aspects of family life, structures, and roles in different cultures and in many eras (e.g., ▸ medieval families, matrilineal families in Africa, extended families in China) BD (BE,36;KE,60,61;NI,2,3)

- Knows about life in urban areas and communities of various cultures of the world at various times in their history (e.g., ▸ Rome, Tenochtitlán, Timbuktu, a medieval European city) BD (BE,36;KE,60,61)

- Knows significant historical achievements of various cultures of the world (e.g., ▸ the Hanging Gardens of Babylon, the Taj Mahal in India, pyramids in Egypt, temples in ancient Greece, bridges and aqueducts in ancient Rome) BD (BE,36;KE,60,61)

- Knows about the migrations of large groups in the past and recently (e.g., Native American ancestors across the Bering land bridge; the Bantu migrations in Africa; the movement of Europeans and Africans to the Western Hemisphere; the exodus of Vietnamese boat people, Haitians, and Cubans) BD (BE,37;KE,62;NI,3)

Codes (right side of page):   BD = Benchmark, Declarative; BP = Benchmark, Procedural; BC = Benchmark, Contextual

1st letter of each code in parentheses	*2nd letter of code*	*Number*
B = NCHS: basic edition	E = Explicitly stated in document	Page number of cited document
K = NCHS: K-4 History, expanded edition	I = Implied in document	
N = NAEP: Provisional Item Specifications		

Symbol

▸ material appears only in NCHS expanded edition

● material appears in both NCHS editions

BD (BE,37;KE,62,63;NI,2,3,5)

- Knows about European explorers of the 15th and 16th centuries, their reasons for exploring, the information gained from their journeys, and what happened as a result of their travels (e.g., Christopher Columbus, Marco Polo, Eric the Red, Zheng He ▸ Ferdinand Magellan, Vasco de Gama, Jacques Cartier)

BD (BE,37;KE,62,63;NI,5)

- Knows about the various crops, foods, and animals that were transported from the Western Hemisphere and from the Eastern Hemisphere as a result of the "Columbian Exchange" (e.g., ▸ tomato, corn, cassava, potato; horse, cattle, sugar cane)

BD (KE,63)

▸ Understands the different perspectives and major arguments surrounding the Columbian encounter

(BE,37;KE,64)

8. Understands major discoveries in science and technology, some of their social and economic effects, and the major scientists and inventers responsible for them

Level I (Grades K-2)

BD (BE,37;KE,64)

- Understands differences between hunters and gatherers and people who cultivated plants and raised domesticated animals for food (e.g., ▸ in family life, the amounts of land necessary for support, ability to acquire surplus food for storage and trading)

BD (BE,38;KE,64;NE,24,25,26)

- Knows the accomplishments of major scientists and inventors (e.g., ▸ George Washington Carver, Galileo, Marie Curie, Louis Pasteur, Alexander Graham Bell)

BD (BE,38;KE,66)

- Knows basic information about marine transportation (e.g., ▸ the technology and activities of people along the Erie Canal)

BD (BE,38;KE,67;NI,34)

- Knows the ways people communicate with each other now and long ago, and the technological developments that facilitated communication (e.g., ▸ speaking by gestures, transmitting stories orally, pictographs, hieroglyphics, different alphabets, writing by hand, printing techniques, the invention of the telegraph and telephone, satellite transmission of messages)

BD (BE,38;KE,67)

- Knows various systems of long-distance communication and their effects (e.g., runners, the

---

Codes (right side of page):   BD = Benchmark, Declarative; BP = Benchmark, Procedural; BC = Benchmark, Contextual
1st letter of each code in parentheses   *2nd letter of code*   *Number*
B = NCHS: basic edition   E = Explicitly stated in document   Page number of cited document
K = NCHS: K-4 History, expanded edition   I = Implied in document
N = NAEP: Provisional Item Specifications

Symbol
▸ material appears only in NCHS expanded edition
● material appears in both NCHS editions

"talking drums" of Africa, smoke signals of Native Americans, the pony express, the telegraph, telephones, satellite systems)

- Understands differences in the methods of travel from various times in human history and the advantages and disadvantages of each (e.g., ▸ the use of animals such as horses and camels; nonmotorized vehicles such as chariots and hot air balloons; motorized vehicles such as railroads, automobiles, and airplanes; modern space advancements) BD (BI,38;KE,66;NI,18,26,35)

Level II (Grades 3-4)

- Knows about the development of the wheel and its early uses in ancient societies BD (BE,37;KE,64)

- Understands the development and the influence of basic tools on work and behavior BD (BE,37;KE,64)

- Knows various technological developments to control fire, water, wind, and soil, and to utilize natural resources (e.g., trees, coal, oil, gas) in order to satisfy basic human needs for food, water, clothing, and shelter BD (BE,37;KE,64)

- Knows about technological inventions and developments that evolved during the 19th century and the influence of these changes on the lives of workers BD (BE,37;KE,64;NE,25,26)

- Knows the different forms of transportation and their developments over time BD (BE,38;KE,66;NI,18,26,35)

- Understands the development in marine vessels constructed by people from ancient times until today (e.g., ▸ early dugout Phoenician ships, Native American canoes, the Portuguese caravel, the Chinese vessels used by Zheng He, the Arab dhow, the Norse long ships, currachs used in the British Isles, square riggers, aircraft carriers, submarines, bathyscaphs) BD (BE,38;KE,66;NI,4)

- Understands the development of extensive road systems (e.g., the Roman system of roads; the trade routes by camel caravan linking East Asia, Southwest Asia, and Africa during the ancient and early Middle Ages; the network of roads and highways of the Inca in Peru; the interstate highway system), the travel and communication difficulties encountered by people over vast expanses of territory, and the social and economic effects of these developments BD (BE,38;KE,66,67)

- Knows the developments in rail transportation beginning in the 19th century and the effects of national systems of railroad transport on the lives of people BD (BE,38;KE,66;NI,26)

Codes (right side of page):	BD = Benchmark, Declarative; BP = Benchmark, Procedural; BC = Benchmark, Contextual	
1st letter of each code in parentheses	*2nd letter of code*	*Number*
B = NCHS: basic edition	E = Explicitly stated in document	Page number of cited document
K = NCHS: K-4 History, expanded edition	I = Implied in document	
N = NAEP: Provisional Item Specifications		
	Symbol	
	▸ material appears only in NCHS expanded edition	
	● material appears in both NCHS editions	

- BD (BE,38;KE,66;NE,34)
  Understands the design and development of aircraft and rocketry, and the people involved

- BD (BE,38;KE,66,67;NE,29,34)
  Knows about people who have made significant contributions in the field of transportation (e.g., ▸ Henry Ford, Amelia Earhart, John Glenn, Sally Ride)

- BD (BE,38;KE,67,68)
  Understands the origins and changes in methods of writing over time and how the changes made communications between people more effective (e.g., ▸ pictographs, cuneiform, hieroglyphics, alphabets)

- BD (BE,38;KE,67,68)
  Understands the significance of the printing press, the computer, and electronic developments in communication and their impact on the spread of ideas

- BD (BE,38;KE,67,68;NE,34,35)
  Knows about people who have made significant contributions in the field of communications (e.g., ▸ the inventors of the telegraph, telephone, the Braille alphabet, radio, television, the computer, satellite communication)

- BD (KE,65)
  ▸ Knows the significant scientific and technological achievements of various historical societies (e.g., the invention of paper in China, Mayan calendars, mummification in Egypt, astronomical discoveries in the Moslem world, the invention of the steam engine in England)

Codes (right side of page): BD = Benchmark, Declarative; BP = Benchmark, Procedural; BC = Benchmark, Contextual
1st letter of each code in parentheses *2nd letter of code* *Number*
B = NCHS: basic edition E = Explicitly stated in document Page number of cited document
K = NCHS: K-4 History, expanded edition I = Implied in document
N = NAEP: Provisional Item Specifications

Symbol
▸ material appears only in NCHS expanded edition
● material appears in both NCHS editions

Summary of Standards for United States History

Era 1 Three Worlds Meet (Beginnings to 1620)
1. Understands the characteristics of societies in the Americas, Western Europe, and Western Africa that increasingly interacted after 1450
2. Understands cultural and ecological interactions among previously unconnected people resulting from early European exploration and colonization

Era 2 Colonization and Settlement (1585-1763)
3. Understands why the Americas attracted Europeans, why they brought enslaved Africans to their colonies, and how Europeans struggled for control of North America and the Caribbean
4. Understands how political, religious, and social institutions emerged in the North American colonies
5. Understands how the values and institutions of European economic life took root in the colonies and how slavery reshaped European and African life in the Americas

Era 3 Revolution and the New Nation (1754-1820s)
6. Understands the causes of the American Revolution, the ideas and interests involved in shaping the revolutionary movement, and reasons for the American victory
7. Understands the impact of the American Revolution on politics, economy, and society
8. Understands the institutions and practices of government created during the revolution and how these elements were revised between 1787 and 1815 to create the foundation of the American political system based on the U.S. Constitution and the Bill of Rights

Era 4 Expansion and Reform (1801-1861)
9. Understands the United States territorial expansion between 1801 and 1861, and how it affected relations with external powers and Native Americans
10. Understands how the industrial revolution, increasing immigration, the rapid expansion of slavery, and the westward movement changed American lives and led to regional tensions
11. Understands the extension, restriction, and reorganization of political democracy after 1800
12. Understands the sources and character of cultural, religious, and social reform movements in the antebellum period

Era 5 Civil War and Reconstruction (1850-1877)
13. Understands the causes of the Civil War
14. Understands the course and character of the Civil War and its effects on the American people
15. Understands how various reconstruction plans succeeded or failed

Era 6 The Development of the Industrial United States (1870-1900)
16. Understands how the rise of corporations, heavy industry, and mechanized farming transformed American society
17. Understands massive immigration after 1870 and how new social patterns, conflicts, and ideas of national unity developed amid growing cultural diversity

18. Understands the rise of the American labor movement and how political issues reflected social and economic changes
19. Understands federal Indian policy and United States foreign policy after the Civil War

Era 7 The Emergence of Modern America (1890-1930)
20. Understands how Progressives and others addressed problems of industrial capitalism, urbanization, and political corruption
21. Understands the changing role of the United States in world affairs through World War I
22. Understands how the United States changed between the post-World War I years and the eve of the Great Depression

Era 8 The Great Depression and World War II (1929-1945)
23. Understands the causes of the Great Depression and how it affected American society
24. Understands how the New Deal addressed the Great Depression, transformed American federalism, and initiated the welfare state
25. Understands the causes and course of World War II, the character of the war at home and abroad, and its reshaping of the U.S. role in world affairs

Era 9 Postwar United States (1945 to early 1970s)
26. Understands the economic boom and social transformation of post-World War II United States
27. Understands how the Cold War and conflicts in Korea and Vietnam influenced domestic and international politics
28. Understands domestic policies in the post-World War II period
29. Understands the struggle for racial and gender equality and for the extension of civil liberties

Era 10 Contemporary United States (1968 to the present)
30. Understands developments in foreign and domestic policies between the Nixon and Clinton presidencies
31. Understands economic, social, and cultural developments in the contemporary United States

(BE,77;AE,35)

1. Understands the characteristics of societies in the Americas, Western Europe, and Western Africa that increasingly interacted after 1450

Level II (Grades 5-6)

BD (BE,77;AE,40-41;LE,55;LI,55-56;NI,39)
- Understands the migration and settlement patterns of peoples in the Americas (e.g., the archaeological and geological evidence that explains the movement of people from Asia to the Americas, the spread of human societies and the rise of diverse cultures from hunter-gatherers to urban dwellers, ► use of the Bering land bridge)

BD (BE,77;AE,40;LE,55;LI,56)
- Understands the significance of beliefs held by both Native Americans and Europeans (e.g., Native American beliefs about their origins in America, ► ideas of land use held by Native Americans and Europeans)

BD (BE,77;AE,43;LI,55;NI,84)
- Understands social, economic, and cultural characteristics of European society (e.g., the customary European family organization, gender roles, property holding, education and literacy, linguistic diversity, religion)

BD (BE,78;AE,44;LI,56)
- Knows the geographic characteristics of Western and Central Africa and understands the impact of geography on settlement patterns, cultural traits, and trade (e.g., ► in political kingdoms such as Mali, Songhai, and Benin; in urban centers such as Timbuktu and Jenne)

BC (BE,78;AE,40)
- Compares political, social, economic, and religious systems of Africans, Europeans, and Native Americans who converged in the western hemisphere after 1492 (e.g., concepts of political authority, civic values, and the organization and practice of government; population levels, urbanization, family structure, and modes of communication; systems of labor, trade, concepts of property, and exploitation of natural resources; dominant ideas and values including religious beliefs and practices, gender roles, and attitudes toward nature)

BD (AE,40;LE,55-56)
► Understands the economic, social, and cultural influence of location and physical geography on different Native American societies (e.g., Iroquois and Pueblo, Northwest and Southeast societies)

BD (AE,41;LI,55)
► Understands how the Mohawk, Oneida, Onondaga, Cayuga, and Seneca united to form the

---

Codes (right side of page):	BD = Benchmark, Declarative; BP = Benchmark, Procedural; BC = Benchmark, Contextual	
1st letter of each code in parentheses	*2nd letter of code*	*Number*
B = NCHS: basic edition	E = Explicitly stated in document	Page number of cited document
A = NCHS: U.S. History, expanded edition	I = Implied in document	
L = Lessons From History		
N = NAEP: Provisional Item Specifications	*Symbol*	
	■ material appears only in NCHS basic edition	
	► material appears only in NCHS expanded edition	
	● material appears in both NCHS editions	

Iroquois nation and to solve conflicts peaceably

BD (AE,43;LI,55)
▸ Knows legends of pre-Columbus explorations and the technological, scientific, and geographic factors that led to the age of exploration in the Americas

Level III (Grades 7-8)

BD (BE,77;AI,40)
● Understands the rise and decline of the Mississippian mound-building society

BD (BE,77;AE,43)
● Understands the role of religion in Western Europe during the age of exploration (e.g., the causes and consequences of European Crusades in Iberia, connections between the Christian crusading tradition and European overseas exploration, dissent within the Catholic Church and beliefs and ideas of leading religious reformers)

BD (BE,78;AE,44)
● Understands the influence of Islam in Western Africa in the 15th and 16th centuries (e.g. interactions between Islam and local religious beliefs)

BD (AE,43;LE,55)
▸ Understands the geographic, technological, and scientific factors that contributed to the European age of exploration and settlement in the Americas

BD (AE,43;LI,56)
▸ Understands European perspectives of different cultures during the period of exploration and early settlement (e.g., European attitudes toward property and the environment)

Level IV (Grades 9-12)

BD (BE,77;LI,57-58;NI,85,85)
■ Understands economic changes in Western Europe in the age of exploration (e.g., major institutions of capitalism; the effects of the emerging capitalist economy on agricultural production, manufacturing, and the uses of labor)

BC (BE,77;AE,41;LE,55;LI,55-56)
● Understands the similarities and differences among Native American societies (e.g., gender roles; patterns of social organization; cultural traditions; economic organization; political culture; ▸ among Hopi, Zuni, Algonkian, Iroquoian, Moundbuilder, and Mississippian cultures)

Codes (right side of page):   BD = Benchmark, Declarative; BP = Benchmark, Procedural; BC = Benchmark, Contextual
1st letter of each code in parentheses   *2nd letter of code*   *Number*
B = NCHS: basic edition   E = Explicitly stated in document   Page number of cited document
A = NCHS: U.S. History, expanded edition   I = Implied in document
L = Lessons From History
N = NAEP: Provisional Item Specifications   *Symbol*
      ■ material appears only in NCHS basic edition
      ▸ material appears only in NCHS expanded edition
      ● material appears in both NCHS editions

MREL

BD (BE,77;AE,43)

- Understands the social, economic, and political factors that stimulated overseas exploration (e.g., the rise of centralized states, the development of urban centers, the expansion of commerce, ▸ the spirit of individualism and how it affected cross-cultural contacts with new peoples)

BD (BE,78;AE,45;LI,56;NE,85)

- Understands the characteristics of Western African societies, such as Mali, Songhai, and Benin, in the 15th and 16th centuries (e.g., the economic importance of the trans-Saharan slave trade; the response of African states to early European coastal trading and raiding; general features of family organization, labor division, agriculture, manufacturing, trade)

BD (AE,40-41;LE,55)

▸ Understands how values and beliefs in Native American origin stories explain other facets of Native American culture (e.g., migration, settlement, interactions with the environment)

BD (AE,41;LI,56)

▸ Understands different European perceptions of Native American societies during the years of exploration (e.g., John White's vs. Theodore deBry's)

(BE,79;AE,46)

2. **Understands cultural and ecological interactions among previously unconnected people resulting from early European exploration and colonization**

Level II (Grades 5-6)

BD (BE,79;AE,46,52;LI,56-57,63-66;NE,41,43;NI,39)

- Knows the features of the major European explorations that took place between the 15th and 17th centuries (e.g., the routes and motives of Spanish, French, Dutch, and English explorers; ▸ the goals and achievements of major expeditions; problems encountered on the high seas; fears and superstitions of the times; what sailors expected to find when they reached their destinations)

BD (BE,79;AE,48;LI,55-57;NE,41,42)

- Understands aspects of the Spanish exploration, conquest, and immigration to the Americas in the centuries following Columbus (e.g., Spanish interactions with the Aztec, Inca, and Pueblo; ▸ the expeditions of Cabeza de Vaca and Francisco Vasquez de Coronado in the American Southwest; the conquest of Spanish America)

Codes (right side of page):	BD = Benchmark, Declarative; BP = Benchmark, Procedural; BC = Benchmark, Contextual	
1st letter of each code in parentheses	*2nd letter of code*	*Number*
B = NCHS: basic edition	E = Explicitly stated in document	Page number of cited document
A = NCHS: U.S. History, expanded edition	I = Implied in document	
L = Lessons From History		
N = NAEP: Provisional Item Specifications	*Symbol*	
	■ material appears only in NCHS basic edition	
	▸ material appears only in NCHS expanded edition	
	● material appears in both NCHS editions	

MREL

Level III (Grades 7-8)

- BD (BE,79;AE,47;LI,56-57;NI,39)

  Understands the immediate and long-term impact of Columbus' voyages on Native populations and on colonization in the Americas (e.g., Columbus' interactions with indigenous peoples, the Columbian Exchange, ▸ religious influences)

- BD (BE,79;AE,48;LI,55-57)

  Understands characteristics of the Spanish and Portuguese exploration and conquest of the Americas (e.g., the social composition of early settlers of America and their motives for exploration and colonization, connections between silver mined in Peru and Mexico and the rise of global trade and the price revolution in 16th century Europe, ▸ methods the Spanish used to conquer the Aztec and Incan empires, societies the Spanish explorers encountered in the Aztec and Incan settlements)

- ▸ BD (AE,53;LI,63-64;NE,43)

  Understands how motives differed among English colonizers and between the English and the Spanish, French, and Dutch colonizers

Level IV (Grades 9-12)

- BD (BE,79;AE,47,53;LE,60,63;LI,55;NI,89)

  Understands the political and religious factors that influenced English, Spanish, French, and Dutch colonization of the Americas (e.g., ▸ the enclosure movement; the accession of Elizabeth I to the throne in England; how the Spanish "Black Legend" was used to motivate and justify English colonization of North America; to what extent the "Black Legend" was Protestant propaganda; to what extent it was a valid description of the Spanish conquest)

- BD (BE,79;AE,49;LI,58;NI,86)

  Understands the economic characteristics of the early Spanish and Portuguese empires in the Americas (e.g., *encomienda* system and the evolution of labor systems, the origin and expansion of the African slave trade in the Americas)

- ▸ BD (AE,47)

  Understands how interpretations of Columbus' voyages and his interactions with indigenous peoples have changed (e.g., between 1892 and 1992)

- ▸ BD (AE,47;LI,53)

  Understands the long-range social and ecological impact of the Columbian Exchange (e.g., how the horse, the pig, and the dandelion brought about changes in the land; how the sugar trade affected Caribbean slaves, Indian laborers, and European urban proletarians)

BD (AE,49;LI,55-58)

▸ Understands characteristics of Spanish conquest and settlement in the Americas (e.g., the social composition of early Spanish settlers in the Americas in terms of age, gender, class, and its consequences for Latin America; how Cortes and Pizarro were able to conquer the Aztec and Inca; the role of religious beliefs in perceptions the Aztec and Spanish held of one another; Spanish attempts at justification for their treatment of Native Americans)

(BE,81;AI,51)

3. **Understands why the Americas attracted Europeans, why they brought enslaved Africans to their colonies and how Europeans struggled for control of North America and the Caribbean**

Level II (Grades 5-6)

BD (BE,81;LE,63-64;NE,43)

■ Understands the lives of free and indentured immigrants who came to North America and the Caribbean from Europe (e.g., religious, political, and economic motives of free immigrants from different parts of Europe; why indentured servants risked the hardships of bound labor overseas; opportunities and challenges encountered by European immigrants)

BD (BE,81;AE,53;LE,65,68)

● Understands growth and change in the European colonies during the two centuries following their founding (e.g., the arrival of Africans in the European colonies in the 17th century, the rapid increase of slave importation in the 18th century)

BD (BE,81;AE,56;LI,62,64;NI,41)

● Understands peaceful and conflictory interaction between English settlers and Native Americans in the New England, Mid-Atlantic, Chesapeake, and lower South colonies (e.g., ▸ how Native American and European societies influenced one another, differing European and Native American views of the land and its use)

BC (AE,52;LI,63;NE,43)

▸ Understands the similarities and differences in backgrounds, motivations, and occupational skills between people in the English settlements and those in the French and Spanish settlements

Level III (Grades 7-8)

BD (BE,81,82;AE,57;LI,62,64;NI,42)

● Understands the cultural and environmental impacts of European settlement in North

---

Codes (right side of page):	BD = Benchmark, Declarative; BP = Benchmark, Procedural; BC = Benchmark, Contextual	
1st letter of each code in parentheses	*2nd letter of code*	*Number*
B = NCHS: basic edition	E = Explicitly stated in document	Page number of cited document
A = NCHS: U.S. History, expanded edition	I = Implied in document	
L = Lessons From History		
N = NAEP: Provisional Item Specifications	*Symbol*	
	■ material appears only in NCHS basic edition	
	▸ material appears only in NCHS expanded edition	
	● material appears in both NCHS editions	

America (e.g., friendly and conflictory relations between English, French, Spanish, and Dutch settlers and Native Americans; how various Native American societies changed as a result of the expanding European settlements and how they influenced European societies; ► the impact of the fur trade on the environment)

BD (BE,82;AE,57;LI,72-73)

● Understands the events that culminated in the English victory over the French in the Seven Years War, and why the war and its outcomes were significant

Level IV (Grades 9-12)

BD (BE,81;AE,53;LE,65,68;LI,63,67-68;NI,89)

● Understands social and economic characteristics of European colonization in the 17th and 18th centuries (e.g., ► changing immigration and settlement patterns of Puritans, Quakers, Germans, and Scots-Irish; the slave trade and chattel slavery in the Spanish, English, and French Caribbean, Louisiana, the Dutch West Indies, and Chesapeake)

BD (BE,82;AE,57)

● Understands the events and consequences of the Seven Years War (e.g., ► the significance of the Peace of Paris, options left to Native Americans)

BD (BE,82;AE,57)

● Understands the nature of the interaction between Native Americans and various settlers (e.g., Native American involvement in the European wars for control between 1675 and 1763, ► how Native American societies responded to European land hunger and expansion)

(BE,82;AE,58)

4. **Understands how political, religious, and social institutions emerged in the English colonies**

Level II (Grades 5-6)

BD (BE,83)

■ Understands the influence of Enlightenment ideas on American society (e.g., Benjamin Franklin's experiments with electricity)

BD (BE,82;AE,58;LE,63;NE,42;NI,42)

● Understands the development of colonial governments (e.g., how early colonies differed in the way they were established and governed, ► how characteristics of colonial self-

---

Codes (right side of page):	BD = Benchmark, Declarative; BP = Benchmark, Procedural; BC = Benchmark, Contextual

1st letter of each code in parentheses   *2nd letter of code*   *Number*

B = NCHS: basic edition   E = Explicitly stated in document   Page number of cited document

A = NCHS: U.S. History, expanded edition   I = Implied in document

L = Lessons From History

N = NAEP: Provisional Item Specifications   *Symbol*

    ■ material appears only in NCHS basic edition

    ► material appears only in NCHS expanded edition

    ● material appears in both NCHS editions

MREL

government such as the right to vote and hold office were reflected in the Mayflower Compact)

- Understands Puritanism in colonial America (e.g., how Puritanism shaped New England communities, the changes in Puritanism during the 17th century, ▸ opposition to King James I, why Puritans came to America, the Puritan family structure) BD (BE,82;AE,60;LI,61-62)

- Understands how and why family and community life differed in various regions of colonial North America (e.g., ▸ Williamsburg, Philadelphia, Boston, New York, French Quebec, Santa Fe) BD (BE,83;AE,54)

Level III (Grades 7-8)

- Understands ideas that influenced religious and political aspects of colonial America (e.g., how the growth of individualism contributed to participatory government, challenged inherited ideas of hierarchy, and affected the ideal of community; ▸ whether political rights in colonial society reflected democratic ideas; how Benjamin Franklin's thirteen virtues in his *Autobiography* compare to Puritan ideas and values) BD (BE,82-83;AE,58-59;LI,67;NE,42)

- Understands the concepts that contributed to the "rights of Englishmen" (e.g., ▸ as found in the Magna Carta, English Common law, the English Bill of Rights [1689]) BD (BE,82;AE,58;LI,64)

- Understands the impact of the English Civil War and the Glorious Revolution on the colonies BD (BE,82;AE,58;LI,64)

- Understands how political, social, and economic tensions led to violent conflicts between the colonists and their governments (e.g. ▸ Bacon's rebellion, the Paxton Boys Massacre) BD (BE,82;AE,63)

- Understands the role of religion in the English colonies (e.g., the evolution of religious freedom, ▸ treatment of religious dissenters such as Anne Hutchison, the concept of the separation of church and state) BD (BE,82;AE,60;LI,61-62,67;NE,43,44)

- ▸ Understands how family and gender roles of different regions of colonial America changed across time (1600-1700) BD (AE,54)

Codes (right side of page):	BD = Benchmark, Declarative; BP = Benchmark, Procedural; BC = Benchmark, Contextual
1st letter of each code in parentheses	*2nd letter of code*	*Number*

Codes (right side of page):
1st letter of each code in parentheses
B = NCHS: basic edition
A = NCHS: U.S. History, expanded edition
L = Lessons From History
N = NAEP: Provisional Item Specifications

BD = Benchmark, Declarative; BP = Benchmark, Procedural; BC = Benchmark, Contextual
2nd letter of code
E = Explicitly stated in document
I = Implied in document

Number
Page number of cited document

Symbol
■ material appears only in NCHS basic edition
▸ material appears only in NCHS expanded edition
● material appears in both NCHS editions

Level IV (Grades 9-12)

- BD (BE,82;AE,59,63;LI,64-65)

  Understands influences on the development of representative government in colonial America (e.g., conflicts between legislative and executive branches in Virginia, New York, and Massachusetts; ▸ how different colonies adopted different laws and governmental frameworks; how demography influenced different forms of government in the colonies; the influence of colonial institutions; how an abundance of land, devotion to private property, and a competitive entrepreneurial spirit influenced the idea of participatory government)

- BD (BE,82;AE,59)

  Understands how gender, property ownership, religion, and legal status affected political rights (e.g., ▸ that women were not allowed to vote even if they held property and met religious requirements)

- BD (BE,82;AE,61;LI,61-62,67-68;NE,90;NI,90)

  Understands characteristics of religious development in colonial America (e.g., the presence of diverse religious groups and their contributions to religious freedom; the political and religious influence of the Great Awakening; ▸ the major tenets of Puritanism and its legacy in American society; the dissension of Anne Hutchison and Roger Williams, and Puritan objections to their ideas and behavior)

- BD (BE,83;AE,54;NI,90)

  Understands characteristics of the social structure of colonial America (e.g., the property rights of single, married, and widowed women; public education in the New England colonies and how it differed from the southern colonies, ▸ different patterns of family life; different ideals among diverse religious groups, social classes, and cultures; different roles and status of men and women)

- ▸ BC (AE,59;LI,61-62)

  Understands the similarities and differences in colonial concepts of community (e.g., Puritan's covenant community, Chesapeake colonial emphasis on individualism)

- ▸ BD (AE,63)

  Understands the elements of ethnic, class, and race relations in conflicts between backwoodsmen and planters of colonial America (e.g., Bacon's Rebellion, Leisler's Rebellion, the Carolina Regulators and Paxton Boys revolts)

Codes (right side of page):   BD = Benchmark, Declarative; BP = Benchmark, Procedural; BC = Benchmark, Contextual

1st letter of each code in parentheses   *2nd letter of code*   *Number*

B = NCHS: basic edition   E = Explicitly stated in document   Page number of cited document

A = NCHS: U.S. History, expanded edition   I = Implied in document

L = Lessons From History

N = NAEP: Provisional Item Specifications   *Symbol*

    ■ material appears only in NCHS basic edition

    ▸ material appears only in NCHS expanded edition

    ● material appears in both NCHS editions

139

MREL

(BE,83;AE,64)

5. Understands how the values and institutions of European economic life took root in the colonies and how slavery reshaped European and African life in the Americas

Level II (Grades 5-6)

BD (BE,83;AE,64;NE,45)
- Understands the factors that shaped the economic system in the colonies and the Americas (e.g., labor systems, ► natural resources, relations with other countries and the home country)

BD (BE,83;AE,66;LI,65,68;NE,44,45)
- Understands economic life in the New England, Chesapeake, and southern colonies (e.g., environmental and human factors; ► the work people did; the crops that plantation, yeoman, and family farmers grew; the New England merchant's trading triangle)

BD (BE,84;AE,68;LI,65,68)
- Understands elements of African slavery during the colonial period in North America (e.g., relocation of enslaved Africans to the Caribbean and North America, ► the slave trade and "the middle passage")

Level III (Grades 7-8)

BD (BE,83;AE,64)
- Understands mercantilism and how it influenced patterns of economic activity (e.g., ► the advantages and disadvantages of mercantilism for the mother country and its colonies; the value of the regions that produced sugar, rice, tobacco, timber, coffee, grains, fish and minerals to the mother country)

BD (BE,83;AE,66)
- Understands the environmental and legislative impacts on economic growth in different regions of the English colonies (e.g., the connection between the Navigation Acts and mercantilism; ► the influence of climate, land fertility, water resources, access to markets)

BD (BE,84;AE,67;LI,65,68;NE,45)
- Understands patterns of indentured servitude and influences on slavery (e.g. ► why indentured servitude was prevalent in the mid-Atlantic, Chesapeake, and southern colonies; the Virginia and Massachusetts' laws that institutionalized slavery)

BD (BE,84;AE,68;LE,68;LI,68)
- Understands the social, cultural, and political events that shaped African slavery in colonial America (e.g., how slavery in African societies differed from chattel racial slavery in English

---

Codes (right side of page):   BD = Benchmark, Declarative; BP = Benchmark, Procedural; BC = Benchmark, Contextual
1st letter of each code in parentheses   *2nd letter of code*   *Number*
B = NCHS: basic edition   E = Explicitly stated in document   Page number of cited document
A = NCHS: U.S. History, expanded edition   I = Implied in document
L = Lessons From History
N = NAEP: Provisional Item Specifications   *Symbol*
    ■ material appears only in NCHS basic edition
    ► material appears only in NCHS expanded edition
    ● material appears in both NCHS editions

colonies, influence of African heritage on efforts to develop a new African American culture, incidents of resistance to slavery, ► the introduction of crops by African slaves)

Level IV (Grades 9-12)

BD (BE,83;AE,64-65)
● Understands the characteristics of mercantilism in colonial America (e.g., the Atlantic economy and triangular trade, ► overseas trade and the Navigation Acts, economic development in French, English, and Spanish colonies)

BD (BE,83;AE,67)
● Understands factors that influenced economic life in the North American and West Indian colonies (e.g., the development of a consumer society and the imitation of English culture)

BD (BE,84;AE,67;LI,65,68)
● Understands elements of slavery in the colonies in the 17th century (e.g., the emergence of chattel slavery in Virginia and Maryland, ► why free labor and chattel slavery did not provide an alternative for labor in the Chesapeake colonies before 1675)

BD (BE,84;AE,69)
● Understands the contributions of African slaves to economic development in the Americas (e.g., ► contributions of rice cultivation and cattle raising in South Carolina) and the transmission of African cultural heritage (e.g., ► through religious practices, dances, and work songs)

(BE,86;AE,72)
6. Understands the causes of the American Revolution, the ideas and interests involved in shaping the revolutionary movement, and reasons for the American victory

Level II (Grades 5-6)

BD (BE,86;AE,72;LI,72-73)
● Understands the major consequences of the Seven Years War (e.g., ► the English victory, the removal of the French as a power in North America, the reduced need of the colonists for the protection of the mother country)

BD (BE,86;AE,72;LE,73;LI,74;NE,46,51)
● Understands the events that contributed to the outbreak of the American Revolution and the earliest armed conflict of the Revolutionary War (e.g., opponents and defenders of England's

---

Codes (right side of page):   BD = Benchmark, Declarative; BP = Benchmark, Procedural; BC = Benchmark, Contextual
1st letter of each code in parentheses   *2nd letter of code*   *Number*
B = NCHS: basic edition   E = Explicitly stated in document   Page number of cited document
A = NCHS: U.S. History, expanded edition   I = Implied in document
L = Lessons From History
N = NAEP: Provisional Item Specifications   *Symbol*
      ■ material appears only in NCHS basic edition
      ► material appears only in NCHS expanded edition
      ● material appears in both NCHS editions

141   MREL

new imperial policy, ▸ the idea of "taxation without representation," the battle at Lexington and Concord)

- BD (BE,86,87;AE,74;LI,73-74;NE,48,50)
  Understands the major ideas in the Declaration of Independence, their sources, and how they became unifying ideas of American democracy (e.g., ▸ major terms, why the document was written, what the signers risked)

- BD (BE,87;AE,76;LE,74,75;NE,46;LI,75-76)
  Understands the major developments and chronology of the Revolutionary War and the roles of its political, military, and diplomatic leaders (e.g., George Washington, ▸ Benjamin Franklin, Thomas Jefferson, John Adams, Samuel Adams, John Hancock, Richard Henry Lee)

- BD (BE,87;AE,76;LI,74-75;NE,49,51)
  Understands perspectives of and the roles played in the American Revolution by various groups of people (e.g., men, women, white settlers, free and enslaved African-Americans, and Native Americans)

- BD (BE,87;AE,78;LI,74-76)
  Understands the United States relationships with European countries and the contributions of each European power to the outcome of the Revolution (e.g., relations with France, Holland and Spain; consequences of the Treaty of Paris; ▸ Ben Franklin's negotiations with the French)

Level III (Grades 7-8)

- BD (BE,86;AE,72-73;LE,73;LI,70-71,74;NE,46;NI,46,50)
  Understands how political, ideological, and religious ideas joined economic interests to bring about the "shot heard round the world" (e.g., ▸ leaders of resistance to imperial policy; the English tax on the colonists to help pay for the Seven Years War; the interests and positions of different economic groups, such as northern merchants, southern rice and tobacco planters, yeoman farmers, and urban artisans)

- BD (BE,86;AE,74)
  Understands contradictions between the Declaration of Independence and the institution of chattel slavery

- BD (BE,87;AE,76-77;LI,74-75)
  Understands the strategic elements of the Revolutionary War (e.g., how the Americans won the war against superior British resources, ▸ American and British military leaders, major military campaigns)

Codes (right side of page):	BD = Benchmark, Declarative; BP = Benchmark, Procedural; BC = Benchmark, Contextual	
1st letter of each code in parentheses	*2nd letter of code*	*Number*
B = NCHS: basic edition	E = Explicitly stated in document	Page number of cited document
A = NCHS: U.S. History, expanded edition	I = Implied in document	
L = Lessons From History		
N = NAEP: Provisional Item Specifications	*Symbol*	
	■ material appears only in NCHS basic edition	
	▸ material appears only in NCHS expanded edition	
	● material appears in both NCHS editions	

- Understands the impact of European countries and individual Europeans on the American victory (e.g., ▸ interest, goals, and actions of France, Holland, and Spain; contributions of European individuals)

  BD (BE,87;AE,78;LI,74-76)

- Understands the terms of the Treaty of Paris and implications for U.S. relationships with Native Americans and European powers who still held interests and territory in North America

  BD (BE,87;AE,78;LI,74-76;NI,51)

- ▸ Understands the creation of the Declaration of Independence (e.g., historical antecedents that contributed to the document, individuals who struggled for independence)

  BD (AE,74;LE,75;LI,73-74;NE,47,NI,46)

Level IV (Grades 9-12)

- Understands the social, political, and religious aspects of the American Revolution (e.g., decisions leading to crisis of revolution; ▸ efforts by Parliament and colonies to prevent revolution; ideas of different religions; economic and social differences of Loyalists, Patriots, and neutrals)

  BD (BE,86;AE,73;LE,73;LI,71-74)

- Understands how the principles of the Declaration of Independence justified American independence

  BD (BE,87;AE,74;LI,73-74;NI,94)

- Understands differences and similarities between the Declaration of Independence and other documents on government (e.g., the French Declaration of the Rights of Man and Citizen, ▸ John Locke's Two Treatises on Government)

  BC (BE,87;AE,75;LI,73-74;NI,94)

- Understands the major political and strategic factors that led to the American victory in the Revolutionary War (e.g., ▸ the importance of the Battle of Saratoga, the use of guerilla and conventional warfare, the importance of King's Mountain in defining the war)

  BD (BE,87;AE,77;LE,75;LI,74;NI,93-94)

- Understands the social and economic impact of the Revolutionary War (e.g., problems of financing the war, wartime inflation, hoarding and profiteering; ▸ personal impact and economic hardship on families involved in the war)

  BD (BE,87;AE,76;LI,75-76)

- Understands contributions of European nations during the American Revolution and how their involvement influenced the outcome and aftermath (e.g., ▸ the assistance of France and

  BD (BE,87;AE,78-79;LI,74-76)

Codes (right side of page):	BD = Benchmark, Declarative; BP = Benchmark, Procedural; BC = Benchmark, Contextual	
1st letter of each code in parentheses	*2nd letter of code*	*Number*
B = NCHS: basic edition	E = Explicitly stated in document	Page number of cited document
A = NCHS: U.S. History, expanded edition	I = Implied in document	
L = Lessons From History		
N = NAEP: Provisional Item Specifications	*Symbol*	
	■ material appears only in NCHS basic edition	
	▸ material appears only in NCHS expanded edition	
	● material appears in both NCHS editions	

Spain in the war, how self-interests of France and Spain differed from those of the United States after the war, the effect of American diplomatic initiatives and the contributions of the European military leaders on the outcome of the war)

BD. (BE,87;AE,79;LI,74-76;NI,98)

- Understands how the Treaty of Paris influenced U.S. relations with other countries and indigenous peoples (e.g., ▸ the resulting boundary disputes with Spain; influences on economic and strategic interests of the United States, Native Americans, Spain, England, and France; the impact of the Jay Gardoqui Treaty of 1786)

BD (AE,75;LI,75)

▸ Understands the arguments of advocates and opponents of slavery from different regions of the country during the revolutionary period (e.g., ▸ how pro-slavery Americans justified their defense of slavery with their espousal of inalienable rights to freedom, how enslaved African Americans employed revolutionary ideals to obtain their freedom)

BD (AE,77;LI,74)

▸ Understands the military and diplomatic factors that helped produce the Treaty of Paris

(BE,87;AI,80)

7.   Understands the impact of the American Revolution on politics, economy, and society

Level II (Grades 5-6)

BD (BE,87;AE,82;LE,76;LI,76,81-82;NE,46)

- Understands the major political issues in the thirteen colonies after their independence from England (e.g., arguments over the Articles of Confederation, ▸ arguments over how to govern themselves)

BD (BE,88;AE,84;LE,82;NE,48)

- Understands the factors that led to Shay's Rebellion

BD (BE,88;AE,80-81;LI,75-76;NE,49)

- Understands the social, political, and economic effects of the American revolutionary victory on different groups (e.g., rural farmers, wealthy merchants, enslaved and free African Americans, abolitionists, ▸ women who contributed to the war effort)

Codes (right side of page):	BD = Benchmark, Declarative; BP = Benchmark, Procedural; BC = Benchmark, Contextual	
1st letter of each code in parentheses	*2nd letter of code*	*Number*
B = NCHS: basic edition	E = Explicitly stated in document	Page number of cited document
A = NCHS: U.S. History, expanded edition	I = Implied in document	
L = Lessons From History		
N = NAEP: Provisional Item Specifications	*Symbol*	
	■ material appears only in NCHS basic edition	
	▸ material appears only in NCHS expanded edition	
	● material appears in both NCHS editions	

144

KREL

Level III (Grades 7-8)

- BD (BE,87,88;AE,82;LE,76;LI,76,81-82;NE,46)
  Understands political and economic issues addressed by the Continental Congress (e.g., the accomplishments and failures of the Continental Congress, the Northwest Ordinance of 1787, revolutionary war debt, the dispute over the sale of western lands)

- BD (BE,88;AE,80-81;75-76;NE,49)
  Understands how the ideals of the American Revolution influenced the goals of various groups of people during and after the war (e.g., African Americans, Native Americans, Loyalists, women, ▸ young people)

Level IV (Grades 9-12)

- BD (BE,87;AE,82,83)
  Understands the differences among several state constitutions (e.g., various applications of 18th-century republicanism, such as virtue in government, balancing the interests of different social groups, service to the common good, representation, separation of powers, judicial independence, and the legitimacy of slavery)

- BD (BE,88;LE,76;LI,81-82;NE,96)
  Understands the efforts of the Continental Congress and the states to rebuild the economy after the American Revolution (e.g., by addressing issues of foreign and internal trade, banking, and taxation)

- BD (BE,88;AE,81;LE,75;LI,75-76;NI,96)
  Understands the goals of different groups of people after the Revolution (e.g., the importance of African American leaders and institutions in shaping free black communities in the North, ▸ the influence of the American victory in advancing or retarding goals of different groups, the degree to which women were able to enter the public realm after 1776)

Codes (right side of page):	BD = Benchmark, Declarative; BP = Benchmark, Procedural; BC = Benchmark, Contextual	
1st letter of each code in parentheses	*2nd letter of code*	*Number*
B = NCHS: basic edition	E = Explicitly stated in document	Page number of cited document
A = NCHS: U.S. History, expanded edition	I = Implied in document	
L = Lessons From History		
N = NAEP: Provisional Item Specifications	*Symbol*	
	■ material appears only in NCHS basic edition	
	▸ material appears only in NCHS expanded edition	
	● material appears in both NCHS editions	

MREL

(BE,89;AE,82)

8. Understands the institutions and practices of government created during the Revolution and how these elements were revised between 1787 and 1815 to create the foundation of the American political system based on the U.S. Consitution and the Bill of Rights

Level II (Grades 5-6)

BD (BE,89;AE,84;LE,82;NE,48)

- Understands the factors involved in calling the Constitutional Convention (e.g., ▸ Shay's Rebellion)

BD (BE,89;AE,84;LI,81-82;NE,46;NI,49)

- Understands the issues and ideas supported and opposed by delegates at the Consitutional Convention (e.g., enduring features of the Constitution, such as the separation of powers, and checks and balances; ▸ the Virginia Plan; the New Jersey Plan; the Conneticut Compromise; abolition)

BD (BE,89;AE,86;LI,83)

- Understands the significance of the Bill of Rights and its specific guarantees (e.g., ▸ the relevance of the Bill of Rights in today's society)

BD (BE,90;AE,88;LE,83)

- Understands the differences in leaders (e.g., ▸ Alexander Hamilton and Thomas Jefferson) and the social and economic composition of each political party in the 1790s

BD (AE,88)

▸ Understands the issues that impacted the lives of farmers in western Pennsylvania during the Whiskey Rebellion

Level III (Grades 7-8)

BD (BE,89;AE,82,84,85;LE,82;LI,81-82;NE,46;NI,48)

- Understands events that led to and shaped the Constitutional Convention (e.g., alternative plans and major compromises considered by delegates, ▸ the grievances of the debtor class and the fears of wealthy creditors involved in Shay's Rebellion, the accomplishments and failures of the Articles of Confederation)

BD (BE,89;AE,86;LE,80;NI,46)

- Understands arguments over the necessity of a Bill of Rights (e.g., ▸ Anti-Federalist arguments for its inclusion in the Constitution) and Madison's role in securing its adoption

---

by the First Congress

- BD (BE,90;AE,90;LE,84;LI,84;NE,47,52)
  Understands the establishment of power and significant events in the development of the U.S. Supreme Court (e.g., the role of Chief Justice Marshall in the growth of the court, ▸ Article III of the Constitution, Judiciary Act of 1789, *Marbury* v. *Madison*)

- BD (BE,90;AE,88;LI,78,83-84;NE,47)
  Understands the development and impact of the American party system (e.g., social, economic, and foreign policy issues of the 1790s; influence of the French Revolution on American politics; ▸ the rise of the Federalist and Democratic-Republican parties; the election of 1800; the appointment of the "midnight judges")

- BD (AE,88;LI,83-84)
  Understands the role of ordinary people in the Whiskey Rebellion and in demonstrations against Jay's Treaty (e.g., the causes of the rebellion, similarities and differences between rebellion against the whiskey tax and British taxation during the revolutionary period, why western farmers objected to Jay's Treaty)

Level IV (Grades 9-12)

- BD (BE,89;AE,85;LE,81-82;LI,82,83;NI,93)
  Understands influences on the ideas established by the Constitution (e.g., the ideas behind the distribution of powers and the system of checks and balances; ▸ the influence of 18th-century republican ideals and the economic and political interests of different regions on the compromises reached in the Constitutional Convention)

- BD (BE,89;AE,85;LI,83)
  Understands how Federalists and Anti-Federalists differed (e.g., their arguments for and against the Constitution of 1787, their relevance in late 20th century politics, ▸ their backgrounds, service during the Revolution, political experience)

- BD (BE,89;AE,87;LE,80,83-84)
  Understands the Bill of Rights and various challenges to it (e.g., arguments by Federalists and Anti-Federalists over the need for a Bill of Rights, the Alien and Sedition Acts, recent court cases involving the Bill of Rights)

- BD (BE,90;AE,89;NI,93,94)
  Understands the significance of Chief Justice Marshall's decisions on the development of the Supreme Court (e.g., ▸ *Marbury* v. *Madison* [1803]; *Dartmouth College* v. *Woodward* [1819]; *Gibbons* v. *Ogden* [1824]; *McCulloch* v. *Maryland*)

Codes (right side of page):   BD = Benchmark, Declarative; BP = Benchmark, Procedural; BC = Benchmark, Contextual
1st letter of each code in parentheses   *2nd letter of code*   *Number*
B = NCHS: basic edition   E = Explicitly stated in document   Page number of cited document
A = NCHS: U.S. History, expanded edition   I = Implied in document
L = Lessons From History
N = NAEP: Provisional Item Specifications   *Symbol*
■ material appears only in NCHS basic edition
▸ material appears only in NCHS expanded edition
● material appears in both NCHS editions

BD (BE,90;AE,89;LI,93)

- Understands how the stature and significance of the federal judiciary changed during the 1790s and early 19th century, and the influence of the Supreme Court today

BD (BE,90;AE,89;LI,83-84)

- Understands the factors that led to the development of the two-party system (e.g., the emergence of an organized opposition party led by Thomas Jefferson, ▸ Hamilton's financial plan)

BD (AE,89;LI,83-84)

▸ Understands the factors that led to the Whiskey Rebellion (e.g., the extent to which the rebellion was a confrontation between the haves and the have-nots; the government's reaction; similarities and differences between grievances of the Whiskey Rebels and those of the Regulators, the Paxton Boys, and the Shaysites)

(BE,92;AE,94)

9. Understands the United States territorial expansion between 1801 and 1861, and how it affected relations with external powers and Native Americans

Level II (Grades 5-6)

BD (BE,92;AE,94,96;LI,101-102;NI,53)

- Understands the factors that led to U.S. territorial expansion in the Western Hemisphere (e.g., Napoleon's reasons for selling the Lousiana Territory, ▸ expeditions of American explorers and mountain men)

BD (BE,92;AE,95)

- Understands the War of 1812 (e.g., causes, sectional divisions, Native American support of the British, ▸ defining the war)

BD (BE,93;AE,94;NI,57)

- Knows the foreign territorial claims in the Western Hemisphere in 1800 and the impact on American foreign policy (e.g., the origins and provisions of the Monroe Doctrine; ▸ the claims of Spain, France, Britain, and Russia; nations that declared their independence in 1823; how President Monroe dealt with European attempts to reestablish control)

BD (BE,93;AE,97,98;LI,100-101,103)

- Understands the impact of territorial expansion on Native American tribes (e.g., the Cherokee, Chickasaw, Choctaw, Creek and Seminole removals, ▸ the significance of the Trail of Tears, the original lands held by various tribes of the Southeast and those held in the Old Northwest territory)

Codes (right side of page):	BD = Benchmark, Declarative; BP = Benchmark, Procedural; BC = Benchmark, Contextual	
1st letter of each code in parentheses	*2nd letter of code*	*Number*
B = NCHS: basic edition	E = Explicitly stated in document	Page number of cited document
A = NCHS: U.S. History, expanded edition	I = Implied in document	
L = Lessons From History		
N = NAEP: Provisional Item Specifications	*Symbol*	
	▪ material appears only in NCHS basic edition	
	▸ material appears only in NCHS expanded edition	
	● material appears in both NCHS editions	

BD (BE,93,AE,99)

- Understands the origins of Manifest Destiny and its influence on the westward expansion of the United States (e.g., its role in the resolution of the Oregon dispute with Great Britian, how it led to the Mexican-American war)

BD (BE,93;AE,99;LI,99;NI,57)

- Understands elements of the relationship between Texas and Mexico in the mid-19th century (e.g., the Texas War for Independence, ► American settlement in Mexico's Texas, the American defeat at the Alamo)

BD (BE,93;AE,99;LI,102;NI,57)

- Understands events that led to the Mexican-American war (e.g., the idea of Manifest Destiny, ► U.S. annexation of Texas, the invasion of Mexico by U.S. troops) and the consequences of the Treaty of Guadalupe Hidalgo

Level III (Grades 7-8)

BD (BE,92;AE,95;LI,93;LE,90,98,100-101;NI,53)

- Understands the short-term political and long-term cultural impacts of the Louisiana Purchase (e.g., those who opposed and supported the acquisition, ► the impact on Native Americans between 1801 and 1861)

BD (BE,93;E,97,98;LI,99,101,103)

- Understands how early state and federal policy influenced various Native American tribes (e.g., survival strategies of Native Americans, ► environmental differences between Native American homelands and resettlement areas, the Black Hawk War and removal policies in the Old Northwest)

BD (BE,93;AE,99,100;LI,99,102;NI,57)

- Understands the social and political impact of the idea of Manifest Destiny (e.g., ► how it fueled the controversy over the Oregon territory, how it was reflected in the Treaty of Guadalupe Hidalgo, its appeal to 19th century American industrial workers and small farmers)

BD (BE,93;AE,99;LI,102)

- Understands the diplomatic and political developments that led to the resolution of conflicts with Britain and Russia in the period 1815 to 1850

BD (AE,95;LE,102)

► Understands the significance of the Lewis and Clark expedition (e.g., its role as a scientific expedition, its contributions to friendly relations with Native Americans)

BD (AE,95)

► Understands the major events of U.S. foreign policy during the early 19th century (e.g.,

---

Codes (right side of page):   BD = Benchmark, Declarative; BP = Benchmark, Procedural; BC = Benchmark, Contextual
1st letter of each code in parentheses   *2nd letter of code*   *Number*
B = NCHS: basic edition   E = Explicitly stated in document   Page number of cited document
A = NCHS: U.S. History, expanded edition   I = Implied in document
L = Lessons From History
N = NAEP: Provisional Item Specifications   *Symbol*
    ■ material appears only in NCHS basic edition
    ► material appears only in NCHS expanded edition
    ● material appears in both NCHS editions

differences between the Monroe Doctrine and earlier foreign policy; renewed English-French hostilities; whether the War of 1812 was a war of independence, expansion, or maritime rights)

Level IV (Grades 9-12)

BD (BE,92;AE,96;LI,102;NI,100)
- Understands the impact of the Louisiana Purchase (e.g., its influence on politics, economic development, and the concept of Manifest Destiny; how it affected relations with Native Americans and the lives of French and Spanish inhabitants of the Louisiana Territory; ▸ how the purchase of the Louisiana Territory was justified)

BD (BE,93;AE,96;NI,104)
- Understands the major provisions of the Monroe Doctrine (e.g., ▸ the extent to which its major purpose was to protect the newly won independence of Latin American states or to serve notice of U.S. expansionist intentions in the hemisphere, why the U.S. and other countries ignored the provisions of the doctrine for so long, its impact today)

BD (BE,93;AE,98;LI,101,103)
- Understands shifts in federal and state policy toward Native Americans in the first half of the 19th century (e.g., arguments for and against removal policy, ▸ changing policies from assimilation to removal and isolation after 1825)

BD (BE,93;AE,100)
- Understands the religious, political, and social ideas that contributed to the 19th century belief in Manifest Destiny (e.g., the influence of U.S. trading interests in the Far East on continental expansion to the Pacific, ▸ "City Upon a Hill" and subsequent Protestant belief in building a model Christian community, millennialism and the Great Awakening, Republicanism, the urge to keep foreign enemies from gaining control of the Pacific Coast, the belief in America's duty to uplift "less civilized" peoples in the West)

BD (BE,93;AE,100;LI,99,102;NI,104)
- Understands the initiating factors and outcomes of the Mexican-American War (e.g., ▸ the extent to which President Polk bore responsibility for initiating the war, whether the war was justified, arguments for and against the war, the impact of the Treaty of Guadalupe Hidalgo on the U.S. and Mexico)

BD (BE,93;AE,100;NI,105)
- Understands Mexican and American perspectives of events leading to the Mexican-American War (e.g., ▸ the Alamo, the treatment of Mexicans and Cherokees loyal to the Texas Revolution in the Lone Star Republic prior to 1846)

Codes (right side of page):	BD = Benchmark, Declarative; BP = Benchmark, Procedural; BC = Benchmark, Contextual	
1st letter of each code in parentheses	*2nd letter of code*	*Number*
B = NCHS: basic edition	E = Explicitly stated in document	Page number of cited document
A = NCHS: U.S. History, expanded edition	I = Implied in document	
L = Lessons From History		
N = NAEP: Provisional Item Specifications	*Symbol*	
	■ material appears only in NCHS basic edition	
	▸ material appears only in NCHS expanded edition	
	● material appears in both NCHS editions	

BD (AE,96;LI,84,93,101)

► Understands political interests and views regarding the War of 1812 (e.g., U.S. responses to shipping harassments prior to the war; interests of Native American and white settlers of the Northwest Territory during the war; congressional positions for and against the war resolution of June 3, 1812)

(BE,94;AE,101)

10. **Understands how the industrial revolution, increasing immigration, the rapid expansion of slavery, and the westward movement changed American lives and led to regional tensions**

Level II (Grades 5-6)

BD (BE,95;LE,91-92;NI,54)

■ Understands the lives of immigrants in American society during the antebellum period (e.g., factors that led to increased immigration from China, Ireland, and Germany; how immigrants adapted to life in the United States and to hostility from the nativist movement and the "Know- Nothing" party)

BD (BE,94;AE,101;LE,90,91;LI,91;NI,56)

● Understands the major technological developments that influenced land and water transportation, the economy, international markets, and the environment between 1801 and 1860 (e.g., ► the importance of the spinning jenny, steam locomotive, and telegraph; the development of the canal system after 1825 and railroad system after 1860)

BD (BE,94;AE,102,104;LE,91;LI,87,90;NI,56)

● Understands social and economic elements of urban and rural life in the early and mid-19th centuries (e.g., the impact of the factory system on gender roles and the daily life of men, women, and children; factors that caused rapid urbanization; city life in the 1840s; ► differences in urban and rural childrens' lives, life in New England mill towns in the early 1800s, the impact of the canal and railroad on the locations and size of cities after 1820)

BD (BE,94;AE,104-105;LI,86,92)

● Understands popular and high culture in growing urban areas during the 19th century (e.g., ► novels, theater, minstrel shows, P.T. Barnum's "American Museum")

BD (BE,95;AE,106,107;LE,110;LI,110-111;NI,55)

● Understands how slavery shaped social and economic life in the South after 1800 (e.g., how the cotton gin and the opening of new lands in the South and West led to increased demands for slaves; differences in the lives of plantation owners, poor free black and white families,

---

Codes (right side of page):   BD = Benchmark, Declarative; BP = Benchmark, Procedural; BC = Benchmark, Contextual

1st letter of each code in parentheses   *2nd letter of code*   *Number*

B = NCHS: basic edition   E = Explicitly stated in document   Page number of cited document

A = NCHS: U.S. History, expanded edition   I = Implied in document

L = Lessons From History

N = NAEP: Provisional Item Specifications   *Symbol*

                                       ■ material appears only in NCHS basic edition

                                       ► material appears only in NCHS expanded edition

                                       ● material appears in both NCHS editions

and slaves; methods of passive and active resistance to slavery; ► escaped slaves and the Underground Railroad)

BD (BE,95,96;AE,108;LE,98,100-101,103;LI,102)

● Understands elements of early western migration (e.g., the lure of the West and the reality of life on the frontier; motivations of various settlers; Mormon contributions to the settlement of the West; differences in the settlement of California and Oregon in the late 1840s and 1850s; ► routes taken by settlers of the Western U.S.; interactions between settlers and Native Americans and Mexicans in the western territories)

Level III (Grades 7-8)

BD (BE,95;LE,91-92;NI,54)

■ Understands how immigration affected American society in the antebellum period (e.g., the connection between industrialization and immigration, how immigration intensified ethnic and cultural conflict and complicated the forging of a national identity)

BD (BE,94;AE,101-102;LI,93)

● Understands the role of government in various areas of public service in the early 1800s (e.g., national and state policies regarding protective tariffs and a national bank, the controversy over federally funded internal improvements)

BD (BE,94;AE,101-102;LI,90,91-92;NE,56)

● Understands the social and economic impacts of the factory system (e.g., its role in developing a labor movement in the antebellum period, perspectives of owners and workers, ► child labor in New England mills)

BD (BE,94;AE,104;LE,91,92)

● Understands influences on urban life in the early and late 19th century (e.g., how rapid urbanization, immigration, and industrialization affected the social fabric of cities; individuals who contributed to the development of free black communities in the cities; the rise of racial hostility)

BD (BE,95;AE,106-107,114;LE,110;LI,110-111;NI,54)

● Understands different economic, cultural, and social characteristics of slavery after 1800 (e.g., the influence of the Haitian Revolution and the ending of the Atlantic slave trade, how slaves forged their own culture in the face of oppression, ► the role of the plantation system in shaping slaveholders and the enslaved, the experiences of escaped slaves)

BD (BE,95,96;AE,108-109;LE,99,100-101,103;LI,94)

● Understands characteristics of life on the western frontier in the 19th century (e.g., cultural interactions between diverse groups in the trans-Mississippi region, ► how the Mormons

---

Codes (right side of page):   BD = Benchmark, Declarative; BP = Benchmark, Procedural; BC = Benchmark, Contextual

1st letter of each code in parentheses   *2nd letter of code*   *Number*

B = NCHS: basic edition   E = Explicitly stated in document   Page number of cited document

A = NCHS: U.S. History, expanded edition   I = Implied in document

L = Lessons From History

N = NAEP: Provisional Item Specifications   *Symbol*

      ■ material appears only in NCHS basic edition

      ► material appears only in NCHS expanded edition

      ● material appears in both NCHS editions

established the Church of Latter Day Saints and their communities)

- BD (AE,101-102;LE,91;LI,90,91)

  Understands how major technological and economic developments influenced various groups (e.g., business owners, farmers, workers in different regions)

Level IV (Grades 9-12)

- BD (BE,94;AE,103;LE,88,93)

  Understands policies affecting regional and national interests during the early 19th century (e.g., how expansion-based economic policies, including northern dominance of locomotive transportation, contributed to growing political and sectional differences; ‣ the cheap price for the sale of western lands to residents of the North, South, and West; Andrew Jackson's veto of the Bank Recharter Bill of 1832)

- BD (BE,94;AE,101,103;LE,91-92,93;LI,85-86,92,93)

  Understands characteristics of economic development during the 19th century (e.g., patterns of economic development in different regions of the country during the first half of the 19th century; ‣ how early 19th century court cases promoted the market revolution; the causes and results of economic depressions of 1819, 1837, and 1857)

- BD (BE,95;AE,107)

  Understands how slavery influenced economic and social elements of Southern society (e.g., how slavery hindered the emergence of capitalist institutions and values, ‣ the influence of slavery on the development of the middle class, the influence of slave revolts on the lives of slaves and freed slaves)

- BD (BE,96;AE,109;LE,101,103;LI,94,103)

  Understands significant religious, cultural, and social changes in the American West (e.g., the degree to which political democracy influenced social and political conditions on the frontier, ‣ cultural characteristics of diverse groups, the impact of the Second Great Awakening and religious revivals on Mormon migration to the West, the lives of women in the West)

- BD (AE,103;LE,90-91;LI,88,92)

  Understands the impact of the Industrial Revolution during the early and later 19th century (e.g., ‣ the growth and spread of the factory system in New England, the effects of ethnic, religious, and racial tensions on the emergence of a unified labor movement)

- BD (AE,105)

  Understands the social and cultural influence of former slaves in cities of the North (e.g., their leadership of African American communities, how they advanced the rights and

---

Codes (right side of page):   BD = Benchmark, Declarative; BP = Benchmark, Procedural; BC = Benchmark, Contextual
1st letter of each code in parentheses   *2nd letter of code*   *Number*
B = NCHS: basic edition   E = Explicitly stated in document   Page number of cited document
A = NCHS: U.S. History, expanded edition   I = Implied in document
L = Lessons From History
N = NAEP: Provisional Item Specifications   *Symbol*
                                                                          ■ material appears only in NCHS basic edition
                                                                          ‣ material appears only in NCHS expanded edition
                                                                          ● material appears in both NCHS editions

MREL

interests of African Americans)

(BE,96;AE,110)

11. Understands the extension, restriction, and reorganization of political democracy after 1800

Level II (Grades 5-6)

BD (BE,96;AE,111;LE,92;NI,52)
- Understands elements of suffrage in the antebellum years (e.g., contradictions between the movement for universal white male suffrage and disenfranchisement of free African Americans and women, the influence of the West and western politicians in supporting equality in the political process)

BD (BE,96;AE,110)
- Understands why the election of Andrew Jackson was considered a victory for the "common man (e.g., ▸ the "spoils system," Jackson's interest in providing the "common man" with opportunities to serve in the government)

BD (BE,96;AE,112;LE,111-112)
- Understands divisive issues prior to the Civil War (e.g., the Missouri Compromise and its role in determining slave and non-slave land areas, ▸ the issues that divided the North and the South)

Level III (Grades 7-8)

BD (BE,96;AE,111;LE,92,93;NI,52)
- Understands political influences and views after 1800 (e.g., the impact of changes in electoral qualifications for white males on local, state, and national politics; how President Jackson's position on the bank recharter and nullification issues contributed to the rise of the Whig party)

BD (BE,96,97;AE,112;LE,111-112;LI,88)
- Understands the major events and issues that promoted sectional conflicts and strained national cohesiveness in the antebellum period (e.g., support and opposition of the Missouri Compromise of 1820, the debate over slavery from the late 1830s to the Compromise of 1850)

Codes (right side of page):　　　　　　BD = Benchmark, Declarative; BP = Benchmark, Procedural; BC = Benchmark, Contextual
1st letter of each code in parentheses　　　*2nd letter of code*　　　　　　　　　*Number*
B = NCHS: basic edition　　　　　　　　E = Explicitly stated in document　　　Page number of cited document
A = NCHS: U.S. History, expanded edition　　I = Implied in document
L = Lessons From History
N = NAEP: Provisional Item Specifications　　*Symbol*
　　　　　　　　　　　　　　　　　　　　■ material appears only in NCHS basic edition
　　　　　　　　　　　　　　　　　　　　▸ material appears only in NCHS expanded edition
　　　　　　　　　　　　　　　　　　　　● material appears in both NCHS editions

- Understands how tariff policy and issues of state's rights influenced party development and promoted sectional differences (e.g., ▸ the political positions of Whigs and Democrats on important issues in 1832, how platform issues had special appeal to different sections of the country) ^{BD (BE,96;AE,112;LE,93)}

Level IV (Grades 9-12)

- Understands increased political activity in the first half of the 19th century (e.g., the importance of state and local issues, the rise of interest-group politics, and the style of campaigning in increasing voter participation; factors that affected the vitality of the National Republican, Democratic, Whig, and "Know-Nothing" parties) ^{BD (BE,96;AE,110,111;LE,92,93)}

▸ Understands the positions of northern antislavery advocates and southern proslavery spokesmen on a variety of issues (e.g., race, chattel slavery, the nature of the Union, states' rights) ^{BD (AE,113;LE,111-112)}

12. Understands the sources and character of cultural, religious, and social reform movements in the antebellum period ^(BE,97;AE,114)

Level II (Grades 5-6)

- Understands how literary and artistic movements fostered a distinct American identity among different groups and in different regions ^{BD (BE,96;LI,95;NI,54)}

- Understands the major characteristics of the abolition movement in the antebellum period (e.g., different viewpoints within the abolitionist movement, ▸ arguments of those opposed to and those who supported slavery, the Underground Railroad) ^{BD (BE,97;AE,114-115;LE,95;LI,94-96)}

- Understands the religious revivals that swept the nation in the early 19th century (e.g., the importance of the Second Great Awakening, the messages of Great Awakening leaders such as Charles Finney and Peter Cartwright) ^{BD (BE,97;AE,116;LE,94)}

Codes (right side of page):   BD = Benchmark, Declarative; BP = Benchmark, Procedural; BC = Benchmark, Contextual
1st letter of each code in parentheses   *2nd letter of code*   *Number*
B = NCHS: basic edition   E = Explicitly stated in document   Page number of cited document
A = NCHS: U.S. History, expanded edition   I = Implied in document
L = Lessons From History
N = NAEP: Provisional Item Specifications   *Symbol*
    ■ material appears only in NCHS basic edition
    ▸ material appears only in NCHS expanded edition
    • material appears in both NCHS editions

- BD (BE,98;AE,118;LE,95-96;NE,55)
  Understands the role of women in the reform movements in antebellum America (e.g., the contributions of individuals of different racial and social groups, the types of reforms women sought, ▸ how fashion became a part of the movement for women's rights)

Level III (Grades 7-8)

- BD (BE,97;AE,114-115;LI,96)
  Understands perspectives that influenced slavery in the antebellum period (e.g., changing ideas about race, the reception of proslavery and antislavery ideologies in the North and South, ▸ arguments used to defend slavery in the 18th and 19th centuries)

- BD (BE,97;AE,116,117;LE,94-96;LI,88,93,95)
  Understands the significant religious, philosophical, and social movements of the 19th century and their impacts on American society and social reform (e.g., the impact of the Second Great Awakening on issues such as public education, temperance, women's suffrage, and abolitionism; Transcendentalism and the literary works of its central leaders; Transcendentalist ideas about the individual, society, and nature)

- BD (BE,98;AE,118-119;LE,96;LI,89;NE,54;NI,53)
  Understands how women influenced reform movements and American society during the antebellum period (e.g., the Seneca Falls "Declaration of Sentiments" of 1848, ▸ the leadership role women played in major reform movements, how the public at large viewed these women)

Level IV (Grades 9-12)

- BD (BE,97;AE,115;LE,94-95)
  Understands elements of slavery in both the North and South during the antebellum period (e.g., similarities and differences between African American and white abolitionists, ▸ defense of chattel slavery by slaveholders, growing hostility toward free blacks in the North, how African American leaders fought for rights)

- BD (BE,97;AE,117;LE,94-95;NI,102)
  Understands the social impact of the Second Great Awakening (e.g., ▸ how Great Awakening leaders affected ordinary people; how the belief in individual responsibility for salvation and millenialism influenced reform movements; the role of moral suasion, social control, and compromise in reform)

- BD (BE,97;AE,117;LI,88,95)
  Understands the ideas of Transcendentalism (e.g., ▸ views of Transcendentalists about good

---

Codes (right side of page):	BD = Benchmark, Declarative; BP = Benchmark, Procedural; BC = Benchmark, Contextual	
1st letter of each code in parentheses	*2nd letter of code*	*Number*
B = NCHS: basic edition	E = Explicitly stated in document	Page number of cited document
A = NCHS: U.S. History, expanded edition	I = Implied in document	
L = Lessons From History		
N = NAEP: Provisional Item Specifications	*Symbol*	
	■ material appears only in NCHS basic edition	
	▸ material appears only in NCHS expanded edition	
	● material appears in both NCHS editions	

and evil, authority, tradition, and reform; similarities and differences between Transcendentalists and evangelical Protestants)

BD (BE,97;AE,117)
- Understands the development of Utopian communities (e.g., ► origins, beliefs, size, how their ideas compared to Transcendentalists)

BD (BE,97,98;AE,118,119;LE,96)
- Understands changing gender roles in the antebellum period (e.g., men and women's occupations, legal rights, and social status in the North, South and West; ► how gender roles were influenced by class, ethnic, racial, and religious lines)

BD (BE,98;AE,118,119;LI,89,96)
- Understands the ideas associated with women's rights during the antebellum period (e.g., the goals and ideas of the antebellum women's movement for equality compared to 20th-century feminism, ► how the Seneca Falls "Declaration of Sentiments" relates to the ideas of the Declaration of Independence, the connection between the evangelical movement and the idea of southern woman, and the extent to which southern women endorsed the "Declaration of Sentiments")

(BE,100;AE,122)

13. Understands the causes of the Civil War

Level II (Grades 5-6)

BD (BE,100;AE,122;LE,94-95,110,111;NE,58)
- Understands slavery prior to the Civil War (e.g., the importance of slavery as a principal cause of the Civil War, ► the growing influence of abolitionists, childrens' roles and family life under slavery)

BD (AE,122;LI,90,110)
► Knows the locations of the southern and northern states and their economic resources (e.g., the industries and small family farms of the industrial North, the agricultural economy and slavery of the South)

Level III (Grades 7-8)

BD (BE,100;AE,123;LI,110-111;NI,60)
- Understands the economic, social, and cultural differences between the North and South

---

Codes (right side of page):   BD = Benchmark, Declarative; BP = Benchmark, Procedural; BC = Benchmark, Contextual

1st letter of each code in parentheses	*2nd letter of code*	*Number*
B = NCHS: basic edition	E = Explicitly stated in document	Page number of cited document
A = NCHS: U.S. History, expanded edition	I = Implied in document	
L = Lessons From History		
N = NAEP: Provisional Item Specifications	*Symbol*	
	■ material appears only in NCHS basic edition	
	► material appears only in NCHS expanded edition	
	● material appears in both NCHS editions	

(e.g., how the free labor system of the North differed from that of the South)

- Understands the development of sectional polarization and secession prior to the Civil War ^{BD (BE,100;AE,123;LE,112;LI,111-112;NI,58)} (e.g., how events after the Compromise of 1850 and the Dred Scott decision impacted sectional differences, southern justification for secession, ► the presidential leadership of Buchanan and Lincoln during the secession crisis)

- Understands issues other than slavery that led to the Civil War (e.g., the appeal of the ^{BD (BE,100;AE,123;LE,112)} Northern "free labor" ideology in preventing the further extension of slavery in the new territories; cultural differences, conflicting economic issues, ► opposing constitutional perspectives)

Level IV (Grades 9-12)

- Understands the reasons for the disruption of the second American party system and how this ^{BD (BE,100;AE,123)} led to the ascent of the Republican party in the 1850s

► Understands events that fueled the political and sectional conflicts over slavery and ^{BD (AE,123;LI,112)} ultimately polarized the North and the South (e.g., the Missouri Compromise, the Wilmot Proviso, the Kansas-Nebraska Act)

(BE,100;AE,124)

14.   Understands the course and character of the Civil War and its effects on the American people

Level II (Grades 5-6)

- Understands the technological, social, and strategic aspects of the Civil War (e.g., the impact ^{BD (BE,101;AE,124;LE,113;NI,61)} of innovations in military technology; turning points of the war; leaders of the Confederacy and Union; ► conditions, characteristics, and armies of the Confederacy and Union; major areas of Civil War combat)

- Understands the provisions and significance of the Emancipation Proclamation (e.g., reasons ^{BD (BE,101;AE,124;LI,113;NI,59)}

Codes (right side of page):   BD = Benchmark, Declarative; BP = Benchmark, Procedural; BC = Benchmark, Contextual
1st letter of each code in parentheses   *2nd letter of code*   *Number*
B = NCHS: basic edition   E = Explicitly stated in document   Page number of cited document
A = NCHS: U.S. History, expanded edition   I = Implied in document
L = Lessons From History
N = NAEP: Provisional Item Specifications   *Symbol*
                                                                         ■ material appears only in NCHS basic edition
                                                                         ► material appears only in NCHS expanded edition
                                                                         ● material appears in both NCHS editions

McREL

Abraham Lincoln issued it, ▸ public reactions to it in the North and the South)

- Understands the impact of the Civil War on social and gender issues (e.g., the roles of women on the home front and on the battlefield; the human and material costs of the war; the degree to which the war united the nation; ▸ how it changed the lives of women, men, and children)
  BD (BE,101;AE,126;LE,107,114)

Level III (Grades 7-8)

- Understands the circumstances that shaped the Civil War and its outcome (e.g., differences between the economic, technological, and human resources of both sides; ▸ the impact of the Emancipation Proclamation on the outcome of the war)
  BD (BE,101;AE,125;LE,113;NE,59;NI,61)

- Understands how different groups of people shaped the Civil War (e.g., the motives and experiences of Confederate and white and African American Union soldiers, ▸ different perspectives on conscription, the effects of divided loyalties)
  BD (BE,101;AE,126-127;LE,114;LI,113;NE,59;NI,61)

Level IV (Grades 9-12)

- Understands military events that influenced the outcome of the Civil War (e.g., ▸ the "hammering campaigns" of Generals Grant and Sherman, the wartime leadership of Jefferson Davis and Abraham Lincoln)
  BD (BE,101;AE,125;LE,113)

- Understands the influence of Abraham Lincoln's ideas on the Civil War (e.g., the Gettysburg Address, ▸ how the Emancipation Proclamation transformed the goals of the Civil War)
  BD (BE,101;AE,125)

- Understands the impact of the Civil War on Native Americans (e.g., the positions of major Indian nations during the Civil War and the effect of the war on these nations, ▸ the internal conflicts among the "Five Civilized Tribes" regarding their support for the Union or Confederacy, the long-term consequences for Native Americans)
  BD (BE,101;AE,125)

- Understands how the Civil War influenced Northern and Southern society on the home front (e.g., the New York City draft riots of July 1863, the Union's reasons for curbing civil liberties in wartime, ▸ Lincoln's suspension of the writ of habeas corpus during the war)
  BD (BE,101;AE,127)

Codes (right side of page): BD = Benchmark, Declarative; BP = Benchmark, Procedural; BC = Benchmark, Contextual
1st letter of each code in parentheses *2nd letter of code* *Number*
B = NCHS: basic edition E = Explicitly stated in document Page number of cited document
A = NCHS: U.S. History, expanded edition I = Implied in document
L = Lessons From History
N = NAEP: Provisional Item Specifications *Symbol*
  ■ material appears only in NCHS basic edition
  ▸ material appears only in NCHS expanded edition
  ● material appears in both NCHS editions

MREL

▸ Understands how the Civil War influenced both military personnel and civilians (e.g., the treatment of African American soldiers in the Union Army and Confederacy, how the war changed gender roles and traditional attitudes toward women in the work force) BD (AE,127;LE,107,114;NI,107)

15. Understands how various reconstruction plans succeeded or failed (BE,101;AE,128)

Level II (Grades 5-6)

● Understands military, political, and social factors affecting the post Civil War period (e.g., the basic provisions of the 13th, 14th, and 15th amendments, and the political and social forces that opposed and supported them, ▸ how the lives of African Americans were changed by these amendments; demobilization of the Union and Confederate armies; how the leadership of Presidents Lincoln and Johnson affected reconstruction) BD (BE,102;AE,128;LE,106,109;LI,113;NE,58;NI,60)

● Understands changes in social relations in the South during Reconstruction (e.g., the role of the Freedmen's Bureau, ▸ the impact of emancipation in the South, how former slaves improved their position in society, how people from the North traveled to aid in Reconstruction) BD (BE,102;AE,130;LE,115;NE,60)

● Understands the lives of African Americans during the Reconstruction era (e.g., the progress of "Black Reconstruction" and the impact of legislative reform programs, ▸ contributions of individual African Americans who served as teachers and political leaders, why some abolition leaders voiced opposition to the 15th amendment) BD (BE,102;AE,132)

● Understands the impact of the Reconstruction period on politics in the South (e.g., the increase in corruption in the post-Civil War period, ▸ the importance of political cartoonists in drawing attention to corruption) BD (BE,102;AE,132;LI,116)

▸ Understands how economic conditions and family life in the North and South changed over the war years BD (AE,132)

Codes (right side of page): BD = Benchmark, Declarative; BP = Benchmark, Procedural; BC = Benchmark, Contextual
1st letter of each code in parentheses *2nd letter of code* *Number*
B = NCHS: basic edition E = Explicitly stated in document Page number of cited document
A = NCHS: U.S. History, expanded edition I = Implied in document
L = Lessons From History
N = NAEP: Provisional Item Specifications *Symbol*
  ■ material appears only in NCHS basic edition
  ▸ material appears only in NCHS expanded edition
  ● material appears in both NCHS editions

160   MREL

Level III (Grades 7-8)

- BD (BE,101,102;AE,128;LE,114-115;NI,60)

  Understands the effect of differing Reconstruction policies and how they were perceived (e.g., plans advocated by President Lincoln, Congressional leaders, and President Johnson; the Compromise of 1877; ▸ different perspectives on the effectiveness of the Reconstruction amendments)

- BD (BE,101;AE,128-129)

  Understands the reasons for and consequences of President Johnson's impeachment and trial (e.g., the escalating conflict between Johnson and Congress, ▸ Johnson's resistance to Congressional authority, the Tenure of Office Act)

- BD (BE,102;AE,130;NI,61)

  Understands the economic and social problems facing the South and their impact on different groups of people at the close of the Civil War

- BD (BE,102;AE,130,131;LI,115;NI,58)

  Understands attempts to improve African American lives during Reconstruction (e.g., African American attempts to improve their economic position, their quest for land ownership; ▸ how the Freedmen's Bureau proposed to deal with abandoned lands in the South)

- BD (BE,102;AE,133;LI,115-116;NE,59,NI,60)

  Understands changes in the political and social structure in different regions during Reconstruction (e.g., changes in political and economic positions of African Americans in the North; changes in gender roles and status in the North, South and West; ▸ contributions of African Americans who served in state and national offices; personal challenges to Freedmen)

Level IV (Grades 9-12)

- BD (BE,101;AE,129;LI,114-115)

  Understands the elements of different plans for Reconstruction (e.g., ▸ how each plan viewed secession, amnesty, pardon, and procedure for readmission to the Union; the influence of the issue of Federalism on the debate over Reconstruction policy; the motives of the Radical Republicans)

- BD (BE,102;AE,129;LI,115;NI,107)

  Understands the 14th and 15th amendments to the Constitution (e.g., ▸ how citizenship was included, why the clauses of "equal protection of the laws" and "due process" were included, why women were excluded in the 15th amendment)

Codes (right side of page):	BD = Benchmark, Declarative; BP = Benchmark, Procedural; BC = Benchmark, Contextual	
1st letter of each code in parentheses	*2nd letter of code*	*Number*
B = NCHS: basic edition	E = Explicitly stated in document	Page number of cited document
A = NCHS: U.S. History, expanded edition	I = Implied in document	
L = Lessons From History		
N = NAEP: Provisional Item Specifications	*Symbol*	
	▪ material appears only in NCHS basic edition	
	▸ material appears only in NCHS expanded edition	
	● material appears in both NCHS editions	

MREL

- Understands events leading to the formation of the Compromise of 1877 (e.g., the role of violence and tactics of the "redeemers" in bringing about the Compromise, the consequences in the South)   BD (BE,102;AE,129;LI,115-116)

- Understands factors that inhibited and fostered African American attempts to improve their lives during Reconstruction (e.g., how foundations were laid for modern black communities, ▸ how traditional values inhibited the role of the Freedmen's Bureau, the struggle between former masters and former slaves, the role of black churches and schools in providing self-help within the African American community)   BD (BE,102;AE,131;LI,115-116)

- Understands social and economic factors during and toward the end of Reconstruction (e.g., how economic expansion and development in the North and South were influenced by Reconstruction, ▸ the impact of fraud and violence on the end of Reconstruction)   BD (BE,102;AE,133)

- Understands different perspectives of Reconstruction (e.g., Reconstruction as an expression of social democratization and perfectionism, ▸ Reconstruction as a revolution)   BD (BE,102;AE,133;LI,115-116)

▸ Understands the extent to which social and political issues were influenced by the Civil War and Reconstruction (e.g., why women's rights leaders felt betrayed by Reconstruction, the extent to which crooked busines deals encouraged corruption in the government)   BD (AE,134)

(BE,104;AE,138)

16. Understands how the rise of corporations, heavy industry, and mechanized farming transformed American society

Level II (Grades 5-6)

- Understands the impact of significant achievements and individuals of the late 19th century (e.g., the effects of major technological, transportation, and communication changes that occurred after 1870; careers of industrial and financial leaders of the late 19th century)   BD (BE,104;AE,138;LE,119;LI,119,122;NE,66,67)

- Understands the economic and social changes that occurred in late 19th century American cities (e.g., where industries and transportation expanded; geographic reasons for building factories, commercial centers, and transportation hubs; why different groups moved from the   BD (BE,104,105;AE,140;LE,124;LI,124;NI,66)

Codes (right side of page):   BD = Benchmark, Declarative; BP = Benchmark, Procedural; BC = Benchmark, Contextual

1st letter of each code in parentheses   *2nd letter of code*   *Number*

B = NCHS: basic edition   E = Explicitly stated in document   Page number of cited document

A = NCHS: U.S. History, expanded edition   I = Implied in document

L = Lessons From History

N = NAEP: Provisional Item Specifications   *Symbol*

■ material appears only in NCHS basic edition

▸ material appears only in NCHS expanded edition

● material appears in both NCHS editions

farms to the big cities and how they adjusted; ▸ living conditions in the growing cities)

- BD (BE,105;AE,142;LE,125,126;LI,125,126;NI,66)

  Understands social development and labor patterns in the late 19th century West (e.g., major technological and geographic influences that affected farming, mining, and ranching; conflicts among farmers, ranchers, and miners during settlement; life on the Great Plains and the idea of "frontier")

- BD (BE,105;AE,144;LE,131;NI,66,67)

  Understands environmental issues of the late 19th century (e.g., environmental costs of pollution and depletion of natural resources; ▸ efforts of reformers to control pollution and promote concern for the natural environment)

Level III (Grades 7-8)

- BD (BE,104;AE,139;LE,119,122;LI,122,124;NE,67;NI,66)

  Understands influences on business and industry in the 19th century (e.g., how business leaders attempted to limit competition and maximize profits, ▸ the role of the government in promoting business, the concept of the "American Dream")

- BD (BE,104-105;AE,140-141;LE,126)

  Understands responses to the challenges of rapid urbanization in the late 19th century (e.g., how urban political machines gained power; the response of urban leaders, such as architects and philanthropists)

- BD (BE,105;AE,142-143;LE,125-126;LI,126;NI,64,66)

  Understands influences on the development of the American West (e.g., cross-cultural encounters and conflicts among different racial and ethnic groups; the daily life of women on the western frontier; ▸ disputes between farmers, ranchers, and miners over water rights and open ranges)

- BD (BE,105;AE,142;LI,125)

  Understands differences in commercial farming in various regions of the United States (e.g., crop production, farm labor, financing, and transportation in the Northeast, South, Great Plains, West; the significance of farm organizations)

- BD (BE,105;AE,144;NI,67)

  Understands various influences on the scenic and urban environment (e.g., how rapid industrialization, extractive mining techniques, and the "gridiron pattern" of urban growth influenced the city and countryside; environmentalism and the conservation movement in the late 19th century)

Level IV (Grades 9-12)

- Understands the development of business in the late 19th century (e.g., types of business organizations that affected the economy; the impact of industrialization on availability of consumer goods, living standards, and redistribution of wealth; how new industries gained dominance in their field; ▸ the changing nature of business enterprise)

  BD (BE,104;AE,139;LE,122;LI,119,120)

- Understands issues associated with urban growth in the late 19th century (e.g., how city residents dealt with urban problems; ▸ demographic, economic, and spatial expansion of cities; how urban bosses won the support of immigrants)

  BD (BE,104-105;AE,141;LE,124,126)

- Understands influences on economic conditions in various regions of the country (e.g., effects of the federal government's land, water and Indian policy; ▸ the extension of railroad lines, increased agricultural productivity and improved transportation facilities on commodity prices; grievances and solutions of farm organizations; the crop lien system in the South, transportation and storage costs for farmers, and the price of staples)

  BD (BE,105;AE,143;LI,125,126)

- Understands the factors leading to the conservation movement of the late 19th century (e.g., ▸ how emphasis on staple crop production, strip mining, lumbering, ranching, and destruction of western buffalo herds led to massive environmental damage)

  BD (BE,105;AE,144-145;NI,115)

- Understands how rapid increase in population and industrial growth in urban areas influenced the environment (e.g., ▸ inefficient urban garbage collection and sewage disposal, how city leaders and residents coped with environmental problems in the city)

  BD (BE,105;AE,144-145;NI,115)

- ▸ Understands the role of class, race, gender, and religion in western communities in the late 19th century (e.g., hardships faced by settlers, how gender and racial roles were defined, the role of religion in stabilizing communities)

  BD (AE,143)

Codes (right side of page):   BD = Benchmark, Declarative; BP = Benchmark, Procedural; BC = Benchmark, Contextual
1st letter of each code in parentheses   *2nd letter of code*   *Number*
B = NCHS: basic edition   E = Explicitly stated in document   Page number of cited document
A = NCHS: U.S. History, expanded edition   I = Implied in document
L = Lessons From History
N = NAEP: Provisional Item Specifications   *Symbol*
    ■ material appears only in NCHS basic edition
    ▸ material appears only in NCHS expanded edition
    ● material appears in both NCHS editions

(BE,106;AE,146)

17. Understands massive immigration after 1870 and how new social patterns, conflicts, and ideas of national unity developed amid growing cultural diversity

Level II (Grades 5-6)

- BD (BE,106;AE,146;LE,123-124;LI,123;NE,64,65)
  Understands patterns of immigrant life after 1870 (e.g., where people came from and where they settled; how immigrants formed a new American culture; the challenges, opportunities, and contributions of different immigrant groups; ▸ ways in which immigrants learned to live and work in a new country)

- BD (BE,106;AE,148;LI,123-124,130;NE,64)
  Understands the experiences of diverse groups and minorities in different regions of the country (e.g., the experiences of African Americans, Asian Americans, and Hispanic Americans; the anti-Chinese movement in the West; the rise of lynching in the South; ▸ the impact of Jim Crow laws on African Americans)

- BD (BE,107;AE,150;NE,64)
  Understands social activities in the late 19th century (e.g., new forms of popular culture and leisure activities at different levels of American society, ▸ entertainment for children)

Level III (Grades 7-8)

- BD (BE,106;AE,147;LI,123;NE,65)
  Understands the background and experiences of immigrants of the late 19th century (e.g., how the immigrants differed from those of the early 19th century in numbers, motives, origins, ethnicity, religion and language; how Catholic and Jewish immigrants responded to discrimination; ▸ attitudes toward immigrants)

- BD (BE,106;AE,148;LE,122-123;NE,64)
  Understands the scientific theories of race and their application to society and politics

- BD (BE,106;AE,150;NI,64)
  Understands changes in American life in the late 19th century (e.g., how regional artists and writers portrayed American life, attitudes, and values; ▸ reasons for the appeal of new sports, entertainment, and recreational activities; changes in lifestyles)

- BD (AE,148;LE,130;LI,123-124,130;NI,63)
  ▸ Understands opposition to discrimination in the late 19th century (e.g., how Asian Americans and Hispanic Americans responded to discriminatory practices, leadership roles of those who

---

Codes (right side of page): BD = Benchmark, Declarative; BP = Benchmark, Procedural; BC = Benchmark, Contextual
1st letter of each code in parentheses   *2nd letter of code*   *Number*
B = NCHS: basic edition   E = Explicitly stated in document   Page number of cited document
A = NCHS: U.S. History, expanded edition   I = Implied in document
L = Lessons From History
N = NAEP: Provisional Item Specifications   *Symbol*
    ■ material appears only in NCHS basic edition
    ▸ material appears only in NCHS expanded edition
    ● material appears in both NCHS editions

165   MREL

spoke out against discrimination)

Level IV (Grades 9-12)

- BD (BE,106;AE,147;LI,123;NI,113)
  Understands challenges immigrants faced in society in the late 19th century (e.g., ▸ experiences of new immigrants from 1870 to 1900, reasons for hositility toward the new immigrants, restrictive measures against immigrants, the tension between American ideals and reality)

- BD (BE,106,107;AE,147)
  Understands the influence of public education on American society after 1870 (e.g., the role of public and parochial schools in integrating immigrants into mainstream America, how the rise of public education and voluntary organizations promoted national unity and American values)

- BD (BE,106;AE,149;LI,122-12;NI,112)
  Understands how scientific theories of race affected society in the late 19th century (e.g., ▸ arguments of advocates and opponents, the impact of these theories on public policy)

- BD (BE,106;AE,148,149;LI,123-124,130)
  Understands the challenges diverse people encountered in late 19th century American society (e.g.,the role of new laws and the federal judiciary in instituting racial inequality; arguments and methods by which various minority groups sought to acquire equal rights and opportunities; ▸ experiences of African American families who migrated from the South to New York City in the 1890s)

- BD (BE,107;AE,151;LI,124)
  Understands changes in social and class development in late 19th century America (e.g.,Victorianism and its impact on architecture, literature, manners and morals)

(BE,107;AE,152)

18. Understands the rise of the American labor movement and how political issues reflected social and economic changes

Level II (Grades 5-6)

- BD (BE,107;AE,152;LE,124;NI,67)
  Understands changes in business and labor practices during the late 19th century (e.g.,

---

Codes (right side of page):
1st letter of each code in parentheses
B = NCHS: basic edition
A = NCHS: U.S. History, expanded edition
L = Lessons From History
N = NAEP: Provisional Item Specifications

BD = Benchmark, Declarative; BP = Benchmark, Procedural; BC = Benchmark, Contextual
2nd letter of code
E = Explicitly stated in document
I = Implied in document

Symbol
■ material appears only in NCHS basic edition
▸ material appears only in NCHS expanded edition
● material appears in both NCHS editions

Number
Page number of cited document

166

McREL

reasons for child labor and it consequences, ► changes in business operation, how workers lives were affected after the Civil War)

- BD (BE,107;AE,154;NE,66)
Understands characteristics of the labor conflicts of the late 19th century (e.g., causes and effects of escalating labor conflicts, ► causes and effects of coal mine strikes, the organizing efforts of Mother Mary Jones)

- BD (BE,108;AE,156;NI,63,67)
Understands major political issues and events of the late 19th century (e.g., the issues and results of the 1896 election, ► why third parties were established, the importance of Thomas Nast's political cartoons, the lives of important political personalities)

Level III (Grades 7-8)

- BD (BE,107;AE,152-153;LE,124;LI,124;NI,66,67)
Understands the conditions affecting employment and labor in the late 19th century (e.g., the change from workshop to factory in different regions; how working conditions changed and how workers responded to new industrial conditions)

- BD (BE,107;AE,154;LI,124;NE,67;NI,63)
Understands reactions to developments in labor in late 19th century America (e.g., how management and industry responded to efforts to organize workers, the response of management and government to labor strife in different regions of the country)

- BD (BE,108;AE,156,157;LI,126;NE,63)
Understands the goals of political parties and individuals in the late 19th century (e.g., how Democrats and Republicans responded to civil service reform, monetary policy, tariffs, and business regulations; political, social, and economic roots of Populism; successes and failures of Populism; ► goals of the Socialist and Populist parties and their leaders; importance of individuals in promoting political reform)

Level IV (Grades 9-12)

- BD (BE,107;AE,153;NI,113)
Understands influences on the workforce during the late 19th century (e.g., gender, race, ethnicity, and skill; ► how big business and the impersonal nature of factory work affected workers; inroads made by women in male-dominated jobs; legal status of women; the type of work children performed; occupations in which children were employed; dangers they faced during the workday)

Codes (right side of page):	BD = Benchmark, Declarative; BP = Benchmark, Procedural; BC = Benchmark, Contextual	
1st letter of each code in parentheses	*2nd letter of code*	*Number*
B = NCHS: basic edition	E = Explicitly stated in document	Page number of cited document
A = NCHS: U.S. History, expanded edition	I = Implied in document	
L = Lessons From History		
N = NAEP: Provisional Item Specifications	*Symbol*	
	■ material appears only in NCHS basic edition	
	► material appears only in NCHS expanded edition	
	● material appears in both NCHS editions	

BD (BE,107;AE,155;NI,116)

- Understands labor issues of the late 19th century (e.g., organizational and agenda differences between reform and trade unions, ▸ the extent of radicalism in the labor movements, labor conflicts of 1894 and their effects)

BD (BE,108;AE,156,157;LI,126; NI,112)

- Understands the appeal of various political parties and the positions they took (e.g., the Populist's Omaha Platform of 1892; ▸ problems that prompted the establishment of the Populist Party; the appeal of the Democratic, Republican, and Greenback Labor parties to different socioeconomic groups)

BD (BE,108;AE,156,157)

- Understands how economic issues influenced American society (e.g., the causes and effects of the depressions of 1873-1879 and 1893-1897, and how government, business, labor, and farmers responded; ▸ the reaction of western and southern farmers to the cycle of falling prices, scarce money, and debt)

BD (BE,108;AE,158)

- Understands the issues and results of the 1896 election (e.g., ▸ the extent to which farmers were unable to adjust to the changing industrial scene and the Populist decision to endorse the Democratic nominee, William Jennings Bryan's "Cross of Gold" speech and how it affected the outcome of the election, arguments and strategies used by William McKinley and Mark Hanna, urban women's support of the Republican party, the major components of the "full dinner pail")

(BE,108;AE,159)

19.   Understands federal Indian policy and United States foreign policy after the Civil War

Level II (Grades 5-6)

BD (BE,108;AE,159;LE,125;NI,64)

- Understands significant events for Native American tribes in the late 19th century and how they responded (e.g., survival strategies of Native American societies during the "second great removal," ▸ movement to reservations in western states, the effect of government policies on Native American nations and Native American land holdings between 1870 and 1900)

BD (BE,108;AE,161;LE,135;NI,68)

- Understands the expansion of U.S. territories in the post-Civil War era (e.g., areas the U.S. annexed, ▸ primary interests in these areas)

Codes (right side of page):	BD = Benchmark, Declarative; BP = Benchmark, Procedural; BC = Benchmark, Contextual	
1st letter of each code in parentheses	*2nd letter of code*	*Number*
B = NCHS: basic edition	E = Explicitly stated in document	Page number of cited document
A = NCHS: U.S. History, expanded edition	I = Implied in document	
L = Lessons From History		
N = NAEP: Provisional Item Specifications	*Symbol*	
	■ material appears only in NCHS basic edition	
	▸ material appears only in NCHS expanded edition	
	● material appears in both NCHS editions	

BD (BE,109;AE,161;LE,139-140;NE,68)

●   Understands critical features of the Spanish-American War (e.g., conditions that led to the war with Spain in 1898, character and outcome of the war, ► leading personalities of the Spanish-American War)

Level III (Grades 7-8)

BD (BE,108;AE,159-160;LI,120;NI,64,65)

●   Understands interaction between Native Americans and white society (e.g., the attitudes and policies of government officials, the U.S. Army, missionaries, and settlers toward Native Americans; the provisions and effects of the Dawes Severalty Act of 1887 on tribal identity, land ownership and assimilation; the legacy of the 19th century federal Indian policy; ► Native American responses to increased white settlement, mining activities, and railroad construction)

BD (BE,109;AE,161,162;LE,139,140;NE,63)

●   Understands the causes and consequences of the Spanish-American War (e.g., ► economic and geographic factors, U.S. justifications, impact of the press on the public opinion, the role of the U.S. in Cuba after the war, the war's effects on U.S. involvement in international relations, constitutional issues raised by the acquisition of new territories)

BD (BE,109;AE,161,162;LE,140;NE,68)

●   Understands factors that influenced U.S. expansionism in the late 19th century (e.g., consequences of the Philippine annexation and Filipino insurrection; ► geographic, economic, and social factors; arguments used to justify expansion; arguments of opponents to expansion)

Level IV (Grades 9-12)

BD (BE,109;AE,162;LE,139-140)

●   Understands factors in the outbreak and outcome of the Spanish-American War (e.g., ► President McKinley's reasons for going to war; changing U.S. attitudes toward Emilio Aguinaldo from 1898 to the issue of warrants for his arrest after the Treaty of Paris)

BD (BE,109;AE,161,162;LE,139;NI,117)

●   Understands elements that contributed to late 19th century expansionist foreign policy (e.g., geopolitics, economic interests, racial ideology, Protestant missionary zeal, nationalism, and domestic tensions)

BD (AE,160;LE,125;NI,113)

►   Understands influences on and perspectives of Native American life in the late 19th century

---

Codes (right side of page):   BD = Benchmark, Declarative; BP = Benchmark, Procedural; BC = Benchmark, Contextual

1st letter of each code in parentheses	*2nd letter of code*	*Number*
B = NCHS: basic edition	E = Explicitly stated in document	Page number of cited document
A = NCHS: U.S. History, expanded edition	I = Implied in document	
L = Lessons From History		
N = NAEP: Provisional Item Specifications	*Symbol*	

■ material appears only in NCHS basic edition
► material appears only in NCHS expanded edition
● material appears in both NCHS editions

(e.g., how the admission of new western states affected relations between the United States and Native American societies; leadership and values of Native American leaders; depiction of Native Americans and whites by 19th century artists)

(BE,111;AE,165)

20.   Understands how Progressives and others addressed problems of industrial capitalism, urbanization, and political corruption

Level II (Grades 5-6)

BD (BE,111;AE,165;LE,131;NI,63)
●   Understands Progressive ideas and reform efforts (e.g., the Progressive idea of a democracy responsive to the needs of an industrial society, Progressive attempts at social and moral reform, ▸ conditions that inspired these reforms)

BD (BE,111,112;AE,167;LE,128,133-134;LI,134;NI,63)
●   Understands political and legislative elements of the Progressive movement (e.g., how the Progressives promoted political change and expanded democracy at state and local levels; the leadership of Presidents Roosevelt, Taft, and Wilson and their ideas for reform; the 16th, 17th, and 18th amendments; ▸ the movement for women's suffrage)

BD (BE,112;AE,169;LE,130,131;NI,63,65)
●   Understands issues and perspectives of different groups during the Progressive era (e.g., African Americans and their alternative programs; ▸ women, Native Americans, organized workers)

BD (AE,165;LI,123-124;NI,63,64)
▸   Understands how migrants from rural areas and immigrants from other lands experienced life in growing urban centers and how they coped (e.g., schools, settlement houses, religious groups, philanthropists)

Level III (Grades 7-8)

BD (BE,111;AE,165-66;LE,123,130-133;NI,63)
●   Understands the spread of Progressive ideas and the successes of the Progressive movement (e.g., how intellectuals, religious leaders, and writers alerted the public to the problems of urban industrial society; Progressive social reforms in education, conservation, and the "Americanization" of immigrants; ▸ contributions of governors such as Hiram Johnson,

---

Codes (right side of page):

	BD = Benchmark, Declarative; BP = Benchmark, Procedural; BC = Benchmark, Contextual	
1st letter of each code in parentheses	*2nd letter of code*	*Number*
B = NCHS: basic edition	E = Explicitly stated in document	Page number of cited document
A = NCHS: U.S. History, expanded edition	I = Implied in document	
L = Lessons From History		
N = NAEP: Provisional Item Specifications	*Symbol*	
	■ material appears only in NCHS basic edition	
	▸ material appears only in NCHS expanded edition	
	● material appears in both NCHS editions	

170   *MREL*

Robert La Follette, and Charles Evans Hughes)

- BD (BE,112;AE,167,168;LE,133-134;LI,134;NI,63)
Understands the influence of events and individuals on the Progressive Movement (e.g., results of the election of 1912; ► movements that led to the 16th, 17th, and 18th amendments; how Roosevelt, Taft, and Wilson were popularly portrayed as leaders of reform)

- BD (BE,112;AE,167;NI,66)
Understands the New Nationalism, New Freedom, and Socialist agendas for change

► BD (AE,169;LE,130;NI,63,65,66)
Understands the issues of those groups who supported and rejected the goals of Progressivism (e.g., how African Americans used Progressive tactics to attempt change, how the goals of the Industrial Workers of the World differed from Progressive programs)

Level IV (Grades 9-12)

- BD (BE,111;AE,166;LE,130,131,132;NI,111,112)
Understands the origins and impact of the Progressive movement (e.g., social origins of Progressives and how these contributed to the success and failure of the movement; Progressive reforms pertaining to big business, and worker's and consumer's rights; ► arguments of Progressive leaders)

- BD (BE,112;AE,168;NI,111,112)
Understands major social and political issues of the Progressive era (e.g., Supreme Court decisions that affected Progressivism; ► the Hetch Hetchy controversy)

- BD (BE,112;AE,169,170;LI,131;NI,111,113)
Understands how the Progressive movement influenced different groups in American society (e.g., counter-Progressive programs of labor organizations compared to social democratic programs in industrial Europe, the response of mainstream Progressives to women's issues, the changing perception of Native American assimilation under Progressivism, ► the founding of the NAACP, how African American women contributed to the movement, how the International Ladies Garment Workers Union provided alternatives, the success of the Progressive movement to groups outside the mainstream)

► BD (AE,166;LE,123-124;NI,111,113)
Understands how racial and ethnic events influenced American society during the Progressive era (e.g., the movement to restrict immigration; how racial and ethnic conflicts contributed to delayed statehood for New Mexico and Arizona; the impact of new nativism; influences on African, Native, Asian, and Hispanic Americans)

Codes (right side of page):   BD = Benchmark, Declarative; BP = Benchmark, Procedural; BC = Benchmark, Contextual
1st letter of each code in parentheses   *2nd letter of code*   *Number*
B = NCHS: basic edition   E = Explicitly stated in document   Page number of cited document
A = NCHS: U.S. History, expanded edition   I = Implied in document
L = Lessons From History
N = NAEP: Provisional Item Specifications   *Symbol*
          ■ material appears only in NCHS basic edition
          ► material appears only in NCHS expanded edition
          ● material appears in both NCHS editions

▸ Understands efforts to achieve women's suffrage in the early twentieth century (e.g., methods used by Carrie Chapman Catt in her leadership of the National Women's Suffrage Association to get the 19th amendment passed and ratified, why President Wilson changed his mind about the amendment, which of Catt's tactics were most successful) BD (AE,168;NI,111)

(BE,112;AE,171)

21. Understands the changing role of the United States in world affairs through World War I

Level II (Grades 5-6)

● Understands various U.S. foreign policies in the early part of the 20th century (e.g., the Open Door policy; ▸ places the U.S. claimed, occupied, or protected in the Caribbean after the Spanish-American War; the importance of the Panama Canal) BD (BE,112;AE,171;LE,135-136,139-140;NI,68,69)

● Understands World War I prior to U.S. intervention (e.g., the causes in 1914, reasons for declaration of U.S. neutrality, ▸ locations of Allied and Central Powers, the extent of war in Europe and the use of new weapons and technology) BD (BE,113;AE,173;LE,141;NI,72-74)

● Understands U.S. involvement in World War I (e.g., how the American Expeditionary Force contributed to the Allied victory, Wilson's Fourteen Points, the negotiation of the Versailles Treaty, the national debate over treaty ratification and the League of Nations) BD (BE,113;AE,175;LE,136,142;NI,74)

Level III (Grades 7-8)

● Understands different types of U.S. diplomacy in the early 20th century and how they were applied (e.g., Theodore Roosevelt's foreign policies, U.S. relations with Japan and the "Gentleman's Agreement," American diplomatic initiatives in East Asia, differences between Taft's dollar diplomacy and Roosevelt's big stick diplomacy) BD (BE,112,113;AE,171;LE,139;LI,135-140;NI,68,69)

● Understands the development of World War I (e.g., the influence of industrial research in aviation and chemical warfare on military strategy and the war's outcome, ▸ how technological developments contributed to the war's brutality, the system of alliances BD (BE,113;AE,173;LI,141;NI,72)

Codes (right side of page):	BD = Benchmark, Declarative; BP = Benchmark, Procedural; BC = Benchmark, Contextual	
1st letter of each code in parentheses	*2nd letter of code*	*Number*
B = NCHS: basic edition	E = Explicitly stated in document	Page number of cited document
A = NCHS: U.S. History, expanded edition	I = Implied in document	
L = Lessons From History		
N = NAEP: Provisional Item Specifications	*Symbol*	
	■ material appears only in NCHS basic edition	
	▸ material appears only in NCHS expanded edition	
	● material appears in both NCHS editions	

through which European nations sought to protect their interests, how nationalism and militarism contributed to the outbreak, how the war expanded to become a world war)

BD (BE,113;AE,173,174;LI,141;NI,72,73)
- Understands the United States' intervention in World War I (e.g., the impact of U.S. public opinion on the Wilson administration's evolving foreign policy during the period 1914 to 1917, Wilson's leadership during the period of neutrality and his reasons for U.S. intervention)

BD (BE,113;AE,175,176;LE,141;NI,73,74)
- Understands the impact of the United States involvement in World War I (e.g., U.S. military and economic mobilizations for war and the role of labor, women, and African Americans in the war effort; ▸ World War I military engagements and the campaigns in which the American Expeditionary Force participated; the impact of the war on American troops; Wilson's goals in recommending the establishment of a League of Nations)

BD (BE,113;AE,175;LI,136;NI,73)
- Understands the significance of the Russian Revolution, its impact on the war and on the foreign policies of the U.S. and Allied powers

Level IV (Grades 9-12)

BD (BE,112-113;AE,172;LE,140-141;LI,139-140;NI,117)
- Understands U.S. foreign policy and involvement in foreign countries in the early 20th century (e.g., Wilson's moral diplomacy and the Mexican Revolution, ▸ the commercial basis of foreign policy in East Asia, the Roosevelt Corollary and its connection to the Monroe Doctrine, the U.S. role in the Panama Revolution of 1903)

BD (BE,113;AE,174;LI,136;NI,123,124)
- Understands the causes, course, and impact of World War I prior to U.S. entry (e.g., ▸ motivations of leading world powers, the relative success of nations in mobilizing their resources and populations, the relative success of their propaganda campaigns to influence neutral nations, the successes of military strategies, the general spirit of disillusionment)

BD (BE,113;AE,176;LI,141;NI,122)
- Understands how the home front influenced and was influenced by U.S. involvement in World War I (e.g., the impact of public opinion and government policies on constitutional interpretation and civil liberties, ▸ the events of Wilson's second term; the role of various organizations in the mobilization effort; the "Great Migration" of African Americans to northern cities)

Codes (right side of page):   BD = Benchmark, Declarative; BP = Benchmark, Procedural; BC = Benchmark, Contextual
1st letter of each code in parentheses   *2nd letter of code*   *Number*
B = NCHS: basic edition   E = Explicitly stated in document   Page number of cited document
A = NCHS: U.S. History, expanded edition   I = Implied in document
L = Lessons From History
N = NAEP: Provisional Item Specifications   *Symbol*
                                                ■ material appears only in NCHS basic edition
                                                ▸ material appears only in NCHS expanded edition
                                                ● material appears in both NCHS editions

173   MREL

BD (AE,176,177;LI,136;NI,119,124)

▸ Understands influences on the outcome of World War I (e.g., how point six of the Fourteen Points dealt specifically with Russia, the effectiveness of the Versailles Treaty)

(BE,114;AE,178)

22.   Understands how the United States changed between the post-World War I years and the eve of the Great Depression

Level II (Grades 5-6)

BD (BE,114;AE,178;LE,144,149;LI,149;NI,70,71)

● Understands efforts to restrict immigrants and diverse groups of people in the post-World War I era (e.g., the closing of the "Golden Door," ▸ nativism and anti-immigrant attitudes)

BD (BE,114;AE,181;LI,144)

● Understands how urban life changed in the 1920s (e.g., how scientific management and technological innovations, including assembly lines, rapid transit, household appliances, and radio, transformed production, work and daily life; ▸ how improvements in steel construction and elevators contributed to the changes; why people prized home ownership; why people left the cities for the suburbs)

BD (BE,114,115;AE,183;LE,146,149;LI,145,147;NI,64,71)

● Understands the rise of a mass culture in the 1920s (e.g., the media and recreation available in the 1920s; how increased leisure time promoted the growth of professional sports, amusement parks, and national parks; ▸ the impact of recreational areas on the local environment)

BD (BE,115;AE,183;LE,146)

● Understands influences on African American culture during the 1920s (e.g., the Harlem Renaissance)

BD (BE,115;AE,185;LI,96,132,144;NI,63,65)

● Understands the effects of women's suffrage on politics (e.g., ▸ the major events of women's suffrage movement from the Seneca Falls Convention of 1848 to the ratification of the 19th amendment; how the 19th Amendment changed political life in America)

BD (AE,178)

▸ Understands how women's lives changed after World War I (e.g., their contributions in schools, hospitals, settlement houses, and social agencies; how the spread of electrification and household appliances improved the life of homemakers)

Codes (right side of page):   BD = Benchmark, Declarative; BP = Benchmark, Procedural; BC = Benchmark, Contextual
1st letter of each code in parentheses   *2nd letter of code*   *Number*
B = NCHS: basic edition   E = Explicitly stated in document   Page number of cited document
A = NCHS: U.S. History, expanded edition   I = Implied in document
L = Lessons From History
N = NAEP: Provisional Item Specifications   *Symbol*
                                                 ■ material appears only in NCHS basic edition
                                                 ▸ material appears only in NCHS expanded edition
                                                 ● material appears in both NCHS editions

> ‣ Understands aspects of Prohibition (e.g., smuggling)

BD (AE,178)

Level III (Grades 7-8)

BD (BE,114;AE,179;LE,149;LI,144,149;NI,69,70,71)

● Understands the various social conflicts that took place in the early 1920s (e.g., state and federal government reactions to the growth of radical political movements, rising racial tensions and the resurgence of the Ku Klux Klan, the Garvey Movement, the clash between traditional moral values and changing ideas as exemplified in the Scopes trial and Prohibition, ‣ how the restriction of European immigration affected Mexican American immigration)

BD (BE,114;AE,181;LI,145;NE,71)

● Understands elements that contributed to the rise of modern capitalist economy (e.g., changes in the modern corporation of the 1920s, including labor policies and the advent of mass advertising and sales techniques; the role of new technology and scientific research in the rise of agribusiness and agricultural productivity; ‣ the impact of advertisement on the desire for new products)

BD (BE,115;AE,183;LE,146;LI,143,145,147;NI,64,71)

● Understands changes in the social and cultural life of American society in the 1920s (e.g., art and literature from the social realists to the "Lost Generation," ‣ how cultural trends were introduced into mainstream society, reasons for increased leisure time in the 1920s)

BD (BE,115;AE,185;NI,63;LI,150)

● Understands events that shaped the political structure of America in the 1920s (e.g., changes in Progressivism during the Harding and Coolidge administrations; foreign policy of the Republican administrations of Harding, Coolidge and Hoover; ‣ U.S. territories and spheres of influence in the 1920s; the extent of support for an Equal Rights Amendment)

BD (AE,179)

> ‣ Understands changing attitudes toward women in the post-World War I era (e.g., changing values and new ideas regarding employment opportunities, appearance standards, leisure activities, and political participation)

Level IV (Grades 9-12)

BD (BE,114;AE,179-180;LE,149;LI,144,149;NI,113,119,120,121)

● Understands the major social issues of 1920s America (e.g., the emergence of the "New Woman" and challenges to Victorian values, ‣ the purpose and goals of the "New Klan," the

---

Codes (right side of page): BD = Benchmark, Declarative; BP = Benchmark, Procedural; BC = Benchmark, Contextual
1st letter of each code in parentheses *2nd letter of code* *Number*
B = NCHS: basic edition E = Explicitly stated in document Page number of cited document
A = NCHS: U.S. History, expanded edition I = Implied in document
L = Lessons From History
N = NAEP: Provisional Item Specifications *Symbol*
■ material appears only in NCHS basic edition
‣ material appears only in NCHS expanded edition
● material appears in both NCHS editions

175

MREL

causes and outcome of Prohibition, the ethnic composition of immigrants and fears these changes represented, the "Red Scare," the Sacco and Vanzetti trial)

- Understands factors that contributed to changes in work, production, and the rise of a consumer culture (e.g., ▸ the "new paternalism" of the modern corporation, how national advertising and sales campaigns affected the American economy)

  BD (BE,114;AE,181,182;LI,147)

- Understands influences on urban life in America during the 1920s (e.g., new downtown business areas, suburbs, transportation, ▸ architecture, the idea of the "civic center")

  BD (BE,114;AE,182;LI,147;NI,114)

- Understands the impact of new cultural movements on American society in the 1920s (e.g., the extension of secondary education to new segments of American society, ▸ the emergence of artists in the postwar period, the origins and development of jazz, how the creation of national parks affected Native American culture)

  BD (BE,114,115;AE,184;LE,146;LI,149;NI,121)

- ▸ Understands how political issues in the 1920s influenced American society (e.g., the goals and effectiveness of the Republican party in the 1920s, the Harding and Coolidge administrations and the effects of World War I on Progressivism)

  BD (AE,186;LI,146,150;NI,111,119)

(BE,117;AE,188)

23.   Understands the causes of the Great Depression and how it affected American society

Level II (Grades 5-6)

- Understands economic aspects of the Great Depression (e.g., the causes and consequences of the stock market crash of 1929; the factors that contributed to the Great Depression; ▸ the effects of the depression on farmers, city workers, and military veterans)

  BD (BE,117;AE,188;LE,155-156;NE,72;NI,72)

- Understands the environmental and social impact of the Great Depression (e.g., the effects of the Great Depression and Dust Bowl on American farm owners, tenants, and sharecroppers; ▸ the effects of the depression on diverse groups and on local communities)

  BD (BE,117;AE,190;LE,156;LI,153-154,156;NI,70-72)

Codes (right side of page):	BD = Benchmark, Declarative; BP = Benchmark, Procedural; BC = Benchmark, Contextual	
1st letter of each code in parentheses	*2nd letter of code*	*Number*
B = NCHS: basic edition	E = Explicitly stated in document	Page number of cited document
A = NCHS: U.S. History, expanded edition	I = Implied in document	
L = Lessons From History		
N = NAEP: Provisional Item Specifications	*Symbol*	
	■ material appears only in NCHS basic edition	
	▸ material appears only in NCHS expanded edition	
	● material appears in both NCHS editions	

Level III (Grades 7-8)

BD (BE,117;AE,189;LE,155-156;NE,72)

● Understands various poltical influences on the Great Depression (e.g., the effectiveness of measures the Hoover administration took to stem the tide of the Great Depression, the central political and economic causes of the Great Depression)

BD (BE,117;AE,190,191;LI,156,158;NE,70,NI,72)

● Understands the social and economic impact of the Great Depression (e.g., the impact of the depression on industry and workers; the response of local and state officials in combating the resulting economic and social crises; the effects of the depression on American families and on ethnic and racial minorities; ▶ the effect on gender roles; the victimization of African Americans and white sharecroppers)

Level IV (Grades 9-12)

BD (BE,117;AE,188,189;LE,155;NI,122)

● Understands influences on the national and global economy in the 1920s and 1930s (e.g., economic policies of the Harding and Coolidge administrations and their impact on wealth distribution, investment, and taxes; the global context of the depression and the reasons for the worldwide economic collapse; ▶ characteristics of the American economy in the 1920s)

BD (BE,118;AE,190,192;LI,157,158;NI,120,121)

● Understands the impact of the Great Depression on American culture (e.g., art, literature, and music, and the government's role in promoting artistic expression; ▶ how the works of various American artists reflected American conditions in the 1930s and influenced the New Deal)

BD (AE,191)

▶ Understands how the Great Depression influenced local, state, and charitable resources in the period 1930-1938

Codes (right side of page):　　BD = Benchmark, Declarative; BP = Benchmark, Procedural; BC = Benchmark, Contextual
1st letter of each code in parentheses　　*2nd letter of code*　　　　*Number*
B = NCHS: basic edition　　　　　E = Explicitly stated in document　　Page number of cited document
A = NCHS: U.S. History, expanded edition　I = Implied in document
L = Lessons From History
N = NAEP: Provisional Item Specifications

　　　　　　　　　　　　　　　　Symbol
　　　　　　　　　　　　　　　　■ material appears only in NCHS basic edition
　　　　　　　　　　　　　　　　▶ material appears only in NCHS expanded edition
　　　　　　　　　　　　　　　　● material appears in both NCHS editions

McREL

(BE,118;AE,193)

24. Understands how the New Deal addressed the Great Depression, transformed American federalism, and initiated the welfare state

Level II (Grades 5-6)

● Understands the background and leadership styles of depression-era presidents (e.g., Herbert Hoover, Franklin D. Roosevelt) ^{BD (BE,118;AE,193)}

● Understands the influences on and impact of the New Deal (e.g., how legislation and policies affected American workers and the labor movement, ▸ the condition of working men and women in the United States in the 1930s, how the New Deal affected the lives of local families, how women contributed to New Deal programs) ^{BD (BE,118;AE,193,195;LE,157,158,159)}

● Understands the significance and legacy of the New Deal (e.g., ▸ major New Deal programs still in effect today, support for and opposition to Roosevelt's "court packing" proposal and why he abandoned this proposal) ^{BD (BE,119;AE,197;LI,157-158)}

Level III (Grades 7-8)

■ Understands renewed efforts to protect the environment during the Great Depression and their success in places such as the Dust Bowl and the Tennessee Valley ^{BD (BE,118)}

● Understands the link between Progressivism and the early New Deal ^{BD (BE,118;AE,193;LI,134,158)}

● Understands the factors contributing to the forging of the Roosevelt coalition in 1936 and its electoral significance in subsequent years ^{BD (BE,118;AE,193;LE,156,159)}

● Understands the labor movement during the New Deal era (e.g., the re-emergence of labor militancy and the struggle between craft and industrial unions; the commitment of labor unions to organize diverse groups and secure equitable conditions and pay for minorities; ▸ the objectives of labor leaders and advocates; how art, photographs, and song lyrics contributed to the emotional appeal to support unions; WPA projects and their impact on local areas) ^{BD (BE,118;AE,195-196;LI,157)}

Codes (right side of page): BD = Benchmark, Declarative; BP = Benchmark, Procedural; BC = Benchmark, Contextual

1st letter of each code in parentheses	*2nd letter of code*	*Number*
B = NCHS: basic edition	E = Explicitly stated in document	Page number of cited document
A = NCHS: U.S. History, expanded edition	I = Implied in document	
L = Lessons From History		
N = NAEP: Provisional Item Specifications	*Symbol*	
	■ material appears only in NCHS basic edition	
	▸ material appears only in NCHS expanded edition	
	● material appears in both NCHS editions	

178

MREL

- Understands various challenges to the New Deal (e.g., arguments of leading opponents, ▸ the roots of opposition to Roosevelt's policies, the ideas of the Townsend Plan and the "Share the Wealth" program of Dr. Francis Townsend and Senator Huey Long)

  BD (BE,119;AE,197;LE,159)

- ▸ Understands the personal and political reasons for Herbert Hoover's and Franklin D. Roosevelt's responses to the depression

  BD (AE,193-194;LI,156,157)

- ▸ Understands the contributions of Eleanor Roosevelt to the New Deal (e.g., specific efforts the First Lady made in response to the crisis)

  BD (AE,193-194;LE,159)

- ▸ Understands how the New Deal influenced public opinion (e.g., the public's belief in the responsibility of government to deliver public services)

  BD (AE,197;LI,156-159)

Level IV (Grades 9-12)

- Understands the first and second New Deals (e.g., the success of the relief, recovery, and reform measures associated with each)

  BD (BE,118;AE,193,194;LI,156,157-158)

- Understands how the New Deal influenced the civil and political rights of diverse groups (e.g., the involvement of women and minorities in the New Deal and its impact upon them, ▸ FDR's commitment to advancing the civil and political rights of African Americans, how African Americans planted the seeds of a civil rights revolution during the 1930s, how the Indian Reorganization Act of 1934 affected Native Americans, the role of John Collier in securing a "new deal" for Native Americans)

  BD (BE,118;AE,193-194;LI,158;LE,159)

- Understands how the New Deal influenced labor and employment (e.g., the impact of the New Deal on non-union workers; ▸ factors contributing to the success of the CIO leadership in organizing the rubber, auto, and steel workers in the period 1937 1941; labor's commitment to organizing; causes, strategies, and leadership of major strikes during the New Deal; the effects of the New Deal agricultural programs on farm laborers)

  BD (BE,118;AE, 195,196)

- Understands influences on the New Deal (e.g., Supreme Court cases related to the New Deal and Roosevelt's response to the rulings; ▸ the class basis for support and opposition to the New Deal in the Northeast, South, Midwest, and Far West)

  BD (BE,119;AE,198;LI,156-157;NI,120)

Codes (right side of page):   BD = Benchmark, Declarative; BP = Benchmark, Procedural; BC = Benchmark, Contextual
1st letter of each code in parentheses   *2nd letter of code*   *Number*
B = NCHS: basic edition   E = Explicitly stated in document   Page number of cited document
A = NCHS: U.S. History, expanded edition   I = Implied in document
L = Lessons From History
N = NAEP: Provisional Item Specifications   *Symbol*
    ■ material appears only in NCHS basic edition
    ▸ material appears only in NCHS expanded edition
    ● material appears in both NCHS editions

MREL

▸ Understands the significance and ideology of FDR and the New Deal (e.g., whether the New Deal was able to solve the problems of depression, who the New Deal helped the most and the least; how the New Deal changed the relationship between state and federal government)
BD (AE,198;LI,158,159)

▸ Understands the proposals of Upton Sinclair's EPIC campaign in California (e.g., groups that opposed it, why it failed, the reasons for the growth of the American Communist Party during the 1930s, to whom the party most appealed)
BD (AE,198)

25. **Understands the causes and course of World War II, the character of the war at home and abroad, and its reshaping of the U.S. role in world affairs**
(BE,119;AE,199)

Level II (Grades 5-6)

● Understands events leading to U.S. involvement in World War II (e.g., reasons for American isolationist sentiment and its effects on international relations and diplomacy; American responses to German, Italian, and Japanese aggression in Europe, Africa, and Asia from 1935 to 1941, ▸ global involvement of nations and people before World War II; the location of Pearl Harbor and events that brought the U.S. into the war)
BD (BE,119;AE,199;LE,161,166;LI,142;NE,73,74;NI,73)

● Understands significant military aspects of World War II (e.g., major turning points of the war; Axis and Allied military campaigns in the European and Pacific theaters; the financial, material, and human costs of the war and their economic consequences for the Allies and the Axis powers; ▸ the locations of the major theaters of war in North Africa, Europe, and the Pacific; the diverse contributions of men and women during the war)
BD (BE,119,120;AE,201;LE,163-165;LI,167)

● Understands events on the U.S. home front during World War II (e.g., economic and military mobilization; the internment of Japanese Americans and the implications for civil liberties)
BD (BE,120;AE,203;LE,167;NE,70;NI,72)

Level III (Grades 7-8)

● Understands the development of new political thinking and forms of government in Europe between World War I and World War II (e.g., the rise of fascism, national socialism, and
BD (BE,119;AE,199;LE,161,166;NI,73,74)

Codes (right side of page):
1st letter of each code in parentheses
B = NCHS: basic edition
A = NCHS: U.S. History, expanded edition
L = Lessons From History
N = NAEP: Provisional Item Specifications

BD = Benchmark, Declarative; BP = Benchmark, Procedural; BC = Benchmark, Contextual
2nd letter of code   *Number*
E = Explicitly stated in document   Page number of cited document
I = Implied in document

Symbol
■ material appears only in NCHS basic edition
▸ material appears only in NCHS expanded edition
● material appears in both NCHS editions

180   MЯEL

communism)

- Understands how the outcome of World War I contributed to the outbreak of World War II (e.g., lack of support for the League of Nations, the breakdown of the Versailles settlement in the 1930s)

  BD (BE,119;AE,199,200;LI,142,150;NI,73,74)

- Understands U.S. international relations prior to its entrance into World War II (e.g., the events that caused growing tensions between the U.S. and Japan, the bombing of Pearl Harbor)

  BD (BE,119;AE,199,200;LE,166;LI,142,159;NE,73;NI,73)

- Understands military strategies used during World War II (e.g., ▸ the non-aggression pact between Germany and the USSR in 1939; the "Battle for Britain"; Japanese strategy in East Asia and the Pacific; Roosevelt's strategy for an aggressive war against the Axis powers and a defensive war in Asia; the North Africa, Sicily, and Normandy invasions)

  BD (BE,119;AE, 201,202;LE,166-167)

- Understands the dimensions of Hitler's "final solution" and the Allies' response to the Holocaust and war crimes (e.g., ▸ human costs of Nazi genocide, Roosevelt's immigration policy toward Jewish refugees from Hitler's Germany)

  BD (BE,119;AE,201,202)

- Understands the legacy of World War II (e.g., the decision to use the atomic bomb against Japan during World War II, how military experiences fostered American identity and cross-cultural interaction, the purpose and organization of the United Nations)

  BD (BE,120;AE,202;LE,164-165;LI,167;NI,74)

- Understands how World War II influenced American society (e.g., how the war fostered cultural exchange and promoted nationalism and American identity, the effects on gender roles and the American family)

  BD (BE,120;AE,203-204;NI,70-72)

- Understands how minority groups were affected by World War II (e.g., how minority groups organized to gain access to wartime jobs and discrimination they faced, ▸ factors that led to the internment of Japanese Americans)

  BD (BE,120;AE,203-204;LE,167;NE,70;NI,72)

Level IV (Grades 9-12)

- Understands the influence of international events on U.S. policies and political developments (e.g., Roosevelt's foreign policy toward Latin America and the reasons for the Good

  BD (BE,119;AE,200;NI,123)

Codes (right side of page):

1st letter of each code in parentheses
B = NCHS: basic edition
A = NCHS: U.S. History, expanded edition
L = Lessons From History
N = NAEP: Provisional Item Specifications

BD = Benchmark, Declarative; BP = Benchmark, Procedural; BC = Benchmark, Contextual

2nd letter of code
E = Explicitly stated in document
I = Implied in document

Number
Page number of cited document

Symbol
■ material appears only in NCHS basic edition
▸ material appears only in NCHS expanded edition
● material appears in both NCHS editions

181

MREL

Neighbor Policy; ▸ the effect of the Nazi-Soviet Non-Aggression Pact of 1939 on the U.S. Communist Party)

●   Understands events that led to the Japanese attack on Pearl Harbor (e.g., ▸ why Japan set up the East Asian Co-Prosperity Sphere, U.S. reasons for cutting off oil to Japan, U.S. response to the November 10 proposal from Japan)

BD (BE,119;AE,200;NI,123)

●   Understands President Roosevelt's ideas and policies during World War II (e.g., Roosevelt's administration's wartime diplomacy among the Allied powers, ▸ the ideas presented in his Four Freedoms speech)

BD (BE,119;AE,201,202;LE,168;NI,123)

●   Understands how World War II influenced the home front (e.g., the impact on science, medicine, and technology; how Americans viewed their achievements and global responsibilities at the war's end; ▸ how minorities contributed to the war effort and the contradiction between their treatment at home and the goals that they were fighting for in Europe; the effects of the relocation centers on Japanese American families)

BD (BE,120;AE,204;LI,162,167;NI,120,122)

▸   Understands characteristics of the end of World War II (e.g., why there was a delay in creating a second front in Europe, the Soviet Union's role in helping to defeat the Axis Powers and the reasons for the success of D-Day)

BD (AE,202;LE,167;LI,167)

(BE,122;AE,206)

26. Understands the economic boom and social transformation of post-World War II United States

Level II (Grades 5-6)

■   Understands the impact of postwar scientific research on contemporary society (e.g., the work of pioneers in modern scientific research, the significance of research and scientific breakthroughs in promoting the U.S. space program)

BD (BE,123;LI,172;NI,79)

●   Understands how the American economy changed in the post-World War II period (e.g., reasons for sustained economic growth, ▸ economic opportunities for members of the armed forces)

BD (BE,122;AE,206;LE,169-170;NI,78)

Codes (right side of page):   BD = Benchmark, Declarative; BP = Benchmark, Procedural; BC = Benchmark, Contextual
1st letter of each code in parentheses   *2nd letter of code*   *Number*
B = NCHS: basic edition   E = Explicitly stated in document   Page number of cited document
A = NCHS: U.S. History, expanded edition   I = Implied in document
L = Lessons From History
N = NAEP: Provisional Item Specifications   *Symbol*
          ■ material appears only in NCHS basic edition
          ▸ material appears only in NCHS expanded edition
          ● material appears in both NCHS editions

- Understands influences on American society during the post-World War II years (e.g., the effects of the G.I. Bill, the influence of popular culture and the mass media)
  BD (BE,122,123;AE,208;NE,77)

Level III (Grades 7-8)

- Understands agricultural innovation and consolidation in the postwar period and their impact on the world economy
  BD (BE,123;LI,169)

- Understands the immediate social, political, and economic impacts on America after World War II (e.g., the economic and political effects of demobilization and reconversion; the growth and impact of opportunities in the service, white collar, and professional sectors in government and business; the growth of the middle class)
  BD (BE,122;AE, 206,207)

- Understands how American society changed after World War II (e.g., reasons for the "return to domesticity" and the effect on family life and women's careers)
  BD (BE,123;AE,208,209;LE,170;NI,77)

Level IV (Grades 9-12)

- Understands scientific and technological developments in America after World War II (e.g., the new system of scientific research and development, advances in medical science and how they improved the standard of living and changed demographic patterns, the global influence of the communications revolution ushered in by American technology)
  BD (BE,123;LI,169,172;NE,129)

- Understands influences on the American economy after World War II (e.g., the impact of the Cold War, ▸ increased defense spending, the U.S. economy in relation to Europe and Asian economies)
  BD (BE,122;AE,207;LI,169-170,173;NI,129,130)

- Understands the socioeconomic factors of the post-World War II period in America (e.g., the gap between poverty and the rising affluence of the middle class, ▸ the extent of poverty in post-World War II America)
  BD (BE,122;AE,206,207)

- Understands social, religious, cultural, and economic changes at the onset of the Cold War era (e.g., the causes and results of new governmental spending on educational programs, the expansion of suburbanization and the impact of the "crabgrass frontier," the role of religion,
  BD (BE,122-123;AE,208-209;NI,129)

Codes (right side of page):   BD = Benchmark, Declarative; BP = Benchmark, Procedural; BC = Benchmark, Contextual

1st letter of each code in parentheses	*2nd letter of code*	*Number*
B = NCHS: basic edition	E = Explicitly stated in document	Page number of cited document
A = NCHS: U.S. History, expanded edition	I = Implied in document	
L = Lessons From History		
N = NAEP: Provisional Item Specifications	*Symbol*	
	■ material appears only in NCHS basic edition	
	▸ material appears only in NCHS expanded edition	
	● material appears in both NCHS editions	

▸ the impact of the GI Bill on higher education, how the Cold War influenced the lives and roles of women, how artists and writers portrayed the effects of alienation on the individual and society after 1945)

(BE,123;AE,214)

27. Understands how the Cold War and conflicts in Korean and Vietnam influenced domestic and international politics

Level II (Grades 5-6)

- BD (BE,123;AE,214;LI,169;NI,80)
  Understands influences on international relations after World War II (e.g., the "flawed peace" resulting from World War II, the effectiveness of the United Nations in reducing international tensions and conflict)

- BD (BE,124;AE,216)
  Understands shifts in international relations after World War II (e.g., effects of popular uprisings against communist governments in Eastern Europe on U.S. foreign policy, U.S. relations with Israel and how Arab-Israeli crises influenced U.S. foreign policy, ▸ how the modern state of Israel became an independent country after World War II)

- BD (BE,124;AE,218;LE,179;LI,180)
  Understands the characteristics and impact of the Vietnam War (e.g., the war's effect on Vietnamese and Americans; effects on postwar politics and culture; ▸ the location of the war in Southeast Asia; how the war escalated during the 1960s)

Level III (Grades 7-8)

- BD (BE,123,124;AE,214,215;LI,169;NE,80)
  Understands major events in U.S.foreign policy during the early Cold War period (e.g., the origins of the Cold War and the advent of nuclear politics, U.S. response to the Chinese Revolution, causes of the Korean War and resulting international tensions, the implementation of the U.S. containment policy, ▸ the circumstances that led to the Marshall Plan and its accomplishments)

- BD (BE,124;AE,216;LI,178-179;NI,81)
  Understands the differences between the foreign policies of Kennedy and Johnson (e.g., changes in U.S. foreign policy toward the Soviet Union and the reasons for these changes,

Codes (right side of page):   BD = Benchmark, Declarative; BP = Benchmark, Procedural; BC = Benchmark, Contextual
1st letter of each code in parentheses   *2nd letter of code*   *Number*
B = NCHS: basic edition   E = Explicitly stated in document   Page number of cited document
A = NCHS: U.S. History, expanded edition   I = Implied in document
L = Lessons From History
N = NAEP: Provisional Item Specifications   *Symbol*
     ■ material appears only in NCHS basic edition
     ▸ material appears only in NCHS expanded edition
     ● material appears in both NCHS editions

184   McREL

changing foreign policy toward Latin America, ▸ the Kennedy administration's Cuban policy)

BD (BE,124;AE,218;LI,170,179-180;NI,75)
● Understands political and social characteristics of the Vietnam War (e.g., the Vietnam policy of the Kennedy, Johnson, and Nixon administrations and shifts of public opinion about the war; the role of the Nixon administration in the Paris Peace Accord of 1973; ▸ early U.S. involvement in Vietnam following World War II and policies of the Truman and Eisenhower administrations)

BD (AE,216;LI,170;NI,80)
▸ Understands the Truman and Eisenhower doctrines of foreign policy in terms of the international tensions that prompted each

Level IV (Grades 9-12)

BD (BE,124;AE,216-217;LI,169,178-179;NI,131,132)
● Understands U.S. foreign policy from the Truman adminstration to the Johnson administration (e.g., American policies toward independence movements in Africa, Asia, Latin America, and the Middle East; ▸ U.S. policy regarding the British mandate over Palestine and the establishment of the state of Israel; Kennedy's response to the Bay of Pigs and the Cuban Missile crises; how the Korean War affected the premises of U.S. foreign policy; the Kennedy-Johnson response to anti-colonial movements in Africa)

BD (BE,124;AE,218,219;LI,179-180;NI,132)
● Understands the political elements of the Vietnam War (e.g., the constitutional issues involved in the Vietnam War, the legacy of the war)

BD (BE,124;AE,218,219;LI,179-180)
● Understands the social issues that resulted from U.S. involvement in the Vietnam War (e.g., the composition of American forces recruited in the war, ▸ why the Vietnam War contributed to a generational conflict and concomitant lack of respect for traditional authority figures)

BD (AE,214-215;LE,169;NE,131)
▸ Understands factors that contributed to the development of the Cold War (e.g., the mutual suspicions and divisions fragmenting the Grand Alliance at the end of World War II, U.S. support for "self-determination" and the U.S.S.R's desire for security in Eastern Europe, the practice of "atomic diplomacy")

Codes (right side of page):   BD = Benchmark, Declarative; BP = Benchmark, Procedural; BC = Benchmark, Contextual

1st letter of each code in parentheses   *2nd letter of code*   *Number*

B = NCHS: basic edition   E = Explicitly stated in document   Page number of cited document

A = NCHS: U.S. History, expanded edition   I = Implied in document

L = Lessons From History

N = NAEP: Provisional Item Specifications   *Symbol*

                           ■ material appears only in NCHS basic edition

                           ▸ material appears only in NCHS expanded edition

                           ● material appears in both NCHS editions

185   McREL

(BE,125;AE,210)

28. Understands domestic policies in the post-World War II period

Level II (Grades 5-6)

BD (BE,125;AE,210;LI,170)
- Understands the civil rights movement during President Truman's presidency (e.g., his support of civil rights, the effect on the Democratic party)

BD (BE,125;AE,212;LI,177;LE,177;NI,79)
- Understands the impact of the Kennedy and Johnson administrations on domestic affairs (e.g., the domestic policies of the "New Frontier," legislation and programs enacted during Johnson's presidency, ▸ how Jacqueline Kennedy developed the Camelot images to depict her husband's presidency)

Level III (Grades 7-8)

BD (BE,125;AE,210,214-215;LI,170)
- Understands the domestic policies of Presidents Truman and Eisenhower (e.g., Eisenhower's "Modern Republicanism," ▸ Truman's Fair Deal program for securing fair employment practices, desegregation, civil rights, and race relations)

BD (BE,125;AE,214,215;LI,170)
- Understands the role of McCarthyism in the early Cold War period (e.g., the rise of McCarthysim, the effect of McCarthyism on civil liberties, and McCarthy's fall from power; the connection between post-war Soviet espionage and internal security and loyalty programs under Truman and Eisenhower)

BD (BE,125;AE,212;LI,177;NI,79)
- Understands the legacy of the New Frontier and Great Society domestic programs (e.g., the effectiveness of the Great Society programs, the second environmental movement, ▸ how the two programs differed, the impact of the Kennedy assassination on the passage of reform legislation during the Johnson administration, how Kennedy's and Johnson's leadership styles differed, factors that contributed to greater public support for Great Society)

BD (AE,212)
▸ Understands the major issues of the 1960 presidential campaign and Kennedy's stance on each (e.g., the central domestic and foreign issues that divided Kennedy and Nixon, the extent to which religion was an issue in the campaign, how Kennedy responded to the Cold War issues)

Codes (right side of page):   BD = Benchmark, Declarative; BP = Benchmark, Procedural; BC = Benchmark, Contextual
1st letter of each code in parentheses   *2nd letter of code*   *Number*
B = NCHS: basic edition   E = Explicitly stated in document   Page number of cited document
A = NCHS: U.S. History, expanded edition   I = Implied in document
L = Lessons From History
N = NAEP: Provisional Item Specifications   *Symbol*
     ■ material appears only in NCHS basic edition
     ▸ material appears only in NCHS expanded edition
     ● material appears in both NCHS editions

MREL

Level IV (Grades 9-12)

- Understands different social and economic elements of the Truman and Eisenhower administrations (e.g.Truman's policies in labor relations, housing, education and health; ▸ postwar reaction to the labor movement, how Eisenhower's domestic and foreign policy priorities contrasted with his predecessors)

  BD (BE,125;AE,210,211;LI,170;NI,125)

- Understands characteristics of the Kennedy presidency (e.g., the role of the media in the election of 1960; ▸ Kennedy's commitment to liberalism and his ideas about citizenship, rights, and responsibilities)

  BD (BE,125;AE,212-213;LI,177;NE,127)

- ▸ Understands the various anti-communist movements after World War II (e.g., causes and consequences of the second "Red Scare" that emerged after World War II)

  BD (AE,215;LI,170)

- ▸ Understands characteristics of the Johnson presidency (e.g., how Johnson's presidential leadership contrasted with and was affected by the Kennedy legacy)

  BD (AE,213; LI,177;NI,127)

(BE,125;AE,220)

29. Understands the struggle for racial and gender equality and for the extension of civil liberties

Level II (Grades 5-6)

- Understands the development of the civil rights movement (e.g., the Supreme Court case *Brown* v. *Board of Education* and its significance in advancing civil rights; the resistance to civil rights in the South between 1954 and 1965; ▸ how the "freedom ride," "civil disobedience," and "non-violent resistance" were important to the civil rights movement; Martin Luther King Jr.'s "I Have a Dream" speech in the context of major events)

  BD (BE,126;AE,220;LE,177-178;NI,75;NE,75)

- Understands the involvement of diverse groups in the civil rights movement (e.g., the agendas, strategies, and effectiveness of African, Asian, Latino, and Native Americans, as well as the disabled, in advancing the movement for civil and equal rights; ▸ regional issues important to diverse groups and their efforts to attain equality and civil rights after World War II)

  BD (BE,126;AE,222;LI,178)

Codes (right side of page):   BD = Benchmark, Declarative; BP = Benchmark, Procedural; BC = Benchmark, Contextual
1st letter of each code in parentheses   *2nd letter of code*   *Number*
B = NCHS: basic edition   E = Explicitly stated in document   Page number of cited document
A = NCHS: U.S. History, expanded edition   I = Implied in document
L = Lessons From History
N = NAEP: Provisional Item Specifications   *Symbol*
                                 ■ material appears only in NCHS basic edition
                                 ▸ material appears only in NCHS expanded edition
                                 ● material appears in both NCHS editions

- BD (BE,126;AE,224;LI,178;NI,75)

  Understands the development of the post-World War II women's movement (e.g., the major issues affecting women and the conflicts these issues engendered, ▸ the emergence of the National Organization for Women, post-World War II attitudes toward women)

- BD (BE,126;AE,226;NI,75)

  Understands the Warren Court's interpretation of freedom of religion (e.g., ▸ the importance of the separation of church and state and freedom of religion in contemporary American society, local and regional issues regarding religious freedom)

Level III (Grades 7-8)

- BD (BE,125-126;AE,220,221;LI,175,177-178; NI,75,LE,170)

  Understands individual and institutional influences on the civil rights movement (e.g., the origins of the postwar civil rights movement; the role of the NAACP in the legal assualt on segregation; the leadership and ideologies of Martin Luther King, Jr. and Malcolm X; the effects of the constitutional steps taken in the executive, judicial, and legislative branches of government; the shift from *de jure* to *de facto* segregation; ▸ important milestones in the civil rights movement between 1954 and 1965; Eisenhower's reasons for dispatching federal troops to Little Rock in 1957)

- BD (BE,126;AE,224;LI,178)

  Understands factors that shaped the women's rights movement after World War II (e.g., the factors that contributed to the development of modern feminism; the ideas, agendas, and strategies of feminist and counter-feminist organizations; ▸ conflicts originating from within and outside of the women's movement)

- BD (AE,226;NI,75)

  ▸ Understands conflicts raised by the Warren Court decisions (e.g., why the *Engel* v. *Vitale* decision provoked widespread opposition)

Level IV (Grades 9-12)

- BD (BE,126;AE,222,223;LI,178)

  Understands how diverse groups united during the civil rights movement (e.g., the escalation from civil disobedience to more radical protest, ▸ issues that led to the development of the Asian Civil Rights Movement and the Native American Civil Rights Movement, the issues and goals of the farm labor movement and La Raza Unida)

- BD (BE,126;AE,224,225)

  Understands conflicting perspectives on different issues addressed by the women's rights

---

Codes (right side of page):	BD = Benchmark, Declarative; BP = Benchmark, Procedural; BC = Benchmark, Contextual	
1st letter of each code in parentheses	*2nd letter of code*	*Number*
B = NCHS: basic edition	E = Explicitly stated in document	Page number of cited document
A = NCHS: U.S. History, expanded edition	I = Implied in document	
L = Lessons From History		
N = NAEP: Provisional Item Specifications	*Symbol*	
	■ material appears only in NCHS basic edition	
	▸ material appears only in NCHS expanded edition	
	● material appears in both NCHS editions	

188   MREL

movement (e.g., the Equal Rights Amendment, Title VII, and *Roe* v. *Wade*)

BD (BE,126;AE,226,227;NI,126,127)

- Understands how various Warren Court decisions influenced society (e.g., the Warren Court's expansion of due process rights for the accused and criticisms of this extension; Warren Court's reasoning in establishing the "one man, one vote" principle; the effectiveness of the judiciary in promoting civil liberties and equal opportunities)

BD (AE,220,221;LE,177;NI,126,127)

▸ Understands significant influences on the civil rights movement (e.g., the social and constitutional issues involved in *Plessy* v. *Ferguson* (1896) and *Brown* v. *Board of Education* (1954) court cases; the connection between legislative acts, Supreme Court decisions, and the civil rights movement; the role of women in the civil rights movement and in shaping the struggle for civil rights)

(BE,128;AE,229)

30. Understands developments in foreign policy and domestic politics between the Nixon and Clinton presidencies

Level II (Grades 5-6)

BD (BE,128;AE,229)

- Understands domestic politics from Nixon to Carter (e.g., the effectiveness of different social and environmental programs under the Nixon, Ford, and Carter administrations; the Nixon administration's involvement in Watergate, and the role of the media in exposing the scandal; ▸ how "law and order," the "Silent Majority," and the "New Federalism" were used by the Nixon administration)

BD (BE,128;AE,231,232;LI,183;NI,79,81)

- Understands elements of both the Reagan and Bush presidencies (e.g., the impact of the "Reagan Revolution" on federalism and public perceptions of the role of government, ▸ reasons for Reagan's popularity, how each administration dealt with major domestic problems)

BD (BE,129;AE,234;LI,184,185;NI,80)

- Understands the events that influenced U.S. foreign policy from the Carter to the Bush administrations (e.g., Reagan's efforts to reassert American military power and rebuild American prestige; ▸ crisis areas around the world and some of the major peace initiatives made during the Carter administration; geographic changes after the fall of the U.S.S.R and

---

Codes (right side of page):   BD = Benchmark, Declarative; BP = Benchmark, Procedural; BC = Benchmark, Contextual

1st letter of each code in parentheses	*2nd letter of code*	*Number*
B = NCHS: basic edition	E = Explicitly stated in document	Page number of cited document
A = NCHS: U.S. History, expanded edition	I = Implied in document	
L = Lessons From History		
N = NAEP: Provisional Item Specifications	*Symbol*	

■ material appears only in NCHS basic edition
▸ material appears only in NCHS expanded edition
● material appears in both NCHS editions

189

MREL

communist states in eastern Europe; places in the Middle East, Central America, the Caribbean, Africa, and Asia where U.S. advisers and military forces were involved during the Reagan and Bush years)

Level III (Grades 7-8)

- BD (BE,128;AE,231,232;LE,183;NE,79)

  Understands the domestic problems facing Presidents Bush and Reagan and the programs their administrations presented to deal with these issues (e.g., supply-side economic strategies, ▸ Reagan's environmental program and the views of its supporters and opponents, how the Bush administration dealt with the recession, the effectiveness of the Republican administration in dealing with the Democratic congress)

- BD (BE,128,129;AE,234,235;LI,184,185;NI,80,81)

  Understands major foreign policy events and how they influenced public opinion of the administrations from Nixon to Clinton (e.g., U.S. policies toward arms limitations; Nixon's policy of detente with the U.S.S.R. and the People's Republic of China; reasons for the collapse of communist governments in Eastern Europe and the U.S.S.R; ▸ President Carter's role in the Camp David Accords; the Iranian hostage crisis; the foreign policy of the Reagan administration and domestic and foreign reactions to it; foreign policy goals of the Bush and Clinton administrations and their effectiveness)

▸ BD (AE,230;LI,182)

  Understands the impact of the Nixon administration's ideas and policies on American society (e.g., factors that caused so many Americans to support Nixon and his 'law and order" stance, Nixon's advocacy of family assistance and employment opportunity programs, the events of Watergate)

▸ BD (AE,231)

  Understands key domestic issues of the post-Nixon years (e.g., President Ford's pardon of Richard Nixon; the successes and failures of the Carter administration)

▸ BD (AE,232)

  Understands the principal issues and legislation affecting organized labor in the post-World War II era (e.g., terms such as "open shop," "closed shop," "featherbedding," "right to work" laws; how the general public has perceived labor unions; the relationship between the Reagan-Bush administrations and organized labor)

Codes (right side of page): BD = Benchmark, Declarative; BP = Benchmark, Procedural; BC = Benchmark, Contextual
1st letter of each code in parentheses *2nd letter of code* *Number*
B = NCHS: basic edition E = Explicitly stated in document Page number of cited document
A = NCHS: U.S. History, expanded edition I = Implied in document
L = Lessons From History
N = NAEP: Provisional Item Specifications *Symbol*
  ■ material appears only in NCHS basic edition
  ▸ material appears only in NCHS expanded edition
  ● material appears in both NCHS editions

Level IV (Grades 9-12)

- BD (BE,128;AE,229,230,232;LE,182;LI,183;NI,127)

  Understands how the Nixon, Ford, and Carter administrations dealt with major domestic issues (e.g., policies for dealing with problems of recession and inflation; ▸ the Nixon administration's "southern strategy;" Carter's program for dealing with the energy crisis)

- BD (BE,128;AE,229,230,232;LI,182)

  Understands the events and legacy of the Watergate break-in (e.g., the constitutional issues raised by the affair and the effects of Watergate on public opinion; ▸ the involvement of the Nixon administration in the cover-up; how Presidents Ford and Carter addressed the concept of the "imperial presidency" after Watergate and attempted to restore credibility to the presidency)

- BD (BE,128;AE,231,232,233;LI,182-183;NI,132)

  Understands the impact of the Reagan presidency on relations with other countries (e.g., the issues raised in the Iran-Contra affair, ▸ Reagan's view of the Soviet Union as an "evil empire" and how that shaped defense policy, the Reagan administration's policy toward South Africa)

- BD (BE,128;AE,231,233;LI,183)

  Understands the major economic issues from the Reagan through the Clinton presidencies (e.g., why labor unions declined in recent decades, the impact of recession and the growing national debt on the Bush and Clinton administration's domestic agendas, ▸ the impact of Reagan's tax policies on the national economy)

- BD (BE,129;AE,234-236;LI,184,185;NE,132;NI,131-133)

  Understands the influence of U.S. foreign policy on international events from Nixon to Clinton (e.g., the U.S.'s role in the evolving political struggles in the Middle East, Africa, Asia, and Latin America; foreign policy in the post-Cold War era; ▸ U.S. goals and objectives in the Middle East; the pros and cons of U.S. intervention in the Persian Gulf under Reagan and Bush; how human rights has been used in American foreign policy)

(BE,129;AE,237)

31. Understands economic, social, and cultural developments in the contemporary United States

Level II (Grades 5-6)

BD (BE,129;AE,244;LI,183,184;NI,79,80)
- Understands changes in the contemporary workplace (e.g., how scientific and technological changes and the computer revolution affect the economy and nature of work, ▸ kinds of education and skills required for available jobs)

BD (BE,129;AE,240;LI,180;NI,78)
- Understands the factors that prompted new immigration in contemporary American society (e.g., new immigration policies after 1965, ▸ areas of the world from which most immigrants have come)

BD (BE,130;AE,242;LI,181;LE,181;NI,77,78)
- Understands influences on religion in contemporary society (e.g., how changing immigration patterns affected religious diversity, ▸ issues related to religious belief)

BD (BE,130;AE,245;LI,176;NI,77)
- Understands aspects of contemporary American culture (e.g., the international influence of American culture, increased popularity of professional sports, influence of spectator sports on popular culture, ▸ sports and entertainment figures who advertise specific products)

BD (BE,130;AE,237;NI,75)
- Understands contemporary issues concerning gender and ethnicity (e.g., the range of women's organizations, the changing goals of the women's movement, and the issues currently dividing women; ▸ issues involving justice and common welfare; how interest groups attempted to achieve their goals of equality and justice; how African, Asian, Hispanic, and Native Americans have shaped American life and retained their cultural heritage)

Level III (Grades 7-8)

BD (BE,129;AE,244;LI,183,184;NI,79)
- Understands changes in the workplace and the economy in contemporary America (e.g., the effects of a sharp increase in labor force participation of women and new immigrants; the shift of the labor force from manufacturing to service industries)

BD (BE,129-130;AE,240;LI,180;NI,78)
- Understands demographic shifts and the influences on recent immigration patterns (e.g., the

---

Codes (right side of page):	BD = Benchmark, Declarative; BP = Benchmark, Procedural; BC = Benchmark, Contextual	
1st letter of each code in parentheses	*2nd letter of code*	*Number*
B = NCHS: basic edition	E = Explicitly stated in document	Page number of cited document
A = NCHS: U.S. History, expanded edition	I = Implied in document	
L = Lessons From History		
N = NAEP: Provisional Item Specifications	*Symbol*	
	■ material appears only in NCHS basic edition	
	▸ material appears only in NCHS expanded edition	
	● material appears in both NCHS editions	

flow from cities to suburbs, reasons for internal migrations from the "Rustbelt" to the "Sunbelt" and its impact on politics, implications of the shifting age structure of the population)

- BD (BE,130;AE,242;LI,181)
  Understands the growth of religious issues in contemporary society (e.g., the growth of the Christian evangelical movement and its use of modern telecommunications, ▸ issues regarding the guarantee of no establishment of religion and the free exercise clauses of the First Amendment, the significance of religious groups in local communities and their approaches to social issues)

- BD (BE,130;AE,245;NI,77,78)
  Understands various influences on American culture (e.g., the desegregation of education and its role in the creation of private white academies; the influence of the media on contemporary American culture; ▸ how ethnic art, food, music, and clothing are incorporated into mainstream culture and society)

- BD (BE,130,131;AE,238;NI,75)
  Understands how different groups attempted to achieve their goals (e.g., the grievances of racial and ethnic minorities and their reference to the nation's charter documents to rectify past injustices, ▸ local community efforts to adapt facilities for the disabled)

Level IV (Grades 9-12)

- BD (BE,129;AE,244;LI,183,184;NI,129,130)
  Understands how changes in the national and global economy have influenced the workplace (e.g., sluggishness in the overall rate of economic growth, the relative stagnation of wages since 1973, the social and political impact of an increase in income disparities, the effects of increased global trade and competition on the U.S. economy, ▸ the influence of new technology on education and learning, and the relation between education and earnings in the workplace)

- BD (BE,129,130;AE,240,241;NI,77,128,129;LI,181)
  Understands how recent immigration and migration patterns impacted social and political issues (e.g., major issues that affect immigrants and resulting conflicts; changes in the size and composition of the traditional American family; ▸ demographic and residential mobility since 1970)

- BD (BE,130;AE,242,243;LI,181)
  Understands how the rise of religious groups and movements influenced political issues in contemporary American society (e.g., the position of major religious groups on such issues

---

Codes (right side of page):   BD = Benchmark, Declarative; BP = Benchmark, Procedural; BC = Benchmark, Contextual
1st letter of each code in parentheses   *2nd letter of code*   *Number*
B = NCHS: basic edition   E = Explicitly stated in document   Page number of cited document
A = NCHS: U.S. History, expanded edition   I = Implied in document
L = Lessons From History
N = NAEP: Provisional Item Specifications   *Symbol*
■ material appears only in NCHS basic edition
▸ material appears only in NCHS expanded edition
● material appears in both NCHS editions

as abortion, gay rights, women in the clergy, and educational issues; ▸ the causes and significance of religious evangelism and its effect on American political and religious culture in the 1980s; how Supreme Court decisions since 1968 have affected the meaning and practice of religious freedom)

- BD (BE,130;AE,245,LE,186)
  Understands the influence of social change and the entertainment industry in shaping views on art, gender, and culture (e.g., how social change and renewed ethnic diversity affects artistic expression in contemporary American society, ▸ the reflection of values in popular TV shows, the effects of women's participation in sports on gender roles and career choices)

- BD (BE,130-131;AE,237,238,239;NI,125-126;NE,128)
  Understands major contemporary social issues and the groups involved (e.g., the current debate over affirmative action and to what degree affirmative action policies have reached their goals; the evolution of government support for the rights of the disabled; the emergence of the Gay Liberation Movement and civil rights of gay Americans; continuing debates over multiculturalism, bilingual education, and group identity and rights vs. individual rights and identity; ▸successes and failures of the modern feminist movement)

Codes (right side of page):	BD = Benchmark, Declarative; BP = Benchmark, Procedural; BC = Benchmark, Contextual
1st letter of each code in parentheses	*2nd letter of code* *Number*

Codes (right side of page):   BD = Benchmark, Declarative; BP = Benchmark, Procedural; BC = Benchmark, Contextual
1st letter of each code in parentheses   *2nd letter of code*   *Number*
B = NCHS: basic edition   E = Explicitly stated in document   Page number of cited document
A = NCHS: U.S. History, expanded edition   I = Implied in document
L = Lessons From History
N = NAEP: Provisional Item Specifications   *Symbol*
    ■ material appears only in NCHS basic edition
    ▸ material appears only in NCHS expanded edition
    ● material appears in both NCHS editions

McREL

Summary of Standards for World History

Era 1 The Beginnings of Human Society
1. Understands the biological and cultural processes that shaped the earliest human communities
2. Understands the processes that contributed to the emergence of agricultural societies around the world

Era 2 Early Civilizations and the Rise of Pastoral Peoples, 4000-1000 BCE
3. Understands the major characteristics of civilization and the development of civilizations in Mesopotamia, Egypt, and the Indus Valley
4. Understands how agrarian societies spread and new states emerged in the third and second millennia BCE
5. Understands the political, social, and cultural consequences of population movements and militarization in Eurasia in the second millennium BCE
6. Understands major trends in Eurasia and Africa from 4000 to 1000 BCE

Era 3 Classical Traditions, Major Religions, and Giant Empires, 1000 BCE-300 CE
7. Understands technological and cultural innovation and change from 1000 to 600 BCE
8. Understands how Aegean civilization emerged and how interrelations developed among peoples of the eastern Mediterranean and Southwest Asia from 600 to 200 BCE
9. Understands how major religious and large-scale empires arose in the Mediterranean Basin, China, and India from 500 BCE to 300 CE
10. Understands how early agrarian civilizations arose in Mesoamerica
11. Understands major global trends from 1000 BCE to 300 CE

Era 4 Expanding Zones of Exchange and Encounter, 300-1000 CE
12. Understands the Imperial crises and their aftermath in various regions from 300 to 700 CE
13. Understands the causes and consequences of the development of Islamic civilization between the 7th and 10th centuries
14. Understands major developments in East Asia and Southeast Asia in the era of the Tang Dynasty from 600 to 900 CE
15. Understands the political, social, and cultural redefinitions in Europe from 500 to 1000 CE
16. Understands the development of agricultural societies and new states in tropical Africa and Oceania
17. Understands the rise of centers of civilization in Mesoamerica and Andean South America in the first millennium CE
18. Understands major global trends from 300 to 1000 CE

Era 5 Intensified Hemispheric Interactions 1000-1500 CE
19. Understands the maturation of an interregional system of communication, trade, and cultural exchange during a period of Chinese economic power and Islamic expansion
20. Understands the redefinition of European society and culture from 1000 to 1300 CE

21. Understands the rise of the Mongol empire and its consequences for Eurasian peoples from 1200 to 1350
22. Understands the growth of states, towns, and trade in Sub-Saharan Africa between the 11th and 15th centuries
23. Understands patterns of crisis and recovery in Afro-Eurasia between 1300 and 1450
24. Understands the expansion of states and civilizations in the Americas between 1000 and 1500
25. Understands major global trends from 1000 to 1500 CE

Era 6 Global Expansion and Encounter, 1450-1770
26. Understands how the transoceanic interlinking of all major regions of the world between 1450 and 1600 led to global transformations
27. Understands how European society experienced political, economic, and cultural transformations in an age of global intercommunication between 1450 and 1750
28. Understands how large territorial empires dominated much of Eurasia between the 16th and 18th centuries
29. Understands the economic, political, and cultural interrelations among peoples of Africa, Europe, and the Americas between 1500 and 1750
30. Understands transformations in Asian societies in the era of European expansion
31. Understands major global trends from 1450 to 1770

Era 7 An Age of Revolutions, 1750-1914
32. Understands the causes and consequences of political revolutions in the late 18th and early 19th centuries
33. Understands the causes and consequences of the agricultural and industrial revolutions from 1700 to 1850
34. Understands how Eurasian societies were transformed in an era of global trade and the emergence of European power from 1750 to 1870
35. Understands patterns of nationalism, state-building, and social reform in Europe and the Americas from 1830 to 1914
36. Understands patterns of global change in the era of Western military and economic domination from 1850 to 1914
37. Understands major global trends from 1750 to 1914

Era 8 A Half-Century of Crisis and Achievement, 1900-1945
38. Understands reform, revolution, and social change in the world economy in the early century
39. Understands the causes and global consequences of World War I
40. Understands the search for peace and stability throughout the world in the 1920s and 1930s
41. Understands the causes and global consequences of World War II
42. Understands major global trends from 1900 to the end of World War II

Era 9   The 20th Century Since 1945: Promises and Paradoxes

43.   Understands how post-World War II reconstruction occurred, new international power relations took shape, and colonial empires broke up

44.   Understands the search for community, stability, and peace in an interdependent world

45.   Understands major global trends since Word War II

World History Across the Eras

46.   Understands long-term changes and recurring patterns in world history

(BE,138;WE,41)

1. Understands the biological and cultural processes that shaped the earliest human communities

Level II (Grades 5-6)

- BD (BE,138;R;WE,41;LI,197)
Understands scientific evidence regarding early hominid evolution in Africa (e.g., daily life of individuals and communities in early hunter-gatherer populations; ▸ major anthropological discoveries, their locations, and their discoverers)

- BD (BE,138;C;WE,43)
Understands the social and cultural characteristics of hunter-gatherer communities in various continental regions (e.g., similarities and differences between hunter-gatherer communities in Africa, Eurasia, and the Americas and their responses to local environments; characteristics of Cro-Magnon communities of western Eurasia; ▸ location and composition of archaeological discoveries and what understanding these bring to Neanderthal culture and community life)

Level III (Grades 7-8)

- BD (BE,138;R;WE,41,42)
Understands early hominid development and scientific methods used to determine the dates and evolution of different human communities (e.g., methods employed by archaeologists, geologists, and anthropologists to study hominid evolution; the approximate chronology, sequence, and territorial range of early hominid evolution in Africa from the *Australopithecines* to *Homo erectus*)

- BD (BE,138;C;WE,43,44;LE,197)
Understands the role of the environment in the development of different human communities (e.g., current and past theories regarding the emergence of *Homo sapiens sapiens* and the processes by which human groups populated the major world regions; how environmental conditions in the last Ice Age possibly affected changes in the economy, culture, and organization of human communities)

- BD (BE,138;C;WE,43,44)
Understands how different human communities expressed their beliefs (e.g., theories regarding the relationship between linguistic and cultural development; ▸ possible social, cultural, and/or religious meanings inferred from late paleolithic cave paintings found in

---

Codes (right side of page):   BD = Benchmark, Declarative; BP = Benchmark, Procedural; BC = Benchmark, Contextual

1st letter of each code in parentheses	*2nd letter of code*	*Number*
B = NCHS: basic edition	E = Explicitly stated in document	Page number of cited document
W = NCHS: World History, expanded ed.	I = Implied in document	
L = Lessons from History		
C = Core material	*Symbol*	
R = Related material	■ material appears only in NCHS basic edition	
	▸ material appears only in NCHS expanded edition	
	● material appears in both NCHS editions	

Spain and France; theories about the ways in which hunter-gatherers may have communicated, maintained memory of past events, and expressed religious feelings)

Level IV (Grades 9-12)

BD (BE,138;R;WE,42)

● Understands methods by which early human communities are studied and what these studies reveal (e.g., ▸ the way in which newly discovered sites and investigative techniques used to examine them affect the study and understanding of human evolution, how common refuse can be studied to make inferences about earlier communities)

BD (BE,138;C;WE,44)

● Understands how different kinds of evidence are used to determine the cultural characteristics of early human communities (e.g., ▸ how archaeological evidence demonstrates the influences of climate, geographic location, and economic specialization on everyday life; how non-verbal evidence such as burials, carvings, and paintings can indicate the presence of religion)

BD (R;WE,42;LE,197)

▸ Understands physical, social, and cultural characteristics of different human communities (e.g., the possible types of early hominid communities; characteristics of skeletal remains of non-hominid, primate, hominid, and *Homo sapiens* and how to classify them chronologically; major features of flora, fauna, and climate associated with different hominid communities)

BD (C;WE,44)

▸ Understands environmental, biological, and cultural influences on early human communities (e.g., how language helped early humans hunt, establish roles, rules, and structure within communities; the proposition that Mesolithic peoples were the first to take advantage of a changing climate; biological and cultural relationships between Neanderthal and *Homo sapiens sapiens*)

Codes (right side of page): BD = Benchmark, Declarative; BP = Benchmark, Procedural; BC = Benchmark, Contextual

1st letter of each code in parentheses	*2nd letter of code*	*Number*
B = NCHS: basic edition	E = Explicitly stated in document	Page number of cited document
W = NCHS: World History, expanded ed.	I = Implied in document	
L = Lessons from History		
C = Core material	*Symbol*	
R = Related material	■ material appears only in NCHS basic edition	
	▸ material appears only in NCHS expanded edition	
	● material appears in both NCHS editions	

(BE,139;WE,45)

2. Understands the processes that contributed to the emergence of agricultural societies around the world

Level II (Grades 5-6)

BD (BE,139;C;WE,45)
● Understands the role of agriculture in early settled communities (e.g., how archaeological evidence explains the technology, social organization, and cultural life of settled farming communities in Southwest Asia; ▸ differences between wild and domestic plants and animals; how patterns of settlement were influenced by agricultural practices)

BD (BE,139;R;WE,47;LE,198)
● Understands the development of early agricultural communities in different regions of the world (e.g., differences between hunter-gatherer, fishing, and agrarian communities; social, cultural, and economic characteristics of large agricultural settlements and their unique problems; ▸ the development of tropical agriculture in Southeast Asia)

Level III (Grades 7-8)

BD (BE,139;C;WE,45,46;LI,198)
● Understands immediate and long-term impacts and influences of early agricultural communities (e.g., areas in Southwest Asia and the Nile valley where early farming communities first appeared, the effect of new tools and other objects on early farming settlements, ▸ whether fishing was considered a nomadic or agricultural way of life)

BD (BE,139;R;WE,47)
● Understands influences on the spread of agricultural communities (e.g., how local needs and conditions affected food plant domestication and world-wide patterns of settlement)

BD (BE,139;R;WE,47;LE,198;LI,199)
● Understands what archaeological evidence reveals about the social and cultural conditions of agricultural societies (e.g., the emergence of social class divisions, occupational specialization, differences in gender roles; long distance trade routes in Southwest Asia; ▸ the importance of obsidian to this trade)

BD (C;WE,45;LE,198)
▸ Understands inherent disadvantages and advantages of hunter-gatherer and early farming styles

---

Codes (right side of page):   BD = Benchmark, Declarative; BP = Benchmark, Procedural; BC = Benchmark, Contextual

1st letter of each code in parentheses   *2nd letter of code*   *Number*
B = NCHS: basic edition   E = Explicitly stated in document   Page number of cited document
W = NCHS: World History, expanded ed.   I = Implied in document
L = Lessons from History
C = Core material   *Symbol*
R = Related material   ■ material appears only in NCHS basic edition
▸ material appears only in NCHS expanded edition
● material appears in both NCHS editions

McREL

►   Understands the bases for the argument that agricultural life was an advance in human social development

BD (R;WE,48;LI,198)

Level IV (Grades 9-12)

●   Understands how agricultural communities maintained their produce and livestock (e.g., methods used by scholars to reconstruct the early history of domestication and agricultural settlement, how and why human groups domesticated wild grains and animals after the last Ice Age, ► the importance of controlling food supplies and storing them in the "Neolithic revolution")

BD (BE,139;C;WE,45-46)

●   Understands what archaeological evidence has revealed about the cultural beliefs of early agricultural societies (e.g., the emergence of complete belief systems, including female deity worship)

BD (BE,139;R;WE,47)

►   Understands social and cultural factors that define agricultural communities (e.g., archaeological evidence that distinguishes hunter-gatherer from agricultural sites, the relationship between agricultural production and cultural change)

BD (C;WE,46)

►   Understands what environmental and architectural evidence reveals about different types of large agricultural communities (e.g., the locations of different types of communities between 10,000 and 4,000 BCE; how patterns of layout, fortification, and standardization in large settlements helped transform human culture)

BD (R;WE,47-48;LI,198)

►   Understands why some groups developed and accepted complete sedentary agriculture and others retained earlier subsistence methods

BD (R;WE,48)

Codes (right side of page):   BD = Benchmark, Declarative; BP = Benchmark, Procedural; BC = Benchmark, Contextual

1st letter of each code in parentheses	*2nd letter of code*	*Number*
B = NCHS: basic edition	E = Explicitly stated in document	Page number of cited document
W = NCHS: World History, expanded ed.	I = Implied in document	
L = Lessons from History		
C = Core material	*Symbol*	
R = Related material	■ material appears only in NCHS basic edition	
	► material appears only in NCHS expanded edition	
	● material appears in both NCHS editions	

201

MREL

(BE,141;WE,52)

3.   Understands the major characteristics of civilization and the development of civilizations in Mesopotamia, Egypt, and the Indus Valley

Level II (Grades 5-6)

BD (BE,141;C;WE,52;LI,199,207)

- Understands influences on the development of various civilizations in the 4th and 3rd millennia BCE (e.g., how the natural environment of the Tigris-Euphrates, Nile, and Indus Valleys shaped the early development of civilization; different characteristics of urban development in Mesopotamia, Egypt, and the Indus Valley)

BD (BE,142;C;WE,52;LE,200,205,207)

- Understands the characteristics of writing forms in Mesopotamia, Egypt, and the Indus Valley and how written records shaped political, legal, religious, and cultural life

BD (BE,142;R;WE,54;LE,199,206)

- Understands how economic, political, and environmental factors influenced the civilizations of Mesopotamia, Egypt, and the Indus Valley (e.g., the impact of trade networks connecting various regions of Southwest Asia on Mesopotamian civilization; the importance of commercial, cultural, and political connections between Egypt and peoples of Nubia along the upper Nile; ▸ how geography and climate affected trade in the Nile Valley)

Level III (Grades 7-8)

BD (BE,141,142;C;WE,53;LE,199,203)

- Understands environmental and cultural factors that shaped the development of Mesopotamia, Egypt and the Indus Valley (e.g., development of religious and ethical belief systems and how they legitimized political and social order; ▸ demands of the natural environment; how written records such as the Epic of Gilgamesh reflected and shaped the political, religious, and cultural life of Mesopotamia)

BD (BE,142;R;WE,54)

- Understands the role of economics in shaping the development of Mesopotamia, Egypt, and the Indus Valley (e.g., the economic and cultural significance of the trade routes between Egypt, India, and Mesopotamia in the 3rd millennium, ▸ the importance of traded goods to each society)

Codes (right side of page):   BD = Benchmark, Declarative; BP = Benchmark, Procedural; BC = Benchmark, Contextual
1st letter of each code in parentheses   *2nd letter of code*   *Number*
B = NCHS: basic edition   E = Explicitly stated in document   Page number of cited document
W = NCHS: World History, expanded ed.   I = Implied in document
L = Lessons from History
C = Core material   *Symbol*
R = Related material   ■ material appears only in NCHS basic edition
                                        ▸ material appears only in NCHS expanded edition
                                        ● material appears in both NCHS editions

Level IV (Grades 9-12)

BD (BE,142;C;WE,52,53;LE,199,200,207)
- Understands influences on the social and economic framework of Mesopotamia, Egypt, and the Indus Valley (e.g., the characteristics of government and military in Egypt and Mesopotamia and the ways in which central authorities commanded labor and taxes from peasant farmers; how architectural, artistic, technological, and scientific achievements of these civilizations affected the economics of daily life)

BD (BE,142;C;WE,53)
- Understands how written codes and stories reflect social conditions in Mesopotamia, Egypt, and the Indus Valley (e.g., ▸ how the code of Hammurabi illustrated the ethical values, social hierarchy and attitudes, and roles of women in Mesopotamia; how the biblical account of Genesis and the Enuma Elish from Babylon reflect contrasting beliefs)

BD (BE,142;R;WE,55;LI,202,208)
- Understands features of trading networks in Mesopotamia, Egypt, and the Indus Valley (e.g., ▸ those geographical characteristics that encouraged Mesopotamia to engage in trade and those which made trade difficult, shifting political relationships between trading partners in the 1st and 2nd millennia BCE and sources of conflict between them, the breadth of the Indus trade network)

(BE,142;WE,56)
4. Understands how agrarian societies spread and new states emerged in the 3rd and 2nd millennia BCE

Level II (Grades 5-6)

BD (BE,142;C;WE,56)
- Understands how the development of different types of tools influenced Chinese civilization (e.g., the uses and significance of bronze tool-making technology, weapons, and luxury goods in the 3rd and 2nd millennia BCE; ▸ the unique nature of Chinese writing tools, surfaces, and styles in the 2nd millennium BCE)

BD (BE,142,143;C;WE,56;LE,208,209;LI,208)
- Understands significant characteristics of early Chinese society and religion (e.g., the influence of the natural environment on Huang He [Yellow River] civilization compared to its impact on Mesopotamia, Egypt, and the Indus Valley; early Chinese urban societies and how they compare to those of Mesopotamia and the Indus Valley, ▸ the nature of Shang

---

Codes (right side of page):   BD = Benchmark, Declarative; BP = Benchmark, Procedural; BC = Benchmark, Contextual
1st letter of each code in parentheses   *2nd letter of code*   *Number*
B = NCHS: basic edition   E = Explicitly stated in document   Page number of cited document
W = NCHS: World History, expanded ed.   I = Implied in document
L = Lessons from History
C = Core material   *Symbol*
R = Related material   ■ material appears only in NCHS basic edition
                                           ▸ material appears only in NCHS expanded edition
                                           ● material appears in both NCHS editions

ancestor worship and what it illustrates about concepts of life and death in Shang society)

- Understands the role of technology in early agrarian societies (e.g., how the advent of the plow influenced new agrarian societies in Southwest Asia, the Mediterranean basin, and temperate Europe; how megalithic stone buildings, such as Stonehenge, indicate the emergence of complex agrarian societies in Europe; ▸ changes for humankind and civilization brought on by the bow and arrow and by pottery; what physical evidence indicated about the characteristics of the agrarian society of ancient Egypt and the life of the Pharaoh)

  BD (BE,143;R;WE,58;LE,198)

Level III (Grades 7-8)

- Understands the rise of urban and complex agrarian societies in the 3rd and 2nd millennium BCE (e.g., how the Minoan civilization emerged on Crete and its significant cultural achievements; ▸ the origins and possible purpose of Stonehenge and the effort made to create it)

  BD (BE,143;R;WE,58)

▸ Understands how the natural environment shaped Huang He civilization (e.g., how changes in the course of the Huang He river challenged citizens and government)

  BD (C;WE,56;LE,208;LI,208)

▸ Understands what archaeological evidence (e.g., oracle bone inscriptions, bronze vessels) reveals about Chinese history during the Shang Dynasty

  BD (C;WE,57;LI,208)

▸ Understands the significance of advancements in tool and weapon technology (e.g., the technology of bronze casting and why bronze weapons were superior to those made of stone; how the development of the plow, bow and arrow, and pottery affected early man and led to changes in gender roles)

  BD (R;WE,58)

Level IV (Grades 9-12)

- Understands the social, cultural, and political characteristics of the Shang Dynasty (e.g., the development of royal government under the Shang Dynasty and the development of social hierarchy, religious institutions, and writing; the role that Chinese peasants played in sustaining the wealth and power of the Shang political centers)

  BD (BE,142,143;C;WE,57)

Codes (right side of page):	BD = Benchmark, Declarative; BP = Benchmark, Procedural; BC = Benchmark, Contextual	
1st letter of each code in parentheses	*2nd letter of code*	*Number*
B = NCHS: basic edition	E = Explicitly stated in document	Page number of cited document
W = NCHS: World History, expanded ed.	I = Implied in document	
L = Lessons from History		
C = Core material	*Symbol*	
R = Related material	■ material appears only in NCHS basic edition	
	▸ material appears only in NCHS expanded edition	
	● material appears in both NCHS editions	

BD (BE,143;R;WE,58,59)

- Understands interaction between urban centers of Southwest Asia, Egypt, and the Aegean Basin, and the Eastern Mediterranean coast (e.g., the important urban centers of Southwest Asia, Egypt, and the Aegean Basin; the role of cities along the Mediterranean coast as commercial bridges between the trading networks of Southwest Asia, Egypt, and the Mediterranean)

BD (BE,143;R;WE,58,59)

- Understands how different agrarian societies developed (e.g., what archaeological evidence suggests about the growth of agricultural societies in West Africa and Southeast Asia, ▸ the origins of domesticated rice in Southeast Asia and the routes of its spread throughout the rest of Asia)

BD (C;WE,57;LI,208)

▸ Understands how environmental conditions such as the prevailing wind, current, and flooding patters, influenced civilizations in the Tigris, Nile, and Huang He valleys

BD (C;WE,57)

▸ Understands evidence of social and cultural development of Chinese civilization in the 3rd and 2nd millennium BCE (e.g., evidence that the Chinese had developed urbanization, sophisticated social cooperation, and written language before 1700 BCE; the physical evidence that highlights possible cultural contact between China and other centers of civilization in antiquity)

BD (R;WE,58)

▸ Understands the impact of various technologies (e.g., the wheel, pottery, the sail, weaving, bronze casting, the plow) upon social organization and the political and economic power of the groups that used them

BD (R;WE,59)

▸ Understands influences on the cultural and economic conditions of Minoan and Egyptian civilizations (e.g., the nature and extent of cultural contact between Minoan and Egyptian civilizations, the extent of Minoan trade and its impact on the development of Minoan civilization)

Codes (right side of page):   BD = Benchmark, Declarative; BP = Benchmark, Procedural; BC = Benchmark, Contextual

1st letter of each code in parentheses	*2nd letter of code*	*Number*
B = NCHS: basic edition	E = Explicitly stated in document	Page number of cited document
W = NCHS: World History, expanded ed.	I = Implied in document	
L = Lessons from History		
C = Core material	*Symbol*	
R = Related material	■ material appears only in NCHS basic edition	
	▸ material appears only in NCHS expanded edition	
	● material appears in both NCHS editions	

(BE,143;WE,60)

5. **Understands the political, social, and cultural consequences of population movements and militarization in Eurasia in the second millennium BCE**

Level II (Grades 5-6)

BD (BE,143;C;WE,60)
- Understands how the rise of pastoral societies was linked to the climate and geography of the Central Asian steppes, and how kinship-based pastoral society differed from the social organization of agrarian states

BD (BE,144;C;WE,62)
- Understands how the invention of the chariot affected Southwest Asian societies (e.g., how the chariot changed transportation, the development of chariot warfare, ▸ how the chariot contributed to the spread of new ideas and technology)

BD (BE,144;R;WE,64)
- Understands characteristics of Mycenaean Greek society and culture (e.g., the political and social organization of the Mycenaean Greeks as revealed in archaeological and written records, ▸ how geography influenced the development of Mycenaean society, the significance of the story of the siege of Troy)

BD (BE,144;R;WE,65)
- Understands possible causes of the decline and collapse of Indus Valley civilization (e.g., ▸ possible causes for the disappearance of cities such as Mohenjo-Daro, the role environmental changes played in the fall of Indus cities)

Level III (Grades 7-8)

BD (BE,143;C;WE,60-61)
- Understands the development of Indo-European language (e.g., the probable geographic homeland of speakers of early Indo-European languages and the spread of the language to other parts of Eurasia, ▸ languages which developed from the Indo-European root language)

BD (BE,144;C;WE,62)
- Understands the origins of the Hittite people, their empire in Anatolia, and major cultural and political achievements of this society

BD (BE,144;C;WE,62)
- Understands significant individuals and events in Egyptian civilization (e.g., the extent of Egyptian expansion during the Old, Middle, and New Kingdoms, and some of the factors that

---

Codes (right side of page):   BD = Benchmark, Declarative; BP = Benchmark, Procedural; BC = Benchmark, Contextual

1st letter of each code in parentheses	*2nd letter of code*	*Number*
B = NCHS: basic edition	E = Explicitly stated in document	Page number of cited document
W = NCHS: World History, expanded ed.	I = Implied in document	
L = Lessons from History		
C = Core material	*Symbol*	
R = Related material	■ material appears only in NCHS basic edition	
	▸ material appears only in NCHS expanded edition	
	● material appears in both NCHS editions	

206

MREL

made this expansion possible; ▸ major political and cultural achievements of Thutmose III, Ramses II, and Queen Hatshepsut in Egypt)

BD (BE,144;R;WE,64)
- Understands significant events in the development of Mycenaean culture (e.g., the cultural influences of Egypt, Minoan Crete, and Southwest Asian civilizations on the Mycenaeans; ▸ the story of the Trojan war through different sources)

BD (BE,144;R;WE,65)
- Understands characteristics of Aryan culture (e.g., the reasons for the migration of Indo-Aryan and Mycenaean-speaking peoples into India, the Eastern Mediterranean, and the Iranian Plateau; ▸ the belief system embraced by the Aryan people; odes from the Vedas that praise major Vedic gods and what they illustrate about Aryan values; potential conflict and tension among Aryan tribes as they began to settle down in the Indo-Gangetic plain)

BD (R;WE,65)
▸ Understands potential sources for the decline in trade, the overcrowding, and eventual collapse of Mohenjo-Daro and other Indus cities

Level IV (Grades 9-12)

BD (BE,144;C;WE,60,61)
- Understands characteristics of pastoral and agrarian societies (e.g., economy, social relations, and political authority among pastoral peoples; women's social equality with men in pastoral societies as opposed to agrarian societies)

BD (BE,144;C;WE,63)
- Understands the beliefs and accomplishments of Mesopotamian and Egyptian rulers (e.g., the religious ideas of Akenaton [Amenhotep IV] and the viewpoint that Atonism was an early form of monotheism, ▸ the accomplishments of Sargon and Akenaton [Amenhotep IV])

BD (BE,144;R;WE,64)
- Understands characteristics of Mycenaean society (e.g., the impact of Mycenaean expansion and city-building on commerce and political life in the Eastern Mediterranean; ▸ society, trade, and government in Mycenae; comparisons of Mycenaean and Minoan societies from archaeological remains)

BD (BE,144;R;WE,66)
- Understands cultural elements of the Aryan civilization (e.g., Aryan culture in India as denoted in linguistic, literary, and archaeological materials; ▸ beliefs expressed in the Vedic hymns; the root of the word "Aryan," those people who came to be called Indo-Aryan)

Codes (right side of page):   BD = Benchmark, Declarative; BP = Benchmark, Procedural; BC = Benchmark, Contextual

1st letter of each code in parentheses	*2nd letter of code*	*Number*
B = NCHS: basic edition	E = Explicitly stated in document	Page number of cited document
W = NCHS: World History, expanded ed.	I = Implied in document	
L = Lessons from History		
C = Core material	*Symbol*	
R = Related material	■ material appears only in NCHS basic edition	
	▸ material appears only in NCHS expanded edition	
	● material appears in both NCHS editions	

▸ Knows the migration routes of Indo-European language speakers and the approximate dates of their arrivals in new locations during the second millenium BCE
BD (C;WE,61)

▸ Understands the emergence and militarization of new kingdoms (e.g., what visual and written sources suggest about the impact of chariot warfare on the battlefield; the boundaries of major states in Southwest Asia, Egypt, and the Eastern Mediterranean in the later part of the 2nd millennium BCE and why wars and diplomatic relations among these states may have represented the first era of "internationalism" in world history)
BD (C;WE,63)

▸ Understands the decline of the Indus valley civilization in comparison to that of other peoples such as the Sumerians
BD (R;WE,66)

▸ Understands the reliability of epics as historic sources and the aspects of these works historians have determined actually reflect contemporary or later culture (e.g., the Iliad, the Odyssey, the Mahabarata, and the Ramayana)
BD (R;WE,66;LE,223)

(BE,145)

6. Understands major trends in Eurasia and Africa from 4000 to 1000 BCE

Level II (Grades 5-6)

■ Knows areas of Eurasia and Africa where cities and dense farming populations appeared between 4000 and 1000 BCE, and understands the connection between the spread of agriculture and the acceleration of world population growth
BD (BE,145;LE,193-195)

■ Understands how new ideas, products, techniques, and institutions spread from one region to another and the conditions under which people assimilated or rejected new ideas or adapted them to cultural traditions
BD (BE,145,LI,195)

Level III (Grades 7-8)

■ Understands the emergence of civilizations in Southwest Asia, the Nile valley, India, China, and the Eastern Mediterranean and how they represented a decisive transformation in human
BD (BE,145;LI,193)

Codes (right side of page):   BD = Benchmark, Declarative; BP = Benchmark, Procedural; BC = Benchmark, Contextual

1st letter of each code in parentheses	*2nd letter of code*	*Number*
B = NCHS: basic edition	E = Explicitly stated in document	Page number of cited document
W = NCHS: World History, expanded ed.	I = Implied in document	
L = Lessons from History		
C = Core material	*Symbol*	
R = Related material	■ material appears only in NCHS basic edition	
	▸ material appears only in NCHS expanded edition	
	● material appears in both NCHS editions	

208

MREL

history

- Understands why geographic, environmental, and economic conditions favored hunter-gatherer, pastoral, and small-scale agricultural ways of life rather than urban civilizations in many parts of the world $\qquad$ BD (BE,145)

- Knows the fundamental inventions, discoveries, techniques, and institutions that appeared from 4000 to 1000 BCE, and understands the significance of bronze technology for economic, cultural, and political life $\qquad$ BD (BE,145;LI,193-195,209)

- Understands the concept of a patriarchal society and the ways in which the legal and customary positions of aristocratic, urban, or peasant women may have changed in early civilizations $\qquad$ BD (BE,145)

- Understands the concept of "civilization" (e.g., the various criteria used to define "civilization;" fundamental differences between civilizations and other forms of social organization, such as hunter-gatherer bands, Neolithic agricultural societies, and pastoral nomadic societies; ▸ how Mohenjo-Daro meets criteria for defining civilization) $\qquad$ BD (BE,145;C;WE,52-53;LI,193-195)

Level IV (Grades 9-12)

- Understands connections between the cultural achievements of early civilizations and the development of political and economic institutions (e.g., state authority, aristocratic power, taxation systems, and institutions of coerced labor, including slavery) $\qquad$ BD (BE,145;LI,194)

- Understands the role of pastoral peoples in Eurasia and Africa up to 1000 BCE, and understands the relationship of conflict and mutual dependence between herding and agrarian societies $\qquad$ BD (BE,144;C;WE,60,61)

Codes (right side of page):	BD = Benchmark, Declarative; BP = Benchmark, Procedural; BC = Benchmark, Contextual	
1st letter of each code in parentheses	*2nd letter of code*	*Number*
B = NCHS: basic edition	E = Explicitly stated in document	Page number of cited document
W = NCHS: World History, expanded ed.	I = Implied in document	
L = Lessons from History		
C = Core material	*Symbol*	
R = Related material	■ material appears only in NCHS basic edition	
	▸ material appears only in NCHS expanded edition	
	● material appears in both NCHS editions	

(BE,147;WE,70)

7.   Understands technological and cultural innovation and change from 1000 to 600 BCE

Level II (Grades 5-6)

- BD (BE,147;C;WE,70)
Understands patterns of Phoenician political organization, culture, and trade in the Mediterranean basin (e.g., dominant trade routes, traded goods of major Phoenician port cities such as Carthage)

- BD (BE,148;C;WE,70)
Understands the development of Greek city-states (e.g., common features of Greek city-states in the Aegean region; the political, social, and legal character of the polis; ► how geography influenced the location and development of Greek city-states)

- BD (BE,148;C;WE,72;LE,201;LI,201)
Understands elements of Judaism and how it compares to other religions (e.g., the differences between Jewish monotheism and the polytheism of Southwest Asia, ► the ethical teachings of Judaism illustrated in stories from the Hebrew Scriptures, the major events in the early history of Judaism through the Babylonian Captivity)

- BD (BE,148;R;WE,74)
Understands major technological, military, and political events in the development of Kushite society (e.g., the importance of Nile Valley trade and the decline of the New Kingdom as factors in the rise of the Kushite state in the 1st millennium BCE, ► how iron was used in Kushite society and which uses were most important to the kingdom)

- BD (BE,149;R;WE,76)
Understands characteristics of pastoral nomadic societies (e.g., the importance of the horse to the development of pastoral nomadism and cavalry warfare; reasons for conflict and economic interdependence between pastoral nomadic peoples of Central Asia and major agrarian states of Eurasia, ► the location and range of nomadic peoples in the 1st millennium BCE and how they moved their herds and belongings)

- ► BD (R;WE,74)
Understands geographical and architectural features of Egypt and Kush (e.g., the locations of Egypt and Kush on the African continent and the geographic features that either assisted or hampered communication between these two kingdoms, what architectural evidence suggests about the relationship between Egypt and Kush)

Codes (right side of page):   BD = Benchmark, Declarative; BP = Benchmark, Procedural; BC = Benchmark, Contextual
1st letter of each code in parentheses   *2nd letter of code*   *Number*
B = NCHS: basic edition   E = Explicitly stated in document   Page number of cited document
W = NCHS: World History, expanded ed.   I = Implied in document
L = Lessons from History
C = Core material   *Symbol*
R = Related material   ■ material appears only in NCHS basic edition
                                             ► material appears only in NCHS expanded edition
                                             ● material appears in both NCHS editions

Level III (Grades 7-8)

- Understands the role of technology in societies of Southwest Asia and the Mediterranean region (e.g., the fundamentals of iron-making technology and consequences of iron tools and weapons to those societies) BD (BE,147;C;WE,71)

- Understands characteristics of the Assyrian and Babylonian Empires (e.g., the geographic extent of the Assyrian and Babylonian Empires and sources of their power and wealth, ▸ the significance of geographic features to the success of these empires, what Assyrian art indicates about Assyrian culture and society) BD (BE,147;C;WE,70,71)

- Knows the locations of significant Greek city-states and colonies in the Black Sea, Northern Africa, and the Western Mediterranean basin and reasons for their establishment BD (BE,148;C;WE,71)

- Understands social development and religious beliefs of Jewish civilization (e.g., the course of development of the Jewish kingdoms and the Jews' maintenance of religious and cultural traditions despite destruction of these kingdoms, ▸ the significance of the Torah in Judaism) BD (BE,148;C;WE,72;LI,201)

- Understands cultural elements of Kush society and their interaction with Egyptian civilization (e.g., the linguistic, architectural, and artistic achievements of Kush in the Meroitic period; how Assyrian and Kushite invasions affected Egyptian society; ▸ the social and political consequences of economic contacts between Kush and Egypt) BD (BE,148;R;WE,74;LE,206;LI,206)

- Understands the importance of maritime trade to the kingdom of Askum (e.g., ▸ the goods traded in this kingdom, and the situation that enabled Askum to play a role in long-distance trade) BD (BE,148;C;WE,122,123)

- Understands elements of different pastoral nomadic peoples in Central Asia (e.g., what archaeological and other evidence has revealed about Scythian and Xiongnu society and culture; ▸ the geography of arid lands of the Eastern Hemisphere, aspects of social relations between peoples of these desert and steppe lands, and how individual communities adapted to the land) BD (BE,149;R;WE,76)

Codes (right side of page):   BD = Benchmark, Declarative; BP = Benchmark, Procedural; BC = Benchmark, Contextual

1st letter of each code in parentheses	*2nd letter of code*	*Number*
B = NCHS: basic edition	E = Explicitly stated in document	Page number of cited document
W = NCHS: World History, expanded ed.	I = Implied in document	
L = Lessons from History		
C = Core material	*Symbol*	
R = Related material	■ material appears only in NCHS basic edition	
	▸ material appears only in NCHS expanded edition	
	● material appears in both NCHS editions	

Level IV (Grades 9-12)

- BD (BE,149;C;WE,70;LE,216)
  Understands how the implementation of laws and the spread of language influenced societies of the Mediterranean Basin and Southwest Asia (e.g., the social and cultural effects of the spread of alphabetic writing in Southwest Asia and the Mediterranean Basin, ▸ social sources of and differences in laws created by early lawmakers)

- BD (BE,148;C;WE,73)
  Understands events that led to the spread of Judaism (e.g., the significance of the Babylonian captivity for the subsequent history and survival of Judaism, the significance of the Jewish diaspora for the transmission of Judaism in the Mediterranean region and Southwest Asia)

- BD (BE,148;R;WE,75)
  Understands how Kush culture interacted with or reflected characteristics of other civilizations (e.g., the importance of political, commercial, and cultural relations between Egypt and Kush; ▸ how Kush could be viewed as a cultural satellite of Egypt, or its own distinctive civilization or both, and the evidence used to support such arguments; how Kushite achievements during the Meroitic period might have been seen by contemporaries in the Nile Delta, Sub-Saharan Africa, and Assyria)

- BD (BE,148;R;WE,75)
  Understands the emergence of states south of the Sahara desert and the influence of metal technology in Sub-Saharan and West Africa (e.g., theories about the spread of iron technology in West and East Africa, ▸ whether iron technology was brought to West Africa or developed in this region independently, what archaeological evidence such as Nok terra cotta figures and metal implements illustrate about the society and culture of their West African creators)

- BD (BE,149;R;WE,76,77)
  Understands the interaction between pastoral nomadic societies, warrior states, and agrarian states in Central Asia (e.g., how the Scythian and Xiongnu warrior states arose among the pastoral nomadic peoples on the Central Asian steppes, ▸ the circumstances and trade that led to interdependence and conflict between pastoral nomadic and agrarian societies such as Xiongnu and China)

Codes (right side of page):   BD = Benchmark, Declarative; BP = Benchmark, Procedural; BC = Benchmark, Contextual

1st letter of each code in parentheses	*2nd letter of code*	*Number*
B = NCHS: basic edition	E = Explicitly stated in document	Page number of cited document
W = NCHS: World History, expanded ed.	I = Implied in document	
L = Lessons from History		
C = Core material	*Symbol*	
R = Related material	■ material appears only in NCHS basic edition	
	▸ material appears only in NCHS expanded edition	
	● material appears in both NCHS editions	

(BE,149;WE,78)

8. Understands how Aegean civilization emerged and how interrelations developed among peoples of the Eastern Mediterranean and Southwest Asia from 600 to 200 BCE

Level II (Grades 5-6)

BD (BE,149;C;WE,78;LE,216,217)
● Understands the social and political characteristics of Greek city-states (e.g., significant similarities and differences between Athenian democracy and Spartan military aristocracy; hierarchical relationships in Greek societies and the civic, economic, and social tasks performed by men and women of different classes; ▸ the location and political structure of the major Greek city-states)

BD (BE,150;R;WE,80;LE,216)
● Understands the major cultural elements of Greek society (e.g., the major characteristics of Hellenic sculpture, architecture, and pottery and how they reflected or influenced social values and culture; ▸ characteristics of Classical Greek art and architecture and how they are reflected in modern art and architecture; Socrates' values and ideas as reflected in his trial; how Greek gods and goddesses represent non-human entities, and how gods, goddesses, and humans interact in Greek myths)

BD (BE,150;R;WE,82)
● Understands significant military developments of the Persian Empire (e.g., major events of the wars between Persia and the Greek city-states; reasons for Persia's failure to conquer the Aegean region; ▸ the growth of and geographic influences on the Persian Empire, from the reign of Cyrus I through the wars with Greece; sources of the conflict between the Greeks and the Persians; the four major battles of the Persian wars)

BD (BE,150;C;WE,84;LE,218)
● Understands Alexander's achievements as a military and political leader (e.g., reasons for the disintegration of the empire into smaller areas after his rule; ▸ the campaigns, battles, and cities founded in Alexander's imperial conquests)

Level III (Grades 7-8)

BD (BE,149;C;WE,79)
● Understands the political framework of Athenian society (e.g., the influence of Athenian political ideals on public life; major changes made to the Athenian political organization between the initial monarchy and the governments of Solon and Cleisthenes; ▸ the role of

---

Codes (right side of page):   BD = Benchmark, Declarative; BP = Benchmark, Procedural; BC = Benchmark, Contextual

1st letter of each code in parentheses	*2nd letter of code*	*Number*
B = NCHS: basic edition	E = Explicitly stated in document	Page number of cited document
W = NCHS: World History, expanded ed.	I = Implied in document	
L = Lessons from History		
C = Core material	*Symbol*	
R = Related material	■ material appears only in NCHS basic edition	
	▸ material appears only in NCHS expanded edition	
	● material appears in both NCHS editions	

213

MREL

women in Athenian society, their rights under the law, and possible reasons why Athenian democracy was limited solely to males)

- BD (BE,150;R;WE,80;LE,216)
  Understands the role of art, literature, and mythology in Greek society (e.g., major works of Greek drama and mythology and how they reveal ancient moral values and civic culture; ▸ how the arts and literature reflected cultural traditions in ancient Greece)

- BD (BE,150;R;WE,82)
  Understands the characteristics of Persian founding, expansion, and political organization (e.g., ▸ the political structure of Persia under Darius the Great, and how the Persian Empire ruled diverse ethnic populations; the leadership organization of Darius I, and why his "chain of command" was so effective; the effects of the Persian Wars upon the daily lives of the people of Persia and Greece)

- BD (BE,150;C;WE,84;LE,218)
  Understands elements of Alexander of Macedon's legacy (e.g., the scope and success of his imperial conquests; ▸ his rise to power, methods used to unite the empire)

- BD (BE,150;C;WE,84,85)
  Understands the impact and achievements of the Hellenistic period (e.g., major lasting achievements of Hellenistic art, mathematics, science, philosophy, and political thought; ▸ the impact of Hellenism on Indian art; how architecture in West Asia after the conquests of Alexander reflected Greek and Macedonian influence)

- ▸ BD (C;WE,79;LE,216)
  Understands the evolution, inherent advantages, and disadvantages of major governmental systems in Greek city-states in the 6th and 5th centuries BCE

- ▸ BC (R,WE,80;LE,216)
  Understands comparisons of the creation myths of Sumer, Babylon, Egypt, Greece, and nationalized China and the similarities and differences in world view they suggest

Level IV (Grades 9-12)

- BD (BE,149;C;WE,78,79;LE,216)
  Understands the legacy of Greek thought and government (e.g., the importance of participatory government in Greek city-states for the development of Western political thought and institutions; ▸ essential ideas in Plato's Republic and the influence of this work on modern political thought; Athenian ideas and practices related to political freedom, national security, and justice; how the maturing democratic institutions in Greece resulted in greater restrictions on the rights and freedoms of women)

Codes (right side of page):   BD = Benchmark, Declarative; BP = Benchmark, Procedural; BC = Benchmark, Contextual

1st letter of each code in parentheses	*2nd letter of code*	*Number*
B = NCHS: basic edition	E = Explicitly stated in document	Page number of cited document
W = NCHS: World History, expanded ed.	I = Implied in document	
L = Lessons from History		
C = Core material	*Symbol*	
R = Related material	■ material appears only in NCHS basic edition	
	▸ material appears only in NCHS expanded edition	
	● material appears in both NCHS editions	

- Knows significant Greek writings, literature, and mythology (e.g., the prominent ideas of Greek philosophers; the significance and major works of Greek historians; ▸ significant Greek tragedies and comedies, and the values and lessons they transmitted; aspects of daily life in Greece between 600 and 200 BCE as they are represented by playwrights of the time)
  BD (BE,150;R;WE,80-81;LE,216,218;LI,216)

- Understands the major events and the significance of the Persian Wars (e.g., ▸ the long-term effects of the Persian Wars upon Greece, how the internal political and military structure of the two antagonists in the Persian Wars dictated their strategies, how the Greek city-states were able to defeat the "monolithic" Persian armies and navies, Herodotus' version of the key events of the Persian Wars and how reliable this account might be)
  BD (BE,150;R;WE,83)

- Understands Persian religious beliefs (e.g., the basic teachings of Zoroastrianism; ▸ the relationship between religion and politics in Persian society and the place of Zoroastrianism within the various levels of Persian society)
  BD (BE,150;R;WE,82-83)

- Understands how conquest influenced cultural life during the Hellenistic era (e.g., the cultural diffusion of Greek, Egyptian, Persian, and Indian art and architecture through assimilation, conquest, migration, and trade; ▸ the benefits and costs of Alexander's conquests on numerous cultures, and the extent to which these conquests brought about cultural mixing and exchange)
  BD (BE,150;C;WE,84,85;LI,221)

- Understands the characteristics of religion, gender, and philosophy in the Hellenistic era (e.g., the significance of the interaction of Greek and Jewish traditions for the emergence of Rabbinic Judaism and early Christianity; ▸ the changes in the status of women during the Hellenistic era, their new opportunities, and greater restrictions; what different Greek philosophers considered to be a "good life")
  BD (BE,150;C;WE,84,85;LI,221)

- ▸ Understands how Sumerian, Egyptian, and Greek societies saw themselves in relation to their gods and how attitudes towards women are indicated in representations of their goddesses
  BD (R;WE,81)

Codes (right side of page):   BD = Benchmark, Declarative; BP = Benchmark, Procedural; BC = Benchmark, Contextual

1st letter of each code in parentheses	*2nd letter of code*	*Number*
B = NCHS: basic edition	E = Explicitly stated in document	Page number of cited document
W = NCHS: World History, expanded ed.	I = Implied in document	
L = Lessons from History		
C = Core material	*Symbol*	
R = Related material	■ material appears only in NCHS basic edition	
	▸ material appears only in NCHS expanded edition	
	● material appears in both NCHS editions	

McREL

(BE,151;WE,86)

9. Understands how major religious and large-scale empires arose in the Mediterranean Basin, China, and India from 500 BCE to 300 CE

Level II (Grades 5-6)

BD (BE,151;C;WE,86,88;LE,218,219;LI,220)
- Understands the origins and social framework of Roman society (e.g., the geographic location of different ethnic groups on the Italian peninsula in the late 6th century BCE and their influences on early Roman society and culture, ▸ how legends of the founding of Rome describe ancient Rome and reflect the beliefs and values of its citizens, what life was like for the common people living in Rome and Pompeii)

BD (BE,151;C;WE,86;LE,219)
- Understands shifts in the political and social framework of Roman society (e.g., political and social institutions of the Roman Republic and reasons for its transformation from Republic to Empire; ▸ how values changed from the early Republic to the last years of the Empire as reflected through the lives of such Romans as Cincinnatus, Scipio Africanus, Tiberius Gracchus, Cicero, Julius Caesar, Augustus, Nero, Marcus Aurelius, and Constantine)

BD (BE,151;C;WE,88)
- Understands the significance of Jesus of Nazareth (e.g., the story of the life of Jesus, the messages of Jesus' prominent parables)

BD (BE,151;C;WE,88;LE,221)
- Understands events in the rise of Christianity (e.g., the life of Paul the Apostle and his contribution to the spread of Christian beliefs, how Christianity spread widely in the Roman Empire, ▸ how the New Testament illustrates early Christian beliefs)

BD (BE,152;C;WE,90;LE,225)
- Understands the fundamental elements of Chinese society under the early imperial dynasties (e.g., policies and achievements of the Qin emperor Shi Huangdi, the life of Confucius and the fundamentals of Confucianism and Daoism, ▸ what life was like for ordinary people in ancient China as illustrated in Chinese folktales)

BD (BE,152;C;WE,90;LE,222)
- Understands the commercial and cultural significance of the trans-Eurasian "silk roads" to the Roman and Chinese Empires and the peoples of Central Asia

BD (BE,152;C;WE,92;LE,223,224)
- Understands the origins of Buddhism and fundamental Buddhist beliefs (e.g., the life story of Buddha and his essential teachings; how the Buddhist teachings were a response to the

---

Codes (right side of page):   BD = Benchmark, Declarative; BP = Benchmark, Procedural; BC = Benchmark, Contextual

1st letter of each code in parentheses	*2nd letter of code*	*Number*
B = NCHS: basic edition	E = Explicitly stated in document	Page number of cited document
W = NCHS: World History, expanded ed.	I = Implied in document	
L = Lessons from History		
C = Core material	*Symbol*	
R = Related material	■ material appears only in NCHS basic edition	
	▸ material appears only in NCHS expanded edition	
	● material appears in both NCHS editions	

Brahmanic system; the contributions of the emperor Ashoka to the expansion of Buddhism in India; ▸ how Indian epic stories reflect social values, and how the Jakata tales reveal Buddhist teachings)

Level III (Grades 7-8)

- BD (BE,151;C;WE,86,87)
Understands the significant individuals and achievements of Roman society (e.g., the major legal, artistic, architectural, technological, and literary achievements of the Roman Republic; the influence of Hellenistic cultural traditions; ▸ the accomplishments of different, famous Roman citizens [Cincinnatus, the Gracchi, Cicero, Constantine, Nero, Marcus Aurelius)

- BD (BE,151;C;WE,87;LE,219,220)
Understands influences on the economic and political framework of Roman society (e.g., how Roman unity contributed to the growth of trade among lands of the Mediterranean basin; the importance of Roman commercial connections with Sub-Saharan Africa, India, and East Asia; ▸ the history of the Punic Wars and the consequences of the wars for Rome; the major phases of Roman expansion, including the Roman occupation of Britain)

- BD (BE,151,152;C;WE,91;LE,226;LI,225)
Understands fundamental social, political, and cultural characteristics of Chinese society under early imperial dynasties (e.g., the importance of the "Mandate of Heaven" to the success of the Zhou Dynasty and its development of imperial rule; the literary and artistic achievements of early imperial dynasties; the development and consequences of iron technology and the family division of labor system; ▸ comparisons between the Shang, Zhou, Quin, and Han Empires in areas they controlled and methods of government; the composition and stratification of Chinese society, and factors that gave individuals status; imperial attitudes and actions toward nomadic peoples along the borders of the kingdom)

- BD (BE,152;C;WE,92;LI,223)
Understands the major religious beliefs and social framework in India during the Gangetic states and the Mauryan Empire (e.g., the major beliefs and practices of Brahmanism in India; how Buddhism spread in India, Ceylon, and Central Asia; ▸ aspects of social structure of India during the Mauryan Empire; what advice the animal stories of the Panchantantra offer to people with little power, how this advice was used by Chandragupta; how the teachings of Shvetaketu from the Chandogya Upanishad compare to the Buddhist idea of nirvana)

- BD (C;WE,87)
▸ Understands the status and role of women in Roman society

Codes (right side of page): BD = Benchmark, Declarative; BP = Benchmark, Procedural; BC = Benchmark, Contextual
1st letter of each code in parentheses   *2nd letter of code*   *Number*
B = NCHS: basic edition   E = Explicitly stated in document   Page number of cited document
W = NCHS: World History, expanded ed.   I = Implied in document
L = Lessons from History
C = Core material   *Symbol*
R = Related material   ■ material appears only in NCHS basic edition
    ▸ material appears only in NCHS expanded edition
    ● material appears in both NCHS editions

217

McREL

BD (C;WE,88;LE,221)

►   Understands the influence of Christian beliefs on political, social, and cultural aspects of society (e.g., ► how Jesus' moral teachings utilized and expanded upon the prohibitions of the Ten Commandments in the Hebrew Torah, the locations of centers of the Christian church, the impact of Christianity upon the Roman Empire, the values and stories expressed in early Christian religious art)

Level IV (Grades 9-12)

BD (BE,151;C;WE,86,87;LE,219;LI,219)

●   Understands shifts in the political framework of Roman society (e.g., major phases in the empire's expansion through the 1st century CE; how imperial rule over a vast area transformed Roman society, economy, and culture; ► the causes and consequences of the transition from Republic to Empire under Augustus in Rome; how Rome governed its provinces from the late Republic to the Empire; how innovations in ancient military technology affected patterns of warfare and empire building)

BD (BE,151;C;WE,89;LI,221)

●   Understands the spread of Christianity and how it related to other belief systems (e.g., the extent and consequences of Christian expansion in Asia, Africa, and Europe to the 4th century; ► the events and circumstances, including the role of the martyr, that helped this expansion; comparisons between Jewish and Christian approaches to monotheism; the influence of other faiths upon the development of Christianity and those teachings that are distinctive to Christianity)

BD (BE,152;C;WE,91;LE,226;LI,225)

●   Understands the political and cultural characteristics of the Han Dynasty (e.g., the political and ideological contributions of the Han to the development of the imperial bureaucratic state and imperial expansion, ► how contemporaneous art reflects the history and philosophy of China through the end of the Han Dynasty)

BD (BE,152;C;WE,92-93;LE,223)

●   Understands how Buddhism and Brahmanism influenced one another and Indian society (e.g., how Brahmanism responded to challenges posed by Buddhism and other reform movements; ► how Buddha's reforms contributed to the spread of Buddhism within and beyond India, how the Upinshads reflected Brahmanic teachings and how these compared with Buddhist teachings)

BD (BE,152;C;WE,92)

●   Understands the growth of the Mauryan Empire in the context of rivalries among Indian states

---

▸ Understands the political, commercial, and cultural uses of Latin and Greek as universal languages of the Roman Empire $\qquad$ BD (C;WE,87)

▸ Understands the political legacy of Roman society (e.g., influences of the Roman Constitution on the modern U.S. political system) $\qquad$ BD (C;WE,87)

▸ Understands the role and status of women in the Confucian tradition $\qquad$ BD (C;WE,91;LI,225)

▸ Understands how art and literature reflect different aspects of Indian society (e.g., how literature such as the Ramayana can reflect the status and role of women in ancient cultures, how Indian art reflects a Persian or Greek influence) $\qquad$ BD (C;WE,93)

(BE,152;WE,94)

10.   Understands how early agrarian civilizations arose in Mesoamerica

Level II (Grades 5-6)

● Understands the major characteristics and contributions of Olmec civilization (e.g, how maize cultivation influenced the development of the Olmec civilization, the major contributions of Olmec civilization to Mesoamerican civilization, ▸ the achievements of Olmec civilization circa 1200 to 400 BCE, how geography influenced the development of Olmec civilization, the essential aspects of the Olmec civilization) $\qquad$ BD (BE,152,153;C;WE,94;LE,209;LI,209)

Level III (Grades 7-8)

● Understands methods used to study Olmec civilization (e.g., what archaeological evidence indicates about the development of Olmec civilization in the 2nd and 1st millennia BCE, ▸ clues about political and economic structure found in the monumental Olmec stone heads) $\qquad$ BD (BE,153;C;WE,95)

▸ Understands characteristics of Olmec agriculture (e.g., the social and environmental impacts, and the methods of Olmec agriculture; how farming in Mesoamerica differed from that of other agrarian societies in the ancient world) $\qquad$ BD (C;WE,95)

MREL

Level IV (Grades 9-12)

BD (BE,153;C;WE,95;LE,209;LI,209)

● Understands the framework of Olmec society and the influence of Olmec civilization on other civilizations (e.g., the cultural influence of the Olmec on the development of Zapotec and Mayan civilizations; ▸ the role of trade in the diffusion of this culture; the political, economic, and social structure of Olmec society and Olmec beliefs, and how this knowledge has been acquired in spite of undeciphered written records)

(BE,153)

11. Understands major global trends from 1000 BCE to 300 CE

Level II (Grades 5-6)

BD (BE,153;LE,219)

■ Knows the different forms of slavery or coerced labor in various empires (e.g., the Han empire, the Maurya empire, the Greek city-states, the Roman empire)

BD (BE,153;LI,212-214)

■ Understands how new religious or ethical systems contributed to cultural integration of large regions of Afro-Eurasia

Level III (Grades 7-8)

BD (BE,153;LI,211)

■ Understands the concept and importance of "classical civilizations" (e.g., the enduring importance of ideas, institutions, and art forms that emerged in the classical periods; the significance of Greek or Hellenistic ideas and cultural styles in the history of the Mediterranean basin, Europe, Southwest Asia, and India)

BD (BE,153;LE,211-213)

■ Understands the development of large regional empires (e.g., the significance of military power, state bureaucracy, legal codes, belief systems, written languages, and communications and trade networks; how trade networks, merchant communities, state power, tributary systems of production, and other factors contributed to the economic integration of large regions of Afro-Eurasia)

Codes (right side of page):   BD = Benchmark, Declarative; BP = Benchmark, Procedural; BC = Benchmark, Contextual

1st letter of each code in parentheses	*2nd letter of code*	*Number*
B = NCHS: basic edition	E = Explicitly stated in document	Page number of cited document
W = NCHS: World History, expanded ed.	I = Implied in document	
L = Lessons from History		
C = Core material	*Symbol*	
R = Related material	■ material appears only in NCHS basic edition	
	▸ material appears only in NCHS expanded edition	
	● material appears in both NCHS editions	

Level IV (Grades 9-12)

■ Knows the fundamentals of iron metallurgy and understands the economic, cultural, and political significance of iron technology in Eurasia and Africa
BD (BE,153;LI,212)

■ Understands patterns of social and cultural continuity in various societies (e.g., ways in which peoples maintained traditions and resisted external challenges in the context of increasing interregional contacts)
BD (BE,153)

(BE,156;WE,100)

12. **Understands the Imperial crises and their aftermath in various regions from 300 to 700 CE**

Level II (Grades 5-6)

● Understands possible reasons for the decline of the Roman and Han Empires (e.g., possible factors that motivated nomadic peoples to move into the Roman Empire and China, common patterns of decline and fall in the Roman and Han Empires, ▶ the chronological order of significant historical events for Rome from the late Empire through the reign of Justinian, how differences in architecture can illustrate unity and alienation between the Eastern and Western halves of the Roman Empire)
BD (BE,156;C;WE,100)

● Understands various characteristics of Christianity and Buddhism (e.g., methods used to spread the two religions to new areas and people; ▶ possible aspects of Christianity and Buddhism that appealed to people living between the 3rd and 5th centuries CE; the approximate geographical realms of Buddhism, Christianity, Hinduism, and Confucianism until the 5th century CE)
BD (BE,156;C;WE,102;LE,222,223;LI,224)

● Understands fundamental Hindu beliefs (e.g., ▶ how the concept of dharma reflects a social value for the ideal king, husband and wife, brother and friend; the concepts of Brahma, dharma, and karma, the caste system, ritual sacrifice, and reincarnation)
BD (BE,156;C;WE,104)

● Understands significant religious and cultural features of the Gupta era (e.g., Gupta achievements in art, literature, and mathematics; ▶ the relationship among various religions
BD (BE,157;C;WE,104;LE,224;LI,224)

---

in India during Gupta times)

- Understands the influence of Hinduism and Buddhism in East and Southeast Asia (e.g., the role of trade in spreading these religions; ▸ the geographical limits of Hindu and Buddhist influence; the presence and influence of Hinduism and Buddhism in India, Malaysia, and Southeast Asia; how ocean currents affected cultural contact between India and Southeast Asia, and the evidence for this contact)

  BD (BE,157;R;WE,106)

Level III (Grades 7-8)

- Understands political events that may have contributed to the decline of the Roman and Han Empires (e.g., the consequences of nomadic military movements in China and the western part of the Roman Empire; ▸ the nomadic invasions of the Roman Empire as described in the accounts of Orosius, Ammianus Marcellinus, Priscus, and secondary sources; significant battles, internal divisions, political changes, and invasions between the 3rd and 7th centuries CE that led to the fall of the Roman and Han Empires; the relative strengths and weaknesses of the Roman, Byzantine, and Han Empires)

  BD (BE,156;C;WE,101;LI,220)

- Understands how the spread of Buddhism and Christianity influenced different regions (e.g., the spread of the two religions in the context of change and crisis in the Roman and Han empires; the importance of monasticism in the growth of Christianity and Buddhism and the participation of men and women in monastic life and missionary activity; ▸ the importance of universal salvation to the early history of these two religions; the locations of new centers of Buddhism and Christianity and the major routes used to spread the faith beyond these centers; the efforts and successes of Ashoka and Constantine to legitimize Buddhism and Christianity and spread them throughout India and Europe respectively)

  BD (BE,156;C;WE,102)

- Understands political events that shaped the Gupta Empire (e.g., factors that contributed to the Gupta Empire's stability and economic prosperity, how Hinduism prevailed as the dominant faith in India, ▸ possible reasons for the alliance of the Gupta Empire with Brahmanism and the fall of the Mauryan-Buddhist power, how and why Guptan kings promoted Hinduism while simultaneously fostering Buddhist culture and integrating marginal groups into the political system)

  BD (BE,156-157;C;WE,105)

- Understands the basis of social relationships in India during the Gupta era (e.g., the social

  BD (BE,157;C;WE,104,105)

Codes (right side of page):	BD = Benchmark, Declarative; BP = Benchmark, Procedural; BC = Benchmark, Contextual	
1st letter of each code in parentheses	*2nd letter of code*	*Number*
B = NCHS: basic edition	E = Explicitly stated in document	Page number of cited document
W = NCHS: World History, expanded ed.	I = Implied in document	
L = Lessons from History		
C = Core material	*Symbol*	
R = Related material	▪ material appears only in NCHS basic edition	
	▸ material appears only in NCHS expanded edition	
	● material appears in both NCHS editions	

222

MREL

and legal position of women and men, ▸ restrictions upon women and their place within the caste system, different social perspectives on the advantages and disadvantages of the caste system)

- Understands how the spread of trade and religion influenced Southeast Asia and Polynesian areas (e.g., the impact of Indian civilization on state-building in mainland Southeast Asia and the Indonesian archipelago, the nature of monumental religious architecture as evidence for the spread of Buddhist and Hindu belief and practice in Southeast Asia, ▸ the function of Hindu and Buddhist clerics in the spread of their religions and trade to Southeast Asia and Malayo- Polynesia by the end of the 1st millennium BCE, the locations and geographic challenges of potential and actual trade routes in the Southeast Asian and Polynesian areas)

BD (BE,157;R;WE,106,107)

BD (C;WE,103)

▸ Understands the changing status of women in early Christian and Buddhist societies

BD (C;WE,105;LE,224)

▸ Understands major achievements in technology, astronomy, and medicine in the Gupta period

Level IV (Grades 9-12)

BD (BE,156;C;WE,101)

- Understands political and social elements during the decline of the Roman and Han Empires and the rise of the Byzantine Empire (e.g., the strengths and weaknesses of the Eastern and Western Roman Empires and the factors that enabled the Byzantine Empire to continue as Rome fell; how Constantine selectively supported aspects of Western rule with Eastern institutions to create a new, independent, Byzantine state in the 4th century CE; ▸ the links between military, social, and economic causes for the decline in the Han and Roman Empires; the impact of barbarian movements on the regions of Europe, China, and India by the end of the 7th century CE; the life of Germanic peoples and society including the status and role of women)

BD (BE,157;C;WE,105,108;LE,224;LI,224)

- Understands the significant social, political, and cultural characteristics of Gupta society (e.g., the Gupta decline and the importance of Hun invasions in the empire's disintegration; ▸ the Gupta golden age under Chandragupta II; centers of learning in India in the 4th and 5th centuries CE, and the role of Buddhist monks in education and higher learning; types of evidence available for understanding Gupta India; the route of the Hun invasion of India, and the revival of the golden age of the Guptas)

Codes (right side of page):   BD = Benchmark, Declarative; BP = Benchmark, Procedural; BC = Benchmark, Contextual

1st letter of each code in parentheses	*2nd letter of code*	*Number*
B = NCHS: basic edition	E = Explicitly stated in document	Page number of cited document
W = NCHS: World History, expanded ed.	I = Implied in document	
L = Lessons from History		
C = Core material	*Symbol*	
R = Related material	■ material appears only in NCHS basic edition	
	▸ material appears only in NCHS expanded edition	
	● material appears in both NCHS editions	

BD (BE,157;R;WE,107)

●   Understands Indian contributions to Southeast Asia (e.g., the adaptation of Buddhist-Hindu culture in Southeast Asia , ▸ how art and architecture revealed the spread of Indian influence in Southeast Asia, the Indian concept of ideal kingship and its introduction and spread throughout the emerging states of Southeast Asia)

BD (C;WE,103)

▸   Understands how the spread of different religions influenced political and social conditions in various regions (e.g., the spread of religious Daoism and Buddhism in China; possible causal relationships between the spread of Christianity and Buddhism, and the expansion of international trade; royal patronage of religion and the desires of a growing middle class for "peace" to enable commercial expansion)

BD (C;WE,103)

▸   Understands shifts in the status of women from pagan Roman society to Christian society (e.g., the shifting importance of social class, marital status)

BD (C;WE,105)

▸   Understands the resurgence of Hinduism in India and its spread to South India (e.g., as reflected in the growth of temple towns and the development of South Indian temple architecture such as the temple of Maduri)

BD (R;WE,107)

▸   Understands the significance of Pandyas and Pallavas (e.g., the history of Pandyas and Pallavas in South India; trade relationships with West Asia, Greece, Rome, and Southeast Asia; how Pallavas helped spread Hindu and Buddhist thought to Southeast Asia)

(BE,157;WE,108)

13.   Understands the causes and consequences of the development of Islamic civilization between the 7th and 10th centuries

Level II (Grades 5-6)

BD (BE,157;C;WE,108;LE,233,234)

●   Understands the spread of Islam in Southwest Asia and the Mediterranean region (e.g., the life of Muhammad, his devotion to God, and the basic beliefs and values he preached; how Islam spread in Southwest Asia and the Mediterranean and evidence for its influence; ▸ the importance to Islam of the Hegira [Hirjah], the Ka'abah, the Qur'an, the Sunnah, the Hajj, the daily prayer [Salat], the poor due [Zakat] and Ramadan)

Codes (right side of page):   BD = Benchmark, Declarative; BP = Benchmark, Procedural; BC = Benchmark, Contextual

1st letter of each code in parentheses	*2nd letter of code*	*Number*
B = NCHS: basic edition	E = Explicitly stated in document	Page number of cited document
W = NCHS: World History, expanded ed.	I = Implied in document	
L = Lessons from History		
C = Core material	*Symbol*	
R = Related material	■ material appears only in NCHS basic edition	
	▸ material appears only in NCHS expanded edition	
	● material appears in both NCHS editions	

- BD (BE,158;C;WE,110;LE,234)
  Understands the influence of Islamic ideas and practices on other cultures and social behavior (e.g., the origin and development of Islamic law; the influence of Islamic law and Muslim practice on family life, morals, marriage, inheritance, and slavery; the possible appeal of Islam to culturally diverse non-Muslims across Afro-Eurasia in the Abbasid era)

- BD (BE,158;R;WE,112)
  Understands how the Byzantine state withstood attacks between the 8th and 10th centuries (e.g., ▸ military technology and the successful defense of Byzantium against Arab Muslim attacks)

- BD (C;WE,108)
  Understands the effect of geography on different groups and their trade practices (e.g., nomads, town-dwellers, trade practices on the Arabian peninsula; the goods traded and the origins of these goods)

- BD (C;WE,110;LE,235)
  Understands the significance of Baghdad (e.g., the trade network and goods traded, its role as a center of commerce in the 8th to 10th centuries CE)

- BD (C;WE,110)
  Understands the impact of the invention of paper on various cultures (e.g., Chinese, Muslim, later European culture) and its route from its source through Muslim lands to Europe)

Level III (Grades 7-8)

- BD (BE,157-158;C;WE,108,109;LE,234;LI,234)
  Understands how the Muslims spread Islamic beliefs and established their empire (e.g., how Muslim forces overthrew the Byzantines in Syria and Egypt and the Sassanids in Persia and Iraq; Arab Muslim success in founding an empire stretching from Western Europe to India and China; the diverse religious, cultural, and geographic factors that influenced the ability of the Muslim government to rule; ▸ how Islam attracted new converts)

- BD (BE,158;C;WE,110)
  Understands significant aspects of Islamic civilization (e.g., the emergence of Islamic civilization in Iberia and its economic and cultural achievements, ▸ how family life and gender relations were prescribed in Islamic society)

- BD (BE,158;C;WE,110;LE,236)
  Understands significant aspects of Abbasid culture (e.g., sources of Abbasid wealth and the economic and political importance of various forms of slavery; why the Abbasid state became a center of Afro-Eurasian commercial exchange; how the Abbasids promoted and preserved Greek learning and contributed to science, mathematics, and medicine; ▸ the

---

Codes (right side of page):	BD = Benchmark, Declarative; BP = Benchmark, Procedural; BC = Benchmark, Contextual	
1st letter of each code in parentheses	*2nd letter of code*	*Number*
B = NCHS: basic edition	E = Explicitly stated in document	Page number of cited document
W = NCHS: World History, expanded ed.	I = Implied in document	
L = Lessons from History		
C = Core material	*Symbol*	
R = Related material	■ material appears only in NCHS basic edition	
	▸ material appears only in NCHS expanded edition	
	● material appears in both NCHS editions	

contributions of specific individuals to the Abbasid advancement of scientific knowledge)

- Understands how the Byzantine Empire defended itself against various invaders (e.g., ▸ variations in maritime technology and ship design in the 9th century and the role of the navy in Byzantine defense against Arab Muslim attacks; weapons, fortification, and military preparedness of the Byzantine Empire and explanations for its successful defense against Bulgar and Arab invaders) BD (BE,158;R;WE,112)

- Understands the Byzantine role in preserving and transmitting ancient Greek learning BD (BE,158;R;WE,112)

Level IV (Grades 9-12)

- Understands the political, social, and religious problems confronting the Byzantine and Sassanid Persian Empires in the 7th century and the commercial role of Arabia in the Southwest Asian economy BD (BE,157;C;WE,109)

- Understands challenges to Muslim civilization (e.g., the transformation of the Arab Caliphate into a Southwest Asian and Mediterranean Empire under the Umyyad Dynasty, and why the Muslim community divided into Sunni and Shi'ite factions; ▸ the significance of the Battle of Tours of 733 as interpreted by Muslim and Christian sources and changing historiographical views of the event) BD (BE,158;C;WE,109)

- Understands the strengths and weaknesses of the Abbasid, Byzantine, and Sassanid Persian governments and military institutions BD (BE,157;C;WE,111)

- Understands the social structure of the Abbasid Empire (e.g., the treatment and legal status of non-Muslims and their cultural and social contributions to society; ▸ the lives of prominent women and factors that facilitated and mitigated their rise to prominence; the role and status of royal bureaucrats, landowning nobles, peasants, urban artisans, and slaves; what Islamic conversion and adherence meant for social status) BD (BE,157;C;WE,111;LE,235)

- Understands political and economic systems of the Byzantine state (e.g., Byzantium's imperial political system compared to that of the Abbasid state; ▸ understands patterns of economic, political, and military power in the manufacturing and trading centers of Constantinople and Baghdad) BD (BE,158;R;WE,112)

Codes (right side of page):   BD = Benchmark, Declarative; BP = Benchmark, Procedural; BC = Benchmark, Contextual

1st letter of each code in parentheses	*2nd letter of code*	*Number*
B = NCHS: basic edition	E = Explicitly stated in document	Page number of cited document
W = NCHS: World History, expanded ed.	I = Implied in document	
L = Lessons from History		
C = Core material	*Symbol*	
R = Related material	■ material appears only in NCHS basic edition	
	▸ material appears only in NCHS expanded edition	
	● material appears in both NCHS editions	

- Understands how the spread of Greek Orthodox Christianity affected different regions (e.g., the patterns of the spread of Greek Orthodox Christianity into the Balkans, Ukraine, and Russia between the 9th and 11th centuries; ▸ explanations for the preference of Greek over Latin Christianity in the Slavic world; the story of Vladimir of Kiev in the Russian Chronicle, and the nature of the church/state relationship in Kievan Russia) _{BD (BE,159;R;WE,113)}

▸ Understands significant social and cultural changes in Islamic civilization between the 7th and 10th centuries (e.g., the changing position of women in the new Islam, how Muslim mosque architecture physically reflects the relationship between people, spiritual leaders, and God in Islam; the process through which Arabic became a common language in the early Islamic centuries; what branches of. scholarship developed out of the efforts of Muslim leaders and scholars to record the Qur'an and Hadith) _{BD (C;WE,109;LE,234,235)}

▸ Understands possible motivations behind the Byzantine preservation of ancient Greek and Hellenistic scholastic works _{BD (R;WE,112)}

_(BE,159;WE,114)

14. Understands major developments in East Asia and Southeast Asia in the era of the Tang Dynasty from 600 to 900 CE

Level II (Grades 5-6)

- Understands geographic and political features of Tang China (e.g., the imperial conquests of the empire in Southeast and Central Asia; the locations of major cities in Tang China and their attraction for diverse people of differing religions; ▸ major geographical features of the area incorporated by the Tang Dynasty, the location of the network of canals, and how the Great Canal changed life in China; features of government and administration of Tang China) _{BD (BE,159;C;WE,114;LE,243)}

- Understands characteristics of Japanese society through the imperial period (e.g., aspects of the indigenous development of Japanese society until the 7th century CE; the establishment of the imperial state in Japan and the role of the emperor in government; the political, social, and cultural role of women and their contributions to the court of Heian; ▸ how the geography of Japan affected its development and its relations with China and Korea) _{BD (BE,159;R;WE,116;LI,244)}

BD (BE,160;R;WE,117)

- Understands the importance of the commercial state of Srivijava and the Straits of Malacca in Southeast Asia as a trade link between India and China (e.g., ▸ how the monsoon winds and geography of the strait contributed to Srivijava's wealth and power)

Level III (Grades 7-8)

BD (BE,159,160;R;WE,117)

- Understands China's influence on other cultures (e.g., relations with pastoral peoples of Inner Asia in the Tang period and long-term patterns of interaction along China's grassland frontier; how Korea assimilated Chinese ideas and institutions yet preserved its political independence; China's colonization of Vietnam and the effects of Chinese rule on Vietnamese society, including resistance to Chinese domination)

BD (BE,159;C;WE,114)

- Understands how Buddhism was introduced from Tang China to Korea and Japan (e.g., ▸ why the Korean emperor encouraged Japan to adopt this religion)

BD (BE,159;C;WE,114,115;LE,243)

- Understands the culture and technological achievements of Tang China (e.g., the ideals and values of everyday life expressed in the poetry, landscape, painting, and pottery of the Tang Dynasty; ▸ the system of roads and canals in Tang China; the extent of the Tang Empire, the trade routes used by the empire, and the products exchanged; major technologies developed under the Tang Dynasty, how these technologies influenced Tang society and spread to other regions)

BD (BE,159;R;WE,116,117;LE,244)

- Understands events that shaped Japanese culture (e.g., the influence of Chinese culture on Japanese society from the 7th to the 11th century; ▸ use of Chinese as the lingua franca in East Asia in the late 1st millennium; major contributions and developments of early cultures of Japan from 10,000 B.C.E. to circa 200 CE; the influence of Buddhism on Japan between the 8th and 9th centuries, how it changed Japanese society, and reasons for its restriction by the emperor in Heian)

BD (R;WE,116,117)

▸ Understands basic beliefs in Japanese culture (e.g., the legends of creation of Japan and what these legends reveal about Japanese history, the basic beliefs of Shinto and how art and literature reflect Shinto's impact, courtly life and ideals in Heian)

Codes (right side of page):   BD = Benchmark, Declarative; BP = Benchmark, Procedural; BC = Benchmark, Contextual

1st letter of each code in parentheses	*2nd letter of code*	*Number*
B = NCHS: basic edition	E = Explicitly stated in document	Page number of cited document
W = NCHS: World History, expanded ed.	I = Implied in document	
L = Lessons from History		
C = Core material	*Symbol*	
R = Related material	■ material appears only in NCHS basic edition	
	▸ material appears only in NCHS expanded edition	
	● material appears in both NCHS editions	

Level IV (Grades 9-12)

BD (BE,159;C;WE,115)

● Understands social and political characteristics of the reunification of China (e.g., the process of political centralization and economic reforms that marked China's reunification under the Sui and Tang dynasties, ▸ the roles of women and family)

BD (C;WE,115)

▸ Understands features of cultural life in various regions of China (e.g., differences between the lifestyles and living conditions in rural areas and urban communities during the Tang Dynasty, and how urban centers influenced growth in the arts; the significance of Chinese popular culture from the Tang Dynasty onward; the place of poetry and painting in the lives of scholar-officials in China, the values of the Chinese elite, and attitudes of poets toward the common people)

BD (R;WE,117)

▸ Understands the influence of Chinese culture on different countries (e.g., the political and cultural influence of Tang China in East Asian countries such as Korea, Vietnam, and Japan; the uniqueness of the Chinese writing system and how Japan adapted this system to fit the spoken language of Japan)

BD (R;WE,117;LE,245)

▸ Understands the importance of women as authors at the Japanese court of the Heian period (e.g., the courtly roles and values reflected in works by female authors, such as the *Diary of Muraski Shikibu* and *The Pillow Book* by Sei Shonagon)

(BE,159;WE,118)

15. Understands the political, social, and cultural redefinitions in Europe from 500 to 1000 CE

Level II (Grades 5-6)

BD (BE,160;C;WE,118;LI,242)

● Understands the influence of the monastery in European development (e.g., the importance of monasteries, convents, and missionaries from Britain and Ireland in the Christianizing of Western and Central Europe; ▸ the individual duties of monks and nuns)

BD (BE,160;C;WE,118;LI,240)

● Understands the development of the Merovingian and Carolingian states (e.g., their success at maintaining public order and local defense in western Europe)

● Understands the significance of Norse migrations and invasions (e.g., how Norse explorations stimulated the emergence of independent lords and the knightly class; ► locations of Norse settlements, including routes to North America, Russia, Western Europe, and the Black Sea)

BD (BE,160;R;WE,120)

► Understands the significance of Charlemagne (e.g., his government, laws, conquests, personal values)

BD (C;WE,118;LI,240)

► Knows the life story and major achievements of King Alfred of England, and understands how he earned the title "Alfred the Great"

BD (R;WE,120)

Level III (Grades 7-8)

■ Understands the importance of monasteries and convents as centers of political power, economic productivity, and communal life

BD (BE,160;LI,242)

● Understands the influence of the Carolingian Empire on the development of European civilization (e.g., how Charlemagne's royal court, monasteries, and convents preserved Greco-Roman and early Christian learning and contributed to the emergence of European civilization; changing political relations between the papacy and the secular rulers of Europe; ► extent and causes of the Carolingian influence in Europe and reasons for its decline; how the Rules of St. Benedict shaped Medieval Europe; how secular leaders such as Charlemagne influenced political order within Europe)

BD (BE,160;C;WE,118-119;LE,242;LI,240)

● Understands social class and gender roles in Medieval Europe (e.g., changes in the legal, social, and economic status of peasants in the 9th and 10th centuries; ► how the political fragmentation of Europe after Charlemagne affected their lives; the responsibilities of women with different social status)

BD (BE,160;R;WE,120;LE,241,242)

► Understands the significance of Clovis (e.g., the major conquests of Clovis, how his conversion to Christianity was influenced by his wife, Clothilde; how his conversion affected the Frankish and Saxon peoples)

BD (C;WE,119)

► Understands the role of Norse peoples in the development of Europe (e.g., Nordic contributions to long-distance trade and exploration, the failure of Norse settlements in

BD (R;WE,120)

Codes (right side of page):	BD = Benchmark, Declarative; BP = Benchmark, Procedural; BC = Benchmark, Contextual	
1st letter of each code in parentheses	*2nd letter of code*	*Number*
B = NCHS: basic edition	E = Explicitly stated in document	Page number of cited document
W = NCHS: World History, expanded ed.	I = Implied in document	
L = Lessons from History		
C = Core material	*Symbol*	
R = Related material	■ material appears only in NCHS basic edition	
	► material appears only in NCHS expanded edition	
	● material appears in both NCHS editions	

Newfoundland and Greenland)

Level IV (Grades 9-12)

- Understands significant religious events that shaped medieval society (e.g., the successes of ^BD (BE,160;C;WE,119)^ the Latin Catholic and Byzantine churches in introducing Christianity and Christian culture to Eastern Europe; ▸ similarities and differences in governance and worship in the Latin Catholic and Byzantine churches; how the Anglo-Saxon Boniface was an exemplar for other missionaries, and how he represented the "romanization of Europe")

- Understands shifts in political power during 9th and 10th century Europe (e.g., how royal officials such as counts and dukes transformed delegated powers into hereditary, autonomous power over land and people)

- Understands the significance of different empires in Europe (e.g., the size, wealth, and political organization of Charlemagne's empire compared to Byzantium, the Abbasid empire, and the Islamic caliphate of Iberia; the extent of the Frankish Empire under Clovis, the eventual division of imperial territory among his four sons, and the consequences of this division)

- Understands central and peripheral reasons for the failure of the Carolingian Empire to endure after the death of Charlemagne (e.g., the independent power of nobles; the advantage of the Magyar cavalry and Viking longboat)

(BE,161;WE,122)

16. Understands the development of agricultural societies and new states in tropical Africa and Oceania

Level II (Grades 5-6)

- Knows the routes by which migrants settled the Pacific Islands and New Zealand and the navigational techniques they used on long distance voyages

---

Codes (right side of page):   BD = Benchmark, Declarative; BP = Benchmark, Procedural; BC = Benchmark, Contextual
1st letter of each code in parentheses   *2nd letter of code*   *Number*
B = NCHS: basic edition   E = Explicitly stated in document   Page number of cited document
W = NCHS: World History, expanded ed.   I = Implied in document
L = Lessons from History
C = Core material   *Symbol*
R = Related material   ■ material appears only in NCHS basic edition
       ▸ material appears only in NCHS expanded edition
       ● material appears in both NCHS editions

Level III (Grades 7-8)

BD (BE,161;C;WE,122,123;LE,246,247)
- Understands influences on state-building in West Africa (e.g., how the natural environments of West Africa defined agricultural production, and the importance of the Niger River in promoting agriculture, commerce, and state-building; the growth of the Ghana empire; how Islam, labor specialization, regional commerce and the trans-Saharan camel trade promoted urbanization in West Africa; ▸ the governing system of the royal court in Ghana, and how the effectiveness of imperial efforts was aided by a belief in the king's divinity)

BD (BE,161;R;WE,106)
- Understands the establishment of agricultural societies on the Pacific Islands and New Zealand (e.g., the plants and animals that early migrants carried with them; ▸ how these "introductions" affected the existing island flora and fauna; possible links between the cultures of Southeast Asia, the Pacific Islands, and New Zealand)

BD (C;WE,122,123)
▸ Understands the role of oral history in understanding West African history (e.g., the griot "keeper of tales" and other sources used to understand history)

Level IV (Grades 9-12)

BD (BE,161)
■ Understands the origins and development of societies in Oceania (e.g., theories using linguistic, biological, and cultural evidence to explain migration patterns to the Pacific Islands and New Zealand; how complex social structures, religions, and states developed in Oceania)

BD (BE,161;C;WE,123)
- Understands economic, social, and religious influences on Ghana society (e.g., what archaeological evidence indicates about the development of Jenn,-jeno and Kumbi-Saleh into important early commercial cities; ▸ the agriculture, trade, standard of living, expansionary tendencies and role of religious ideas in Ghana)

BD (BE,161;C;WE,122,123;LE,246,247)
- Understands settlement patterns in different regions of Africa (e.g., causes and consequences of the settling of East, Central, and Southern Africa by Bantu-speaking farmers and cattle herders until 1000 CE)

Codes (right side of page):   BD = Benchmark, Declarative; BP = Benchmark, Procedural; BC = Benchmark, Contextual
1st letter of each code in parentheses   *2nd letter of code*   *Number*
B = NCHS: basic edition   E = Explicitly stated in document   Page number of cited document
W = NCHS: World History, expanded ed.   I = Implied in document
L = Lessons from History
C = Core material   *Symbol*
R = Related material   ■ material appears only in NCHS basic edition
                                             ▸ material appears only in NCHS expanded edition
                                             ● material appears in both NCHS editions

(BE,162;WE,124)

17. Understands the rise of centers of civilization in Mesoamerica and Andean South America in the 1st millennium CE

Level II (Grades 5-6)

BD (BE,162;C;WE,124)
- Understands the significant features of Mayan civilization (e.g., locations of Mayan city-states, road systems, and sea routes in Mesoamerica and the influence of the environment on these developments; the role and status of elite women and men in Mayan society as indicated by their portrayal in Mayan monumental architecture; ▸ the importance of religion in Mayan society; the structure and purpose of Mayan pyramids; ceremonial games among the Mayans)

BD (BE,162;R;WE,126)
- Understands different farming methods of Teotihuacán and Moche civilization (e.g., agricultural methods, water utilization, and herding methods used by the Teotihuacán and Moche peoples, and how the natural environment of the Andes helped to influence these methods)

BD (R;WE,126)
▸ Understands methods used to study Zapotec, Teotihuacán, and Moche civilizations (e.g., locations of these communities and their major archaeological remains, what archaeological evidence such as clay pottery and figures reveal about Moche civilization, what remains of planned cities reveal about the structure of Zapotec and Teotihuacán civilization)

Level III (Grades 7-8)

BD (BE,162;C;WE,125;LI,249)
- Understands the economic and agricultural elements of Mayan society (e.g., the extent, importance, and composition of Mayan trade; the adaptability and importance of Mayan agricultural techniques and their connection to the rise of Mayan city-states)

BD (BE,162;C;WE,124,125)
- Understands social features of Mayan culture (e.g., differing views concerning the causes for the decline of Mayan civilization, ▸ ways that Mayan myths reflect social values and daily survival skills)

BD (BE,162;R;WE,126,127)
- Understands what art and architecture reveal about early Mesoamerica and Andean societies

---

(e.g., what art and architecture reflects about the character of the Zapotec state in the valley of Oaxaca; what art and artifacts indicate about the interests, occupations, and religious concerns of the Moche people; ▸ what murals infer about Mayan and Teotihuacán societies)

BD (R;WE,127)

▸ Understands social features of Andean societies (e.g., different agriculture practices in the Moche/Andean region; kinship groups, regulated family and community life in Andean societies)

Level IV (Grades 9-12)

BD (BE,162;C;WE,125;LI,249)

● Understands ways in which the Mayan world view and cultural life were portrayed (e.g., the Mayan cosmic world view and the role of Mayan deities as revealed in art and architecture, ▸ the descriptions of social and religious life inferred in Mayan [Bonampak] glyphs and murals, what the Popul Vuh tells about the Mayan world view and creation myth and its reliability as an account of the Mayan world view)

BD (BE,162;C;WE,125)

● Understands Mayan achievements in astronomy, mathematics, and the development of a calendar (e.g., ▸ the place of archaeological evidence such as the "Long Count" calendar in the interpretation of Mayan history, how achievements in astronomy affected Mayan society, the value of mathematical innovations and the calendar to farmers)

BD (BE,162;R;WE,127)

● Understands relationships between Mesoamerican and Andean societies (e.g., the growth of urban society centered on Teotihuacán and the importance of this city as a transmitter of Mesoamerican cultural traditions to later societies; ▸ comparisons between Mayan, Moche, and Teotihuacán religions and rituals; the basic structure, economy, and ritual of Andean societies such as the Moche, Tihuanaco, and Chimu; the basic construction and variations of Mesoamerican calendars; possible methods of contact between Mesoamerican and Andean societies and the cultural diffusion seen in areas such as agriculture, societal structure, and artisan crafts)

BD (C;WE,125;LI,249)

▸ Understands urban planning in Mayan culture (e.g., patterns and significance of architectural planning and city planning in Mayan culture and the religious factors that affected these layouts)

Codes (right side of page):   BD = Benchmark, Declarative; BP = Benchmark, Procedural; BC = Benchmark, Contextual

1st letter of each code in parentheses	*2nd letter of code*	*Number*
B = NCHS: basic edition	E = Explicitly stated in document	Page number of cited document
W = NCHS: World History, expanded ed.	I = Implied in document	
L = Lessons from History		
C = Core material	*Symbol*	
R = Related material	■ material appears only in NCHS basic edition	
	▸ material appears only in NCHS expanded edition	
	● material appears in both NCHS editions	

(BE,162)

18.   Understands major global trends from 300 to 1000 CE

Level II (Grades 5-6)

BD (BE,163;LE,228-229)
■   Understands major changes in the religious map of Eurasia and Africa between 300 and 1000 CE (e.g., the success of Christianity, Buddhism, Hinduism, and Islam in making converts among peoples of differing ethnic and cultural traditions)

BD (BE,163;LE,229-230)
■   Knows the maritime and overland trade routes linking regions of Afro-Eurasia and understands the importance of international trade for African and Eurasian societies

Level III (Grades 7-8)

BD (BE,162-163;LI,212,227)
■   Understands the factors that contributed to the weakening of empires in world history from 300 to 1000 CE (e.g., the migratory and military movements of pastoral nomadic peoples from Central Asia and the Arabian Peninsula and the consequences of these movements for empires and agrarian civilizations of Eurasia and Africa)

BD (BE,163;LE,229-230)
■   Understands the growth of economic and cultural exchanges among different regions from 300 to 1000 CE (e.g., the importance of Muslim civilization in mediating long-distance commercial, cultural, intellectual, and food crop exchange across Eurasia and parts of Africa; migrations of farming peoples to new regions of Europe, Sub-Saharan Africa, China, Oceania, and Mesoamerica; connections between new settlements and the development of towns, trade, and greater cultural complexity in these regions)

Codes (right side of page):   BD = Benchmark, Declarative; BP = Benchmark, Procedural; BC = Benchmark, Contextual

1st letter of each code in parentheses	*2nd letter of code*	*Number*
B = NCHS: basic edition	E = Explicitly stated in document	Page number of cited document
W = NCHS: World History, expanded ed.	I = Implied in document	
L = Lessons from History		
C = Core material	*Symbol*	
R = Related material	■ material appears only in NCHS basic edition	
	▸ material appears only in NCHS expanded edition	
	● material appears in both NCHS editions	

235

MREL

(BE,166;WE,132)

19. Understands the maturation of an interregional system of communication, trade, and cultural exchange during a period of Chinese economic power and Islamic expansion

Level II (Grades 5-6)

BD (BE,166;C;WE,132)
- Understands the impact of urbanization and commercial expansion on Chinese society between the 10th and 13th centuries (e.g., the effects of major technological and scientific inventions in the Song era on Chinese life, China's trade with Southeast Asia and the lands rimming the Indian Ocean, ▸how this trade affected China internally)

BD (BE,166;R;WE,134;LE,245)
- Understands different elements of Japanese feudal society (e.g., Japanese government during the Kamakura and Ashikaga periods, and whether it was feudalism; the rise of the warrior class in feudal Japan and the values it prescribed; how the economic and social status of women and peasants changed in feudal Japanese society; how art and aesthetic values were cherished in the warrior culture in Japan and what this art reveals about Japanese values; ▸ how the Japanese successfully defended themselves against Mongol invasions in the 13th century)

BD (BE,167;C;WE,136;LE,235)
- Understands the cultural characteristics of Islamic society (e.g., the importance of scientific, literary, and artistic contributions made by the Islamic civilization between the 11th and 13th centuries; ▸ how these contributions helped communication between different Islamic peoples; the diverse, multiethnic character of the Islamic state)

BD (BE,167;R;WE,138;LE,247;LI,247)
- Understands features of trade routes in Asia, Europe, and Africa (e.g., how goods traveled from East Asia to Europe and the importance of the Indian Ocean to the societies of Asia, East Africa, and Europe; the usefulness of the camel in desert transportation and trade)

Level III (Grades 7-8)

BD (BE,166;C;WE,133)
- Understands how Confucianism changed between the 10th and 13th centuries (e.g., the impact of major dynastic changes in China on Confucianism; ▸ the synthesis of Confucianism, Buddhism, and Daoism created by Zhu Xi to form neo-Confucianism)

Codes (right side of page):   BD = Benchmark, Declarative; BP = Benchmark, Procedural; BC = Benchmark, Contextual
1st letter of each code in parentheses   *2nd letter of code*   *Number*
B = NCHS: basic edition   E = Explicitly stated in document   Page number of cited document
W = NCHS: World History, expanded ed.   I = Implied in document
L = Lessons from History
C = Core material   *Symbol*
R = Related material   ■ material appears only in NCHS basic edition
                                            ▸ material appears only in NCHS expanded edition
                                            ● material appears in both NCHS editions

- BD (BE,166;C;WE,132,133)

  Understands the social and economic elements of Song China (e.g., how improved agricultural production and increased trade helped the growth of cities and the merchant class in Song China; ▸ the traditional social attitudes of China toward merchants and commercial activity; significant achievements and developments of the Song Dynasty, the rigors and class restrictions of the civil service examination in Song China)

- BD (BE,166;R;WE,133,134;LE,240,245)

  Understands government and politics of the Kamakura period (e.g., ▸ similarities and differences between feudalism in Japan and medieval Europe; significant political events in the history of the Kamakura period)

- BD (BE,166;R;WE,134,135;LI,245)

  Understands influences on the development of Buddhist sects in Japan (e.g., how unique forms of Buddhism [sects] developed under the influence of social, political, and religious forces; ▸ the impact of the warrior culture on the lives of common people and the development of Buddhist sects)

- BD (BE,166;R;WE,134)

  Understands the development of Southeast Asian states (e.g., how Champa, Angkor, and Dai Vet accumulated power and wealth; the influence of Confucianism, Buddhism, and Hinduism on these states)

- BD (BE,167;C;WE,136;LE,236)

  Understands the expansion of Islam and daily life in Islamic regions (e.g., how Turkic migration from Turkestan into Southwest Asia and India helped Islam expand and forced the retreat of Byzantium and Greek Christian civilization, ▸ what life in Egypt was like for Jewish and Christian communities, what student life was like in Islamic regions)

- BD (BE,167;R;WE,138;LI,248)

  Understands elements of trade in different regions (e.g., the importance of Cairo and other major cities as centers of international trade and culture; how the spread of Islam was connected to trade in Central Asia, East Africa, West Africa, the coasts of India, and Southeast Asia; ▸ the importance to individual societies of goods traded between Asia, Africa, and Europe; the consequences placed on maritime trade by the seasonal monsoon winds in the Indian Ocean; features and functions of caravansaries and khans in Central Asian and Middle Eastern cities; which ships were most successfully used for trade in the Indian Ocean and why)

Codes (right side of page): BD = Benchmark, Declarative; BP = Benchmark, Procedural; BC = Benchmark, Contextual

1st letter of each code in parentheses *2nd letter of code* *Number*

B = NCHS: basic edition E = Explicitly stated in document Page number of cited document

W = NCHS: World History, expanded ed. I = Implied in document

L = Lessons from History

C = Core material *Symbol*

R = Related material ■ material appears only in NCHS basic edition

▸ material appears only in NCHS expanded edition

● material appears in both NCHS editions

MREL

Level IV (Grades 9-12)

■ Understands the struggle for Vietnamese independence from China and the subsequent reconstruction of Vietnamese society and government
BD (BE,167)

● Understands religious, social, and political aspects of the Song Dynasty (e.g., the importance of women of gentry families in preserving and transmitting Chinese cultural values; ▸ Chinese advancements in alchemy, astronomy, and medicine; the values of Confucianism, Taoism, and Buddhism as reflected in Song art; changes in the social and moral status of women as reflected in the practice of foot binding; the attitudes of typical Chinese gentlemen toward women, family, servants, tenants, and social inferiors; the debate during the Song Dynasty about how the government should respond to rapid social and economic change)
BD (BE,166;C;WE,132,133)

● Understands how different religious movements influenced various cultures between the 11th and 13th centuries (e.g., the origins and growth of the North African Islamic reform movements; ▸ the impact of Christian campaigns of the Crusades on the societies and Muslim populations of Cairo, Damascus, and Sicily)
BD (BE,167;C;WE,137;LE,249;LI,237)

● Understands the significance of Sufism (e.g., the basic beliefs of Sufism and Sufism's role in the spread of Islam, ▸ how society and Sufi ideas are described and exemplified in Islamic literature, the roles and social position of Sufi orders in rural and urban areas)
BD (BE,167;C;WE,137;LI,236)

● Understands how interregional trade and communication affected Eurasia and Africa (e.g., ▸ how international trade encouraged the rise of city-states along the East African coast, and helped end the isolation of African societies below the Saharan desert; the impact of economic and commercial expansion of Song China on communication and trade in Eurasia)
BD (BE,167;R;WE,139;LI,248)

▸ Understands significant religious and economic aspects of Chinese society between the 10th and 13th centuries (e.g., the impact of economic growth on Chinese society and how it affected the gentry class; how Zhu Xi's basic ideas of Neo-Confucianism affected Chinese society, government, and education)
BD (C;WE,133)

▸ Understands different social classes and gender roles in Japanese society (e.g., the influence of Buddhist sects on the samurai class; the role of social class, area, time, and age in determining women's experiences)
BD (R;WE,135)

Codes (right side of page):   BD = Benchmark, Declarative; BP = Benchmark, Procedural; BC = Benchmark, Contextual

1st letter of each code in parentheses	*2nd letter of code*	*Number*
B = NCHS: basic edition	E = Explicitly stated in document	Page number of cited document
W = NCHS: World History, expanded ed.	I = Implied in document	
L = Lessons from History		
C = Core material	*Symbol*	
R = Related material	■ material appears only in NCHS basic edition	
	▸ material appears only in NCHS expanded edition	
	● material appears in both NCHS editions	

BD (R;WE,135;LI,246)

▸ Understands the significance of art and philosophy in Japanese and Cambodian society (e.g., philosophical values and traditions presented in Noh drama, how diverse Japanese art forms from the Kamakura and Ashikaga periods reflect Shinto and Buddhist philosophy, Indian and Southeast Asian influences on the architecture of the 12th-century temple of Angkor Wat in Cambodia, what art and literature reveal about the lives of people in Japan in the Kamakura and Ashikaga periods)

BD (R;WE,135)

▸ Understands how the wars with the Mongols influenced Japanese society (e.g., the defeat of the Mongols, the samurai revolt against the Kamakura shogunate and the negative economic impact of these conflicts)

BD (C;WE,136,137;LI,237)

▸ Understands cultural and political aspects of the Turkic Empires (e.g., the way of life of Turkic peoples such as the Seljuks, the origins and growth of the militaristic Seljuk and Ghazanavid Empires)

(BE,168;WE,140)

20.   Understands the redefinition of European society and culture from 1000 to 1300 CE

Level II (Grades 5-6)

BD (BE,168;LE,230-231)

■ Understands the significance of developments in medieval English legal and constitutional practice and their importance for modern democratic thought and institutions

BD (BE,168;C;WE,140,142;LI,241)

● Understands the systems of feudalism and manorialism (e.g., the principles of feudalism, manorialism, and serfdom, and their widespread use in parts of Europe in the 11th century; how population growth and agricultural expansion affected the legal, economic, and social position of peasant men and women; ▸ how the lives of peasants and serfs differed; how their lives were affected by the manors and castles)

BD (BE,168;C;WE,142;LE,241;LI,241)

● Understands the influence of Christianity in Medieval Europe (e.g., how successful the Christian states were in overthrowing Muslim powers in Central and Southern Iberia, the reasons for and consequences of the European Crusades against Syria and Palestine)

BD (BE,169;R;WE,144;LE,242)

● Understands the lives of different groups of people in Medieval Europe (e.g., life in Jewish

---

Codes (right side of page):   BD = Benchmark, Declarative; BP = Benchmark, Procedural; BC = Benchmark, Contextual

1st letter of each code in parentheses	*2nd letter of code*	*Number*
B = NCHS: basic edition	E = Explicitly stated in document	Page number of cited document
W = NCHS: World History, expanded ed.	I = Implied in document	
L = Lessons from History		
C = Core material	*Symbol*	
R = Related material	■ material appears only in NCHS basic edition	
	▸ material appears only in NCHS expanded edition	
	● material appears in both NCHS editions	

communities and what Jews added to the cultural and economic development of Europe; the influence of ideals of chivalry and courtly love on feudal society; ▸ how the status of women changed in medieval European life)

BD (BE,169;R;WE,144;LE,242)

● Understands the significance of the university in Medieval Europe (e.g., how universities contributed to literacy, learning, and scientific advancement; ▸ why universities were founded in certain parts of Europe; the meaning of the word "university")

BD (C;WE,140)

▸ Understands the significance of William the Conqueror in English society (e.g., why William invaded England; how he won control of England after the Battle of Hastings; what changes he made in governing England)

BD (R;WE,144)

▸ Understands aspects of the architecture of Medieval Europe (e.g., different architectural styles from this period; how some elements may still be seen in local, modern architecture)

Level III (Grades 7-8)

BD (BE,168;C;WE,140,141;LE,242;LI,240,242)

● Understands political events that shaped the development of European governments (e.g., how European monarchies expanded their power at the expense of feudal lords, and the growth and limitations of representative institutions in these monarchies; how the political relationship between the Roman Catholic Church and secular states changed from the Early Middle Ages to the High Middle Ages; ▸ the conflict that led to the Battle of Hastings; the political changes William initiated after his victory, and the long-term cultural and social changes in England following the Norman conquest)

BD (BE,168;C;WI,140,141;LI,240)

● Understands the importance of inheritance laws, arranged marriages, dowries, and family alliances for dynastic and aristocratic politics

BD (BE,168;C;WE,142)

● Understands the connection between agricultural technology and increased agricultural production and population growth in Europe between 1000 and 1300 CE

BD (BE,168;C;WE,143;LE,241)

● Understands Christian efforts for the Reconquest of Spain from Muslim powers

BD (BE,168;C;WE,142)

● Understands the consequences of German expansion into Poland and the Baltic region

---

Codes (right side of page):   BD = Benchmark, Declarative; BP = Benchmark, Procedural; BC = Benchmark, Contextual

1st letter of each code in parentheses	*2nd letter of code*	*Number*
B = NCHS: basic edition	E = Explicitly stated in document	Page number of cited document
W = NCHS: World History, expanded ed.	I = Implied in document	
L = Lessons from History		
C = Core material	*Symbol*	
R = Related material	■ material appears only in NCHS basic edition	
	▸ material appears only in NCHS expanded edition	
	● material appears in both NCHS editions	

240

MREL

- Understands art, architecture, and education in medieval Christian and Spanish Muslim society (e.g., how major works of art, architecture, and literature reflect values and attitudes of medieval Christian society; ▸ poetry of Muslim Spain and Christian Europe; the origins, organization, and studies of Christian universities in Europe, and the influence of Muslim scholarship and universities; how Gothic cathedrals reflect central aspects of European society) BD (BE,169;R;WE,144,145;LI,242)

- ▸ Understands the roles and motivations of squires, saints, and soldiers in Christian Europe (e.g., aspects of training, rights, and responsibilities required of young men from noble families wishing to become squires; the role played by saints in the spread of Christianity; why Muslim and Christian soldiers may have joined the Crusades) BD (C;WE,142,143)

Level IV (Grades 9-12)

- Understands the role of feudalism and manorialism in European society (e.g., ▸ how different feudal institutions assisted monarchies in centralizing power; how manorialism could be considered an economic system, and the rights, roles, and obligations of manorial inhabitants; the relative success of European monarchies at establishing security and political legitimacy for feudalism) BD (BE,168;C;WE,141)

- Understands the development of English government and its legal and political system (e.g., ▸ the Magna Carta and its tenets of the rule of the law and constitutional liberties; the structural differences, powers of, and participants in the representative governmental bodies of the English Parliament and French Estates-General) BD (BE,168;C;WE,141;LE,240)

- Understands the rise of the city-state in Italy and northern Europe (e.g., how city-states differed from centralizing monarchies; ▸ common features and activities that allowed city-states such as Genoa, Venice, and Bruges to become commercial, financial, and economic leaders of Europe and maintain their independence) BD (BE,168;C;WE,141)

- Understands the effects of urbanization in Europe and the Mediterranean region (e.g., urban growth in the Mediterranean region and Northern Europe, and causes for expansion of manufacturing, interregional trade, and a money economy in Europe; ▸ the growth in economy, population, and urbanization in Europe in global context) BD (BE,168;C;WE,143;LI,236)

Codes (right side of page):   BD = Benchmark, Declarative; BP = Benchmark, Procedural; BC = Benchmark, Contextual

1st letter of each code in parentheses	*2nd letter of code*	*Number*
B = NCHS: basic edition	E = Explicitly stated in document	Page number of cited document
W = NCHS: World History, expanded ed.	I = Implied in document	
L = Lessons from History		
C = Core material	*Symbol*	
R = Related material	■ material appears only in NCHS basic edition	
	▸ material appears only in NCHS expanded edition	
	● material appears in both NCHS editions	

MREL

- Understands the spread of philosophy to Europe (e.g., the importance of the Islamic states of Iberia and Sicily as well as the Byzantine Empire in transmitting scientific and philosophical knowledge to Western and Central Europe; ▸ how classical works such as those of Aristotle and Plato became part of medieval philosophy in Western Europe, and the attitude of the Church toward these non-Christian philosophies)
  BD (BE,169;R;WE,145;LE,242)

- Understands comparisons of church-state relations and religious authority between Orthodox Christianity in the East and Latin Christianity in the West
  BD (BE,169;R;WE,145)

▸ Understands the social elements of feudalism (e.g., the daily life of serfs, knights, and lords as feudalism developed late in the 1st millennium CE; how their lives and duties were interrelated, and what diverse sources illustrate about this life and this time)
  BD (C;WE,143)

▸ Understands how women influenced medieval politics (e.g., the roles and duties of women in 14th century political and home life; the opportunities available to upper class women and the obstacles they faced)
  BD (C;WE,141)

▸ Understands the influence of religious beliefs on various regions (e.g., the presence and motivation behind anti-Semitism in Western Europe during the Crusades; the correlations between commercial and naval domination by Latin Christian states over Muslim states in the Mediterranean and Black Sea basins and an increase in Christian political strength between the 11th and 13th centuries)
  BD (C;WE,143;LE,242)

▸ Understands the rise of guilds as economic and social institutions and their efforts to promote economic growth, product quality, and workers' rights
  BD (C;WE,143)

▸ Understands how women's experiences in Europe were determined by social class, area, time, and stage of life and how these experiences are reflected in different types of literature (e.g., Treasure of City of Ladies by Catherine of Pisan and Art of Courtly Love)
  BD (C;WE,145;LE,242)

Codes (right side of page):   BD = Benchmark, Declarative; BP = Benchmark, Procedural; BC = Benchmark, Contextual

1st letter of each code in parentheses	*2nd letter of code*	*Number*
B = NCHS: basic edition	E = Explicitly stated in document	Page number of cited document
W = NCHS: World History, expanded ed.	I = Implied in document	
L = Lessons from History		
C = Core material	*Symbol*	
R = Related material	■ material appears only in NCHS basic edition	
	▸ material appears only in NCHS expanded edition	
	● material appears in both NCHS editions	

McREL

(BE,169;WE,146)

21. Understands the rise of the Mongol Empire and its consequences for Eurasian peoples from 1200 to 1350

Level II (Grades 5-6)

BD (BE,169;C;WE,146;LE,237)
- Understands the significance of Chinggis Khan (e.g., the major achievements of Chinggis Khan, the geographical extent of Chinggis Khan's conquests, the role military technology may have played in the success of Mongol military campaigns)

BD (BE,170;R;WE,148)
- Understands Mongol interaction with different cultures (e.g., how Mongol rule affected economy, society, and culture in China and Korea; how Southeast Asians and Japanese resisted incorporation into the Mongol empire; ▸ how citizens responded to Mongol rule)

Level III (Grades 7-8)

BD (BE,169;C;WE,146,147;LE,237)
- Understands political, social, and cultural features of the Mongol Empire (e.g., the chronology and consequences of the Mongol conquests of 1206 to 1279 on China, Southeast Asia, Russia, and Southwest Asia; ▸ the relative strengths and weaknesses of the nomadic Mongol lifestyle with regard to social, political, and economic organization, and why the Mongols prevailed; what legend and fact reveal about Mongol conquest and Mongol warriors)

BD (BE,170;R;WE,148)
- Understands the influence of the "Golden Horde" in various regions (e.g., the impact of the "Golden Horde" rule on the peoples of Eastern Europe and Russia, ▸ the major accomplishments of Batu)

Level IV (Grades 9-12)

BD (BE,169;C;WE,147)
- Understands the political features of the Mongol Empire and its influence on other regions (e.g., the political character of Mongol rule in China, Central Asia, southwest Asia, and Russia; the significance of the "Pax Mongolica" and how long-distance communication and trade led to cultural and technological diffusion across Eurasia; ▸ how Mongol military

---

Codes (right side of page):   BD = Benchmark, Declarative; BP = Benchmark, Procedural; BC = Benchmark, Contextual

1st letter of each code in parentheses   *2nd letter of code*   *Number*
B = NCHS: basic edition   E = Explicitly stated in document   Page number of cited document
W = NCHS: World History, expanded ed.   I = Implied in document
L = Lessons from History
C = Core material   *Symbol*
R = Related material   ■ material appears only in NCHS basic edition
    ▸ material appears only in NCHS expanded edition
    ● material appears in both NCHS editions

243

MREL

organization and techniques led to victory in their conquests between 1206 and 1279)

- Understands factors that contributed to the division and eventual decline of the Mongol Empire after the death of Chinggis Kahn (e.g., ▸ disputes over succession, the absence of a bureaucracy, conflicts between nomadic traditions and the ideas of conquered urban cultures)

  BD (BE,169;C;WE,147;LI,237)

- Understands the interaction between the Mongols and cultures of Mongol domination (e.g., the Islamization of the Golden Horde and the Khanate of Persian-Iraq; why the Mongols did not conquer the Mamluks in Northern Africa; ▸ comparisons between Mongol and Muslim society and culture; the extent of Mongol control of Southwest Asia; relations between Chinese artists and the Mongol court during the Yuan Dynasty; the advantages of living under Mongol rule for the Chinese, Russians, and Southwest Asians)

  BD (BE,170;R;WE,148,149;LI,244)

▸ Knows the trade routes that emerged under Mongol domination, and the goods traded along these routes

  BD (C;WE,147;LI,237)

▸ Understands the usefulness of foreign sources in recording the history in areas of Mongol domination (e.g., the travels of Marco Polo, John of Plano Carpini, and Ibn Battuta)

  BD (C;WE,147;LI,244)

▸ Knows the consequences of the death of the Great Khan Ogodei for the Mongol enterprise in Eastern Europe and that of the Great Khan Mongke for the Mongol plans to invade Egypt

  BD (R;WE,148)

(BE,170;WE,150)

22. Understands the growth of states, towns, and trade in Sub-Saharan Africa between the 11th and 15th centuries

Level II (Grades 5-6)

- Understands influences on the economic development of Sub-Saharan empires (e.g., the importance of agriculture, gold production, and the trans-Saharan caravan trade to the growth of the Mali and Songhay Empires; ▸ the importance of trade within the major city-states and populations of Sub-Saharan Africa)

  BD (BE,170;C;WE,150;LE,248)

- Understands social and religious features of West Africa (e.g., what art reveals about the

  BD (BE,170;C;WE,150;LI,249)

Codes (right side of page):   BD = Benchmark, Declarative; BP = Benchmark, Procedural; BC = Benchmark, Contextual

1st letter of each code in parentheses	*2nd letter of code*	*Number*
B = NCHS: basic edition	E = Explicitly stated in document	Page number of cited document
W = NCHS: World History, expanded ed.	I = Implied in document	
L = Lessons from History		
C = Core material	*Symbol*	
R = Related material	■ material appears only in NCHS basic edition	
	▸ material appears only in NCHS expanded edition	
	● material appears in both NCHS editions	

societies and rulers of Benin and Ile-Ife, ▸ the story of Solomon and Sheba and the role of Sheba in African history)

BD (BE,170;R;WE,152;LI,249)

● Understands the emergence of commercial towns on the East African coast and the significance of Swahili as the language of trade

Level III (Grades 7-8)

BD (BE,170;C;WE,151;LE,248)

● Understands the development of the empires of Mali and Songhay (e.g., the importance of Islamic expansion in the political and cultural life of Mali and Songhay; ▸ the economic, social, and religious characteristics of the two empires; the observations of Ibn Battua and Leo Africanus in Mali and Songhay; the importance of the Monarch Mansa Musa in Mali)

BD (BE,170;C;WE,151)

● Understands religious aspects of Ethiopian society (e.g., the expansion of the Christian Ethiopian kingdom and its search for wider connections in the Christian world, ▸ the major achievements of the Zagwe Dynasty in Ethiopia and how this dynasty affected both Coptic Christians and Muslims)

BD (BE,170;R;WE,152;LI,247,249)

● Understands significant features of the major population centers of Bantu and the East African coastal region in the 2nd millennium CE (e.g., influences on the economic and cultural life of Kilwa and other East African coastal cities, the Bantu state of Great Zimbabwe and its links to the Indian Ocean trade, ▸ consequences of the contact between Bantu farmers and Khoisan hunter-gatherers in the early 2nd millennium)

BD (C;WE,151;LI,249)

▸ Understands how architecture (e.g., the churches of Lalaibela and of Kalash in Ellora, India) reveals the influence of foreign states and the end of African isolation

Level IV (Grades 9-12)

BD (BE,170;C;WE,151;LI,249)

● Understands how art and architecture reveal elements of Ile-Ife, Benin, and other African societies (e.g., ▸ the role of the ruler, political power, gender differences, foreign contact, technology)

BD (C;WE,151)

▸ Understands the political, social, economic, and religious development of the West African

---

Codes (right side of page):   BD = Benchmark, Declarative; BP = Benchmark, Procedural; BC = Benchmark, Contextual

1st letter of each code in parentheses	*2nd letter of code*	*Number*
B = NCHS: basic edition	E = Explicitly stated in document	Page number of cited document
W = NCHS: World History, expanded ed.	I = Implied in document	
L = Lessons from History		
C = Core material	*Symbol*	
R = Related material	■ material appears only in NCHS basic edition	
	▸ material appears only in NCHS expanded edition	
	● material appears in both NCHS editions	

Sudan and the East African coast between the 8th and 13th centuries (e.g., how these areas were affected by outside influences, the role of commerce in their development)

BD (C;WE,151;LE,248)
▸ Understands the influence of religion on African culture (e.g., Islamic and Christian expansion in Africa and why Islam was successful there; the differences between Coptic and Latin Christianity and how Coptics adapted African traditions to Christianity; the Zagwe Dynasty's achievements through patronage of Christian art and architecture, and characteristics of Ethiopian art and rock churches)

BD (R;WE,152,153)
▸ Understands the role of language in shaping African society (e.g., class structure and cultural influence of Swahili-speaking towns of East Africa; relationships among modern Bantu languages and what these relationships reveal about migrations of Bantu-speaking peoples; the interaction of religion with wealth, language, and country of origin in influencing social status)

BD (R;WE,152;LE,247)
▸ Understands the network of trade between East Africa, Southeast Asia, and the Persian Gulf (e.g., sources of traded items, controlling parties), the goods traded, and the importance of city-states such as Kilwa in this network

(BE,171;WE,154)
23. Understands patterns of crisis and recovery in Afro-Eurasia between 1300 and 1450

Level II (Grades 5-6)

BD (BE,171;C;WE,154;LI,242)
● Understands the origins and impact of the plague (e.g., how the plague started and spread across Eurasia and North Africa; ▸ the impact of the plague on daily life in urban Southwest Asia and Europe; how Christian and Muslim communities responded to the plague, and how the plague changed the lives of survivors)

BD (BE,171;C;WE,156)
● Understands major changes in the social, political, and cultural characteristics of European society after the 14th century (e.g., the effect of population decline on European agrarian and commercial economies; causes of and major figures in the Hundred Years War; the causes of peasant rebellions in Europe between 1300 and 1500; how the techniques of painting, sculpting, and architecture changed in this period)

Codes (right side of page):   BD = Benchmark, Declarative; BP = Benchmark, Procedural; BC = Benchmark, Contextual
1st letter of each code in parentheses   *2nd letter of code*   *Number*
B = NCHS: basic edition   E = Explicitly stated in document   Page number of cited document
W = NCHS: World History, expanded ed.   I = Implied in document
L = Lessons from History
C = Core material   *Symbol*
R = Related material   ■ material appears only in NCHS basic edition
                        ▸ material appears only in NCHS expanded edition
                        ● material appears in both NCHS editions

- Understands the origins and early expansion of the Ottoman Empire up to the capture of Constantinople in 1453
  BD (BE,172;R;WE,158)

Level III (Grades 7-8)

- Understands how the plague influenced economic, social, and political conditions in various regions (e.g., ► how the spread of disease relates to geography, social reaction to the plague in rural and urban Europe and Southwest Asia, the increase in mortality rates by the plague between the 14th and 15th centuries, the impact of the plague on young people)
  BD (BE,171;C;WE,154;LI,242)

- Understands causes for changes in social, political, and religious events in Europe after the 14th century (e.g., how the population decreased after the Great Plague; the effect of the crises in the Catholic Church on its organization, prestige, and power; ► increased wage levels and what governments did to discourage these increases)
  BD (BE,171;C;WE,156)

- Understands the "humanism" that emerged in Italy in the 14th and 15th centuries, and how new studies (e.g., Greco-Roman antiquity, critical text analysis) encouraged new forms of literature, philosophy, and education
  BD (BE,171;C;WE,156;LE,256)

- Understands the Zheng He maritime expeditions of the early 15th century, and why the Ming state initiated, then terminated, these voyages
  BD (BE,172;C;WI,182)

- Understands the significance of Timur the Lame (Tamerlane) (e.g., the impact of conquests in Southwest Asia, India, and Central Asia; how Timur's rule encouraged a flourishing of cultural life in Samarkand and the role his government played in the support of arts and sciences)
  BD (BE,172;R;WE,158)

Level IV (Grades 9-12)

- Knows ways in which long-term climatic change contributed to Europe's economic and social crisis in the 14th century
  BD (BE,171;C;WE,154)

- Understands religious and political changes in post 14th-century Europe (e.g., the resurgence of centralized monarchies and economically powerful city-states in Western Europe in the
  BD (BE,172;C;WE,156,157;LE,243)

Codes (right side of page):   BD = Benchmark, Declarative; BP = Benchmark, Procedural; BC = Benchmark, Contextual

1st letter of each code in parentheses	*2nd letter of code*	*Number*
B = NCHS: basic edition	E = Explicitly stated in document	Page number of cited document
W = NCHS: World History, expanded ed.	I = Implied in document	
L = Lessons from History		
C = Core material	*Symbol*	
R = Related material	■ material appears only in NCHS basic edition	
	► material appears only in NCHS expanded edition	
	● material appears in both NCHS editions	

15th century, ▸ the elements and consequences of the "Great Western Schism")

● Understands characteristics of 15th century Italian humanism (e.g.,▸ reasons for its emergence in this time and place, which social populations it most significantly affected)

BD (BE,171;C;WE,157;LE,256)

● Understands shifts in the leadership and political climate in China (e.g., the events that led to the collapse of Mongol rule in China; the reconstitution of the Mongol Empire under the Chinese Ming Dynasty; ▸ economic and political reforms and other achievements of the Hongwu emperor in China, and how these reforms restored for the Ming Dynasty continuity with pre-Yuan Empires)

BD (BE,172;R;WE,158;LE,244)

▸ Understands perceptions of the Black Death from diverse, contemporaneous sources (e.g., from Boccaccio in Europe and Ibn Battuta in Egypt and Syria)

BD (C;WE,155)

▸ Understands events and consequences of Jewish scapegoating in Europe during the Great Plague (e.g., the cremation of Strasbourg Jews, pogroms in the Holy Roman Empire, Jewish flight to Poland and Russia) and the attitudes and values these events represent

BD (C;WE,155;LE,242)

▸ Understands immediate and long-term consequences of the plague on European society (e.g., the medical, administrative, and psychological measures taken to cope with the plague in the 14th century; long-term consequences of recurrent pandemics in the 14th and 15th centuries on Europe society)

BD (C;WE,155;LE,242)

▸ Understands how economic conditions influenced the political and social climate in post 14th- century Europe (e.g., the impact of climatic change on the European agricultural system and the social and political consequences; how decreasing revenues led to competition between nobles for other sources of income, which increased the occurrence of civil wars)

BD (C;WE,157;LI,242)

▸ Understands the significance of Joan of Arc (e.g., her role in the Hundred Years War; her subsequent trial and execution; the Church's review of her trial 25 years later, and her revered image as a patron saint of France)

BD (C;WE,157)

▸ Understands Timur the Lame's patronage of scholars, artists, and scientists at Samarkand; the extent to which the "Republic of Letters" was a widespread phenomenon; and evidence of cross-cultural communication among scholars and artists

BD (R;WE,159)

Codes (right side of page):   BD = Benchmark, Declarative; BP = Benchmark, Procedural; BC = Benchmark, Contextual
1st letter of each code in parentheses   *2nd letter of code*   *Number*
B = NCHS: basic edition   E = Explicitly stated in document   Page number of cited document
W = NCHS: World History, expanded ed.   I = Implied in document
L = Lessons from History
C = Core material   *Symbol*
R = Related material   ■ material appears only in NCHS basic edition
    ▸ material appears only in NCHS expanded edition
    ● material appears in both NCHS editions

> Understands what accounts for the success of the Ottoman empire

BD (R;WE,159;LE,237)

(BE,172;WE,160)

24. Understands the expansion of states and civilizations in the Americas between 1000 and 1500

Level II (Grades 5-6)

BD (BE,172;C;WE,160;LE,249)

● Understands how the Aztec Empire arose in the 14th century (e.g., major aspects of Aztec government, society, religion and culture; ► the construction of Tenochtitlán, the "Foundation of Heaven")

BD (BE,172;C;WE,162;LE,250)

● Understands social and political elements of Incan society (e.g., Incan methods for expansion and unification of their empire, ► daily life for different people in Incan society, the food plants that formed the basis of Incan as compared with Aztec agriculture)

BD (C;WE,160)

► Understands what archaeological, artistic, and written sources can illustrate about pre-European life in the Americas

Level III (Grades 7-8)

BD (BE,172;C;WE,160;LE,250)

● Understands social and cultural features of Aztec society (e.g., ► the characteristics of Tenochtitlán that made it a unique city, gender roles in Aztec society and what these indicate about Aztec culture)

BD (BE,172;C;WE,160)

● Understands cultural and economic elements of North American and Mesoamerican civilizations (e.g., the major characteristics of Toltecs, Anasazi, Pueblo, and North American mound-building peoples; patterns of long-distance trade centered in Mesoamerica)

BD (BE,172;C;WE,162;LE,250;LI,250)

● Understands major political and social features of Incan society (e.g., the development of Incan social and political institutions, ► the chronology of Incan imperial expansion from 1230 to 1525 and the difficulties posed by its geographically an climatically diverse territories, the location and major features of Machu Picchu and what this site reveals about

---

Codes (right side of page):   BD = Benchmark, Declarative; BP = Benchmark, Procedural; BC = Benchmark, Contextual
1st letter of each code in parentheses   *2nd letter of code*   *Number*
B = NCHS: basic edition   E = Explicitly stated in document   Page number of cited document
W = NCHS: World History, expanded ed. I = Implied in document
L = Lessons from History
C = Core material   *Symbol*
R = Related material   ■ material appears only in NCHS basic edition
                                      ► material appears only in NCHS expanded edition
                                      ● material appears in both NCHS editions

Incan civilization)

BC (BE,172;C;WE,162;LE,250)

● Understands the similarities and differences between Incan and Aztec society (e.g., the essential differences between Aztec and Incan government, economy, religion, and social organization; ▸ how Incan and Aztec art and architecture reveal cultural achievements in their societies)

BD (C;WE,160)

▸ Understands how the natural environment affected the organization of developing societies of the North American plains, Southwestern deserts, and the tropical forests of the Yucatan

Level IV (Grades 9-12)

BD (BE,172;C;WE,161;LI,249)

● Understands political, social, and economic features of Aztec society (e.g., ▸ the locations and geographic limits of different phases of the Aztec Empire, the role and status of women in Aztec society and how this compares to the Incan and Mayan societies, the complex structure and features of the Aztec city of Tenochtitlán)

BD (C;WE,161,162)

▸ Understands the significance of the mound centers located in the Mississippi valley, such as the mound center at Cahokia in Illinois

BD (C;WE,162)

▸ Understands gender roles in Caribbean, Mesoamerican, and Andean societies and how these are reflected in images, myths, and individual qualities of their gods

BD (C;WE,163;LE,250)

▸ Knows the technology (e.g., engineering of roads, bridges, irrigation systems) and urbanism of the Incas (in Cuzco), the Aztecs (in Tenochtitlán), and of North American mound-builders

(BE,173)

25.   Understands major global trends from 1000 to 1500 CE

Level II (Grades 5-6)

BD (BE,173;LI,229-230)

■ Understands influences on the growth of long-distance exchanges between different regions (e.g., the continuing spread of Islam, and the importance of Muslim civilization in mediating

Codes (right side of page):   BD = Benchmark, Declarative; BP = Benchmark, Procedural; BC = Benchmark, Contextual

1st letter of each code in parentheses	*2nd letter of code*	*Number*
B = NCHS: basic edition	E = Explicitly stated in document	Page number of cited document
W = NCHS: World History, expanded ed.	I = Implied in document	
L = Lessons from History		
C = Core material	*Symbol*	
R = Related material	■ material appears only in NCHS basic edition	
	▸ material appears only in NCHS expanded edition	
	● material appears in both NCHS editions	

250

MREL

long-distance commercial, cultural, and intellectual exchanges; why new ports, manufacturing centers, merchant communities, and long-distance trade routes emerged in the region of the "Southern Seas," from the Arabian Sea to the coasts of China)

Level III (Grades 7-8)

■ Understands how major migratory and military movements of pastoral peoples of Asia and Africa affected agrarian states and societies of Eurasia and Africa
BD (BE,173;LI,227-228)

■ Understands economic, political, and cultural differences and similarities between Europe and Asia (e.g., causes and consequences of productive growth, commercialization, urbanization, and technological or scientific innovation in Europe and China; society, economy, and political organization of Europe and Japan, and causes of economic growth, urbanization, and cultural innovation in the two regions)
BC (BE,173;LI,231)

■ Understands the impact of interaction between Christians and Muslims in the Mediterranean region (e.g., how their encounters, both hostile and peaceful, affected political, economic, and cultural life in Europe, North Africa, and Southwest Asia)
BD (BE,173;LI,228-229)

■ Understands the concept of capitalism and the emergence of capitalistic institutions and productive methods in Europe and other parts of Afro-Eurasia
BD (BE,173;LI,252)

■ Understands differences and similarities between the Inca and Aztec empires and empires of Afro-Eurasia (e.g., political institutions, warfare, social organizations, cultural achievements)
BC (BE,173;LE,249-250)

Level IV (Grades 9-12)

■ Understands demographic changes in various regions from 1000 to 1500 CE (e.g., the growth, decline, and recovery of the overall population of Afro-Eurasia; ways in which large demographic swings affected economic, social, and cultural life in various regions)
BD (BE,173)

Codes (right side of page): BD = Benchmark, Declarative; BP = Benchmark, Procedural; BC = Benchmark, Contextual

1st letter of each code in parentheses	*2nd letter of code*	*Number*
B = NCHS: basic edition	E = Explicitly stated in document	Page number of cited document
W = NCHS: World History, expanded ed.	I = Implied in document	
L = Lessons from History		
C = Core material	*Symbol*	
R = Related material	■ material appears only in NCHS basic edition	
	▸ material appears only in NCHS expanded edition	
	● material appears in both NCHS editions	

(BE,176;WE,168)

26. Understands how the transoceanic interlinking of all major regions of the world between 1450 and 1600 led to global transformations

Level II (Grades 5-6)

BD (BE,176;C;WE,168)
- Understands the interregional trading system that linked peoples of Africa, Asia, and Europe on the eve of the European overseas voyages

BD (BE,176;C;WE,168)
- Understands what contributed to increasing oceanic travel in the 15th and 16th centuries (e.g., major Spanish and Portuguese technological innovations in shipbuilding, navigation, and naval warfare; navigational inventions such as the compass, astrolabe, and quadrant; ▸ trade routes of prominent Asian and European explorers and how prevailing wind currents influenced these routes; the features of Chinese and Arab sailing vessels that made long-distance travel easier)

BD (BE,176;C;WE,170;LI,258)
- Understands the character and impact of Portuguese maritime expansion to Africa, India, and Southeast Asia upon local populations (e.g., ▸ relations between King Affonso II of the Kongo and Portuguese, why Bartholomew de las Casas was considered the "defender of the Indians")

BD (BE,176;C;WE,170;LI,258)
- Understands features of Spanish exploration and conquest (e.g., why the Spanish wanted to invade the Incan and Aztec Empires, and why these empires collapsed after the conflict with the Spanish; ▸ interaction between the Spanish and indigenous populations such as the Inca and the Aztec; different perspectives on Cortés' journey into Mexico)

BD (BE,177;R;WE,172;LI,258)
- Understands the cultural and biological exchange between the Americas and Afro-Eurasia in the late 15th and 16th centuries (e.g., the exchange of animals between the Americas and Afro-Eurasia; how the exchange of plants between the Americas and other countries affected societies and commerce; ▸ the roots of "cowboy" culture in the Americas)

BD (C;WE,168)
- ▸ Knows the major accomplishments of Columbus (e.g., his voyages off the coast of Africa and to North America)

Codes (right side of page):   BD = Benchmark, Declarative; BP = Benchmark, Procedural; BC = Benchmark, Contextual

1st letter of each code in parentheses	*2nd letter of code*	*Number*
B = NCHS: basic edition	E = Explicitly stated in document	Page number of cited document
W = NCHS: World History, expanded ed.	I = Implied in document	
L = Lessons from History		
C = Core material	*Symbol*	
R = Related material	■ material appears only in NCHS basic edition	
	▸ material appears only in NCHS expanded edition	
	● material appears in both NCHS editions	

252

McREL

Level III (Grades 7-8)

BD (BE,176;C;WE,169)
- Understands the impact of the exploratory and commercial expeditions in the 15th and 16th centuries (e.g., the motives and short-term significance of the Portuguese and Spanish military and commercial expeditions to Sub-Saharan Africa, Asia, and the Americas; ▸ technologies that advanced international, seaborne trade in the latter part of the century; the connotations of the words "conquest," "exchange," and "discovery" used to describe Columbus' travels to North America and his encounters with indigenous populations)

BD (BE,176;C;WE,170)
- Understands how the Ottoman, Indian, Chinese, Japanese, Vietnamese, and Siamese powers restricted European commercial, military, and political penetration in the 16th century

BD (BE,176;C;WE,170,171;LI,258)
- Understands cultural interaction between various societies in the late 15th and 16th centuries (e.g., how the Church helped administer Spanish and Portuguese colonies in the Americas; ▸ reasons for the fall of the Incan Empire to Pizarro; how the Portuguese dominated seaborne trade in the Indian Ocean basin in the 16th century; the relations between pilgrims and indigenous populations in North and South America, and the role different religious sects played in these relations; how the presence of Spanish conquerors affected the daily lives of Aztec, Maya, and Inca peoples)

BD (BE,177;R;WE,173,LI,258)
- Understands the impact of the exchange of flora, fauna, and pathogens on the Americas and the global population (e.g., the spread of disease throughout the world, and how new disease microorganisms in the Americas devastated indigenous populations; ▸ population decline in parts of the Americas within the context of global population trends and growth in Europe and East Asia in the 16th and 17th centuries, origins and routes of flora and fauna exchanged across the globe)

BD (C;WE,169)
▸ Understands the significance and cultural impact of migrations of the Muslims and Jews after their expulsion from Spain

BD (R;WE,173)
▸ Knows which crops in Spanish and Portuguese regions of the Americas were domestic and which were commercial, and knows what resources commercial crops demanded

---

Codes (right side of page):   BD = Benchmark, Declarative; BP = Benchmark, Procedural; BC = Benchmark, Contextual

1st letter of each code in parentheses	*2nd letter of code*	*Number*
B = NCHS: basic edition	E = Explicitly stated in document	Page number of cited document
W = NCHS: World History, expanded ed.	I = Implied in document	
L = Lessons from History		
C = Core material	*Symbol*	
R = Related material	■ material appears only in NCHS basic edition	
	▸ material appears only in NCHS expanded edition	
	● material appears in both NCHS editions	

253

McREL

Level IV (Grades 9-12)

- Understands features of Portuguese overseas trade and exploration (e.g., ▸ the goals of the Portuguese trading policy as established by King João II, and his reasons for refusing to finance Columbus' expedition west; the impact of maritime technologies on the quality of Portuguese sailing in the 15th century)

  BD (BE,176;C;WE,169;LI,257)

- Understands significant social, economic, political, and cultural features of European society (particularly Spain and Portugal) that stimulated exploration and conquest overseas

  BD (BE,1176;C;WE,168;LE,257)

- Understands the consequences of Portuguese military conflicts and interaction with other cultures (e.g., ▸ the origins and consequences of Ottoman-Portuguese military conflicts in the Red Sea, Arabian Sea, and Ethiopia in the early 16th century; the political and economic impact of Portuguese presence on the peoples of West and East Africa in the late 15th and 16th centuries)

  BD (BE,176;C;WE,171;LI,258)

- Understands the consequences of the spread of disease globally and regionally (e.g., ▸ which diseases spread through colonization and exploration in the 16th and 17th centuries, how they were spread, and the effects of these diseases on individual societies, world trade, political expansion, and political control; fundamental plantation systems brought to the New World and how these may be connected to the spread of disease on the continents)

  BD (BE,177;R;WE,173;LE,258)

- Understands the effects that knowledge of the peoples, geography, and natural environments of the Americas had on European religious and intellectual life (e.g., ▸ through such ideas as the romanticized "noble savage," systems of human classification, natural history, and cartography)

  BD (BE,177;R;WE,173;LE,258)

▸ Knows the extent of Chinese naval and commercial activities in the Indian Ocean in the 15th century, and understands what these activities reveal about Chinese wealth, technology, and its use of tributes as a means of trade

  BD (C;WE,169)

▸ Understands measures that restricted Muslims and Jews in the 15th and 16th centuries (e.g., the moral and religious justifications used by the Spanish for the expulsion of Jews and Muslims from Spain, and possible consequences of the Spanish conquest of Grenada in 1492; how the organization of overseas trades in the Iberian states prohibited Mudehar Muslims, converts, and Jews from settling in the Americas)

  BD (C;WE,169)

Codes (right side of page):　　BD = Benchmark, Declarative; BP = Benchmark, Procedural; BC = Benchmark, Contextual

1st letter of each code in parentheses	*2nd letter of code*	*Number*
B = NCHS: basic edition	E = Explicitly stated in document	Page number of cited document
W = NCHS: World History, expanded ed.	I = Implied in document	
L = Lessons from History		
C = Core material	*Symbol*	
R = Related material	■ material appears only in NCHS basic edition	
	▸ material appears only in NCHS expanded edition	
	● material appears in both NCHS editions	

BD (C;WE,171;LI,258)

▸ Understands how various cultures responded to European presence in the 15th and 16th centuries (e.g., how practitioners of free trade along the northern rim of the Indian Ocean responded to European penetration; relations between the church and native populations; Asian responses to European naval encroachments)

BD (C;WE,171;LI,258)

▸ Knows the dynamics of the encomienda system of colonial government and labor, and how this compares to European manorial systems

BD (R;WE,173)

▸ Knows the routes of exchange of specific flora and fauna (e.g., corn, cassava, sugar; horses, cattle, pigs) throughout the world between the 15th and 18th centuries, and the impact of these exchanges on the world economy

(BE,177;WE,174)

27. Understands how European society experienced political, economic, and cultural transformations in an age of global intercommunication between 1450 and 1750

Level II (Grades 5-6)

BD (BE,177;C;WE,174;LI,258)

● Understands the social characteristics of European society from 1450 to 1750 (e.g., how lifestyles were different among varied social classes in early modern Europe, changes in institutions of serfdom, ▸ changes in the social status of women)

BD (BE,177;C;WE,176;LE,256;LI,258)

● Understands significant contributions of the Renaissance and Reformation to European society (e.g., major achievements in literature, music, painting, sculpture, and architecture in 16th-century Europe; ▸ the life and accomplishments of select figures from the Renaissance to the Reformation)

BD (BE,178;C;WE,178;LE,260)

● Understands the English civil war and the Revolution of 1688 (e.g., how these events affected government, religion, economy, and society in England; how the English Revolution influenced political institutions and attitudes in the English colonies and the outbreak of the American Revolution; ▸ new freedoms granted to the English people after 1688)

BD (BE,178-179;C;WE,180;LE,261;LI,261)

● Understands the significance of the Scientific Revolution and the Age of Enlightenment (e.g., the impact of astronomical discoveries from Copernicus to Newton; principal ideas of the

---

Codes (right side of page): BD = Benchmark, Declarative; BP = Benchmark, Procedural; BC = Benchmark, Contextual
1st letter of each code in parentheses *2nd letter of code* *Number*
B = NCHS: basic edition E = Explicitly stated in document Page number of cited document
W = NCHS: World History, expanded ed. I = Implied in document
L = Lessons from History
C = Core material *Symbol*
R = Related material ■ material appears only in NCHS basic edition
  ▸ material appears only in NCHS expanded edition
  ● material appears in both NCHS editions

255

MREL

Enlightenment, from rationalism to theories of education; ▸ the word "revolution" and what is meant by the term "Scientific Revolution"; the lives and achievements of significant figures of the Scientific Revolution; how Diderot's encyclopedia contributed to the Age of Enlightenment)

▸ Understands the role of gunpowder in changing European warfare (e.g., through the necessary redesign of fortifications)
    BD (C;WE,178)

Level III (Grades 7-8)

■ Understands early influences on the Scientific Revolution and the Enlightenment (e.g., connections between the Scientific Revolution and its antecedents, such as Greek rationalism, medieval theology, Muslim science, Renaissance humanism, and new global knowledge; connections between the Enlightenment and its antecedents, such as Roman republicanism, the Renaissance, and the Scientific Revolution)
    BD (BE,178,179;LE,252,261-262)

● Understands changes in urban and rural Europe between the 15th and 18th centuries (e.g., social and economic consequences of population growth and urbanization in Europe between the 15th and 18th centuries; ▸ the growth pattern of European cities between the 17th and 18th centuries, and the major urban centers of this period; causes and effects of the "agrarian revolution" on Western and Eastern European society)
    BD (BE,177;C;WE,174;LE,257;LI,257)

● Understands significant social and cultural changes that took place during the Renaissance (e.g., advances in printing press technology, the connections between the Italian Renaissance and the development of Humanist ideals in Europe north of the Alps, ▸ positive and negative changes in the status of women during the Renaissance and Reformation, the legacy of Renaissance architecture, changes in European art and architecture between the Middle Ages and the High Renaissance)
    BD (BE,177;C;WE,176,177;LE,256,257)

● Understands origins of the Reformation and Catholic Reformation (e.g., why many Europeans were unhappy with the late medieval Catholic Church, and how the beliefs and ideas of leading Protestant reformers reflected this discontent; what the Catholic Reformation sought to achieve, and the effect of religious reforms and divisions on Europeans; ▸ the patterns of religious affiliation in Europe in the early 17th century and factors that led some populations to embrace the Protestant Reformation while others rejected it)
    BD (BE,178;C;WE,176-177;LE,257,259;LI,258-259)

Codes (right side of page):   BD = Benchmark, Declarative; BP = Benchmark, Procedural; BC = Benchmark, Contextual
1st letter of each code in parentheses   *2nd letter of code*   *Number*
B = NCHS: basic edition   E = Explicitly stated in document   Page number of cited document
W = NCHS: World History, expanded ed.   I = Implied in document
L = Lessons from History
C = Core material   *Symbol*
R = Related material   ■ material appears only in NCHS basic edition
    ▸ material appears only in NCHS expanded edition
    ● material appears in both NCHS editions

BD (BE,178;C;WE,178;LE,260;LI,260)

- Understands the emergence of strong individual leaders, monarchies, and states in Europe between the 16th and 18th centuries (e.g., the character, development, and sources of wealth of strong bureaucratic monarchies; the significance of Peter the Great's westernizing reforms; the emergence of the Dutch Republic as a powerful European state; ► the reign of Elizabeth I and her efficacy as a leader and builder of a strong nation-state; the governmental policies of Catherine the Great; why St. Petersburg was called the "window on the West")

BD (BE,178;C;WE,180,181;LE,261;LI,261)

- Understands contributions of the Scientific Revolution to European society (e.g., the importance of discoveries in mathematics, physics, biology, and chemistry to 17th-and 18th-century Europe; the significance of the principles of the scientific method advanced by Francis Bacon and René Descartes; ► the trial of Galileo and arguments and evidence used to prove him "innocent" or "guilty"; the major features of the Scientific Revolution in major fields of endeavor)

BD (BE,179;C;WE;180;LI,262)

- Understands the short and long-term impact of Enlightenment ideas (e.g., how Enlightenment-era thought contributed to the reform of church and state, the reform programs of absolutist monarchs of Central Europe and Russia, the influence of Enlightenment ideas on the development of modern nationalism and democratic thought and institutions)

BD (C;WE,174)

► Understands the effects on world trade of the Spanish silver trade from America

BD (C;WE,178)

► Understands the role of gunpowder in the development of strong European leadership (e.g., how gunpowder came to Europe from China, and how it helped establish and maintain the power of state leaders in Europe)

BD (C;WE,179;LE,260)

► Understands the long and short-term causes of the "Glorious" revolution of 1688 and how it earned this title

Level IV (Grades 9-12)

BD (BE,177;C;WE,175;LE,258)

- Understands shifts in the European economy, trade, and labor systems in the 16th century (e.g., aspects of manufacturing and production in the 16th century's emerging capitalist economy, developments that affected men's and women's work options in this period, ► trends in worldwide trade in the 16th century, how the Dutch and English merchant classes

---

Codes (right side of page):   BD = Benchmark, Declarative; BP = Benchmark, Procedural; BC = Benchmark, Contextual
1st letter of each code in parentheses   *2nd letter of code*   *Number*
B = NCHS: basic edition   E = Explicitly stated in document   Page number of cited document
W = NCHS: World History, expanded ed.   I = Implied in document
L = Lessons from History
C = Core material   *Symbol*
R = Related material   ■ material appears only in NCHS basic edition
                                          ► material appears only in NCHS expanded edition
                                          ● material appears in both NCHS editions

MREL

established a significant presence in the world market)

- Understands causes and the major political, social, and economic consequences of the religious wars in Europe in the 16th and 17th centuries, and the legacy of these wars in modern Europe

  BD (BE,178;C;WE,177;LI,259)

- Understands the accomplishments of significant European leaders between the 16th and 18th centuries (e.g., the success of Russian expansion in the Caucasus, Central Asia, and Siberia, and the success of the tsars in transforming the Duchy of Moscow into a Eurasian empire; ▸ the life and achievements of Louis XIV, and elements of absolutist power during this period; how Peter the Great and Catherine the Great expanded Russian territory; major achievements in the reigns of Frederick the Great, Catherine the Great, and Joseph II, and which of these leaders displayed the features of an "Enlightened Despot")

  BD (BE,178;C;WE,179;LE,260)

- Understands influences on the spread of scientific ideas and Enlightenment thought (e.g., the importance of royal societies and other international networks in disseminating scientific ideas and methods; how academies, salons, and popular publishing spread Enlightenment thought; ▸ how the salons of aristocratic and bourgeois Parisian women influenced French political affairs, and why men eventually created their own salons; how Chinese humanist philosophy influenced the ideas of major Enlightenment writers and thinkers)

  BD (BE,179;C;WE,181)

- Understands features of the conflict between religious beliefs and scientific thought during the Scientific Revolution (e.g., the coexistence of the new scientific rationalism in 17th-and 18th-century Europe with traditional learning and rituals; ▸ Galileo's ideas about the solar system, and why he hesitated to apply scriptural passages to science-related problems; the fundamental ideas of Descartes' *Discourse on Method*, and the methods he used to ascertain the "truth")

  BD (BE,179;C;WE,180,181;LI,261)

- Understands the role of the Enlightenment in shaping European society (e.g., the impact of Europe's growing knowledge of other regions on the development of concepts of universalism, tolerance, and world history; ▸ the connection between the Enlightenment and the Scientific Revolution, and arguments supporting the notion that one was dependent upon the other)

  BD (BE,179;C;WE,181;LE,261;LI,261)

▸ Understands significant individuals and ideologies that emerged during the Renaissance and Reformation (e.g., the basic arguments in *The Prince* by Machiavelli; works of Renaissance

  BD (C;WE,177;LE,256,259;LI,256)

Codes (right side of page):   BD = Benchmark, Declarative; BP = Benchmark, Procedural; BC = Benchmark, Contextual

1st letter of each code in parentheses   *2nd letter of code*   *Number*
B = NCHS: basic edition   E = Explicitly stated in document   Page number of cited document
W = NCHS: World History, expanded ed.   I = Implied in document
L = Lessons from History
C = Core material   *Symbol*
R = Related material   ■ material appears only in NCHS basic edition
                                               ▸ material appears only in NCHS expanded edition
                                               ● material appears in both NCHS editions

writers and elements of Humanism in these works; individuals and factors that contributed to the revival of Greco-Roman art, architecture, and scholarship; differing ideas on women's roles in the Protestant household; social oppression and conflict in Europe during the Renaissance, as contrasted with humanist principles of the time)

BD (C;WE,179)
▸ Understands sources of military buildup of the 17th and 18th centuries (e.g., how they compare with the advice of Machiavelli on the use of mercenaries)

BD (C;WE,179)
▸ Understands the complaints, goals, and issues of the Cavaliers and Roundheads in the English Civil War

BD (C;WE,179;LE,260)
▸ Understands factors that influenced the economic and political development of the Dutch Republic, England, and France (e.g., characteristics of the Dutch Republic that affected commerce and religion, and enabled Amsterdam to gain commercial supremacy over the northern Italian city-states in the late 16th century; factors that led England to develop a Parliamentary government and led to absolutism in France under Louis XIV)

(BE,179;WE,182)
28. Understands how large territorial empires dominated much of Eurasia between the 16th and 18th centuries

Level II (Grades 5-6)

BD (BE,179;C;WE,182)
● Understands the power and limit of imperial absolutism under the Ming Dynasty (e.g., ▸ variations in control over society and the bureaucracy)

BD (BE,180;C;WE,182)
● Understands how China viewed its role in the world during the Ming Dynasty (e.g., why China's attitude toward external political and commercial relations changed after the Zheng He voyages from 1405 to 1433, ▸ the Chinese belief that other countries had a tributary relationship to the celestial empire)

BD (BE,180;C;WE,184)
● Understands political and cultural achievements of the Ottoman Empire (e.g., the significance of the capture of Constantinople for Christians and Ottomans; how the Ottoman military succeeded against various enemies; artistic, architectural, and literary achievements

---

Codes (right side of page):   BD = Benchmark, Declarative; BP = Benchmark, Procedural; BC = Benchmark, Contextual

1st letter of each code in parentheses	*2nd letter of code*	*Number*
B = NCHS: basic edition	E = Explicitly stated in document	Page number of cited document
W = NCHS: World History, expanded ed.	I = Implied in document	
L = Lessons from History		
C = Core material	*Symbol*	
R = Related material	■ material appears only in NCHS basic edition	
	▸ material appears only in NCHS expanded edition	
	● material appears in both NCHS editions	

of the Ottoman Empire in the 15th and 16th centuries; ‣ achievements of Sulieman the Magnificent; the extent of the Byzantine and Ottoman Empires in the 14th and 15th centuries)

BD (BE,180;R;WE,186)
- Understands political achievements of the Safavid and Mughal Empires (e.g., how Persia was unified by the Turkic Safavids, the political and cultural achievements of the Safavid Golden Age under Shah Abbas I, the Mughal conquest of India and how the Turkic warrior class united diverse peoples of the Indian continent)

BD (BE,180;R;WE,186)
- Understands the network of Afro-Eurasian trade in the 16th and 17th centuries (e.g., the importance of Indian textiles, spices, and other products in the trade; ‣ how spices brought to Europe by Vasco da Gama initiated the spice trade between India and Europe)

Level III (Grades 7-8)

BD (BE,179;C;WE;182)
- Understands interactions between China and other countries during the Ming Dynasty (e.g., the Chinese view of itself as the "Middle Kingdom;" political, commercial, and cultural relations with Korea, Vietnam, and other societies of East and Southeast Asia)

BD (BE,180;C;WE,182,183)
- Understands features of class structure and sources of social change in China (e.g., the effects of American crops and silver on demographic, economic, and social change in China; ‣ the stratification of Chinese society under Ming rule)

BD (BE,180;C;WE,184,185)
- Understands cultural, political, and economic factors that influenced the development of the Ottoman Empire (e.g., the development of the Ottoman Empire among diverse religious and ethnic groups, ‣ the Christian European view of the Ottoman seizure of Constantinople in 1453, trade routes within the Ottoman Empire and how trade was affected by the development of a sea route around Africa)

BD (BE,180;R;WE,187;LE,269)
- Understands political and religious influences on the development of the Mughal Empire (e.g., relations between Muslims and Hindus in the empire, the effectiveness of Akbar's governing methods and religious ideas in comparison to other Mughal emperors)

BD (C;WE,182-183)
‣ Understands changes in the political structure of the Ming Dynasty (e.g., how the power of the Ming emperor changed over time, the source of political threat to the Ming Empire and

---

Codes (right side of page):   BD = Benchmark, Declarative; BP = Benchmark, Procedural; BC = Benchmark, Contextual

1st letter of each code in parentheses	*2nd letter of code*	*Number*
B = NCHS: basic edition	E = Explicitly stated in document	Page number of cited document
W = NCHS: World History, expanded ed.	I = Implied in document	
L = Lessons from History		
C = Core material	*Symbol*	
R = Related material	■ material appears only in NCHS basic edition	
	‣ material appears only in NCHS expanded edition	
	● material appears in both NCHS editions	

the role of defense in their military strategy)

- Understands factors that influenced the development and expansion of the Safavid Empire ^{BD (R;WE,186,187)} (e.g., key urban areas of the empire, and factors that contributed to the success of Safavid rule; how the city of Isfahan developed under the reign of Shah Abbas I)

- Knows how the popularity of Indian textiles in Europe undermined the efforts of the East ^{BD (R;WE,187)} India Company to sell more British goods in India than it imported

Level IV (Grades 9-12)

- Understands influences on the Chinese economy and social structure (e.g., the effects of ^{BD (BE,179-180;C;WE,183;LE,267)} commercialization on social relations among gentry elites, urban merchants, and peasants; ▸ how the Chinese central government controlled various aspects of peoples' lives)

- Understands significant cultural and social features of the Ming Dynasty (e.g., the role of ^{BD (BE,180;C;WE,183;LI,266)} Neo-Confucianism, Buddhism, and Daoism in Ming government and society; ▸ how the Ming Dynasty brought cultural unity to China; the imperial examination system in China established under Ming rule)

- Understands the social, economic, and cultural features of the Ottoman Empire (e.g., how ^{BD (BE,180;C;WE,184-185;LE,269)} Muslim, Orthodox, Catholic, and Jewish peoples interacted in southeastern Europe under Ottoman rule, ▸ the role and legal status of women within the Ottoman Empire, sources of revenue and patterns in state spending in the Ottoman Empire)

- Understands cultural and religious influences on Mughal social and cultural conditions (e.g., ^{BD (BE,180;R;WE,187;LE,269)} the Indian, Persian, and European influences on Mughal artistic, architectural, literary, and scientific achievements; ▸ how Akbar unified diverse cultures and encouraged religious tolerance within his Mughal Empire; the synthesis of Muslim and Hindu influences in art of the Mughal Empire)

- Understands major political events in the rise and decline of the Ottoman Empire (e.g., the ^{BD (C;WE,185;LE,269)} emergence of the Ottomans as a regional and world power between 1450 and 1650, the Ottoman Empire in the context of the Byzantine and Roman Empires, Austrian and Russian responses to Ottoman aggression, significant events in the expansion and recession of the

---

Codes (right side of page):   BD = Benchmark, Declarative; BP = Benchmark, Procedural; BC = Benchmark, Contextual
1st letter of each code in parentheses   *2nd letter of code*   *Number*
B = NCHS: basic edition   E = Explicitly stated in document   Page number of cited document
W = NCHS: World History, expanded ed.   I = Implied in document
L = Lessons from History
C = Core material   *Symbol*
R = Related material   ■ material appears only in NCHS basic edition
    ▸ material appears only in NCHS expanded edition
    ● material appears in both NCHS editions

261   MᴄREL

Ottoman Empire from the 15th to the 17th centuries)

▶ Understands the origins and development of the Safavid Empire (e.g., how Ismail created the Safavid Empire with the support of Qizilbash nomadic tribesmen; the evolution of Safavid social and political system from the nomadic-warrior years of Ismail to the golden age of Shah Abbas I)

BD (R;WE,187)

▶ Knows similarities and differences between major empires and leaders (e.g., comparisons between the Ottoman, Safavid, and Mughal Empires; differences and similarities in government, military, and religious patterns of the six major Mughal emperors)

BC (R;WE,187;LE,269)

(BE,181;WE,188)

29. Understands the economic, political, and cultural interrelations among peoples of Africa, Europe, and the Americas between 1500 and 1750

Level II (Grades 5-6)

● Understands European influence in the Americas between the 16th and 18th centuries (e.g., European activity and control in the Americas in the form of territorial empires, trading-post empires, plantation colonies, and settler colonies; how the Netherlands, England, and France became naval, commercial, and political powers in the Atlantic basin; ▶ the locations of the British and French in the Americas, and their interest in trade there; the concept of mercantilism and its advantages and disadvantages for the colonies and the mother country)

BD (BE,181;C;WE,188)

● Understands features of the labor system and economy in the Americas (e.g., why sugar, tobacco, coffee, tea, and other crops grown in the colonies became so important in the world economy; ▶ different jobs performed by indigenous peoples in the Americas)

BD (BE,181;C;WE,190;LI,262)

● Understands elements of the trans-Atlantic African slave trade (e.g., how slaves were transported to the Americas via the "middle passage"; how European firms and governments organized and financed the slave trade; conditions of slave life on plantations in the Caribbean, Brazil, and British North America; how slaves resisted servitude and preserved their African heritage)

BD (BE,182;C;WE,190;LI,262)

Codes (right side of page):   BD = Benchmark, Declarative; BP = Benchmark, Procedural; BC = Benchmark, Contextual

1st letter of each code in parentheses	*2nd letter of code*	*Number*
B = NCHS: basic edition	E = Explicitly stated in document	Page number of cited document
W = NCHS: World History, expanded ed.	I = Implied in document	
L = Lessons from History		
C = Core material	*Symbol*	
R = Related material	■ material appears only in NCHS basic edition	
	▶ material appears only in NCHS expanded edition	
	● material appears in both NCHS editions	

BD (BE,182;R;WE,192;LE,262;LI,262)

● Understands elements of the slave trade in Africa (e.g., how the Atlantic slave trade affected population, economic systems, family life, polygynous marriage, and the use of male and female slave labor in West and Central Africa; ▸ what narratives reveal about the experience of Africans sold into slavery)

Level III (Grades 7-8)

BD (BE,181;C;WE,188,189;LI,263)

● Understands the consequences of European interaction with indigenous populations of the Americas (e.g., the moral, political, and cultural role of Catholic and Protestant Christianity in the European colonies in America; the Seven Years War and its consequences for Britain, France, Spain, and the indigenous peoples of the American colonial territories; ▸ the political relationships between American Indian nations and Holland, France, and England)

BD (BE,181-182;C;WE,191;LE,262;LI,262,265)

● Understands features of and participants in the slave trade (e.g., ways in which entrepreneurs and colonial governments exploited American Indian labor, and the use of African slave labor for commercial agriculture; the treatment of slaves in the Western Hemisphere as opposed to those in the Islamic lands, Christian Europe, and West Africa; the organization of long-distance trade in West and Central Africa and circumstances under which African governments, elites, and merchants participated in the sale of slaves to Europeans; ▸ treatment of slaves and forms of resistance used in the "middle passage")

BD (BE,182;R;WE,192)

● Understands factors that contributed to the development of various African societies (e.g., the importance of trade, slavery, and an expanding world economy to the development of such African states as Ashanti, Dahomey, Benin, Lunda, and Kongo; ▸ different forms of slave resistance and the founding of Maroon societies; how Ashanti concepts of monarchical power compare to those of Europeans)

BD (BE,182;R;WE,192)

● Knows the causes and consequences of encounters among Khoisan groups, Bantu-speaking peoples, and European settlers in South Africa in the 17th and 18th centuries

BD (C;WE,188,189)

▸ Understands the differences in the demands and purposes of European colonies in different areas of the Western Hemisphere (e.g., how European colonies in Peru differed from those in the Great Lakes region, Barbados, or Massachusetts)

Codes (right side of page):   BD = Benchmark, Declarative; BP = Benchmark, Procedural; BC = Benchmark, Contextual

1st letter of each code in parentheses	*2nd letter of code*	*Number*
B = NCHS: basic edition	E = Explicitly stated in document	Page number of cited document
W = NCHS: World History, expanded ed.	I = Implied in document	
L = Lessons from History		
C = Core material	*Symbol*	
R = Related material	■ material appears only in NCHS basic edition	
	▸ material appears only in NCHS expanded edition	
	● material appears in both NCHS editions	

Level IV (Grades 9-12)

- BD (BE,181;C;WE,189;LE,264,265;LI,264)
  Understands economic and political features of various European colonies between the 16th and 18th centuries (e.g., the administrative system of the Spanish viceroyalties of Peru and Mexico, and the importance of Indian agriculture and silver production to Spanish colonial economy; ▸ the fundamental ideas of mercantilism and differences in how it was practiced by the Netherlands, France, and England; diversity in colonial governments, economies, the military, and social organization in European colonies)

- BD (BE,182;C;WE,190;LI,265)
  Knows reasons for the emergence of social hierarchies based on race and gender in both the Iberian Empire and the British colonies in the Americas

- BD (BE,182;R;WE,193)
  Understands the development of different African societies (e.g., the development, characteristics, and decline of the Songhay Empire in the 16th century, ▸ the regional and international circumstances under which large new states such as Lunda and Buganda emerged in East and Central Africa, the history of the African kingdom of Palmares in Brazil)

- ▸ BD (C;WE,189;LE,264)
  Understands characteristics of the development of European colonies in the Americas (e.g., the appeal of the Americas for European colonists in the 16th and 17th centuries, why Europeans were able to establish large colonies on these continents, and why they did not assert this type of control in Africa and Asia)

- ▸ BD (C;WE,189)
  Understands possible reasons why Catholics were generally more successful than Protestants in converting non-Europeans between the 16th and 18th centuries

- ▸ BD (C;WE,191;LE,264)
  Understands the development of different colonial labor systems and their impact on indigenous populations (e.g., the evolution of labor systems from the encomienda to the hacienda in North and South America from the 16th to the 17th centuries, the impact of the encomienda system on indigenous peoples and how it compares to slavery)

- ▸ BD (C;WE,191)
  Understands the "Black Legend," how it helped build opposition toward Spain, and how it illustrates Spain's unique dealings with aboriginal populations

- ▸ BD (C;WE,191)
  Understands how slavery was defined by different groups of people (e.g., key differences between the understanding of "slavery" by Africans and by European settlers in the

---

Codes (right side of page):   BD = Benchmark, Declarative; BP = Benchmark, Procedural; BC = Benchmark, Contextual

1st letter of each code in parentheses	*2nd letter of code*	*Number*
B = NCHS: basic edition	E = Explicitly stated in document	Page number of cited document
W = NCHS: World History, expanded ed.	I = Implied in document	
L = Lessons from History		
C = Core material	*Symbol*	
R = Related material	▪ material appears only in NCHS basic edition	
	▸ material appears only in NCHS expanded edition	
	● material appears in both NCHS editions	

264

McREL

Americas; how slavery was practiced in ancient, medieval, and early modern societies)

BD (R;WE,192,193;LI,262)

▸ Understands how the African slave trade influenced the lives of slaves in the Western Hemisphere (e.g., the institutions, beliefs, and practices of slaves working on plantations in the Western Hemisphere; the history of open slave rebellion and resistance in the Western Hemisphere; how the English and Spanish subdued slave rebellion in their colonies)

(BE,182;WE,194)

30. Understands transformations in Asian societies in the era of European expansion

Level II (Grades 5-6)

BD (BE,182;C;WE,194;LE,270)

● Understands the impact of European military and commercial involvement in Asia (e.g., how the Netherlands, England, and France became naval and commercial powers in the Indian Ocean basin in the 17th and 18th centuries; the impact of British and French commercial and military penetration on politics, economy, and society in India; why the Dutch wanted military and commercial influence in Indonesia and how this imperialism affected the region's economy and society; ▸ why Asian trade was so important within the British economic and political structure)

BD (BE,183;C;WE,196;LE,267,268)

● Understands social and political features of Japanese society under the Tokugawa shogunate (e.g., centralized feudalism in Japan and how Japan achieved political stability, economic growth, and cultural dynamism; the nature of the relationship between Japan and European powers between the 16th and 18th centuries)

BD (R;WE,198)

▸ Understands the role of art in conveying ideas in China and Japan (e.g., how nature is portrayed in Chinese and Japanese brush paintings)

BD (R;WE,198)

▸ Knows what groups of people in India most frequently converted to Islam between the 16th and 18th centuries, and the major vehicle for conversion

---

Codes (right side of page):   BD = Benchmark, Declarative; BP = Benchmark, Procedural; BC = Benchmark, Contextual
1st letter of each code in parentheses   *2nd letter of code*   *Number*
B = NCHS: basic edition   E = Explicitly stated in document   Page number of cited document
W = NCHS: World History, expanded ed.   I = Implied in document
L = Lessons from History
C = Core material   *Symbol*
R = Related material   ■ material appears only in NCHS basic edition
                                                            ▸ material appears only in NCHS expanded edition
                                                            ● material appears in both NCHS editions

265   M*REL*

Level III (Grades 7-8)

- BD (BE,183;C;WE,196;LE,270)
  Understands political, economic, and social aspects of Chinese society during the era of European expansion (e.g., how the Manchus overthrew the Ming Dynasty and the consequences of this event; ▸ demands and consequences of increasing population growth, agricultural output, commerce, and European trading networks in the Manchu Empire; treatment and opportunities open to women in 17th-and 18th-century China)

- BD (BE,183;C;WE,194,195,196)
  Understands trade patterns and relations between Europe and China (e.g., how well the Chinese government was able to control European trade within its borders and the extent of European commercial penetration; ▸ trade routes and major port cities used by the Europeans in their trade with China, and why Gangzhou [Canton] was central in this trade; the trade relationship between Britain and China in the 18th century)

- BD (BE,183;R;WE,198)
  Understands how the spread of different religions affected various Asian countries (e.g., how and why Islam continued to expand in India, Southeast Asia, and China)

▸ BD (C;WE,197;LE,268)
  Understands features in the development of Korean and Japanese culture (e.g., why Korea was called the "Hermit Kingdom" before 1800, the role and status of women in Tokugawa Japan, the roots and development of 17th-century Japanese art forms)

▸ BD (R;WE,198)
  Understands the spread of Confucianism in various Asian cultures (e.g., how the rising popularity of Confucianism among the elites in Korea and Japan contributed to changes in the roles of women; how Confucianism was influenced by government and society in China, Korea, Japan, and Vietnam)

▸ BD (R;WE,198)
  Understands the evolution, recurring themes, and foreign influence in Japanese art and artists (e.g., Nikko and Katsuru rikyu, Sotabu screens, brush painting, works of Shiba Kokan) and how they reflected society

Level IV (Grades 9-12)

- BD (BE,183;C;WE,195;LE,270;LI,270)
  Understands the economic and cultural consequences of European involvement in other countries (e.g., the significance of Christian missionary activity in India, Vietnam, and the Philippines, and how people of other religions - Buddhism, Hinduism, and Islam - responded

---

Codes (right side of page):   BD = Benchmark, Declarative; BP = Benchmark, Procedural; BC = Benchmark, Contextual
1st letter of each code in parentheses   *2nd letter of code*   *Number*
B = NCHS: basic edition   E = Explicitly stated in document   Page number of cited document
W = NCHS: World History, expanded ed.   I = Implied in document
L = Lessons from History
C = Core material   *Symbol*
R = Related material   ■ material appears only in NCHS basic edition
                                             ▸ material appears only in NCHS expanded edition
                                             ● material appears in both NCHS editions

to these efforts; ▸ Joseph Francois Dupleix's theory of "divide and rule" in South India for the French, and how this policy affected relations between the British East India Company and Indian peasants; how the French, Dutch, and British attempted to remedy unfavorable trade balances in Asia between 1500 and 1800)

● Understands the impact of the Seven Years War on the relative power of Britain and France in Asia

BD (BE,183;C;WE,194)

● Knows the events that led to the demise of centralized control by the imperial Mughals and the ascent of Maratha and Sikh power in India

BD (BE,183;C;WE,197;LE,270)

● Understands the cultural, economic, and social structure of China during the period of European commercial expansion (e.g., cultural and economic achievements of the Chinese during the reigns of the Kangzi and Qianlong emperors; ▸ the major differences in the trading policies of the Ming and Manchu, the factors that contributed to these changes, and European products desired by the Chinese; aspects of life of the elite in China; the family and its role in Chinese society)

BD (BE,183;C;WE,196,197)

● Understands the spread of different religions throughout the world (e.g., the varieties of Buddhism and Hindu practice and teaching that developed in Asia and their influence on social and cultural life; ▸ major world religions in the mid-18th century, their relative sizes, and their degrees of success at winning new converts; how the development of Buddhism in Japan compared to that in China)

BD (BE,183;R;WE,199)

● Understands how art, literature, and architecture reflect features of different cultures and religions (e.g., the influence of new currents in both Confucianism and Chinese art, architecture, and literature on cultural life in Korea, Vietnam, and Japan in the 17th and 18th centuries; ▸ the role of women in the Bhati movement of the 16th century, as reflected in the poetry of Mirabai; the Islamic and Hindu influences in the poetry of Kabir)

BD (BE,183;R;WE,199)

▸ Understands Mughal responses to the expansion of European commercial and maritime power in Asia (e.g., Mughal efforts to control the expansion and influence of European trading centers in India, and how these compared to similar efforts by the Chinese and Japanese to regulate foreign trade and influence within their borders; the catalysts behind the military buildup of Emperor Aurazngzeb in 1700 and how he responded to growing maritime strength of the British and French)

BD (C;WE,195;LI,270)

Codes (right side of page):   BD = Benchmark, Declarative; BP = Benchmark, Procedural; BC = Benchmark, Contextual

1st letter of each code in parentheses	*2nd letter of code*	*Number*
B = NCHS: basic edition	E = Explicitly stated in document	Page number of cited document
W = NCHS: World History, expanded ed.	I = Implied in document	
L = Lessons from History		
C = Core material	*Symbol*	
R = Related material	■ material appears only in NCHS basic edition	
	▸ material appears only in NCHS expanded edition	
	● material appears in both NCHS editions	

▸ Understands foreign influences on Japanese and Chinese economies (e.g., the impact of American silver upon the Japanese and Chinese economies between the 16th and 18th centuries, the role the Portuguese and Dutch played in Japanese trade, and why Japan limited trade to the West but not to Asia)

BD (C;WE,197;DE,63.4)

▸ Understands how the unification of Japan and the centralization of feudalism under Tokugawa rule compared to the rise of nation states in early modern Europe

BD (C;WE,197;LE,267)

(BE,184;WE,200)

31.   Understands major global trends from 1450 to 1770

Level II (Grades 5-6)

● Understands major shifts in world demography and urbanization between 1450 and 1770 and reasons for these changes

BD (BE,184;R;WE,200)

● Understands the major changes in world political boundaries that took place between 1450 and 1770, and how far European nations had extended political and military influence in Africa, Asia, and the Americas as of the mid-18th century

BD (BE,184;R;WE,200)

● Understands how the acceleration of scientific and technological innovations in this era affected social, economic, and cultural life in various parts of the world (e.g., ▸ the broad effects of navigational and ship-building innovations such as astrolabe and lateen sails)

BD (BE,184;R;WE,200)

Level III (Grades 7-8)

● Knows ways in which expanding capitalistic enterprise and commercialization affected relations among states and contributed to changing class and race relations

BD (BE,184;R;WE,200)

● Understands the influence of technological advancements on society (e.g., how innovations in military technology and tactics changed the balance of naval military power and affected empire building around the globe; ▸ countries that benefited and suffered as a result of military innovations)

BD (BE,184;R;WE,201)

Codes (right side of page):   BD = Benchmark, Declarative; BP = Benchmark, Procedural; BC = Benchmark, Contextual
1st letter of each code in parentheses   *2nd letter of code*   *Number*
B = NCHS: basic edition   E = Explicitly stated in document   Page number of cited document
W = NCHS: World History, expanded ed.   I = Implied in document
L = Lessons from History
C = Core material   *Symbol*
R = Related material   ■ material appears only in NCHS basic edition
                                                             ▸ material appears only in NCHS expanded edition
                                                             ● material appears in both NCHS editions

- Knows how Buddhism, Islam, and Christianity spread between 1450 and 1750 (e.g., the location and geographical area of influence, the rate of growth of practitioners, reasons for growth) _{BD (BE,184;R;WE,201)}

- Understands patterns of social and cultural continuity in various societies (e.g., ways in which peoples maintained traditions and resisted external challenges in the context of a rapidly changing world) _{BD (BE,184;R;WE,200)}

Level IV (Grades 9-12)

▸ Understands the catalysts behind the shift of economic power from the Mediterranean basin to Northern Europe during the 16th century _{BD (R;WE,201)}

▸ Understands the emergence of capitalism in India and Europe (e.g., the expanding capitalist system, the rise of the middle class, and changes in the textile industry in India after 1700; why modern capitalism successfully developed in England, Holland, and France but failed to take root in Italy, Spain, or Portugal; the rise of Western European capitalism and its effects on the rest of the world) _{BD (R;WE,201)}

▸ Understands how the Ming and Qing rulers viewed the European merchants, Christian missionaries, and military personnel who sought trading privileges in China _{BD (R;WE,201)}

- Understands how traditional Puritan and Confucian attitudes toward profit making affected commerce and trading practices in China and the early New England colonies _{BD (R;WE,201)}

32. Understands the causes and consequences of political revolutions in the late 18th and early 19th centuries _(BE,187;WE,206)

Level II (Grades 5-6)

- Understands the ideas and events that shaped the Revolution in France (e.g., the causes, character, and consequences of the American and French revolutions; the meaning of the _{BD (BE,187;C;WE,206;LE,275)}

Codes (right side of page):   BD = Benchmark, Declarative; BP = Benchmark, Procedural; BC = Benchmark, Contextual
1st letter of each code in parentheses   *2nd letter of code*   *Number*
B = NCHS: basic edition   E = Explicitly stated in document   Page number of cited document
W = NCHS: World History, expanded ed.   I = Implied in document
L = Lessons from History
C = Core material   *Symbol*
R = Related material   ■ material appears only in NCHS basic edition
          ▸ material appears only in NCHS expanded edition
          ● material appears in both NCHS editions

revolutionary slogan in France, "Liberty, Equality, Fraternity," and the social ideals it embodied; the legacy of leading ideas of the revolution; how the wars of the revolutionary and Napoleonic periods changed Europe and Napoleon's effects on the aims and outcomes of the revolution; connections between political events in the Americas and France between 1770 and 1815)

BD (BE,188;C;WE,208;LI,276,277)
● Understands the origins and development of Latin American independence movements (e.g., how the American, French, and Haitian revolutions and South American rebellions influenced the development of independence movements in Latin America; the political and ideological objectives, and the success of the independence movements between 1808 and 1830; ► how the colonial powers and independent countries of Latin America changed between 1790 and 1828; the role of geography in the outcome of the Latin American independence movements)

Level III (Grades 7-8)

BD (BE,187;C;WE,206)
● Understands the diverse factors (e.g., the Seven Years War, Enlightenment-era thought, the American Revolution, escalating internal economic crisis) that affected social and political conditions in Old Regime France

BD (BE,187;C;WE,207)
● Understands events and ideas that influenced the course of the French Revolution (e.g., how the revolution developed from constitutional monarchy to democratic despotism to the Napoleonic empire; ► the organization of the Estates-General and its merits and limitations; central ideas and origins of the Declaration of Rights of Man and Citizen)

BD (BE,187;C;WE,206,207)
● Understands how the French Revolution changed social conditions in France (e.g., how the revolution changed political and religious institutions, social relations, education, family life, and the legal and political position of women; ► how territorial changes were made in Europe between 1789 and 1815 and their consequences for diverse social groups such as clergy, nobility, peasantry, bourgeoisie, and sans-culottes)

BD (BE,188;C;WE,208)
● Knows the consequences of Napoleon's invasions (e.g., the impact of Napoleon's invasion of Iberia and growing British power in the Atlantic basin on the independence movements in Latin America, ► the events surrounding Napoleon's invasion of Portugal, the flight of the Portuguese court to Brazil)

Codes (right side of page):	BD = Benchmark, Declarative; BP = Benchmark, Procedural; BC = Benchmark, Contextual	
1st letter of each code in parentheses	*2nd letter of code*	*Number*
B = NCHS: basic edition	E = Explicitly stated in document	Page number of cited document
W = NCHS: World History, expanded ed.	I = Implied in document	
L = Lessons from History		
C = Core material	*Symbol*	
R = Related material	■ material appears only in NCHS basic edition	
	► material appears only in NCHS expanded edition	
	● material appears in both NCHS editions	

BD (BE,188;C;WE,208)

- Understands the political and ideological objectives of Latin American independence movements (e.g., ▸ knows who supported Father Miguel Hidalgo, his role in the Mexican Revolution of 1810; knows the role of Agustín de Iturbide in the Creole-dominated revolt of 1821)

BD (C;WE,207)

▸ Knows the leading figures and issues of the Congress of Vienna

BD (C;WE,208)

▸ Understands elements of the Haitian revolution (e.g., the role of Touissant L'Overture, Haiti's social and economic conditions under French rule)

Level IV (Grades 9-12)

BD (BE,188;C;WE,207;LI,277)

- Understands the impact of the Haitian Revolution (e.g., connections between the French and Haitian Revolutions, the impact of this event on race relations and slavery in the Americas and the French Empire)

BD (BE,188;C;WE,209;LE,276,277)

- Understands comparisons between the Latin American revolutions and those in America, France, and Haiti (e.g., ▸ pre-independence social and political conditions, opposed regimes/policies, justifications of the revolutionaries, class representation, extent of revolution)

BD (BE,188;C;WE,209)

- Understands the status of women and other social classes during and following the Latin American independence movements (e.g., the political roles of Creole elites, the Catholic Church, and mestizo, mulatto, and Indian populations; ▸ social and racial divisions in most of Latin America; how independence changed the status of women in Latin America and affected mestizo, mulatto, and Indian populations; roles played by prominent women before the wars of independence in Latin America)

BD (C;WE,207;LI,276)

▸ Understands the political beliefs and writings that emerged during the French Revolution (e.g., characteristics and actions of radical, liberal, moderate, conservative, and reactionary thinking; the ideas in the "Declaration of the Rights of Man and the Citizen" and Olympe de Gouge's "Declaration of the Rights of Women and the Female Citizen"; the implications of the "Code Napoleon" for Protestant and Catholic Clergy, property owners, workers, and women)

Codes (right side of page):   BD = Benchmark, Declarative; BP = Benchmark, Procedural; BC = Benchmark, Contextual

1st letter of each code in parentheses	*2nd letter of code*	*Number*
B = NCHS: basic edition	E = Explicitly stated in document	Page number of cited document
W = NCHS: World History, expanded ed.	I = Implied in document	
L = Lessons from History		
C = Core material	*Symbol*	
R = Related material	■ material appears only in NCHS basic edition	
	▸ material appears only in NCHS expanded edition	
	● material appears in both NCHS editions	

MREL

BD (C;WE,209;LE,276,277)
► Understands the ideas and issues during and after the Latin American independence movement (e.g., how the Brazilian independence movement differed from the rest, issues that concerned New Granada after independence, the provisions of the Monroe Doctrine and Latin American response to it)

(BE,188;WE,210)
33. **Understands the causes and consequences of the agricultural and industrial revolutions from 1700 to 1850**

Level II (Grades 5-6)

BD (BE,188;C;WE,210)
● Understands the emergence and impact of industrialism in 18th-century England (e.g., the effects of the agricultural revolution on population growth, industrialization, and patterns of land-holding; major characteristics of industrialization; ► how the industrial revolution affected population shifts; how the industrial revolution in the textile industry changed the way people worked; how figures such as John Kay, James Hargreaves, James Watt, Edmund Cartwright, and Richard Arkwright contributed to industrialization in England)

BD (BE,189;C;WE,212;LE,277-278)
● Understands the impact of the industrial revolution in Europe and the Atlantic Basin (e.g., connections between population growth, industrialization, and urbanization; the quality of life in early 19-century cities; the effects of urbanization on the development of class distinctions, family life, and the daily working lives of men, women, and children; ► advances made in communication and transportation; effects upon the political and economic status of women)

BD (BE,189;R;WE,214)
● Understands aspects of the abolition movement in the 18th and 19th centuries (e.g., the organization and arguments of movements in Europe and the Americas that sought to end slavery, and how the trans-Atlantic slave trade was suppressed; ► why and how the slave trade continued after it had been outlawed; major accomplishments of the American abolitionist Frederick Douglass)

Codes (right side of page):   BD = Benchmark, Declarative; BP = Benchmark, Procedural; BC = Benchmark, Contextual
1st letter of each code in parentheses   *2nd letter of code*   *Number*
B = NCHS: basic edition   E = Explicitly stated in document   Page number of cited document
W = NCHS: World History, expanded ed.   I = Implied in document
L = Lessons from History
C = Core material   *Symbol*
R = Related material   ■ material appears only in NCHS basic edition
    ► material appears only in NCHS expanded edition
    ● material appears in both NCHS editions

Level III (Grades 7-8)

- Understands why industrialization flourished in Britain (e.g., Britain's commercial connections with foreign markets in the early industrial revolution; Britain's unique combination of geography, location, natural resources, economy, technology, and political tendencies)
  BD (BE,188;C;WE,211;LI,277)

- Understands the effect of the industrial revolution on social and political conditions in various regions (e.g., connections between industrialization, labor unions, and movements for political and social reform in England, Western Europe, and the United States; ▸ the pace and extent of industrialization in Great Britain and the United States in the latter half of the 19th century; Robert Owen's New Lanark System and its role in dealing with societal problems caused by the industrial revolution; changes affected by the "Great Reform" bill of 1832, and how it addressed problems of the industrial revolution)
  BD (BE,189;C;WE,212;LI,278)

- Understands the status of slavery and slaves throughout the 19th century (e.g., how contract labor migration and other forms of coerced labor compare with slavery as methods of organizing commercial agriculture in the Americas in the later 19th century; the degree to which emancipated slaves and their descendants achieved social equality and economic advancement in various countries of the Western Hemisphere; ▸ locations of legal slavery around the world in 1800, 1830, and 1880, and how changes in the legal status could be linked to revolution ideology and economics)
  BD (BE,189;R;WE,214)

- ▸ Understands the importance and consequences of new technologies (e.g., seed drill, crop rotation, stock breeding, three piece iron) in the agricultural revolution
  BD (C;WE,211)

- ▸ Understands the impact of new technology that emerged during the industrial revolution (e.g., technological innovations that propelled the textile industry to the forefront of the industrial revolution; the roles of interchangeable parts and mass production in the industrial revolution)
  BD (C;WE,211)

- ▸ Knows new patterns in world manufacturing production that developed among the nations of Great Britain, United States, Germany, France, Russia, and Italy between 1800 and 1900
  BD (C;WE,212)

- ▸ Understands the discourse surrounding the abolition of slavery (e.g., the debate over abolition of slavery in the context of the French Revolution, the different strategies to resist

---

slavery employed by peoples in the Americas)

► Understands significant individuals in the abolition movement (e.g., prominent women from the abolitionist movement in America and their major accomplishments, including Harriet Tubman, Sojourner Truth, the Grimké sisters, Lucretia Mott; the story of Olaudah Equiana [Gustavus Vasa], his experience during the "middle passage," and his efforts to bring an end to the slave trade) BD (R;WE,214)

Level IV (Grades 9-12)

● Understands the effect of economic conditions and theories on the development of industrialization (e.g., the relationship between the expanding global market of the16th to18th century and the development of industrialization, ► the effect of new economic theories on industrial policies and practices) BD (BE,188;C;WE,211)

● Understands how industrialization shaped social class and labor organizations (e.g., connections between industrialization and the rise of new types of labor organizations and mobilization; ► what 19th-century literature reveals about the emergence and conditions of new social classes during the industrial period; conditions for children employed by 19th-century England before and after major legislation passed in 1833, 1842, and 1847; the wide variety of organizations created by working-class peoples in England, Western Europe, and the United States in response to the conditions of industrial labor) BD (BE,189;C;WE,213)

● Understands reasons why various countries abolished slavery (e.g., the importance of Enlightenment thought, Christian piety, democratic revolutions, slave resistance, and changes in the world economy in bringing about the abolition of the slave trade and emancipation of the slaves in the Americas; ► evangelical arguments against slavery, and the economic, evangelical, and "Enlightened" reasons for Britain's abolition of slavery; why Brazil was the last nation to abolish slavery and the slave trade; the consequences of the Haitian Revolution for the slave trade) BD (BE,189;R;WE,215)

► Understands the realities and romanticized visions of pre-industrial England (e.g., as reflected in the paintings of Constable and Turner) BD (C;WE,211;LE,278)

► Understands the relationship between improvements in agriculture, population increase, the BD (C;WE,211)

Codes (right side of page):　　BD = Benchmark, Declarative; BP = Benchmark, Procedural; BC = Benchmark, Contextual

1st letter of each code in parentheses	*2nd letter of code*	*Number*
B = NCHS: basic edition	E = Explicitly stated in document	Page number of cited document
W = NCHS: World History, expanded ed.	I = Implied in document	
L = Lessons from History		
C = Core material	*Symbol*	
R = Related material	■ material appears only in NCHS basic edition	
	► material appears only in NCHS expanded edition	
	● material appears in both NCHS editions	

rise of the textile industry, the enclosure movement, urbanization, and industrialization in 18th century England

- ▸ Knows the strengths and weaknesses of Adam Smith's analysis of capitalism in the The Wealth of Nations (e.g., his principle of the "Invisible Hand," the role of free enterprise, the profit motive, and competition; his "pin" story)

  BD (C;WE,213)

- ▸ Understands how and why industrialization developed differently in Britain than it did on the continent

  BD (C;WE,213;LI,277)

- ▸ Understands different perspectives regarding the nature of the African slave trade (e.g., how the African slave trade might be compared to the migration of Chinese workers to North and South America, and Indian workers to the Caribbean in the 19th century; the significance of the book *The Interesting Narrative of the Life of Olaudah Equiano or Gustavus Vasa, Written by Himself* about the slave trade)

  BD (R;WE,215)

- ▸ Knows the extent of slave imports to Brazil, Spanish America, the British West Indies, the French West Indies, British North America, and the U.S. and how the influx of slaves differed in the periods 1701 to 1810 and 1811 to 1871

  BD (R;WE,214)

(BE,190;WE,216)

34. **Understands how Eurasian societies were transformed in an era of global trade and the emergence of European power from 1750 to 1870**

Level II (Grades 5-6)

- ● Understands changes in social and political elements of the Ottoman Empire during the 18th and 19th centuries (e.g., reasons for the empire's retreat from the Balkans and Black Sea region; ▸ the lives of different members of Ottoman society such as the janissary, attendees of the Palace School, the role of women)

  BD (BE,190;C;WE,216)

- ● Understands political characteristics of Egypt (e.g., the impact of the French invasion of Egypt in 1798, the reign and major accomplishments of Muhammad Ali of Egypt, ▸ why he was known as the "father of modern Egypt")

  BD (BE,190;C;WE,216)

Codes (right side of page):   BD = Benchmark, Declarative; BP = Benchmark, Procedural; BC = Benchmark, Contextual

1st letter of each code in parentheses	*2nd letter of code*	*Number*
B = NCHS: basic edition	E = Explicitly stated in document	Page number of cited document
W = NCHS: World History, expanded ed.	I = Implied in document	
L = Lessons from History		
C = Core material	*Symbol*	
R = Related material	■ material appears only in NCHS basic edition	
	▸ material appears only in NCHS expanded edition	
	● material appears in both NCHS editions	

- Understands aspects of Russian expansion and settlement in the late 18th and 19th centuries (e.g., why Russia was successful in wars of expansion against the Ottoman empire; why and how Russia expanded across Asia into Alaska, and along the California coast; ► what archaeological evidence reveals about daily life in the Russian settlements at Sitka and Bogeda Bay)

  BD (BE,190;R;WE,218)

- Understands the advance of British power in India up to 1850, its social and economic impact, and the efforts of Indians to resist European conquest and achieve cultural renewal

  BD (BE,190;C;WE,220;LI,282)

- Understands Chinese policies toward foreign trade and immigration to other countries (e.g., why China resisted political contact and trade with Europeans, and how the opium trade contributed to European penetration of Chinese markets; ► motivations behind the Chinese trading policy and China's desire to keep out foreigners; motivations behind Chinese immigration to the U.S. and Southeast Asia)

  BD (BE,191;C;WE,222;LI,286)

- Understands events and ideas that led to the modernization of Japan (e.g., the internal and external causes of the Meiji Restoration; the goals and policies of the Meiji state, and the impact of these upon Japan's modernization; ► what Commodore Matthew Perry accomplished in Japan in the 1850s and what his voyage meant for the Japanese)

  BD (BE,191;C;WE,224;LE,285)

► Understands the emergence of European trading companies and their impact on Indian culture (e.g., the origins of both the French and British East India companies, what their charters enabled them to do, and how the home countries viewed the role of these companies in India; the trading relationship between the East India companies and Indian rulers)

  BD (C;WE,220;LE,282)

Level III (Grades 7-8)

- Understands the decline of the Ottoman Empire in the 19th century (e.g., the defensive reform programs of Selim III and Mahmud II, and the challenges they faced in resolving the empire's political and economic crisis; ► sources of weakness of the Ottoman Empire in the late 19th century; the military training and equipment of the Janissary Corps; how and when territory of the Ottoman Empire changed during the first half of the 19th century; causes of the Crimean War, the main events, nations involved, and forms of warfare employed)

  BD (BE,190;C;WE,216)

- Understands political conditions in Russia during the reign of Catherine the Great (e.g., the

  BD (BE,190;R;WE,218)

Codes (right side of page): BD = Benchmark, Declarative; BP = Benchmark, Procedural; BC = Benchmark, Contextual

1st letter of each code in parentheses	*2nd letter of code*	*Number*
B = NCHS: basic edition	E = Explicitly stated in document	Page number of cited document
W = NCHS: World History, expanded ed.	I = Implied in document	
L = Lessons from History		
C = Core material	*Symbol*	
R = Related material	■ material appears only in NCHS basic edition	
	► material appears only in NCHS expanded edition	
	● material appears in both NCHS editions	

McREL

effects of the French Revolution, Napoleonic invasion, and world economy on Russian absolutism; the significance of imperial reforms and popular opposition movements in the late 19th century; ▸ the extent of Russian expansion into Eastern Europe and Central Asia; how Poland was partitioned in 1772, 1793, and 1795, and the location and significance of Russian ports on the White and Black Seas and the Baltic)

BD (BE,191;C;WE,220,221)

● Understands the impact of foreign trade and politics on Indian culture (e.g., major trade routes that linked China, India, and Europe, and the impact of this trade on Indian agriculture and industry; ▸ the decline of the Mughal empire and the rise of British political and military influence in India between 1750 and 1858; the competitive policies of the British and the French in India, and why the British East India Company was able to prevail; the goods imported to and exported from India)

BD (BE,191;C;WE,222)

● Understands the economic and social consequences of rapid population growth in China between the 17th and 19th centuries

BD (BE,191;C;WE,222;LI,286)

● Understands causes of political and social turmoil in China in the 18th and 19th centuries (e.g., causes of governmental breakdown, political conflict, and social disintegration in China in the late 18th and 19th centuries; ▸ the main events surrounding the Boxer Rebellion and the Opium War)

BD (BE,191;C;WE,224;LI,285)

● Understands the origins of Japanese modernization and Japan's changing policies toward Western influences (e.g., the impact of Western ideas and the role of Confucianism and Shinto traditional values on Japan in the Meiji period, ▸ the role of the samurai in the events leading up to the Mejii Restoration)

BD (R;WE,218)

▸ Understands the general political, social, and economic structure of Russia in the 1800s

BD (C;WE,220)

▸ Understands significant cultural and political changes in India in the 18th and 19th centuries (e.g., changing linguistic and religious diversity in India between the early 18th and late 19th centuries, the significant changes in political control and boundaries in India between 1798 and 1850)

BD (C;WE,220,221)

▸ Understands Dutch involvement in various regions (e.g., changes in Dutch influence and control in South Asia between 1815 and 1850, how the Dutch ruled their colonies in the East Indies and what types of goods were traded by the Dutch in this region)

Codes (right side of page):   BD = Benchmark, Declarative; BP = Benchmark, Procedural; BC = Benchmark, Contextual

1st letter of each code in parentheses	*2nd letter of code*	*Number*
B = NCHS: basic edition	E = Explicitly stated in document	Page number of cited document
W = NCHS: World History, expanded ed.	I = Implied in document	
L = Lessons from History		
C = Core material	*Symbol*	
R = Related material	■ material appears only in NCHS basic edition	
	▸ material appears only in NCHS expanded edition	
	● material appears in both NCHS editions	

277

McREL

Level IV (Grades 9-12)

- Understands the social structure of the Ottoman Empire in the early and middle 19th century (e.g., the effects of population growth and European commercial penetration on Ottoman society and government; ▸ the roles of janissaries and Jewish and Christian merchants and landowners changed by the middle of the 19th century; the relative presence and the location of diverse religious and ethnic groups within the Ottoman Empire in 1800, and the prevailing Ottoman policy toward religion; the success and reception of the reforms of 1856 in the Hatt-I-Humayun issued by Abdul-Mejid) BD (BE,190;C;WE,217;LI,284)

- Understands events that shaped the social structure of Russia in the 19th century (e.g., relations between the Russian peasantry and land-owning aristocracy, and the persistence of serfdom; ▸ the czarist reform movements of the 1820s and how they appealed to different social sectors; Czar Nicholas I's positions on the creation of a constitution, freedom of the press, the Decembrist uprising, the Polish rebellion, and the process of Russification) BD (BE,190;R;WE,218,219)

- Understands how Western culture influenced Asian societies (e.g., British policies in India compared to Dutch colonial practices in the East Indies; the lives of indigenous elites under these regimes; ▸ aspects of indigenous cultures that were embraced by Europeans; the major accomplishments of Ram Mohan Roy and his central ideas regarding Western influence in India) BD (BE,191;C;WE,221)

- Understands causes and consequences of the Taiping Rebellion (e.g., ▸ how Christianity, rural class relations, and rural poverty contributed to the Taiping rebellion) BD (BE,191;C;WE,223;LE,286)

- Understands China's relations with Western countries (e.g., reasons for the Chinese diaspora in Southeast Asia and the Americas, the role of overseas Chinese in attempts to reform the Qing, ▸ the Chinese and British positions on opium sales and trade within China, prominent Chinese views on China's relations with the West and challenges presented to the West) BD (BE,191;C;WE,223)

- Understands Japan's political and social transformation in the 19th century (e.g., Japan's transformation from a hereditary social system to a middle-class society; how Japan's relations with China and the Western powers changed from the 1850s to the 1890s; ▸ the goals of the new imperial government, as outlined in the Charter Oath of 1868; reasons for Japan's rapid industrialization and its response to Western commerce; aspects of Western society that appealed to 19th-century Japanese; who benefitted and suffered in the initial BD (BE,191;C;WE,224;LE,285)

Codes (right side of page):   BD = Benchmark, Declarative; BP = Benchmark, Procedural; BC = Benchmark, Contextual

1st letter of each code in parentheses   *2nd letter of code*   *Number*

B = NCHS: basic edition   E = Explicitly stated in document   Page number of cited document

W = NCHS: World History, expanded ed.   I = Implied in document

L = Lessons from History

C = Core material   *Symbol*

R = Related material   ■ material appears only in NCHS basic edition

     ▸ material appears only in NCHS expanded edition

     ● material appears in both NCHS editions

decades of industrialization and nation building)

▸ Knows the individual motivations and relative military strength of the English, French, and Ottomans in the Crimean War, as well as the significance of the outcome of the war for each of these participants

BD (C;WE,217)

▸ Understands events that shaped the expansion and development of Russia in the 19th century and early 20th century (e.g., the causes of the Crimean War and its consequences for Russia, the Ottoman Empire, Britain, and France; the limits of Russian expansion eastward across Siberia and southward beyond the Caspian Sea; why Russia invaded the Ottoman territory in the early 1850s; how the Crimean War led to political and social reform for Russia; how Pan-Slavism affected Russian foreign policy in the late 19th century; what the Trans-Siberian and other railroad routes tell about Russian development and expansion from 1801 to 1914)

BD (R;WE,219;LE,284)

▸ Understands how the British presence and British policies shaped Indian society (e.g., the attitude of Muslim and upper-class Hindus toward the British presence in India; Britain's "modernizing" policies in India under the administration of Lord Dalhousie, and the social and political impact of the railroad on India; the central issues surrounding the supposition that the British "unified" India)

BD (C;WE,221;LE,282)

▸ Understands how the Treaties of Nanking (1842) and Shimonoseki (1895) illustrate the advent of late 19th-century Chinese imperialism

BD (C;WE,223;LI,286)

▸ Understands social conditions and change in Meiji Japan (e.g., the nature of living conditions for factory workers, aspects of education and social change, comparisons between the Meiji restoration and the French and American revolutions, the meaning and significance of various Meiji slogans)

BD (C;WE,224,225;LI,285-286)

Codes (right side of page):   BD = Benchmark, Declarative; BP = Benchmark, Procedural; BC = Benchmark, Contextual

1st letter of each code in parentheses   *2nd letter of code*   *Number*
B = NCHS: basic edition   E = Explicitly stated in document   Page number of cited document
W = NCHS: World History, expanded ed.   I = Implied in document
L = Lessons from History
C = Core material   *Symbol*
R = Related material   ■ material appears only in NCHS basic edition
    ▸ material appears only in NCHS expanded edition
    ● material appears in both NCHS editions

279   MℝEL

(BE,192;WE,226)

35. Understands patterns of nationalism, state-building, and social reform in Europe and the Americas from 1830 to 1914

Level II (Grades 5-6)

BD (BE,192;C;WE,226;LI,279)

- Understands the emergence of nationalist movements in Italy and Germany (e.g., the major leaders of unification and nationalism in Italy and Germany, and why these movements succeeded; ▸ the appeal of Garibaldi's nationalist Redshirts to Italians)

BD (BE,192;C;WE,228)

- Understand causes of large-scale population movements from rural areas to cities in continental Europe and how these movements affected the domestic and working lives of men and women

BD (BE,193;R;WE,230)

- Understands the impact of cultural achievements on 19th-century Europe and America (e.g., movements in literature, music, and the visual arts, and ways in which they shaped or reflected social and cultural values)

BD (BE,193;R;WE,232)

- Understands the political and social changes in 19th-century Latin America (e.g., where democracy failed and succeeded in Latin American nations after independence was achieved, ▸ how geography possibly influenced nation-building in Latin America, the class system in Latin America and its racial core)

BD (R;WE,230)

▸ Understands aspects of education in 19th-century Europe (e.g., aspects of the basic school day for male and female students in the 19th century; how significantly education, or lack thereof, affected the lives and prospects of 19th century Europeans; differences in the daily lives of children from working, middle class, and upper class families)

BD (R;WE,232)

▸ Understands how major events in the United States affected the rest of the hemisphere

Level III (Grades 7-8)

BD (BE,192;C;WE,226,227;LI,279)

- Understands the ideas that influenced the nationalist movements (e.g., major characteristics of 19th-century European nationalism, and connections between nationalist ideology, the

---

Codes (right side of page): BD = Benchmark, Declarative; BP = Benchmark, Procedural; BC = Benchmark, Contextual

1st letter of each code in parentheses	*2nd letter of code*	*Number*
B = NCHS: basic edition	E = Explicitly stated in document	Page number of cited document
W = NCHS: World History, expanded ed.	I = Implied in document	
L = Lessons from History		
C = Core material	*Symbol*	
R = Related material	■ material appears only in NCHS basic edition	
	▸ material appears only in NCHS expanded edition	
	● material appears in both NCHS editions	

280

French Revolution, Romanticism, and liberal reform movements; ▸ the extent to which Garibaldi reflected 19th-century Romanticism; the purpose of Bismarck's "Blood and Iron" speech, and previous attempts at unification to which he refers; the chronology of significant events in the unifications of Italy and Germany)

BD (BE,192;C;WE,228;LI,278)

● Understands movements and ideas that contributed to social change in 19th-century North America and Europe (e.g., the leading ideas of Karl Marx and the impact of Marxist beliefs and programs on politics, industry, and labor relations in Europe; the origins of women's suffrage in North America and Europe, leading figures on both continents, and their success until World War I)

BD (BE,193;R;WE,230;LI,278)

● Understands social change and the emergence of new social class culture in 19th-century Europe (e.g., the elements of the distinctive middle-class and working class culture that developed in industrial Europe; ▸ how the average standard of living changed in Europe in the 19th century and the factors that accounted for this change; broad-ranging benefits and disadvantages of attending school for children from peasant, middle class, craft, and urban factory-working families)

BD (BE,193;R;WE,232)

● Understands influences on the government structure in Latin America and Mexico (e.g., the effects of foreign intervention and liberal government policies on social and economic change in Mexico; ▸ the advent of the caudillo ruler in Latin America, his supporters, and the methods by which he maintained power)

BD (BE,193;R;WE,232)

● Understands expansion and nation-building in the United States and Canada in the 19th century (e.g., the factors that contributed to nation-building in Canada; ▸ the territorial expansions of the United States in the 19th century, how new territories were acquired, and from whom)

BD (C;WE,228)

▸ Understands trends in immigration within and out of Europe in the 19th century

BD (R;WE,230,231;LI,278)

▸ Understands cultural trends in 19th-century Europe (e.g., how leisure activity and popular culture changed throughout the 19th century, activities associated with "high culture," types of entertainment that were open to the middle and working classes)

Codes (right side of page):   BD = Benchmark, Declarative; BP = Benchmark, Procedural; BC = Benchmark, Contextual

1st letter of each code in parentheses	*2nd letter of code*	*Number*
B = NCHS: basic edition	E = Explicitly stated in document	Page number of cited document
W = NCHS: World History, expanded ed.	I = Implied in document	
L = Lessons from History		
C = Core material	*Symbol*	
R = Related material	■ material appears only in NCHS basic edition	
	▸ material appears only in NCHS expanded edition	
	● material appears in both NCHS editions	

Level IV (Grades 9-12)

- Understands the causes and results of the revolutions of 1848 (e.g., why these revolutions failed to achieve nationalist and democratic objectives; ▸ where revolutions occurred in 1848, how they were a chain reaction, and the goals and motivating spirit of each; the major accomplishments of prominent figures in the revolutionary era)

  BD (BE,192;C;WE,226,227;LI,279)

- Understands the role of nationalism in conflicts within different nations (e.g., how nationalism fostered tension and conflict in the Austro-Hungarian and Ottoman Empires, ▸ the importance of Greek nationalists' and Europeans' roles in the struggle for Greek independence from the Ottomans)

  BD (BE,192;C;WE,227)

- Understands factors that led to social and political change in 19th-century Europe (e.g., the interconnections between labor movements, various forms of socialism, and political or social changes in Europe; the influence of industrialization, democratization, and nationalism on popular 19th-century reform movements; the extent to which Britain, France, and Italy become broadly liberal and democratic societies in the 19th century; ▸ the broad beneficial and detrimental effects of the industrial revolution on specific European countries)

  BD (BE,192;C;WE,228,229)

- Understands the status of different groups in 19th-century Europe (e.g., the changing roles and status of European Jews and the rise of new forms of anti-Semitism; ▸ the goals of the women's movement in the 19th century, and the essential ideas outlined by Mary Wollstonecraft in Vindication of the Rights of Women; support for and opposition to women's suffrage in the late 19th century)

  BD (BE,192;C;WE,228,229)

- Understands the status of education in 19th-century Europe (e.g., how expanded educational opportunities and literacy contributed to changes in European society and cultural life, ▸ what countries enacted compulsory education by the end of the 19th century, how school attendance figures were affected by the industrial age)

  BD (BE,193;R;WE,231)

- Understands the emergence of new social thought in the 19th century (e.g., ways in which trends in philosophy and the new social sciences challenged and reshaped traditional patterns of thought, religious understanding, and understanding of social organization)

  BD (BE,193;R;WE,231)

- Understands how political and economic change influenced Latin American society in the 19th century (e.g., Latin America's growing dependence on the global market economy, as

  BD (BE,193;R;WE,232,233)

Codes (right side of page):   BD = Benchmark, Declarative; BP = Benchmark, Procedural; BC = Benchmark, Contextual

1st letter of each code in parentheses	*2nd letter of code*	*Number*
B = NCHS: basic edition	E = Explicitly stated in document	Page number of cited document
W = NCHS: World History, expanded ed.	I = Implied in document	
L = Lessons from History		
C = Core material	*Symbol*	
R = Related material	■ material appears only in NCHS basic edition	
	▸ material appears only in NCHS expanded edition	
	● material appears in both NCHS editions	

well as the effects of international trade and investment on the power of landowners and the urban middle class; the consequences of economic development, elite domination, and the abolition of slavery for peasants, indigenous populations, and immigrant laborers in Latin America; the impact of the expansion of secular education upon women's legal and political rights; ▸ the roles and perspectives of the caudillo, military official, landowner, urban bourgeoisie, or church official in post-independence Latin America; attitudes toward nationalism and cultural identity in 19th-century Latin America)

▸ Understands the chronology, major events, and outcomes of the Franco-Prussian War (e.g., how it impacted the British, Bavarians, and French; how the French were agitated into war by the edited Ems telegram)
BD (C;WE,227)

▸ Understands the definition of realpolitik and how Cavour and Bismarck exemplified this political philosophy
BD (C;WE,227)

▸ Understands how different movements and ideas influenced society in the 19th century (e.g., the effect of the continental revolutions on the Chartist movement in England, and how the ruling classes reacted to Chartist demands; the essential ideas outlined in Marx and Engel's Communist Manifesto and their meaning in the context of late 19th-century economic, political, and social conditions)
BD (C;WE,229)

▸ Knows the events and issues of the Dreyfus affair in France (e.g., why the French military establishment refused to pardon Dreyfus in the face of overwhelming evidence proving his innocence, how this affair became a political conflict between conservatives and progressives)
BD (C;WE,229)

▸ Understands sources that illustrate social conditions and cultural identity in 19th-century Europe (e.g., how primary sources such as diaries reflect the life experiences of middle and working class men and women in 19th-century Europe; the characteristics of popular, diverse 19th-century art styles, such as Romanticism, Realism, and Impressionism; how Europeans shaped their identity through their view of "other" peoples and cultures)
BD (R;WE,231)

Codes (right side of page):   BD = Benchmark, Declarative; BP = Benchmark, Procedural; BC = Benchmark, Contextual
1st letter of each code in parentheses   *2nd letter of code*   *Number*
B = NCHS: basic edition   E = Explicitly stated in document   Page number of cited document
W = NCHS: World History, expanded ed.   I = Implied in document
L = Lessons from History
C = Core material   *Symbol*
R = Related material   ■ material appears only in NCHS basic edition
  ▸ material appears only in NCHS expanded edition
  ● material appears in both NCHS editions

283   McREL

(BE,194;WE,234)

36. Understands patterns of global change in the era of Western military and economic dominance from 1800 to 1914

Level II (Grades 5-6)

BD (BE,194;R;WE,230;LI,277,278)

- Understands the impact of new inventions and technological developments in various regions of the world (e.g., how new inventions transformed patterns of global communication, trade, and state power; how new machines, fertilizers, transport systems, and commercialization affected agricultural production; ▸ significant inventions and inventors in 19th-century Europe and America)

BD (BE,194;R;WE,234)

- Understands the experiences and motivations of European migrants and immigrants in the 19th century (e.g., why migrants left Europe in large numbers in the 19th century and regions of the world where they settled; the consequences of encounters between European migrants and indigenous peoples in such regions as the United States, Canada, South Africa, Australia, and Siberia; ▸ the general appeal of Canada to European immigrants in the second half of the 19th century)

BD (BE,195;C;WE,236;LI,280)

- Understands factors that contributed to European imperialist expansion between 1850 and 1914 (e.g., advances in transportation, medicine, and weaponry that helped European imperial expansion in the late 19th century)

BD (BE,195;C;WE,238)

- Understands political and economic changes in Japanese society in the 19th and 20th centuries (e.g., Japan's rapid industrialization, technological advancement, and national integration in the late 19th and 20th centuries; ▸ the death of the Meiji emperor in 1912 and the main achievements of Meiji Japan)

BD (BE,196;C;WE,240;LE,281)

- Understands events that shaped African relations with other countries (e.g., the rise of the Zulu empire and its effects on African societies and European colonial settlements; how the discovery of gold and diamonds in South Africa affected British investors and race relations among Africans, Afrikaners, and British colonial authorities; ▸ the relationship between European and African merchants and the types of products traded between the two in the period after slavery ended)

Codes (right side of page):   BD = Benchmark, Declarative; BP = Benchmark, Procedural; BC = Benchmark, Contextual

1st letter of each code in parentheses   *2nd letter of code*   *Number*

B = NCHS: basic edition   E = Explicitly stated in document   Page number of cited document

W = NCHS: World History, expanded ed.   I = Implied in document

L = Lessons from History

C = Core material   *Symbol*

R = Related material   ■ material appears only in NCHS basic edition

                                        ▸ material appears only in NCHS expanded edition

                                        ● material appears in both NCHS editions

BD (BE,196;C;WE,240)

● Understands major changes in the political geography of Africa between 1880 and 1914

BD (R;WE,234)

▸ Understands trends in the population of Europe for the last three and a half centuries, and at what time Europe had the greatest number of inhabitants

BD (C;WE,238;LI,286)

▸ Knows the causes, course, and consequences of the Boxer Rebellion

Level III (Grades 7-8)

BD (BE,194;R;WE,230,231;LI,278)

● Understands major developments in science and the industrial economy (e.g., the social significance of the work of scientists, including Maxwell, Darwin, and Pasteur; how new forms of generative power contributed to Europe's "second industrial revolution;" the role of the state in different countries in directing or encouraging industrialization; ▸ the social, economic, and cultural impact of the railroad)

BD (BE,194;R;WE,234)

● Understands influences on European migration, immigration, and emigration patterns throughout the world between 1846 and 1932 (e.g., the geographical, political, economic, and epidemiological factors that contributed to the success of European colonial settlements in various regions; ▸ possible connections of the rise of the Zulu Empire in South Africa to European settlements in the Cape Region; relations between migrating European and African peoples that laid the foundation for the apartheid system in the 20th century; how technology such as the steamship and the railroad facilitated emigration)

BD (BE,195;C;WE,236;LI,279)

● Understands European motives and ideology that justified extending imperial power into African and Asian countries (e.g., the motives that impelled several European powers to undertake imperial expansion against peoples of Africa, Southeast Asia, and China; ▸ achievements of Cecil Rhodes and his motives and goals in the "scramble for Africa")

BD (BE,195;C;WE,236)

● Knows the causes and course of the Spanish-American War, and how this related to U.S. participation in Western imperial expansion

BD (BE,195;C;WE,238;LI,282-283)

● Understands the extent of British rule in India, and British reaction to Indian nationalism (e.g., the economic and political impact of British rule on India in the 19th century; the social, economic, and intellectual sources of Indian nationalism; the British reaction to Indian nationalism; ▸ the causes of the Uprising of 1857)

Codes (right side of page):   BD = Benchmark, Declarative; BP = Benchmark, Procedural; BC = Benchmark, Contextual

1st letter of each code in parentheses	*2nd letter of code*	*Number*
B = NCHS: basic edition	E = Explicitly stated in document	Page number of cited document
W = NCHS: World History, expanded ed.	I = Implied in document	
L = Lessons from History		
C = Core material	*Symbol*	
R = Related material	■ material appears only in NCHS basic edition	
	▸ material appears only in NCHS expanded edition	
	● material appears in both NCHS editions	

- BD (BE,195;C;WE,238)

  Understands political and social elements of Chinese society in the late 19th and early 20th centuries (e.g., Chinese efforts to reform government and society after 1895, as well as related causes for revolution in 1911; ▸ how the Chinese reacted to the presence and activities of foreigners in their country in the late 1890s)

- BD (BE,195;C;WE,240)

  Understands the role of trade in shaping political and social conditions in various regions (e.g., how West African economies changed after the end of the trans-Atlantic slave trade; how trade helped make empire-builders such as Zanzibar and Tippu Tip; ▸ the effect trade had on resistance to European imperialism; the location of the Suez Canal, how and why it was created, and what it did for world trade and political alliances)

- BD (R;WE,235)

  Understands the diverse factors (e.g., variations in birth and death rates, infant mortality rates) that contributed to the peaking and then leveling off of European population growth from the 17th to the 20th centuries

- BD (C;WE,238)

  Understands the geographic location of European interests in South, Southeast, and East Asia in the late 19th century

- BD (C;WE,240;LI,281)

  Understands the accomplishments and goals of specific African resistance movements (e.g., Abd al-Qadir in Algeria, Samori Ture in West Africa, the Mahdist state in the Sudan, Memelik II in Ethiopia, the Zulus in South Africa)

Level IV (Grades 9-12)

- BD (BE,194)

  Knows the factors that transformed the character of cities in various parts of the world

- BD (BE,194;R;WE,235)

  Understands influences on and consequences of European immigration and settlement (e.g., ▸ how European settlements affected the politics and economy of the local regions, as well as resources, labor, the flow of goods, and markets; the diverse motivations behind resettlement for specific groups of immigrants; the impact of new immigrants upon the environment and indigenous populations of Australia; how substantial European immigration in the 19th century had economic consequences for cities in the United States)

- BD (BE,194;C;WE,237)

  Understands the influence of European imperial expansion on political and social facets of African and Indian society (e.g., ideas of Social Darwinism and scientific racism in

---

Codes (right side of page):	BD = Benchmark, Declarative; BP = Benchmark, Procedural; BC = Benchmark, Contextual

1st letter of each code in parentheses   *2nd letter of code*   *Number*

B = NCHS: basic edition   E = Explicitly stated in document   Page number of cited document

W = NCHS: World History, expanded ed.   I = Implied in document

L = Lessons from History

C = Core material   *Symbol*

R = Related material   ■ material appears only in NCHS basic edition

    ▸ material appears only in NCHS expanded edition

    ● material appears in both NCHS editions

19th-century Europe and how these encouraged European imperial expansion in Africa and Asia; ‣ the major chain of events in Europe and Africa that led to the "scramble" for African territory, and the role of particular African governments or peoples in the partition of Africa by the Europeans; the impact of European expansion on legal, familial, and gender relations in Indian and African village life)

- Understands the effects of the Sino-Japanese War, the Russo-Japanese War, and the colonization of Korea on Japan's status as a world power, and how Japan justified its imperial expansion

  BD (BE,195;C;WE,236-237)

- Knows where the British and French expanded into mainland Southeast Asia, how their colonial policies differed, and how Thailand avoided colonization

  BD (BE,195;C;WE,239)

- Understands economic, social, and religious influences on African society (e.g., the impact of religious and political revolutions in Sudan on state-building, Islamization, and European imperial conquest; ‣ how and why slavery and the slave trade flourished in both West and East Africa even after the end of the trans-Atlantic slave trade; the relative strengths of Islam and Christianity in Africa at the beginning of the 20th century, types of rivalries among Christian denominations, and the links between both of these and the interests of the government)

  BD (BE,195;C;WE,241)

- Understands African resistance movements against the British during the period of European imperial expansion (e.g., the successes and failures of prominent African resistance movements in West Africa, Sudan, Ethiopia, and South Africa; ‣ the nature of the Sudanese resistance to the British, as well as the general success of Mahdi Muhammad Ahmed and the Mahdi uprising against British imperialism)

  BD (BE,196;C;WE,241;LI,281)

‣ Understands the debate on the westward movement in North America in the 19th century: whether this movement was unique, or simply part of a larger pattern of European overseas settlement, and what consequences the expansion had for indigenous peoples

  BD (R;WE,235)

‣ Understands the advantages and disadvantages of imperialism (e.g., the chief benefits and costs of the introduction of new political institutions, and advances in communication, technology, and medicine to countries under European imperialist rule; how medical advances, steam power, and military technology were used in European imperialism)

  BD (C;WE,237;LE,280)

Codes (right side of page):   BD = Benchmark, Declarative; BP = Benchmark, Procedural; BC = Benchmark, Contextual

1st letter of each code in parentheses	*2nd letter of code*	*Number*
B = NCHS: basic edition	E = Explicitly stated in document	Page number of cited document
W = NCHS: World History, expanded ed.	I = Implied in document	
L = Lessons from History		
C = Core material	*Symbol*	
R = Related material	■ material appears only in NCHS basic edition	
	‣ material appears only in NCHS expanded edition	
	● material appears in both NCHS editions	

McREL

▸ Knows the locations, history, and source of funding of major national and international rail lines in Africa and Eurasia constructed in the late 19th and early 20th centuries, and understands the benefits they provided to imperial powers and indigenous economies
BD (C;WE,237)

▸ Understands the European intellectual justifications for imperialism (e.g., the French notion of mission civilisatrice, the German concept of Kultur, and British imperialism as reflected in Rudyard Kipling's *White Man's Burden*)
BD (C;WE,237;LE,280)

▸ Knows the causes and impact of the Indian Uprising of 1857 (e.g., British imposed religious policies, the participants in the uprising, the varied reactions to the revolt on the part of Sikhs, Hindus, Muslims, and Indian royalty who had made alliances with the East India Company)
BD (C;WE,238;LI,282)

▸ Understands significant political events in 20th-century China (e.g., reasons for initial Chinese imperial support for the Boxer Rebellion, the major achievements of Sun Yatsen, the role overseas Chinese played in the 1911 revolution)
BD (C;WE,238)

▸ Understands Western influence on Japanese society in the 19th century (e.g., the chronology of major social, economic, and technological changes derived from the West in 19th-century Japan; the political and symbolic role of the emperor of Meiji Japan and how that role compared to those of British and other Western monarchs of the time)
BD (C;WE,239;LI,285)

(BE,196;WE,242)

37. Understands major global trends from 1750 to 1914

Level II (Grades 5-6)

● Understands major shifts in world population and urbanization in this era and how factors such as industrialization, migration, changing diets, and scientific and medical advances affected worldwide demographic trends (e.g., ▸ the changes large cities around the world went through during this period, such as Guangzhou [Canton], Cairo, Tokyo, Buenos Aires, Bombay, San Francisco, and London)
BD (BE,196;R;WE,242)

▸ Understands the experiences of immigrants to North and South America in the 19th century
BD (R;WE,242)

Codes (right side of page):   BD = Benchmark, Declarative; BP = Benchmark, Procedural; BC = Benchmark, Contextual
1st letter of each code in parentheses   *2nd letter of code*   *Number*
B = NCHS: basic edition   E = Explicitly stated in document   Page number of cited document
W = NCHS: World History, expanded ed.   I = Implied in document
L = Lessons from History
C = Core material   *Symbol*
R = Related material   ■ material appears only in NCHS basic edition
     ▸ material appears only in NCHS expanded edition
     ● material appears in both NCHS editions

Level III (Grades 7-8)

● Understands industrialization and its social impact in Great Britain, France, Germany, the United States, Russia, Japan, and other countries (e.g., ▸ conditions for rural families, the roles of women and children, the daily lives of working class men and women) _{BD (BE,196;R;WE,243)}

● Understands major patterns of long-distance migration of Europeans, Africans, and Asians, as well as causes and consequences of these movements (e.g., ▸ migrations from Asia and Africa between 1750 and 1900) _{BD (BE,196;R;WE,242)}

● Understands major changes in world political boundaries during this era (e.g., why a few European states achieved extensive military, political, and economic power in the world) _{BD (BE,196;R;WE,242)}

● Understands where Christianity and Islam grew in this era, and understands the causes of 19th-century reform movements or renewal in Buddhism, Christianity, Hinduism, Islam, and Judaism _{BD (BE,196;R;WE,243)}

▸ Understands trends in world population between 1500 and 1900, where the greatest increases occurred, and possible factors for this growth _{BD (R;WE,243)}

Level IV (Grades 9-12)

● Understands the importance of ideas associated with republicanism, liberalism, socialism, and constitutionalism on 19th-century political life in such states as Great Britain, France, the United States, Germany, Russia, Mexico, Argentina, the Ottoman Empire, China, or Japan (e.g., ▸ how these movements were tied to new or old-class interests) _{BD (BE,196;R;WE,243)}

● Understands patterns of social and cultural continuity in various societies, and how people maintained and resisted external changes in an era of expanding Western hegemony and rapid industrial and urban change (e.g., ▸ the efforts of people such as Jamal al-Din, al-Afghani, Rashid Rida, and Muhammad Abdul) _{BD (BE,196;R;WE,243)}

▸ Understands the process of educational reform in various Muslim regions during the 19th century (e.g., the new institutions that were established, the effect of this reform on women, those areas that wholly embraced Western values, and those that rejected them) _{BD (R;WE,243)}

Codes (right side of page):   BD = Benchmark, Declarative; BP = Benchmark, Procedural; BC = Benchmark, Contextual
1st letter of each code in parentheses   *2nd letter of code*   *Number*
B = NCHS: basic edition   E = Explicitly stated in document   Page number of cited document
W = NCHS: World History, expanded ed.   I = Implied in document
L = Lessons from History
C = Core material   *Symbol*
R = Related material   ■ material appears only in NCHS basic edition
                                               ▸ material appears only in NCHS expanded edition
                                               ● material appears in both NCHS editions

(BE,199;WI,248)

38. **Understands reform, revolution, and social change in the world economy of the early 20th century**

Level II (Grades 5-6)

BD (BE,199;C;WE,248;LI,293)

- Understands factors that transformed American and European society in the early 20th century (e.g., how industrial development affected the culture and working lives of middle and working class people in the United States, Japan, and Europe; ▸ major scientific, medical, and technological advances in Europe and the United States at the turn of the century; popular attitudes regarding material progress and the West's global leadership)

BD (BE,200;R;WE,250;LE,303;LI,295,310)

- Understands the consequences of the significant revolutions of the early 20th century (e.g., the prominent figures in the Mexican Revolution and its significance as the first 20th century movement in which peasants played a prominent role)

BD (R;WE,250;LE,303)

▸ Understands why Dr. Sun Yatsen is considered an important figure in the history of modern China

Level III (Grades 7-8)

BD (BE,199;C;WE,255;LI,293)

- Understands the industrial power of Great Britain, France, Germany, Japan, and the United States in the early 20th century (e.g., ▸ how the nations compare statistically, the importance and potential of industrialization)

BD (BE,199;C;WE,255;LI,293)

- Understands prominent features and ideas of liberalism, social reformism, conservatism, and socialism in the early 20th century (e.g., ▸ the "welfare state" promoted by liberal ideals; the influential ideas of leading Europeans such as Stanley Baldwin, Ramsay MacDonald, Emmeline Pankhurst, Jean Jaur,s, Raymond Poncar, Peter Stolypin, Alfred Krupp, or Rosa Luxemborg)

BD (BE,199-200;R;WE,250;LI,295,303)

- Understands events that led to revolutions in the early 20th century (e.g., causes, events, and consequences of the Russian "Bloody Sunday" in 1905, and the ensuing revolution; the promises of China's 1911 republican revolution and the New Culture movement and why

---

Codes (right side of page):   BD = Benchmark, Declarative; BP = Benchmark, Procedural; BC = Benchmark, Contextual

1st letter of each code in parentheses	*2nd letter of code*	*Number*
B = NCHS: basic edition	E = Explicitly stated in document	Page number of cited document
W = NCHS: World History, expanded ed.	I = Implied in document	
L = Lessons from History		
C = Core material	*Symbol*	
R = Related material	■ material appears only in NCHS basic edition	
	▸ material appears only in NCHS expanded edition	
	● material appears in both NCHS editions	

290

MREL

they failed to address China's political, economic, and social problems; ▸ what the peasantry and middle class fought for and against in the Mexican Revolution)

BD (C;WE,248,249;LI,302)

▸ Understands the consequences of changes inside Japan in the early 20th century (e.g., Japan's economic development, national integration, and political ideologies around the turn of the century; how Japanese territorial expansion affected the industrialization and economic development of Japan)

Level IV (Grades 9-12)

BD (BE,199;C;WE,249)

● Understands the diverse factors that contributed to the industrialization of various countries (e.g., how entrepreneurs, scientists, technicians, and urban workers in Asia, Africa, and Latin America participated in world trade and industrialization; ▸ how changes in land ownership policy, new technology, and government subsidies encouraged industrial development in Japan)

BD (BE,199;C;WE,249)

● Understands why European colonial territories and Latin American countries continued to maintain largely agricultural and mining economies in the early 20th century (e.g.,▸ restrictive policies of the European countries regarding industrialization in the colonies)

BD (BE,199;R;WE,257)

● Understands elements of the South African (Anglo-Boer) War (e.g., the causes, course, and consequences of the war for Boers, British, and African populations; the degree to which it was an example of "total war;" ▸ the attitude of the British toward non-British people and colonial troops at the time of the Boer War)

BD (BE,199;R;WE,257)

● Understands the diverse events that led to and resulted from the Russian Revolution of 1905 (e.g., ▸ the Russo-Japanese War, "Bloody Sunday," the October Manifesto, groups agitating for political reform and those supporting radical changes)

BD (BE,199;R;WE,257)

● Understands the reforms of Ottoman government and society advocated by the Young Turk movement, its origins, and possible reasons for its success

BD (BE,200;R;WE,257;LI,310)

● Understands the role of the peasantry in the Mexican Revolution (e.g., ▸ the aspects of nationalism expressed in the works of the Mexican Revolution by muralists Jos, Clemente Orozco, David Siquieros, and Diego Riviera, and how these murals fostered support for the

---

Codes (right side of page):   BD = Benchmark, Declarative; BP = Benchmark, Procedural; BC = Benchmark, Contextual

1st letter of each code in parentheses	*2nd letter of code*	*Number*
B = NCHS: basic edition	E = Explicitly stated in document	Page number of cited document
W = NCHS: World History, expanded ed.	I = Implied in document	
L = Lessons from History		
C = Core material	*Symbol*	
R = Related material	■ material appears only in NCHS basic edition	
	▸ material appears only in NCHS expanded edition	
	● material appears in both NCHS editions	

Revolution among the peasantry; the impact of the Mexican Revolution on the peasantry)

BD (R;WE,257;LI,303)
▸ Understands events and ideas that led to China's revolutionary movements in the early 20th century (e.g., social and cultural conditions in China that led to the New Culture, or May Fourth movement; the four points of Sun Yatsen's Manifesto for the Revolutionary Alliance [Tong Meng Hui] and to whom these revolutionary goals appealed)

(BE,200;WE,252)

39. Understands the causes and global consequences of World War I

Level II (Grades 5-6)

BD (BE,200;C;WE,252;LE,293,294)
● Understands the origins and significant features of World War I (e.g., the precipitating causes of the war; the factors that led to military stalemate in some areas; ▸ which countries joined each of the two alliances - the Allied Powers and the Central Powers - and the advantages and disadvantages for the formation of alliances; major areas of combat in Europe and Southwest Asia)

BD (BE,200;C;WE,254)
● Understands the immediate and long-term consequences of World War I (e.g., the principal theaters of conflict in World War I in Europe, Southeast Asia, Sub-Saharan Africa, East Asia, and the South Pacific; major turning points in the war; the short-term demographic, social, economic, and environmental consequences of the war's violence and destruction; ▸ the hardships of trench warfare)

BD (BE,201;C;WE,256;LE,295)
● Understands the roles of significant individuals, and the events that led to the Russian Revolution of 1917 (e.g., causes of the Russian Revolution of 1917 and how the revolutionary government progressed from moderate to radical; ▸ the historical importance of Russian leaders such as Tsar Nicholas II, Rasputin, and Lenin)

BD (BE,201;C;WE,256;LE,295)
● Understands the rise of Joseph Stalin, and his impact on the Soviet Union (e.g., how Joseph Stalin came to and maintained power in the Soviet Union, and how his projects [collectivization, the first Five Year Plan] disrupted and transformed Soviet society in the 1920s and 1930s; ▸ what life was like for common people under Stalin's rule)

Codes (right side of page):   BD = Benchmark, Declarative; BP = Benchmark, Procedural; BC = Benchmark, Contextual
1st letter of each code in parentheses   *2nd letter of code*   *Number*
B = NCHS: basic edition   E = Explicitly stated in document   Page number of cited document
W = NCHS: World History, expanded ed.   I = Implied in document
L = Lessons from History
C = Core material   *Symbol*
R = Related material   ■ material appears only in NCHS basic edition
                                             ▸ material appears only in NCHS expanded edition
                                             ● material appears in both NCHS editions

BD (C;WE,254)

▸ Understands how the homefront contributed to World War I (e.g., how massive industrial production and innovations in military technology affected strategy and tactics, and the scale, duration, brutality, and efficiency of the war)

Level III (Grades 7-8)

BD (BE,200;C;WE,252)

● Understands events that contributed to the outbreak of World War I (e.g., diverse long-range causes of World War I, such as political and economic rivalries, ethnic and ideological conflicts, militarism, imperialism, and nationalism; ▸ how nationalism threatened the balance of power among the Great Powers in Europe, and why it was considered one of the causes of World War I)

BD (BE,200;C;WE,252)

● Understands ways in which popular faith in science, technology, and material progress affected attitudes toward the possibility of war among European states

BD (BE,200;C;WE,254,255;LE,294)

● Understands the role of the U.S. and other countries in World War I (e.g., how the Russian Revolution and the entry of the United States affected the course and outcome of the war, ▸ motivations behind the entrance of the U.S. into the war)

BD (BE,201;C;WE,257;LE,295;LI,295)

● Understands the influence of Lenin and Stalin on the government, economy, and social conditions in Russia and the Soviet Union after the Revolution of 1917 (e.g., the effects of Lenin's New Economic Policy on Soviet society, economy, and government; ▸ why and how Stalin changed Lenin's policy and forced collectivization, and the consequences of resistance to this policy for the kulaks; how people who were persecuted survived during Stalin's purges)

BD (C;WE,252-253;LI,294;LE,294)

▸ Understands how different countries were aligned during World War I (e.g., the systems of alliances through which Europe organized itself into World War I, the role militarism played in these alliances, and the reasons for the war's expansion beyond European boundaries to become a world war; immediate causes for the entry of different nations into World War I)

BD (C;WE,256)

▸ Understands the role of Tsar Nicholas II and Rasputin prior to and during the Russian Revolution of 1917 (e.g., the biography of Tsar Nicholas III and his family, including how they died; the role the monk Rasputin played in determining Russian policy, and his influence on the royal court)

Codes (right side of page):   BD = Benchmark, Declarative; BP = Benchmark, Procedural; BC = Benchmark, Contextual
1st letter of each code in parentheses   *2nd letter of code*   *Number*
B = NCHS: basic edition   E = Explicitly stated in document   Page number of cited document
W = NCHS: World History, expanded ed.   I = Implied in document
L = Lessons from History
C = Core material   *Symbol*
R = Related material   ■ material appears only in NCHS basic edition
                                 ▸ material appears only in NCHS expanded edition
                                 ● material appears in both NCHS editions

Level IV (Grades 9-12)

- Understands arguments and theories regarding the causes of World War I (e.g., the role of social and class conflict leading to World War I; ▸ how primary and secondary sources illustrate the arguments presented by leaders on the eve of the Great War; why and how political leaders in European nations felt aggressive foreign policy, and the advocation of war, would help subdue domestic discontent and disorder; the arguments for and against war used by diverse political groups and figures in European countries) BD (BE,200;C;WE,253;LI,293,294)

- Understands the extent to which different sources supported the war effort (e.g., how nationalism and propaganda helped mobilize civilian populations to support "total war;" ways in which colonial peoples contributed to the war effort of the Allies and the Central Powers by providing military forces and supplies, and what this effort might have meant to colonial subjects; ▸ the effectiveness of propaganda to gain support from neutral nations; how and why original support and enthusiasm to support the war deteriorated) BD (BE,200;C;WE,253,255;LI,294)

- Understands Lenin's ideology and policies and their impact on Russia after the Revolution of 1917 (e.g., Lenin's political ideology and how the Bolsheviks adapted Marxist ideas to conditions particular to Russia; ▸ why Lenin declined to follow Marxist economic philosophy; the platforms and promises of Kerenksy and Lenin in 1917, the impact of war upon Kerensky's program, and the importance of Lenin's promise, "land, bread, peace"; how statistics on women in the labor force and education contradict Lenin's statements concerning women's equality) BD (BE,201;C;WE,257;LI,295)

- Understands the impact of the Russian Revolution on other countries (e.g., the challenge that revolutionary Russia posed to Western governments; the impact of the Bolshevik victory on world labor movements; ▸ how the Red Russians, White Russians, British, French, and Japanese viewed the Russian Revolution) BD (BE,201;C;WE,257)

- Understands the role of Stalin in the emerging Soviet Union (e.g., ▸ to what degree Stalin was able to accomplish his goal of bringing the USSR to industrial parity with the West, the unique problems in industrialization Stalin faced, and how this model differed from those of Western nations; what primary sources reveal about the human cost of Stalinist totalitarianism in the USSR in the 1920s and 1930s) BD (BE,201;C;WE,257)

- ▸ Understands the Schlieffen Plan and whether it contributed to a military stalemate BD (C;WE,253)

Codes (right side of page):   BD = Benchmark, Declarative; BP = Benchmark, Procedural; BC = Benchmark, Contextual

1st letter of each code in parentheses	*2nd letter of code*	*Number*
B = NCHS: basic edition	E = Explicitly stated in document	Page number of cited document
W = NCHS: World History, expanded ed.	I = Implied in document	
L = Lessons from History		
C = Core material	*Symbol*	
R = Related material	■ material appears only in NCHS basic edition	
	▸ material appears only in NCHS expanded edition	
	● material appears in both NCHS editions	

294

McREL

► Understands the strategies of the Allied and Central Powers at the beginning of the war, when these strategies changed, and how
BD (C;WE,255)

► Understands the human cost and social impact of World War I (e.g., what sources, such as letters and books, illustrate about the mental and physical costs of the war to soldiers around the world; how the casualty figures for World War I compare to other wars, and reasons for the high casualty rate; the changes in women's roles during the Great War)
BD (C;WE,255)

(BE,201;WE,258)

40. Understands the search for peace and stability throughout the world in the 1920s and 1930s

Level II (Grades 5-6)

● Understands treaties and other efforts to achieve peace and recovery from World War I (e.g., the conflicting aims and aspirations of the conferees at Versailles, and how the major powers responded to the terms of the settlement; why and how the League of Nations was founded, and its initial goals and limitations; ► the nations that were and were not invited to participate in the League of Nations; changes made to political boundaries after the peace treaties ending World War I, and which countries were winners or losers)
BD (BE,201;C;WE,258;I,F,294)

● Understands how the settlements of World War I influenced the Middle East, Africa, Asia, and Latin America (e.g., the mandate system created by the League of Nations and how it changed European rule in the Middle East and Africa, how World War I settlements contributed to the rise of both Pan-Arabism and nationalist struggles for the independence in the Middle East, ► how the readjustment of national borders in Africa after World War I affected people in East and West Africa)
BD (BE,202;C;WE,260)

● Understands the emergence of a new mass and popular culture between 1900 and 1940 (e.g., how new modes of transportation affected world commerce, international migration, and work and leisure habits; how the new media - newspapers, magazines, commercial advertising, film, and radio - contributed to the rise of mass culture around the world; ► the new approaches to visual art represented by the works of Pablo Picasso and Henri Matisse; the types of leisure activity and sports people enjoyed; changes in clothing fashions for men
BD (BE,202-203;R;WE,262;LE,301)

Codes (right side of page):   BD = Benchmark, Declarative; BP = Benchmark, Procedural; BC = Benchmark, Contextual
1st letter of each code in parentheses   *2nd letter of code*   *Number*
B = NCHS: basic edition   E = Explicitly stated in document   Page number of cited document
W = NCHS: World History, expanded ed.   I = Implied in document
L = Lessons from History
C = Core material   *Symbol*
R = Related material   ■ material appears only in NCHS basic edition
     ► material appears only in NCHS expanded edition
     ● material appears in both NCHS editions

and women, and how they reflected changes in social attitudes and values)

- BD (BE,203;R;WE,264)
Understands the economic and social impact of the Great Depression (e.g., how the Great Depression affected industrialized economies and societies around the world; the human cost of the depression; how governments, businesses, social groups, families and individuals coped with hardships of world depression)

Level III (Grades 7-8)

- BD (BE,201;C;WE,259;LI,294)
Understands the immediate and long-term political and social effects of World War I (e.g., the objectives and achievements of the women's movements in the context of World War I and its aftermath, the causes and effects of the U.S. isolationist policies on world politics and international relations in the 1920s, ▸ the agreements on reparation payments made at the Conference of Versailles and how these agreements corresponded to Woodrow Wilson's Fourteen Points)

- BD (BE,202;C;WE,260)
Understands internal shifts in the political conditions of China and Japan in the 1920s and 1930s (e.g., the factors that influenced the struggle for dominance in China between the Kuomintang and the Communist Party, how militarism and fascism derailed parliamentary democracy in Japan)

- BD (BE,202;C;WE,260)
Understands the goals and policies of European colonial rule in India, Africa, and Southeast Asia, and how these policies affected indigenous societies and economies (e.g., ▸ the response to the Moroccan resistance movement against the Spanish led by Abd al Quadir)

- BD (BE,202;R;WE,263,LI,301)
Understands major discoveries in science and medicine in the first half of the 20th century (e.g., those made by Curie, Einstein, Freud) and how they affected the quality of life and traditional views of nature, the cosmos, and the psyche

- BD (BE,202-203;R;WE,262)
Understands influences on art and culture in Europe and around the world in the early 20th century (e.g., the social and cultural dimensions of mass consumption of goods; the impact and aftermath of World War I on literature, art, and intellectual life in Europe and the U.S.; the impact of innovative movements in Western art and literature on other regions of the world; the influence of African and Asian art forms in Europe)

Codes (right side of page):	BD = Benchmark, Declarative; BP = Benchmark, Procedural; BC = Benchmark, Contextual	
1st letter of each code in parentheses	*2nd letter of code*	*Number*
B = NCHS: basic edition	E = Explicitly stated in document	Page number of cited document
W = NCHS: World History, expanded ed.	I = Implied in document	
L = Lessons from History		
C = Core material	*Symbol*	
R = Related material	■ material appears only in NCHS basic edition	
	▸ material appears only in NCHS expanded edition	
	● material appears in both NCHS editions	

● Understands how the Great Depression affected economies and systems of government globally (e.g., how the Depression contributed to the growth of communist, fascist, and socialist movements, and how it affected capitalist economic theory and practice among leading Western industrial powers; ▸ how the depression affected countries dependent on foreign markets and foreign capital investment)
BD (BE,203;R;WE,264)

▸ Understands the reflections of Depression-era hunger and poverty in the works of such artists as Käthe Kollwitz, José Clemente Orozco, and Dorothea Lange, and their impact upon society
BD (R;WE,264)

Level IV (Grades 9-12)

● Understands how the collapse of the German, Hapsburg, and Ottoman Empires and the creation of new states affected international relations in Europe and the Middle East
BD (BE,201;C;WE,259;LI,294)

● Understands how World War I influenced demographics and the international economy (e.g., the impact of the war on the international economy and the effects of industrial conversion from war to peace in Britain, France, Italy, and Germany; ▸ significant refugee populations created as a result of World War I, and their movements and dispersion)
BD (BE,201;C;WE,257,258,259)

● Understands reasons for the shifts in the political conditions in nations around the world after World War I (e.g., how social and economic conditions of colonial rule, and ideals of liberal democracy and national autonomy contributed to the rise of nationalist movements in India, Africa, and Southeast Asia; the successes and failures of democratic government in Latin America in the context of class divisions, economic dependency, and U.S. intervention; ▸ how Japan's domestic democracy may have fallen victim to its imperialist foreign policy)
BD (BE,202;C;WE,261)

● Understands the impact of scientific and technological innovations on early 20th century society (e.g., major medical successes in the treatment of infectious diseases, the causes and social costs of the world influenza pandemic of 1918-1919, how new forms of communication affected the relationship of government to citizens and bolstered the power of new authoritarian regimes)
BD (BE,202,203)

● Understands how the emergence of new art, literature, music, and scientific theories influenced society in the early 20th century (e.g., the impact of innovative movements in art,
BD (BE,203;R;WE,262,263;LE,301)

Codes (right side of page): BD = Benchmark, Declarative; BP = Benchmark, Procedural; BC = Benchmark, Contextual
1st letter of each code in parentheses   *2nd letter of code*   *Number*
B = NCHS: basic edition   E = Explicitly stated in document   Page number of cited document
W = NCHS: World History, expanded ed.   I = Implied in document
L = Lessons from History
C = Core material   *Symbol*
R = Related material   ■ material appears only in NCHS basic edition
                                                ▸ material appears only in NCHS expanded edition
                                                ● material appears in both NCHS editions

architecture, and literature, such as Cubism, Surrealism, Expressionism, Socialist Realism, and jazz; ▸ reflections of war in such movements as Dadaism, and the literary works of Remarque, Spender, Brooke, and Hemingway; the major themes of writers of the "Lost Generation" in the post-World War I era; prominent musicians and composers of the first half of the century and the cultural impact of their music around the world; how Freud's psychoanalytic method and theories of the unconscious changed views of human motives and human nature)

● Understands the causes of the Great Depression and its immediate and long-term BD (BE,203;R;WE,264,265) consequences for the world (e.g., the financial, economic, and social causes of the Great Depression, and its global impact; how the Depression affected colonial peoples of Africa and Asia, and how it contributed to the growth of nationalist movements; ▸ how the Great Depression affected the Middle East under British and French mandates; to what degree Britain, Germany, Japan, the Soviet Union, and the United States employed the military-industrial complex to stimulate recovery from the Great Depression)

▸ Understands how the treaties ending World War I and the League of Nations addressed BD (C;WE,259) different groups of people (e.g., how treaties ending World War I accorded with Woodrow Wilson's Fourteen Points and the processes by which the treaties were established, the varied reactions of the Chinese to the provisions of the Versailles Peace Treaty, the goals and failures of the "racial equality clause" in the preamble to the Covenant of the League of Nations)

▸ Understands post-World War I shifts in geographic and political borders in Europe and the BD (C;WE,259;LE,305) Middle East (e.g., how the postwar borders in Southern Europe and the Middle East were created, including influence of local opinion, prewar "spheres of influence," long-and short-term interests; how Ataturk worked to modernize Turkey, how Turkish society and international society responded)

▸ Understands elements of social and political change in China in the early 20th century (e.g., BD (C;WE,261) which populations supported the Kuomintang and the Chinese Communist Party, and how the Japanese invasion of China in the 1930s changed viewpoints regarding these two parties; how Mao Zedong adapted Marxism to Chinese needs and how he viewed the peasantry as a revolutionary force; the goals and outcomes of the three major revolutions in China in the first half of the century)

> ► Understands the conditions of the Hussein-McMahon correspondence and the Sykes-Picot agreement, how they differed from the conditions of the treaties of Versailles and San Remo, and what each party sought to gain from these efforts
>
> BD (R;WE,261)

> ► Understands the origins and consequences for international trade of the U.S. Smoot-Hawley Tariff (e.g., how international trade was affected by the depression, how other nations reacted to the tariff)
>
> BD (R;WE,265)

(BE,204;WE,266)

41. Understands the causes and global consequences of World War II

Level II (Grades 5-6)

● Understands the rise of fascism and Nazism in Europe and Japan (e.g., the ideologies of fascism and Nazism, and how fascist regimes seized power and gained mass support in Germany, Italy, Spain, and Japan; German, Italian, and Japanese military conquests and drives for empires in the 1930's; ► how Hitler, Franco, and Mussolini rose to power; the causes of the Spanish Civil War and how this war coincided with the rise of fascism in Europe; what Nazi oppression in Germany was like)

BD (BE,204;C;WE,266;LE,296)

● Understands influences on the outcome of World War II (e.g., the major turning points in the war; the principal theaters of conflict in Western Europe, Eastern Europe, the Soviet Union, North Africa, Asia, and the Pacific; the political and diplomatic leadership of individuals such as Churchill, Roosevelt, Hitler, Mussolini, and Stalin)

BD (BE,204;C;WE,268;LI,296,297)

► Understands the human costs of World War II (e.g., how and why the Nazi regime forged a "war against the Jews," and the devastation suffered by Jews and other groups in the Nazi Holocaust; ► social problems as a consequence of the war)

BD (C;WE,268;LI,296)

Level III (Grades 7-8)

● Understands events that led to the outbreak of World War II (e.g., the importance of the legacy of World War I, the depression, ethnic and ideological conflicts, imperialism, and

BD (BE,204;C;WE,267;LI,296,302)

Codes (right side of page):   BD = Benchmark, Declarative; BP = Benchmark, Procedural; BC = Benchmark, Contextual

1st letter of each code in parentheses	*2nd letter of code*	*Number*
B = NCHS: basic edition	E = Explicitly stated in document	Page number of cited document
W = NCHS: World History, expanded ed.	I = Implied in document	
L = Lessons from History		
C = Core material	*Symbol*	
R = Related material	■ material appears only in NCHS basic edition	
	► material appears only in NCHS expanded edition	
	● material appears in both NCHS editions	

traditional political or economic rivalries as underlying causes of World War II; the precipitating causes of the war and the reasons for early German and Japanese victories between 1939 and 1942; ▸ how Hitler capitalized on the despair of the German people to rise to power)

BD (BE,204;C;WE,267;LI,297)
● Understands the positions of the major powers Britain, France, the U.S., and the Soviet Union on fascist aggression, and the consequences of their failure to take forceful measures to stop this aggression

BD (BE,204;C;WE,269;LI,298)
● Understands the influence of Nazism on European society and Jewish culture (e.g., ▸ European and Jewish resistance movements to the Nazis and their policies, discrepancies between Nazi public announcements concerning Jews and the actual experiences of Jews between 1941 and 1944)

BD (C;WE,269)
▸ Understands the impact of World War II on civilian populations and soldiers (e.g., the roles of women and children during the war and how they differed in Allied and Axis countries, the hardships of the war on soldiers from both sides)

Level IV (Grades 9-12)

BD (BE,204;C;WE,267;LI,297)
● Understands motives and consequences of the Soviet nonaggression pacts with Germany and Japan (e.g., ▸ the Munich Agreement in 1938, what it meant for Stalin, and how it lead to the Nazi-Soviet Non-Aggression Pact of 1939)

BD (BE,204;C;WE,269;LE,296)
● Understands the Holocaust and its impact on Jewish culture and European society (e.g., ▸ the chronology of the Nazi "war on the Jews," and the geography and scale of Jewish deaths resulting from this policy; personal reasons for resistance to or compliance with Nazi policies and orders; the brutality of Nazi genocide in the Holocaust as revealed in personal stories of the victims)

BD (BE,204;C;WE,269)
● Understands the overall effect of World War II on various facets of society (e.g., the impact on industrial production, political goals, communication, national mobilization, technological innovations, and scientific research, and how these in turn made an impact upon war strategies, tactics, and levels of destruction; the consequences of World War II as a "total war")

Codes (right side of page):   BD = Benchmark, Declarative; BP = Benchmark, Procedural; BC = Benchmark, Contextual
1st letter of each code in parentheses   *2nd letter of code*   *Number*
B = NCHS: basic edition   E = Explicitly stated in document   Page number of cited document
W = NCHS: World History, expanded ed.   I = Implied in document
L = Lessons from History
C = Core material   *Symbol*
R = Related material   ■ material appears only in NCHS basic edition
                                        ▸ material appears only in NCHS expanded edition
                                        ● material appears in both NCHS editions

▸ Understands the rise of Nazism and how it was received by society (e.g., the essence and elements of Nazi ideology as represented in Mein Kampf and the Nazi party platform, and their use of terror against "enemies of the state"; the propaganda techniques employed by the Nazis to promote their ideas; political debate and opposition to the Nazi and Fascist movements in Germany and Italy in the 1920s and 1930s)

BD (C;WE,267;LE,296)

▸ Understands the exceptional violence of the Spanish Civil War (e.g., as described in works by George Orwell and Ernest Hemingway) and understands how foreign intervention affected the outcome of this war

BD (C;WE,267)

▸ Understands the argument that the severity of the Treaty of Versailles caused unavoidable revolt against the nations that imposed it

BD (C;WE,267)

▸ Understands Japan's "greater East Asia co-prosperity" sphere and the support of this idea in European colonies in East Asia

BD (C;WE,267;LI,297)

▸ Understands the climax and moral implications of World War II (e.g., the moral implications of military technologies and techniques used in the war, statistics of population displacement caused by the war, debates surrounding the use of the atomic bomb to end the war with Japan)

BD (C;WE,269;LI,297)

(BE,205)

42. Understands major global trends from 1900 to the end of World War II

Level II (Grades 5-6)

■ Understands major shifts in world geopolitics between 1900 and 1945, and understands the growing role of the United States in international affairs

BD (BE,205;LI,287-288)

■ Understands how new technologies and scientific breakthroughs both benefitted and imperiled humankind

BD (BE,205;LI,288-289)

Codes (right side of page):   BD = Benchmark, Declarative; BP = Benchmark, Procedural; BC = Benchmark, Contextual
1st letter of each code in parentheses   *2nd letter of code*   *Number*
B = NCHS: basic edition   E = Explicitly stated in document   Page number of cited document
W = NCHS: World History, expanded ed.   I = Implied in document
L = Lessons from History
C = Core material   *Symbol*
R = Related material   ■ material appears only in NCHS basic edition
                                         ▸ material appears only in NCHS expanded edition
                                         ● material appears in both NCHS editions

MREL

Level III (Grades 7-8)

■ Understands the nature and extent of Western military, political, and economic power in the world in 1945 compared with 1900
BD (BE,205;LI,298)

■ Understands the ideologies, policies, and governing methods of 20th century totalitarian regimes compared to those of contemporary democracies and absolutist states of earlier centuries
BD (BE,205;LI,295-296)

■ Understands influences on the emergence of movements for national self-rule or sovereignty in Africa and Asia (e.g., world war, depression, nationalist ideology, labor organizations, communism, liberal democratic ideals)
BD (BE,205;LE,307-309)

■ Understands ways in which secular ideologies (e.g., nationalism, fascism, communism, materialism) challenged or were challenged by established religions and ethical systems
BD (BE,205;LI,301-302)

■ Understands patterns of social and cultural continuity in various societies (e.g., ways in which peoples maintained traditions, sustained basic loyalties, and resisted external challenges in an era of recurrent world crises)
BD (BE,205;LI,292)

Level IV (Grades 9-12)

■ Understands how revolutionary movements in such countries as Mexico, Russia, and China either drew upon or rejected liberal, republican, and constitutional ideals of 18th and 19th century revolutions
BD (BE,205;LE,295,303,310)

■ Understands why mass consumer economies developed in some industrialized countries of the world but not in others
BD (BE,205)

Codes (right side of page):   BD = Benchmark, Declarative; BP = Benchmark, Procedural; BC = Benchmark, Contextual
1st letter of each code in parentheses   *2nd letter of code*   *Number*
B = NCHS: basic edition   E = Explicitly stated in document   Page number of cited document
W = NCHS: World History, expanded ed.   I = Implied in document
L = Lessons from History
C = Core material   *Symbol*
R = Related material   ■ material appears only in NCHS basic edition
    ▸ material appears only in NCHS expanded edition
    ● material appears in both NCHS editions

(BE,208;WE,270)

43. Understands how post-World War II reconstruction occurred, new international power relations took shape, and colonial empires broke up

Level II (Grades 5-6)

BD (BE,208,C;WE,270;LE,300;LI,303)

● Understands the shift in political and economic conditions after World War II (e.g., why and how the United Nations was established, where it has been active in the world, and how successful it has been as a peacekeeper; the United States' economic position and international leadership post-World War I and post-World War II; ▸ aspects of social and political conflict in China in the period following the war)

BD (BE,208-209;C;WE,270;LE,298;LI,298-300)

● Understands the development of the Cold War (e.g., how political, economic, and military conditions in the mid-1940's led to the Cold War; the significance of international Cold War crises such as the Berlin blockade, the Korean War, the Polish worker's protest, the Hungarian revolt, the Suez crisis, the Cuban missile crisis, the Indonesian civil war, and the Soviet invasion of Czechoslovakia; ▸ how the United States and the Soviet Union competed for power and influence in Europe)

BD (BE,209;C;WE,272;LI,307)

● Understands political and social change in the developing countries of the Middle East, Africa, and Asia after World War II (e.g., how Israel was created, and why persistent conflict developed between Israel and both Arab Palestinians and neighboring states; ▸ the African experience under European colonial rule; major social and economic forces that compelled many Vietnamese to seek refuge in foreign countries)

BD (C;WE,272)

▸ Understands the position of women in developing countries (e.g., as compared to their position in industrialized countries, how change has occurred in different societies)

Level III (Grades 7-8)

BD (BE,208-209;C;WE,270,271;LE,298;LI,298)

● Understands factors that brought about the political and economic transformation of Western and Eastern Europe after World War II (e.g., how Western European countries and Japan achieved rapid economic recovery after the war; the impact of the Marshall Plan, the European Economic Community, government planning, and the growth of welfare states

---

Codes (right side of page): BD = Benchmark, Declarative; BP = Benchmark, Procedural; BC = Benchmark, Contextual

1st letter of each code in parentheses	*2nd letter of code*	*Number*
B = NCHS: basic edition	E = Explicitly stated in document	Page number of cited document
W = NCHS: World History, expanded ed.	I = Implied in document	
L = Lessons from History		
C = Core material	*Symbol*	
R = Related material	■ material appears only in NCHS basic edition	
	▸ material appears only in NCHS expanded edition	
	● material appears in both NCHS editions	

303

MREL

upon the political stabilization of Western Europe;▸ the formations of the Warsaw Pact and the North Atlantic Treaty Organization after the war, and which countries have participated in each of these pacts; why Germany and Berlin were divided after the 1948 crisis, and the resulting problems)

- Understands post-war relations between the Soviet Union, Europe, and the United States
  BD (BE,208,209)
  (e.g., differences in the political ideologies and values of the Western democracies and the Soviet bloc; the impact of Soviet domination in Eastern Europe; interconnections between superpower rivalries and the development of new military, nuclear, and space technology)

- Understands the rise of the Communist Party in China between 1936 and 1949, the factors
  BD (BE,209;C;WE,270)
  leading to Mao's programs (e.g., the Great Leap Forward, the Cultural Revolution) and their results (e.g., ▸ effects on economic development, human suffering)

- Understands nationalist movements and other attempts by colonial countries to achieve
  BD (BE,209;C;WE,272;LI,308,309)
  independence after World War II (e.g., the impact of Indian nationalism on other movements in Africa and Asia, and reasons for the division of the subcontinent; how World War II and postwar global politics affected the mass nationalist movements in colonial Africa and Southeast Asia; factors that enabled some African and Asian countries to achieve independence through constitutional devolution of power, while others used armed revolution; ▸ the methods used by Indians to achieve independence from British rule and the effects of Mohandas Ghandi's call for nonviolent action)

▸ Understands political conditions in Africa after World War II (e.g., the moral, social,
  BD (C;WE,273)
  political, and economic implications of apartheid; the diverse leadership and governing styles of African regimes through the second half of the 20th century)

▸ Understands important events in the struggle between Israelis and Palestinians since 1948
  BD (C;WE,273;LI,308)
  and the argument on each side for rights to the disputed land

Level IV (Grades 9-12)

■ Understands political shifts in Europe and Asia following World War II (e.g., why fascism
  BD (BE,208;LI,298-299)
  was discredited after World War II; how popular democratic institutions were established in such countries as Italy, the German Federal Republic, Greece, India, Spain, and Portugal

---

Codes (right side of page):   BD = Benchmark, Declarative; BP = Benchmark, Procedural; BC = Benchmark, Contextual
1st letter of each code in parentheses   *2nd letter of code*   *Number*
B = NCHS: basic edition   E = Explicitly stated in document   Page number of cited document
W = NCHS: World History, expanded ed.   I = Implied in document
L = Lessons from History
C = Core material   *Symbol*
R = Related material   ■ material appears only in NCHS basic edition
                                             ▸ material appears only in NCHS expanded edition
                                             ● material appears in both NCHS editions

between 1945 and 1975)

- Understands the impact of relations between the United States and the Soviet Union during the Cold War (e.g., the effects of United States and Soviet competition for influence or dominance upon such countries as Egypt, Iran, the Congo, Vietnam, Chile, and Guatemala; the impact of the Cold War on art, literature, and popular culture around the world)

  BD (BE,209;C;WE,270,271)

- Understands reasons for the division of the Indian subcontinent (e.g., ► events that led to the dispute over Kashmir and the resulting partition of the Indian subcontinent, and the role of the United Nations in the mediation of the dispute; how the withdrawal of the British and the division between Muslims and Hindus affected the division of the Indian subcontinent into two nations)

  BD (BE,209;C;WE,273;LI,309)

- Understands the impact of independence movements in various countries and whether they were successful (e.g., the connections between the rise of independence movements in Africa and Southeast Asia and social transformations such as accelerated population growth, urbanization, and new Western-educated elites; ► the chronology of the Algerian struggle for independence, the role of domestic and international public opinion in the actions of the government, and how the French presence influenced the outcome; how diverse independence movements in Asia and Africa succeeded)

  BD (BE,209;C;WE,272)

- Understands reasons for the shift in government in Africa and how Africans responded (e.g., reasons for the replacement of parliamentary-style governments with military regimes and one-party states in much of Africa, ► how Africans survived and resisted apartheid)

  BD (BE,209;C;WE,272)

► Understands factors that influenced political conditions in China after World War II (e.g., how much of the Communist success in the Chinese civil war was the result of Mao Zedong's leadership or Jiang Jieshi's lack of leadership, why rifts developed in the relationships between the U.S.S.R. and China in spite of the common bond of Communist-led government)

  BD (C;WE,271)

► Understands the strategic role of the Muslim countries during the Cold War (e.g., the importance of geography, economy, and population) and the change in the region's role since the breakup of the Soviet Union

  BD (C;WE,271)

► Understands similarities between the stance of Buddhist priests against the Diem regime in

  BC (C;WE,273)

Codes (right side of page):	BD = Benchmark, Declarative; BP = Benchmark, Procedural; BC = Benchmark, Contextual	
1st letter of each code in parentheses	*2nd letter of code*	*Number*
B = NCHS: basic edition	E = Explicitly stated in document	Page number of cited document
W = NCHS: World History, expanded ed.	I = Implied in document	
L = Lessons from History		
C = Core material	*Symbol*	
R = Related material	■ material appears only in NCHS basic edition	
	► material appears only in NCHS expanded edition	
	● material appears in both NCHS editions	

McREL

Vietnam and the Muslim stance against the Kukarn regime in Indonesia

> ▸ Understands how the Balfour Declaration affected British policy toward Palestine and the political goals of the Arab League and the Zionist Movement, and how the White Paper Reports affected Jewish and Arab inhabitants of Palestine
>
> BD (C;WE,273;LE,305,306)

(BE,210;WI,274)

44. Understands the search for community, stability, and peace in an interdependent world

Level II (Grades 5-6)

- Understands global influences on the environment (e.g., how population growth, urbanization, industrialization, warfare, and the global market economy have contributed to environmental alterations; how effective governments and citizens' groups have been at protecting the global natural environment)

  BD (BE,210;C;WE,274)

- Understands the impact of increasing economic interdependence in different regions of the world (e.g., how global communications and changing international labor demands have shaped new patterns of world migration since World War II, the effects of the European Economic Community and its growth on economic productivity and political integration in Europe, the emergence of the Pacific Rim economy and economic growth in South Korea and Singapore in recent decades, ▸ the effects of new transport and communications technology on patterns of world trade and finance)

  BD (BE,210;C;WE,276)

- Understands efforts to improve political and social conditions around the world (e.g., the progress of human and civil rights around the globe since the 1948 U.N. Declaration of Human Rights; how the apartheid system was dismantled in South Africa and the black majority won voting rights; the progress made since the 1970s in resolving conflict between Israel and neighboring states)

  BD (BE,211,212;C;WE,278,280;LI,300,304-306)

- Understands how feminist movements and social conditions have affected the lives of women around the world, and the extent of women's progress toward social equality, economic opportunity, and political rights in various countries

  BD (BE,211;C;WE,278)

Codes (right side of page):   BD = Benchmark, Declarative; BP = Benchmark, Procedural; BC = Benchmark, Contextual

1st letter of each code in parentheses	*2nd letter of code*	*Number*
B = NCHS: basic edition	E = Explicitly stated in document	Page number of cited document
W = NCHS: World History, expanded ed.	I = Implied in document	
L = Lessons from History		
C = Core material	*Symbol*	
R = Related material	■ material appears only in NCHS basic edition	
	▸ material appears only in NCHS expanded edition	
	● material appears in both NCHS editions	

McREL

BD (BE,212;R;WE,282)

- Understands scientific and technological trends of the second half of the 20th century (e.g, worldwide implications of the revolution in nuclear, electronic, and computer technology; the social and cultural implications of medical successes such as the development of antibiotics and vaccines and the conquest of smallpox; ▸ the "consumer societies" of industrialized nations compared with those in predominantly agrarian nations)

BD (BE,213;R;WE,282;LI,306)

- Understands cultural trends of the second half of the 20th century (e.g., the influence of television, the Internet, and other forms of electronic communication on the creation and diffusion of cultural and political information worldwide; how the world's religions have responded to challenges and uncertainties in society and the world)

Level III (Grades 7-8)

BD (BE,210;C;WE,274;LI,306)

- Understands the causes and effects of population growth and urbanization (e.g., why population growth rate is accelerating around the world, and connections between population growth and economic and social development in many countries; the global proliferation of cities and the rise of the megalopolis, as well as the impact of urbanization on family life, standards of living, class relations, and ethnic identity; why scientific, technological, and medical advances have improved living standards but have failed to eradicate hunger, poverty, and epidemic disease)

BD (BE,210-211;C;WE,277;LI,299,305)

- Understands influences on economic development around the world (e.g., why economic disparities between industrialized and developing nations have persisted or increased, how neo-colonialism and authoritarian political leadership have affected development in African and Asian countries, the continuing growth of mass consumption of commodities and resources since World War II)

BD (BE,211;C;WE,278,279;LE,300)

- Understands events that led to an easing of Cold War tensions from the 1970s to the early 1990s (e.g., why the Cold War eased in the 1970s and how the Helsinki Accords, the Soviet invasion of Afghanistan, and Reagan-Gorbachev "summit diplomacy" affected progress toward detente; the collapse of the government of the Soviet Union and other communist governments around the world in the late 1980s and 1990s; ▸ the internal and external forces that led to changes within the USSR and in its relations with Eastern European countries)

BD (BE,211-212;R;WE,280;LI304,306)

- Understands instances of political conflict and terrorism in modern society (e.g., the changes

---

Codes (right side of page):   BD = Benchmark, Declarative; BP = Benchmark, Procedural; BC = Benchmark, Contextual

1st letter of each code in parentheses	*2nd letter of code*	*Number*
B = NCHS: basic edition	E = Explicitly stated in document	Page number of cited document
W = NCHS: World History, expanded ed.	I = Implied in document	
L = Lessons from History		
C = Core material	*Symbol*	
R = Related material	■ material appears only in NCHS basic edition	
	▸ material appears only in NCHS expanded edition	
	● material appears in both NCHS editions	

MREL

continuing urban protest and reformist economic policies have caused in post-Mao China under authoritarian rule; the causes, consequences, and moral implications of mass killings or famine in different parts of the world; ▸ possible factors in modern society that facilitate politically motivated terrorism and random forms of violence; world events that gave rise to the 1989 movement in China and led to the Tiannamen Square protest, the government response to this movement, and the international reaction)

BD (BE,212;R;WE,281)

- Understands the definition of "fundamentalism," and the political objectives of militant religious movements in various countries of the world, as well as the social and economic factors that contribute to the growth of these movements

BD (BE,213;R;WE,282,283;LI,301)

- Understands the emergence of a global culture (e.g., connections between electronic communications, international marketing, and the rise of a popular "global culture" in the late 20th century; ▸ how modern arts have expressed and reflected social transformations, political changes, and how they have been internationalized)

BD (C;WE,275)

▸ Understands the importance or meaning of the natural environment for societies around the world

BD (C;WE,285)

▸ Understands the role and difficulties of the present day migrant worker (e.g., the Southeast Asian domestic in the Persian Gulf, the American oil executive in Saudi Arabia, the Moroccan factory worker in France)

BD (C;WE,279)

▸ Understands the motivations, moral imperatives, and goals of specific separatist movements around the globe and the potential impact on the affected populations

BD (R;WE,283)

▸ Understands the effects of modern communication on consumer tastes and demands in different parts of the world

Level IV (Grades 9-12)

BD (BE,212;LE,301-302)

■ Understands the influences on and impact of cultural trends in the second half of the 20th century (e.g., the impact of World War II and its aftermath on literature, art, and intellectual life in Europe and other parts of the world; the meaning and social impact of innovative movements in literature and the arts such as Existentialism, Abstract Expressionism, or Pop

---

Codes (right side of page):   BD = Benchmark, Declarative; BP = Benchmark, Procedural; BC = Benchmark, Contextual

1st letter of each code in parentheses	*2nd letter of code*	*Number*
B = NCHS: basic edition	E = Explicitly stated in document	Page number of cited document
W = NCHS: World History, expanded ed.	I = Implied in document	
L = Lessons from History		
C = Core material	*Symbol*	
R = Related material	■ material appears only in NCHS basic edition	
	▸ material appears only in NCHS expanded edition	
	● material appears in both NCHS editions	

308

MREL

Art; ways in which art, literature, religion, and traditional customs have expressed or strengthened national or other communal loyalties in recent times)

- BD (BE,210-211;C;WE,276,277)
Understands rates of economic development and the emergence of different economic systems around the globe (e.g., systems of economic management in communist and capitalist countries, as well as the global impact of multinational corporations; the impact of black markets, speculation, and trade in illegal products on national and global markets; ► patterns of inward, outward, and internal migration in the Middle East and North Africa, types of jobs involved, and the impact of the patterns upon national economies; the rapid economic development of East Asian countries in the late 20th century, and the relatively slow development of Sub-Saharan African countries)

- BD (BE,210;C;WE,276)
Understands major reasons for the great disparities between industrialized and developing nations (e.g., ► disparities in resources, production, capital investment, labor, or trade; possible programs and measures to help equalize these disparities)

- BD (BE,211;C;WE,276-277)
Understands the oil crisis and its aftermath in the 1970s (e.g., how the oil crisis revealed the extent and complexity of global economic interdependence; ► events that have affected world oil prices since 1950; relationships between U.S. domestic energy policy and foreign policy in oil producing regions since 1970)

- BD (BE,211;C;WE,279)
Understands the role of political ideology, religion, and ethnicity in shaping modern governments (e.g., the strengths of democratic institutions and civic culture in different countries and challenges to civil society in democratic states; how successful democratic reform movements have been in challenging authoritarian governments in Africa, Asia, and Latin America; ► the implications of ethnic, religious, and border conflicts on state-building in the newly independent republics of Africa; significant differences among nationalist movements in Eastern Europe that have developed in the 20th century, how resulting conflicts have been resolved, and the outcomes of these conflicts)

- BD (BE,212;R;WE,280-281)
Understands the role of ethnicity, cultural identity, and religious beliefs in shaping economic and political conflicts across the globe (e.g., why terrorist movements have proliferated and the extent of their impact on politics and society in various countries; ► the tensions and contradictions between globalizing trends of the world economy and assertions of traditional cultural identity and distinctiveness, including the challenges to the role of religion in contemporary society; the meaning of jihad and other Islamic beliefs that are relevant to

---

Codes (right side of page):	BD = Benchmark, Declarative; BP = Benchmark, Procedural; BC = Benchmark, Contextual	
1st letter of each code in parentheses	*2nd letter of code*	*Number*
B = NCHS: basic edition	E = Explicitly stated in document	Page number of cited document
W = NCHS: World History, expanded ed.	I = Implied in document	
L = Lessons from History		
C = Core material	*Symbol*	
R = Related material	■ material appears only in NCHS basic edition	
	► material appears only in NCHS expanded edition	
	● material appears in both NCHS editions	

military activity, how these compare to the Geneva Accords, and how such laws and principles apply to terrorist acts)

- Understands the impact of population pressure, poverty, and environmental degradation on the breakdown of state authority in various countries in the 1980s and 1990s, and international reaction to the deterioration of these states
  BD (BE,212;R;WE,280)

- Understands how trends in science have influenced society (e.g., interconnections between space exploration and developments since the 1950s in scientific research, agricultural productivity, consumer culture, intelligence gathering, and other aspects of contemporary life; the changing structure and organization of scientific and technological research, including the role of governments, corporations, international agencies, universities and scientific communities)
  BD (BE,212;R;WE,283;LE,301)

▸ Understands influences on population growth, and efforts to control such growth in modern society (e.g., how statistics from specific, diverse nations illustrate the relationship between scientific, medical, and technological advancements and population growth; China's population growth from the 1700s to 1990, why the population growth increased dramatically, and the effects of the "one-child" policy of the 1990s; issues and objections raised at the 1994 Cairo Conference on World Population and the difficulty of arriving at a consensus document on population growth)
  BD (C;WE,275;LI,304)

▸ Understands the effectiveness of United Nations programs (e.g., improvements in health and welfare, whether UN programs have been cost-effective, whether programs fulfilled the purpose for which they were created, reasons for economic and arms embargoes sponsored by U.N. resolutions and the political and economic consequences for the sanctioned countries)
  BD (C;WE,275,281)

▸ Understands common arguments of opposition groups in various countries around the world, common solutions they offer, and the position of these ideas with regard to Western economic and strategic interests
  BD (C;WE,279)

▸ Understands gender roles across the globe (e.g., conflicts in the perception of gender roles in various religions, especially the role of women; how the legal status of women varies around the world in Muslim societies, and how the status of women from different classes has changed in the past century)
  BD (C;WE,279;LI,307)

Codes (right side of page):   BD = Benchmark, Declarative; BP = Benchmark, Procedural; BC = Benchmark, Contextual

1st letter of each code in parentheses   *2nd letter of code*   *Number*
B = NCHS: basic edition   E = Explicitly stated in document   Page number of cited document
W = NCHS: World History, expanded ed.   I = Implied in document
L = Lessons from History
C = Core material   *Symbol*
R = Related material   ▪ material appears only in NCHS basic edition
                                              ▸ material appears only in NCHS expanded edition
                                              ● material appears in both NCHS editions

BD (R;WE,283)

► Understands how global political change has altered the world economy (e.g., what participation in the world economy can mean for different countries; the relationship between demands for democratic reform and the trend toward privatization and economic liberalization in developing economies and former communist states, and how multilateral aid organizations and multinational corporations have supported or challenged these trends)

BD (R;WE,290;LE,304)

► Understands how specific countries have implemented social and cultural changes (e.g., the different manifestations of China's contingency quest for a "new culture" throughout the 20th century, and what the Cultural Revolution meant for Chinese people in the late 1960s; models for family life, the economy, and social and political institutions suggested by modern Muslim intellectuals)

BD (R;WE,283)

► Understands "liberation theology" and the ideological conflicts that have surrounded this philosophy

(BE,213)

45. Understands major global trends since World War II

Level II (Grades 5-6)

BD (BE,213)

■ Understands the causes, consequences, and major patterns of international migration in the late 20th century compared to world population movements of the 19th century and the first half of the 20th

BD (BE,213;LE,288)

■ Understands the advancement of human rights and democratic ideals and practices in the world during the 20th century

Level III (Grades 7-8)

BD (BE,213;LI,288)

■ Understands the changing configuration of political boundaries in the world since 1900 and connections between nationalist ideology and the proliferation of sovereign states

BD (BE,213;LE,300)

■ Understands the origins and decline of the Cold War and its significance as a 20th-century

---

Codes (right side of page):   BD = Benchmark, Declarative; BP = Benchmark, Procedural; BC = Benchmark, Contextual

1st letter of each code in parentheses	*2nd letter of code*	*Number*
B = NCHS: basic edition	E = Explicitly stated in document	Page number of cited document
W = NCHS: World History, expanded ed.	I = Implied in document	
L = Lessons from History		
C = Core material	*Symbol*	
R = Related material	■ material appears only in NCHS basic edition	
	► material appears only in NCHS expanded edition	
	● material appears in both NCHS editions	

event

■ Understands the causes and consequences of the world's shift from bipolar to multipolar
centers of economic, political, and military power
BD (BE,213;LI,289)

Level IV (Grades 9-12)

■ Understands the usefulness of the concept of "postindustrial society" in comparing the late
20th century with the period from the industrial revolution to 1950
BD (BE,213)

■ Understands causes of economic imbalances and social inequalities among the world's
peoples and efforts made to close these gaps
BD (BE,213;LI,310)

■ Understands connections between globalizing trends in economy, technology, and culture
and dynamic assertions of traditional cultural identity and distinctiveness
BD (BE,213)

(BE,214)

46.   Understands long-term changes and recurring patterns in world history

Level II (Grades 5-6)

■ Understands why humans have built cities and how the character, function, and number of
cities have changed over time
BD (BE,214)

■ Understands major patterns of long-distance trade from ancient times to the present and how
trade has contributed to economic and cultural change in particular societies or civilizations
BD (BE,214;LI,195,253)

■ Understands the economic and social importance of slavery and other forms of coerced labor
in various societies
BD (BE,214;LI,219)

■ Understands how ideals and institutions of freedom, equality, justice, and citizenship have
changed over time and from one society to another
BD (BE,214)

■ Understands ways in which human action has contributed to long-term changes in the natural
BD (BE,215)

Codes (right side of page):   BD = Benchmark, Declarative; BP = Benchmark, Procedural; BC = Benchmark, Contextual
1st letter of each code in parentheses   *2nd letter of code*   *Number*
B = NCHS: basic edition   E = Explicitly stated in document   Page number of cited document
W = NCHS: World History, expanded ed.   I = Implied in document
L = Lessons from History
C = Core material   *Symbol*
R = Related material   ■ material appears only in NCHS basic edition
                                            ▸ material appears only in NCHS expanded edition
                                            ● material appears in both NCHS editions

environment in particular regions or worldwide

Level III (Grades 7-8)

- Understands major changes in world population from paleolithic times to the present (e.g., why these changes occurred, the effects of major disease pandemics)

  BD (BE,214)

- Understands the emergence of capitalism (e.g., the origins, development, and characteristics of capitalism; capitalist systems compared with other systems for organizing production, labor, and trade)

  BD (BE,214;LI,252)

- Understands the development of the nation-state and how nation-states differ from empires or other forms of political organization

  BD (BE,214)

- Understands political revolutionary movements of the past three centuries and their idcologics, organization, and successes or failures

  BD (BE,215;LI,254,273,289-290)

Level IV (Grades 9-12)

- Understands the importance of the revolutions in tool-making, agriculture, and industrialization as major turning points in human history

  BD (BE,214;LI,195,273)

- Understands the circumstances under which European countries came to exercise temporary military and economic dominance in the world in the late 19th and 20th centuries

  BD (BE,214;LI,272-273,287)

Codes (right side of page):   BD = Benchmark, Declarative; BP = Benchmark, Procedural; BC = Benchmark, Contextual

1st letter of each code in parentheses	*2nd letter of code*	*Number*
B = NCHS: basic edition	E = Explicitly stated in document	Page number of cited document
W = NCHS: World History, expanded ed.	I = Implied in document	
L = Lessons from History		
C = Core material	*Symbol*	
R = Related material	■ material appears only in NCHS basic edition	
	▸ material appears only in NCHS expanded edition	
	● material appears in both NCHS editions	

LANGUAGE
ARTS

10. Language Arts

The following process was used to identify standards and benchmarks for the language arts:

Identification of Significant Reports
This category deals with basic knowledge and skill in reading, writing, and language. As described in Chapter 2, the federally funded efforts to develop language arts standards were never completed. Specifically, federal funding halted for the Standards Projects for the English Language Arts (SPELA) as of March 1994. One complete draft document survived that effort, the *Incomplete Work of the Task Forces of the Standards Project for English Language Arts* (1994). It identified standards in five broad areas referred to as strands. The document was the product of a joint effort of the Center for the Study of Reading (CSR) at the University of Illinois, the International Reading Association (IRA), and the National Council of Teachers of English (NCTE). When funding for SPELA was halted in 1994, NCTE and IRA continued their joint effort to produce language arts standards. In 1996, NCTE and IRA published their unsponsored standards in the work *Standards for the English Language Arts*. It identified 12 broadly articulated standards that cover such skills and abilities as reading a wide range of literature, using a variety of writing strategies, developing an appreciation for differing language patterns and dialects, and applying knowledge of such conventions as spelling and punctuation to create texts. However, the document does not identify specific elements of information and skill as benchmarks for the standards. Rather, the benchmarks that define the specific content within each standard must be inferred from four documents that provide vignettes of how the standards might be addressed at different grade levels.

> * *Standards in Practice*: *Grades K-2* (Crafton, 1996)
> * *Standards in Practice*: *Grades 3-5* (Sierra-Perry, 1996)
> * *Standards in Practice*: *Grades 6-8* (Wilhelm, 1996)
> * *Standards in Practice*: *Grades 9-12* (Smagorinsky, 1996)

In addition to these works, NCTE has developed the *Standards Exemplar Series* (1997). Thus far, the series includes *Grades 6-8* (eds., Miles Myers and Elizabeth Spalding) and *Assessing Student Performance: Grades 9-12* (eds., Miles Myers and Elizabeth Spalding). The K-5 edition is scheduled to be published in August 1997. These guides provide performance standards that include rubrics for different types of writing and are connected to the NCTE content standards.

In addition to the NCTE/IRA documents, a number of other documents contain explicit and implicit descriptions of language arts standards; together, they provided a rather comprehensive source of information for identifying standards in the English language arts. The most explicit of these are documents produced by the National Assessment of Educational Progress (NAEP) as a part of its 1992 assessment efforts. In the area of writing, NAEP has produced the *Description of Writing Achievement Levels—Setting Process and Proposed Achievement Level Definitions* (1992). This document provides descriptions of basic, proficient, and advanced levels of performance at three levels: grade 4, grade 8, and grade 12. The performance levels represent fairly straightforward descriptions of what students should know and be able to do in writing. In reading, NAEP has produced the *Assessment and Exercise Specifications: NAEP Reading Consensus Project: 1992 NAEP Reading Assessment* (1990). This document provides explicit statements of what students should know and be able to do relative to the process of reading and identifies the types of materials students should be able to read at various levels. Other sources of explicit descriptions of knowledge and skills students should acquire within the language arts include documents from the Edison Project (1994a, 1994b, 1994c), selected language arts frameworks from various states (Mississippi, Texas, Utah, and Virginia), the language arts standards framework from Australia (Australian Education Council, 1994), documents from the New Standards Project (New Standards, 1997), the language arts curriculum documents from the International Baccalaureate program (1992,1995d), and standards from the Speech Communication Association (1996).

All of the standards documents mentioned thus far discuss the critical role of literature in developing students' expertise in the skills of language arts. To obtain a comprehensive view of the various perspectives regarding the literature with which students should be familiar, a number of sources were consulted. These included: a list of recommended readings from the New England Association of Teachers of English (Stotsky, Anderson, and Beierl, 1989); recommended readings from the California State Department of Education (California State Department of Education, 1989); lists of "best books" by Gillespie (1991a, 1991b); recommended literature by Ravitch and Finn (1987), reading lists from the New Standards Project (1997), lists of recommended literature by the International Baccalaureate Organisation (May,1996a, 1996b), E.D. Hirsch (Hirsch, 1987, 1993a, 1993b, 1993c, 1993d, 1993e, 1993f), and the Edison Project (1994a, 1994b, 1994c).

In addition to documents that have a specific focus on the language arts, the document *Expectations of Excellence: Curriculum Standards for Social Studies* (NCSS, 1994) has explicit and implicit standards that deal with reading and writing in enough detail to be useful to this effort.

Selection of Reference Documents and Identification of Standards
Although the standards developed by NCTE and IRA are certainly considered the "official" language arts standards, neither this document nor its related works were amenable to the level of specificity and detail necessary to this study. Given the lack of appropriateness of the NCTE/IRA documents for this effort, different reference documents were identified for different aspects of the English language arts. Two NAEP documents were identified as reference documents for reading and writing since they contained the most explicit statements of standards. Specifically, the reference document selected for the general area of writing was the *Description of Writing Achievement Levels—Setting Process and Proposed Achievement Level Definitions*. The reference document selected for the general area of reading was *Assessment and Exercise Specifications: NAEP Reading Consensus Project: 1992 NAEP Reading Assessment*. Both of these documents contain a level of detail sufficient to provide a strong basis for identifying standards in the areas of writing and reading. The reference document identified for the area of listening and speaking was the standards framework developed by the Australian Education Council, *English: A Curriculum Profile for Australian Schools* (Australian Education Council, 1994). Although listening and speaking were addressed to some extent within other sources (e.g., the New Standards Project), the Australian

Framework was deemed the most comprehensive treatment of this area.

No single source was used as the reference document for the literary works found in the appendix for the language arts standards. The literature cited in the various sources mentioned previously was organized into fairly traditional categories (e.g., nursery rhymes, fairy tales, folk tales, fiction, Greek and Roman mythology).

Summary of Standards for Language Arts

Writing

1. Demonstrates competence in the general skills and strategies of the writing process
2. Demonstrates competence in the stylistic and rhetorical aspects of writing
3. Uses grammatical and mechanical conventions in written compositions
4. Gathers and uses information for research purposes

Reading

5. Demonstrates competence in the general skills and strategies of the reading process
6. Demonstrates competence in general skills and strategies for reading a variety of literary texts
7. Demonstrates competence in the general skills and strategies for reading a variety of informational texts

Listening and Speaking

8. Demonstrates competence in speaking and listening as tools for learning

(AI,10,11;NS1,2,3I,20,21;SP1,2,3,4E,ix;TE,8,21,35;VE,59)

1. Demonstrates competence in the general skills and strategies of the writing process

Level I (Grades K-2)

BP (AE,39;SP1E,25;TE,10;U2E,08;VE,63)
- **Prewriting**: Uses prewriting strategies to plan written work (e.g., discusses ideas with peers, draws pictures to generate ideas, writes key thoughts and questions, rehearses ideas, records reactions and observations)

BP (AE,39;E1E,25;NS1E,26;SP1E,25,63;TE,10;U2E,08;VE,63)
- **Drafting and Revising**: Uses strategies to draft and revise written work (e.g., rereads; rearranges words, sentences, and paragraphs to improve or clarify meaning; varies sentence type; adds descriptive words and details; deletes extraneous information; incorporates suggestions from peers and teachers; sharpens the focus)

BP (E1E,25;NS1E,26;SP1E,25,63;TE,10;U2E,08;VE,63)
- **Editing and Publishing**: Uses strategies to edit and publish written work (e.g., proofreads using a dictionary and other resources; edits for grammar, punctuation, capitalization, and spelling at a developmentally appropriate level; incorporates illustrations or photos; shares finished product)

BP (E1E,25;NS1E,26;SP1E,25;TE,10)
- Evaluates own and others' writing (e.g., asks questions and makes comments about writing, helps classmates apply grammatical and mechanical conventions)

BP (AE,38;E1I,25;NWI,23;SP1I,25;TI,8;VE,63)
- Dictates or writes with a logical sequence of events (e.g., includes a beginning, middle, and ending)

BP (AE,38;E1E,25;VE,62)
- Dictates or writes detailed descriptions of familiar persons, places, objects, or experiences

BP (NS1I,24;U2E,07;VE,63)
- Writes in response to literature

BP (AI,38;SP1E,25;TE,9;U2E,08;VE,63)
- Writes in a variety of formats (e.g., picture books, letters, stories, poems, information pieces)

Level II (Grades 3-5)

BP (AE,39;SP2E,61-62;TE,10,22;U5E,07;VE,64,67)
- **Prewriting**: Uses prewriting strategies to plan written work (e.g., uses graphic organizers, story maps, and webs; groups related ideas; takes notes; brainstorms ideas)

Codes (right side of page):	BD = Benchmark, Declarative; BP = Benchmark, Procedural; BC = Benchmark, Contextual

1st letter(s) of each code in parentheses | *2nd letter of code* | *Number*
A = Australian Education Council | E = Explicitly stated in document | Page number of cited document
E1,2,3 = Edison Proj: Primary, Elem., Junior | I = Implied in document | *or, for Utah document:*
ES1,2,3 = NCTE: Exemplar Series: 6-8, 9-12 | | Standard number
IA,IA1 = Int'l Bacc.: Middle, A1 Guide
M = Mississippi: English Language Arts | SS = NCSS: Curric. Standards for Social Studies
NR = NAEP: 1992 Reading Assessment | T = Texas: English Language Arts and Reading
NS1,2,3 = New Standards: Elem., Middle, High | UK-12 = Utah Core Curriculum: Language Arts
NW = NAEP: Writing Achiev. Levels-Setting Proc. | V = Board of Ed., Commonwealth of Virginia: Standards of Learning
S = Speech Communication Association | AP = See appendix immediately following the Language Arts Standards
SP1,2,3,4 = NCTE: Standards in Practice

319

McREL

- ***Drafting and Revising***: Uses strategies to draft and revise written work (e.g., elaborates on a central idea; writes with attention to voice, audience, word choice, tone, and imagery; uses paragraphs to develop separate ideas)
  BP (E2I,36;NS1,2E,26;SP2E,30,35;TE,10;U5E,07;VE,66,67)

- ***Editing and Publishing***: Uses strategies to edit and publish written work (e.g., edits for grammar, punctuation, capitalization, and spelling at a developmentally appropriate level; considers page format [paragraphs, margins, indentations, titles]; selects presentation format; incorporates photos, illustrations, charts, and graphs)
  BP (AE,39;SP2E,69;U5E,07;VE,67)

- Evaluates own and others' writing (e.g., identifies the best features of a piece of writing, determines how own writing achieves its purposes, asks for feedback, responds to classmates' writing)
  BP (E2E,36;NS1,2E,26;SP2E,30,35;TE,10)

- Writes stories or essays that show awareness of intended audience
  BP (AI,39;E2E,36;NS1,2I,24;NWE,23;SP2E,35;TE,9,21;U5E,06)

- Writes stories or essays that convey an intended purpose (e.g., to record ideas, to describe, to explain)
  BP (AE,38,39;E2I,36;NS1,2I,24;NWE,23;SP2E,35;TE,9,21;U5E,06;VE,67)

- Writes expository compositions (e.g., identifies and stays on the topic; develops the topic with simple facts, details, examples, and explanations; excludes extraneous and inappropriate information)
  BP (E2E,36;IAE,15;MI,34;NS1,2E,24;NWI,23;U5I,06)

- Writes narrative accounts (e.g., engages the reader by establishing a context and otherwise developing reader interest; establishes a situation, plot, point of view, setting, and conflict; creates an organizational structure that balances and unifies all narrative aspects of the story; uses sensory details and concrete language to develop plot and character; uses a range of strategies such as dialogue and tension or suspense)
  BP (AE,38;IAI,14;MI,32;NS1,2E,24;U5E,06;VE,66)

- Writes autobiographical compositions (e.g., provides a context within which the incident occurs, uses simple narrative strategies, provides some insight into why this incident is memorable)
  BP (E2E,36;IAI,15;NS1,2E,24)

- Writes expressive compositions (e.g., expresses ideas, reflections, and observations; uses an individual, authentic voice; uses narrative strategies, relevant details, and ideas that enable
  BP (IAI,14;NS1I,24;NWI,23-25;TI,9,21;VI,64,66)

Codes (right side of page):	BD = Benchmark, Declarative; BP = Benchmark, Procedural; BC = Benchmark, Contextual
1st letter(s) of each code in parentheses	*2nd letter of code* — *Number*
A = Australian Education Council	E = Explicitly stated in document — Page number of cited document
E1,2,3 = Edison Proj: Primary, Elem., Junior	I = Implied in document — *or, for Utah document:*
ES1,2,3 = NCTE: Exemplar Series: 6-8, 9-12	Standard number
IA,IA1 = Int'l Bacc.: Middle, A1 Guide	
M = Mississippi: English Language Arts	SS = NCSS: Curric. Standards for Social Studies
NR = NAEP: 1992 Reading Assessment	T = Texas: English Language Arts and Reading
NS1,2,3 = New Standards: Elem., Middle, High	UK-12 = Utah Core Curriculum: Language Arts
NW = NAEP: Writing Achiev. Levels-Setting Proc.	V = Board of Ed., Commonwealth of Virginia: Standards of Learning
S = Speech Communication Association	AP = See appendix immediately following the Language Arts Standards
SP1,2,3,4 = NCTE: Standards in Practice	

320

McREL

the reader to imagine the world of the event or experience)

- Writes in response to literature (e.g., advances judgments; supports judgments with references to the text, other works, other authors, nonprint media, and personal knowledge)

  BP (MI,34;NS1,2E,24;TE,5;U5I,06)

- Writes personal letters (e.g., includes the date, address, greeting, and closing; addresses envelopes)

  BP (IAI,15;ME,33;SP2E,72-73;U5E,07;VE,64)

Level III (Grades 6-8)

- **Prewriting**: Uses a variety of prewriting strategies (e.g., makes outlines, uses published pieces as writing models, constructs critical standards, brainstorms, builds background knowledge)

  BP (AI,61;SP3E,22;TE,22,23;U8E,01-1;VE,71)

- **Drafting and Revising**: Uses a variety of strategies to draft and revise written work (e.g., analyzes and clarifies meaning, makes structural and syntactical changes, uses an organizational scheme, uses sensory words and figurative language, rethinks and rewrites for different audiences and purposes, checks for a consistent point of view and for transitions between paragraphs, uses direct feedback to revise compositions)

  BP (AE,61;E3E,35;NS2E,26;SP3I,33;TE,22;U8E,02-1;VE,71)

- **Editing and Publishing**: Uses a variety of strategies to edit and publish written work (e.g., eliminates slang; edits for grammar, punctuation, capitalization, and spelling at a developmentally appropriate level; proofreads using reference materials, word processor, and other resources; edits for clarity, word choice, and language usage; uses a word processor to publish written work)

  BP (AE,61;E3E,35;NS2E,26;SP3I,33;TE,22;U8E,03-1;VE,70,71)

- Evaluates own and others' writing (e.g., applies criteria generated by self and others, uses self-assessment to set and achieve goals as a writer, participates in peer response groups)

  BP (NS2E,26;SP3E,33;TE,23;U8E,02-1)

- Uses style and structure appropriate for specific audiences (e.g., public, private) and purposes (e.g., to entertain, to influence, to inform)

  BP (AE,60;NS2E,24;NWE,25;TE,21;U8I,01-2)

- Writes expository compositions (e.g., presents information that reflects knowledge about the topic of the report; organizes and presents information in a logical manner)

  BP (ES2I,11;IAE,15,16;MI,34;NS2E,24;VE,71)

Codes (right side of page):   BD = Benchmark, Declarative;   BP = Benchmark, Procedural;   BC = Benchmark, Contextual

1st letter(s) of each code in parentheses	2nd letter of code	Number
A = Australian Education Council	E = Explicitly stated in document	Page number of cited document
E1,2,3 = Edison Proj: Primary, Elem., Junior	I = Implied in document	or, for Utah document:
ES1,2,3 = NCTE: Exemplar Series: 6-8, 9-12		Standard number
IA,IA1 = Int'l Bacc.: Middle, A1 Guide		

M = Mississippi: English Language Arts   SS = NCSS: Curric. Standards for Social Studies
NR = NAEP: 1992 Reading Assessment   T = Texas: English Language Arts and Reading
NS1,2,3 = New Standards: Elem., Middle, High   UK-12 = Utah Core Curriculum: Language Arts
NW = NAEP: Writing Achiev. Levels-Setting Proc.   V = Board of Ed., Commonwealth of Virginia: Standards of Learning
S = Speech Communication Association   AP = See appendix immediately following the Language Arts Standards
SP1,2,3,4 = NCTE: Standards in Practice

- Writes narrative accounts (e.g., engages the reader by establishing a context and otherwise developing reader interest; establishes a situation, plot, persona, point of view, setting, and conflict; creates an organizational structure that balances and unifies all narrative aspects of the story; uses sensory details and concrete language to develop plot and character; excludes extraneous details and inconsistencies; develops complex characters; uses a range of strategies such as dialogue, tension or suspense, naming, and specific narrative action such as movement, gestures, and expressions)

  BP (AE,60,82;IAE,14,15;NS2E,24;U8E,02-2;VE,71)

- Writes compositions about autobiographical incidents (e.g., explores the significance and personal importance of the incident; uses details to provide a context for the incident; reveals personal attitude towards the incident; presents details in a logical manner)

  BP (E3I,34;ES3I,2;IAI,15;NS2E,24;NWI,23,25;SSI,149)

- Writes biographical sketches (e.g., illustrates the subject's character using narrative and descriptive strategies such as relevant dialogue, specific action, physical description, background description, and comparison or contrast to other people; reveals the significance of the subject to the writer; presents details in a logical manner)

  BP (E3I,34;ES3I,7;IAI,14,15;MI,35;NS2E,24;NWI,23;U8E,02-2,02-3)

- Writes persuasive compositions (e.g., engages the reader by establishing a context, creating a persona, and otherwise developing reader interest; develops a controlling idea that conveys a judgment; creates and organizes a structure appropriate to the needs and interests of a specific audience; arranges details, reasons, examples, and/or anecdotes persuasively; excludes information and arguments that are irrelevant; anticipates and addresses reader concerns and counterarguments; supports arguments with detailed evidence, citing sources of information as appropriate)

  BP (AE,82;ES2I,19;IAI,15;NS2E,24;U8E,02-4;VE,71)

- Writes compositions that speculate on problems/solutions (e.g., identifies and defines a problem in a way appropriate to the intended audience, describes at least one solution, presents logical and well-supported reasons)

  BP (E3I,34;ES3I,15;IAI,15)

- Writes in response to literature (e.g., anticipates and answers a reader's questions, responds to significant issues in a log or journal, answers discussion questions, writes a summary of a book, describes an initial impression of a text, connects knowledge from a text with personal knowledge)

  BP (ES3I,22;IAI,16;NS2E,24;SP3E,64)

Codes (right side of page):	BD = Benchmark, Declarative; BP = Benchmark, Procedural; BC = Benchmark, Contextual	
1st letter(s) of each code in parentheses	*2nd letter of code*	*Number*
A = Australian Education Council	E = Explicitly stated in document	Page number of cited document
E1,2,3 = Edison Proj: Primary, Elem., Junior	I = Implied in document	*or, for Utah document:*
ES1,2,3 = NCTE: Exemplar Series: 6-8, 9-12		Standard number
IA,IA1 = Int'l Bacc.: Middle, A1 Guide		
M = Mississippi: English Language Arts	SS = NCSS: Curric. Standards for Social Studies	
NR = NAEP: 1992 Reading Assessment	T = Texas: English Language Arts and Reading	
NS1,2,3 = New Standards: Elem., Middle, High	UK-12 = Utah Core Curriculum: Language Arts	
NW = NAEP: Writing Achiev. Levels-Setting Proc.	V = Board of Ed., Commonwealth of Virginia: Standards of Learning	
S = Speech Communication Association	AP = See appendix immediately following the Language Arts Standards	
SP1,2,3,4 = NCTE: Standards in Practice		

McREL

- Writes business letters and letters of request and response (e.g., uses business letter format; states purpose of the letter; relates opinions, problems, requests, or compliments; uses precise vocabulary)

  BP (IAI,15;ME,33;U8E,02-5)

Level IV (Grades 9-12)

- ***Prewriting***: Uses a variety of prewriting strategies (e.g., develops a focus, plans a sequence of ideas, uses structured overviews, uses speed writing, creates diagrams)

  BP (AE,83,107;U12E,01-1;VE,75,76)

- ***Drafting and Revising***: Uses a variety of strategies to draft and revise written work (e.g., rethinks content, organization, and style; checks accuracy and depth of information; redrafts for readability and needs of readers; reviews writing to ensure that content and linguistic structures are consistent with purpose)

  BP (AE,83,107;ES3I,66;MI,35;NS3E,26;SP4I,14,102;TE,36;U12I,02-1;VE,74-76)

- ***Editing and Publishing***: Uses a variety of strategies to edit and publish written work (e.g., uses a checklist to guide proofreading; edits for grammar, punctuation, capitalization, and spelling at a developmentally appropriate level; refines selected pieces to publish for general and specific audiences; uses technology to publish written work)

  BP (AE,107;ES3I,66;TE,36;U12E,03-1;VE,76)

- Evaluates own and others' writing (e.g., accumulates a body of written work to determine strengths and weaknesses as a writer, makes suggestions to improve writing)

  BP (NS3E,26;TE,36;VE,74)

- Writes compositions that are focused for different audiences (e.g., includes explanations and definitions according to the audience's knowledge of the topic, adjusts formality of style, considers interests of potential readers)

  BP (AE,82;NS3E,23;NWI,26;SP4E,viii-ix;TE,35;U12E,01-1;VE,75,76)

- Writes compositions that fulfill different purposes (e.g., to reflect, to analyze, to persuade)

  BP (IAI,15,16;NS3E,23;NWE,26;SP4E,viii-ix;TE,35;VE,76)

- Writes expository compositions (e.g., synthesizes and organizes information from first- and second-hand sources, including books, magazines, computer data banks, and the community; uses a variety of techniques to develop the main idea [names, describes, or differentiates parts; compares or contrasts; examines the history of a subject; cites an anecdote to provide an example; illustrates through a scenario; provides interesting facts about the subject])

  BP (IAE,15;NS3E,23;TE,35;VE,76)

- BP (AE,82;ES3I,2;IAI,15,16;ME,35;NS3E,24;SP4I,16;U12E,02-1;VE,73)
  Writes fictional, biographical, autobiographical, and observational narrative compositions (e.g., narrates a sequence of events; evaluates the significance of the incident; provides a specific setting for scenes and incidents; provides supporting descriptive detail [specific names for people, objects, and places; visual details of scenes, objects, and places; descriptions of sounds, smells, specific actions, movements, and gestures; the interior monologue or feelings of the characters]; paces the actions to accommodate time or mood changes)

- BP (AE,82;ES3I,11;IAI,15,16;MI,32,35;NS3E,22,24,27;TI,37;U12I,02-3;VE,75)
  Writes persuasive compositions that evaluate, interpret, and speculate about problems/solutions and causes and effects (e.g., articulates a position through a thesis statement; anticipates and addresses counterarguments; backs up assertions using specific rhetorical devices [appeals to logic, appeals to emotion, uses personal anecdotes]; develops arguments using a variety of methods such as examples and details, commonly accepted beliefs, expert opinion, cause-and- effect reasoning, comparison-contrast reasoning)

- BP (AE,82,106;ES3I,6,7;IAI,15,16;ME,35)
  Writes descriptive compositions (e.g., uses concrete details to provide a perspective on the subject being described; uses supporting detail [concrete images, shifting perspectives and vantage points, sensory detail, and factual descriptions of appearance])

- BP (AI,82;ES3I,48;IAI,15,16;NS3E,24;SP4E,38;TE,37)
  Writes reflective compositions (e.g., uses personal experience as a basis for reflection on some aspect of life, draws abstract comparisons between specific incidents and abstract concepts, maintains a balance between describing incidents and relating them to more general abstract ideas that illustrate personal beliefs, moves from specific examples to generalizations about life)

- BP (ES3I,15,24;IAI,16;NS3E,23;SP4E,83;TE,31;U12E,02-4;VE,74)
  Writes in response to literature (e.g., suggests an interpretation; recognizes possible ambiguities, nuances, and complexities in a text; interprets passages of a novel in terms of their significance to the novel as a whole; focuses on the theme of a literary work; explains concepts found in literary works)

- BP (IAE,15;ME,33-34;U9E,01-5;VE,75)
  Writes personal and business correspondence (e.g., informal letters, memos, job application letters, resumes)

(P1,2,3I,20-21;TI,8,21,35;VI,59)

2.   Demonstrates competence in the stylistic and rhetorical aspects of writing

Level I (Grades K-2)

BP (NWI,23;SP1I,25;TI,8;U2E,07;VI,62)
- Uses general, frequently used words to convey basic ideas

Level II (Grades 3-5)

BP (AI,38;NWE,23;TI,22;U5I,06;VE,64;VI,67)
- Uses descriptive language that clarifies and enhances ideas (e.g., describes familiar people, places, or objects)

BP (ME,32;NS1E,26;VE,66;U5I,06)
- Uses paragraph form in writing (e.g., indents the first word of a paragraph, uses topic sentences, recognizes a paragraph as a group of sentences about one main idea, writes several related paragraphs)

BP (NWE,24;TE,22;VE,67)
- Uses a variety of sentence structures

Level III (Grades 6-8)

BP (E3I,34;NWI,25;TI,21;U8I,03-1;VE,70)
- Uses descriptive language that clarifies and enhances ideas (e.g., establishes tone and mood, uses figurative language)

BP (MI,32;NS2E,26;NWE,24,25;U8E,03-1)
- Uses paragraph form in writing (e.g., arranges sentences in sequential order, uses supporting and follow-up sentences)

BP (ES2I,2;NWE,25;TE,22;U8I,03-1;VE,68)
- Uses a variety of sentence structures to express expanded ideas

BP (ES2I,7;NS2I,24;NWE,25;U8E,03-1;VI,71)
- Uses some explicit transitional devices

Level IV (Grades 9-12)

BP (NWI,26;SP4I,58;TE,35;U12I,02-1;VE,74)
- Uses descriptive language that clarifies and enhances ideas (e.g., stimulates the imagination of the reader, translates concepts into simpler or more easily understood terms)

Codes (right side of page):   BD = Benchmark, Declarative; BP = Benchmark, Procedural; BC = Benchmark, Contextual
1st letter(s) of each code in parentheses   *2nd letter of code*   *Number*
A = Australian Education Council   E = Explicitly stated in document   Page number of cited document
E1,2,3 = Edison Proj: Primary, Elem., Junior   I = Implied in document   *or, for Utah document:*
ES1,2,3 = NCTE: Exemplar Series: 6-8, 9-12   Standard number
IA,IA1 = Int'l Bacc.: Middle, A1 Guide
M = Mississippi: English Language Arts   SS = NCSS: Curric. Standards for Social Studies
NR = NAEP: 1992 Reading Assessment   T = Texas: English Language Arts and Reading
NS1,2,3 = New Standards: Elem., Middle, High   UK-12 = Utah Core Curriculum: Language Arts
NW = NAEP: Writing Achiev. Levels-Setting Proc. V = Board of Ed., Commonwealth of Virginia: Standards of Learning
S = Speech Communication Association   AP = See appendix immediately following the Language Arts Standards
SP1,2,3,4 = NCTE: Standards in Practice

- Uses paragraph form in writing(e.g., arranges paragraphs into a logical progression, uses clincher or closing sentences) BP (ME,32;NS3E,26;U12E,03-1;VE,73)

- Uses a variety of sentence structures and lengths BP (AE,107;NWI,26,27;SP4I,58;TI,36;U12I,03-1;VE,74)

- Uses a variety of transitional devices (e.g., phrases, sentences, paragraphs) BP (NS3I,24;NWI,26;TE,36;U12E,03-1)

- Uses technical terms and notations in writing BP (U12I,02-3;VI,76)

- Uses a variety of techniques to provide supporting detail (e.g., analogies, anecdotes, restatements, paraphrases, examples, comparisons) BP (NS3I,24;NWI,26)

- Organizes ideas to achieve cohesion in writing BP (AI,83;IA1E,4;NWI,26,27;VI,76)

- Uses a variety of techniques to convey a personal style and voice BP (NWI,25-27;TE,35)

3. Uses grammatical and mechanical conventions in written compositions

(NS1,2,3E,21;SP1,2,3,4E,ix;TI,8,21,35;VI,59)

Level I (Grades K-2)

- Forms letters in print and spaces words and sentences BP (AE,23,39;ME,5,6;TE,8,9;UE,07;VE,62)

- Uses complete sentences in written compositions BP (MI,27;NS1I,26;NWI,23;TE,9;UI,07;VE,62)

- Uses declarative and interrogative sentences in written compositions BP (MI,30;TI,9;VE,63)

- Uses nouns in written compositions (e.g., nouns for simple objects, family members, community workers, and categories) BP (ME,22,23;NS1I,26;SP1I,47;TI,9;VI,63)

- Uses verbs in written compositions (e.g., verbs for a variety of situations, action words) BP (E1E,25;ME,23,24;NS1I,26;SP1I,47;TE,9;VI,63)

- Uses adjectives in written compositions (e.g., uses descriptive words) BP (MI,25;NS1I,26;NWI,23;SP1I,47;TI,9;VI,63)

Codes (right side of page):   BD = Benchmark, Declarative; BP = Benchmark, Procedural; BC = Benchmark, Contextual

1st letter(s) of each code in parentheses	*2nd letter of code*	*Number*
A = Australian Education Council	E = Explicitly stated in document	Page number of cited document
E1,2,3 = Edison Proj: Primary, Elem., Junior	I = Implied in document	*or, for Utah document:*
ES1,2,3 = NCTE: Exemplar Series: 6-8, 9-12		Standard number
IA,IA1 = Int'l Bacc.: Middle, A1 Guide		
M = Mississippi: English Language Arts	SS = NCSS: Curric. Standards for Social Studies	
NR = NAEP: 1992 Reading Assessment	T = Texas: English Language Arts and Reading	
NS1,2,3 = New Standards: Elem., Middle, High	UK-12 = Utah Core Curriculum: Language Arts	
NW = NAEP: Writing Achiev. Levels-Setting Proc.	V = Board of Ed., Commonwealth of Virginia: Standards of Learning	
S = Speech Communication Association	AP = See appendix immediately following the Language Arts Standards	
SP1,2,3,4 = NCTE: Standards in Practice		

BP (MI,25;NS1I,26;NWI,23;SP1I,47;TI,9;VI,63)

- Uses adverbs in written compositions (i.e., uses words that answer how, when, where, and why questions)

BP (E1E,25;MI,8;NS1I,26;NWI,23;SP1I,47;TE,9;UE,07;VE,63)

- Uses conventions of spelling in written compositions (e.g., spells high frequency, commonly misspelled words from appropriate grade-level list; uses a dictionary and other resources to spell words; spells own first and last name)

BP (AI,23;ME,15;NS1I,26;NWI,23;SP1I,47;TE,9;UE,07;VE,63)

- Uses conventions of capitalization in written compositions (e.g., first and last names, first word of a sentence)

BP (AI,23;E1E,25;MI,17,18;NS1I,26;NWI,23;SP1I,47;TE,9;UE,07;VE,62,63)

- Uses conventions of punctuation in written compositions (e.g., uses periods after declarative sentences, uses questions marks after interrogative sentences, uses commas in a series of words)

Level II (Grades 3-5)

BP (ME,6;TE,22;U5I,06;VE,64)

- Writes in cursive

BP (ME,30)

- Uses exclamatory and imperative sentences in written compositions

BP (AE,39;E2I,36;MI,25;NS1I,26;NWI,24;SP2I,35;U5I,06;VI,66,67)

- Uses pronouns in written compositions (e.g., substitutes pronouns for nouns)

BP (ME,23;NS1I,26;SP2I,35;VI,67)

- Uses nouns in written compositions (e.g., uses plural and singular naming words; forms regular and irregular plurals of nouns; uses common and proper nouns; uses nouns as subjects)

BP (ME,23,24;NS1I,26;SP2I,35;U5E,06;VE,66)

- Uses verbs in written compositions (e.g., uses a wide variety of action verbs, past and present verb tenses, simple tenses, forms of regular verbs, verbs that agree with the subject)

BP (E2I,36;MI,25,28;NS1I,26;NWI,24;SP2I,35;U5I,06;VI,67)

- Uses adjectives in written compositions (e.g., indefinite, numerical, predicate adjectives)

BP (E2I,36;MI,26;NS1I,26;NWI,24;SP2I,35;U5I,06;VI,67)

- Uses adverbs in written compositions (e.g., to make comparisons)

BP (AE,39;E2I,36;MI,27;NS1I,26;NWI,24;SP2I,35;U5I,06;VI,67)

- Uses coordinating conjunctions in written compositions (e.g., links ideas using connecting

---

Codes (right side of page):	BD = Benchmark, Declarative; BP = Benchmark, Procedural; BC = Benchmark, Contextual	
1st letter(s) of each code in parentheses	*2nd letter of code*	*Number*
A = Australian Education Council	E = Explicitly stated in document	Page number of cited document
E1,2,3 = Edison Proj: Primary, Elem., Junior	I = Implied in document	*or, for Utah document:*
ES1,2,3 = NCTE: Exemplar Series: 6-8, 9-12		Standard number
IA,IA1 = Int'l Bacc.: Middle, A1 Guide		
M = Mississippi: English Language Arts	SS = NCSS: Curric. Standards for Social Studies	
NR = NAEP: 1992 Reading Assessment	T = Texas: English Language Arts and Reading	
NS1,2,3 = New Standards: Elem., Middle, High	UK-12 = Utah Core Curriculum: Language Arts	
NW = NAEP: Writing Achiev. Levels-Setting Proc.	V = Board of Ed., Commonwealth of Virginia: Standards of Learning	
S = Speech Communication Association	AP = See appendix immediately following the Language Arts Standards	
SP1,2,3,4 = NCTE: Standards in Practice		

words)

- Uses negatives in written compositions (e.g., avoids double negatives) ^BP (NS1I,26;TI,9,22;VE,66)

- Uses conventions of spelling in written compositions (e.g., spells high frequency, commonly misspelled words from appropriate grade-level list; uses a dictionary and other resources to spell words; uses initial consonant substitution to spell related words; uses vowel combinations for correct spelling) ^BP (E2E,36;ME,8;NS1I,26;NWI,24;SP2I,78;TI,9,22;U5E,06;VI,67)

- Uses conventions of capitalization in written compositions (e.g., titles of people; proper nouns [names of towns, cities, counties, and states; days of the week; months of the year; names of streets; names of countries; holidays]; first word of direct quotations; heading, salutation, and closing of a letter) ^BP (E2I,36;ME,15;NS1I,26;NWI,24;SP2E,69;TI,9;U5E,06;VI,67)

- Uses conventions of punctuation in written compositions (e.g., uses periods after imperative sentences and in initials, abbreviations, and titles before names; uses commas in dates and addresses and after greetings and closings in a letter; uses apostrophes in contractions and possessive nouns; uses quotation marks around titles and with direct quotations; uses a colon between hour and minutes) ^BP (E2I,36;ME,17;NS1I,26;NWI,24;SP2I,78-79;TI,9;U5E,06;VE,66,67)

Level III (Grades 6-8)

- Uses simple and compound sentences in written compositions ^BP (ME,30;NS2I,26;NWI,25;VI,68,70)

- Uses pronouns in written compositions (e.g., relative, demonstrative, personal [i.e., possessive, subject, object]) ^BP (E3I,34;ES2I,2;MI,25;NS2I,26;NWI,25;TI,22;U8I,03-1;VI,71)

- Uses nouns in written compositions (e.g., forms possessives of nouns; forms irregular plural nouns) ^BP (ES2I,2;ME,23;NS2I,26;TI,22;VI,71)

- Uses verbs in written compositions (e.g., uses linking and auxiliary verbs, verb phrases, and correct forms of regular and irregular verbs) ^BP (ES2I,2;ME,24;SP3I,98;U8I,03-1;VI,71)

- Uses adjectives in written compositions (e.g., pronominal, positive, comparative, superlative) ^BP (E3I,34;ES2I,2;MI,25,26;NS2I,26;NWI,25;U8I,03-1;VE,71)

Codes (right side of page):	BD = Benchmark, Declarative; BP = Benchmark, Procedural; BC = Benchmark, Contextual
1st letter(s) of each code in parentheses	*2nd letter of code* *Number*
A = Australian Education Council	E = Explicitly stated in document Page number of cited document
E1,2,3 = Edison Proj: Primary, Elem., Junior	I = Implied in document *or, for Utah document:*
ES1,2,3 = NCTE: Exemplar Series: 6-8, 9-12	Standard number
IA,IA1 = Int'l Bacc.: Middle, A1 Guide	
M = Mississippi: English Language Arts	SS = NCSS: Curric. Standards for Social Studies
NR = NAEP: 1992 Reading Assessment	T = Texas: English Language Arts and Reading
NS1,2,3 = New Standards: Elem., Middle, High	UK-12 = Utah Core Curriculum: Language Arts
NW = NAEP: Writing Achiev. Levels-Setting Proc.	V = Board of Ed., Commonwealth of Virginia: Standards of Learning
S = Speech Communication Association	AP = See appendix immediately following the Language Arts Standards
SP1,2,3,4 = NCTE: Standards in Practice	

- Uses adverbs in written compositions (e.g., chooses between forms of adjectives and adverbs)

  BP (E3I,34;ES2I,2;MI,26;NS2I,26;NWI,25;U8I,03-1;VE,71)

- Uses prepositions and coordinating conjunctions in written compositions (e.g., uses prepositional phrases, combines and embeds ideas using conjunctions)

  BP (AE,61;E3I,34;ES2I,2;MI,27;NS2I,26;NWI,25;VE,68)

- Uses interjections in written compositions

  BP (ME,27;VI,71)

- Uses conventions of spelling in written compositions (e.g., spells high frequency, commonly misspelled words from appropriate grade-level list, uses a dictionary and other resources to spell words, uses common prefixes and suffixes as aids to spelling, applies rules for irregular structural changes)

  BP (AE,61;E3I,34;ES2I,2;MI,8;NS2I,26;NWI,25;TI,22;U8I,03-1;VI,71)

- Uses conventions of capitalization in written compositions (e.g., titles [books, stories, poems, magazines, newspapers, songs, works of art], proper nouns [team names, companies, schools and institutions, departments of government, religions, school subjects], proper adjectives, nationalities, brand names of products)

  BP (E3I,34;ES2I,2;ME,15;NS2I,26;NWI,25;TE,22;U8I,03-1;VI,71)

- Uses conventions of punctuation in written compositions (e.g., uses exclamation marks after exclamatory sentences and interjections; uses periods in decimals, dollars, and cents; uses commas with nouns of address and after mild interjections; uses quotation marks with poems, songs, and chapters; uses colons in business letter salutations; uses hyphens to divide words between syllables at the end of a line)

  BP (E3I,34;ES2I,2;MI,17-22;NS2I,26;NWI,25;TE,22;U8I,03-1;VI,71)

- Uses standard format in written compositions (e.g., includes footnotes, uses italics [for titles of books, magazines, plays, movies])

  BP (AE,61;E3E,35 NS2I,24;SSI,148)

Level IV (Grades 9-12)

- Uses complex and compound-complex sentences in written compositions

  BP (ME,30)

- Uses pronouns in written compositions (e.g., reflexive, indefinite, interrogative, compound personal)

  BP (ME,25;NS3I,26;NWI,26;SP4I,58;TI,35;U12I,03-1;VI,76)

Codes (right side of page):   BD = Benchmark, Declarative; BP = Benchmark, Procedural; BC = Benchmark, Contextual

1st letter(s) of each code in parentheses   *2nd letter of code*   *Number*
A = Australian Education Council   E = Explicitly stated in document   Page number of cited document
E1,2,3 = Edison Proj: Primary, Elem., Junior   I = Implied in document   *or, for Utah document:*
ES1,2,3 = NCTE: Exemplar Series: 6-8, 9-12   Standard number
IA,IA1 = Int'l Bacc.: Middle, A1 Guide
M = Mississippi: English Language Arts   SS = NCSS: Curric. Standards for Social Studies
NR = NAEP: 1992 Reading Assessment   T = Texas: English Language Arts and Reading
NS1,2,3 = New Standards: Elem., Middle, High   UK-12 = Utah Core Curriculum: Language Arts
NW = NAEP: Writing Achiev. Levels-Setting Proc.   V = Board of Ed., Commonwealth of Virginia: Standards of Learning
S = Speech Communication Association   AP = See appendix immediately following the Language Arts Standards
SP1,2,3,4 = NCTE: Standards in Practice

MREL

- Uses nouns in written compositions (e.g., collective nouns, compound nouns, noun clauses, noun phrases)

  BP (MI,23;NS3I,26;SP4I,58;TI,35;VI,76)

- Uses verbs in written compositions (e.g., present perfect, past perfect, and future perfect verb tenses; progressive verb forms, compound verbs)

  BP (ME,24;TI,35;U12I,03-1;VI,76)

- Uses adjectives in written compositions (e.g., adjective clauses, adjective phrases; relocates adjectives following nouns they modify)

  BP (MI,25,26;NS3I,26;NWI,26;SP4I,58;TI,35;U12I,03-1;VI,76)

- Uses adverbs in written compositions (e.g., adverb clauses, adverb phrases)

  BP (MI,26;NS2I,26;NWI,26;SP4I,58;TI,35;U12I,03-1;VI,76)

- Uses conjunctions in written compositions (e.g., correlative and subordinating conjunctions, conjunctive adverbs)

  BP (AE,83;MI,27,31;NS3I,26;NWI,26;SP4I,58;TI,35;VI,76)

- Uses conventions of spelling in written compositions (e.g., spells high frequency, commonly misspelled words from appropriate grade-level list; uses a dictionary and other resources to spell words)

  BP (AI,83;MI,8;NS3I,26;NWI,26;TI,35;U12I,03-1;VI,76)

- Uses conventions of capitalization in written compositions (e.g., within divided quotations; for historical periods and events, geological eras, religious terms, scientific terms)

  BP (MI,15,16;NS3I,26;NWI,26;TI,35;U12I,-03-1;VI,76)

- Uses conventions of punctuation in written compositions (e.g., uses commas with nonrestrictive clauses and contrasting expressions, uses quotation marks with ending punctuation, uses colons before extended quotations, uses hyphens for compound adjectives, uses semicolons between independent clauses, uses dashes to break continuity of thought)

  BP (AE,83;MI,17-22;NS3I,26;NWI,26;TI,35;U12I,03-1;VI,76)

- Uses commonly confused terms in written compositions (e.g., *affect* and *effect*)

  BP (NS3I,26;NWI,26;TI,35;VI,76)

- Uses standard format in written compositions (e.g., includes footnotes, uses italics [for works of art, for foreign words and phrases], uses bold or underlined headings)

  BP (AE,83;NS3I,24;SSI,148)

Codes (right side of page):	BD = Benchmark, Declarative; BP = Benchmark, Procedural; BC = Benchmark, Contextual	
1st letter(s) of each code in parentheses	*2nd letter of code*	*Number*
A = Australian Education Council	E = Explicitly stated in document	Page number of cited document
E1,2,3 = Edison Proj: Primary, Elem., Junior	I = Implied in document	*or, for Utah document:*
ES1,2,3 = NCTE: Exemplar Series: 6-8, 9-12		Standard number
IA,IA1 = Int'l Bacc.: Middle, A1 Guide		
M = Mississippi: English Language Arts	SS = NCSS: Curric. Standards for Social Studies	
NR = NAEP: 1992 Reading Assessment	T = Texas: English Language Arts and Reading	
NS1,2,3 = New Standards: Elem., Middle, High	UK-12 = Utah Core Curriculum: Language Arts	
NW = NAEP: Writing Achiev. Levels-Setting Proc.	V = Board of Ed., Commonwealth of Virginia: Standards of Learning	
S = Speech Communication Association	AP = See appendix immediately following the Language Arts Standards	
SP1,2,3,4 = NCTE: Standards in Practice		

4. Gathers and uses information for research purposes

(SP1,2,3,4E,ix;SSE,149;VE,59)

Level I (Grades K-2)

- Generates questions about topics of personal interest

  BC (SP1E,81;TE,6;VI,61)

- Uses books to gather information for research topics (e.g., uses table of contents, examines pictures and charts)

  BP (SPE,25;TE,6;VE,63)

Level II (Grades 3-5)

- Uses a variety of strategies to identify topics to investigate (e.g., brainstorms, lists questions, uses idea webs)

  BP (SP2E,39;TE,6,23;VE,66)

- Uses encyclopedias to gather information for research topics

  BP (ME,35;SP2I,53;SSE,148;TE,6;U5I,02;VE,65)

- Uses dictionaries to gather information for research topics

  BP (SP2I,53;SSE,148;TI,6;U5I,02;VE,65)

- Uses key words, indexes, cross-references, and letters on volumes to find information for research topics

  BP (SSE,148;TI,6)

- Uses multiple representations of information (e.g., maps, charts, photos) to find information for research topics

  BP (SP2I,53;TE,6)

- Uses graphic organizers to gather and record information for research topics (e.g., notes, charts, graphs)

  BP (IAI,15;SP2E,47;TE,10,23;U5I,02;VE,67)

- Compiles information into written reports or summaries

  BP (SP2I,48;SSE,148;TE,10;VE,66)

Level III (Grades 6-8)

- Gathers data for research topics from interviews (e.g., prepares and asks relevant questions, makes notes of responses, compiles responses)

  BP (NS2I,24;SPI,93;SSE,148;VE,69,70)

Codes (right side of page):   BD = Benchmark, Declarative; BP = Benchmark, Procedural; BC = Benchmark, Contextual
1st letter(s) of each code in parentheses   *2nd letter of code*   *Number*
A = Australian Education Council   E = Explicitly stated in document   Page number of cited document
E1,2,3 = Edison Proj: Primary, Elem., Junior   I = Implied in document   *or, for Utah document:*
ES1,2,3 = NCTE: Exemplar Series: 6-8, 9-12   Standard number
IA,IA1 = Int'l Bacc.: Middle, A1 Guide
M = Mississippi: English Language Arts   SS = NCSS: Curric. Standards for Social Studies
NR = NAEP: 1992 Reading Assessment   T = Texas: English Language Arts and Reading
NS1,2,3 = New Standards: Elem., Middle, High   UK-12 = Utah Core Curriculum: Language Arts
NW = NAEP: Writing Achiev. Levels-Setting Proc.   V = Board of Ed., Commonwealth of Virginia: Standards of Learning
S = Speech Communication Association   AP = See appendix immediately following the Language Arts Standards
SP1,2,3,4 = NCTE: Standards in Practice

MREL

- Uses the card catalog to locate books for research topics

BP (ME,35;SP3I,93;SSE,148;TI,19;U8I,01-3;VI,70)

- Uses the Reader's Guide to Periodical Literature and other indexes to gather information for research topics

BP (SP3I,93;SSE,148;TI,19;U8I,01-3;VE,69,72)

- Uses a computer catalog to gather information for research topics

BP (SP3I,93;SSE,148;TI,19;VI,70,72)

- Uses a variety of resource materials to gather information for research topics (e.g., magazines, newspapers, dictionaries, schedules, journals, phone directories, globes, atlases, almanacs)

BP (MI,34,35;SP3I,93;SSE,148;VE,69,72)

- Determines the appropriateness of an information source for a research topic

BP (AI,105;SSE,148;TE,19)

- Organizes information and ideas from multiple sources in systematic ways (e.g., time lines, outlines, notes, graphic representations)

BP (IAI,15;MI,34;SP3I,64;SSE,148;TE,23;UI,01,02;VE,70)

- Writes research papers (e.g., separates information into major components based on a set of criteria, examines critical relationships between and among elements of a research topic, integrates a variety of information into a whole)

BP (AI,58;IAI,16;MI,34;SP3E,93,113;SSE,148,149;TE,23;VI,70)

Level IV (Grades 9-12)

- Uses government publications to gather information for research topics

BP (AI,81;SSE,148;TI,33;VI,75)

- Uses microfiche to gather information for research topics

BP (SSE,148;TI,33;U12I,01-2;VI,73,76)

- Uses a variety of news sources to gather information for research topics (e.g., newspapers, news magazines, television, radio, videotapes, artifacts)

BP (AE,81;SSE,148;TI,37;VI,75)

- Uses telephone information services found in public libraries to gather information for research topics

BP (SSE,148;TI,33,37;VI,75)

- Synthesizes a variety of types of visual information, including pictures and symbols, for research topics

BP (TI,37)

Codes (right side of page):	BD = Benchmark, Declarative; BP = Benchmark, Procedural; BC = Benchmark, Contextual	
1st letter(s) of each code in parentheses	*2nd letter of code*	*Number*
A = Australian Education Council	E = Explicitly stated in document	Page number of cited document
E1,2,3 = Edison Proj: Primary, Elem., Junior	I = Implied in document	*or, for Utah document:*
ES1,2,3 = NCTE: Exemplar Series: 6-8, 9-12		Standard number
IA,IA1 = Int'l Bacc.: Middle, A1 Guide		
M = Mississippi: English Language Arts	SS = NCSS: Curric. Standards for Social Studies	
NR = NAEP: 1992 Reading Assessment	T = Texas: English Language Arts and Reading	
NS1,2,3 = New Standards: Elem., Middle, High	UK-12 = Utah Core Curriculum: Language Arts	
NW = NAEP: Writing Achiev. Levels-Setting Proc.	V = Board of Ed., Commonwealth of Virginia: Standards of Learning	
S = Speech Communication Association	AP = See appendix immediately following the Language Arts Standards	
SP1,2,3,4 = NCTE: Standards in Practice		

- Uses a variety of primary sources to gather information for research topics ^BP (TE,33,37;VI,75)

- Considers the motives, credibility, and perspectives of the authors of primary sources ^BP (TE,33)

- Determines the validity and reliability of primary and secondary source information and uses information accordingly in reporting on a research topic ^BP (SP4I,113;SSI,148;TE,33,37;U12E,01-2;VE,76)

- Synthesizes information from multiple research studies to draw conclusions that go beyond those found in any of the individual studies ^BP (IAI,16;TE,37;U12I,01-2)

- Identifies and defends research questions and topics that may be important in the future ^BP (TI,33)

- Writes research papers (e.g., includes a thesis statement; synthesizes information into a logical sequence) ^BP (AI,81;ES3I,51,70;IAI,16;ME,36;SP4E,113;SSE,148;TE,33;U12I,01-2;VE,76)

- Creates bibliographies for research topics (e.g., uses a style sheet format, such as the *Modern Language Association* or the *American Psychological Association*) ^BP (ME,36;SSE,148;U12E,02-2;VE,75,76)

5. Demonstrates competence in the general skills and strategies of the reading process
(AI,8,9;NS1,2,3E,20;SP1,2,3,4E,viii;SSE,148;TE,1,14,29;VE,59)

Level I (Grades K-2)

- Understands that print conveys meaning ^BD (SP1I,107;TE,1;U2I,01;VE,61)

- Understands how print is organized and read (e.g., identifies front and back covers, title page, and author; follows words from left to right and from top to bottom; recognizes the significance of spaces between words) ^BD (TE,1;UKE,01;VE,60,62)

- Creates mental images from pictures and print ^BP (U2E,01)

- Uses picture clues and picture captions to aid comprehension and to make predictions about content ^BP (SP1E,119;SSE,148;TI,4;U2I,04;VE,61-63)

Codes (right side of page):   BD = Benchmark, Declarative; BP = Benchmark, Procedural; BC = Benchmark, Contextual

1st letter(s) of each code in parentheses	*2nd letter of code*	*Number*
A = Australian Education Council	E = Explicitly stated in document	Page number of cited document
E1,2,3 = Edison Proj: Primary, Elem., Junior	I = Implied in document	*or, for Utah document:*
ES1,2,3 = NCTE: Exemplar Series: 6-8, 9-12		Standard number
IA,IA1 = Int'l Bacc.: Middle, A1 Guide		
M = Mississippi: English Language Arts	SS = NCSS: Curric. Standards for Social Studies	
NR = NAEP: 1992 Reading Assessment	T = Texas: English Language Arts and Reading	
NS1,2,3 = New Standards: Elem., Middle, High	UK-12 = Utah Core Curriculum: Language Arts	
NW = NAEP: Writing Achiev. Levels-Setting Proc.	V = Board of Ed., Commonwealth of Virginia: Standards of Learning	
S = Speech Communication Association	AP = See appendix immediately following the Language Arts Standards	
SP1,2,3,4 = NCTE: Standards in Practice		

- Decodes unknown words using basic elements of phonetic analysis (e.g., common letter/sound relationships) and structural analysis (e.g., syllables, basic prefixes, suffixes, root words)

  BP (NS1E,22;SP1E,119;SSE,148;TE,2-4;U2E,03;VE,63)

- Uses a picture dictionary to determine word meaning

  BP (TE,4;VE,62)

- Uses self-correction strategies (e.g., searches for cues, identifies miscues, rereads)

  BP (NS1E,22;SP1I,47;TE,3;U2E,04;VE,63)

- Reads aloud familiar stories, poems, and passages with attention to rhythm, flow, and meter

  BP (NS1E,22;SP1I,39,47;TE,3;U2E,05;VE,62)

Level II (Grades 3-5)

- Previews text (e.g., skims material; uses pictures, textual clues, and text format)

  BP (SP2E,8;TE,3;VE,64)

- Establishes a purpose for reading

  BP (SP2I,8;SSI,148;TE,4;VE,64)

- Represents concrete information (e.g., persons, places, things, events) as explicit mental pictures

  BP (NRI,4;TE,16;U5E,01)

- Makes, confirms, and revises simple predictions about what will be found in a text

  BP (SP2E,8;SSI,148;TE,4,16;U5E,01;VE,64)

- Decodes words not recognized immediately by using phonetic and structural analysis techniques, the syntactic structure in which the word appears, and the semantic context surrounding the word

  BP (NRI,39;NS1E,22;SP2I,9,24;TE,3,14,15;U5E,03;VE,64)

- Decodes unknown words using a variety of context clues (e.g., draws on earlier reading, reads ahead)

  BP (NS1E,22;SP2E,9,24;SSE,148;TE,3,15;U5E,02,03;VE,64)

- Determines the meaning of unknown words using a glossary, dictionary, and thesaurus

  BP (SP2I,9;SSE,148;TE,15;U5E,02;VE,66)

- Monitors own reading strategies and makes modifications as needed (e.g., recognizes when he or she is confused by a section of text, questions whether the text makes sense)

  BP (NRI,32,33;NS1I,22;SP2E,8;TE,16;U5I,03;VE,64)

- Adjusts speed of reading to suit purpose and difficulty of the material

  BP (NS1I,22;SSE,148;U5I,02,04)

Codes (right side of page): BD = Benchmark, Declarative; BP = Benchmark, Procedural; BC = Benchmark, Contextual

1st letter(s) of each code in parentheses	*2nd letter of code*	*Number*
A = Australian Education Council	E = Explicitly stated in document	Page number of cited document
E1,2,3 = Edison Proj: Primary, Elem., Junior	I = Implied in document	*or, for Utah document:*
ES1,2,3 = NCTE: Exemplar Series: 6-8, 9-12		Standard number
IA,IA1 = Int'l Bacc.: Middle, A1 Guide		
M = Mississippi: English Language Arts	SS = NCSS: Curric. Standards for Social Studies	
NR = NAEP: 1992 Reading Assessment	T = Texas: English Language Arts and Reading	
NS1,2,3 = New Standards: Elem., Middle, High	UK-12 = Utah Core Curriculum: Language Arts	
NW = NAEP: Writing Achiev. Levels-Setting Proc.	V = Board of Ed., Commonwealth of Virginia: Standards of Learning	
S = Speech Communication Association	AP = See appendix immediately following the Language Arts Standards	
SP1,2,3,4 = NCTE: Standards in Practice		

- Identifies the author's purpose (e.g., to persuade, to inform) BP (NRI,5,17;VE,65)

Level III (Grades 6-8)

- Generates interesting questions to be answered while reading BP (SP3E,42;U6E,01;VE,68)

- Establishes and adjusts purposes for reading (e.g., to understand, interpret, enjoy, solve problems, predict outcomes, answer a specific question, form an opinion, skim for facts) BP (AE,59;IAI,14;SSE,148;TE,14,16)

- Represents abstract information (e.g., concepts, generalizations) as explicit mental pictures BP (NRI,4,16;SP3I,64;TE,16;U6E,01)

- Uses a variety of strategies to define and extend understanding of word meaning (e.g., applies knowledge of word origins and derivations, analogies, idioms, similes, metaphors) BP (TE,15;U6E,03,04;VE,70)

- Uses specific strategies to clear up confusing parts of a text (e.g., pauses, rereads the text, consults another source, draws upon background knowledge, asks for help) BP (AE,59;NRI,32,33;TE,16;U6E,01)

- Identifies specific devices an author uses to accomplish his or her purpose (e.g., persuasive techniques, style, literary form) BP (NRI,5,17,18;NS2E,22;U8I,01-4;VI,69)

- Reflects on what has been learned after reading and formulates ideas, opinions, and personal responses to texts BP (SP3I,64;TI,17;U8I,01-1)

Level IV (Grades 9-12)

- Determines figurative, idiomatic, and technical meanings of terms through context BP (AI,81;SP4I,83;TE,30)

- Extends general and specialized reading vocabulary (e.g., meaning of codes, symbols, abbreviations, and acronyms) BP (IAI,15;TI,33;VE,75)

- Uses a range of automatic monitoring and self-correction methods (e.g., rereading, slowing down, subvocalizing) BP (AE,81;NRI,32,33;TE,31)

Codes (right side of page):	BD = Benchmark, Declarative; BP = Benchmark, Procedural; BC = Benchmark, Contextual

1st letter(s) of each code in parentheses	*2nd letter of code*	*Number*
A = Australian Education Council	E = Explicitly stated in document	Page number of cited document
E1,2,3 = Edison Proj: Primary, Elem., Junior	I = Implied in document	*or, for Utah document:*
ES1,2,3 = NCTE: Exemplar Series: 6-8, 9-12		Standard number
IA,IA1 = Int'l Bacc.: Middle, A1 Guide		
M = Mississippi: English Language Arts	SS = NCSS: Curric. Standards for Social Studies	
NR = NAEP: 1992 Reading Assessment	T = Texas: English Language Arts and Reading	
NS1,2,3 = New Standards: Elem., Middle, High	UK-12 = Utah Core Curriculum: Language Arts	
NW = NAEP: Writing Achiev. Levels-Setting Proc.	V = Board of Ed., Commonwealth of Virginia: Standards of Learning	
S = Speech Communication Association	AP = See appendix immediately following the Language Arts Standards	
SP1,2,3,4 = NCTE: Standards in Practice		

McREL

- BP (NRI,17-20;U12I,01-5;U9E,01-2,01-4;VE,74)
  Recognizes the effectiveness of writing techniques in accomplishing an author's purpose

- BD (AE,80;SP4E,37-38;U12I,01-1)
  Understands influences on a reader's response to a text (e.g., personal values, perspectives, and experiences)

- BC (AI,81;TI,31)
  Represents key ideas and supporting details in outline or graph form

- BP (NRI,4,16)
  Identifies and analyzes the philosophical assumptions and basic beliefs underlying an author's work

(NS1,2,3E,20;SP1,2,3,4E,viii;SSE,148;TI,1,14,29;VE,59)

6. Demonstrates competence in the general skills and strategies for reading a variety of literary texts

Level I (Grades K-2)

- BP (MI,12-14;NS1I,22;SP1E,10;TE,3;U2E,05,06;VE,63;[AP,344-348])
  Applies reading skills and strategies to a variety of familiar literary passages and texts (e.g., fairy tales, folktales, fiction, nonfiction, legends, fables, myths, poems, picture books, predictable books)

- BP (SP1I,10;TI,3;U2E,04)
  Identifies favorite books and stories

- BP (MI,13;NS1E,26;TE,6;U2E,04;VE,63)
  Identifies setting, main characters, main events, and problems in stories

- BP (NS1E,26;SP1E,47;TE,4;U2I,02)
  Makes simple inferences regarding the order of events and possible outcomes

- BP (NS1E,26;TE,4;U2E,02;VE,62,63)
  Identifies the main ideas or theme of a story

- BP (SP1E,11;TE,7;U2E,01;VE,63)
  Relates stories to personal experiences

Level II (Grades 3-5)

- BP (MI,12-14;NRE,3;NS1I,22;SP2E,24;TI,3,14;U5E,04;VE,64-66;[AP,349-355])
  Applies reading skills and strategies to a variety of literary passages and texts (e.g., fairy tales, folktales, fiction, nonfiction, myths, poems, fables, fantasies, historical fiction,

---

Codes (right side of page):   BD = Benchmark, Declarative; BP = Benchmark, Procedural; BC = Benchmark, Contextual

1st letter(s) of each code in parentheses   *2nd letter of code*   *Number*

A = Australian Education Council   E = Explicitly stated in document   Page number of cited document

E1,2,3 = Edison Proj: Primary, Elem., Junior   I = Implied in document   *or, for Utah document:*

ES1,2,3 = NCTE: Exemplar Series: 6-8, 9-12   Standard number

IA,IA1 = Int'l Bacc.: Middle, A1 Guide

M = Mississippi: English Language Arts   SS = NCSS: Curric. Standards for Social Studies

NR = NAEP: 1992 Reading Assessment   T = Texas: English Language Arts and Reading

NS1,2,3 = New Standards: Elem., Middle, High   UK-12 = Utah Core Curriculum: Language Arts

NW = NAEP: Writing Achiev. Levels-Setting Proc.   V = Board of Ed., Commonwealth of Virginia: Standards of Learning

S = Speech Communication Association   AP = See appendix immediately following the Language Arts Standards

SP1,2,3,4 = NCTE: Standards in Practice

biographies, autobiographies)

- Knows the defining characteristics of a variety of literary forms and genres (e.g., fairy tales, folktales, fiction, nonfiction, myths, poems, fables, fantasies, historical fiction, biographies, autobiographies)

  BD (NS1E,26;TE,5,17;VE,64,66)

- Selects reading material based on personal criteria (e.g., personal interest, knowledge of authors and genres, text difficulty, recommendations of others)

  BP (AE,37;TE,3)

- Understands the basic concept of plot

  BD (AI,36;MI,12;NRI,4;NS1I,26;U5E,02;VE,66)

- Identifies similarities and differences among literary works in terms of settings, characters, and events

  BP (NRI,4,14;NS1E,22,26;TE,4;U5E,02;VE,64)

- Makes inferences regarding the qualities and motives of characters and the consequences of their actions

  BP (AE,36;IAI,14;NS1E,26;TE,6;VI,66)

- Understands simple dialogues and how they relate to a story

  BD (NRI,4)

- Identifies recurring themes across literary works

  BP (NS1E,26;SP2I,52;TE,4,17)

- Makes connections between characters or simple events in a literary work and people or events in his or her own life

  BC (AI,36;NRI,15;NS1I,22;SP2E,24;TE,20;U5I,01;VI,64)

- Shares responses to literature with peers

  BC (SP2I,24,27;U5I,05)

Level III (Grades 6-8)

- Applies reading skills and strategies to a variety of literary passages and texts (e.g., fiction, nonfiction, myths, poems, fantasies, biographies, autobiographies, science fiction, tall tales, supernatural tales)

  BP (NRE,3;NS2I,22;TE,14;VE,68-70;MI,12-14;SP3I,48,64;U8E,01-1;[AP,356-361])

- Knows the defining characteristics of a variety of literary forms and genres (e.g., fiction, nonfiction, myths, poems, fantasies, biographies, autobiographies, science fiction, tall tales,

  BD (AE,59;NS2E,26;VE,70;TE,17)

Codes (right side of page):   BD = Benchmark, Declarative;   BP = Benchmark, Procedural;   BC = Benchmark, Contextual

1st letter(s) of each code in parentheses   *2nd letter of code*   *Number*

A = Australian Education Council   E = Explicitly stated in document   Page number of cited document

E1,2,3 = Edison Proj: Primary, Elem., Junior   I = Implied in document   *or, for Utah document:*

ES1,2,3 = NCTE: Exemplar Series: 6-8, 9-12   Standard number

IA,IA1 = Int'l Bacc.: Middle, A1 Guide

M = Mississippi: English Language Arts   SS = NCSS: Curric. Standards for Social Studies

NR = NAEP: 1992 Reading Assessment   T = Texas: English Language Arts and Reading

NS1,2,3 = New Standards: Elem., Middle, High   UK-12 = Utah Core Curriculum: Language Arts

NW = NAEP: Writing Achiev. Levels-Setting Proc.   V = Board of Ed., Commonwealth of Virginia: Standards of Learning

S = Speech Communication Association   AP = See appendix immediately following the Language Arts Standards

SP1,2,3,4 = NCTE: Standards in Practice

supernatural tales)

- Identifies specific questions of personal importance and seeks to answer them through literature BP (VI,68)

- Recognizes complex elements of plot (e.g., cause-and-effect relationships, conflicts, resolutions) BP (AE,58,59;ME,12;NRI,24;TE,18;U6E,02;VE,70)

- Recognizes devices used to develop characters in literary texts (e.g., character traits, motivations, changes, and stereotypes) BP (AE,58;NS2E,26;TE,18;U8E,01-1;VE,68,70)

- Makes inferences and draws conclusions about story elements (e.g., main and subordinate characters, events, setting, theme, missing details) BP (AE,58;NRI,4,14;NS2E,22,26;SP3E,33;TI,18;U8E,01-1;VE,70)

- Understands complex, extended dialogues and how they relate to a story BD (AE,59;NRI,4;NS2E,26;VI,71)

- Recognizes the use of specific literary devices (e.g., foreshadowing, flashback, progressive and digressive time, suspense, figurative language, description, metaphor) BP (NRI,4;NS2E,26;TE,18;VE,70)

- Understands the effects of the author's style on a literary text (e.g., how it elicits an emotional response from the reader) BD (TE,18;VE,68,69)

- Identifies point of view in a literary text (e.g., distinguishes between first and third person) BP (NS2E,26;TE,16;VE,68)

- Explains how the motives of characters or the causes for complex events in texts are similar to and different from those in his or her own life BC (NRI,15;NS2I,26;SP3E,33;TE,20;U6E,02)

- Understands that people respond differently to literature BD (AI,58;SP3I,39;U8I,01-1;VI,71)

Level IV (Grades 9-12)

- Applies reading skills and strategies to a variety of literary texts (e.g., fiction, nonfiction, myths, poems, biographies, autobiographies, science fiction, supernatural tales, satires, parodies, plays, American literature, British literature, world and ancient literature) BP (ES3I,40;NRE,4;MI,12-14;NS3I,22;SP4I,57;TE,30;U12I,01-4;VE,74,76;[AP,362-373])

Codes (right side of page):	BD = Benchmark, Declarative; BP = Benchmark, Procedural; BC = Benchmark, Contextual	
1st letter(s) of each code in parentheses	*2nd letter of code*	*Number*
A = Australian Education Council	E = Explicitly stated in document	Page number of cited document
E1,2,3 = Edison Proj: Primary, Elem., Junior	I = Implied in document	*or, for Utah document:*
ES1,2,3 = NCTE: Exemplar Series: 6-8, 9-12		Standard number
IA,IA1 = Int'l Bacc.: Middle, A1 Guide		
M = Mississippi: English Language Arts	SS = NCSS: Curric. Standards for Social Studies	
NR = NAEP: 1992 Reading Assessment	T = Texas: English Language Arts and Reading	
NS1,2,3 = New Standards: Elem., Middle, High	UK-12 = Utah Core Curriculum: Language Arts	
NW = NAEP: Writing Achiev. Levels-Setting Proc.	V = Board of Ed., Commonwealth of Virginia: Standards of Learning	
S = Speech Communication Association	AP = See appendix immediately following the Language Arts Standards	
SP1,2,3,4 = NCTE: Standards in Practice		

- BD (AI,81;NS3E,26;SP4E,55,83;TE,32;VE,72,73,76)
  Knows the defining characteristics of a variety of literary forms and genres (e.g.,fiction, nonfiction, myths, poems, biographies, autobiographies, science fiction, supernatural tales, satires, parodies, plays, American literature, British literature, world and ancient literature, the Bible)

- BP (AI,104;ME,12;NRI,14,24;TE,32)
  Analyzes the effectiveness of complex elements of plot (e.g., time frame, cause-and-effect relationships, conflicts, resolutions)

- BP (AI,105;NRI,4,14,24;U12I,01-1)
  Identifies the simple and complex actions (e.g., internal/external conflicts) between main and subordinate characters in texts containing complex character structures

- BP (ME,11;TE,32;VE,73,74)
  Recognizes archetypes and symbols across literary texts (e.g., heroes, beneficence of nature, "dawn")

- BP (AE,104;IA1I,4;MI,13;NS3E,26;TE,32;U12I,01-1;VE,73,74,76)
  Makes connections among literary works based on theme (e.g., universal themes in literature of different cultures, major themes in American literature)

- BD (AE,81;IA1I,4;NRI,4,16,19;NS3E,26;SP4I,38;TE,32,33;U12E,01-4,5;VE,72)
  Understands the effects of complex literary devices and techniques on the overall quality of a work (e.g., tone, irony, mood, figurative language, allusion, diction, dialogue, symbolism, point of view, style)

- BD (NS3E,26;TE,32;VE,72,74,76)
  Understands historical and cultural influences on literary works

- BC (AI,104;NRI,15;NS3I,22;SP4I,16)
  Makes abstract connections between his or her own life and the characters, events, motives, and causes of conflict in texts

- BP (AI,80;IA1I,4)
  Relates personal response to the text with that seemingly intended by the author

---

Codes (right side of page): BD = Benchmark, Declarative; BP = Benchmark, Procedural; BC = Benchmark, Contextual

1st letter(s) of each code in parentheses	*2nd letter of code*	*Number*
A = Australian Education Council	E = Explicitly stated in document	Page number of cited document
E1,2,3 = Edison Proj: Primary, Elem., Junior	I = Implied in document	*or, for Utah document:*
ES1,2,3 = NCTE: Exemplar Series: 6-8, 9-12		Standard number
IA,IA1 = Int'l Bacc.: Middle, A1 Guide		
M = Mississippi: English Language Arts	SS = NCSS: Curric. Standards for Social Studies	
NR = NAEP: 1992 Reading Assessment	T = Texas: English Language Arts and Reading	
NS1,2,3 = New Standards: Elem., Middle, High	UK-12 = Utah Core Curriculum: Language Arts	
NW = NAEP: Writing Achiev. Levels-Setting Proc.	V = Board of Ed., Commonwealth of Virginia: Standards of Learning	
S = Speech Communication Association	AP = See appendix immediately following the Language Arts Standards	
SP1,2,3,4 = NCTE: Standards in Practice		

(NRI,4;NS1,2,3I,20;SP1,2,3,4I,viii;TI,1,14,29;VI,59)

7. Demonstrates competence in the general skills and strategies for reading a variety of informational texts

Level I (Grades K-2)

BP (NS1E,22;SP1I,10;TE,3;U2E,05;VE,63)
- Applies reading skills and strategies to a variety of informational books

BD (TE,4;U2E,04;VE,63)
- Understands the main idea of simple expository information

BP (NS1E,22;TE,4;U2E,04;VI,63)
- Summarizes information found in texts (e.g., retells in own words)

BP (AE,20,21;NS1E,22;TE,4;U2E,01;VE,63)
- Relates new information to prior knowledge and experience

Level II (Grades 3-5)

BP (NRE,4-6;NS1E,22;SP2I,52;TE,3;U5E,04,05;VI,67)
- Applies reading skills and strategies to a variety of informational texts (e.g., textbooks, biographical sketches, letters, diaries, directions, procedures, magazines)

BD (NRE,5;TE,17)
- Knows the defining characteristics of a variety of informational texts (e.g., textbooks, biographical sketches, letters, diaries, directions, procedures, magazines)

BP (SSE,148;TE,19;U5E,02;VE,67)
- Uses text organizers (e.g., headings, topic and summary sentences, graphic features) to determine the main ideas and to locate information in a text

BP (SSE,148;TE,6;U5E,02)
- Identifies and uses the various parts of a book (index, table of contents, glossary, appendix) to locate information

BP (NRI,5-6,18 NS1E,22;SSE,148;TE,4;SP2E,8;U5E,02;VE,65)
- Summarizes and paraphrases information in texts (e.g., identifies main ideas and supporting details)

BP (AI,36;NRI,18,19;NS1I,22;U5E,01;VE,64)
- Uses prior knowledge and experience to understand and respond to new information

BP (NRI,5)
- Identifies the author's viewpoint in an informational text

Codes (right side of page):	BD = Benchmark, Declarative; BP = Benchmark, Procedural; BC = Benchmark, Contextual
1st letter(s) of each code in parentheses	*2nd letter of code* *Number*
A = Australian Education Council	E = Explicitly stated in document Page number of cited document
E1,2,3 = Edison Proj: Primary, Elem., Junior	I = Implied in document *or, for Utah document:*
ES1,2,3 = NCTE: Exemplar Series: 6-8, 9-12	Standard number
IA,IA1 = Int'l Bacc.: Middle, A1 Guide	
M = Mississippi: English Language Arts	SS = NCSS: Curric. Standards for Social Studies
NR = NAEP: 1992 Reading Assessment	T = Texas: English Language Arts and Reading
NS1,2,3 = New Standards: Elem., Middle, High	UK-12 = Utah Core Curriculum: Language Arts
NW = NAEP: Writing Achiev. Levels-Setting Proc.	V = Board of Ed., Commonwealth of Virginia: Standards of Learning
S = Speech Communication Association	AP = See appendix immediately following the Language Arts Standards
SP1,2,3,4 = NCTE: Standards in Practice	

Level III (Grades 6-8)

- BP (AE,58;MI,12;NRE,5,6;NS2E,22;SP3I,83;TE,14;U8I,01-1,01-5;VE,69,71)

  Applies reading skills and strategies to a variety of informational texts (e.g., textbooks, biographical sketches, letters, diaries, directions, procedures, magazines, essays, primary source historical documents, editorials, news stories, periodicals, bus routes, catalogs)

- BD (IAI,15;NRE,5;TE,17;VI,69)

  Knows the defining characteristics of a variety of informational texts (e.g., textbooks, biographical sketches, letters, diaries, directions, procedures, magazines, essays, primary source historical documents, editorials, news stories, periodiocals, bus routes, catalogs)

- BP (AE,58;IAI,14,15;NRI,5,18,19;TE,16;VE,69;U6E,02)

  Summarizes and paraphrases complex, explicit hierarchic structures in informational texts

- BD (SP3I,64;U6I,02;VE,68)

  Identifies information-organizing strategies that are personally most useful

- BP (NRI,18,19;NS2E,22;TI,17;U6E,01)

  Uses new information to adjust and extend personal knowledge base

- BP (NRI,16,17;TI,16;VE,69)

  Identifies techniques used to convey viewpoint (e.g., word choice, language structure, context)

- BC (U6I,05)

  Seeks peer help to understand information

- BP (NRI,18;TE,16;U6I,02;VE,68)

  Draws conclusions and makes inferences based on explicit and implicit information in texts

- BP (SSE,148;TE,16;U8E,01-3;VE,69)

  Differentiates between fact and opinion in informational texts

Level IV (Grades 9-12)

- BP (ES3I,40;MI,12;NRE,5-7;NS3E,22;SP4I,113;TE,30;U12E,01-5;VI,76)

  Applies reading skills and strategies to a variety of informational texts (e.g., textbooks, biographical sketches, letters, diaries, directions, procedures, magazines, essays, primary source historical documents, editorials, news stories, periodiocals, catalogs, job-related materials, schedules, speeches, memoranda)

- BD (IAI,15;NRE,5;TI,32)

  Knows the defining characteristics of a variety of informational texts (e.g., textbooks, biographical sketches, letters, diaries, directions, procedures, magazines, essays, primary source historical documents, editorials, news stories, periodiocals, catalogs, job-related

---

Codes (right side of page):	BD = Benchmark, Declarative; BP = Benchmark, Procedural; BC = Benchmark, Contextual

1st letter(s) of each code in parentheses
A = Australian Education Council
E1,2,3 = Edison Proj: Primary, Elem., Junior
ES1,2,3 = NCTE: Exemplar Series: 6-8, 9-12
IA,IA1 = Int'l Bacc.: Middle, A1 Guide
M = Mississippi: English Language Arts
NR = NAEP: 1992 Reading Assessment
NS1,2,3 = New Standards: Elem., Middle, High
NW = NAEP: Writing Achiev. Levels-Setting Proc.
S = Speech Communication Association
SP1,2,3,4 = NCTE: Standards in Practice

2nd letter of code
E = Explicitly stated in document
I = Implied in document

Number
Page number of cited document
or, for Utah document:
Standard number

SS = NCSS: Curric. Standards for Social Studies
T = Texas: English Language Arts and Reading
UK-12 = Utah Core Curriculum: Language Arts
V = Board of Ed., Commonwealth of Virginia: Standards of Learning
AP = See appendix immediately following the Language Arts Standards

materials, schedules, speeches, memoranda)

- Scans a passage to determine whether it contains relevant information
  BP (AE,81;IAI,14;VE,73)

- Summarizes and paraphrases complex, implicit hierarchic structures in informational texts, including the relationships among the concepts and details in those structures
  BP (AE,105;IAI,15;NRI,5,18,19;NS3E,22;U12E,01-2)

- Uses new information from texts to clarify or refine understanding of academic concepts
  BP (NRI,18,19;VE,75)

- Determines the effectiveness of techniques used to convey viewpoint
  BP (NRI,16,17;U12E,01-5;VE,75)

- Uses discussions with peers as a way of understanding information
  BP (AE,81)

- Reorganizes the concepts and details in informational texts in new ways and describes the advantages and disadvantages of the new organization
  BC (NRI,18,19)

- Evaluates the clarity and accuracy of information
  BP (TI,33;U12E,01-2;VE,72,76)

- Supports inferences about information in texts by referring to text features (e.g., vocabulary, text structure)
  BP (AE,81;NRI,18)

8. Demonstrates competence in speaking and listening as tools for learning
(AI,6,7;NS1,2,3E,21;SP1,2,3,4I,viii;TE,12,25,40;VE,59)

Level I (Grades K-2)

- Recognizes the characteristic sounds and rhythms of language
  BD (AI,19;NS1I,22;VE,61-62)

- Makes contributions in class and group discussions (e.g., recounts personal experiences, reports on personal knowledge about a topic, initiates conversations)
  BP (AE,18;NS1E,25;SP1E,11;TI,12;U2E,10;VE,63)

- Asks and responds to questions
  BP (AE,18;19;NS1E,25;SP1I,11;UI,10;VE,61)

- Follows rules of conversation (e.g., takes turns, raises hand to speak, stays on topic, focuses
  BP (AE,18,19;NS1E,25;TE,12;UE,10;VE,60,61)

Codes (right side of page):   BD = Benchmark, Declarative;   BP = Benchmark, Procedural;   BC = Benchmark, Contextual

1st letter(s) of each code in parentheses   *2nd letter of code*   *Number*

A = Australian Education Council   E = Explicitly stated in document   Page number of cited document

E1,2,3 = Edison Proj: Primary, Elem., Junior   I = Implied in document   *or, for Utah document:*

ES1,2,3 = NCTE: Exemplar Series: 6-8, 9-12   Standard number

IA,IA1 = Int'l Bacc.: Middle, A1 Guide

M = Mississippi: English Language Arts   SS = NCSS: Curric. Standards for Social Studies

NR = NAEP: 1992 Reading Assessment   T = Texas: English Language Arts and Reading

NS1,2,3 = New Standards: Elem., Middle, High   UK-12 = Utah Core Curriculum: Language Arts

NW = NAEP: Writing Achiev. Levels-Setting Proc.   V = Board of Ed., Commonwealth of Virginia: Standards of Learning

S = Speech Communication Association   AP = See appendix immediately following the Language Arts Standards

SP1,2,3,4 = NCTE: Standards in Practice

MREL

attention on speaker)

- Uses different voice level, phrasing, and intonation for different situations

  BP (AE,19;NS1I,25;SPE,47,81;VE,60,61)

- Listens and responds to oral directions

  BP (AE,18;SI,6;TE,12;UE,11;VE,63)

- Listens to and recites familiar stories, poems, and rhymes with patterns

  BP (AE,18;SP1E,46,62;TE,13;UE,10;VE,60,61)

- Listens and responds to a variety of media (e.g., books, audiotapes, videos)

  BP (VE,61;SI,6)

- Identifies differences between language used at home and language used in school

  BC (AE,18;SP1I,63;U2I,12)

Level II (Grades 3-5)

- Contributes to group discussions

  BP (AE,34;NS1E,25;SP2I,24;TI,12;U5E,10;VE,66)

- Asks questions in class (e.g., when he or she is confused, to seek others' opinions and comments)

  BP (AE,35;NS1E,25;UE,10;VE,64,65)

- Responds to questions and comments (e.g., gives reasons in support of opinions)

  BP (NS1E,25;SI,6;U5I,10;VE,64,65)

- Listens to classmates and adults (e.g., does not interrupt, faces the speaker, asks questions, paraphrases to confirm understanding, gives feedback)

  BP (AE,34,35;NS1E,25;SI,6;TE,25,26;U5I,10;VE,64)

- Makes some effort to have a clear main point when speaking to others

  BP (AE,35;NS1I,25;U5I,10;VE,66)

- Reads compositions to the class

  BP (AI,34;NS1E,25;U5E,10;VE,64)

- Makes eye contact while giving oral presentations

  BP (AI,34;NS1E,25;U5E,10;VE,66)

- Organizes ideas for oral presentations (e.g., includes content appropriate to the audience, uses notes or other memory aids, summarizes main points)

  BP (AE,34,35;NS1E,25;SI,2;U5E,10;VE,66)

- Listens to and identifies persuasive messages (e.g., television commercials, commands and

  BP (NS1I,25;SI,6;TE,12)

Codes (right side of page):   BD = Benchmark, Declarative; BP = Benchmark, Procedural; BC = Benchmark, Contextual

1st letter(s) of each code in parentheses	*2nd letter of code*	*Number*
A = Australian Education Council	E = Explicitly stated in document	Page number of cited document
E1,2,3 = Edison Proj: Primary, Elem., Junior	I = Implied in document	*or, for Utah document:*
ES1,2,3 = NCTE: Exemplar Series: 6-8, 9-12		Standard number
IA,IA1 = Int'l Bacc.: Middle, A1 Guide		

M = Mississippi: English Language Arts	SS = NCSS: Curric. Standards for Social Studies
NR = NAEP: 1992 Reading Assessment	T = Texas: English Language Arts and Reading
NS1,2,3 = New Standards: Elem., Middle, High	UK-12 = Utah Core Curriculum: Language Arts
NW = NAEP: Writing Achiev. Levels-Setting Proc.	V = Board of Ed., Commonwealth of Virginia: Standards of Learning
S = Speech Communication Association	AP = See appendix immediately following the Language Arts Standards
SP1,2,3,4 = NCTE: Standards in Practice	

requests, pressure from peers)

- Identifies the use of nonverbal cues used in conversation BD (AE,34;TI,12;VI,66)

- Identifies specific ways in which language is used in real-life situations (e.g., buying BD (AE,34) something from a shopkeeper, requesting something from a parent, arguing with a sibling, talking to a friend)

Level III (Grades 6-8)

- Plays a variety of roles in group discussions (e.g., active listener, discussion leader, BP (AI,56,57;IAI,15;NS2I,25;SP3E,113;VE,68) facilitator)

- Asks questions to seek elaboration and clarification of ideas BP (AI,57;NS2E,25;VE,69)

- Listens in order to understand a speaker's topic, purpose, and perspective BP (AE,56,57;NS2I,25;SI,6;TE,26)

- Conveys a clear main point when speaking to others and stays on the topic being discussed BP (AE,78;NS2E,25;VI,69)

- Presents simple prepared reports to the class BP (AE,56;IAI,16;NS2E,25)

- Uses explicit techniques for oral presentations (e.g., modulation of voice, inflection, tempo, BP (AE,79;IAI,16;NS2E,25;SE,5;U8I,05;VE,69) enunciation, physical gestures, eye contact, posture)

- Identifies strategies used by speakers in oral presentations (e.g., persuasive techniques, verbal BP (AE,79;IAI,16;SE,5;TE,25-27;VE,68,69) and nonverbal messages, the use of fact and opinion)

- Listens to and understands the impact of nonprint media on media consumers (e.g., BP (AE,80;NS2E,25;SI,6;U8I,07;VE,69) persuasive messages and advertising in media, the presence of media in people's daily lives, the role of the media in forming opinions, media as a source of entertainment and information)

- Identifies the ways in which language differs across a variety of social situations BP (AI,56;IAI,14;SP3E,33)

Codes (right side of page):	BD = Benchmark, Declarative; BP = Benchmark, Procedural; BC = Benchmark, Contextual

1st letter(s) of each code in parentheses — *2nd letter of code* — *Number*

A = Australian Education Council — E = Explicitly stated in document — Page number of cited document
E1,2,3 = Edison Proj: Primary, Elem., Junior — I = Implied in document — *or, for Utah document:*
ES1,2,3 = NCTE: Exemplar Series: 6-8, 9-12 — Standard number
IA,IA1 = Int'l Bacc.: Middle, A1 Guide
M = Mississippi: English Language Arts — SS = NCSS: Curric. Standards for Social Studies
NR = NAEP: 1992 Reading Assessment — T = Texas: English Language Arts and Reading
NS1,2,3 = New Standards: Elem., Middle, High — UK-12 = Utah Core Curriculum: Language Arts
NW = NAEP: Writing Achiev. Levels-Setting Proc. — V = Board of Ed., Commonwealth of Virginia: Standards of Learning
S = Speech Communication Association — AP = See appendix immediately following the Language Arts Standards
SP1,2,3,4 = NCTE: Standards in Practice

Level IV (Grades 9-12)

- BC (AE,119;NS3E,25;TE,42;VE,74,76)
  Evaluates own and others' effectiveness in group discussions and in formal presentations (e.g., evaluates accuracy, relevance, and organization of information; evaluates clarity of delivery; evaluates relationships among purpose, audience, and content; identifies types of arguments used)

- BP (NS3E,25;SP4I,31)
  Asks questions as a way to broaden and enrich classroom discussions

- BP (AI,119;NS3E,25;SI,5;TE,40,42;VE,76)
  Adjusts message wording and delivery to particular audiences and for particular purposes (e.g., to defend a position, to entertain, to inform, to persuade)

- BP (AE,118;NS3E,25;TE,40,41;VE,72,76)
  Makes formal presentations to the class (e.g., includes definitions for clarity; supports main ideas using anecdotes, examples, statistics, analogies, and other evidence; uses visual aids or technology)

- BP (AI,119;IAI,16;NS3I,25;SE,5;TI,40;VE,72)
  Uses a variety of explicit techniques for presentations (e.g., modulation of voice, inflection, tempo, enunciation, physical gestures) and demonstrates poise and self-control while presenting

- BP (NS3I,25;SI,6;TE,41,42;VE,72,74,76)
  Responds to questions and feedback about own presentations (e.g., defends ideas, expands on a topic, uses logical arguments)

- BP (AE,119;NS3E,25;SI,6)
  Makes informed judgments about nonprint media (e.g., detects elements of persuasion and appeal in advertisements; recognizes the impact of pace, volume, tone, and images on media consumers)

- BC (AI,78;IAI,14;SP4I,54-55;TI,41)
  Compares form, meaning, and usefulness of different kinds of language

- BD (AI,118;SP4I,50)
  Understands influences on language use (e.g., political beliefs, positions of social power, culture)

Appendix for Language Arts: Level I (Primary)

Nursery Rhymes

"A Diller, A Dollar" (H1,17)
"Baa, Baa, Black Sheep" (H1,17)
"Chinese Mother Goose Rhymes" by
     Robert Wyndham (CS,15)
"Diddle, Diddle, Dumpling" (H1,17)
"Early to Bed" (H1,17)
"Georgie Porgie" (H1,18)
"Here We Go Round the Mulberry Bush"
     (H1,19)
"Hey, Diddle, Diddle" (H1,18)
"Hickory, Dickory, Dock" (H1,18)
"Hot Cross Buns!" (H1,18)
"Humpty Dumpty" (H1,19)
"Jack Sprat" (H,181;H1,17)
"Jack, Be Nimble" (H,181;H1,19)
"Jack and Jill" (H,181;H1,18)
"Ladybug, Ladybug"(H1,17)
"Little Bo Peep" (H,184;H1,21)
"Little Miss Muffett" (H,184;H1,20)
"Little Jack Horner" (H,184;H1,21)
"Little Boy Blue" (H,184;H1,19)
"London Bridge Is Falling Down" (H1,19)
"Mary Had a Little Lamb" (H1,20)
"Mary, Mary, Quite Contrary" (H1,20)
"Old King Cole" (H,193;H1,20)
"Old Mother Hubbard" (H,193;H1,23)

"One, Two, Buckle My Shoe" (H1,21)
"Pat-a-Cake" (H1,21)
"Rain, Rain, Go Away" (H1,24)
"Ride a Cock Horse" (H,200;H1,23)
"Ring Around the Rosey" (Hl,21)
"Rock-a-bye, Baby" (H1,23)
"Roses are Red" (H1,24)
"Rub-a-dub-dub" (H1,24)
"See-Saw, Margery Daw" (H1,23)
"Simple Simon" (H,204;H1,25)
"Sing a Song of Sixpence" (H1,24)
"Star Light, Star Bright" (H1,23)
"The Owl and the Pussycat" (H1,22)
"There Was an Old Woman Who Lived in a
     Shoe" (H1,26)
"There Was A Little Girl" (H1,25)
"This Little Pig Went to Market" (H1,26)
"Three Blind Mice" (H1,25)
"Tom, Tom, the Piper's Son" (H1,23)
*Tortillitas para mama; And Other Spanish
     Nursery Rhymes* by Griego, Margot
     C., and others (CS,11)
"Twinkle, Twinkle, Little Star" (H1,25)
"Wynken, Blynken, and Nod"
     (H,215;H1,18)

Fairy Tales

Andersen, Hans Christian (H,154)
     "Cinderella" (CS,9;RF,270;H1,29)
     "Princess and the Pea" (H,197;H1,43)
     "The Emperor's New Clothes" (H,170)
"Beauty and the Beast" (H,157;H2,18)
"Chicken Little" (CS,10;H1,28)
"Goldilocks and The Three Bears" (H,209;H1,31)
Grimm brothers (H,176)

McREL

"Hansel and Gretel" (H,176;H2,29)
"Snow White" (H,204;H1,52)
The Bremen Town Musicians (CS,12)
The Shoemaker and the Elves (CS,12)
"Jack and the Beanstalk" (CS,11;E1,19;H,181;H1,32)
"Red Riding Hood" (H,184)
"Pied Piper of Hamelin" (H,195;H1,40)
"Pinocchio" (H,195;H1,42)
"Puss-in-Boots" (H,199;H1,44)
"Rumpelstiltskin" (H1,46)
"Rupunzel" (H1,46)
"Sleeping Beauty" (H,204;H1,50)
"The Little Red Hen" (CS,10;H,184;H1,34)
"The Three Little Pigs" (H,209;H1,54)
"The Emperor's New Clothes" (H2,27)
"The Three Billy Goats Gruff" (CS,11;H1,65)
"The Ugly Duckling" (II1,55;NS1,23)
"The Three Bears" (CS,11)

Folktales and Legends

Aardema, Verna *Why Mosquitoes Buzz in People's Ears: A West African Tale* (CS,8)
Aardema, Verna *Bringing the Rain to Kapiti Plain* (CS,8)
"Aladdin and the Wonderful Lamp" (H,53)
"Anansi" (E1,19;H1,27)
Brown, Marica *Once a Mouse* (CS,9)
Carpenter, Frances *Tales of a Korean Grandmother* (CS,9)
DePoala, Tomie *Strega Nona* (CS,10)
"El Pajaro Cu" (H2,25)
"From Tiger to Anansi" (H2,48)
Gerson, Mary-Joan "Why the Sky is Far Away: A Nigerian Folktale" (E1,18)
Haley, Gail E. *A Story, a Story* (CS,12)
Hodges, Margaret *The Wave* (CS,12)
Hogrogian, Nonny "One Fine Day" (CS,13;E1,18)
Hong, Lily "How the Ox Star Fell From Heaven" (E1,18)
"Inktomi Lost His Eyes" (H2,31)
Leaf, Munro "The Story of Ferdinand" (E1,18)

C = California Recommended Readings, K-8
CS = California Recommended Literature, 9-12
E1,2,3 = Edison Proj.: Primary,Elem.,Junior Acad.
GJ = Gillespie: Best Books for Junior High Readers
GS = Gillespie: Best Books for Senior High Readers
H = Hirsch: Cultural Literacy
H1 - H6 = Hirsch: Core Knowledge Series, Grades 1-6

IE,IW = Int'l Bacc.: English A1, World Lit.
IEA,IWA= Int'l Bacc.: English A1, World Lit. (author citation)
NE = New England Association of Teachers of English
NS1,2,3 = New Standards: Elem., Middle, High
NS1A,2A,3A = New Standards: Elem., Middle, High (author
    citation)
RF = Ravitch & Finn: What Do Our 17-Year-Olds Know?

347

MREL

Lindgren, Aastrid "The Tomten" (E1,18)
Lobel, Arnold "Frog and Toad are Friends" (E1,18)
"Medio Pollito" (H1,37)
"One-Inch Fellow" (H2,36)
"Peter Pan" (H2,43)
Roland, Donna *Grandfather's Stories - Cambodia* (CS,14)
Roland, Donna *More of Grandfather's Stories* (CS,14)
"St. George and the Dragon" (H,202)
Steptoe, John "Mufaro's Beautiful Daughters: An African Tale" (E1,18;NS1,23)
"The Blind Men and the Elephant" (H2,20)
"The Fable of Brer Rabbit and the Tar Baby" (H1,68)
"The Tiger and the Brahmin" (E1,19)
Uchida, Yoshiko *The Magic Listening Cap: More Folktales from Japan* (CS,15)
Van Allsburg, Chris "Jumanji" (E1,18)
"Why the Owl Has Big Eyes" (H1,56)
Wolkstein, Dian *The Banza* (CS,15)
Yashima, Taro *Umbrella* (CS,16)
Young, Ed "Lon Po Po: A Red Riding Hood Story from China" (E1,18)

Fables and Myth
Aesop's fables (RF,272; E1,18;H,152)
      "The Boy Who Cried Wolf" (H,159;H1,59)
      "Tortoise and Hare" (RF,271;H,176;H1,62)
      "The Dog in the Manger" (H1,60)
      "The Wolf in Sheep's Clothing" (H1,60)
      "The Maid and the Milk Pail" (H1,61)
      "The Fox and the Grapes" (H1,62)
      "The Goose and the Golden Eggs" (H1,63)
      "King Midas" (E1,19)
Mythology--Introducing Some Gods and Goddesses (i.e., Zeus, Hera, Apollo, Poseidon, Aphrodite and Eros, Ares, Hermes, Hephaestos, Athena, Hades) (H2,52-55)
      "Demeter and Persephone" (H2,56)
      "Prometheus and Pandora" (H2,58)
      "The Quest of the Golden Fleece" (H2,59)
      "Sailing with the Argonauts" (H2,60)
      "Finding the Fleece" (H2,61)

C = California Recommended Readings, K-8
CS = California Recommended Literature, 9-12
E1,2,3 = Edison Proj.: Primary,Elem.,Junior Acad.
GJ = Gillespie: Best Books for Junior High Readers
GS = Gillespie: Best Books for Senior High Readers
H = Hirsch: Cultural Literacy
H1 - H6 = Hirsch: Core Knowledge Series, Grades 1-6

IE,IW = Int'l Bacc.: English A1, World Lit.
IEA,IWA= Int'l Bacc.: English A1, World Lit. (author citation)
NE = New England Association of Teachers of English
NS1,2,3 = New Standards: Elem., Middle, High
NS1A,2A,3A = New Standards: Elem., Middle, High (author citation)
RF = Ravitch & Finn: What Do Our 17-Year-Olds Know?

"The Legend of Oedipus and the Sphinx" (H1,66)
"The Legend of the Minotaur, Daedalus, and Icarus" (H1,67)

Novels

Dickens, Charles *A Christmas Carol* (H2,22;IEA,1,2)
Hahn, Jae Hyun, and Han Hahn *Special Korean Birthday* (CS,32)
Lionni, Leo *Alexander and the Wind-up Mouse* (CS,19)
Lobel, Arnold *Frog and Toad Are Friends* (CS,20)
Milne, A. A. *Winnie the Pooh* (H,214)
Peet, Bill *Big Bad Bruce* (CS,20)
Potter, Beatrix *Peter Rabbit* (E1,18; H1,38)
Seuss, Dr. *And to Think That I Saw It on Mulberry Street* (CS,21)
Steig, William *Sylvester and the Magic Pebble* (CS,21)
Yashima, Mitsu and Taro *Momo's Kitten* (CS,22;E1,18)
Zolotow, Charlotte *Mr. Rabbit and the Lovely Present* (CS,22)

Poetry

Adoff, Arnold *Outside-Inside Poems* (CS,23)
Livingston, Myra C., ed. *Listen, Children, Listen: An Anthology of Poems for the Very Young* (CS,26)
Blake, William "Spring" (E1,18;IEA,1)
Chippewa Indians, North America *The Approach of the Storm* (E1,18)
De Reniers, Beatrice Schenk *Keep a Poem in Your Pocket* (E1,18)
Farjean, Eleanor *Eleanor Farjeon's Poems for Children* (E1,18)
Giovanni, Nikki "Because" (E1,18;NS1A,23)
Hopkins, Lee Bennett "Poetry Time" (E1,18)
                        Surprises (CS,28)
Koriyama, Naoshi *"Unfolding Bud"* (E1,18)
Kuskin, Karla *"Take a Word like a Cat"* and *"Honey, I Love You"* (E1,18)
Longfellow, Henry Wadsworth *"Paul Revere's Ride"* (H2,38;RF,273;NS3A,23)
Moore, Clement C. *"'Twas the Night Before Christmas"* (H2,33)

C = California Recommended Readings, K-8
CS = California Recommended Literature, 9-12
E1,2,3 = Edison Proj.: Primary,Elem.,Junior Acad.
GJ = Gillespie: Best Books for Junior High Readers
GS = Gillespie: Best Books for Senior High Readers
H = Hirsch: Cultural Literacy
H1 - H6 = Hirsch: Core Knowledge Series, Grades 1-6

IE,IW = Int'l Bacc.: English A1, World Lit.
IEA,IWA= Int'l Bacc.: English A1, World Lit. (author citation)
NE = New England Association of Teachers of English
NS1,2,3 = New Standards: Elem., Middle, High
NS1A,2A,3A = New Standards: Elem., Middle, High (author citation)
RF = Ravitch & Finn: What Do Our 17-Year-Olds Know?

Nonfiction

Baylor, Byrd *The Desert Is Theirs* (CS,41)

Boynton, Sandra *A is for Angry: An Animal and Adjective Alphabet* (E1,18)

Lauber, Patricia *Seeds: Pop Stick Glide* and *What's Hatching Out of That Egg* (CS,41)

Price, Christine *Dancing Masks of Africa* (CS,44)

C = California Recommended Readings, K-8	IE,IW = Int'l Bacc.: English A1, World Lit.
CS = California Recommended Literature, 9-12	IEA,IWA= Int'l Bacc.: English A1, World Lit. (author citation)
E1,2,3 = Edison Proj.: Primary,Elem.,Junior Acad.	NE = New England Association of Teachers of English
GJ = Gillespie: Best Books for Junior High Readers	NS1,2,3 = New Standards: Elem., Middle, High
GS = Gillespie: Best Books for Senior High Readers	NS1A,2A,3A = New Standards: Elem., Middle, High (author
H = Hirsch: Cultural Literacy	citation)
H1 - H6 = Hirsch: Core Knowledge Series, Grades 1-6	RF = Ravitch & Finn: What Do Our 17-Year-Olds Know?

350

Appendix for Language Arts: Level II (Upper Elementary)

Mythology from Around the World
Norse Mythology
> "Balder and Loki" (H3,46)
> "How the Norse Gods Lived" (H3,44)
> "How the Days of the Week Got Their Names" (H3,42)
> "How the Gods' Home, Asgard, Was Built" (H3,45)
> "The Enemies of the Gods" (H3,44)
> "Why the Universe Doesn't Fall Down" (H3,47)

Myths from Medieval England
> "Guinevere" (H4,59)
> "How Arthur Became King: the Sword in the Stone" (H4,56)
> "Merlin and the Lady of the Lake" (H4,61)
> "Sir Launcelot" (H4,62)
> "The Sword Excalibur and the Lady of the Lake" (H4,58)
> "The Legend of King Arthur and the Knights of the Round Table" (H4,55)

Classical Greek Mythology
> Background information on *The Iliad* and *The Odyssey* (H5,28)
> D'Aulaire, Ingri, and Edgar P. D'Aulaire *D'Aulaires' Book of Greek Myths* (CS,10;NS2A,23)
> from *The Iliad*
>> "Epilogue to the Iliad" (H5,39)
>> "Hector and Andromache" (H5,34)
>> "The Arming of Achilles" (H5,36)
>> "The Combat Between Menelaus and Paris" (H5,35)
>> "The Death of Hector" (H5,38)
>> "The Judgment of Paris" (H5,28)
>> "The Quarrel Between Agamemnon and Achilles" (H5,31)
> from *The Odyssey*
>> Background to T*he Odyssey* (H5,40)
>> "Odysseus and the Cyclops" (H5,41)

Adaptations from the Classics
"A Voyage to Lilliput" (H4,3)
"Adventures of Sherlock Homes: The Red-Headed League" (H5,14)

C = California Recommended Readings, K-8
CS = California Recommended Literature, 9-12
E1,2,3 = Edison Proj.: Primary,Elem.,Junior Acad.
GJ = Gillespie: Best Books for Junior High Readers
GS = Gillespie: Best Books for Senior High Readers
H = Hirsch: Cultural Literacy
H1 - H6 = Hirsch: Core Knowledge Series, Grades 1-6

IE,IW = Int'l Bacc.: English A1, World Lit.
IEA,IWA= Int'l Bacc.: English A1, World Lit. (author citation)
NE = New England Association of Teachers of English
NS1,2,3 = New Standards: Elem., Middle, High
NS1A,2A,3A = New Standards: Elem., Middle, High (author citation)
RF = Ravitch & Finn: What Do Our 17-Year-Olds Know?

MREL

"Aladdin and the Wonderful Lamp" (H3,12)

"Ali Baba and the Forty Thieves" (H3,15)

"Alice's Adventures in Wonderland" (H3,17)

Andersen, Hans Christian *The Ugly Duckling* Retold by Lorinda B. Cauley (CS,17)

Beauty and the Beast Retold by Marianna Mayer (CS,9)

"Dr. Jekyll and Mr. Hyde" (H5,23)

"Julius Caesar" (H5,8)

"On Thin Ice" from *Little Women* (H4,13)

"Pollyanna" (H3,25;E2,37)

"Rip Van Winkle" (H4,17;RF,270)

"Robinson Crusoe" (H4,8)

"The Adventures of Don Quixote" (H5,19)

"The Adventures of Tom Sawyer" (H5,5;RF,272)

"The Glittering Cloud" from *On the Banks of Plum Creek* (H4,37)

"The Legend of Sleepy Hollow" (H4,21)

"Treasure Island" (H4,30)

Folktales

Aesop *Aesop's Fables* (CS,8)

Asbjornsen, Peter Christian, and Jorgen E. Moe *East of the Sun and West of the Moon and Other Tales* (CS,8)

Blair, Walter *Tall Tale America* (CS,9;NS2,23)

Brown, Marcia *Once a Mouse* (CS,9)

Chase, Richard *The Jack Tales* (CS,10)

"Coyote Goes to the Land of the Dead" (H5,2)

Dayrell, Elphinstone *Why the Sun and Moon Live in the Sky* (CS,10)

DePaola, Tomie *Strega Nona* (CS,10)

Fleischman, Sid *Humbug Mountain* (CS,11)

Gag, Wanda *Tales from Grimm* (CS,11)

Granfa' Grig Had a Pig and Other Rhymes Without Reason from Mother Goose (CS,11)

Grimm, Jacob, and Wilhelm Grimm *Little Red Riding Hood* (CS,12)

Rapunzel (CS,12)

Snow-White and the Seven Dwarfs (CS,12)

Jaquith, Priscilla *Bo Rabbit Smart for True: Folktales from the Gullah* (CS,13)

Keats, Ezra Jack *John Henry: An American Legend* (CS,13)

Louie, Ai-Lang *Yeh Shen: A Cinderella Story from China* (CS,13;NS1,23)

C = California Recommended Readings, K-8

CS = California Recommended Literature, 9-12

E1,2,3 = Edison Proj.: Primary,Elem.,Junior Acad.

GJ = Gillespie: Best Books for Junior High Readers

GS = Gillespie: Best Books for Senior High Readers

H = Hirsch: Cultural Literacy

H1 - H6 = Hirsch: Core Knowledge Series, Grades 1-6

IE,IW = Int'l Bacc.: English A1, World Lit.

IEA,IWA= Int'l Bacc.: English A1, World Lit. (author citation)

NE = New England Association of Teachers of English

NS1,2,3 = New Standards: Elem., Middle, High

NS1A,2A,3A = New Standards: Elem., Middle, High (author citation)

RF = Ravitch & Finn: What Do Our 17-Year-Olds Know?

Luenn, Nancy *The Dragon Kite* (CS,13;NS1,23)
North American Legends Virginia Havland, ed. (CS,14)
Paul Bunyan Retold by Steven Kellogg (CS,14)
Steptoe, John *The Story of Jumping Mouse, a Native American Legend* (CS,15)
"Talk" (H3,36)
"The People Could Fly" (H3,24)
The Sleeping Beauty by the Brothers Grimm (CS,15)
"The Quillwork Girl and Her Seven Brothers" (H3,32)
"The Sun Dance" (H4,25)
"The Tongue-cut Sparrow" (H4,6)
"Three Words of Wisdom" (H3,34)
Two Brothers and Their Magic Gourds Edward B. Adams, ed. (CS,15)
Yagawa, Sumiko *The Crane Wife* (CS,16)

Unabridged Fiction

Andersen, Hans Christian *The Nightingale* (CS,17)
Atkinson, Mary *Maria Teresa* (CS,29)
Baylor, Byrd *Amigo* (E2,36)
Bernstein, Margery and Janet Kobrin *Coyote Goes Hunting for Fire: A California Indian Myth* (E2,37)
Brenner, Barbara *Wagon Wheels* (CS,36)
Bryan, Ashley *Beat the Story Drum, Pum-Pum* (CS,9;E2,37;NS2,23)
Cameron, Eleanor *The Court of the Stone Children* (CS,18)
Cleary, Beverly *Ramona and Her Father* (CS,30;NS1,23)
Clifton, Lucille *The Boy Who Didn't Believe in Spring* (E2,36)
Dahl, Roald *James and the Giant Peach* (CS,18;NS1,23)
Dalgliesh, Alice *The Courage of Sarah Noble* (CS,36)
DeClements, Barthe *Nothing's Fair in Fifth Grade* (E2,36)
DePaola, Tomie *Nana Upstairs and Nana Downstairs* (CS,30)
DuBois, William P. *Lion* (CS,18)
Estes, Eleanor *The Hundred Dresses* (CS,30)
Galbraith, Claire K. *Victor* (CS,31)
Gates, Doris *Blue Willow* (CS,31)
Grahame, Kenneth *Wind in the Willows* (E2,37;NS1,23)
Greene, Bette *Philip Hall Likes Me, I Reckon Maybe* (CS,31;NS2A,23)
Hahn, Jae, Hyun *Seven Korean Sisters* (CS,31;E2,37)

C = California Recommended Readings, K-8	IE,IW = Int'l Bacc.: English A1, World Lit.
CS = California Recommended Literature, 9-12	IEA,IWA= Int'l Bacc.: English A1, World Lit. (author citation)
E1,2,3 = Edison Proj.: Primary,Elem.,Junior Acad.	NE = New England Association of Teachers of English
GJ = Gillespie: Best Books for Junior High Readers	NS1,2,3 = New Standards: Elem., Middle, High
GS = Gillespie: Best Books for Senior High Readers	NS1A,2A,3A = New Standards: Elem., Middle, High (author
H = Hirsch: Cultural Literacy	citation)
H1 - H6 = Hirsch: Core Knowledge Series, Grades 1-6	RF = Ravitch & Finn: What Do Our 17-Year-Olds Know?

353

MREL

Haley, Gail *Jack Jouett's Ride* (CS,37)

Hall, Donald *The Ox-Cart Man* (CS,37)

Hamilton, Virginia *Zeely* (CS,32;NS1,23;NS2A,23)

Han, Mieko *Turtle Power - Vietnamese* (CS,18)

Konigsburg, E. L. *From the Mixed-Up Files of Mrs. Basil E. Frankweiler* (CS,32)

Lasker, Joe *He's My Brother* (E2,36)

Lawson, Robert *Ben and Me* (CS,19)

L'Engle, Madeleine *A Wrinkle in Time* (CS,19;E2,37;NS2,23)

Lewis, Thomas P. *Hill of Fire* (CS,37)

Lobel, Arnold *Fables* (CS,20)

Lord, Bette B. *In the Year of the Boar and Jackie Robinson* (CS,37;NS1,23)

Lowry, Lois *Anastasia Krupnik* (CS,33)

MacLachlan, Patricia *Arthur, for the Very First Time* (CS,33)

Sarah, Plain and Tall (CS,38)

Maury, Inex *My Mother the Mail Carrier* (CS,33)

Meadowcroft, Enid *By Secret Railway* (CS,38)

Miles, Miska *Annie and the Old One* (CS,33)

Milne, A.A. *Winnie-the-Pooh* (CS,20)

Monjo, F. N. *The Drinking Gourd* (CS,38)

Ness, Evaline *Sam, Bangs, and Moonshine* (CS,33)

O'Brien, Robert C. *Mrs. Frisby and the Rats of NIMH* (E2,36)

Robinson, Marc *Cock-a-Doodle-Doo! What Does It Sound Like to You?* (E2,36)

Sendak, Maurice *Where the Wild Things Are* (CS,21)

Seuss, Dr. *Five Hundred Hats of Bartholomew Cubbins* (CS,21)

Shub, Elizabeth *The White Stallion* (CS,39)

Speare, Elizabeth G. *The Sign of the Beaver* (CS,39;E2,36;NS1,23)

Sperry, Armstrong *Call It Courage* (CS,39;E2,36)

Steig, William *Abel's Island* (CS,21)

Steptoe, John *Stevie* (CS,34)

Spyri, Johanna *Heidi* (E2,36)

Turkle, Brinton *Do Not Open* (CS,21)

Turner, Ann *Nettie's Trip South* (E2,36)

Uchida, Yoshiko *Journey to Topaz* (CS,39)

Van Allsburg, Chris *Jumanji* (CS,21;NS1,23)

Williams, Margery *The Velveteen Rabbit* (CS,22)

Williams, Vera B. *A Chair for My Mother* (CS,34;E2,36)

White, E. B. *Charlotte's Web* (CS,22;NS1,23)

Wilder, Laura I. *Little House in the Big Woods* (CS,40)
Yashima, Taro *Crow Boy* (CS,34)

Poetry
A Book of Animal Poems Selected by William Cole (CS,24)
Amon, Aline *The Earth is Sore: Native Amricans on Nature* (CS,24)
Angelou, Maya "Life Doesn't Frighten Me" (H4,50;IEA,2)
Anonymous "Monday's Child Is Fair of Face" (H4,43)
Anonymous "Solomon Grundy" (H4,43)
Baylor, Byrd *When Clay Sings* (CS,24)
Cricket Songs: Japanese Haiku Translated by Harry Behn (CS,24)
Belloc, Hilaire "The Frog" (H4,44)
Benet, Rosemary, and Stephen Vincent Benet *A Book of Americans* (CS,24)
Blake, William "The Tiger" (E2,37;H5,50;RF,277;IEA,1)
Brooks, Gwendolyn "Narcissa" (H5,58)
Burgess, Gelett "The Purple Cow" (H4,47)
Carroll, Lewis "Jabberwocky" (H5,53)
Carroll, Lewis "The Crocodile" (H4,45)
Crazy to Be Alive in Such a Strange World Edited by Nancy Larrick (CS,24)
Cullen, Countee "Incident" (H5,59)
Dickinson, Emily "A Bird Came Down the Walk" (H5,48;IEA,1)
Fisher, Aileen *Out in the Dark and Daylight* (CS,25)
Froman, Robert *Seeing Things: A Book of Poems* (CS,25)
Greenfield, Eloise "Things" (H4,52;NS1A,23;NS2A,23)
How to Eat a Poem and Other Morsels Selected by Rose Agree (CS,25)
Howard, Coralie *The Firt Book of Short Verse* (CS,25)
Howe, Julia Ward "Battle Hymn of the Republic" (H5,54)
Hughes, Langston "Dreams" (E2,37;H4,46;IEA,1)
Hughes, Langston "I, Too" (H5,57;IEA,1)
Hughes, Langston *The Dream Keeper* (E2,37;IEA,1)
Kilmer, Sergeant Joyce "Trees" (H5,49)
Knock on a Star: A Child's Introduction to Poetry Edited by X.J. Kennedy and Dorothy
    Kennedy (CS,26)
Lear, Edward *How Pleasant to Know Mr. Lear!* (CS,26)
Lear, Edward "The Pobble Who Has No Toes" (H4,49)
Livingston, Myra C. *Circle of Seasons* (CS,26)
Longfellow, Henry Wadsworth "The Arrow and the Song" (H5,58;NS3A,23)

McCord, David *One at a Time* (CS,26)

Merriam, Eve *There is No Rhyme for Silver* (CS,26)

Millay, Edna St. Vincent "Afternoon on a Hill" (E2,37;H4,53)

Moore, Lilian *Something New Begins* (CS,26)

My Song Is A Piece of Jade: Poems of Ancient Mexico in English and Spanish Edited by Toni de Gerez (CS,26)

My Tang's Tungled and Other Ridiculous Situations Compiled by Sara Brewton (CS,26)

Nash, Ogden "The Rhinoceros" (H4,44)

O'Neill, Mary *Hailstones and Halibut Bones* (CS, 27)

Perkins, Useni Eugene "Ballad of John Henry" (H5,54)

Piping Down the Valleys Wild Edited by Nancy Larrick (CS,27)

Poem Stew Edited by William Cole (CS,27)

Richards, Edward Hersey "A Wise, Old Owl" (H5,50)

Sandburg, Carl "Fog" (H5,48)

Silverstein, Shel "Clarence" (H4,48;NS1A,23)

Stuckey, Elma "Humanity" (H4,46)

Sutherland, Zena, and Myra Livingston *The Scott, Foresman Anthology of Children's Literature* (CS,28)

Tennyson, Alfred "The Eagle" (H5,51)

Thackeray, William Makepeace "The Tragic Story" (H4,47)

Thayer, Ernest Lawrence "Casey at the Bat" (H5,51)

Whitman, Walt "I Hear America Singing" (E2,37;H5,56;IEA,1)

Whitman, Walt "O Captain! My Captain!" (H5,56;IEA,1)

Wilbur, Richard "Some Opposites" (H5,59;NS3A,23)

Nonfiction - Information

Aliki *Corn is Maize: The Gift of the Indians* and *The Story of Johnny Appleseed* (C,40;NS1,23)

Ancona, George *Bananas: From Manolo to Margie* (C,41)

Baylor, Byrd *The Way to Start a Day* (C,41;NS1,23)

Charlip, Remy, and Marybeth *Handtalk: An ABC of Finger Spelling and Sign Language* (C,42)

Chief Joseph "I Will Fight No More Forever" (H5,45)

DePaola, Tomie *The Quicksand Book* (C,42)

"Give Me Liberty or Give Me Death!" (H3,40)

Isenbart, Hans-Heinrich *A Duckling is Born* (C,42)

Kohl, Herbert and Judith *The View from the Oak* (C,42)

Krementz, Jill *A Very Young Rider* (C,43)

C = California Recommended Readings, K-8	IE,IW = Int'l Bacc.: English A1, World Lit.
CS = California Recommended Literature, 9-12	IEA,IWA= Int'l Bacc.: English A1, World Lit. (author citation)
E1,2,3 = Edison Proj.: Primary,Elem.,Junior Acad.	NE = New England Association of Teachers of English
GJ = Gillespie: Best Books for Junior High Readers	NS1,2,3 = New Standards: Elem., Middle, High
GS = Gillespie: Best Books for Senior High Readers	NS1A,2A,3A = New Standards: Elem., Middle, High (author
H = Hirsch: Cultural Literacy	citation)
H1 - H6 = Hirsch: Core Knowledge Series, Grades 1-6	RF = Ravitch & Finn: What Do Our 17-Year-Olds Know?

Kuskin, Karla *The Philharmonic Gets Dressed* (C,43)
Lincoln, Abraham *Gettysburg Address* (H5,46)
Meyers, Susan *Pearson, a Harbor Seal Pup* (C,43;NS2,23)
Patterson, Francine *Koko's Kitten* (C,44)
Price, Christine *Dancing Masks of Africa* (C,44)
Rockwell, Anne *The Toolbox* (C,44)
Selsam, Millicent E. *Cotton* and *The Maple Tree* and *See Through the Forest* (C,44,45)
Truth, Sojourner "Ain't I a Woman" (H4,40)

Nonfiction - Biography
Aliki *A Weed Is a Flower: The Life of George Washington Carver* (C,46)
Barnard, Jacqueline *Voices from the Southwest: Antonio Jose Martinez, Elfego Baca, and Reies Lopez Tijerina* (C,46)
Fritz, Jean *And Then What Happened, Paul Revere?* and *What's the Big Idea, Ben Franklin?* and *Where Was Patrick Henry on the 29th of May?* (C,47,48;NS1,23)
Meltzer, Milton *Dorothea Lange: A Photographer's Life* (C,49)
Monjo, Ferdinand N. *Me and Willie an Pa* and *The One Bad Thing About Father* (C,49)
Provensen, Alice, and Martin *The Glorious Flight Across the Channel with Louis Bleriot* (C,49)
Tobias, Tobi *Isamu Noguchi: The Life of a Sculptor* (C,50)

C = California Recommended Readings, K-8
CS = California Recommended Literature, 9-12
E1,2,3 = Edison Proj.: Primary,Elem.,Junior Acad.
GJ = Gillespie: Best Books for Junior High Readers
GS = Gillespie: Best Books for Senior High Readers
H = Hirsch: Cultural Literacy
H1 - H6 = Hirsch: Core Knowledge Series, Grades 1-6

IE,IW = Int'l Bacc.: English A1, World Lit.
IEA,IWA= Int'l Bacc.: English A1, World Lit. (author citation)
NE = New England Association of Teachers of English
NS1,2,3 = New Standards: Elem., Middle, High
NS1A,2A,3A = New Standards: Elem., Middle, High (author citation)
RF = Ravitch & Finn: What Do Our 17-Year-Olds Know?

McREL

Appendix for Language Arts: Level III (Middle School)

Greek and Roman Mythology

Aphrodite/Venus (H,154;RF,271)

"Apollo and Daphne" (H6,52)

Apollo/Mars (H,154;RF,273)

Artemis/Diana (H,155)

Athena/Minerva (H,155)

Atlas (RF,272)

Cupid/Eros (H,165)

"Cupid and Psyche" (H6,58)

Dionysus/Bacchus (H,167)

"Echo and Narcissus" (H6,55)

Elysian Fields (H,169)

Eros/Cupid (H,170)

Furies (H,173)

Hera/Juno (H,177)

Hercules (H,177)

Hermes/Mercury (H,177)

Janus (H,181)

Lord of the Sky: Zeus by Doris Gates
    (CS,11)

Medusa (H,187)

"Orpheus and Eurydice" (H6,53)

Pandora's box (RF,272)

Posieden/Neptune (H,197)

Prometheus (RF,275)

Pygmalion (H6,57)

Romulus and Remus (H,201)

Sirens (H,204)

Styx (H,206)

Classic American Literature

Alcott, Louisa May *Little Women* (H,153;GJ,17)

Cooper, James Fennimore *The Last of the Mohicans* (GJ,17;H,164)

Crane, Stephen *The Red Badge of Courage* (GJ,17)

Hale, E. E. *The Man Without a Country and Other Stories* (GJ,17)

Henry, O. "The Gift of the Magi" (GJ,17)

Irving, Washington *The Legend of Sleepy Hollow and Other Selections* (GJ,18)

London, Jack (E3,38;RF,272)

      Call of the Wild (NE,6;NS2,23)

      "To Build a Fire" (NE,6)

      Sea Wolf (GJ,18)

      White Fang (GJ, 18)

Poe, Edgar Allan (GJ,18)

      "The Black Cat" (NE,10)

      The Complete Tales and Poems of Edgar Allan Poe (GJ,18)

      Tales of Terror (GJ,18)

Twain, Mark (E3,38;GJ,18;IEA,2)

      The Adventures of Tom Sawyer (NE,6;GJ,18)

      The Adventures of Huckleberry Finn (NE,10;GJ,18;IW,3)

McREL

A Connecticut Yankee in King Arthur's Court (GJ,18;NS3,23)
    The Prince and the Pauper (GJ,18)
    Pudd'nhead Wilson (GJ,18)
    Tom Sawyer Abroad (GJ,18)
    Tom Sawyer, Detective (GJ,18)
Steinbeck, John *Of Mice and Men* (NE,6;IEA,2;IW,3)
    The Pearl (NE,6)
    The Red Pony (NE,6)
Hemingway, Ernest *The Old Man and the Sea* (NE,6;IEA,2)
Wilder, Thornton *Our Town* (NE,10;NS3A,23)

Classic British Literature

Barrie, J. M. *Peter Pan* (GJ,16)
Shelley, Mary W. *Frankenstein* (GJ,17)
Stevenson, Robert Louis *Dr. Jeckyl and Mr. Hyde* (GJ,17;NS2A,23)
Swift, Jonathan *Gulliver's Travels* (GJ,17;IEA,1;IW,5)
Orwell, George *Animal Farm* (H6,20;NE,6;IEA,2)
Burnett, Frances H. *The Secret Garden* (GJ,16)
Defoe, Daniel *Robinson Crusoe* (GJ,16;IW,5)
Dickens, Charles (GJ,16-17;IEA,1,2)
    David Copperfield (GJ,16)
    Oliver Twist (GJ,16)
    A Christmas Carol (NE,6)
    Great Expectations (NE,10;IW,5)
    A Tale of Two Cities (NE,10)
Eliot, George *Silas Marner* (GJ,17;IEA,1)
Doyle, Arthur Conan *Sherlock Holmes: The Complete Novels and Stories* (GJ,17)
Kipling, Rudyard *Captains Courageous, Kim* (GJ,17)
Tennyson, Alfred (GJ,17)
Wilde, Oscar *The Canterville Ghost* (GJ,17;IEA,2)
Bronte, Charlotte *Jane Eyre* (GJ,16;IEA,1;IW,4)
Bronte, Emily *Wuthering Heights* (GJ,16;IEA,2;IW,6)
Shakespeare, William *The Taming of the Shrew* (NE,6;IEA,2;IW,4)
    Romeo and Juliet (NE,6;IE,1;IW,6;NS3,23)
    Julius Caesar (NE,10;IW,4;NS3,23)
    A Midsummer Night's Dream (NE,10;NS2,23)

C = California Recommended Readings, K-8
CS = California Recommended Literature, 9-12
E1,2,3 = Edison Proj.: Primary,Elem.,Junior Acad.
GJ = Gillespie: Best Books for Junior High Readers
GS = Gillespie: Best Books for Senior High Readers
H = Hirsch: Cultural Literacy
H1 - H6 = Hirsch: Core Knowledge Series, Grades 1-6

IE,IW = Int'l Bacc.: English A1, World Lit.
IEA,IWA= Int'l Bacc.: English A1, World Lit. (author citation)
NE = New England Association of Teachers of English
NS1,2,3 = New Standards: Elem., Middle, High
NS1A,2A,3A = New Standards: Elem., Middle, High (author citation)
RF = Ravitch & Finn: What Do Our 17-Year-Olds Know?

Classic World Literature

Cervantes, Miguel de *The Adventures of Don Quixote de la Mancha* (GJ,16)

Dumas, Alexandre *The Count of Monte Cristo, The Three Musketeers* (GJ,16)

Frank, Anne *The Diary of a Young Girl* (H6,25;NE,6;NS2,23)

Maupassant, Guy de *Best Short Stories* (GJ,16)

Verne, Jules *Around the World in Eighty Days* (GJ, 16)

     Journey to the Center of the Earth (GJ,16)

     Twenty Thousand Leagues Under the Sea (GJ,16;NS3,23)

Wyss, Johann *The Swiss Family Robinson* (GJ,16)

Adapted/Retold and Exerpted Literature

Angelou, Maya *I Know Why the Caged Bird Sings* (H6,27;IEA,2;IW,3;NS1,22)

Oliver Twist (H6,7)

Romeo and Juliet (H6,2;IW,6;NS3,23)

The Secret Garden (H6,12)

Modern/Contemporary Fiction

Hien, Nguyen Thai Duc *Doi song moi/Tren dat moi: A New Life in a New Land* (CS,12)

Adams, Edward B., ed. *Two Brothers and Their Magic Gourds* (CS,15)

Armstrong, William H. *Sounder* (NE,10;GJ,18;NS2,23)

Borland, Hal *When the Legends Die* (NE,10)

Bradbury, Ray *Fahrenheit 451* (NE,10;NS2A,23)

Bradbury, Ray *All Summer in a Day* (NE,10;NS2,23)

Buck, Pearl S. *The Good Earth* (E3,79)

Burch, Robert *Queenie Peavy* (CS,29)

Byers, Betsy *The Summer of Swans* (CS,30)

Clapp, Patricia *I'm Deborah Sampson: A Soldier in the War of the Revolution* (CS,36)

Cleary, Beverly *Dear Mr. Henshaw* (CS,30)

Cormier, Robert *8+1* (NE,10)

Cormier, Robert *I Am the Cheese* (NE,10;NS2,23)

Cormier, Robert *The Chocolate War* (NE,6)

Craven, Margaret *I Heard the Owl Call My Name* (NE,10)

Dorris, Michael *Morning Girl* (E3,39)

Fletcher, Lucille *Sorry, Wrong Number* (NE,10)

Forbes, Esther *Johnny Tremain* (NE,6)

C = California Recommended Readings, K-8

CS = California Recommended Literature, 9-12

E1,2,3 = Edison Proj.: Primary,Elem.,Junior Acad.

GJ = Gillespie: Best Books for Junior High Readers

GS = Gillespie: Best Books for Senior High Readers

H = Hirsch: Cultural Literacy

H1 - H6 = Hirsch: Core Knowledge Series, Grades 1-6

IE,IW = Int'l Bacc.: English A1, World Lit.

IEA,IWA= Int'l Bacc.: English A1, World Lit. (author citation)

NE = New England Association of Teachers of English

NS1,2,3 = New Standards: Elem., Middle, High

NS1A,2A,3A = New Standards: Elem., Middle, High (author citation)

RF = Ravitch & Finn: What Do Our 17-Year-Olds Know?

Fox, Paula *One-Eyed Cat* (CS,31)
George, Jean Craighead *Julie of the Wolves* (E3,39;NE,10)
Gibson, William *The Miracle Worker* (E3,39;NE,10;NS2,23)
Gipson, Fred *Old Yeller* (NE,6)
Golding, William *Lord of the Flies* (NE,6;NS3,22)
Hamilton, Virginia *The House of Dies Drear* (NS1A,23;NS2A,23)
Hansberry, Lorraine *A Raisin in the Sun* (NE,6;NS3,23)
Hautzig, Esther *A Gift for Mama* (CS,37)
Hinton, S. E. *Tex* (NE,10)
Hinton, S. E. *The Outsiders* (NE,6;NS2,23)
Keyes, Daniel *Flowers for Algernon* (NE,6)
Knowles, John *A Separate Peace* (NE,6;NS3,22)
Kroeber, Theodora *Ishi, Last of His Tribe* (E3,39)
Lawrence, Jerome and Robert Lee *Inherit the Wind* (NE,10;NS2,23)
Lee, Harper *To Kill a Mockingbird* (NE,6;NS3,22)
L'Engle, Madeleine *A Wrinkle in Time* (CS,19;NS2,23)
Lewis, C. S. *The Lion, the Witch and the Wardrobe* (CS,19;NS1,23)
Mathis, Sharon B. *The Hundred Penny Box* (CS,33)
O'Dell, Scott *Island of the Blue Dolphins* (CS,38;NS1,23)
Orgel, Doris *Ariadne, Awake!* (E3,39)
Orlev, Uri *The Island on Bird Street* (CS,38)
Paulsen, Gary *The River* (E3,39;NS3A,22)
Paterson, Katherine *Bridge to Terabithia* (CS,33)
Peck, Robert Newton *A Day No Pigs Would Die* (NE,6)
Rawlings, Marjorie Kinnan *The Yearling* (NE,10)
Rawls, Wilson *Where the Red Fern Grows* (CS,34;E3,39;NE,6)
Richter, Conrad *The Light in the Forest* (NE,10)
Rose, Reginald *Twelve Angry Men* (NE, 10;NS3,23)
Saint-Exupery, Antoine de *The Little Prince* (CS,30;NS1,23)
Salinger, J. D. *Catcher in the Rye* (NE,6)
Saroyan, William *The Human Comedy* (NE,10)
Schaeffer, Jack *Shane* (NE,6;NS2,23)
Soto, Gary *Local News* (E3,39)
Speare, Elizabeth *The Witch of Blackbird Pond* (CS,39;NE,6)
Taylor, Theodore *The Cay* (NE,10)
Taylor, Mildred D. *Roll of Thunder, Hear My Cry* (CS,39;E3,39;NE,6)
Thurber, James "The Secret Life of Walter Mitty" (RF,275;H,203)

C = California Recommended Readings, K-8
CS = California Recommended Literature, 9-12
E1,2,3 = Edison Proj.: Primary,Elem.,Junior Acad.
GJ = Gillespie: Best Books for Junior High Readers
GS = Gillespie: Best Books for Senior High Readers
H = Hirsch: Cultural Literacy
H1 - H6 = Hirsch: Core Knowledge Series, Grades 1-6

IE,IW = Int'l Bacc.: English A1, World Lit.
IEA,IWA= Int'l Bacc.: English A1, World Lit. (author citation)
NE = New England Association of Teachers of English
NS1,2,3 = New Standards: Elem., Middle, High
NS1A,2A,3A = New Standards: Elem., Middle, High (author citation)
RF = Ravitch & Finn: What Do Our 17-Year-Olds Know?

Tolkien, J. R. R. *The Hobbit* (NE,7;NS2,23)
Uchida, Yoshiko *A Jar of Dreams* (E3,39)
White, T.H. *The Once and Future King* (E3,38;NS3,23)
Yep, Laurence *Dragonwings* (E3,39;NS2A,23)
Yep, Laurence *Child of the Owl* (CS,35;NS1,23)
Zindel, Paul *The Pigman* (NE,6;NS2,23)

Poetry and Poets
Angelou, Maya "Caged Bird", "Woman Work" (H6,47, 49;IEA,2)
Austin, Mary, translator "A Song of Greatness" a Chippewa song (H6,38)
Brewton, Sara, and John Brewton, eds. *America Forever New: A Book of Poems* (CS,23)
Brooks, Gwendolyn "The Bean Eaters" (E3,39)
Carroll, Lewis "Father William" (H6,41)
Dickinson, Emily "I Like to See It Lap the Miles" (H6,41;IEA,1)
Dunbar, Paul Laurence "Sympathy" (H6,47)
Dunning, Stephen, ed. *Reflections on a Gift of Watermelon Pickle* (NE,6)
Frost, Robert "Stopping by the Woods on a Snowy Evening," "The Road Not Taken"
      (H6,39,50;IEA,1)
Hughes, Langston *Don't You Turn Back* (CS,25;IEA,1)
            "Harlem," "Life is Fine," "The Negro Speaks of Rivers" (H6,35,50,51)
Johnson, James Weldon "Lift Ev'ry Voice and Sing" (H6,38)
Longfellow, Henry Wadsworth "A Psalm of Life" (H6,36;NS3A,23)
            "Song of Hiawatha" (H,166;NS3A,23)
Ortiz, Simon "My Father's Song" (E3,39)
Plotz, Helen, ed. *The Gift Outright: America to Her Poets* (CS,25)
Poe, Edgar Allan "Annabel Lee," "The Raven" (H6,43;RF,271)
Sandburg, Carl (GJ,18)
Shakespeare, William "All the World's a Stage" from *As You Like It* (H6,40;IE,1)
Tennyson, Alfred "The Lady of Shallot" (GJ,17)
Williams, William Carlos "This is Just to Say" (H6,42;IEA,2)

Nonfiction - Information
Beatty, Patricia *Lupita Mañana* (C,41)
Brenner, Barbara *On the Frontier with Mr. Audubon* (C,41)
De Garza, Patricia *Chicanos: The Story of Mexican-Americans* (C,41)

C = California Recommended Readings, K-8
CS = California Recommended Literature, 9-12
E1,2,3 = Edison Proj.: Primary,Elem.,Junior Acad.
GJ = Gillespie: Best Books for Junior High Readers
GS = Gillespie: Best Books for Senior High Readers
H = Hirsch: Cultural Literacy
H1 - H6 = Hirsch: Core Knowledge Series, Grades 1-6

IE,IW = Int'l Bacc.: English A1, World Lit.
IEA,IWA= Int'l Bacc.: English A1, World Lit. (author citation)
NE = New England Association of Teachers of English
NS1,2,3 = New Standards: Elem., Middle, High
NS1A,2A,3A = New Standards: Elem., Middle, High (author
      citation)
RF = Ravitch & Finn: What Do Our 17-Year-Olds Know?

Demuth, Patricia *Joel: Growing Up on Farm Man* (C,41)
Kennedy, John. F. Inaugural Address (H6,30;NS3A,22)
King, Martin Luther, Jr. "I Have a Dream" (H6,32)
St. George, Judith *The Brooklyn Bridge: They Said It Couldn't Be Built* (C,45)

Nonfiction - Biography
Franchere, Ruth *Cesar Chaves* (C,47)
Greenfield, Howard *Marc Chagall: An Introduction* (C,48)
Hunter, Edith Fisher *Child of the Silent Night: The Story of Laura Bridgman* (C,48)
Jackson, Jesse *Make a Joyful Noise Unto the Lord: The Life of Mahalia Jackson, Queen of Gospel Singers* (C,48)
Kohn, Bernice *Talking Leaves: The Story of Sequoyah* (C,48)
Kroeber, Theodora *Ishi, Last of His Tribe* (C,48)
McCunn, Ruthanne L. *Thousand Pieces of Gold: A Biographical Novel* (C,48)
McGovern, Ann *The Secret Soldier: The Story of Deborah Sampson* (C,49;NS1,23)
Nhuong, Huynh Quang *Land I Lost* (C,49)
Reiss, Johanna *The Upstairs Room* (C,50;NS2,23)

C = California Recommended Readings, K-8
CS = California Recommended Literature, 9-12
E1,2,3 = Edison Proj.: Primary,Elem.,Junior Acad.
GJ = Gillespie: Best Books for Junior High Readers
GS = Gillespie: Best Books for Senior High Readers
H = Hirsch: Cultural Literacy
H1 - H6 = Hirsch: Core Knowledge Series, Grades 1-6

IE,IW = Int'l Bacc.: English A1, World Lit.
IEA,IWA= Int'l Bacc.: English A1, World Lit. (author citation)
NE = New England Association of Teachers of English
NS1,2,3 = New Standards: Elem., Middle, High
NS1A,2A,3A = New Standards: Elem., Middle, High (author citation)
RF = Ravitch & Finn: What Do Our 17-Year-Olds Know?

Appendix for Language Arts: Level IV (High School)

CLASSIC AMERICAN LITERATURE

Poetry
Dickinson, Emily (H,167;RF,271;IEA,1;NS3A,23)
Whitman, Walt *Leaves of Grass* (H,183;RF,275;IEA,1)

Fiction
Alcott, Louisa May *Little Women* (GS,21)
Alger, Horatio (H,153)
Anderson, Sherwood *Winesburg, Ohio* (GS,21)
Cather, Willa (GS,21;H,161)
     My Antonia (CS,23;NE,4;RF,276)
     O Pioneers! (RF,276)
     Death Comes for the Archbishop (RF,276)
Chopin, Kate *The Awakening* (NE,5;IW,3)
Cooper, James Fennimore *The Last of the Mohicans* (GS,21)
Crane, Stephen
     Red Badge of Courage (CS,24;GS,21;H,199;NE,4;RF,272)
     Maggie: A Girl of the Streets (NE,5)
Harte, Bret "Outcasts of Poker Flat" (CS,44;GS,22;H,176)
Hawthorne, Nathanial (GS,22;H,176;IEA,1)
     "Rappucini's Daughter" (RF,274)
     The House of Seven Gables (GS,22)
     "The Minister's Black Veil" (RF,274)
     The Scarlet Letter (CS,25;H,202;NE,4;RF,272;NS3,22)
     "Young Goodman Brown" (CS,44;RF,274)
Henry, O. "Gift of the Magi" (GS,22)
Holmes, Oliver Wendell (H,177)
Irving, Washington "The Devil and Tom Walker" (CS,44;GS,22)
James, Henry (GS,22;H,181;IEA,1)
     Daisy Miller (RF,276)
     Portrait of a Lady (GS,22;RF,276)
     The Turn of the Screw (CS,26)
Lewis, Sinclair *Babbitt* (CS,27;H,155)
London, Jack *Call of the Wild* (CS,27;GS,22;NS2,23)
Melville, Herman (GS,22,25)

C = California Recommended Readings, K-8	IE,IW = Int'l Bacc.: English A1, World Lit.
CS = California Recommended Literature, 9-12	IEA,IWA= Int'l Bacc.: English A1, World Lit. (author citation)
E1,2,3 = Edison Proj.: Primary,Elem.,Junior Acad.	NE = New England Association of Teachers of English
GJ = Gillespie: Best Books for Junior High Readers	NS1,2,3 = New Standards: Elem., Middle, High
GS = Gillespie: Best Books for Senior High Readers	NS1A,2A,3A = New Standards: Elem., Middle, High (author
H = Hirsch: Cultural Literacy	citation)
H1 - H6 = Hirsch: Core Knowledge Series, Grades 1-6	RF = Ravitch & Finn: What Do Our 17-Year-Olds Know?

MCREL

"Bartleby" (RF,275)
"Benito Cereno" (NE,5;RF,275)
"Billy Budd" (CS,27;NE,7;RF,275)
Moby Dick (H,153;NE,4;RF,272,275)
Norris, Frank *McTeague* (GS,22;NE,9)
Poe, Edgar Allan (H,196;RF,270)
　　　"Fall of the House of Usher" (GS,22;H,171;RF,270)
　　　"Pit and Pendulum" (RF,270)
Stowe, Harriet Beecher *Uncle Tom's Cabin* (H,206;RF,271)
Twain, Mark (RF,270;IEA,2)
　　　Huckleberry Finn (CS,30;GS,22;H,178;NE,4;RF,270)
　　　Pudd'nhead Wilson (NE,9)
　　　The Prince and the Pauper (NE,10)
Wharton, Edith *Ethan Frome* (CS,30;H,213;NE,4;IEA,1)

Nonfiction

Declaration of Independence (RF,271;H,166)
Douglass, Frederick *Narrative of the Life of Frederick Douglass* (NE,8)
Edwards, Jonathan (H,169)
Emerson, Ralph Waldo (H,170)
Franklin, Ben *Poor Richard's Almanack* (H,196;RF,274)
Lincoln, Abraham (H,184)
　　　Gettysburg Address (RF,271)
　　　"With malice toward none..." (RF,274)
The Constitution, Preamble (RF,272)
Thoreau, Henry David *Walden* (H,209;NE,5;RF,274)

MODERN/CONTEMPORARY AMERICAN LITERATURE

Poetry

cummings, e.e. (H,165;NS3A,23)
Frost, Robert "The Road Not Taken" (H6,39,173;NE,8;RF,272;IEA,7)
Hughes, Langston (RF,275;IEA,1;NS3A,23)

Fiction

Anaya, Rudolfo A. *Bless Me, Ultima* (CS,22;NS2,23)

Baldwin, James *Go Tell It on the Mountain* (CS,22;IEA,2)

Borland, Hal *When the Legends Die* (CS,22)

Bradbury, Ray *Fahrenheit 451* and *The Martian Chronicles* (CS,23;NE,7,8;NS3,23)

Bryant, Dorothy *Miss Giardino* (CS,23)

Buck, Pearl *The Good Earth* (CS,23)

Cisneros, Sandra *The House on Mango Street* (CS,23;IEA,2;NS3,22)

Clark, Walter Van Tilburg *Ox-bow Incident* (CS,23;NS3,22)

Clavell, James *The Children's Story* (NE,10)

Cormier, Robert *After the First Death, I Am the Cheese, The Chocolate War* (CS,23;NE,5,7;NS2,23)

Craven, Margaret *I Heard the Owl Call My Name* (CS,24)

Dos Passos, John (GS,21;H,168)

Ellison, Ralph *Invisible Man* (CS,24;NE,4;H,169;RF,276;IEA,2)

Faulkner, William *The Light in August, The Bear* (CS,24;H,171;NE,8;RF,276;IEA,2;IWA,3)

Fitzgerald, F. Scott *The Great Gatsby* (CS,24;H,175;NE,4;RF,273;IEA,2;IW,3)

Gaines, Ernest J. *The Autobiography of Miss Jane Pittman* (CS,24;NS2A,23)

Gardner, John *Grendel* (NE,5)

Gibson, William *The Miracle Worker* (NE,4;NS2,23)

Guest, Judith *Ordinary People* (NE,8)

Hailey, Alex *Roots* (H,214)

Hale, E. E. (GS,22)

Hemingway, Ernest (H,176;GS,22;IEA,2)

       A Farewell to Arms (NE,4;IW,3)

       For Whom the Bell Tolls (RF,272;NS3,22)

       The Sun Also Rises (H,207;NE,8;RF,272;IW,3)

       The Old Man and the Sea (CS,25;NE,4;RF,274)

       In Our Time (NE,8)

       "In Another Country" (RF,276)

       "The Short Happy Life of Francis Macomber" (RF,276)

       "The Killers" (RF,276)

Heller, Joseph *Catch 22* (CS,25;NE,5)

Hersey, John *Hiroshima* (NE,5,7)

Hinton, S. E. *The Outsiders* (CS,25;NE,8;NS2,23)

Hurston, Zora Neale *Their Eyes Were Watching God* (CS,25;NE,5;IEA,2)

Kesey, Ken *One Flew Over the Cuckoo's Nest* (NE,4)

C = California Recommended Readings, K-8	IE,IW = Int'l Bacc.: English A1, World Lit.
CS = California Recommended Literature, 9-12	IEA,IWA= Int'l Bacc.: English A1, World Lit. (author citation)
E1,2,3 = Edison Proj.: Primary,Elem.,Junior Acad.	NE = New England Association of Teachers of English
GJ = Gillespie: Best Books for Junior High Readers	NS1,2,3 = New Standards: Elem., Middle, High
GS = Gillespie: Best Books for Senior High Readers	NS1A,2A,3A = New Standards: Elem., Middle, High (author citation)
H = Hirsch: Cultural Literacy	
H1 - H6 = Hirsch: Core Knowledge Series, Grades 1-6	RF = Ravitch & Finn: What Do Our 17-Year-Olds Know?

Keyes, Daniel *Flowers for Algernon* (CS,26)

Kim, Richard *Martyred* (CS,26)

Kincaid, Jamaica *Annie John* (CS,26;IEA,2)

Knowles, John *A Separate Peace* (CS,26;NE,4;NS3,22)

Lee, Harper *To Kill a Mockingbird* (CS,26;NE,5;RF,273;NS3,22)

Malamud, Bernard *The Assistant* (NE,8)

Marshall, Paule *Brown Girl, Brownstones* (CS,27)

McCullers, Carson *The Heart is a Lonely Hunter, The Ballad of the Sad Cafe: The Novels and Stories of Carson McCullers* (CS,27;GS,58;NS3,22)

Mitchell, Margaret *Gone with the Wind* (H,175)

Momaday, N. Scott *House Made of Dawn* (CS,27;NS1,23)

Morrison, Toni *Beloved, Song of Solomon, Sula, The Bluest Eye* (CS,27;NE,5;IEA,2)

Naylor, Gloria *The Women of Brewster Place* (NE,5)

Neihardt, John *Black Elk Speaks* (NE,8)

O'Connor, Flannery (RF,277)

Okada, John *No-No Boy* (CS,28)

Peck, Richard *Remembering the Good Times* (CS,28)

Peck, Robert Newton *A Day No Pigs Would Die* (CS,28;NE,5)

Plath, Sylvia *The Bell Jar* (NE,8;IEA,1,2)

Porter, Katherine Anne *Noon Wine* (CS,28)

Potok, Chaim *The Chosen* (CS,28;NE,5;NS3,22)

Rawlings, Marjorie Kinnan *The Yearling* (CS,28)

Richter, Conrad *Light in the Forest* (CS,28)

Rivera, Tomas *And the Earth Did Not Part* (CS,29)

Ronyoung, Kim *Clay Walls* (CS,29)

Salinger, J. D. *Catcher in the Rye* (CS,29;H,161;NE,4;RF,276)

Saroyan, William *The Human Comedy* (CS,29)

Schaeffer, Jack *Shane* (NE,8)

Steinbeck, John (GS,22;H,175;IEA,2)

    The Grapes of Wrath (NE,4;RF,275)

    Of Mice and Men (CS,29;NE,4)

    The Pearl (NE,4)

Uchida, Yoshiko *Picture Bride* (CS,30)

Updike, John *Centaur* (CS,30)

Vonnegut, Kurt *Slaughterhouse Five, Cat's Cradle* (NE,8)

Walker, Alice *The Color Purple* (NE,5,7;IEA,2)

Warren, Robert Penn *All the King's Men* (NE,5)

C = California Recommended Readings, K-8
CS = California Recommended Literature, 9-12
E1,2,3 = Edison Proj.: Primary,Elem.,Junior Acad.
GJ = Gillespie: Best Books for Junior High Readers
GS = Gillespie: Best Books for Senior High Readers
H = Hirsch: Cultural Literacy
H1 - H6 = Hirsch: Core Knowledge Series, Grades 1-6

IE,IW = Int'l Bacc.: English A1, World Lit.
IEA,IWA= Int'l Bacc.: English A1, World Lit. (author citation)
NE = New England Association of Teachers of English
NS1,2,3 = New Standards: Elem., Middle, High
NS1A,2A,3A = New Standards: Elem., Middle, High (author citation)
RF = Ravitch & Finn: What Do Our 17-Year-Olds Know?

MREL

Welty, Eudora (RF,277;NS3A,22)

Wiesel, Elie *Night* (NE,5)

Wright, Richard *Native Son* and *Black Boy* (CS,30;H,158,191;NE,4,8;RF,276;IEA,2;NS1,23)

Zindel, Paul *The Pigman* (CS,30;NE,8;NS2,23)

Drama

Agee, James *Death in the Family* (CS,10)

Albee, Edward *American Dream, Zoo Story, Who's Afraid of Virginia Woolf*
    (CS,7;GS,151;NE,8;IEA,2)

Anderson, Robert *I Never Sang for My Father* (CS,7)

Chin, Frank *The Chickencoop Chinaman and The Year of the Dragon: Two Plays* (CS,8)

Elder, Lonne *Ceremonies in Dark Old Men* (CS,8)

Fugard, Athol *Master Harold and the Boys* (CS,8;NE,5;IEA,2;IW,2)

Goodrich, Frances, and Albert Hackett *Diary of Anne Frank* (CS,8)

Gibson, William *The Miracle Worker* (CS,8;GS,151;NS2,23)

Hansberry, Lorraine *A Raisin in the Sun* (CS,8;NE,4;RF,273;NS3,23)

Hellman, Lillian *The Little Foxes* (CS,8)

Laurents, Arthur *West Side Story* (NE,8)

Lawrence, Jerome and Robert E. Lee
    Inherit the Wind, The Night Thoreau Spent in Jail (CS,9;GS,152;NE,4,9;NS2,23)

Lum, Wing Tek *Oranges are Lucky* (CS,9)

McCullers, Carson *The Member of the Wedding* (CS,9;NS3,23)

Medoff, Mark *Children of a Lesser God* (CS,9)

Miller, Arthur *Death of a Salesman, The Crucible* (CS,9;GS,153;H,166;NE,4;RF,273;IEA,2;I
    W,3,5)

O'Neill, Eugene *Anna Christie, The Emperor Jones, The Hairy Ape, The Iceman Cometh, Long
    Day's Journey Into Night* (CS,9;GS,153;H,192;IEA,2)

Rose, Reginald *Twelve Angry Men* (CS,9)

Sakamoto, Edward *In the Alley* (CS,9)

Simon, Neil *Barefoot in the Park, Brighton Beach Memoirs, Broadway Bound, The Odd Couple,
    They're Playing Our Song* (GS,154)

Valdez, Luis *Zoot Suit* (CS,10)

Vidal, Gore *A Visit to a Small Planet* (CS,10)

Wilder, Thornton *Our Town* (CS,10;H,193;NE,4;NE,9;RF,272;NS3A,23)

Williams, Tennessee *A Streetcar Named Desire, The Glass Menagerie, Cat on a Hot Tin Roof*
    (CS,10;GS,154;H,20;NE4,5;RF,276;IEA,2;IW,3,6)

Wilson, August *Fences* (CS,10)

Nonfiction
Angelou, Maya *I Know Why the Caged Bird Sings* (NE,4;IEA,2;IW,3;NS1,22;NS3A,23)
Capote, Truman *In Cold Blood* (NE,7)
Friedan, Betty (H,173)
King, Martin Luther, Jr. "I Have a Dream" (RF,270)
Menken, H.L. (H,188)
Roosevelt, Franklin D. "The only thing we have to fear is fear itself" and "Yesterday, Dec. 7, 1941,--a date which will live in infamy" (RF,273)
Turkel, Studs *Working* (NE,9)

BRITISH LITERATURE

Poetry
Auden, W. H. *Collected Poems* (GS,158;IEA,2)
Browning, Elizabeth Barrett *The Poetical Works of Elizabeth Barrett Browning* and *Sonnets from the Portuguese* (GS,158)
Browning, Robert *Robert Browning's Poetry: Authoritative Texts, Criticism* (GS,158;H,159;IEA,2)

Burns, Robert *The Poetical Works of Burns* (GS,158;H,160)
Byron, George Gordon "Don Juan" (GS,158;H,168;RF,274)
Chaucer, Geoffrey *Canterbury Tales* (GS,19;H,160;NE,4;RF,275)
Coleridge, Samuel Taylor *The Rime of the Ancient Mariner* (H,162;NE,8;IEA,2)
Donne, John *The Complete Works of John Donne* (GS,160;H,168;IEA,7)
Eliot, T. S. "The Hollow Men," "The Love Song of J. Alfred Prufrock," *The Waste Land* (H,169,213;RF,274;IEA,1)
Gray, Thomas "Elegy Written in a Country Churchyard" (H,169)
Hardy, Thomas *The Complete Poems of Thomas Hardy* (GS,159;IEA,2)
Hopkins, Gerard Manley *The Complete Poems of Gerard Manley Hopkins* (GS,159;IEA,1,2)
Houseman, A. E. *The Complete Poems of A. E. Houseman* (GS,159)
Joyce, James "Araby" and "Eveline" (RF,277)
Keats, John "Ode on a Grecian Urn" (GS,159;H,192;RF,274;IEA,1)
Kipling, Rudyard "Gunga Din" (H,176)
Milton, John *Paradise Lost* (GS,160;H,193;RF,275)
Pope, Alexander (H,196)

C = California Recommended Readings, K-8	IE,IW = Int'l Bacc.: English A1, World Lit.
CS = California Recommended Literature, 9-12	IEA,IWA= Int'l Bacc.: English A1, World Lit. (author citation)
E1,2,3 = Edison Proj.: Primary,Elem.,Junior Acad.	NE = New England Association of Teachers of English
GJ = Gillespie: Best Books for Junior High Readers	NS1,2,3 = New Standards: Elem., Middle, High
GS = Gillespie: Best Books for Senior High Readers	NS1A,2A,3A = New Standards: Elem., Middle, High (author citation)
H = Hirsch: Cultural Literacy	
H1 - H6 = Hirsch: Core Knowledge Series, Grades 1-6	RF = Ravitch & Finn: What Do Our 17-Year-Olds Know?

369   MREL

Shakespeare, William *Sonnets* (RF,273;GS,160;IEA,2)
Shelley, Percy Bysshe *The Poetical Works of Shelley* (GS,16;H,204)
Spender, S. *Collected Poems* (GS,160)
Tennyson, Alfred "Charge of the Light Brigade" (GS,160;H,162)
Thomas, Dylan *The Poems of Dylan Thomas* (GS,160;IEA,2)
Wordsworth, William *The Poetical Works of Wordsworth* (GS,160;H,214;RF,274;IEA,2)
Yeats, William Butler "The Second Coming" (H,215;RF,275;IEA,1)

Fiction

Austen, Jane *Pride and Prejudice* (CS,22;GS,18;H,156;NE,4;RF,275;IEA,1;IW,4)
Bennett, Arnold *The Old Wives' Tale* (GS,19)
Blackmore, R. D. *Lorna Doone* (GS,19)
Bronte, Charlotte *Jane Eyre* (CS,23;GS,19;H,159;NE,4;IEA,1)
Bronte, Emily *Wuthering Heights* (CS,23;H,159;NE,4;RF,275;IEA,2)
Bunyan, John *Pilgrim's Progress* (GS,19;H,1915;RF,277)
Butler, Samuel *The Way of All Flesh* (GS,19)
Carroll, Lewis *Alice in Wonderland* (CS,23;NS3,22)
Christie, Agatha (H,162;NS3A,23)
Clarke, Arthur C. *Childhood's End* (CS,23;NS3,23)
Collins, Wilkie *The Moonstone, The Woman in White* (GS,19)
Conrad, Joseph (GS,19;H,164;RF,276;IEA,2)
    The Heart of Darkness (CS,23;GS,19;NE,4;IW,5)
    Lord Jim (GS,19;RF,275)
Defoe, Daniel *Robinson Crusoe* (GS,19)
Dickens, Charles (GS,19;H,167;IEA,2)
    Oliver Twist (H,193;NE,8;RF,271)
    A Tale of Two Cities (CS,24;NE,4;RF,273)
    Great Expectations (H,175;NE,4)
    Hard Times (NE,7;RF,271)
    David Copperfield (H,166)
Doyle, Sir Arthur Conan *Hound of the Baskervilles* (GS,20;H,164;RF,271)
Eliot, George *The Mill on the Floss* and *Silas Marner* (GS,20;NE,4;IEA,1)
Fielding, Henry *Tom Jones* (GS,20;H,172;IEA,2)
Forster, E.M. *Passage to India* (CS,24;IEA,1,2;IW,7)
Golding, William *Lord of the Flies* (CS,24;NE,4;RF,275;IW,5;NS3,22)
Greene, Graham *The Power and the Glory* (CS,25;NE,9;IWA,5)

C = California Recommended Readings, K-8
CS = California Recommended Literature, 9-12
E1,2,3 = Edison Proj.: Primary,Elem.,Junior Acad.
GJ = Gillespie: Best Books for Junior High Readers
GS = Gillespie: Best Books for Senior High Readers
H = Hirsch: Cultural Literacy
H1 - H6 = Hirsch: Core Knowledge Series, Grades 1-6

IE,IW = Int'l Bacc.: English A1, World Lit.
IEA,IWA= Int'l Bacc.: English A1, World Lit. (author citation)
NE = New England Association of Teachers of English
NS1,2,3 = New Standards: Elem., Middle, High
NS1A,2A,3A = New Standards: Elem., Middle, High (author citation)
RF = Ravitch & Finn: What Do Our 17-Year-Olds Know?

370

Hardy, Thomas (RF,276;IEA,2)
  Jude the Obscure (GS,20)
  Return of the Native (GS,20;NE,8;RF,276)
  Tess of the D'Urbervilles (GS,20;NE,8;RF,276;IW,4)
  The Mayor of Casterbridge (CS,25;GS,20;NE,8;RF,276)
Huxley, Aldous *Brave New World* (CS,25;H,178;NE,7)
Joyce, James (H,182;IEA,1,2)
  Ulysses, A Portrait of the Artist As a Young Man (CS,26;RF,277)
Kipling, Rudyard *Captains Courageous, Kim,* and *The Man Who Would Be King* (GS,20)
Lawrence, D.H. "The Rocking Horse Winner" and *Sons and Lovers*
  (CS,26;GS,20;RF,276;IEA,1;IW,6)
Munro, H. H. *The Complete Works of Saki* (GS,21)
Orwell, George *1984* and *Animal Farm* (CS,28;H,193;NE,4;RF,275;IEA;2;IW,5;NS3,22)
Shelley, Mary *Frankenstein* (GS,20;NE,7;RF,271)
Sillitoe, Alan *Loneliness of the Long Distance Runner* (NE,8)
Sterne, Laurence *Tristam Shandy* (GS,21)
Stevenson, Robert Louis *The Strange Case of Dr. Jekyll and Mr. Hyde, The Black Arrow,* and
  Kidnapped (GS,21;H,168;NS2A,23)
Swift, Jonathan *Gulliver's Travels* and "A Modest Proposal"
  (CS,29;GS,21;H,176,188,207;NE,7;RF,272)
Thackeray, William M. *Vanity Fair* (GS,21)
Tolkien, J.R.R. *The Hobbit* (NE,7;NS2,23)
Trollope, Anthony *Barchester Towers* (CS,30;GS,21)
White, T. H. *The Once and Future King* (NE,8;NS3,23)
Wilde, Oscar *The Picture of Dorian Gray* (GS,21;IEA,2)
Woolf, Virginia (H,214;IEA,2)

Drama

Bolt, Robert *A Man for All Seasons* (CS,7)
Congreve, William *The Way of the World* (GS,149)
Coward, Noel *Blithe Spirit, Hay Fever, Private Lives* (GS,149)
Eliot, T. S. *Murder in the Cathedral, The Family Reunion, The Cocktail Party* (GS,149)
Marlowe, Christopher *Doctor Faustus* (GS,149;IEA,2)
Shakespeare, William (CS,9;GS,150;IEA,2)
  Romeo and Juliet (GS,151;H,201;NE,4;RF,270;IE,1;IW,6;NS3,23)
  Hamlet (GS,150;H,176;NE,4;RF,270;IE,1;IW,6)

C = California Recommended Readings, K-8
CS = California Recommended Literature, 9-12
E1,2,3 = Edison Proj.: Primary,Elem.,Junior Acad.
GJ = Gillespie: Best Books for Junior High Readers
GS = Gillespie: Best Books for Senior High Readers
H = Hirsch: Cultural Literacy
H1 - H6 = Hirsch: Core Knowledge Series, Grades 1-6

IE,IW = Int'l Bacc.: English A1, World Lit.
IEA,IWA= Int'l Bacc.: English A1, World Lit. (author citation)
NE = New England Association of Teachers of English
NS1,2,3 = New Standards: Elem., Middle, High
NS1A,2A,3A = New Standards: Elem., Middle, High (author
  citation)
RF = Ravitch & Finn: What Do Our 17-Year-Olds Know?

Julius Caesar (H,170;NE,4;RF,271,274;IW,4;NS3,23)
Macbeth (GS,150H,185;NE,4;RF,274;IE,1;IW,4)
Antony and Cleopatra (H,154;IE,1;IW,4)
The Tempest (GS,150;H,208;IE,1;IW,5)
Othello (GS,151;H,193;IE,1)
King Lear (GS,150;H,182;NE,8;IE,1;IW,6)
Merchant of Venice (H,189;NE,8;IE,1)
The Taming of the Shrew (GS,150;NE,8;IW,4)
Twelfth Night (GS,150;IE,1)
A Midsummer Night's Dream (GS,151;IE,1;NS2,23)
Shaw, George Bernard *Androcles and the Lion, Arms and the Man, Caesar and Cleopatra,*
    Major Barbara, Pygmalian, Saint Joan (CS,10;GS,150;RF,275;IEA,2)
Sheridan, Richard B. *The Rivals* and *The School for Scandal* (GS,150;IEA,2)
Thomas, Dylan *Under Milkwood: A Play for Voices* (CS,10;IEA,2)
Wilde, Oscar *The Importance of Being Earnest* (GS,150;H,214;NE,5;IEA,2)

Nonfiction
Churchill, Winston "Blood, toil, tears, and sweat" speech and "From Stettin in the Baltic to
    Trieste in the Adriatic, an Iron Curtain has descended across the continent" (RF,273)

WORLD LITERATURE

Achebe, Chinua *Things Fall Apart* (NE,5;IEA,2;IW,2,5,6)
Alain-Fournier, Henri *The Wanderer* (GS,17)
Anouilh, Jean *Antigone* (CS,7;IW,4)
Azuela, Mariano *The Underdogs* (CS,22;IW,7)
Balzac, Honore de *Old Goriot* (GS,17;IW,6)
Beckett, Samuel *Waiting for Godot* (CS,7;IEA,2;IW,5)
Beowulf (RF,274;NE,7)
Brecht, Bertold *Mother Courage and Her Children* (CS,7;G,158;IW,4)
Camus, Albert *The Stranger, The Plague* (CS,23;NE,4,8;IWA,5)
Cervantes *Don Quixote* (GS,17;RF,274)
Chekhov, Anton *The Cherry Orchard* (CS,7;GS17,148;H,162;IW,3,6)
Confucius (H,164)
Dante *The Divine Comedy* (H,167;RF,276)

Descartes (H,167)

Dostoevsky, F. *The Brothers Karamazov, Crime and Punishment, The Idiot*
(CS,24;GS,17;H,165;NE,4;RF,277;IW,3)

Dumas, Alexandre *The Count of Monte Cristo, The Man in the Iron Mask, The Three Musketeers*
(GS,17,18)

Everyman (NE,7)

Flaubert, Gustave *Madame Bovary* (CS,24;GS,17;IW,4)

Frankl, Victor *Man's Search for Meaning* (NE,9)

Garcia Lorca, Federico *Blood Wedding* (CS,8,IW,6)

Garcia Marquez, Gabriel *Love in the Time of Cholera* (CS,24;IWA,2,5)

Giraudoux, Jean *The Madwoman of Chaillot* (GS,148;IWA,7)

Goethe, Johann Wolfgang von *Faust* (H,171;IWA,4)

Hesse, Hermann *Siddhartha, Beneath the Wheel* (CS,25;NE,8)

Hitler, Adolph *Mein Kampf* (H,187)

Hugo, Victor *The Hunchback of Notre Dame, Les Miserables* (CS,25;GS,18;H,178)

Ibsen, Henrik *A Doll's House, An Enemy of the People, Hedda Gabler, The Master Builder, The
Wild Duck* (CS,8;GS,148;H,168;NE,7;RF,276;IW,4,5,6)

Ionesco, Eugene *Rhinoceros* (CS,8)

Kafka, Franz (H,182) *Metamorphosis* (NE,8;IW,5)

Kawabata, Yasunari *Snow Country* (CS,26;IWA,3)

Khayyam, Omar *The Rubaiyat* (H,192)

Machiavelli *The Prince* (H,197)

Mansfield, Katherine *Miss Brill* (NE,8)

Maupassant, Guy de *Selected Short Stories* (GS,17)

Mishima, Yukio *The Sound of Waves* (CS,27;IWA,3)

Mo, Timothy *Sour Sweet* (CS,27)

Moliere, Jean *The Misanthrope and Other Plays* (GS,148)

Montaigne (H,188)

O Yong-Jin and others *Wedding day and Other Korean Plays* (CS,9)

Paton, Alan *Cry, the Beloved Country* (CS,28;NE,5;IW,2,5)

Proust, Marcel (H,108)

Rabelais (H,199)

Racine, Jean Baptiste *Phaedra* (GS,149)

Remarque, Erich Maria *All Quiet on the Western Front* (CS,28;NE,4)

Rostand, Edmond *Cyrano de Bergerac* (CS,9;GS,149;NS3,23)

Rousseau, Jean Jacques *Confessions* (H,164)

Saint-Exupery, Antoine de *The Little Prince* (CS,29;NS1,23)

C = California Recommended Readings, K-8
CS = California Recommended Literature, 9-12
E1,2,3 = Edison Proj.: Primary,Elem.,Junior Acad.
GJ = Gillespie: Best Books for Junior High Readers
GS = Gillespie: Best Books for Senior High Readers
H = Hirsch: Cultural Literacy
H1 - H6 = Hirsch: Core Knowledge Series, Grades 1-6

IE,IW = Int'l Bacc.: English A1, World Lit.
IEA,IWA= Int'l Bacc.: English A1, World Lit. (author citation)
NE = New England Association of Teachers of English
NS1,2,3 = New Standards: Elem., Middle, High
NS1A,2A,3A = New Standards: Elem., Middle, High (author
    citation)
RF = Ravitch & Finn: What Do Our 17-Year-Olds Know?

373

MREL

Sartre, Jean-Paul *No Exit* (GS,149;H,202;IW,7)
Solzhenitsyn, Alexander *One Day in the Life of Ivan Denisovich* (CS,29;NE,8;IW,3,5)
St. Augustine's *Confessions* (H,164)
Tocqueville, Count Alexis de *Democracy in America* (RF,277)
Tolstoy, A. *Anna Karenina, The Death of Ivan Ilyich, War and Peace*
(CS,29;GS,18;H,209;IW,3,4,5)
Turgenev, Ivan *Fathers and Sons* (GS,18;IW,3,6)
Verne, Jules *Around the World in Eighty Days, 20,000 Leagues under the Sea*
(GS,18;H,212;NS3,23)
Voltaire *Candide* (GS,18;H,160)
Zola, Emile (H,215;IWA,4)

CLASSICAL/ANCIENT LITERATURE

Aeschylus *Oresteian Trilogy* (CS,7;IWA,4,6)
Aristophanes *Lysistrata* (GS,148;IW,4)
Aristotle *Nichomachean Ethics* (H,155)
Cicero (H,162)
Euripedes *Medea* (CS,8;H,170;NE,8)
Homer *The Iliad* and *The Odyssey* (GS,158;NE,4;RF,271,274;IW,4)
Horace (H,178)
Ovid *Metamorphoses* (GS,158;H,193;IW,4)
Plato *The Republic, The Last Days of Socrates* [*Euthyphro, The Apology, Crito, Phaedo*]
(GS,158;RF,270)
Sophocles *Antigone, Oedipus at Colonus,Oedipus Rex*
(CS,10;GS,149;H,154;NE,4;RF,273,275;IW,4,6)
Virgil *Aeneid* (GS,158;H,152;IW,4)

THE BIBLE AS LITERATURE

23rd Psalm, "The Lord is my Shepherd..." 3 lines (RF,270)
Abraham and Isaac (H,152)
Beatitudes (H,157)
Cain and Abel (RF,271)
Daniel in the Lion's Den (H,166)
David and Goliath (H,166;RF,270)

C = California Recommended Readings, K-8
CS = California Recommended Literature, 9-12
E1,2,3 = Edison Proj.: Primary,Elem.,Junior Acad.
GJ = Gillespie: Best Books for Junior High Readers
GS = Gillespie: Best Books for Senior High Readers
H = Hirsch: Cultural Literacy
H1 - H6 = Hirsch: Core Knowledge Series, Grades 1-6

IE,IW = Int'l Bacc.: English A1, World Lit.
IEA,IWA= Int'l Bacc.: English A1, World Lit. (author citation)
NE = New England Association of Teachers of English
NS1,2,3 = New Standards: Elem., Middle, High
NS1A,2A,3A = New Standards: Elem., Middle, High (author
    citation)
RF = Ravitch & Finn: What Do Our 17-Year-Olds Know?

Exodus (H,171)
Gospel according to St. Matthew (G,187)
Gospel according to St. Luke (H,185)
Gospel according to St. John (H,181)
Jacob and Esau (H,181)
Jeremiah (H,181)
Jesus betrayed for 30 pieces of silver (H,209;RF,271)
Job (H,181;RF,275)
King Solomon's wisdom (RF,272)
Lucifer (as another name for Satan) (RF,271)
Moses, the Ten Commandments (RF,270)
Noah, the ark (RF,270)
Revelations (H,200)
Salome (H,202)
Samson and Delilah (H,202;RF,271)
Sermon on the Mount (H,203)
Sodom and Gomorrah (H,205;RF,276)
The Garden of Eden (H,169)
The Crucifixion (H,165)
The Second Coming (H,203)
The Prodigal Son (RF,273)
The story of Creation in Genesis (H,174;RF,270)
Tower of Babel (H,210)
"To every thing there is a season..." (RF,274)

C = California Recommended Readings, K-8
CS = California Recommended Literature, 9-12
E1,2,3 = Edison Proj.: Primary,Elem.,Junior Acad.
GJ = Gillespie: Best Books for Junior High Readers
GS = Gillespie: Best Books for Senior High Readers
H = Hirsch: Cultural Literacy
H1 - H6 = Hirsch: Core Knowledge Series, Grades 1-6

IE,IW = Int'l Bacc.: English A1, World Lit.
IEA,IWA= Int'l Bacc.: English A1, World Lit. (author citation)
NE = New England Association of Teachers of English
NS1,2,3 = New Standards: Elem., Middle, High
NS1A,2A,3A = New Standards: Elem., Middle, High (author citation)
RF = Ravitch & Finn: What Do Our 17-Year-Olds Know?

MREL

11. The Arts

The following process was used to identify standards and benchmarks for the arts:

Identification of National Reports
Four reports were identified as important for representing current thinking on knowledge and skills in the arts: *The National Standards for Arts Education* (1994) developed by the Consortium of National Arts Education Associations, the *NAEP Arts Education Assessment Framework* (NAEP, 1994), the *Visual and Performing Arts Framework for California Public Schools: K–12* (California Department of Education, 1989), and *The School Music Program: Description and Standards* (1986) from the Music Educators National Conference. Two curriculum documents from the International Baccalaureate Organization were consulted for citations: *Middle years programme: Arts* (1995a) and *Art/Design* (1996a).

Selection of the Reference Document
The *National Standards for Arts Education* was selected as the reference document for constructing standards in the arts. The developers of the document represented a consortium of arts educators in music, theatre, the visual arts, and dance. The work provides content standards in each arts area, with "achievement standards" described for three levels: K–4, 5–8, and 9–12.

Identification of Standards and Benchmarks
At the standard level, most statements in the national document were retained with some revision to reflect the more content-oriented focus of this model. Additionally, one standard, Art Connections, was formed by combining very similar ideas from across the arts areas, namely, content that addressed the connections among various art forms and other disciplines.

At the benchmark level, there were some aspects in which the material for the arts standards was consistently revised and adapted to fit the model used in this study. This was the case when "achievement standards" in the national document were rewritten to describe specific knowledge and/or skill. For example, under the visual arts content standard "Using knowledge of structures and functions," one 8th-grade achievement standard is:

> a. [Students] generalize about the effects of visual structures and functions and reflect upon these effects in their own work (p. 50)

Because content standards are the focus of this study, material such as the example above was rewritten to describe the knowledge a student should have, rather than to describe an activity that might be used to demonstrate achievement of that knowledge. Additionally, detailed information was added to the benchmark when it was available; primary sources were the NAEP arts framework and a glossary provided in the *National Standards*. Thus, the benchmark was rewritten as:

(AE,50;CI,95-96;IAI,5;IMI,11;NE,110)
- Knows some of the effects of various visual structures (e.g., design elements such as line,

color, shape; principles such as repetition, rhythm, balance) and functions of art

For the example analyzed here, it should be noted that another standard in the visual arts, "Understands the characteristics and merits of one's own artwork and the artwork of others," separately addresses that aspect of the activity that concerns the students' review of their own works.

Integration of Information from Other Documents

As demonstrated above, supplementary documents were used to provide detail (which was the primary use of the NAEP framework) and to provide page references to a well-known curriculum framework; in this case, the California Visual and Performing Arts Framework. Additionally, material from *The School Music Program,* produced by the Music Educators National Conference, was used to provide benchmarks at K–2 in the section on music. In the other arts areas, no documents were found suitable to address this need; consequently, areas other than music are presented at levels found in the arts standards document: K–4, 5–8, and 9–12. The International Baccalaureate arts documents, *Middle Years: Arts* and *Art/Design,* were cited wherever similar knowledge and skills were addressed in those documents and the benchmarks in this report.

Summary of Standards for the Arts

Art Connections
1.   Understands connections among the various art forms and other disciplines

Dance
1.   Identifies and demonstrates movement elements and skills in performing dance
2.   Understands choreographic principles, processes, and structures
3.   Understands dance as a way to create and communicate meaning
4.   Applies critical and creative thinking skills in dance
5.   Understands dance in various cultures and historical periods
6.   Understands connections between dance and healthful living

Music
1.   Sings, alone and with others, a varied repertoire of music
2.   Performs on instruments, alone and with others, a varied repertoire of music
3.   Improvises melodies, variations, and accompaniments
4.   Composes and arranges music within specified guidelines
5.   Reads and notates music
6.   Knows and applies appropriate criteria to music and music performances
7.   Understands the relationship between music and history and culture

Theatre
1.   Demonstrates competence in writing scripts
2.   Uses acting skills
3.   Designs and produces informal and formal productions
4.   Directs scenes and productions
5.   Understands how informal and formal theatre, film, television, and electronic media productions create and communicate meaning
6.   Understands the context in which theatre, film, television, and electronic media are performed today as well as in the past

Visual Arts
1.   Understands and applies media, techniques, and processes related to the visual arts
2.   Knows how to use the structures (e.g., sensory qualities, organizational principles, expressive features) and functions of art
3.   Knows a range of subject matter, symbols, and potential ideas in the visual arts
4.   Understands the visual arts in relation to history and cultures
5.   Understands the characteristics and merits of one's own artwork and the artwork of others

Art Connections

1. Understands connections among the various art forms and other disciplines
(AE,25,28,31,35)

Level II (Grades K-4)

- Uses Knows how visual, aural, oral, and kinetic elements are used in the various art forms
  BD (AE,31;NI,102)

- Knows how ideas (e.g., sibling rivalry, respect) and emotions (e.g., sadness, anger) are expressed in the various art forms
  BD (AE,31;NE,102)

- Knows the similarities and differences in the meanings of common terms used in the various arts (e.g., form, line, contrast)
  BD (AE,28)

- Knows ways in which the principles and subject matter of other disciplines taught in the school are interrelated with those of the arts (e.g., pattern in the arts and in science)
  BD (AI,25,28,35)

Level III (Grades 5-8)

- Understands how the characteristic materials of various arts (e.g., sound in music, visual stimuli in visual arts, movement in dance, human interrelationships in theatre) are used to transform similar events, scenes, emotions, or ideas into distinct works of art
  BD (AE,45)

- Understands characteristics of works in various art forms that share similar subject matter, historical periods, or cultural context
  BD (AE,51;NE,111,112)

- Understands the characteristics and presentation of characters, environments, and actions in the various art forms
  BD (AE,47;NE,95)

- Knows how various concepts and principles are used in the arts and disciplines outside the arts (e.g., balance, shape, pattern)
  BD (AE,41)

- Knows the aesthetic impact of arts performances seen live versus those recorded on audio or video
  BD (AE,41)

- Understands the functions and interaction between performing and visual artists and audience members in theatre, dance, music, and visual arts
  BD (AE,48)

Codes (right side of page):   BD = Benchmark, Declarative; BP = Benchmark, Procedural; BC = Benchmark, Contextual
1st letter of each code in parentheses   *2nd letter of code*   *Number*
A = CNAEA: National Standards for Arts Education   E = Explicitly stated in document   Page number of cited document
C = California Visual/Performing Arts Framework   I = Implied in document
N = NAEP: Arts Education Assessment Framework

Level IV (Grades 9-12)

- Knows ways in which various arts media can be integrated

  BD (AE,66;CI,51)

- Knows how characteristics of the arts vary within a particular historical period or style and how these characteristics relate to ideas, issues, or themes in other disciplines

  BD (AE,62,72)

- Understands how elements, materials, technologies, artistic processes (e.g., imagination, craftsmanship), and organizational principles (e.g., unity and variety, repetition and contrast) are used in similar and distinctive ways in the various art forms

  BD (AE,58,62,72;NE,115)

Codes (right side of page): BD = Benchmark, Declarative; BP = Benchmark, Procedural; BC = Benchmark, Contextual
1st letter of each code in parentheses *2nd letter of code* *Number*
A = CNAEA: National Standards for Arts Education E = Explicitly stated in document Page number of cited document
C = California Visual/Performing Arts Framework I = Implied in document
N = NAEP: Arts Education Assessment Framework

Dance

1. Identifies and demonstrates movement elements and skills in performing dance ^(AE,23)

Level II (Grades K-4)

- Uses basic nonlocomotor/axial movements (e.g., bend, twist, stretch, swing) ^{BP (AE,23;CI,16;NE,83)}

- Uses basic locomotor movements (e.g., walk, hop, leap, gallop, slide, skip) in different directions (e.g., forward, backward, sideward, diagonally, turning) ^{BP (AE,23;CI,16;NE,83)}

- Creates shapes (e.g., body shapes, lines, angles, curves) at low, middle, and high levels (different heights from the floor) ^{BP (AE,23;CE,17)}

- Defines and maintains personal space (e.g., form; distance from others when moving through space as part of a group) ^{BP (AE,23;CE,16;NE,84)}

- Uses movements in straight and curved pathways ^{BP (AE,23;CI,17;NE,83)}

- Moves to a rhythmic accompaniment (e.g., drum beat) and responds to changes in tempo ^{BP (AE,23;CI,17;NE,83)}

- Uses kinesthetic awareness, concentration, and focus in performing movement skills ^{BP (AE,23;CE,22;NE,84)}

- Knows basic actions (e.g., skip, gallop) and movement elements (e.g., height of the dancer in relation to the floor, directions), and how they communicate ideas ^{BD (AE,23;CI,15;NE,84)}

Level III (Grades 5-8)

- Understands various movements and their underlying principles (e.g., alignment, balance, initiation of movement, articulation of isolated body parts, weight shift, elevation and landing, fall and recovery) ^{BD (AE,39;CI,17;NE,86)}

- Knows basic dance steps, body positions, and spatial patterns for dance from various styles or traditions (e.g., ballet, square, Ghanaian, Middle Eastern, modern) ^{BD (AE,39;CE,24;NE,85)}

- Transfers a spatial pattern from the visual to the kinesthetic (e.g., reproduces a pattern drawn on paper by traveling through space) ^{BC (AE,39;CI,15;NE,85)}

- Transfers a rhythmic pattern from the aural to the kinesthetic (e.g., reproduces a rhythmic ^{BC (AE,39;CI,15;NE,85)}

Codes (right side of page): BD = Benchmark, Declarative; BP = Benchmark, Procedural; BC = Benchmark, Contextual
1st letter of each code in parentheses 2nd letter of code Number
A = CNAEA: National Standards for Arts Education E = Explicitly stated in document Page number of cited document
C = California Visual/Performing Arts Framework I = Implied in document
N = NAEP: Arts Education Assessment Framework

pattern beat on a drum by using movement)

- Knows a range of dynamics/movement qualities (e.g., sustained, swing, percussive, collapse; vibratory and effort combinations such as a float, dab, punch, and glide)
  BD (AE,39;CE,17;NE,85)

- Memorizes and reproduces movement sequences
  BP (AE,39;CE,22;NE,85)

- Understands the action and movement elements observed in dance, and knows appropriate movement/dance vocabulary (e.g., level, direction)
  BD (AE,39;CI,23;NE,86)

Level IV (Grades 9-12)

- Uses appropriate skeletal alignment (e.g., relationship of the skeleton to the line of gravity and the base of support), body-part articulation, strength, flexibility, agility, and coordination in locomotor and nonlocomotor/axial movements
  BP (AE,55;CI,16;NE,87)

- Knows complex steps and patterns from various dance styles (e.g., dances of a particular performer, choreographer, period) and traditions (e.g., dances of bharata natyam, noh; folk dances of indigenous peoples of Europe or other areas)
  BD (AE,55;CI,24)

- Understands various complex time elements (e.g., duple and triple meters and tempi varied in relation to a basic pulse)
  BD (AE,55;CE,17)

- Creates and performs combinations and variations in a broad dynamic range (e.g., sustained, percussive, vibratory, swing)
  BP (AE,55;CI,17;NI,86)

- Uses projection in dance (e.g., confident presentation of one's body and energy to communicate movement and meaning to an audience; performance quality; positive sense of involvement)
  BP (AE,55;CI,17)

- Memorizes and reproduces extended movement sequences and rhythmic patterns
  BP (AE,55;CE,22;NE,87)

Codes (right side of page): BD = Benchmark, Declarative; BP = Benchmark, Procedural; BC = Benchmark, Contextual
1st letter of each code in parentheses *2nd letter of code* *Number*
A = CNAEA: National Standards for Arts Education E = Explicitly stated in document Page number of cited document
C = California Visual/Performing Arts Framework I = Implied in document
N = NAEP: Arts Education Assessment Framework

383 MREL

2. Understands choreographic principles, processes, and structures

(AE,24)

Level II (Grades K-4)

- Creates a sequence with a beginning, middle, and ending

  BP (AE,24;CE,19;NE,83)

- Improvises, creates, and performs dances based on personal ideas and concepts from other sources

  BC (AE,24;CI,23;NI,83)

- Knows how improvisation is used to discover and invent movement and to solve movement problems

  BD (AE,24;CI,18)

- Creates a dance phrase (e.g., a brief sequence of related movements that has a sense of rhythmic completion), repeats it, and varies it (e.g., makes changes in the time, space, force/energy)

  BP (AE,24;CE,19;NE,83)

- Uses partner skills such as copying, leading and following, and mirroring

  BP (AE,24;NE,84)

Level III (Grades 5-8)

- Understands the principles of contrast and transition

  BD (AE,40;CE,19;NE,85)

- Understands the processes of reordering (e.g., elements such as specific movements or movement phrases are separated from their original relationship and restructured in a different pattern) and chance (e.g., elements are specifically chosen and defined but randomly structured to create a dance or movement phrase)

  BD (AE,40;NI,85)

- Understands structures or forms such as AB, ABA, canon, call and response, and narrative

  BD (AE,40;CE,19;NE,85)

- Uses partner skills such as creating contrasting and complementary shapes and taking and supporting weight

  BP (AE,40;NE,85)

Level IV (Grades 9-12)

- Knows how improvisation is used to generate movement for choreography

  BD (AE,56;NE,86)

- Understands structures or forms such as palindrome, theme and variation, rondo, round, and contemporary forms

  BD (AE,56;CE,19;NE,87)

Codes (right side of page):   BD = Benchmark, Declarative; BP = Benchmark, Procedural; BC = Benchmark, Contextual
1st letter of each code in parentheses   *2nd letter of code*   *Number*
A = CNAEA: National Standards for Arts Education   E = Explicitly stated in document   Page number of cited document
C = California Visual/Performing Arts Framework   I = Implied in document
N = NAEP: Arts Education Assessment Framework

● Identifies choreographic principles, processes, and structures used in dance ^BP (AI,56;CI,23;NE,87)

3.   Understands dance as a way to create and communicate meaning ^(AE,24)

Level II (Grades K-4)

● Knows how dance is different from other forms of human movement (e.g., sports, everyday gestures) ^BD (AE,24;NE,84)

● Knows how a dance may elicit various interpretations and reactions that differ from the meaning intended by the dancer ^BD (AE,24;CI,23;NI,84)

Level III (Grades 5-8)

● Understands the difference between pantomiming and abstracting a gesture ^BD (AE,40;CI,18)

● Understands how different accompaniment (e.g., sound, music, spoken text) can affect the meaning of a dance ^BD (AE,40)

● Understands how lighting and costuming can contribute to the meaning of a dance ^BD (AE,40)

● Creates dance that communicates topics/ideas of personal significance ^BC (AE,40;CE,18;NE,86)

Level IV (Grades 9-12)

● Understands how movement choices are used to communicate abstract ideas and themes in dance (e.g., isolation, relationships, poverty, the environment) ^BD (AE,56;CI,18;NE,87,88)

● Understands how interpretation of dance can be influenced by personal experience ^BD (AE,56)

4.   Applies critical and creative thinking skills in dance ^(AE,24)

Level II (Grades K-4)

● Knows how a variety of solutions can be used to solve a given movement problem ^BD (AE,24;NE,83)

Codes (right side of page):   BD = Benchmark, Declarative; BP = Benchmark, Procedural; BC = Benchmark, Contextual
1st letter of each code in parentheses   *2nd letter of code*   *Number*
A = CNAEA: National Standards for Arts Education   E = Explicitly stated in document   Page number of cited document
C = California Visual/Performing Arts Framework   I = Implied in document
N = NAEP: Arts Education Assessment Framework

- Knows technical and artistic components of various forms of dance (e.g., body shapes, space, levels, pathways) *BD (AE,24;NE,84)*

Level III (Grades 5-8)

- Knows appropriate audience response to dance performances *BD (AE,40)*

- Knows the critical elements that contribute to a dance in terms of space (e.g., shape, pathways) time (e.g., rhythm, tempo), and force/energy (e.g., movement qualities) *BD (AE,40;NE,86)*

- Knows possible aesthetic criteria that could be used to evaluate dance (e.g., skill of performers, originality, visual and/or emotional impact, variety and contrast) *BD (AE,40;CI,23;NE,86)*

Level IV (Grades 9-12)

- Establishes a set of aesthetic criteria and applies it in evaluating one's own work and that of others *BP (AE,57;CI,19;NE,88)*

- Formulates and answers one's own aesthetic questions (e.g., knows what makes a particular dance unique, how much one can change a dance before it becomes a different dance) *BP (AE,57)*

5. Understands dance in various cultures and historical periods *(AE,24)*

Level II (Grades K-4)

- Knows folk dances from various cultures *BD (AE,24;CI,20,24;NE,84)*

- Knows the cultural and/or historical context of various dances (e.g., colonial America, dances within one's community) *BD (AE,25;CE,21,24;NE,84)*

Level III (Grades 5-8)

- Knows similarities and differences in steps and movement styles among folk dances and classical dances from various cultures *BD (AE,41;CI,20,24;NI,85)*

- Knows folk, social, and theatrical (e.g., jazz, tap) dances from a broad spectrum of 20th-century America *BD (AE,41;CI,21,24)*

Codes (right side of page):   BD = Benchmark, Declarative; BP = Benchmark, Procedural; BC = Benchmark, Contextual
1st letter of each code in parentheses   *2nd letter of code*   *Number*
A = CNAEA: National Standards for Arts Education   E = Explicitly stated in document   Page number of cited document
C = California Visual/Performing Arts Framework   I = Implied in document
N = NAEP: Arts Education Assessment Framework

386   MREL

- Knows the role of dance in various cultures and time periods

  BD (AE,41;CI,21,24;NE,86)

Level IV (Grades 9-12)

- Knows the similarities and differences among various contemporary theatrical forms of dance (e.g., jazz, tap)

  BD (AE,57;CI,24;NE,88)

- Knows traditions and techniques of classical dance forms (e.g., Balinese, ballet)

  BD (AE,57;CI,24;NE,88)

- Understands how dance and dancers are portrayed in contemporary media

  BD (AE,57;CI,21;NE,88)

6. Understands connections between dance and healthful living

(AE,25)

Level II (Grades K-4)

- Knows how healthy practices (e.g., nutrition, safety) enhance the ability to dance

  BD (AE,25)

Level III (Grades 5-8)

- Knows strategies to prevent dance injuries

  BD (AE,41;CE,16)

- Creates personal dance warmup techniques

  BC (AE,41;CI,16;NE,85)

- Creates goals to improve as a dancer

  BC (AE,41)

Level IV (Grades 9-12)

- Knows how lifestyle choices affect the dancer as a professional performer

  BD (AE,58)

- Understands contemporary images of the body in dance and how images of the body vary across cultures and through history

  BD (AE,58)

Codes (right side of page):   BD = Benchmark, Declarative; BP = Benchmark, Procedural; BC = Benchmark, Contextual
1st letter of each code in parentheses   *2nd letter of code*   *Number*
A = CNAEA: National Standards for Arts Education   E = Explicitly stated in document   Page number of cited document
C = California Visual/Performing Arts Framework   I = Implied in document
N = NAEP: Arts Education Assessment Framework

Music

1. Sings, alone and with others, a varied repertoire of music

(AE,26)

Level I (Grades K-2)

- Sings ostinatos (repetition of a short musical pattern), partner songs, and rounds

  BP (AE,26;CE,76;IMI,71;ME,22;NE,90)

Level II (Grades 3-5)

- Sings on pitch and in rhythm, with appropriate timbre, diction, and posture, and maintains a steady tempo

  BP (AE,26;CI,76;MI,23;NE,90)

- Sings expressively, with appropriate dynamics, phrasing, and interpretation

  BP (AE,26;CI,75;MI,23;NE,90)

- Blends vocal timbres, matches dynamic levels, and responds to the cues of a conductor when singing as part of a group

  BP (AE,26;CI,76;IMI,71;ME,24;NE,90)

- Knows songs representing genres (e.g., march, work song, lullaby, Dixieland) and styles (e.g., of various composers, nations) from diverse cultures

  BD (AE,26;CI,78;IMI,69,71;MI,23)

Level III (Grades 6-8)

- Sings with good breath control, expression, and technical accuracy (e.g., appropriate timbre, intonation, and diction; correct pitches and rhythms) at a level that includes modest ranges and changes of tempo, key, and meter

  BP (AE,42;CI,76;IMI,69;ME,33;NE,93)

- Sings music written in two and three parts

  BP (AE,42;CE,76;ME,32;NE,93)

- Knows music that represents diverse genres (e.g., sonata, madrigal, jazz, barbershop) and cultures

  BD (AE,42;CE,78;IMI,71;ME,32)

Level IV (Grades 9-12)

- Sings a varied repertoire of vocal literature with expression and technical accuracy at a moderate level of difficulty (e.g., attention to phrasing and interpretation, various meters and rhythms in a variety of keys)

  BP (AE,59;CI,76;IMI,69;ME,43;NI,97)

Codes (right side of page):   BD = Benchmark, Declarative; BP = Benchmark, Procedural; BC = Benchmark, Contextual
1st letter of each code in parentheses   *2nd letter of code*   *Number*
A = CNAEA: National Standards for Arts Education   E = Explicitly stated in document   Page number of cited document
C = California Visual/Performing Arts Framework   I = Implied in document
IM = Int'l Baccalaureate: Middle Years Arts
M = MENC: The School Music Program
N = NAEP: Arts Education Assessment Framework   388

MREL

- Sings music written in four parts, with and without accompaniment

  BP (AE,59;CI,76;ME,43;NE,97)

- Uses ensemble skills (e.g., balance, intonation, rhythmic unity)

  BP (AE,49;MI,43;NE,97)

2. Performs on instruments, alone and with others, a varied repertoire of music

(AE,26)

Level I (Grades K-2)

- Echoes short rhythms (2-4 measure) and melodic patterns

  BP (AE,26;CE,74;IMI,71;MI,23;NE,90)

Level II (Grades 3-5)

- Performs on pitch, in rhythm, with appropriate dynamics and timbre, and maintains a steady tempo

  BP (AE,26;CE,76;MI,23;NE,90)

- Performs simple rhythmic, melodic, and chordal patterns accurately and independently on rhythmic, melodic, and harmonic classroom instruments (e.g., recorder-type instruments, percussion instruments, keyboard instruments, electronic instruments, fretted instruments such as a guitar or ukulele)

  BP (AE,26;CE,76;IMI,71;MI,23;NE,90,91)

- Knows a varied repertoire of music representing diverse genres and styles

  BD (AE,26;CI,78;IMI,69;MI,23;NI,90)

- Performs in groups (e.g., blends instrumental timbres, matches dynamic levels, responds to the cues of a conductor)

  BP (AE,26;CI,76;IMI,71;ME,24;NE,90)

- Performs independent instrumental parts (e.g., simple rhythmic or melodic ostinatos, contrasting rhythmic lines, harmonic progressions and chords) while others sing or play contrasting parts

  BP (AE,26;CE,76;IMI,71;ME,23;NE,90)

Level III (Grades 6-8)

- Performs on an instrument (e.g., band or orchestra instrument, keyboard instrument, fretted instrument such as guitar, electronic instrument) accurately and independently, alone and in small and large ensembles, with good posture, good playing position, and good breath, bow, or stick control

  BP (AE,42;CI,76;MI,33;NE,94)

Codes (right side of page):   BD = Benchmark, Declarative; BP = Benchmark, Procedural; BC = Benchmark, Contextual
1st letter of each code in parentheses   *2nd letter of code*   *Number*
A = CNAEA: National Standards for Arts Education   E = Explicitly stated in document   Page number of cited document
C = California Visual/Performing Arts Framework   I = Implied in document
IM = Int'l Baccalaureate: Middle Years Arts
M = MENC: The School Music Program
N = NAEP: Arts Education Assessment Framework   389   MREL

- Performs with expression and technical accuracy on a string, wind, percussion, or other classroom instrument a repertoire of instrumental literature that may include modest ranges and changes of tempo, key, and meter
  BP (AE,43;IMI,69;MI,33)

- Performs music representing diverse genres and cultures, with expression appropriate for the work being performed
  BP (AE,43;CE,78;MI,33;NE,94)

- Plays by ear simple melodies (e.g., folk songs) on a melodic instrument and simple accompaniments (e.g., strummed, I, IV, V, vi, ii chords) on a harmonic instrument
  BP (AE,43;CE,76;IMI,71;MI,32;NE,94)

Level IV (Grades 9-12)

- Performs with expression (e.g., appropriate dynamics, phrasing, rubato) and technical accuracy a large and varied repertoire of instrumental literature at a moderate level of difficulty (e.g., attends to phrasing and interpretation, performs various meters and rhythms in a variety of keys)
  BP (AE,59;IMI,69;ME,44;NE,97)

- Uses ensemble skills (e.g., balance, intonation, rhythmic unity) when performing as part of a group
  BP (AE,60;MI,44;NE,97)

3. Improvises melodies, variations, and accompaniments
(AE,27)

Level I (Grades K-2)

- Improvises "answers" in the same style to given rhythmic and melodic phrases
  BP (AE,27;ME,22;NE,89)

Level II (Grades 3-5)

- Improvises simple rhythmic and melodic ostinato (repetition of a short musical pattern) accompaniments
  BP (AE,27;CE,77;ME,23;NE,89)

- Improvises simple rhythmic variations and simple melodic embellishments on familiar melodies
  BP (AE,27;MI,23;NE,89)

- Improvises short songs and instrumental pieces using a variety of sound sources, including traditional sounds (e.g., voices, instruments), nontraditional sounds (e.g., paper tearing,
  BP (AE,27;CE,77;ME,23;NE,89)

Codes (right side of page):   BD = Benchmark, Declarative;   BP = Benchmark, Procedural;   BC = Benchmark, Contextual
1st letter of each code in parentheses   *2nd letter of code*   *Number*
A = CNAEA: National Standards for Arts Education   E = Explicitly stated in document   Page number of cited document
C = California Visual/Performing Arts Framework   I = Implied in document
IM = Int'l Baccalaureate: Middle Years Arts
M = MENC: The School Music Program
N = NAEP: Arts Education Assessment Framework   390   *McREL*

pencil tapping), body sounds (e.g., hands clapping, fingers snapping), and sounds produced by electronic means (e.g., personal computers and basic MIDI devices such as keyboards, sequencers, synthesizers, and drum machines)

Level III (Grades 6-8)

- Improvises simple harmonic accompaniments

  BP (AE,43;ME,32;NE,93)

- Improvises melodic embellishments and simple rhythmic and melodic variations on given pentatonic melodies and melodies in major keys

  BP (AE,43;CI,77;IMI,69;NE,93)

- Improvises short melodies, unaccompanied and over given rhythmic accompaniments, in a consistent style (e.g., classical, blues, folk, gospel), meter (e.g., duple, triple), and tonality (e.g., major, pentatonic)

  BP (AE,43;MI,32;NE,93)

Level IV (Grades 9-12)

- Improvises stylistically appropriate harmonizing parts

  BP (AE,60;NI,96)

- Improvises rhythmic and melodic variations on given pentatonic melodies and melodies in major and minor keys (e.g., folk songs, standard pop songs, hymn tunes)

  BP (AE,60;IMI,69;NE,96)

- Improvises original melodies over given chord progressions in a consistent style, meter, and tonality

  BP (AE,60;CI,77;NI,96)

4.   Composes and arranges music within specified guidelines

(AE,27)

Level I (Grades K-2)

- Uses a variety of sound sources when composing (e.g., classroom instruments, electronic sounds, body sounds)

  BP (AE,27;MI,22;NE,89)

Level II (Grades 3-5)

- Creates and arranges music to accompany readings or dramatizations (e.g., manipulate dimensions such as the variety of sounds, tempo, loudness, mood)

  BP (AE,27;MI,23;NE,89)

Codes (right side of page):   BD = Benchmark, Declarative; BP = Benchmark, Procedural; BC = Benchmark, Contextual
1st letter of each code in parentheses   *2nd letter of code*   *Number*
A = CNAEA: National Standards for Arts Education   E = Explicitly stated in document   Page number of cited document
C = California Visual/Performing Arts Framework   I = Implied in document
IM = Int'l Baccalaureate: Middle Years Arts
M = MENC: The School Music Program
N = NAEP: Arts Education Assessment Framework   391   *MREL*

- Creates and arranges short songs and instrumental pieces within specified guidelines (e.g., a particular style, form, instrumentation, compositional technique)

  BP (AE,27;CI,77;IMI,69;MI,22;NE,89)

Level III (Grades 6-8)

- Knows how the elements of music are used to achieve unity and variety, tension and release, and balance in musical compositions

  BD (AE,43;MI,32;NE,92)

- Composes short pieces within specified guidelines (e.g., ABA form, limited range, simple rhythms)

  BP (AE,43;CI,77;IMI,69;NE,92)

- Arranges simple pieces for voices or instruments other than those for which the pieces originally were written (e.g., a guitar accompaniment for a folk song)

  BP (AE,43;NE,92)

- Uses a variety of traditional and nontraditional sound sources and electronic media (e.g., synthesizer, sequencer) when composing and arranging

  BP (AE,43;MI,32;NE,92)

Level IV (Grades 9-12)

- Composes music in a variety of distinct styles (e.g., classical, folk, pop, jazz, rock)

  BP (AE,60;NE,96)

- Uses the elements of music for expressive effect (e.g., pitch, rhythm, harmony, dynamics, timbre, texture, form)

  BD (AE,60;CI,74-75;IMI,73;MI,44;NE,96)

- Arranges pieces for voices or instruments other than those for which the pieces were written in ways that preserve or enhance the expressive effect of the music (e.g., piano music, 4-part hymns, duets, trios, quartets)

  BP (AE,60;NE,96)

- Composes and arranges music for voices and various acoustic and electronic instruments

  BP (AE,60;CE,77;MI,45;NE,96)

- Understands the ranges and traditional uses of various sound sources (e.g., voices, acoustic instruments, electronic instruments)

  BD (AE,60;MI,43;NE,96)

Codes (right side of page):   BD = Benchmark, Declarative; BP = Benchmark, Procedural; BC = Benchmark, Contextual

1st letter of each code in parentheses   *2nd letter of code*   *Number*

A = CNAEA: National Standards for Arts Education   E = Explicitly stated in document   Page number of cited document

C = California Visual/Performing Arts Framework   I = Implied in document

IM = Int'l Baccalaureate: Middle Years Arts

M = MENC: The School Music Program

N = NAEP: Arts Education Assessment Framework

MREL

(AE,27)

5. Reads and notates music

Level I (Grades K-2)

BD (AE,27;IMI,69;ME,22;NE,91)
• Knows standard symbols used to notate meter (e.g., 2/4, 3/4, 4/4 time signatures), rhythm (e.g., whole, half, dotted half, quarter, eighth notes), pitch (e.g., notes in treble clef), and dynamics (e.g., p, f, <, >) in simple patterns

BP (AE,27;CE,77;IMI,69;ME,22;NE,90,91)
• Uses a system (e.g., syllables, numbers, letters) to read simple pitch notation in the treble clef in major keys

Level II (Grades 3-5)

BP (AE,27;IMI,69;ME,23;NE,90,91)
• Reads whole, half, dotted half, quarter, and eighth notes and rests in 2/4, 3/4, and 4/4 meter signatures

BD (AE,27;IMI,71;MI,22,NE,91)
• Knows symbols and traditional terms referring to dynamics (e.g., piano, forte, crescendo, diminuendo), tempo (e.g., presto, ritard, accelerando), and articulation (e.g., staccato, legato, marcato, accent)

Level III (Grades 6-8)

BP (AE,44;IMI,69;NE,93,94,95)
• Reads sixteenth and dotted notes and rests in 6/8, 3/8, and alla breve (2/2) meter signatures

BP (AE,44;IMI,69;ME,32;NE,93,94)
• Reads at sight simple melodies in both the treble and bass clefs

BD (AE,44;CI,77;IMI,69;ME,32;NE,95)
• Knows standard notation symbols for pitch, rhythm, dynamics (e.g., piano, forte, crescendo, diminuendo), tempo, articulation (e.g., accents, legato, staccato, marcato), and expression (e.g., phrasing)

BP (AE,44;IMI,69;ME,32;NE,93,95,96,99)
• Uses standard notation to record musical ideas

Level IV (Grades 9-12)

BP (AE,61;NE,99)
• Reads an instrumental or vocal score of up to four staves

BP (AE,61;CI,77;MI,43-44;NI,97,98)
• Reads music that contains moderate technical demands, expanded ranges, and varied

---

Codes (right side of page):   BD = Benchmark, Declarative; BP = Benchmark, Procedural; BC = Benchmark, Contextual
1st letter of each code in parentheses   *2nd letter of code*   *Number*
A = CNAEA: National Standards for Arts Education   E = Explicitly stated in document   Page number of cited document
C = California Visual/Performing Arts Framework   I = Implied in document
IM = Int'l Baccalaureate: Middle Years Arts
M = MENC: The School Music Program
N = NAEP: Arts Education Assessment Framework   393   MREL

interpretive requirements

6. Knows and applies appropriate criteria to music and music performances

(AI,28)

Level I (Grades K-2)

- Knows personal preferences for specific musical works and styles

  BD (AE,28;CE,79;IMI,69;MI,22;NE,89,90,91,92)

- Identifies simple music forms (e.g., AB, ABA, call and response) when presented aurally

  BC (AE,28;IME,69;ME,22;NE,91)

- Responds through purposeful movement (e.g., swaying, skipping, dramatic play) to selected prominent music characteristics or to specific music events (e.g., meter changes, dynamic changes, same/different sections)

  BP (AE,28;CI,77;MI,22;NE,91)

Level II (Grades 3-5)

- Knows music of various styles representing diverse cultures

  BD (AE,28;CI,79;IMI,69;MI,23;NE,91)

- Knows appropriate terminology used to explain music, music notation, music instruments and voices, and music performances

  BD (AE,28;IMI,69;ME,23;NE,91)

- Identifies the sounds of a variety of instruments (e.g., orchestral, band, instruments from various cultures) and voices (e.g., male, female, children's voices)

  BD (AE,28;CI,74;IMI,72;ME,23;NE,91)

Level III (Grades 6-8)

- Identifies specific music events (e.g., entry of oboe, change of meter, return of refrain) when listening to music

  BD (AE,44;CI,77;NE,94)

- Understands how the elements of music are used in various genres and cultures

  BD (AE,44;CI,77;IMI,71;MI,32;NE,94)

- Understands the basic principles of meter, rhythm, tonality, intervals, chords, and harmonic progressions

  BD (AE,44;CI,74-75;IMI,69,71;MI,32;NE,94)

- Knows criteria that affect the quality (e.g., use of elements to create unity, variety, tension/release, balance) and effectiveness (e.g., expressive impact) of music performances and compositions

  BD (AE,44;CI,79;MI,32;NE,92,93,94,95)

Codes (right side of page):   BD = Benchmark, Declarative; BP = Benchmark, Procedural; BC = Benchmark, Contextual
1st letter of each code in parentheses   *2nd letter of code*   *Number*
A = CNAEA: National Standards for Arts Education   E = Explicitly stated in document   Page number of cited document
C = California Visual/Performing Arts Framework   I = Implied in document
IM = Int'l Baccalaureate: Middle Years Arts
M = MENC: The School Music Program
N = NAEP: Arts Education Assessment Framework   394   McREL

Level IV (Grades 9-12)

● Understands how the elements of music and expressive devices are used in music from diverse genres and cultures
BD (AE,61;CI,78;IMI,71;NE,98)

● Understands the technical vocabulary of music (e.g., Italian terms, form, harmony, tempo markings)
BD (AE,61;IMI,69;MI,46;NE,98)

● Understands compositional devices and techniques that are used to provide unity and variety and tension and release in a musical work (e.g., motives, imitation, retrograde, inversion)
BD (AE,61;MI,45;NE,98)

● Knows specific criteria that affect the quality and effectiveness of music performances, compositions, arrangements, and improvisations (e.g., considers questions of unity or variety, consistency, appropriate use of resources)
BD (AE,62;CI,79;NE,96,97,98,99)

(AE,28)

7. Understands the relationship between music and history and culture

Level I (Grades K-2)

● Knows characteristics that make certain music suitable for specific uses
BD (AE,29;CE,78;MI,22;NE,92)

● Knows appropriate audience behavior for the context and style of music performed
BD (AE,29;MI,22)

Level II (Grades 3-5)

● Identifies (by genre or style) music from various historical periods and cultures
BC (AE,29;IMI,69;MI,23;NE,92)

● Knows how basic elements of music are used in music from various cultures of the world
BD (AE,29;MI,24;NE,92)

● Understands the roles of musicians (e.g., orchestra conductor, folksinger, church organist) in various music settings and cultures
BD (AE,29;MI,24;NE,92)

Level III (Grades 6-8)

● Understands distinguishing characteristics (e.g., relating to instrumentation, texture, rhythmic qualities, melodic lines, form) of representative music genres and styles from a variety of cultures
BD (AE,45;CI,78;IMI,69;MI,32;NE,95)

Codes (right side of page):   BD = Benchmark, Declarative; BP = Benchmark, Procedural; BC = Benchmark, Contextual
1st letter of each code in parentheses   *2nd letter of code*   *Number*
A = CNAEA: National Standards for Arts Education   E = Explicitly stated in document   Page number of cited document
C = California Visual/Performing Arts Framework   I = Implied in document
IM = Int'l Baccalaureate: Middle Years Arts
M = MENC: The School Music Program
N = NAEP: Arts Education Assessment Framework   395   *MREL*

- Understands characteristics that cause various musical works (e.g., from different genres, styles, historical periods, composers) to be considered exemplary

  BD (AE,45;IMI,69;MI,46;NE,95)

- Understands the functions music serves, roles of musicians (e.g., lead guitarist in a rock band, composer of jingles for commercials, singer in Peking opera), and conditions under which music is typically performed in various cultures of the world

  BD (AE,45;CI,78;NE,95)

Level IV (Grades 9-12)

- Classifies unfamiliar but representative aural examples of music (e.g., by genre, style, historical period, culture)

  BC (AE,63;CI,78,79;IMI,69;MI,46;NE,99)

- Knows sources of American music genres (e.g., swing, Broadway musical, blues), the evolution of these genres, and musicians associated with them

  BD (AE,63;MI,46;NE,99)

- Knows various roles that musicians perform (e.g., entertainer, teacher, transmitter of cultural tradition) and representative individuals who have functioned in these roles

  BD (AE,63;NE,99)

Codes (right side of page):	BD = Benchmark, Declarative; BP = Benchmark, Procedural; BC = Benchmark, Contextual
1st letter of each code in parentheses	*2nd letter of code* *Number*
A = CNAEA: National Standards for Arts Education	E = Explicitly stated in document Page number of cited document
C = California Visual/Performing Arts Framework	I = Implied in document
IM = Int'l Baccalaureate: Middle Years Arts	
M = MENC: The School Music Program	
N = NAEP: Arts Education Assessment Framework	

396

McREL

Theatre

1. Demonstrates competence in writing scripts

(AE,30)

Level II (Grades K-4)

- Selects interrelated characters, environments, and situations for simple dramatizations

  BC (AE,30;NE,101)

- Improvises dialogue to tell stories

  BP (AE,30;IMI,52;NE,101)

- Writes or records dialogue

  BP (AE,30;IMI,50)

- Plans and records improvisations based on personal experience and heritage, imagination, literature, and history

  BC (AE,30;IMI,50)

Level III (Grades 5-8)

- Creates characters, environments (e.g., place, time, atmosphere/mood), and actions that create tension and suspense

  BP (AE,46;CI,45;IMI,49;NE,103)

- Refines and records dialogue and action

  BP (AE,46;IMI,50;NE,103)

- Creates improvisations and scripted scenes based on personal experience and heritage, imagination, literature, and history

  BP (AE,46;IMI,52)

Level IV (Grades 9-12)

- Constructs imaginative scripts that convey story and meaning to an audience

  BP (AE,64;CI,45;IMI,52;NE,104)

- Improvises, writes, and refines scripts based on personal experience and heritage, imagination, literature, and history

  BP (AE,64;IMI,52)

Codes (right side of page):   BD = Benchmark, Declarative; BP = Benchmark, Procedural; BC = Benchmark, Contextual
1st letter of each code in parentheses   *2nd letter of code*   *Number*
A = CNAEA: National Standards for Arts Education   E = Explicitly stated in document   Page number of cited document
C = California Visual/Performing Arts Framework   I = Implied in document
IM = Int'l Baccalaureate: Middle Years Arts
N = NAEP: Arts Education Assessment Framework

MREL

(AE,30)

2.   Uses acting skills

Level II (Grades K-4)

BD (AE,30;NE,101)

- Knows characters in dramatizations, their relationships, and their environments

BP (AE,30;CI,44,47;IMI,49;NE,101)

- Uses variations of locomotor and nonlocomotor movement and vocal pitch, tempo, and tone for different characters

BP (AE,30;IMI,49;NE,101)

- Assumes roles that exhibit concentration and contribute to the action of dramatizations based on personal experience and heritage, imagination, literature, and history

BP (AE,30;IMI,52)

- Knows how to interact in improvisations

Level III (Grades 5-8)

BD (AE,46;NE,103)

- Understands how descriptions, dialogue, and actions are used to discover, articulate, and justify character motivation

BP (AE,46;CE,46;IMI,49,50;NE,103)

- Uses basic acting skills (e.g., sensory recall, concentration, breath control, diction, body alignment, control of isolated body parts) to develop characterizations that suggest artistic choices

BP (AE,46;CI,45;IMI,49;NE,103)

- Invents character behaviors based on the observation of interactions, ethical choices, and emotional responses of people

BP (AE,46;CI,45;IMI,49)

- Interacts as an invented character in improvised and scripted scenes

Level IV (Grades 9-12)

BD (AE,64;IMI,49;NE,105)

- Understands the physical, emotional, and social dimensions of characters found in dramatic texts from various genres and media

BD (AE,64;CE,53;IMI,50)

- Knows various classical and contemporary acting techniques and methods

BP (AE,64;IMI,49;NE,105)

- Develops, communicates, and sustains characters that communicate with audiences in improvisations and informal or formal productions

---

Codes (right side of page):   BD = Benchmark, Declarative; BP = Benchmark, Procedural; BC = Benchmark, Contextual
1st letter of each code in parentheses   *2nd letter of code*   *Number*
A = CNAEA: National Standards for Arts Education   E = Explicitly stated in document   Page number of cited document
C = California Visual/Performing Arts Framework   I = Implied in document
IM = Int'l Baccalaureate: Middle Years Arts
N = NAEP: Arts Education Assessment Framework

McREL

(AE,31)

3.   Designs and produces informal and formal productions

Level II (Grades K-4)

BD (AE,31;CI,49;IMI,49;NE,101)
- Knows how visual elements (e.g., space, color, line, shape, texture) and aural aspects are used to communicate locale and mood

BC (AE,31;CI,50;IME,50;NE,101)
- Selects and organizes available materials that suggest scenery, properties, lighting, sound, costumes, and makeup

BP (AE,31)
- Visualizes and arranges environments for classroom dramatizations

Level III (Grades 5-8)

BD (AE,47;CI,50;IMI,50;NE,103)
- Understands the functions and interrelated nature of scenery, properties, lighting, sound, costumes, and makeup in creating an environment appropriate for the drama

BD (AE,47;IMI,52;NE,103)
- Understands technical requirements for various improvised and scripted scenes

BC (AE,47;IMI,49)
- Develops focused ideas for the environment using visual elements (e.g., line, texture, color, space), visual principles (e.g., repetition, balance, emphasis, contrast, unity), and aural qualities (e.g., pitch, rhythm, dynamics, tempo, expression) from traditional and nontraditional sources

BC (AE,47;CI,50-51;IME,50;NE,103)
- Selects and creates elements of scenery, properties, lighting, and sound to signify environments, and costumes and makeup to suggest character

Level IV (Grades 9-12)

BD (AE,65;CI,50;IMI,50)
- Understands the basic physical and chemical properties of the technical aspects of theatre (e.g., light, color, electricity, paint, makeup)

BD (AE,65;IMI,49;NI,105)
- Understands production requirements for a variety of dramatic texts from cultural and historical perspectives

BC (AE,65;CI,51;IMI,52;NE,105)
- Develops designs that use visual and aural elements to convey environments (e.g., place, time, atmosphere/mood) that clearly support the text

---

Codes (right side of page):   BD = Benchmark, Declarative; BP = Benchmark, Procedural; BC = Benchmark, Contextual
1st letter of each code in parentheses   *2nd letter of code*   *Number*
A = CNAEA: National Standards for Arts Education   E = Explicitly stated in document   Page number of cited document
C = California Visual/Performing Arts Framework   I = Implied in document
IM = Int'l Baccalaureate: Middle Years Arts
N = NAEP: Arts Education Assessment Framework

MREL

- Creates functional scenery, properties, lighting, sound, costumes, and makeup
  BP (AE,65;IME,50;NI,105)

- Conceptualizes and realizes artistic interpretations for informal or formal productions
  BC (AE,65)

- Designs coherent stage management, promotional, and business plans
  BP (AE,65;CE,49;IMI,52;NE,105)

4. Directs scenes and productions

(AE,31)

Level II (Grades K-4)

- Knows various ways of staging classroom dramatizations
  BD (AE,31;CI,48;IMI,52;NE,101)

- Plans and prepares improvisations
  BP (AE,31;IMI,52;NI,101)

Level III (Grades 5-8)

- Plans visual and aural elements for improvised and scripted scenes
  BP (AE,47;IMI,52;NI,103)

- Organizes rehearsals for improvised and scripted scenes
  BP (AE,47;IMI,52)

Level IV (Grades 9-12)

- Develops multiple interpretations and visual and aural production choices for scripts and production ideas
  BP (AE,65;CI,48;IMI,52)

- Justifies selections of text, interpretations, and visual and aural artistic choices (e.g., situation, action, direction, design)
  BC (AE,65;CI,48;IMI,52)

- Communicates directorial choices for improvised or scripted scenes
  BP (AE,65;CI,48;IMI,52;NE,105)

- Organizes and conducts rehearsals for informal or formal productions
  BP (AE,65;IMI,52)

Codes (right side of page):   BD = Benchmark, Declarative;   BP = Benchmark, Procedural;   BC = Benchmark, Contextual
1st letter of each code in parentheses   *2nd letter of code*   *Number*
A = CNAEA: National Standards for Arts Education   E = Explicitly stated in document   Page number of cited document
C = California Visual/Performing Arts Framework   I = Implied in document
IM = Int'l Baccalaureate: Middle Years Arts
N = NAEP: Arts Education Assessment Framework

5. Understands how informal and formal theatre, film, television, and electronic media productions create and communicate meaning

Level II (Grades K-4)

BD (AE,32;NE,102)
- Understands the visual, aural, oral, and kinetic elements of dramatic performances

BD (AE,32;NI,102)
- Understands how the wants and needs of characters are similar to and different from one's own wants and needs

BC (AE,32;NE,102)
- Provides rationales for personal preferences about the whole as well as the parts of dramatic performances

BD (AE,32;IMI,49;NE,102)
- Knows how alternative ideas can be used to enhance character roles, environments, and situations

BD (AE,32;CE,54;IME,50)
- Knows appropriate terminology used in analyzing dramatizations (e.g., intent, structure, effectiveness, worth)

BC (AE,31)
- Identifies people, events, time, and place in classroom dramatizations

Level III (Grades 5-8)

BD (AE,48;NE,104)
- Understands the effect of publicity, study guides, programs, and physical environments on audience response and appreciation of dramatic performances

BC (AE,48;NE,103)
- Articulates the meanings constructed from one's own and others' dramatic performances

BD (AE,48;NE,104)
- Understands the perceived effectiveness of artistic choices found in dramatic performances

BD (AE,48;IMI,52;NE,104)
- Understands the perceived effectiveness of contributions (e.g., as playwrights, actors, designers, directors) to the collaborative process of developing improvised and scripted scenes

BP (AE,47;IMI,49,52)
- Applies research from print and nonprint sources to script writing, acting, design, and directing choices

Codes (right side of page): BD = Benchmark, Declarative; BP = Benchmark, Procedural; BC = Benchmark, Contextual
1st letter of each code in parentheses   *2nd letter of code*   *Number*
A = CNAEA: National Standards for Arts Education   E = Explicitly stated in document   Page number of cited document
C = California Visual/Performing Arts Framework   I = Implied in document
IM = Int'l Baccalaureate: Middle Years Arts
N = NAEP: Arts Education Assessment Framework

401

MREL

Level IV (Grades 9-12)

- Knows how social meanings (aural, oral, and visual symbols with personal and/or social significance) communicated in informal productions, formal productions, and personal performances of different cultures and historical periods can relate to current personal, national, and international issues   BD (AE,67)

- Articulates and justifies personal aesthetic criteria for comparing, for dramatic texts and events, perceived artistic intent with the final aesthetic achievement   BC (AE,67;IMI,49;NE,106)

- Understands how the context in which a dramatic performance is set can enhance or hinder its effectiveness   BD (AE,67;CI,55;NE,106)

- Knows how varying collaborative efforts and artistic choices can affect the performance of informal and formal productions   BD (AE,67;NE,106)

- Identifies and researches cultural, historical, and symbolic clues in dramatic texts   BP (AE,66;CE,52;IMI,49)

- Understands the validity and practicality of cultural, historical, and symbolic information used in making artistic choices for informal and formal productions   BD (AE,66;IMI,50)

6.   Understands the context in which theatre, film, television, and electronic media are performed today as well as in the past   (AE,32)

Level II (Grades K-4)

- Identifies and compares similar characters and situations in stories/dramas from and about various cultures   BC (AE,32;IMI,50;NE,102)

- Understands the various settings and reasons for creating dramas and attending theatre, film, television, and electronic media productions   BD (AE,32)

- Knows ways in which theatre reflects life   BD (AE,32;NE,102)

Level III (Grades 5-8)

- Understands similarities and differences among archetypal characters (e.g., the trickster, the   BC (AE,48;CI,53;IMI,50;NE,104)

Codes (right side of page):   BD = Benchmark, Declarative; BP = Benchmark, Procedural; BC = Benchmark, Contextual
1st letter of each code in parentheses   *2nd letter of code*   *Number*
A = CNAEA: National Standards for Arts Education   E = Explicitly stated in document   Page number of cited document
C = California Visual/Performing Arts Framework   I = Implied in document
IM = Int'l Baccalaureate: Middle Years Arts
N = NAEP: Arts Education Assessment Framework

villain, the warrior, the superhero) and situations in dramas from and about various cultures and historical periods

- Understands the knowledge, skills, and discipline needed to pursue careers and avocational opportunities in theatre, film, television, and electronic media
  BD (AE,48;NE,104)

- Understands the emotional and social impact of dramatic performances in one's own life, in the community, and in other cultures
  BP (AE,48;CE,53;IMI,50;NE,104)

- Knows ways in which theatre reflects a culture
  BD (AE,48;IMI,50)

- Knows how culture affects the content and production values of dramatic performances
  BD (AE,48;IMI,50;NE,104)

- Understands how social concepts such as cooperation, communication, collaboration, consensus, self-esteem, risk taking, sympathy, and empathy apply in theatre
  BD (AE,48;NE,104)

Level IV (Grades 9-12)

- Understands how similar themes are treated in drama from various cultures and historical periods
  BD (AE,67;CI,53;IMI,50;NE,106)

- Understands ways in which theatre can reveal universal concepts
  BD (AE,67;NE,106)

- Understands similarities and differences among the lives, works, and influence of representative theatre artists in various cultures and historical periods
  BD (AE,67;IMI,50;NE,106)

- Knows cultural and historical influences on American theatre and musical theatre
  BD (AE,67;IMI,50;NE,106)

- Understands ways in which personal and cultural experiences can affect an artist's dramatic work
  BD (AE,67;IMI,50;NE,106)

Codes (right side of page):   BD = Benchmark, Declarative; BP = Benchmark, Procedural; BC = Benchmark, Contextual

1st letter of each code in parentheses	*2nd letter of code*	*Number*
A = CNAEA: National Standards for Arts Education	E = Explicitly stated in document	Page number of cited document
C = California Visual/Performing Arts Framework	I = Implied in document	
IM = Int'l Baccalaureate: Middle Years Arts		
N = NAEP: Arts Education Assessment Framework		

Visual Arts

(AE,33)

1. Understands and applies media, techniques, and processes related to the visual arts

Level II (Grades K-4)

- BD (AE,33;CI,98-99;NE,107)
Knows the differences between art materials (e.g., paint, clay, wood, videotape), techniques (e.g., overlapping, shading, varying size or color), and processes (e.g., addition and subtraction in sculpture, casting and constructing in making jewelry)

- BD (AE,33;NE,108)
Knows how different materials, techniques, and processes cause different responses from the viewer

- BD (AE,34;CE,98-99;IMI,11;NE,107,108)
Knows how different media (e.g., oil, watercolor, stone, metal), techniques, and processes are used to communicate ideas, experiences, and stories

- BP (AE,34;IMI,11;NE,107)
Uses art materials and tools in a safe and responsible manner

Level III (Grades 5-8)

- BD (AE,50;IMI,11;NE,110,111)
Understands what makes different art media, techniques, and processes effective (or ineffective) in communicating various ideas

- BD (AE,50;IAI,5;IMI,11)
Knows how the qualities and characteristics of art media, techniques, and processes can be used to enhance communication of experiences and ideas

Level IV (Grades 9-12)

- BP (AE,69;CE,98-99;IAI,5;NE,114)
Applies media, techniques, and processes with sufficient skill, confidence, and sensitivity that one's intentions are carried out in artworks

- BD (AE,69;CI,105;IMI,11;NE,113,114)
Understands how the communication of ideas relates to the media, techniques, and processes one uses

---

Codes (right side of page):   BD = Benchmark, Declarative;   BP = Benchmark, Procedural;   BC = Benchmark, Contextual
1st letter of each code in parentheses   *2nd letter of code*   *Number*
A = CNAEA: National Standards for Arts Education   E = Explicitly stated in document   Page number of cited document
C = California Visual/Performing Arts Framework   I = Implied in document
IA = Int'l Baccalaureate: Art/Design
IM = Int'l Baccalaureate: Middle Years Arts
N = NAEP: Arts Education Assessment Framework   404   MREL

(AE,34)

2. Knows how to use structures (e.g., sensory qualities, organizational principles, expressive features) and functions of art

Level II (Grades K-4)

BD (AE,34;IMI,11;NE,107)
- Knows the differences among visual characteristics (e.g., color, texture) and purposes of art (e.g., to convey ideas)

BD (AE,34;CI,96;IAI,5;IMI,11;NE,108)
- Understands how different compositional, expressive features (e.g., evoking joy, sadness, anger), and organizational principles (e.g., repetition, balance, emphasis, contrast, unity) cause different responses

BP (AE,34;IMI,22)
- Uses visual structures and functions of art to communicate ideas

Level III (Grades 5-8)

BD (AE,50;CI,95-96;IAI,5;IMI,11;NE,110)
- Knows some of the effects of various visual structures (e.g., design elements such as line, color, shape; principles such as repetition, rhythm, balance) and functions of art

BD (AE,50;IAI,5;IMI,16,22;NE,110)
- Understands what makes various organizational structures effective (or ineffective) in the communication of ideas

BD (AE,50;CI,96;IAI,5;IMI,22)
- Knows how the qualities of structures and functions of art are used to improve communication of one's ideas

Level IV (Grades 9-12)

BD (AE,70;NE,113)
- Understands how the characteristics and structures of art are used to accomplish commercial, personal, communal, or other artistic intentions

BD (AE,70;IMI,16)
- Understands the effectiveness of various artworks in terms of organizational structures and functions

BD (AE,70;IAI,5;IMI,11;NE,113)
- Knows how organizational principles and functions can be used to solve specific visual arts problems

---

Codes (right side of page):   BD = Benchmark, Declarative; BP = Benchmark, Procedural; BC = Benchmark, Contextual
1st letter of each code in parentheses   *2nd letter of code*   *Number*
A = CNAEA: National Standards for Arts Education   E = Explicitly stated in document   Page number of cited document
C = California Visual/Performing Arts Framework   I = Implied in document
IA = Int'l Baccalaureate: Art/Design
IM = Int'l Baccalaureate: Middle Years Arts
N = NAEP: Arts Education Assessment Framework   405   MREL

(AE,34)

3. Knows a range of subject matter, symbols, and potential ideas in the visual arts

Level II (Grades K-4)

- BP (AE,34;CI,98;IMI,22;NE,107,108)
  Selects prospective ideas (e.g., formulated thoughts, opinions, concepts) for works of art

- BD (AE,34;IMI,22;NE,107)
  Knows how subject matter, symbols, and ideas are used to communicate meaning

Level III (Grades 5-8)

- BD (AE,50;IMI,20,22;NE,111)
  Knows how visual, spatial, and temporal concepts integrate with content to communicate intended meaning in one's artworks

- BD (AE,50;CI,105;IAI,5;NE,111)
  Knows different subjects, themes, and symbols (through context, value, and aesthetics) which convey intended meaning in artworks

Level IV (Grades 9-12)

- BD (AE,70;CI,103;IAI,5;IMI,18)
  Understands how visual, spatial, temporal, and functional values of artworks are tempered by culture and history

- BP (AE,70)
  Applies various subjects, symbols, and ideas in one's artworks

(AE,34)

4. Understands the visual arts in relation to history and cultures

Level II (Grades K-4)

- BD (AE,34;IAI,5;IMI,18;NE,107)
  Knows that the visual arts have both a history and a specific relationship to various cultures

- BC (AE,34;CE,103,103;IAI,5;IMI,18;NE,108)
  Identifies specific works of art as belonging to particular cultures, times, and places

- BD (AE,34;IAI,5;IMI,18;NE,107)
  Knows how history, culture, and the visual arts can influence each other

---

Codes (right side of page):   BD = Benchmark, Declarative;   BP = Benchmark, Procedural;   BC = Benchmark, Contextual
1st letter of each code in parentheses   *2nd letter of code*   *Number*
A = CNAEA: National Standards for Arts Education   E = Explicitly stated in document   Page number of cited document
C = California Visual/Performing Arts Framework   I = Implied in document
IA = Int'l Baccalaureate: Art/Design
IM = Int'l Baccalaureate: Middle Years Arts
N = NAEP: Arts Education Assessment Framework   406   McREL

Level III (Grades 5-8)

BD (AE,50;CI,106;IAI,5;IMI,18;NE,111,112)
- Understands similarities and differences among the characteristics of artworks from various eras and cultures (e.g., materials; visual, spatial, and temporal structures)

BD (AE,50;IAI,5;IMI,18;NE,111,112)
- Understands the historical and cultural contexts of a variety of art objects

BD (AE,50;CI,102;IMI,18;NE,109,110,112)
- Understands how factors of time and place (e.g., climate, resources, ideas, technology) influence visual, spatial, or temporal characteristics that give meaning or function to a work of art

Level IV (Grades 9-12)

BD (AE,71;IAI,5;IMI,18;NE,115)
- Knows a variety of historical and cultural contexts regarding characteristics and purposes of works of art

BD (AE,71;CI,101;IAI,5;IMI,18;NE,115)
- Knows the function and meaning of specific art objects within varied cultures, times, and places

BD (AE,71;IAI,5;IMI,18;NE,115)
- Understands relationships among works of art in terms of history, aesthetics, and culture

(AE,34)
5. Understands the characteristics and merits of one's own artwork and the artwork of others

Level II (Grades K-4)

BD (AE,34;CI,102;NE,108,109)
- Knows various purposes for creating works of visual art

BD (AE,34;NE,108,109)
- Knows how people's experiences (e.g., cultural background, human needs) can influence the development of specific artworks

BD (AE,34)
- Understands that specific artworks can elicit different responses

---

Codes (right side of page):   BD = Benchmark, Declarative; BP = Benchmark, Procedural; BC = Benchmark, Contextual
1st letter of each code in parentheses   *2nd letter of code*   *Number*
A = CNAEA: National Standards for Arts Education   E = Explicitly stated in document   Page number of cited document
C = California Visual/Performing Arts Framework   I = Implied in document
IA = Int'l Baccalaureate: Art/Design
IM = Int'l Baccalaureate: Middle Years Arts
N = NAEP: Arts Education Assessment Framework   407   MREL

Level III (Grades 5-8)

- Distinguishes among multiple purposes for creating works of art
  BC (AE,51;CI,102;NE,111)

- Understands possible contemporary and historic meanings in specific artworks
  BD (AE,51;CI,101;IAI,5;IMI,18;NE,111,112)

- Understands how one's own artworks, as well as artworks from various eras and cultures, may elicit a variety of responses
  BD (AE,51;IMI,18;NE,112)

Level IV (Grades 9-12)

- Identifies intentions of those creating artworks
  BC (AE,71;CI,102;NE,114,116)

- Understands some of the implications of intention and purpose in particular works of art
  BD (AE,71;NE,114,116)

- Knows how specific works are created and relate to historical and cultural contexts
  BD (AE,71;CI,103;IAI,5;IMI,18;NE,114)

- Understands how various interpretations can be used to understand and evaluate works of visual art
  BD (AE,71;IAI,5;NE,114,116)

Codes (right side of page): BD = Benchmark, Declarative; BP = Benchmark, Procedural; BC = Benchmark, Contextual

1st letter of each code in parentheses   *2nd letter of code*   *Number*

A = CNAEA: National Standards for Arts Education   E = Explicitly stated in document   Page number of cited document

C = California Visual/Performing Arts Framework   I = Implied in document

IA = Int'l Baccalaureate: Art/Design

IM = Int'l Baccalaureate: Middle Years Arts

N = NAEP: Arts Education Assessment Framework   408   M?REL

CIVICS

12. Civics

The following process was used to identify standards and benchmarks for civics:

Identification of Significant Reports
Four reports and a set of teacher's guides were selected for identifying standards in civics: *National Standards for Civics and Government* (1994) from the Center for Civic Education, *Civitas: A Framework for Civic Education* (Quigley & Bahmmeller, 1991), *Civics Framework for the 1998 National Assessment of Educational Progress* (NAEP, n.d.) and *National Standards for Business Education: What America's Students Should Know and be Able to do in Business* (National Business Education Association, 1995). The teacher's guides were comprised of a series of civics units authored and published by Law in a Free Society.

Selection of the Reference Document
The Center for Civic Education's *National Standards for Civics and Government* (1994) was selected as the reference report. The report was developed over two years, using a process that enlisted the participation of more than a thousand teachers and other educators as well as scholars, parents, educators, and representatives of public and private organizations.

Identification of Standards and Benchmarks
For the most part, the *Standards for Civics and Government* document fits well with our model for the identification of standards. Essential ideas in civics are organized under some 70-plus content standards. Each content standard has associated with it a set of key concepts that students should know in order to meet the standard.

In three areas, however, the *Civics and Government* document is not directly compatible with our approach. First, the content standards are often stated and elaborated upon through performance descriptions, that is, tasks that describe a specific demonstration of achievement. These tasks are prefaced with the statement, "To achieve this standard, students should be able to...." What follows are activities that may require the student to identify, describe, or explain an idea, or to take, defend, or evaluate a particular position. The activities also provide important information about the content standard. Since our approach seeks to provide content knowledge that is either declarative, procedural, or contextual (see Section 3), we translated such tasks to benchmark statements of knowledge and skills specifically related to content in civics.

The second area in which the approach used in *National Standards for Civics and Government* differs from our model has to do with the articulation of standards across K–12. While standards appear at levels K–4, 6–8, and 9–12, and many similar ideas are organized beneath each level, there is no articulation across K–12 by standard level. While we believe content information from the reference document should be minimally revised in the process of identifying benchmarks, we consider the standards under which they are found to be more arbitrary in composition (see Section 3). Thus, in order to accomplish the articulation of standards across grade levels, we revised and combined a number of standards and reorganized the benchmarks beneath them.

Finally, our model and the reference document differ concerning the range and number of benchmark levels. The *Standards* document specifies three benchmark levels: K–4, 5–8, and 9–12. Our model recommends four, corresponding to primary, upper elementary, middle, and high school. In this case, then, completion of our benchmark levels depended upon an analysis of supplementary materials that could provide us with further benchmark information, especially at the primary grades (discussed below).

Integration of Information from Other Documents

Supplementary material was consulted both to assist us in confirming our interpretation of the benchmark content deduced from civics activities found in the reference work, and to provide the reader with a pointer to additional materials that are keyed to the benchmarks. The primary work for this citation was Center for Civic Education's source book, *Civitas*. In addition, the *Civics Framework* from NAEP was also cited. Those readers seeking to reduce the amount of content required for Civics instruction might consult the "citation log" associated with each benchmark in order to select those items deemed important both by the Center for Civic Education and the National Assessment for Educational Progress. Civics related content in the *National Standards for Business Education* was also cited. These standards address topics related to the impact of laws and government on business, the consumer, and the citizen.

Additionally, supporting material was used to provide the means for identifying knowledge and skills at the primary level. As noted above, the reference document does not isolate the knowledge and skills that might be especially suitable for the early (K–2) grades. In order to remedy this, we consulted a series of teacher guides available from Law and a Free Society. These books, which focus on the concepts of authority, privacy, justice, and responsibility, allowed us to distinguish information from the standards K–4 level that would be suitable for the primary grades.

Summary of Standards for Civics

What is Government and What Should it Do?

1. Understands ideas about civic life, politics, and government
2. Understands the essential characteristics of limited and unlimited governments
3. Understands the sources, purposes, and functions of law and the importance of the rule of law for the protection of individual rights and the common good
4. Understands the concept of a constitution, the various purposes that constitutions serve, and the conditions that contribute to the establishment and maintenance of constitutional government
5. Understands the major characteristics of systems of shared powers and of parliamentary systems
6. Understands the advantages and disadvantages of federal, confederal, and unitary systems of government
7. Understands alternative forms of representation and how they serve the purposes of constitutional government

What are the Basic Values and Principles of American Democracy?

8. Understands the central ideas of American constitutional government and how this form of government has shaped the character of American society
9. Understands the importance of Americans sharing and supporting certain values, beliefs, and principles of American constitutional democracy
10. Understands the roles of voluntarism and organized groups in American social and political life
11. Understands the role of diversity in American life and the importance of shared values, political beliefs, and civic beliefs in an increasingly diverse American society
12. Understands the relationships among liberalism, republicanism, and American constitutional democracy
13. Understands the character of American political and social conflict and factors that tend to prevent or lower its intensity
14. Understands issues concerning the disparities between ideals and reality in American political and social life

411

How Does the Government Established by the Constitution Embody the Purposes, Values, and Principles of American Democracy?

15. Understands how the United States Constitution grants and distributes power and responsibilities to national and state government and how it seeks to prevent the abuse of power

16. Understands the major responsibilities of the national government for domestic and foreign policy, and understands how government is financed through taxation

17. Understands issues concerning the relationship between state and local governments and the national government and issues pertaining to representation at all three levels of government

18. Understands the role and importance of law in the American constitutional system and issues regarding the judicial protection of individual rights

19. Understands what is meant by "the public agenda," how it is set, and how it is influenced by public opinion and the media

20. Understands the roles of political parties, campaigns, elections, and associations and groups in American politics

21. Understands the formation and implementation of public policy

What is the Relationship of the United States to Other Nations and to World Affairs?

22. Understands how the world is organized politically into nation-states, how nation-states interact with one another, and issues surrounding U.S. foreign policy

23. Understands the impact of significant political and nonpolitical developments on the United States and other nations

What are the Roles of the Citizen in American Democracy?

24. Understands the meaning of citizenship in the United States, and knows the requirements for citizenship and naturalization

25. Understands issues regarding personal, political, and economic rights

26. Understands issues regarding the proper scope and limits of rights and the relationships among personal, political, and economic rights

27. Understands how certain character traits enhance citizens' ability to fulfill personal and civic responsibilities

28. Understands how participation in civic and political life can help citizens attain individual and public goals

29. Understands the importance of political leadership, public service, and a knowledgeable citizenry in American constitutional democracy

1. Understands ideas about civic life, politics, and government

Level I (Grades K-2)

BD (A1E,10-11;NI,42)
- Knows examples of situations in which individuals are acting on their own (e.g., two friends decide to do something) and situations in which individuals' actions are directed by others (e.g., parents tell their children to do something)

BD (A1E,14-15;NI,42;QI,95)
- Knows examples of authority (e.g., a teacher tells a group of students to do something) and power without authority (e.g., an older, larger student tells a group of younger students to do something)

BD (A1E,22;NI,42)
- Knows some of the problems that might result from lack of effective authority (e.g., inability to settle disputes or accomplish necessary tasks)

Level II (Grades 3-5)

BD (CE,15;BI,23;NE,42;QI,331)
- Knows various people and groups who make, apply, and enforce rules and laws for others (e.g., adult family members, teachers, city councils, governors, tribal governments, national governments) and who manage disputes about rules and laws (e.g., courts at all levels)

BD (CE,16;NE,42;NI,43;QE,95)
- Knows the difference between power (e.g., the capacity to direct or control something or someone) and authority (e.g., power that people have the right to use because of custom, law, or the consent of the governed)

BD (CE,16;NI,43;QI,102)
- Knows ways in which authority is used (e.g., parents have authority to direct and control their children, governors of states have the authority to carry out and enforce laws) and ways in which power can be used without authority (e.g., a bully forcing smaller children to give up their lunch money, a robber holding up a bank)

BD (CE,17;NI,42,43)
- Knows possible consequences of the absence of government and rules and laws (e.g., the strong may take advantage of the weak, people may become disorderly or violent, people may feel insecure or be unable to plan for the future)

BD (CE,17;NE,43;QE,14-15)
- Knows the basic purposes of government in the United States (e.g., to protect the rights of individuals, to promote the common good)

Codes (right side of page):   BD = Benchmark, Declarative; BP = Benchmark, Procedural; BC = Benchmark, Contextual

1st letter of each code in parentheses	*2nd letter of code*	*Number*
C = CCE: National Standards for Civics	E = Explicitly stated in document	Page number of cited document
A1 = LFS: Authority, I (elementary)	I = Implied in document	*or, for duplicates,*
B = National Standards for Business Education		Standard number & level of duplicate
J1 = LFS: Justice, I (elementary)		
N = NAEP: Civics Consensus Project	R1 = LFS: Responsibility, I (elementary)	
P1, P2 = LFS: Privacy, I & II (elementary)	D = Duplicated in another standard	
Q = Quigley: Civitas		

- Knows the major things governments do in one's school, community, state, and nation (e.g., make, carry out, and enforce laws; manage conflicts; provide national security)

  BD (CE,18;NE,42;NI,43)

- Knows how government makes it possible for people to work together to accomplish goals they could not achieve individually

  BD (CE,18;NE,43)

Level III (Grades 6-8)

- Distinguishes between private life and civic life (e.g., private life concerns the personal life of the individual such as being with family and friends or practicing one's religious beliefs, civic life concerns taking part in government such as helping to find solutions to problems or helping to make rules and laws)

  BC (CE,45;NI,45;QE,15-17)

- Understands how politics enables people with differing ideas to reach binding agreements (e.g., presenting information and evidence, stating arguments, negotiating, compromising, voting)

  BD (CE,45;NE,44)

- Knows institutions that have the authority to direct or control the behavior of members of a society (e.g., a school board, state legislature, courts, Congress)

  BD (CE,45;BI,23;NE,44)

- Understands major ideas about why government is necessary (e.g., people's lives, liberty, and property would be insecure without government; individuals by themselves cannot do many of the things they can do collectively such as create a highway system, provide armed forces for the security of the nation, or make and enforce laws)

  BD (CE,46;NI,44)

- Understands competing ideas about the purposes government should serve (e.g., whether government should protect individual rights, promote the common good, provide economic security, mold the character of citizens, promote a particular religion)

  BD (CE,46;NE,44;NI,46)

Level IV (Grades 9-12)

- Understands how politics enables a group of people with varying opinions and/or interests to reach collective decisions, influence decisions, and accomplish goals that they could not reach as individuals (e.g., managing the distribution of resources, allocating benefits and

  BD (CE,90)

Codes (right side of page):	BD = Benchmark, Declarative; BP = Benchmark, Procedural; BC = Benchmark, Contextual	
1st letter of each code in parentheses	*2nd letter of code*	*Number*
C = CCE: National Standards for Civics	E = Explicitly stated in document	Page number of cited document
A1 = LFS: Authority, I (elementary)	I = Implied in document	*or, for duplicates,*
B = National Standards for Business Education		Standard number & level of duplicate
J1 = LFS: Justice, I (elementary)		
N = NAEP: Civics Consensus Project	R1 = LFS: Responsibility, I (elementary)	
P1, P2 = LFS: Privacy, I & II (elementary)	D = Duplicated in another standard	
Q = Quigley: Civitas		

burdens, managing conflicts)

- Knows formal institutions that have the authority to make and implement binding decisions (e.g., tribal councils, courts, monarchies, democratic legislatures)
  BD (CE,90;BI,23)

- Understands the nature of political authority (e.g., characteristics such as legitimacy, stability, limitations)
  BD (CE,90;QE,95)

- Understands the sources of political authority (e.g., consent of the governed, birth, knowledge) and its functions (e.g., create and enforce laws)
  BD (CE,90;QE,95)

- Understands why politics is found wherever people gather as a group (e.g., it enables groups to reach collective, binding decisions that can be enforced)
  BD (CE,90)

- Understands major arguments for the necessity of politics and government (e.g., people cannot fulfill their potential without politics and government, people would be insecure or endangered without government, people working collectively can accomplish goals and solve problems they could not achieve alone)
  BD (CE,90)

- Understands some of the major competing ideas about the purposes of politics and government (e.g., achieving a religious vision, glorifying the state, enhancing economic prosperity, providing for a nation's security), and knows examples of past and present governments that serve these purposes
  BD (CE,90-91)

- Understands how the purposes served by a government affect relationships between the individual and government and between government and society as a whole (e.g., the purpose of promoting a religious vision of what society should be like may require a government to restrict individual thought and actions, and place strict controls on the whole of the society)
  BD (CE,91)

Codes (right side of page):   BD = Benchmark, Declarative; BP = Benchmark, Procedural; BC = Benchmark, Contextual

1st letter of each code in parentheses	*2nd letter of code*	*Number*
C = CCE: National Standards for Civics	E = Explicitly stated in document	Page number of cited document
A1 = LFS: Authority, I (elementary)	I = Implied in document	*or, for duplicates,*
B = National Standards for Business Education		Standard number & level of duplicate
J1 = LFS: Justice, I (elementary)		
N = NAEP: Civics Consensus Project	R1 = LFS: Responsibility, I (elementary)	
P1, P2 = LFS: Privacy, I & II (elementary)	D = Duplicated in another standard	
Q = Quigley: Civitas		

McREL

(CE,47)

2. Understands the essential characteristics of limited and unlimited governments

Level I (Grades K-2)

BD (A1,48-50;NI, 44;QE,332)
- Knows that people in positions of authority have limits on their authority (e.g., a crossing guard cannot act as an umpire at a baseball game)

Level II (Grades 3-5)

BD (CE,20;NI,44;QI,330-332)
- Knows the basic conditions necessary to support a limited government (e.g., everyone, including all the people in positions of authority, must obey the laws)

BD (CE,20;NE,44;QI,330-332)
- Knows how laws can limit the power of people in government (e.g., laws that prohibit a teacher from releasing personal information about students to people other than the students' parents or guardians; laws that prohibit governments from discriminating against people because of their religious or political beliefs)

BD (CE,20;BE,105;NE,44;QE,170-171)
- Knows the general characteristics of unlimited government (e.g., a dictatorship in which there are no effective controls over the powers of its rulers; the rulers cannot be easily removed from office by peaceful, legal means)

BD (CE,21;NE,42;QE,170)
- Understands how limited government helps to protect personal rights (e.g., to choose friends, to practice the religion of one's choice), political rights (e.g., to express opinions, to vote), and economic rights (e.g., to own property, to choose the kind of work one pleases)

Level III (Grades 6-8)

BD (CE,47;NE,45;QE,169)
- Knows some of the restraints placed on a limited government's power (e.g., the legal limits placed on the political power of constitutional government)

BD (CE,47;BE,105;NE,45;QE,170-171)
- Understands the basic structure of authoritarian systems and totalitarian systems, and how these systems are considered unlimited governments

---

Codes (right side of page):	BD = Benchmark, Declarative; BP = Benchmark, Procedural; BC = Benchmark, Contextual
1st letter of each code in parentheses	*2nd letter of code* — *Number*
C = CCE: National Standards for Civics	E = Explicitly stated in document — Page number of cited document
A1 = LFS: Authority, I (elementary)	I = Implied in document — *or, for duplicates,*
B = National Standards for Business Education	Standard number & level of duplicate
J1 = LFS: Justice, I (elementary)	
N = NAEP: Civics Consensus Project	R1 = LFS: Responsibility, I (elementary)
P1, P2 = LFS: Privacy, I & II (elementary)	D = Duplicated in another standard
Q = Quigley: Civitas	

416

McREL

Level IV (Grades 9-12)

- Understands what "civil society" is and how it provides opportunities for individuals to associate for social, cultural, religious, economic, and political purposes (e.g., family, friendships, membership in organizations, participation in unions and business enterprises) BD (CE,93;NI,49)

- Understands how civil society allows for individuals or groups to influence government in ways other than voting and elections BD (CE,93;NI,47,49)

- Understands how the individual, social, and economic relationships that make up civil society have been used to maintain limited government BD (CE,93;NE,47)

- Understands how relationships between government and civil society in constitutional democracies differ from those in authoritarian and totalitarian regimes BD (CE,93;NI,47;QI,169-171)

- Knows essential political freedoms (e.g., freedom of religion, speech) and economic freedoms (e.g., freedom to enter into contracts, to choose one's own employment), and understands competing ideas about the relationships between the two (e.g., that political freedom is more important than economic freedom, that political and economic freedom are inseparable) BD (CE,93)

- Understands how political and economic freedoms serve to limit governmental power BD (CE,94)

3. Understands the sources, purposes, and functions of law, and the importance of the rule of law for the protection of individual rights and the common good
(CE,48,92)

Level I (Grades K-2)

- Knows that promoting justice is one of the fundamental purposes of law in American society BD (J1E,1;BI,22;NI,42;QE,374-375)

- Knows that justice means essentially the same thing as fairness BD (J1E,7;BI,22;NI,42;QE,374-375)

- Knows that distributive justice refers to problems of fairness arising over "who gets what" based on the criteria of need, ability, and desert; and knows examples of situations that involve distributive justice (e.g., how much food should different members of a family receive at dinner time) BD (J1E,5,13-16;NI,42;QE,374-375)

Codes (right side of page):   BD = Benchmark, Declarative; BP = Benchmark, Procedural; BC = Benchmark, Contextual

1st letter of each code in parentheses	*2nd letter of code*	*Number*
C = CCE: National Standards for Civics	E = Explicitly stated in document	Page number of cited document
A1 = LFS: Authority, I (elementary)	I = Implied in document	*or, for duplicates,*
B = National Standards for Business Education		Standard number & level of duplicate
J1 = LFS: Justice, I (elementary)		
N = NAEP: Civics Consensus Project	R1 = LFS: Responsibility, I (elementary)	
P1, P2 = LFS: Privacy, I & II (elementary)	D = Duplicated in another standard	
Q = Quigley: Civitas		

BD (J1E,37,41-43;NI,42;QE,374-375)
- Knows that corrective justice deals with problems arising over how to make things right when a wrong or injury has occurred, and knows examples of situations involving corrective justice (e.g., how to deal justly with a child who has stolen something from a classmate)

BD (J1E,55,63;NI,42;QE,374-375)
- Knows that procedural justice refers to problems arising over fair ways to gather information and make just decisions, and knows examples of situations involving procedural justice (e.g., how should a class president go about deciding which games the class will play)

BD (A1E,33-34;NI,43)
- Knows that a good rule or law solves a specific problem, is fair, and "does not go too far"

Level II (Grades 3-5)

BD (CE,18;BI,22;NE,42;QE,331-332)
- Knows common ways in which rules and laws can be used (e.g., to describe how people should behave; to provide order, predictability, and security; to protect rights; to provide benefits; to assign burdens or responsibilities; to limit the power of people in authority)

BD (CE,18;NI,43)
- Knows the characteristics of an effective rule or law (e.g., well designed to achieve its purposes, understandable, possible to follow, fair, designed to protect individual rights and promote the common good)

Level III (Grades 6-8)

BD (CE,48;NI,46;QI,15)
- Understands the difference between the "rule of law" and the "rule of men" (e.g., government decisions and actions made according to established laws vs. arbitrary action or decree)

BD (CE,48;BI,22;NI,46;QI,15)
- Understands how and why the rule of law can be used to restrict the actions of private citizens and government officials

BD (CE,48;NI,46)
- Understands the possible consequences of the absence of a rule of law (e.g., anarchy, arbitrary and capricious rule, absence of predictability, disregard for established and fair procedures)

Codes (right side of page):	BD = Benchmark, Declarative; BP = Benchmark, Procedural; BC = Benchmark, Contextual
1st letter of each code in parentheses	*2nd letter of code* *Number*
C = CCE: National Standards for Civics	E = Explicitly stated in document Page number of cited document
A1 = LFS: Authority, I (elementary)	I = Implied in document *or, for duplicates,*
B = National Standards for Business Education	Standard number & level of duplicate
J1 = LFS: Justice, I (elementary)	
N = NAEP: Civics Consensus Project	R1 = LFS: Responsibility, I (elementary)
P1, P2 = LFS: Privacy, I & II (elementary)	D = Duplicated in another standard
Q = Quigley: Civitas	

Level IV (Grades 9-12)

BD (CE,92;BE,22;NI,48;QE,335-339)
- Knows alternative ideas about the sources of law (e.g., custom, Supreme Being, sovereigns, legislatures) and different varieties of law (e.g., divine law, natural law, common law, statute law, international law)

BD (CE,92;NI,48;QE,330-331)
- Knows alternative ideas about the purposes and functions of law (e.g., regulating relationships among people and between people and their government; providing order, predictability, security, and established procedures for the management of conflict; regulating social and economic relationships in civil society)

(CE,95)
4. Understands the concept of a constitution, the various purposes that constitutions serve, and the conditions that contribute to the establishment and maintenance of constitutional government

Level I (Grades K-2)

BD (CE,49)
- Not appropriate for this level

Level II (Grades 3-5)

BD (CE,49)
- Not appropriate for this level

Level III (Grades 6-8)

BD (CE,49;NI,44;QI,169)
- Knows various uses of the term "constitution" (e.g., as a description of a form of government; as a document; as a higher law limiting the powers of government)

BD (CE,49;QE,169)
- Understands how a government with a constitution but without effective ways to enforce it may still have unlimited power (e.g., former Soviet Union, Nazi Germany, Iraq under Saddam Hussein)

BD (CE,49;QE,170)
- Knows past and present examples of countries with constitutions that actually did limit the power of government (e.g., United States, United Kingdom, Germany, Japan, Botswana, Chile)

Codes (right side of page):   BD = Benchmark, Declarative; BP = Benchmark, Procedural; BC = Benchmark, Contextual
1st letter of each code in parentheses   *2nd letter of code*   *Number*
C = CCE: National Standards for Civics   E = Explicitly stated in document   Page number of cited document
A1 = LFS: Authority, I (elementary)   I = Implied in document   *or, for duplicates,*
B = National Standards for Business Education   Standard number & level of duplicate
J1 = LFS: Justice, I (elementary)
N = NAEP: Civics Consensus Project   R1 = LFS: Responsibility, I (elementary)
P1, P2 = LFS: Privacy, I & II (elementary)   D = Duplicated in another standard
Q = Quigley: Civitas

419   MCREL

- Knows some basic uses of constitutions (e.g., to set forth the purposes of government, to describe the way a government is organized and how power is allocated, to define the relationship between a people and their government)
  BD (CE,49;BE,22;NE,44;QE,169)

- Knows how constitutions have been used to promote the interests of a particular group, class, religion, or political party (e.g., the People's Republic of China, Kenya, Mexico)
  BD (CE,49;NI,44)

- Knows how constitutions have been used to protect individual rights and promote the common good (e.g., First Amendment, Nineteenth Amendment in the United States Constitution)
  BD (CE,49;NI,44;QE,169)

- Knows the type of citizenry needed to establish and maintain constitutional government (e.g., citizens should be educated and enjoy a reasonable standard of living, understand and support the constitution and its values and principles, willingly assume the responsibilities of citizenship, insist that government officials respect limitations the constitution places on their authority)
  BD (CE,50;NI,46,47)

- Knows the type of public servants needed to help establish and maintain constitutional government (e.g., persons serving in government should understand and support the constitution and its values and principles, respect limitations the constitution places on their authority)
  BD (CE,50;NI,46)

Level IV (Grades 9-12)

- Distinguishes between governments with a constitution and constitutional (limited) government
  BD (CE,94;QI,169)

- Understands how constitutions set forth the structure of government, give the government power, and establish the relationship between the people and their government
  BD (CE,95;BE,22;NI,48;QE,169)

- Understands how constitutions may limit government's power in order to protect individual rights and promote the common good
  BD (CE,95;QE,169)

- Understands how constitutions, in the past as well as in the present, have been disregarded or used to promote the interests of a particular group, class, faction, or a government (e.g.,
  BD (CE,95)

Codes (right side of page):	BD = Benchmark, Declarative; BP = Benchmark, Procedural; BC = Benchmark, Contextual

1st letter of each code in parentheses — *2nd letter of code* — *Number*

C = CCE: National Standards for Civics — E = Explicitly stated in document — Page number of cited document

A1 = LFS: Authority, I (elementary) — I = Implied in document — *or, for duplicates,*

B = National Standards for Business Education — Standard number & level of duplicate

J1 = LFS: Justice, I (elementary)

N = NAEP: Civics Consensus Project — R1 = LFS: Responsibility, I (elementary)

P1, P2 = LFS: Privacy, I & II (elementary) — D = Duplicated in another standard

Q = Quigley: Civitas

slavery, exclusion of women from the body politic, prohibition of competing political parties)

- Understands how constitutions can be vehicles for change and for resolving social issues (e.g., use of the Fourteenth Amendment to the United States Constitution in the civil rights movement of the 1950s and 1960s; establishment of the Japanese Constitution after World War II, which provided women the right to vote)

  BD (CE,95;NE,48)

- Understands how constitutions may be used to preserve core values and principles of a political system or society (e.g., prohibition of religious tests for public office, protection of private property by the United States Constitution)

  BD (CE,95;NE,48;QI,169)

- Knows the social, economic, and political conditions that foster constitutional government

  BD (CE,95;QI,130-131)

- Understands reasons why some nations have been successful in establishing constitutional government (e.g., post-World War II Germany, Japan) whereas others have not (e.g., Nigeria, Kenya, Argentina under Peron)

  BD (CE,95)

- Knows responsibilities individual citizens and people serving in government should assume to insure the preservation and improvement of constitutional government

  BD (CE,95;NI,48;QI,13)

5. Understands the major characteristics of systems of shared powers and of parliamentary systems

(CE,97)

Level I (Grades K-2)

- Not appropriate for this level

  BD (CE,51)

Level II (Grades 3-5)

- Not appropriate for this level

  BD (CE,51)

MCREL

Level III (Grades 6-8)

- BD (CE,51;BI,23;NE,45;NI,44)

  Understands the primary responsibilities of each branch of government in a system of shared powers (e.g., legislative, executive, judicial) and ways in which each branch shares the powers and functions of the other branches

- BD (CE,51;BI,105;NE,44;NI,45;QI,170)

  Understands characteristics of systems of shared powers (e.g., in the United States the president and members of the president's Cabinet cannot be members of Congress)

- BD (CE,51;BI,105;NE,44;NI,46;QI,170)

  Understands characteristics of parliamentary systems (e.g., in the United Kingdom a legislature called Parliament assumes authority, the political party or parties that can form a majority in Parliament select the prime minister, and the prime minister selects cabinet members; the prime minister and members of the cabinet must all be members of Parliament)

- BD (CE,51;NE,44;QI,170)

  Understands that in parliamentary systems the prime minster and cabinet direct the administration of the government, but the prime minister and cabinet may be replaced by Parliament if a majority votes "no confidence" in the government

Level IV (Grades 9-12)

- BD (CE,97;BI,105;NE,49;QE,15)

  Understands the major characteristics of systems of shared powers (e.g., in the United States and Brazil the executive, legislative, and judicial branches each have primary responsibility for certain functions and share some of the powers and functions of the other branches)

- BD (CE,97;BI,105;NE,49;QI,170)

  Understands the major characteristics of parliamentary systems (e.g., in the United Kingdom and Israel authority is held by Parliament and the party or parties that form the majority select the prime minister)

- BD (CE,97;NE,49;QI,169-170)

  Understands the relative advantages and disadvantages of the various ways power is distributed, shared, and limited in systems of shared powers and parliamentary systems (e.g., in terms of effectiveness, prevention of the abuse of power, responsiveness to popular will, stability, ability to serve the purposes of constitutional government)

Codes (right side of page):   BD = Benchmark, Declarative; BP = Benchmark, Procedural; BC = Benchmark, Contextual
1st letter of each code in parentheses   *2nd letter of code*   *Number*
C = CCE: National Standards for Civics   E = Explicitly stated in document   Page number of cited document
A1 = LFS: Authority, I (elementary)   I = Implied in document   *or, for duplicates,*
B = National Standards for Business Education   Standard number & level of duplicate
J1 = LFS: Justice, I (elementary)
N = NAEP: Civics Consensus Project   R1 = LFS: Responsibility, I (elementary)
P1, P2 = LFS: Privacy, I & II (elementary)   D = Duplicated in another standard
Q = Quigley: Civitas

(CE,97)

6. Understands the advantages and disadvantages of federal, confederal, and unitary systems of government

Level I (Grades K-2)

BD (CE,52)

- Not appropriate for this level

Level II (Grades 3-5)

BD (CE,52)

- Not appropriate for this level

Level III (Grades 6-8)

BD (CE,52;BI,105;NE,44;NI,46)

- Knows the basic characteristics of a confederal system of government (e.g., sovereign states delegate powers to a national government for specific purposes), and knows examples of this system of government (e.g., the United States under the Articles of Confederation and the Confederate States of America)

BD (CE,52;BI,105;NE,44;QE,170)

- Knows the basic characteristics of a federal system of government (e.g., power is divided and shared between national and state governments), and knows examples of this system of government (e.g., the government of the United States)

BD (CE,52;BI,105;NE,44;NI,46;QE,170)

- Knows the basic characteristics of a unitary system of government (e.g., power is concentrated in a central government; state and local governments can exercise only those powers given to them by the central government), and knows examples of this system of government (e.g., state governments of the United States)

Level IV (Grades 9-12)

BD (CE,98;BI,105;NI,49;QI,170)

- Understands how power is distributed, shared, and limited in confederal, federal, and unitary systems of government (e.g., in terms of effectiveness, prevention of the abuse of power, responsiveness to popular will, stability)

BD (CE,98;BI,105;NE,49)

- Knows the advantages and disadvantages of confederal, federal, and unitary systems in fulfilling the purposes of constitutional government

---

Codes (right side of page):	BD = Benchmark, Declarative; BP = Benchmark, Procedural; BC = Benchmark, Contextual	
1st letter of each code in parentheses	*2nd letter of code*	*Number*
C = CCE: National Standards for Civics	E = Explicitly stated in document	Page number of cited document
A1 = LFS: Authority, I (elementary)	I = Implied in document	*or, for duplicates,*
B = National Standards for Business Education		Standard number & level of duplicate
J1 = LFS: Justice, I (elementary)		
N = NAEP: Civics Consensus Project	R1 = LFS: Responsibility, I (elementary)	
P1, P2 = LFS: Privacy, I & II (elementary)	D = Duplicated in another standard	
Q = Quigley: Civitas		

McREL

(CE,98)

7. Understands alternative forms of representation and how they serve the purposes of constitutional government

Level I (Grades K-2)

BD (CE,98)

- Not appropriate for this level

Level II (Grades 3-5)

BD (CE,98)

- Not appropriate for this level

Level III (Grades 6-8)

BD (CE,98)

- Not appropriate for this level

Level IV (Grades 9-12)

BD (CE,98;NI,49)

- Understands the major arguments for and against representative government as distinguished from direct popular rule

BD (CE,98;NI,49;QI,422-423)

- Knows common bases upon which representation is or has been established (e.g., geographic areas; citizenship; social class or caste; age, sex, or property; religion, race, and ethnicity)

BD (CE,98;NI,49;QI,488)

- Understands differing bases of electoral systems (e.g., winner-take-all systems, proportional systems)

BD (CE,98;NI,49;QI,422-423)

- Understands differing theories of representation (e.g., obligation of a representative to promote the interests of a particular constituency vs. obligation to promote the interests of the society as a whole)

Codes (right side of page):   BD = Benchmark, Declarative; BP = Benchmark, Procedural; BC = Benchmark, Contextual
1st letter of each code in parentheses   *2nd letter of code*   *Number*
C = CCE: National Standards for Civics   E = Explicitly stated in document   Page number of cited document
A1 = LFS: Authority, I (elementary)   I = Implied in document   *or, for duplicates,*
B = National Standards for Business Education   Standard number & level of duplicate
J1 = LFS: Justice, I (elementary)
N = NAEP: Civics Consensus Project   R1 = LFS: Responsibility, I (elementary)
P1, P2 = LFS: Privacy, I & II (elementary)   D = Duplicated in another standard
Q = Quigley: Civitas

424

MREL

(CE,53,100)

8. Understands the central ideas of American constitutional government and how this form of government has shaped the character of American society

Level I (Grades K-2)

BD (DE,4.1.1;J1E,1;QE,21)
- Knows that America has had a historical commitment to the pursuit of justice

Level II (Grades 3-5)

BD (CE,22;DI,9.2.2;NI,44;QE,361)
- Knows the fundamental values of American democracy (e.g., individual rights to life, liberty, property, and the pursuit of happiness; the public or common good; justice; equality of opportunity; diversity; truth; patriotism)

BD (CE,22-23;DI,9.2.2;NI,44;QE,361,378-380)
- Knows the fundamental principles of American democracy (e.g., the people are sovereign; the power of government is limited by law; people exercise their authority directly through voting; people exercise their authority indirectly through elected representatives)

BD (CE,23;DE,9.2.3;NI,44;QE,416-419)
- Knows how fundamental values and principles of American democracy are expressed in documents such as the Declaration of Independence, the Preamble to the United States Constitution, and the Bill of Rights, as well as in American songs, stories, and speeches

BD (CE,23;NI,44;QE,131,362-363)
- Understands the focus on "the individual" in American society (e.g., a primary purpose of government is to protect the rights of the individual to life, liberty, property, and the pursuit of happiness; individuals have the right to differ about politics, religion, or any other matter; the vote of one individual should count as much as another's)

BD (CE,23-24;QI,132)
- Understands the focus on the school, community, state, and nation in American society (e.g., people should try to improve the quality of life in their schools, communities, states, and nation; people should help others who are less fortunate than they and assist them in times of need, emergency, or natural disaster)

BD (CE,24;QE,24-25)
- Understands the importance of equality of opportunity and equal protection of the law as a characteristic of American society (e.g., all people have a right to equal opportunity in education, employment, housing, and to equal access to public facilities; all people have a right to participate in political life by expressing their opinions and trying to persuade others; everyone has the right to be treated equally in the eyes of the law)

- BD (CE,24;QE,15,379)
  Understands the importance of respect for the law as a characteristic of American society (e.g., everyone, including government officials, must obey the law; people have the right to work together to see that laws they consider unfair or unwise are changed by peaceful means)

- BD (CE,24;QE,132)
  Understands the importance of education as a characteristic of American society (e.g., education is essential for informed and effective citizenship; education is important for earning a living; everyone has a right to public education; people with special needs should be provided with appropriate educational opportunities)

- BD (CE,24)
  Understands the importance of work as a characteristic of American society (e.g., work is important to a person's independence and self-esteem; work is important to the well-being of the family, community, state, and nation; all honest work is worthy of respect)

Level III (Grades 6-8)

- BD (CE,53;NI,45;QE,378-380)
  Knows the essential ideas of American constitutional government that are expressed in the Declaration of Independence, the Constitution, and other writings (e.g., the Constitution is a higher law that authorizes a government of limited powers; the Preamble to the Constitution states the purposes of government such as to form a more perfect union, establish justice, provide for the common defense, and promote the general welfare)

- BD (CE,54;NI,45;QE,380)
  Knows how certain provisions of the United States Constitution give government the necessary power to fulfill its purposes (e.g., delegated or enumerated powers as stated in Articles I, II, and III; the general welfare provision as stated in Article I, Section 8; the necessary and proper clause as stated in Article I, Section 8, Clause 18)

- BD (CE,54;NI,45;NE,46;QE,379)
  Understands how the United States Constitution serves to limit the powers of government (e.g., separation and sharing of powers, checks and balances, Bill of Rights)

- BD (CE,54;NI,45;NE,46;QI,169)
  Understands how specific provisions of the United States Constitution (including the Bill of Rights) limit the powers of government in order to protect the rights of individuals (e.g., habeas corpus; trial by jury; ex post facto; freedom of religion, speech, press, and assembly; equal protection of the law; due process of law; right to counsel)

- BD (CE,54)
  Knows opposing positions on current issues involving constitutional protection of individual

Codes (right side of page):	BD = Benchmark, Declarative; BP = Benchmark, Procedural; BC = Benchmark, Contextual	
1st letter of each code in parentheses	*2nd letter of code*	*Number*
C = CCE: National Standards for Civics	E = Explicitly stated in document	Page number of cited document
A1 = LFS: Authority, I (elementary)	I = Implied in document	*or, for duplicates,*
B = National Standards for Business Education		Standard number & level of duplicate
J1 = LFS: Justice, I (elementary)		
N = NAEP: Civics Consensus Project	R1 = LFS: Responsibility, I (elementary)	
P1, P2 = LFS: Privacy, I & II (elementary)	D = Duplicated in another standard	
Q = Quigley: Civitas		

426

MREL

rights such as limits on speech (e.g., "hate speech," advertising), separation of church and state (e.g., school vouchers, prayer in public schools), cruel and unusual punishment (e.g., death penalty), search and seizure (e.g., warrantless searches), and privacy (e.g., national identification cards, wiretapping)

BD (CE,55;NE,46)

- Understands important factors that have helped shape American society (e.g., absence of a nobility or an inherited caste system; religious freedom; abundance of land and widespread ownership of property; large scale immigration; diversity of the population; market economy; relative social equality; universal public education)

Level IV (Grades 9-12)

BD (CE,99;NI,47;QI,330-331)

- Knows major historical events that led to the creation of limited government in the United States (e.g., Magna Carta (1215), common law, and the Bill of Rights (1689) in England; colonial experience, Declaration of Independence (1776), Articles of Confederation (1781), state constitutions and charters, United States Constitution (1787), Bill of Rights (1791) in the United States)

BD (CE,99;NI,47;QI,612)

- Knows how the creation of American constitutional government was influenced by the central ideas of the natural rights philosophy (e.g., all persons have the right to life, liberty, property, and the pursuit of happiness; the major purpose of government is to protect those rights)

BD (CE,100;FE,12;NI,47)

- Knows the major ideas about republican government that influenced the development of the United States Constitution (e.g., the concept of representative government, the importance of civic virtue or concern for the common good)

BD (CE,100;NI,47;QE,14,378)

- Understands the concept of popular sovereignty as a central idea of American constitutional government (e.g., the people as the ultimate source of the power to create, alter, or abolish governments)

BD (CE,100;NI,47;QI,169-170,378-380)

- Understands the necessity for a written Constitution to set forth the organization of government and to grant and distribute its powers (e.g., among different branches of the national government, between the national government and the states, between the people and the government)

Codes (right side of page):	BD = Benchmark, Declarative; BP = Benchmark, Procedural; BC = Benchmark, Contextual	
1st letter of each code in parentheses	*2nd letter of code*	*Number*
C = CCE: National Standards for Civics	E = Explicitly stated in document	Page number of cited document
A1 = LFS: Authority, I (elementary)	I = Implied in document	*or, for duplicates,*
B = National Standards for Business Education		Standard number & level of duplicate
J1 = LFS: Justice, I (elementary)		
N = NAEP: Civics Consensus Project	R1 = LFS: Responsibility, I (elementary)	
P1, P2 = LFS: Privacy, I & II (elementary)	D = Duplicated in another standard	
Q = Quigley: Civitas		

- Understands how various provisions of the Constitution and principles of the constitutional system help to insure an effective government that will not exceed its limits

  BD (CE,100;NI,47;QE,169,378-380)

- Understands how the design of the institutions of government and the federal system works to channel and limit governmental power in order to serve the purposes of American constitutional government

  BD (CE,100;NI,47;QE,379-380)

- Understands how the belief in limited government and the values and principles of the Constitution have influenced American society (e.g., the Constitution has encouraged Americans to engage in commercial and other productive activities)

  BD (CE,100;NI,47;QE,378-380)

- Knows ways in which Americans have attempted to make the values and principles of the Constitution a reality

  BD (CE,100)

- Knows how the distinctive characteristics of American society are similar to and different from the characteristics of other societies

  BD (CE,102;NE,49)

9. Understands the importance of Americans sharing and supporting certain values, beliefs, and principles of American constitutional democracy

(CE,107)

Level I (Grades K-2)

- No material specifically designated for this level

  BD (CE,25)

Level II (Grades 3-5)

- Understands how Americans are united by the values, principles, and beliefs they share rather than by ethnicity, race, religion, class, language, gender, or national origin

  BD (CE,25;DI,11.3.5;NE,42;QI,25-27,361)

- Understands how shared values, principles, and beliefs contribute to the continuation and improvement of American democracy

  BD (CE,25;DI,8.2.1,8.2.2;NE,44;QE,361)

- Knows how specific documents in American history set forth shared values, principles, and beliefs (e.g., Declaration of Independence, United States Constitution and Bill of Rights,

  BD (CE,25;DE,8.2.3;NE,44;QE,416-419)

Codes (right side of page):
1st letter of each code in parentheses
C = CCE: National Standards for Civics
A1 = LFS: Authority, I (elementary)
B = National Standards for Business Education
J1 = LFS: Justice, I (elementary)
N = NAEP: Civics Consensus Project
P1, P2 = LFS: Privacy, I & II (elementary)
Q = Quigley: Civitas

BD = Benchmark, Declarative; BP = Benchmark, Procedural; BC = Benchmark, Contextual
2nd letter of code
E = Explicitly stated in document
I = Implied in document

R1 = LFS: Responsibility, I (elementary)
D = Duplicated in another standard

Number
Page number of cited document
or, for duplicates,
Standard number & level of duplicate

428

McREL

Pledge of Allegiance)

- Knows how various symbols are used to depict Americans' shared values, principles, and beliefs and explain their meaning (e.g., the flag, Statue of Liberty, Statue of Justice, Uncle Sam, great seal, national anthem, oaths of office, mottoes such as *E Pluribus Unum*) BD (CE,25;NE,43)

- Knows how various American holidays reflect the shared values, principles, and beliefs of Americans (e.g., Fourth of July; Labor Day; Memorial Day; Presidents' Day; Columbus Day; Thanksgiving; Veterans Day; Martin Luther King, Jr.'s Birthday) BD (CE,25;NE,43)

- Knows how the values and principles of American democracy can be promoted through respecting the rights of others (e.g., being open to opposing views, not invading others' privacy, not discriminating unfairly against others) BD (CE,27;QE,13)

- Knows how the values and principles of American democracy can be fostered through helping to promote the common good (e.g., volunteer work) BD (CE,27;QE,361-363)

- Knows how the values and principles of American democracy can be promoted through participating in government (e.g., voting, keeping informed about public issues, writing to legislators, serving on juries) BD (CE,27;NI,44;QE,39)

Level III (Grades 6-8)

- Identifies fundamental values and principles that are expressed in basic documents (e.g., Declaration of Independence, United States Constitution), significant political speeches and writings (e.g., The Federalist, King's "I Have a Dream" speech), and individual and group actions that embody fundamental values and principles (e.g., suffrage and civil rights movements) BD (CE,58;NE,45;QI,378-380)

- Understands how certain values (e.g., individual rights, the common good, self government, justice, equality, diversity, openness and free inquiry, truth, patriotism) are fundamental to American public life BD (CE,59;NE,46;QE,361)

- Understands popular sovereignty as opposed to state sovereignty (e.g., ultimate political authority rests with the people who create and can alter or abolish governments; citizens are not the same as subjects), and knows that popular sovereignty is a fundamental principle of BD (CE,59;NI,44;QE,131;378)

Codes (right side of page): BD = Benchmark, Declarative; BP = Benchmark, Procedural; BC = Benchmark, Contextual
1st letter of each code in parentheses *2nd letter of code* *Number*
C = CCE: National Standards for Civics E = Explicitly stated in document Page number of cited document
A1 = LFS: Authority, I (elementary) I = Implied in document *or, for duplicates,*
B = National Standards for Business Education Standard number & level of duplicate
J1 = LFS: Justice, I (elementary)
N = NAEP: Civics Consensus Project R1 = LFS: Responsibility, I (elementary)
P1, P2 = LFS: Privacy, I & II (elementary) D = Duplicated in another standard
Q = Quigley: Civitas

429 MREL

American constitutional democracy

- Knows that constitutional government is a fundamental principle of American democracy (e.g., the rule of law, representative institutions, shared powers, checks and balances, individual rights, separation of church and state, federalism, civilian control of the military)

BD (CE,59;NI,46;QE,131,378-379)

Level IV (Grades 9-12)

- Understands how the institutions of government reflect fundamental values and principles (e.g., justice, equality, the common good, popular sovereignty, checks and balances)

BD (CE,108;QE,380)

- Understands the interdependence among certain values and principles (e.g., individual liberty and diversity)

BD (CE,108;QI,378-80)

- Understands the significance of fundamental values and principles for the individual and society

BD (CE,108;QE,361)

10. **Understands the roles of voluntarism and organized groups in American social and political life**

(CE,102)

Level I (Grades K-2)

- No material specifically designated for this level

BD (CE,55)

Level II (Grades 3-5)

- Understands the importance of voluntarism as a characteristic of American society (e.g., people should volunteer to help others in their family, schools, communities, state, nation, and the world; volunteering is a source of individual satisfaction and fulfillment)

BD (CE,24;QE,16,363)

Level III (Grades 6-8)

- Knows factors that have influenced American voluntarism (e.g., colonial conditions, frontier traditions, religious beliefs)

BD (CE,55;QI,16,363)

Codes (right side of page):	BD = Benchmark, Declarative; BP = Benchmark, Procedural; BC = Benchmark, Contextual	
1st letter of each code in parentheses	*2nd letter of code*	*Number*
C = CCE: National Standards for Civics	E = Explicitly stated in document	Page number of cited document
A1 = LFS: Authority, I (elementary)	I = Implied in document	*or, for duplicates,*
B = National Standards for Business Education		Standard number & level of duplicate
J1 = LFS: Justice, I (elementary)		
N = NAEP: Civics Consensus Project	R1 = LFS: Responsibility, I (elementary)	
P1, P2 = LFS: Privacy, I & II (elementary)	D = Duplicated in another standard	
Q = Quigley: Civitas		

430

McREL

● Knows services that are provided by charitable, religious, and civic groups in the community (e.g., health, child, and elderly care; disaster relief; counseling; tutoring; basic needs such as food, clothing, shelter)
BD (CE,56;QI,16,363)

● Knows volunteer opportunities that exist in one's own school and community
BD (CE,56)

Level IV (Grades 9-12)

● Knows how the Puritan ethic encouraged American voluntarism
BD (CE,102)

● Knows how voluntary associations and other organized groups have been involved in functions usually associated with government (e.g., social welfare, education)
BD (CE,102)

● Knows the extent of voluntarism in American society compared to other countries
BD (CE,102;QI,16,363)

● Understands the relationship between American voluntarism and Americans' ideas about limited government
BD (CE,102;QE,16-17,363)

● Understands issues that arise regarding what responsibilities belong to individuals and groups and the private sector, what responsibilities belong to the government, and how these responsibilities should be shared by the private sector and the government
BD (CE,102;QE,16-17)

● Knows the historical and contemporary role of various organized groups in local, state, and national politics (e.g., unions; professional organizations; religious, charitable, service, and civic groups)
BD (CE,102)

(CE,103)
11. Understands the role of diversity in American life and the importance of shared values, political beliefs, and civic beliefs in an increasingly diverse American society

Level I (Grades K-2)

● No material specifically designated for this level
BD (CE,26)

Codes (right side of page):	BD = Benchmark, Declarative; BP = Benchmark, Procedural; BC = Benchmark, Contextual	
1st letter of each code in parentheses	*2nd letter of code*	*Number*
C = CCE: National Standards for Civics	E = Explicitly stated in document	Page number of cited document
A1 = LFS: Authority, I (elementary)	I = Implied in document	*or, for duplicates,*
B = National Standards for Business Education		Standard number & level of duplicate
J1 = LFS: Justice, I (elementary)		
N = NAEP: Civics Consensus Project	R1 = LFS: Responsibility, I (elementary)	
P1, P2 = LFS: Privacy, I & II (elementary)	D = Duplicated in another standard	
Q = Quigley: Civitas		

Level II (Grades 3-5)

- Understands the concept of diversity

  BD (CE,26;NI,42)

- Knows some common forms of diversity in the United States (e.g., ethnic, racial, religious, class, linguistic, gender, national origin)

  BD (CE,26;NE,42;QE,25-27)

- Knows reasons why diversity is so prevalent in the United States

  BD (CE,26;QE,25-27)

- Knows some of the benefits of diversity (e.g., it fosters a variety of viewpoints, new ideas, and fresh ways of looking at and solving problems; it provides people with choices in the arts, music, literature, and sports; it helps people appreciate cultural traditions and practices other than their own)

  BD (CE,26;NE,44;QE,25-27)

- Knows some of the costs of diversity (e.g., people sometimes discriminate unfairly against others on the basis of age, religious beliefs, race, or disability; members of different groups sometimes misunderstand each other and conflicts subsequently arise)

  BD (CE,26;NE,44;QE,25-27)

- Knows conflicts that are caused by diversity (e.g., unfair discrimination on the basis of race, ethnicity, religion, language, and gender; alienation of one group from another; efforts to impose beliefs and customs on others)

  BD (CE,26;NE,44;QE,25-27)

- Knows ways in which conflicts about diversity can be prevented (e.g., encouraging communication among different groups; identifying common beliefs, interests, and goals; learning about others' customs, beliefs, history, and problems; listening to different points of view; adhering to the values and principles of American democracy)

  BD (CE,26-27;NI,42;QE,25-27)

- Knows ways in which conflicts about diversity can be managed fairly when they occur (e.g., provide opportunities for people to present their points of view; arrange for an impartial individual or group to listen to all sides of a conflict and suggest solutions to problems)

  BD (CE,27;NI,42;QE,25-27)

Level III (Grades 6-8)

- Knows a variety of forms of diversity in American society (e.g., regional, linguistic, socioeconomic)

  BD (CE,56;NI,44;QE,25-27)

- Knows how diversity encourages cultural creativity

  BD (CE,56;NI,44;QE,25-27)

Codes (right side of page):	BD = Benchmark, Declarative; BP = Benchmark, Procedural; BC = Benchmark, Contextual	
1st letter of each code in parentheses	*2nd letter of code*	*Number*
C = CCE: National Standards for Civics	E = Explicitly stated in document	Page number of cited document
A1 = LFS: Authority, I (elementary)	I = Implied in document	*or, for duplicates,*
B = National Standards for Business Education		Standard number & level of duplicate
J1 = LFS: Justice, I (elementary)		
N = NAEP: Civics Consensus Project	R1 = LFS: Responsibility, I (elementary)	
P1, P2 = LFS: Privacy, I & II (elementary)	D = Duplicated in another standard	
Q = Quigley: Civitas		

McREL

- BD (CE,56;NI,44;QE,227-231)
Knows major conflicts in American society that have arisen from diversity (e.g., North/South conflict; conflict about land, suffrage, and other rights of Native Americans; Catholic/Protestant conflicts in the nineteenth century; conflict about civil rights of minorities and women; present day ethnic conflict in urban settings)

- BD (CE,56;NE,46;QE,25-27)
Knows ways in which conflicts about diversity can be resolved in a peaceful manner that respects individual rights and promotes the common good

- BD (CE,57;DI,9.2.1;NI,46;QE,25-27,361)
Knows how an American's identity stems from belief in and allegiance to shared political values and principles, and how this identity differs from that of most other nations, which often base their identity on such things as ethnicity, race, religion, class, language, gender, or national origin

- BD (CE,57;NI,46;QE,361)
Knows basic values and principles that Americans share (e.g., as set forth in documents such as the Declaration of Independence, the United States Constitution, the Gettysburg Address)

- BD (CE,57;NE,46;QE,361)
Knows why it is important to the individual and society that Americans understand and act on their shared political values and principles

Level IV (Grades 9-12)

- BD (CE,103;QE,25-27)
Knows how the racial, religious, socioeconomic, regional, ethnic, and linguistic diversity of American society has influenced American politics through time

- BD (CE,103;QE,25-27)
Knows different viewpoints regarding the role and value of diversity in American life

- BD (CE,103;QE,27-231)
Knows examples of conflicts stemming from diversity, and understands how some conflicts have been managed and why some of them have not yet been successfully resolved

- BD (CE,103;QI,25-27)
Knows why constitutional values and principles must be adhered to when managing conflicts over diversity

- BD (CE,104;NI,49;QE,131)
Knows beliefs that are common to American political culture (e.g., belief in equality of opportunity; mistrust of power, as well as high expectations of what elected officials and government should do; the need to admit to faults or shortcomings in the society; the belief that social, economic, or political problems can be alleviated through collective effort)

MREL

BD (CE,104;QI,416-419)

- Knows how shared ideas and values of American political culture are reflected in various sources and documents (e.g., the Bill of Rights, The Federalist and Anti-federalist writings, Woodrow Wilson's "Fourteen Points," Martin Luther King, Jr.'s "Letter from the Birmingham Jail," landmark decisions of the Supreme Court of the United States)

(CE,106,107)

12. Understands the relationships among liberalism, republicanism, and American constitutional democracy

Level I (Grades K-2)

BD (CE,106)

- Not appropriate for this level

Level II (Grades 3-5)

BD (CE,106)

- Not appropriate for this level

Level III (Grades 6-8)

BD (CE,106)

- Not appropriate for this level

Level IV (Grades 9-12)

BD (CE,106;QE,12)

- Understands that the central idea of liberalism is the belief that the individual has rights that exist independently of government and that ought to be protected by and against government

BD (CE,106;QE,12)

- Knows the general history of liberalism (e.g., ideas of liberalism that emerged in the seventeenth century and developed during the eighteenth-century Enlightenment; relationship between liberalism and the Protestant Reformation and the rise of market economies and free enterprise)

BD (CE,106)

- Knows the difference between the use of the term "liberal" in referring to the American form of government and the use of the terms "liberal" and "conservative" in referring to positions on the spectrum of American politics

---

Codes (right side of page):   BD = Benchmark, Declarative; BP = Benchmark, Procedural; BC = Benchmark, Contextual
1st letter of each code in parentheses   *2nd letter of code*   *Number*
C = CCE: National Standards for Civics   E = Explicitly stated in document   Page number of cited document
A1 = LFS: Authority, I (elementary)   I = Implied in document   *or, for duplicates,*
B = National Standards for Business Education   Standard number & level of duplicate
J1 = LFS: Justice, I (elementary)
N = NAEP: Civics Consensus Project   R1 = LFS: Responsibility, I (elementary)
P1, P2 = LFS: Privacy, I & II (elementary)   D = Duplicated in another standard
Q = Quigley: Civitas

McREL

- BD (CE,106;QI,112)
  Understands that the term "democracy" is derived from the Greek word for "rule by the people," and that the central focus of democracy is the idea that the people are the source of authority for government

- BD (CE,106)
  Knows the difference between the use of the term "democratic" to refer to the American form of government and the use of the term to refer to the Democratic Party in the United States

- BD (CE,106-107;QE,133)
  Understands how the basic premises of liberalism and democracy are joined in the Declaration of Independence, where they are stated as "self-evident Truths" (e.g., "all men are created equal," authority is derived from consent of the governed, people have the right to alter or abolish government when it fails to fulfill its purposes)

- BD (CE,107;QE,362)
  Understands that a "republic" is a state in which the citizenry as a whole is considered sovereign but which is governed by elected representatives rather than directly by the people as in direct democracy

- BD (CE,107;QE,12,362)
  Knows the major ideas of republicanism (e.g., government of a republic seeks the public or common good rather than the good of a particular group or class of society; "civic virtue" of citizens is essential, in which citizens put the public or common good above their private interests)

- BD (CE,107;QI,12)
  Knows how ideas of classical republicanism are reflected in the United States Constitution (e.g., the guarantee to the states of a "republican form of government" in Article IV, Section 4; provisions for the election of representatives to the Congress in Article I, Section 2 and the Seventeenth Amendment)

- BD (CE,107)
  Knows how the use of the term "republican" to refer to the American form of government differs from the use of the term to refer to the Republican Party in the United States

- BD (CE,107;QE,12)
  Understands reasons why classical republicanism and liberalism are potentially in conflict (e.g., on the primary purpose of government as the promotion of the public good or as the promotion of the protection of individual rights)

- BD (CE,107;QE,12)
  Knows various viewpoints regarding the importance of civic virtue for American democracy today

---

Codes (right side of page):   BD = Benchmark, Declarative; BP = Benchmark, Procedural; BC = Benchmark, Contextual

1st letter of each code in parentheses   *2nd letter of code*   *Number*

C = CCE: National Standards for Civics   E = Explicitly stated in document   Page number of cited document

A1 = LFS: Authority, I (elementary)   I = Implied in document   *or, for duplicates,*

B = National Standards for Business Education   Standard number & level of duplicate

J1 = LFS: Justice, I (elementary)

N = NAEP: Civics Consensus Project   R1 = LFS: Responsibility, I (elementary)

P1, P2 = LFS: Privacy, I & II (elementary)   D = Duplicated in another standard

Q = Quigley: Civitas

MREL

13. Understands the character of American political and social conflict and factors that tend to prevent or lower its intensity (CE,104)

Level I (Grades K-2)

- Not appropriate for this level

BD (CE,59)

Level II (Grades 3-5)

- Not appropriate for this level

BD (CE,59)

Level III (Grades 6-8)

BD (CE,59;NE,47;QE,361,416-419)
- Knows conflicts that have arisen regarding fundamental values and principles (e.g., conflicts between liberty and equality, conflicts between individual rights and the common good, conflicts between majority rule and minority rights)

BD (CE,59-60;NI,47)
- Knows how disagreements regarding specific issues may arise between people even though the people agree on values or principles in the abstract (e.g., people may agree on the value of freedom of expression but disagree about the extent to which expression of unpopular and offensive views should be tolerated; people may agree on the value of equality but disagree about affirmative action programs)

BD (CE,57;NI,47;QE,227-234)
- Knows sources of political conflict that have arisen in the United States historically as well as in the present (e.g., geographic and sectional interests, slavery and indentured servitude, national origins, extending the franchise, extending civil rights to all Americans, the role of religion in American public life, engaging in wars)

BD (CE,57;NI,46)
- Knows reasons why most political conflict in the United States has generally been less divisive than in many other nations (e.g., a shared respect for the Constitution and its principles, a sense of unity within diversity, willingness to relinquish power when voted out of office, willingness to use the legal system to manage conflicts, opportunities to improve one's economic condition)

BD (CE,57;BI,125;QE,227-231)
- Knows instances in which political conflict in the United States has been divisive and

---

Codes (right side of page):   BD = Benchmark, Declarative; BP = Benchmark, Procedural; BC = Benchmark, Contextual
1st letter of each code in parentheses   *2nd letter of code*   *Number*
C = CCE: National Standards for Civics   E = Explicitly stated in document   Page number of cited document
A1 = LFS: Authority, I (elementary)   I = Implied in document   *or, for duplicates,*
B = National Standards for Business Education   Standard number & level of duplicate
J1 = LFS: Justice, I (elementary)
N = NAEP: Civics Consensus Project   R1 = LFS: Responsibility, I (elementary)
P1, P2 = LFS: Privacy, I & II (elementary)   D = Duplicated in another standard
Q = Quigley: Civitas

McREL

reasons for this division (e.g., the Civil War, labor unrest, civil rights struggles, opposition to the war in Vietnam)

Level IV (Grades 9-12)

- Understands issues that involve conflicts among fundamental values and principles such as the conflict between liberty and authority

  BD (CE,108;NE,48;QE,416-419)

- Knows why people may agree on values or principles in the abstract but disagree when they are applied to specific issues such as the right to life and capital punishment

  BD (CE,109;NI,48)

- Knows how the rights of organized labor and the role of government in regulating business have created political conflict

  BD (CE,104;BE,125;NI,48)

- Knows how the concept of a loyal opposition and recourse to the legal system to manage conflicts have helped to lessen the divisiveness of political conflict in the United States

  BD (CE,104;NE,48)

- Knows how universal public education and the existence of a popular culture that crosses class boundaries have tended to reduce the intensity of political conflict (e.g., by creating common ground among diverse groups)

  BD (CE,104;NE,48;QI,25-27)

14. Understands issues concerning the disparities between ideals and reality in American political and social life

(CE,109)

Level I (Grades K-2)

- Not appropriate for this level

  BD (CE,60)

Level II (Grades 3-5)

- Not appropriate for this level

  BD (CE,60)

Codes (right side of page):	BD = Benchmark, Declarative; BP = Benchmark, Procedural; BC = Benchmark, Contextual

1st letter of each code in parentheses   *2nd letter of code*   *Number*
C = CCE: National Standards for Civics   E = Explicitly stated in document   Page number of cited document
A1 = LFS: Authority, I (elementary)   I = Implied in document   *or, for duplicates,*
B = National Standards for Business Education   Standard number & level of duplicate
J1 = LFS: Justice, I (elementary)
N = NAEP: Civics Consensus Project   R1 = LFS: Responsibility, I (elementary)
P1, P2 = LFS: Privacy, I & II (elementary)   D = Duplicated in another standard
Q = Quigley: Civitas

Level III (Grades 6-8)

- BD (CE,60;NI,46;QE,131,361)

  Knows some important American ideals (e.g., liberty and justice for all, an informed citizenry, civic virtue or concern for the common good, respect for the rights of others)

- BD (CE,60;QE,361)

  Knows why political and social ideals are important, even if they cannot be fully achieved

- BD (CE,60;NE, 46)

  Knows some of the discrepancies that have arisen between American ideals and the realities of political and social life in the United States (e.g., the ideal of equal justice for all and the reality that the poor may not have equal access to the judicial system)

- BD (CE,60;NE, 46)

  Knows some of the efforts that have been put forth to reduce discrepancies between ideals and the reality of American public life (e.g., abolition, suffrage, civil rights, environmental protection movements)

- BD (CE,60;NE,46;QI,361)

  Knows how various individual actions, social actions, and political actions can help to reduce discrepancies between reality and the ideals of American constitutional democracy

Level IV (Grades 9-12)

- BD (CE,109;QE,361)

  Understands the importance of established ideals in political life and why Americans should insist that current practices constantly be compared with these ideals

- BD (CE,109;NE,49)

  Knows discrepancies between American ideals and the realities of American social and political life (e.g., the ideal of equal opportunity and the reality of unfair discrimination)

- BD (CE,109;NE,49)

  Knows historical and contemporary efforts to reduce discrepancies between ideals and reality in American public life (e.g., union movements, government programs such as Head Start, civil rights legislation and enforcement)

Codes (right side of page):	BD = Benchmark, Declarative; BP = Benchmark, Procedural; BC = Benchmark, Contextual

1st letter of each code in parentheses 2nd letter of code *Number*
C = CCE: National Standards for Civics E = Explicitly stated in document Page number of cited document
A1 = LFS: Authority, I (elementary) I = Implied in document *or, for duplicates,*
B = National Standards for Business Education Standard number & level of duplicate
J1 = LFS: Justice, I (elementary)
N = NAEP: Civics Consensus Project R1 = LFS: Responsibility, I (elementary)
P1, P2 = LFS: Privacy, I & II (elementary) D = Duplicated in another standard
Q = Quigley: Civitas

McREL

(CE, 110)

15. Understands how the United States Constitution grants and distributes power and responsibilities to national and state government and how it seeks to prevent the abuse of power

Level I (Grades K-2)

BD (CE,28)

● No material specifically designated for this level

Level II (Grades 3-5)

BD (CE,28;NI,42;QE,15)

● Understands that the Constitution is a written document which states that the fundamental purposes of American government are to protect individual rights and promote the common good

BD (CE,28;NE,42;QE,378-379)

● Knows that the Constitution describes how the government is organized, defines and limits the powers of government, and is the highest law in the land

BD (CE,28;QE,378-379)

● Knows that the government was created by people who had the following beliefs: the government is established by and for the people, the people have the right to choose their representatives, and the people have the right to change their government and the Constitution

BD (CE,29;NI,43;QI,380)

● Knows that Congress passes laws to protect individual rights (e.g., laws protecting freedom of religion and expression, and preventing unfair discrimination) and promote the common good (e.g., laws providing for clean air, national parks, and the defense of the nation)

BD (CE,29;NI,43;QI,380)

● Knows that the executive branch carries out and enforces laws to protect individual rights (e.g., voting rights, equal opportunities to attain an education) and promote the common good (e.g., enforcement of pure food and drug laws, enforcement of clean air laws)

BD (CE,29;BI,23;DE,18.2.1;NI,43;QI,380)

● Knows that the judicial branch, headed by the Supreme Court, makes decisions concerning the law that aim to protect individual rights (e.g., the right to a fair trial, to vote, to practice one's religious beliefs) and promote the common good (e.g., upholding laws that protect the rights of all people to equal opportunity)

Codes (right side of page):   BD = Benchmark, Declarative; BP = Benchmark, Procedural; BC = Benchmark, Contextual

1st letter of each code in parentheses   *2nd letter of code*   *Number*

C = CCE: National Standards for Civics   E = Explicitly stated in document   Page number of cited document

A1 = LFS: Authority, I (elementary)   I = Implied in document   *or, for duplicates,*

B = National Standards for Business Education   Standard number & level of duplicate

J1 = LFS: Justice, I (elementary)

N = NAEP: Civics Consensus Project   R1 = LFS: Responsibility, I (elementary)

P1, P2 = LFS: Privacy, I & II (elementary)   D = Duplicated in another standard

Q = Quigley: Civitas

MREL

Level III (Grades 6-8)

- BD (CE,61;NI,45;QE,378)
  Understands how the first three words of the Preamble to the Constitution, "We the People...," embodies the principle of the people as the ultimate source of sovereignty

- BD (CE,61-62;BE,22;NE,45;QE,380)
  Understands how the legislative, executive, and judicial branches share power and responsibilities (e.g., each branch has varying degrees of legislative, executive, and judicial powers and responsibilities)

- BD (CE,62;BE,22;NE,45;QE,380)
  Understands how the legislative branch can check the powers of the executive and judicial branches by establishing committees to oversee the executive branch's activities; impeaching the president, other members of the executive branch, and federal judges; overriding presidential vetoes; disapproving presidential appointments; and proposing amendments to the Constitution

- BD (CE,62;BE,22;NE,45;QE,380)
  Understands how the executive branch can check the powers of the legislative and judicial branches by vetoing laws passed by Congress and nominating members of the federal judiciary

- BD (CE,62;BE,22;NE,45;QE,380)
  Understands how the judicial branch can check the powers of the executive and legislative branches by overruling decisions made by lower courts and ruling on the constitutionality of laws made by Congress and the actions of the executive branch

- BD (CE,62;NE,45;QE,392)
  Knows the major parts of the federal system including the national government, state governments, and other governmental units (e.g., District of Columbia, American tribal governments, Virgin Islands)

- BD (CE,62;NI,45;QI,466)
  Knows which powers are primarily exercised by the state governments (e.g., education, law enforcement, roads), which powers are prohibited to state governments (e.g., coining money, conducting foreign relations, interfering with interstate commerce), and which powers are shared by state and national governments (e.g., power to tax, borrow money, regulate voting)

- BD (CE,63;NE,45;NI,46;QI,392)
  Understands how the distribution and sharing of power between the national and state governments increases opportunities for citizens to participate and hold their governments accountable

---

Codes (right side of page):   BD = Benchmark, Declarative; BP = Benchmark, Procedural; BC = Benchmark, Contextual

1st letter of each code in parentheses   *2nd letter of code*   *Number*

C = CCE: National Standards for Civics   E = Explicitly stated in document   Page number of cited document

A1 = LFS: Authority, I (elementary)   I = Implied in document   *or, for duplicates,*

B = National Standards for Business Education   Standard number & level of duplicate

J1 = LFS: Justice, I (elementary)

N = NAEP: Civics Consensus Project   R1 = LFS: Responsibility, I (elementary)

P1, P2 = LFS: Privacy, I & II (elementary)   D = Duplicated in another standard

Q = Quigley: Civitas

Level IV (Grades 9-12)

- BD (CE,110;BI,22;NI,47;QI,378-380)
Understands how the overall design and specific features of the Constitution prevent the abuse of power by aggregating power at the national, state, and local levels to allow government to be responsive; dispersing power among different levels of government to protect individual rights, promote the common good, and encourage citizen participation; and using a system of checks and balances (e.g., separated institutions with shared powers, provisions for veto and impeachment, federalism, judicial review, the Bill of Rights)

- BD (CE,111;NI,47;QI,378-379)
Knows why the framers adopted a federal system in which power and responsibility are divided and shared between a national government and state governments

- BD (CE,111;NI,47;QI,467)
Understands ways in which federalism is designed to protect individual rights to life, liberty, and property and how it has at times made it possible for states to deny the rights of certain groups, (e.g. states' rights and slavery, denial of suffrage to women and minority groups)

- BD (CE,111;NI,47;QI,466)
Understands both the historical and contemporary roles of national and state governments in the federal system and the importance of the Tenth Amendment

- BD (CE,112;BE,22;NI,47;QE,380)
Understands the purposes, organization, and functions of the legislative, executive, and judicial branches and the independent regulatory agencies (e.g., agencies such as the Federal Reserve, Food and Drug Administration, Federal Communications Commission)

- BD (CE,112;NI,47;QI,378-380)
Understands the extent to which each branch of the government reflects the people's sovereignty (e.g., Congress legislates on behalf of the people, the president represents the nation as a whole, the Supreme Court interprets the Constitution on behalf of the people)

- BD (CE,112;BI,22;NI,47;QI,380)
Understands how specific features and the overall design of the Constitution results in tensions among the three branches (e.g., the power of the purse, the power of impeachment, advice and consent, veto power, judicial review), and comprehends the argument that the tensions resulting from separation of powers, checks and balances, and judicial review tend to slow down the process of making and enforcing laws, thus insuring better outcomes

- BD (CE,112)
Knows current issues concerning representation (e.g., term limitations, legislative districting, geographical and group representation)

- BD (CE,112)
Understands how and why beliefs about the purposes and functions of the national

---

Codes (right side of page): BD = Benchmark, Declarative; BP = Benchmark, Procedural; BC = Benchmark, Contextual
1st letter of each code in parentheses *2nd letter of code* *Number*
C = CCE: National Standards for Civics E = Explicitly stated in document Page number of cited document
A1 = LFS: Authority, I (elementary) I = Implied in document *or, for duplicates,*
B = National Standards for Business Education Standard number & level of duplicate
J1 = LFS: Justice, I (elementary)
N = NAEP: Civics Consensus Project R1 = LFS: Responsibility, I (elementary)
P1, P2 = LFS: Privacy, I & II (elementary) D = Duplicated in another standard
Q = Quigley: Civitas

441 MREL

government have changed over time

(CE,112-113)

16. Understands the major responsibilities of the national government for domestic and foreign policy, and understands how government is financed through taxation

Level I (Grades K-2)

BD (CE,63)

- Not appropriate for this level

Level II (Grades 3-5)

BD (CE,63)

- Not appropriate for this level

Level III (Grades 6-8)

BD (CE,63;BI,73;QI,638)

- Understands how and why domestic policies affect American citizens' lives, and knows historical and contemporary examples of important domestic policies (e.g., Pure Food and Drug Act, Environmental Protection Act, civil rights laws, minimum wage laws, Social Security)

BD (CE,63;QI,328-330)

- Understands how and why foreign policies affect the lives of American citizens, and knows historical and contemporary examples of important foreign policies (e.g., Monroe Doctrine, Marshall Plan, immigration acts, arms control, promoting democracy and human rights throughout the world)

BD (CE,63;BE,73)

- Understands why taxation is necessary to pay for government, and knows which provisions of the United States Constitution give the national government the right to collect taxes (i.e., Article One, Sections 7 and 8; Sixteenth Amendment)

BD (CE,64;BE,73)

- Knows major sources of revenue for the national government (e.g., individual income taxes, social insurance receipts such as Social Security and Medicare, borrowing, taxes on corporations and businesses, estate and excise taxes, tariffs on foreign goods)

BD (CE,64;BE,73;QI,482-483)

- Knows major uses of tax revenues received by the national government (e.g. direct payments

---

Codes (right side of page):   BD = Benchmark, Declarative; BP = Benchmark, Procedural; BC = Benchmark, Contextual

1st letter of each code in parentheses	2nd letter of code	Number
C = CCE: National Standards for Civics	E = Explicitly stated in document	Page number of cited document
A1 = LFS: Authority, I (elementary)	I = Implied in document	or, for duplicates,
B = National Standards for Business Education		Standard number & level of duplicate
J1 = LFS: Justice, I (elementary)		
N = NAEP: Civics Consensus Project	R1 = LFS: Responsibility, I (elementary)	
P1, P2 = LFS: Privacy, I & II (elementary)	D = Duplicated in another standard	
Q = Quigley: Civitas		

442

McREL

to individuals such as Social Security, Medicaid, Medicare, and Aid to Families with Dependent Children; national defense; interest on the federal debt; interstate highways)

Level IV (Grades 9-12)

BD (CE,113;QI,328-330)
- Understands how specific foreign policies such as national security and trade policy affect the everyday lives of American citizens and their communities

BD (CE,113;QI,328-330,638)
- Understands competing arguments concerning the role of government in major areas of domestic and foreign policy (e.g., health care, education, child care, regulation of business and industry, foreign aid, intervention abroad)

BD (CE,113;BE,73;QI,482-483)
- Understands the tensions that results from citizens' desire for government services and benefits and their unwillingness to pay taxes for them

BD (CE,113;BI,73)
- Knows the history of taxation in the United States

BD (CE,113;BE,73)
- Understands the equity of various kinds of taxes

(CE,65,114)
17. Understands issues concerning the relationship between state and local governments and the national government and issues pertaining to representation at all three levels of government

Level I (Grades K-2)

BD (CE,30)
- No material specifically designated for this level

Level II (Grades 3-5)

BD (CE,30-31;BI,22;NE,42)
- Knows how to distinguish among national, state, and local governments

BD (CE,30;BI,22;QE,470-473)
- Knows the major responsibilities of the legislative, executive, and judicial branches of his/her state government

BD (CE,30-31;BI,22;NE,42,43;QE,466-467)
- Knows major services provided by national, state, and local governments (e.g., state services such as education and health services and local services such as transportation, education,

---

Codes (right side of page): BD = Benchmark, Declarative; BP = Benchmark, Procedural; BC = Benchmark, Contextual
1st letter of each code in parentheses *2nd letter of code* *Number*
C = CCE: National Standards for Civics E = Explicitly stated in document Page number of cited document
A1 = LFS: Authority, I (elementary) I = Implied in document *or, for duplicates,*
B = National Standards for Business Education Standard number & level of duplicate
J1 = LFS: Justice, I (elementary)
N = NAEP: Civics Consensus Project R1 = LFS: Responsibility, I (elementary)
P1, P2 = LFS: Privacy, I & II (elementary) D = Duplicated in another standard
Q = Quigley: Civitas

443   McREL

recreation, public safety, public utilities), and knows how these services are paid for (e.g., taxes, fees, licenses)

- Knows how state and local government officials are chosen (i.e., by election or appointment) ^{BD (CE,30-31)}

- Knows how people can participate in their state and local government (e.g., being informed, taking part in discussing issues, voting, volunteering their time), and understands why it is important that people participate in their state and local government (e.g., improve the quality of life in their community, gain personal satisfaction, prevent officials from abusing power) ^{BD (CE,30-31;NI,42;QI,39-40)}

- Knows the names of his/her legislators at the state and national levels (e.g., representatives and senators in his/her state legislature and in Congress) and the names of his/her representatives in the executive branches of government at the national, state, and local levels (e.g., mayor, governor, president) ^{BD (CE,32;NE,43)}

- Knows how to contact his/her representatives and which levels of government he/she should contact to express his/her opinions or get help on a specific problem (e.g., the environment, crime, stray or wild animals) ^{BD (CE,32;NE,42)}

Level III (Grades 6-8)

- Understands that his/her state has a constitution because the United States is a federal system ^{BD (CE,64;BI,22;QE,466)}

- Knows the major purposes of his/her state constitution, the process by which citizens can change their state constitution, and the basic similarities and differences between his/her state constitution and the United States Constitution ^{BD (CE,64)}

- Understands why the United States Constitution cannot be violated by state constitutions and state governments ^{BD (CE,64)}

- Understands the process by which citizens can change their state constitution and cite examples of changes ^{BD (CE,64;NI,47)}

- Knows the major responsibilities of his/her state and local governments (e.g., education, welfare, streets and roads, parks, recreation, law enforcement), and understands the organization of his/her state and local governments (e.g., legislative, executive, and judicial ^{BD (CE,65;NI,45)}

Codes (right side of page):	BD = Benchmark, Declarative; BP = Benchmark, Procedural; BC = Benchmark, Contextual	
1st letter of each code in parentheses	*2nd letter of code*	*Number*
C = CCE: National Standards for Civics	E = Explicitly stated in document	Page number of cited document
A1 = LFS: Authority, I (elementary)	I = Implied in document	*or, for duplicates,*
B = National Standards for Business Education		Standard number & level of duplicate
J1 = LFS: Justice, I (elementary)		
N = NAEP: Civics Consensus Project	R1 = LFS: Responsibility, I (elementary)	
P1, P2 = LFS: Privacy, I & II (elementary)	D = Duplicated in another standard	
Q = Quigley: Civitas		

functions at state and local levels)

BD (CE,65;QE,475-476)
- Knows major sources of revenue for state and local governments (e.g., property, sales, and income taxes; fees and licenses; taxes on corporations and businesses; borrowing)

BD (CE,65;NE,44)
- Understands how he/she can contact his/her representatives and why it is important to do so, and knows which level of government he/she should contact to express his/her opinions or to get help on a specific problem (e.g., opinions about a curfew for juveniles, an increase in state sales tax, aid to another country; problems with street lights, driver's license, federal income taxes)

Level IV (Grades 9-12)

BD (CE,114;BI,22;NI,47;QI,466-467)
- Knows the limits the United States Constitution places on the powers of the states (e.g., prohibitions against impairing interstate commerce, restrictions imposed by the Fourteenth Amendment and the Bill of Rights through the process of incorporation) and the limits the Constitution places on the powers of the national government over state governments (e.g., the national government cannot abolish a state, the Tenth Amendment to the Constitution reserves certain powers to the states)

BD (CE,114;NI,47;QE,466)
- Understands that the two kinds of power most commonly associated with state governments are reserved powers, which are powers not delegated to the national government or prohibited to states by the United States Constitution (e.g., legislation regarding public safety, marriage, and divorce; education; the conduct of elections; chartering regional and local governments; licensing drivers, businesses, and professions) and concurrent powers, which are powers jointly held with the national government (e.g., legislating taxation, regulating trade and industry, borrowing money, maintaining courts, protecting the environment)

BD (CE,114)
- Understands criteria for evaluating how the relationship between state and local governments and the national government has changed over time

BD (CE,114;QI,480)
- Understands criteria for evaluating the argument that state and local governments provide significant opportunities for experimentation and innovation

BD (CE,115)
- Understands criteria for evaluating the relationship between his/her state and local

---

Codes (right side of page):
1st letter of each code in parentheses
C = CCE: National Standards for Civics
A1 = LFS: Authority, I (elementary)
B = National Standards for Business Education
J1 = LFS: Justice, I (elementary)
N = NAEP: Civics Consensus Project
P1, P2 = LFS: Privacy, I & II (elementary)
Q = Quigley: Civitas

BD = Benchmark, Declarative; BP = Benchmark, Procedural; BC = Benchmark, Contextual
2nd letter of code
E = Explicitly stated in document
I = Implied in document

R1 = LFS: Responsibility, I (elementary)
D = Duplicated in another standard

Number
Page number of cited document
or, for duplicates,
Standard number & level of duplicate

445

MREL

governments

- Understands how the policies of state and local governments provide citizens with ways to monitor and influence the actions of members of government and hold them responsible for their actions (e.g., requirements of fair and public notice of meetings, meetings of government agencies must be open to the public, public trials, provision of opportunities for citizens to be heard)

BD (CE,115;NI,48)

18. Understands the role and importance of law in the American constitutional system and issues regarding the judicial protection of individual rights

(CE,116,117)

Level I (Grades K-2)

- No material specifically designated for this level

BD (CE,29)

Level II (Grades 3-5)

- Knows that the judicial branch, headed by the Supreme Court, makes decisions concerning the law that aim to protect individual rights (e.g., the right to a fair trial, to vote, to practice one's religious beliefs) and promote the common good (e.g., upholding laws that protect the rights of all people to equal opportunity)

BD (CE,29;BE,23;DE,15.2.6;NI,43;QI,380)

Level III (Grades 6-8)

- Understands the importance of the rule of law in establishing limits on both those who govern and the governed, protecting individual rights, and promoting the common good

BD (CE,66;NE,46;QE,15,379)

- Knows historical and contemporary examples of the rule of law (e.g., Marbury v. Madison, Brown v. Board of Education, U.S. v. Nixon)

BD (CE,66;NI,46)

- Knows principal varieties of law (e.g., constitutional, criminal, civil), and understands how the principal varieties of law protect individual rights and promote the common good

BD (CE,66;BE,22,23;NE,46;QI,332-333)

- Understands criteria for evaluating the strengths and weaknesses of a rule or law by

BD (CE,67;NI,46)

Codes (right side of page):	BD = Benchmark, Declarative; BP = Benchmark, Procedural; BC = Benchmark, Contextual	
1st letter of each code in parentheses	*2nd letter of code*	*Number*
C = CCE: National Standards for Civics	E = Explicitly stated in document	Page number of cited document
A1 = LFS: Authority, I (elementary)	I = Implied in document	*or, for duplicates,*
B = National Standards for Business Education		Standard number & level of duplicate
J1 = LFS: Justice, I (elementary)		
N = NAEP: Civics Consensus Project	R1 = LFS: Responsibility, I (elementary)	
P1, P2 = LFS: Privacy, I & II (elementary)	D = Duplicated in another standard	
Q = Quigley: Civitas		

446

MᴄREL

determining if it is understandable (i.e., clearly written with explicit requirements), possible to follow (i.e., does not demand the impossible), fair, well designed to achieve its purposes, and designed to protect individual rights and to promote the common good

- Understands the process necessary for drafting rules in his/her school or community that meets the criteria for a well-constructed rule or law
  BD (CE,67)

- Understands the basic concept of due process of law (i.e., government must use fair procedures to gather information and make decisions in order to protect the rights of individuals and the interests of society)
  BD (CE,67;FE;619-620;NI,46)

- Understands the importance to individuals and to society of major due process protections such as habeas corpus, presumption of innocence, fair notice, impartial tribunal, speedy and public trials, right to counsel, trial by jury, right against self incrimination, protection against double jeopardy, right of appeal
  BD (CE,67;NI,46;QE,619-620)

- Understands why due process rights in administrative and legislative procedures are essential for the protection of individual rights and the maintenance of limited government (e.g., the right to adequate notice of a hearing that may affect one's interests, the right to counsel in legislative hearings)
  BD (CE,67;NI,46;QE,619-622)

- Understands the advantages and disadvantages of the adversary system and the advantages and disadvantages of alternative means of conflict management (e.g., negotiation, mediation, arbitration, and litigation)
  BD (CE,67-68)

- Knows the basic principles of the juvenile system and the major differences between the due process rights of juveniles and adults
  BD (CE,67)

- Understands current issues regarding judicial protection of the rights of individuals
  BD (CE,68)

Level IV (Grades 9-12)

- Understands how the rule of law makes possible a system of ordered liberty that protects the basic rights of citizens
  BD (CE,116;NI,48;QE,15,379)

- Knows historical and contemporary practices that illustrate the central place of the rule of
  BD (CE,116;BI,22,23;NI,48)

Codes (right side of page):   BD = Benchmark, Declarative; BP = Benchmark, Procedural; BC = Benchmark, Contextual
1st letter of each code in parentheses   *2nd letter of code*   *Number*
C = CCE: National Standards for Civics   E = Explicitly stated in document   Page number of cited document
A1 = LFS: Authority, I (elementary)   I = Implied in document   *or, for duplicates,*
B = National Standards for Business Education   Standard number & level of duplicate
J1 = LFS: Justice, I (elementary)
N = NAEP: Civics Consensus Project   R1 = LFS: Responsibility, I (elementary)
P1, P2 = LFS: Privacy, I & II (elementary)   D = Duplicated in another standard
Q = Quigley: Civitas

law (e.g., submitting bills to legal counsel to insure congressional compliance with constitutional limitations, higher court review of lower court compliance with the law, executive branch compliance with laws enacted by Congress)

- Knows historical and contemporary events and practices that illustrate the absence or breakdown of the rule of law (e.g., events such as vigilantism in the early West, Ku Klux Klan attacks, urban riots, corruption in government and business, police corruption, organized crime; practices such as illegal searches and seizures, bribery, interfering with the right to vote, perjury) BD (CE,116;NI,48)

- Knows historical and contemporary illustrations of the idea of equal protection of the laws for all persons (e.g., the Fourteenth Amendment, Americans with Disabilities Act, equal opportunity legislation) BD (CE,116;NI,48;QE,619-620)

- Understands how the individual's rights to life, liberty, and property are protected by the trial and appellate levels of the judicial process and by the principal varieties of law (e.g., constitutional, criminal, and civil law) BD (CE,116;NI,48;QI,332-333)

- Understands the effects of Americans relying on the legal system to solve social, economic, and political problems rather than using other means, such as private negotiations, mediation, and participation in the political process BD (CE,116)

- Understands the importance of an independent judiciary in a constitutional democracy BD (CE,117;BI,23)

- Knows historical and contemporary instances in which judicial protections have not been extended to all persons and instances in which judicial protections have been extended to those deprived of them in the past BD (CE,117)

- Understands why due process rights in administrative and legislative procedures are essential for protecting individual rights and maintaining limited government BD (CE,117;QI,619-622)

- Knows how state and federal courts' power of judicial reflects the American idea of constitutional government (i.e., limited government) and understands the merits of arguments for and against judicial review BD (CE,117;BE,22;QI,615)

Codes (right side of page):   BD = Benchmark, Declarative; BP = Benchmark, Procedural; BC = Benchmark, Contextual
1st letter of each code in parentheses   *2nd letter of code*   *Number*
C = CCE: National Standards for Civics   E = Explicitly stated in document   Page number of cited document
A1 = LFS: Authority, I (elementary)   I = Implied in document   *or, for duplicates,*
B = National Standards for Business Education   Standard number & level of duplicate
J1 = LFS: Justice, I (elementary)
N = NAEP: Civics Consensus Project   R1 = LFS: Responsibility, I (elementary)
P1, P2 = LFS: Privacy, I & II (elementary)   D = Duplicated in another standard
Q = Quigley: Civitas

19. Understands what is meant by "the public agenda," how it is set, and how it is influenced by public opinion and the media

(CE,118)

Level I (Grades K-2)

BD (CE,68)

- Not appropriate for this level

Level II (Grades 3-5)

BD (CE,68)

- Not appropriate for this level

Level III (Grades 6-8)

BD (CE,68;QE,641)

- Knows that the public agenda consists of those matters that occupy public attention at any particular time (e.g., crime, health care education, child care, environmental protection, drug abuse)

BD (CE,68;BI,23;NI,47;QI,641)

- Knows how the public agenda is shaped by political leaders, interest groups, and state and federal courts; and understands how individual citizens can help shape the public agenda (e.g., by joining interest groups or political parties, making presentations at public meetings, writing letters to government officials and to newspapers)

BD (CE,69;NI,47;QE,539)

- Understands the importance of freedom of the press to informed participation in the political system; and understands the influence of television, radio, the press, newsletters, and emerging means of electronic communication on American politics

BD (CE,69;NI,47;QI,544-545)

- Knows how Congress, the president, the Supreme Court, and state and local public officials use the media to communicate with the citizenry

BD (CE,69;NE,47)

- Understands how citizens can evaluate information and arguments received from various sources so that they can make reasonable choices on public issues and among candidates for political office

BD (CE,69;NI,47;QI,538-539)

- Understands the opportunities that the media provides for individuals to monitor the actions of their government (e.g., televised broadcasts of proceedings of governmental agencies such

---

Codes (right side of page):   BD = Benchmark, Declarative; BP = Benchmark, Procedural; BC = Benchmark, Contextual

1st letter of each code in parentheses	*2nd letter of code*	*Number*
C = CCE: National Standards for Civics	E = Explicitly stated in document	Page number of cited document
A1 = LFS: Authority, I (elementary)	I = Implied in document	*or, for duplicates,*
B = National Standards for Business Education		Standard number & level of duplicate
J1 = LFS: Justice, I (elementary)		
N = NAEP: Civics Consensus Project	R1 = LFS: Responsibility, I (elementary)	
P1, P2 = LFS: Privacy, I & II (elementary)	D = Duplicated in another standard	
Q = Quigley: Civitas		

449

McREL

as Congress and the courts, public officials' press conferences) and communicate their concerns and positions on current issues (e.g., letters to the editor, talk shows, "op-ed pages," public opinion polls)

Level IV (Grades 9-12)

- Understands how political institutions and political parties shape the public agenda
  BD (CE,118;NI,47)

- Understands why issues important to some groups and the nation do not become part of the public agenda
  BD (CE,118;QI,641)

- Understands the concept of public opinion, and knows alternative views of the proper role of public opinion in a democracy
  BD (CE,118;NI,49;QE,569)

- Understands how public opinion is measured, used in public debate, and how it can be influenced by the government and the media
  BD (CE,118;NI,49;QI,570-571)

- Understands the influence that public opinion has on public policy and the behavior of public officials
  BD (CE,118;NI,49;QE,568-570)

- Understands the ways in which television, radio, the press, newsletters, and emerging means of communication influence American politics; and understands the extent to which various traditional forms of political persuasion have been replaced by electronic media
  BD (CE,118;NI,49;QE,645-646)

- Knows how to use criteria such as logical validity, factual accuracy, emotional appeal, distorted evidence, and appeals to bias or prejudice in order to evaluate various forms of historical and contemporary political communication (e.g., Lincoln's "House Divided," Sojourner Truth's "Ain't I a Woman?," Chief Joseph's "I Shall Fight No More Forever," Martin Luther King, Jr.'s "I Have a Dream," campaign advertisements, political cartoons)
  BD (CE,119;NE,49)

Codes (right side of page):	BD = Benchmark, Declarative; BP = Benchmark, Procedural; BC = Benchmark, Contextual	
1st letter of each code in parentheses	*2nd letter of code*	*Number*
C = CCE: National Standards for Civics	E = Explicitly stated in document	Page number of cited document
A1 = LFS: Authority, I (elementary)	I = Implied in document	*or, for duplicates,*
B = National Standards for Business Education		Standard number & level of duplicate
J1 = LFS: Justice, I (elementary)		
N = NAEP: Civics Consensus Project	R1 = LFS: Responsibility, I (elementary)	
P1, P2 = LFS: Privacy, I & II (elementary)	D = Duplicated in another standard	
Q = Quigley: Civitas		

450

McREL

(CE,119)

20. Understands the roles of political parties, campaigns, elections, and associations and groups in American politics

Level I (Grades K-2)

BD (CE,69)

- Not appropriate for this level

Level II (Grades 3-5)

BD (CE,69)

- Not appropriate for this level

Level III (Grades 6-8)

BD (CE,69;NE,45;QE,486-487,502)

- Understands the role of political parties

BD (CE,69;NE,45;QI,486-487)

- Knows the various kinds of elections (e.g., primary and general, local and state, congressional, presidential, recall)

BD (CE,69;NI,45;QE,486-487)

- Understands the ways in which individuals can participate in political parties, campaigns, and elections

BD (CE,69;BI,125;NE,45;QI,503)

- Understands the historical and contemporary roles of prominent associations and groups in local, state, and national politics (e.g., historical associations such as abolitionists, suffragists, labor unions, civil rights groups; religious organizations and contemporary associations such as AFL-CIO, National Education Association, Common Cause, League of Women Voters, Greenpeace, National Association for the Advancement of Colored People)

BD (CE,69;NE,45;QE,503)

- Knows how and why Americans become members of associations and groups, and understands how membership in these associations provides individuals with opportunities to participate in the political process.

Level IV (Grades 9-12)

BD (CE,119;NI,48;QI,488-489,496-497)

- Knows the origins and development of the two party system in the United States, and understands the role of third parties

---

McREL

- Understands how and why American political parties differ from ideological parties in other countries

  BD (CE,119;NI,48,49)

- Knows the major characteristics of American political parties, how they vary by locality, how they reflect the dispersion of power, and how they provide citizens with numerous opportunities for participation

  BD (CE,119;NE,48;QI,487)

- Understands how political parties are involved in channeling public opinion, allowing people to act jointly, nominating candidates, conducting campaigns, and training future leaders; and understands why political parties in the United States are weaker today than they have been at times in the past

  BD (CE,119;NE,48;QE,487,497-498)

- Knows the characteristics of initiatives and referendums

  BD (CE,119;NI,48)

- Understands the significance of campaigns and elections in the American political system, and knows current criticisms of campaigns and proposals for their reform

  BD (CE,119;NI,48;QE,486-487)

- Knows historical and contemporary examples of associations and groups performing functions otherwise performed by the government such as social welfare and education

  BD (CE,120)

- Understands the extent to which associations and groups enhance citizen participation in American political life

  BD (CE,120;NI,49;QE,503)

21. Understands the formation and implementation of public policy

(CE,120)

Level I (Grades K-2)

- Not appropriate for this level

  BD (CE,70)

Level II (Grades 3-5)

- Not appropriate for this level

  BD (CE,70)

MREL

Level III (Grades 6-8)

- BD (CE,70;NI,47;QE,638-639)
Understands what public policy is and knows examples at local, state, and national levels

- BD (CE,70;NI,47;QE,638-639)
Knows how public policies are formed and implemented, and understands how citizens can monitor and influence policies

- BD (CE,70;NI,47;QE,640-641)
Understands why conflicts about values, principles, and interests may make agreement difficult or impossible on certain issues of public policy (e.g., affirmative action, gun control, environmental protection, capital punishment, equal rights)

Level IV (Grades 9-12)

- BD (CE,120;NE,47)
Knows a public policy issue at the local, state, or national level well enough to identify the major groups interested in that issue and explain their respective positions

- BD (CE,120;NI,49;QE,638-639)
Understands the processes by which public policy concerning a local, state, or national issue is formed and carried out

- BD (CE,120;NE,49;QE,638-639)
Knows the points at which citizens can monitor or influence the process of public policy formation

- BD (CE,120;QI,640-641)
Understands why agreement may be difficult or impossible on issues such as abortion because of conflicts about values, principles, and interests

(CE,121-123)
22. Understands how the world is organized politically into nation-states, how nation-states interact with one another, and issues surrounding U.S. foreign policy

Level I (Grades K-2)

- BD (CE,33)
No material specifically designated for this level

Level II (Grades 3-5)

- BD (CE,33;NE,42;QE,279-280)
Knows that the world is divided into many different nations with each one having its own

---

Codes (right side of page):   BD = Benchmark, Declarative; BP = Benchmark, Procedural; BC = Benchmark, Contextual
1st letter of each code in parentheses   *2nd letter of code*   *Number*
C = CCE: National Standards for Civics   E = Explicitly stated in document   Page number of cited document
A1 = LFS: Authority, I (elementary)   I = Implied in document   *or, for duplicates,*
B = National Standards for Business Education   Standard number & level of duplicate
J1 = LFS: Justice, I (elementary)
N = NAEP: Civics Consensus Project   R1 = LFS: Responsibility, I (elementary)
P1, P2 = LFS: Privacy, I & II (elementary)   D = Duplicated in another standard
Q = Quigley: Civitas

MREL

government, and knows that a nation consists of its territory, people, laws, and government

BD (CE,33;QE,278-279)

- Knows that the United States is one nation and that it interacts with every other nation in the world

BD (CE,34;NE,43;QI,280-282)

- Knows the major ways nations interact with each other such as trade, diplomacy, cultural contacts, treaties or agreements, and use of military force

BD (CE,34;NE,44)

- Understands why it is important for nations to try to resolve problems peacefully (e.g., people's standard of living will improve due to increased trade, people's health will improve due to the exchange of medical and scientific knowledge)

Level III (Grades 6-8)

BD (CE,71;NE,45;QE,279-280)

- Knows that the world is divided into nation-states that claim sovereignty over a defined territory and jurisdiction over everyone within it, and understands why the nation-state is the most powerful form of political organization at the international level

BD (CE,71;NI,47;QI,280-282)

- Knows the most important means used by nation-states to interact with one another (e.g., trade, diplomacy, treaties and agreements, humanitarian aid, economic incentives and sanctions, military force and the threat of force)

BD (CE,72;NE,47;QI,280-282)

- Knows reasons for the breakdown of order among nation-states (e.g., conflicts about national interests, ethnicity, and religion; competition for resources and territory; absence of effective means to enforce international law), and understands the consequences of the breakdown of order among nation-states

BD (CE,72;NI,47;QE,328)

- Knows the most important powers the United States Constitution gives to the Congress, president, and federal judiciary in foreign affairs (e.g., Congress can declare war, raise and support armies, provide a navy [Article I, Section 8] and the Senate can approve treaties; the president is Commander in Chief and can make treaties and appoint ambassadors [Article II]; the federal judiciary can decide cases affecting treaties and ambassadors, and those involving treason [Article III])

BD (CE,72;NE,47;QI,280-282)

- Knows various means used to attain the ends of United States foreign policy (e.g., diplomacy; economic, military, and humanitarian aid; treaties; trade agreements; incentives;

Codes (right side of page):	BD = Benchmark, Declarative; BP = Benchmark, Procedural; BC = Benchmark, Contextual
1st letter of each code in parentheses	*2nd letter of code* *Number*
C = CCE: National Standards for Civics	E = Explicitly stated in document Page number of cited document
A1 = LFS: Authority, I (elementary)	I = Implied in document *or, for duplicates,*
B = National Standards for Business Education	Standard number & level of duplicate
J1 = LFS: Justice, I (elementary)	
N = NAEP: Civics Consensus Project	R1 = LFS: Responsibility, I (elementary)
P1, P2 = LFS: Privacy, I & II (elementary)	D = Duplicated in another standard
Q = Quigley: Civitas	

454

McREL

sanctions; military intervention; covert action)

- Knows examples of important current foreign policy issues and the means the United States is using to deal with them
  ^{BD (CE,72)}

- Knows the purposes and functions of major governmental international organizations (e.g., UN, NATO, OAS, World Court) and nongovernmental international organizations (e.g., International Red Cross, World Council of Churches, Amnesty International)
  ^{BD (CE,72;NE,45;QI,300)}

Level IV (Grades 9-12)

- Understands the significance of principal foreign policies and events in the United States' relations with the world (e.g., Monroe Doctrine, World Wars I and II, formation of the United Nations, Marshall Plan, NATO, Korean and Vietnam Wars, end of the Cold War)
  ^{BD (CE,122;NE,47;QI,300)}

- Understands how and why the United States assumed the role of world leader after World War II and what its current leadership role is in the world
  ^{BD (CE,123;NI,47)}

- Understands the major foreign policy positions that have characterized the United States' relations with the world (e.g., isolated nation, imperial power, and world leader)
  ^{BD (CE,123;NE,47;QE,278-279)}

- Knows how the powers over foreign affairs that the Constitution gives to the president, Congress, and the federal judiciary have been used over time; and understands the tension between constitutional provisions and the requirements of foreign policy (e.g., the power of Congress to declare war and the need of the president to make expeditious decisions in times of international emergency, the power of the president to make treaties and the need for the Senate to approve them)
  ^{BD (CE,123;NI,49;QI,328)}

- Understands the process by which United States foreign policy is made, including the roles of federal agencies, domestic interest groups, the media, and the public; and knows the ways in which Americans can influence foreign policy
  ^{BD (CE,123;NE,49;QE,328-330)}

- Understands how and why domestic politics may impose constraints or obligations on the ways in which the United States acts in the world (e.g., long-standing commitments to certain nations, lobbying efforts of domestic groups, economic needs)
  ^{BD (CE,123;NI,49)}

Codes (right side of page):   BD = Benchmark, Declarative; BP = Benchmark, Procedural; BC = Benchmark, Contextual
1st letter of each code in parentheses   *2nd letter of code*   *Number*
C = CCE: National Standards for Civics   E = Explicitly stated in document   Page number of cited document
A1 = LFS: Authority, I (elementary)   I = Implied in document   *or, for duplicates,*
B = National Standards for Business Education   Standard number & level of duplicate
J1 = LFS: Justice, I (elementary)
N = NAEP: Civics Consensus Project   R1 = LFS: Responsibility, I (elementary)
P1, P2 = LFS: Privacy, I & II (elementary)   D = Duplicated in another standard
Q = Quigley: Civitas

MREL

BD (CE,123;NE,49;QI,278-279)

- Understands the idea of the national interest and how it is used as a criterion for shaping American foreign policy

BD (CE,123;NE,49)

- Understands the influence of American constitutional values and principles on American foreign policy (e.g., a commitment to the self-determination of nations), and understands the tensions that might arise among American values, principles, and interests as the nation deals with the practical requirements of international politics (e.g., a commitment to human rights and the requirements of national security)

BD (CE,123;NI,49;QI,288)

- Understands the current role of the United States in peacemaking and peacekeeping

BD (CE,122;NE,48)

- Understands the purposes and functions of major governmental international organizations such as the Organization of American States and major nongovernmental international organizations such as the Roman Catholic Church and multinational corporations

BD (CE,126;NI,48;QI,300)

- Understands the role of the United States in establishing and maintaining principal international organizations (e.g., UN, UNICEF, GATT, NATO, OAS, World Bank, International Monetary Fund)

BD (CE,126)

- Knows some important bilateral and multilateral agreements to which the United States is signatory (e.g., NAFTA, Helsinki Accord, Antarctic Treaty, Most Favored Nation Agreements)

(CE,123-125)

23. Understands the impact of significant political and nonpolitical developments on the United States and other nations

Level I (Grades K-2)

BD (CE,73)

- Not appropriate for this level

Level II (Grades 3-5)

BD (CE,73)

- Not appropriate for this level

Codes (right side of page):	BD = Benchmark, Declarative; BP = Benchmark, Procedural; BC = Benchmark, Contextual	
1st letter of each code in parentheses	*2nd letter of code*	*Number*
C = CCE: National Standards for Civics	E = Explicitly stated in document	Page number of cited document
A1 = LFS: Authority, I (elementary)	I = Implied in document	*or, for duplicates,*
B = National Standards for Business Education		Standard number & level of duplicate
J1 = LFS: Justice, I (elementary)		
N = NAEP: Civics Consensus Project	R1 = LFS: Responsibility, I (elementary)	
P1, P2 = LFS: Privacy, I & II (elementary)	D = Duplicated in another standard	
Q = Quigley: Civitas		

McREL

Level III (Grades 6-8)

- Understands the impact that the American Revolution and the values and principles expressed in the Declaration of Independence, the United States Constitution, and the Bill of Rights has had on other nations

  BD (CE,73;NE,46;QI,133-134)

- Understands the influence that American ideas about rights have had on other nations and international organizations (e.g., French Revolution; democracy movements in Eastern Europe, People's Republic of China, Latin America, South Africa; United Nations Charter; Universal Declaration of Human Rights)

  BD (CE,73;NE,46;QI,134)

- Understands the impact that other nations' ideas about rights have had on the United States (e.g., natural rights in the seventeenth and eighteenth centuries, social and economic rights in the twentieth century)

  BD (CE,73;NE,46;QI,612)

- Understands the impact that current political developments around the world have on the United States (e.g., conflicts within and among other nations, efforts to establish democratic governments)

  BD (CE,73;NE,46)

- Understands the impact of major demographic trends on the United States (e.g., population growth, increase in immigration and refugees)

  BD (CE,73;NE,46;QI,251-252)

- Knows examples of environmental conditions that affect the United States' domestic and foreign policies (e.g., destruction of rain forests and animal habitats, depletion of fishing grounds, air and water pollution)

  BD (CE,73;NE,46;QI,520)

Level IV (Grades 9-12)

- Understands the influence that American ideas about rights have had abroad and how other peoples' ideas about rights have influenced Americans

  BD (CE,124)

- Understands the effects that significant world political developments have on the United States (e.g., the French, Russian, and Chinese Revolutions; rise of nationalism; World Wars I and II; decline of colonialism; terrorism; multiplication of nation-states and the proliferation of conflict within them; the emergence of regional organizations such as the European Union)

  BD (CE,125)

Codes (right side of page):   BD = Benchmark, Declarative; BP = Benchmark, Procedural; BC = Benchmark, Contextual

1st letter of each code in parentheses   *2nd letter of code*   *Number*

C = CCE: National Standards for Civics   E = Explicitly stated in document   Page number of cited document

A1 = LFS: Authority, I (elementary)   I = Implied in document   *or, for duplicates,*

B = National Standards for Business Education   Standard number & level of duplicate

J1 = LFS: Justice, I (elementary)

N = NAEP: Civics Consensus Project   R1 = LFS: Responsibility, I (elementary)

P1, P2 = LFS: Privacy, I & II (elementary)   D = Duplicated in another standard

Q = Quigley: Civitas

McREL

- Understands the effects that significant American political developments have on other nations (e.g., immigration policies; opposition to communism; promotion of human rights; foreign trade; economic, military, and humanitarian aid) *BD (CE,125)*

- Understands why transnational loyalties such as those to ethnic, religious, tribal, or linguistic groups sometimes supersede allegiance to a nation-state (e.g., Communist International, Islam, Christianity) *BD (CE,125)*

- Understands historical and contemporary responses of the American government to demographic and environmental changes that affect the United States *BD (CE,125;QI,251-252,520)*

- Knows some of the principal economic, technological, and cultural effects the United States has had on the world (assembly line manufacturing, research and development in computer technology, popular music, fashion, film, television) *BD (CE,125)*

- Understands the principal effects that economic conditions, technological developments, and cultural developments in other nations have had on American society and the lives of American citizens (e.g., economic conditions such as multinational corporations, migration of labor; technological developments such as fax machines, personal computers, television; cultural developments such as religious movements, resurgence of ethnic consciousness) *BD (CE,125)*

24. Understands the meaning of citizenship in the United States, and knows the requirements for citizenship and naturalization *(CE,127)*

Level I (Grades K-2)

- No material specifically designated for this level *BD (CE,35)*

Level II (Grades 3-5)

- Knows that a citizen is a legally recognized member of the United States who has certain rights and privileges and certain responsibilities (e.g., privileges such as the right to vote and hold public office and responsibilities such as respecting the law, voting, paying taxes, serving on juries) *BD (CE,35;NI,43;QE,611-612)*

Codes (right side of page):	BD = Benchmark, Declarative; BP = Benchmark, Procedural; BC = Benchmark, Contextual
1st letter of each code in parentheses	*2nd letter of code* *Number*
C = CCE: National Standards for Civics	E = Explicitly stated in document Page number of cited document
A1 = LFS: Authority, I (elementary)	I = Implied in document *or, for duplicates,*
B = National Standards for Business Education	Standard number & level of duplicate
J1 = LFS: Justice, I (elementary)	
N = NAEP: Civics Consensus Project	R1 = LFS: Responsibility, I (elementary)
P1, P2 = LFS: Privacy, I & II (elementary)	D = Duplicated in another standard
Q = Quigley: Civitas	

- Knows that citizens owe allegiance or loyalty to the United States and in turn they receive protection and other services from the government

  BD (CE,35;NI,43;QI,237)

- Knows the difference between a citizen and a non-citizen (alien), and knows that people become citizens by birth or naturalization

  BD (CE,36;NI,43)

Level III (Grades 6-8)

- Understands that American citizenship is legally recognized full membership in a self-governing community that confers equal rights under the law; is not dependent on inherited, involuntary groupings such as race, gender, or ethnicity; and confers certain rights and privileges (e.g., the right to vote, to hold public office, to serve on juries)

  BD (CE,74;NE,44)

- Knows that Americans are citizens of both their state and the United States

  BD (CE,74;NI,44)

- Understands what constitutes citizenship by birth in the United States

  BD (CE,74;NI,44)

- Understands the distinction between citizens and noncitizens (aliens) and the process by which noncitizens may become citizens

  BD (CE,74;DE,24.4.1;NI,44)

- Knows how naturalization in the United States compares with naturalization in other nations

  BD (CE,74;DE,24.4.2)

- Knows the criteria established by law that are used for admission to citizenship in the United States such as five years of residence in the U.S.; ability to read, write, and speak English; proof of good moral character; knowledge of the history of the U.S.; knowledge of and support for American constitutional democracy

  BD (CE,74;DE,24.4.3)

Level IV (Grades 9-12)

- Understands the distinction between citizens and noncitizens (aliens) and the process by which aliens may become citizens

  BD (CE,127;DE,24.3.4;NI,47)

- Understands how naturalization in America compares with naturalization in other countries

  BD (CE,127;DE,24.3.5;NI,47)

- Knows the criteria used for admission to citizenship in the United States such as five years

  BD (CE,127;DE,24.3.6;NE,47)

Codes (right side of page):	BD = Benchmark, Declarative; BP = Benchmark, Procedural; BC = Benchmark, Contextual	
1st letter of each code in parentheses	*2nd letter of code*	*Number*
C = CCE: National Standards for Civics	E = Explicitly stated in document	Page number of cited document
A1 = LFS: Authority, I (elementary)	I = Implied in document	*or, for duplicates,*
B = National Standards for Business Education		Standard number & level of duplicate
J1 = LFS: Justice, I (elementary)		
N = NAEP: Civics Consensus Project	R1 = LFS: Responsibility, I (elementary)	
P1, P2 = LFS: Privacy, I & II (elementary)	D = Duplicated in another standard	
Q = Quigley: Civitas		

459

McREL

of residence in U.S.; ability to read, write, and speak English; proof of good moral character; knowledge of the history of the United States; knowledge of and support for the values and principles of American constitutional government

(CE,128-129)

25. Understands issues regarding personal, political, and economic rights

Level I (Grades K-2)

BD (P1E,1;NI,43;QE,18)

- Knows that the right to privacy is a personal right guaranteed by the United States Constitution

BD (P1E,8;QE,18)

- Knows that privacy refers to situations in which one or more persons restrict the access of one or more others to a certain thing or things (the "object" of privacy)

BD (P1E,12-14;QE,18)

- Knows examples of privacy (e.g., writing a letter in private, having a private telephone conversation, telling someone a secret), and knows that objects of privacy can be communications, a person's actions, a person's thoughts and feelings, and a person's space

Level II (Grades 3-5)

BD (CE,36;NI,43;QE,17-18)

- Knows what constitutes personal rights and why they are important (e.g., to associate with whomever one chooses, practice the religion of one's choice)

BD (CE,36;NI,43;QE,18)

- Knows what constitutes political rights and why they are important (e.g., to speak freely, criticize the government, join political parties or organizations that strive to influence government policies, seek and hold political office)

BD (CE,36;BI,73,74;NI,43;QE,18-19)

- Knows what constitutes economic rights and why they are important (e.g., to own property, choose one's work)

BD (CE,36)

- Knows contemporary issues regarding rights (school prayer, equal pay for equal work, welfare)

Codes (right side of page):   BD = Benchmark, Declarative; BP = Benchmark, Procedural; BC = Benchmark, Contextual

1st letter of each code in parentheses	*2nd letter of code*	*Number*
C = CCE: National Standards for Civics	E = Explicitly stated in document	Page number of cited document
A1 = LFS: Authority, I (elementary)	I = Implied in document	*or, for duplicates,*
B = National Standards for Business Education		Standard number & level of duplicate
J1 = LFS: Justice, I (elementary)		
N = NAEP: Civics Consensus Project	R1 = LFS: Responsibility, I (elementary)	
P1, P2 = LFS: Privacy, I & II (elementary)	D = Duplicated in another standard	
Q = Quigley: Civitas		

Level III (Grades 6-8)

BD (CE,75;NE,45;QE,18)
- Knows what constitutes personal rights (e.g., freedom of conscience, freedom to marry whom one chooses, to have children, to associate with whomever one pleases, to live where one chooses, to travel freely, to emigrate) and the major documentary sources of personal rights (e.g., Declaration of Independence, United States Constitution including the Bill of Rights, state constitutions)

BD (CE,75;NE,45;QE,18)
- Understands the importance to individuals and society of such personal rights as freedom of conscience and religion, freedom of expression and association, freedom of movement and residence, and privacy

BD (CE,76;NE,45;QE,18)
- Knows what constitutes political rights (e.g., the right to vote, petition, assembly, freedom of press), and knows the major documentary sources of political rights such as the Declaration of Independence, United States Constitution including the Bill of Rights, state constitutions, and civil rights legislation

BD (CE,76;NE,45;QE,18)
- Understands the importance to individuals and society of such political rights as the right to vote and run for public office and the freedom of speech, press, assembly, and petition

BD (CE,76;BE,73,74;BI,125;NE,45;QE,18-19)
- Knows important economic rights (e.g., the right to own property, choose one's work, change employment, join a labor union, establish a business), and knows statements of economic rights in the United States Constitution (e.g., requirement of just compensation, contracts, copyright, patents)

BD (CE,76;BE,73,74;BI,125;NE,45;QE,18-19)
- Understands the importance to individuals and society of such economic rights as the right to acquire, use, transfer, and dispose of property; choose one's work and change employment; join labor unions and professional associations; establish and operate a business; copyright and patent; and enter into lawful contracts

BD (CE,76;BI,74;NI,45;QI,18-19)
- Understands basic contemporary issues involving personal, political, and economic rights (e.g., personal rights issues such as dress codes, curfews, sexual harassment; political rights issues such as hate speech, fair trial, free press; economic rights issues such as welfare, minimum wage, health care, equal pay for equal work)

Codes (right side of page):	BD = Benchmark, Declarative; BP = Benchmark, Procedural; BC = Benchmark, Contextual	
1st letter of each code in parentheses	*2nd letter of code*	*Number*
C = CCE: National Standards for Civics	E = Explicitly stated in document	Page number of cited document
A1 = LFS: Authority, I (elementary)	I = Implied in document	*or, for duplicates,*
B = National Standards for Business Education		Standard number & level of duplicate
J1 = LFS: Justice, I (elementary)		
N = NAEP: Civics Consensus Project	R1 = LFS: Responsibility, I (elementary)	
P1, P2 = LFS: Privacy, I & II (elementary)	D = Duplicated in another standard	
Q = Quigley: Civitas		

MREL

Level IV (Grades 9-12)

- Understands the importance to individuals and to society of personal rights such as freedom of thought and conscience, privacy and personal autonomy, and the right to due process of law and equal protection of the law _{BD (CE,128;NI,48;QE,18)}

- Understands contemporary issues that involve political rights such as access to classified information and changing the boundaries of congressional and state legislative districts _{BD (CE,129;NI,48;QI,18)}

- Understands the argument that economic responsibilities follow from economic rights _{BD (CE,130;BE,73,74;QE,18-19)}

- Understands contemporary issues that involve economic rights such as consumer product safety, taxation, affirmative action, eminent domain, zoning, copyright, patents _{BD (CE,130;NI,48;QI,18-19)}

- Knows major documentary sources of personal, political, and economic rights such as the Northwest Ordinance, state constitutions and bills of rights, court decisions, and common law _{BD (CE,128-9;BI,23;QI,18-19)}

- Understands how personal, political, and economic rights are secured by constitutional government and by such means as the rule of law, checks and balances, an independent judiciary, and a vigilant citizenry _{BD (CE,129-30;NI,48;QE,14-15)}

26. Understands issues regarding the proper scope and limits of rights and the relationships among personal, political, and economic rights _(CE,130)

Level I (Grades K-2)

- Knows that the consequences of privacy can be both beneficial and costly _{BD (P1E,30)}

- Knows that there are conflicts over the scopes and limits of privacy (e.g., situations in which keeping a secret could be harmful) _{BD (P1E,39-40;QE,18)}

Level II (Grades 3-5)

- Knows criteria necessary for analyzing and evaluating conflicts over privacy (e.g., how and _{BD (CI,36;P2E,39-40)}

Codes (right side of page):	BD = Benchmark, Declarative; BP = Benchmark, Procedural; BC = Benchmark, Contextual	
1st letter of each code in parentheses	*2nd letter of code*	*Number*
C = CCE: National Standards for Civics	E = Explicitly stated in document	Page number of cited document
A1 = LFS: Authority, I (elementary)	I = Implied in document	*or, for duplicates,*
B = National Standards for Business Education		Standard number & level of duplicate
J1 = LFS: Justice, I (elementary)		
N = NAEP: Civics Consensus Project	R1 = LFS: Responsibility, I (elementary)	
P1, P2 = LFS: Privacy, I & II (elementary)	D = Duplicated in another standard	
Q = Quigley: Civitas		

why something is kept secret; possible reasons why it should not be kept secret)

Level III (Grades 6-8)

BD (CE,77;QE,418)
- Understands what is meant by the "scope and limits" of a right (e.g., the scope of one's right to free speech in the United States is extensive and protects almost all forms of political expression, but the right to free speech can be limited if it seriously harms or endangers others)

BD (CE,77;QI,418)
- Understands the argument that all rights have limits, and knows criteria commonly used in determining what limits should be placed on specific rights (e.g., clear and present danger rule, compelling government interest test, national security, libel or slander, public safety, equal opportunity)

BD (CE,77;NI,47)
- Understands different positions on a contemporary conflict between rights (e.g., right of a fair trial and right to a free press; right to privacy and right to freedom of expression)

BD (CE,77;NI,47)
- Understands different positions on a contemporary conflict between rights and other social values and interests (e.g., the right of the public to know what their government is doing versus the need for national security; the right to property versus the protection of the environment)

Level IV (Grades 9-12)

BD (CE,128-9;NI,48;QI,18-19)
- Knows how to distinguish among personal, political, and economic rights (e.g., the right to live where one chooses as distinct from the right to use money to buy personal property as distinct from the right to register to vote)

BD (CE,131;NI,48)
- Understands different positions on a contemporary conflict between rights such as one person's right to free speech versus another person's right to be heard

BD (CE,130)
- Knows examples of situations in which personal, political, or economic rights are in conflict

BD (CE,130)
- Understands the argument that poverty, unemployment, and urban decay serve to limit both political and economic rights

---

Codes (right side of page):	BD = Benchmark, Declarative; BP = Benchmark, Procedural; BC = Benchmark, Contextual	
1st letter of each code in parentheses	*2nd letter of code*	*Number*
C = CCE: National Standards for Civics	E = Explicitly stated in document	Page number of cited document
A1 = LFS: Authority, I (elementary)	I = Implied in document	*or, for duplicates,*
B = National Standards for Business Education		Standard number & level of duplicate
J1 = LFS: Justice, I (elementary)		
N = NAEP: Civics Consensus Project	R1 = LFS: Responsibility, I (elementary)	
P1, P2 = LFS: Privacy, I & II (elementary)	D = Duplicated in another standard	
Q = Quigley: Civitas		

- Understands the argument that personal, political, and economic rights reinforce each other
  BD (CE,130)

- Understands the relationship between political rights and the economic right to acquire, use, transfer, and dispose of property
  BD (CE,130;QI,418)

- Understands the relationship of political rights to economic rights such as the right to choose one's work, to change employment, and to join a labor union and other lawful associations
  BD (CE,130;BI,125;QI,418)

27. Understands how certain character traits enhance citizens' ability to fulfill personal and civic responsibilities
(CE,131-133)

Level I (Grades K-2)

- Knows that a responsibility is a duty to do something or not to do something
  BD (R1E,7;NI,44)

- Knows examples of situations that involve responsibility and the sources of responsibility (e.g., a child obeying his/her parents' request to take care of the family's pet)
  BD (R1E,17)

- Knows some of the benefits of fulfilling responsibilities (e.g., praise and approval from parents, increased confidence and self-esteem)
  BD (R1E,17)

Level II (Grades 3-5)

- Understands why personal responsibility is important, and knows examples of personal responsibility (e.g., taking advantage of the opportunity to be educated)
  BD (CE,37;BI,22;QI,12-13)

- Understands why civic responsibility is important, and knows examples of civic responsibility (e.g., obeying the law, respecting the rights of others)
  BD (CE,37;BE,22;NE,44;QE,611)

- Knows private character traits that contribute to the health of American democracy such as individual responsibility, self-discipline/self-governance, honesty, persistence, and compassion
  BD (CE,37-38;BE,22;QE,13-14)

- Knows public character traits that contribute to the health of American democracy such as
  BD (CE,37-38;BE,22;QE,13-14)

Codes (right side of page):	BD = Benchmark, Declarative; BP = Benchmark, Procedural; BC = Benchmark, Contextual	
1st letter of each code in parentheses	*2nd letter of code*	*Number*
C = CCE: National Standards for Civics	E = Explicitly stated in document	Page number of cited document
A1 = LFS: Authority, I (elementary)	I = Implied in document	*or, for duplicates,*
B = National Standards for Business Education		Standard number & level of duplicate
J1 = LFS: Justice, I (elementary)		
N = NAEP: Civics Consensus Project	R1 = LFS: Responsibility, I (elementary)	
P1, P2 = LFS: Privacy, I & II (elementary)	D = Duplicated in another standard	
Q = Quigley: Civitas		

464

McREL

civility, respect for the rights of other individuals, respect for the law, open mindedness, critical mindedness, negotiation and compromise, civic mindedness, and patriotism

Level III (Grades 6-8)

- BD (CE,78;BE,22;NI,47;QI,13)

  Understands the importance for individuals and society of commonly held personal responsibilities such as taking care of one's self, supporting one's family, accepting responsibility for the consequences of one's actions, adhering to moral principles, considering the rights and interests of others, and behaving in a civil manner

- BD (CE,78;BI,22;NI,47)

  Understands contemporary issues that involve personal responsibilities (e.g., failure to provide adequate support or care for one's children, cheating on examinations, lack of concern for the less fortunate)

- BD (CE,78;BE,22;NI,47;QI,611)

  Understands the importance for individuals and society of commonly held civic responsibilities such as paying taxes, being informed and attentive to public issues, monitoring political leaders and governmental agencies and taking appropriate action if their adherence to constitutional principles is lacking, deciding whether and how to vote, participating in civic groups, performing public service, serving as a juror, and serving in the armed forces

- BD (CE,78;BI,22;NI,47;QI,13,611)

  Understands the meaning of civic responsibilities as distinguished from personal responsibilities, and understands contemporary issues that involve civic responsibilities (e.g., low voter participation, avoidance of jury duty, failure to be informed about public issues)

- BD (CE,78;BI,22;NI,47;QE,13)

  Understands how citizens' responsibilities as Americans could require the subordination of their personal rights and interests to the public good

Level IV (Grades 9-12)

- BD (CE,131;BI,22;NI,48;QI,13,611)

  Understands the distinction between personal and civic responsibilities and the tensions that may arise between them

- BD (CE,131;BI,22;NI,48;QI,13)

  Understands how individuals and society benefit from the fulfillment of personal responsibilities such as supporting one's family and caring for, nurturing, and educating one's

---

Codes (right side of page):	BD = Benchmark, Declarative; BP = Benchmark, Procedural; BC = Benchmark, Contextual

1st letter of each code in parentheses   *2nd letter of code*   *Number*

C = CCE: National Standards for Civics   E = Explicitly stated in document   Page number of cited document

A1 = LFS: Authority, I (elementary)   I = Implied in document   *or, for duplicates,*

B = National Standards for Business Education   Standard number & level of duplicate

J1 = LFS: Justice, I (elementary)

N = NAEP: Civics Consensus Project   R1 = LFS: Responsibility, I (elementary)

P1, P2 = LFS: Privacy, I & II (elementary)   D = Duplicated in another standard

Q = Quigley: Civitas

465

MCREL

children

- Understands the importance of each citizen reflecting on, criticizing, and reaffirming basic constitutional principles
  BD (CE,132;NE,48;QE,13)

- Understands the importance for individuals and society of fulfilling civic responsibilities such as assuming leadership when appropriate, registering to vote, and voting knowledgeably on candidates and issues
  BD (CE,132;NE,48;QI,611)

- Understands whether and when moral obligations or constitutional principles require one to refuse to assume certain civic responsibilities
  BD (CE,132;BI,22;QE,13,611)

- Understands the importance of dispositions that lead citizens to become independent members of society such as self-discipline, self-governance, and individual responsibility (i.e., fulfilling the moral and legal obligations of membership in society)
  BD (CE,133;BE,22;NE,48;QE,13)

- Understands the importance of dispositions that foster respect for individual worth and human dignity such as compassion and respect for the rights and choices of individuals
  BD (CE,133;BE,22;NE,48;QE,13)

- Understands the importance of dispositions that incline citizens toward public affairs such as civic mindedness and patriotism (i.e., loyalty to the principles underlying American constitutional democracy as distinguished from jingoism and chauvinism)
  BD (CE,133;BI,22;NE,48;QE,13)

28. Understands how participation in civic and political life can help citizens attain individual and public goals
(CE,135)

Level I (Grades K-2)

- No material specifically designated for this level
  BD (CE,38)

Level II (Grades 3-5)

- Understands why it is important for citizens to monitor their local, state, and national governments; and knows ways people can monitor the decisions and actions of their government such as reading about public issues, watching television news programs,
  BD (CE,38-39;NE,44;QE,43)

Codes (right side of page):	BD = Benchmark, Declarative; BP = Benchmark, Procedural; BC = Benchmark, Contextual	
1st letter of each code in parentheses	*2nd letter of code*	*Number*
C = CCE: National Standards for Civics	E = Explicitly stated in document	Page number of cited document
A1 = LFS: Authority, I (elementary)	I = Implied in document	*or, for duplicates,*
B = National Standards for Business Education		Standard number & level of duplicate
J1 = LFS: Justice, I (elementary)		
N = NAEP: Civics Consensus Project	R1 = LFS: Responsibility, I (elementary)	
P1, P2 = LFS: Privacy, I & II (elementary)	D = Duplicated in another standard	
Q = Quigley: Civitas		

discussing public issues, and communicating with public officials

BD (CE,39;NE,44;QE,43)

- Knows ways people can influence the decisions and actions of their government such as voting; taking an active role in interest groups, political parties, and other organizations that attempt to influence public policy and elections; attending meetings of governing agencies (e.g., city council, school board); working in campaigns, circulating and signing petitions; taking part in peaceful demonstrations; and contributing money to political parties, candidates, or causes

BD (CE,39;NI,44)

- Knows individuals or groups who monitor and influence the decisions and actions of their local, state, tribal, and national governments (e.g., the media, labor unions, P.T.A., Chamber of Commerce, taxpayer associations, civilian review boards)

Level III (Grades 6-8)

BD (CE,81;NI,45;NE,47;QI,39)

- Understands how participation in civic and political life can help bring about the attainment of individual and public goals (c.g., personal goals such as living in a safe and orderly neighborhood, obtaining a good education, living in a healthy environment; public goals such as increasing the safety of the community, improving local transportation facilities, providing opportunities for education and recreation)

BD (CE,81;NI,45;QI,39)

- Understands the importance of both political and social participation and what distinguishes one from the other (e.g., participating in a campaign to change laws regulating the care of children as opposed to volunteering to care for children), and knows opportunities for both political and social participation in the local community

BD (CE,81;NE,47;QE,43)

- Understands how Americans can use the following means to monitor and influence politics and government at local, state, and national levels: joining political parties, interest groups, and other organizations that attempt to influence public policy and elections; voting; taking part in peaceful demonstrations; circulating and signing petitions

BD (CE,82;BI,125;NI,47)

- Knows historical and contemporary examples of citizen movements seeking to promote individual rights and the common good (e.g., abolition, suffrage, labor and civil rights movements)

BD (CE,82;QE,629-632)

- Understands what civil disobedience is, how it differs from other forms of protest, what its

---

Codes (right side of page):	BD = Benchmark, Declarative; BP = Benchmark, Procedural; BC = Benchmark, Contextual

1st letter of each code in parentheses   *2nd letter of code*   *Number*
C = CCE: National Standards for Civics   E = Explicitly stated in document   Page number of cited document
A1 = LFS: Authority, I (elementary)   I = Implied in document   *or, for duplicates,*
B = National Standards for Business Education   Standard number & level of duplicate
J1 = LFS: Justice, I (elementary)
N = NAEP: Civics Consensus Project   R1 = LFS: Responsibility, I (elementary)
P1, P2 = LFS: Privacy, I & II (elementary)   D = Duplicated in another standard
Q = Quigley: Civitas

consequences might be, and circumstances under which it might be justified

BD (CE,82;DE,29.3.7,29.4.2;NI,7;QE,43)

- Understands why becoming knowledgeable about public affairs and the values and principles of American constitutional democracy and communicating that knowledge to others is a form a political participation

Level IV (Grades 9-12)

BD (CE,135;NI,49;QI,39)

- Understands how individual participation in the political process relates to the realization of the fundamental values of American constitutional democracy

BD (CE,136;NI,49;QI,39)

- Understands what distinguishes participation in government and political life from nonpolitical participation in civil society and private life (e.g., participating in a campaign to change laws regulating nursing homes as opposed to volunteering to work in a nursing home), and understands the importance of both forms of participation to American constitutional democracy

BD (CE,136;NE,49)

- Knows the many ways citizens can participate in the political process at local, state, and national levels, and understands the usefulness of other forms of political participation in influencing public policy (e.g., attending political and governmental meetings, demonstrating, contacting public officials, writing letters, boycotting, community organizing, petitioning, picketing)

BD (CE,136;NI,49)

- Knows historical and contemporary examples of citizen movements seeking to expand liberty, to insure the equal rights of all citizens, and/or to realize other values fundamental to American constitutional democracy (e.g., the suffrage and civil rights movements)

BD (CE,136;NI,49;QE,47)

- Understands the importance of voting as a form of political participation

(CE,136-137)

29. **Understands the importance of political leadership, public service, and a knowledgeable citizenry in American constitutional democracy**

Level I (Grades K-2)

BD (A1I,30;NI,42)

- Knows that a good leader puts the interests of the people ahead of personal interests

---

Codes (right side of page):	BD = Benchmark, Declarative; BP = Benchmark, Procedural; BC = Benchmark, Contextual	
1st letter of each code in parentheses	*2nd letter of code*	*Number*
C = CCE: National Standards for Civics	E = Explicitly stated in document	Page number of cited document
A1 = LFS: Authority, I (elementary)	I = Implied in document	*or, for duplicates,*
B = National Standards for Business Education		Standard number & level of duplicate
J1 = LFS: Justice, I (elementary)		
N = NAEP: Civics Consensus Project	R1 = LFS: Responsibility, I (elementary)	
P1, P2 = LFS: Privacy, I & II (elementary)	D = Duplicated in another standard	
Q = Quigley: Civitas		

- BD (A1E,32;NE,42)
  Knows the characteristics of a good leader (e.g., experience, determination, confidence, a desire to be a leader, the ability to solve problems creatively)

Level II (Grades 3-5)

- BD (CE,39;NI,42)
  Knows what political leaders do and why leadership is necessary in a democracy

- BD (CE, 39;NE,42)
  Knows opportunities for leadership and public service in the student's own classroom, school, community, state, and the nation; and understands why leadership and public service are important to the continuance and improvement of American democracy

- BD (CE,39)
  Understands the importance of individuals working cooperatively with their elected leaders

- BD (CE,40;NI,42)
  Knows the major duties, powers, privileges, and limitations of a position of leadership (e.g., class president, mayor, state senator, tribal chairperson, president of the United States); and knows how to evaluate the strengths and weaknesses of candidates in terms of the qualifications required for a particular leadership role

- BD (CE,40;NE,42;QI,564)
  Knows qualities leaders should have such as commitment to the values and principles of constitutional democracy, respect for the rights of others, ability to work with others, reliability or dependability, courage, honesty, ability to be fair, intelligence, willingness to work hard, and special knowledge or skills

- BD (CE,40;NI, 42;QI,564)
  Knows the criteria necessary for evaluating the strengths and weaknesses of candidates in relation to the qualifications required for a particular leadership role

Level III (Grades 6-8)

- BD (CE,82;NI,46;NE,49)
  Understands the functions of political leadership and why leadership is a vital necessity in a constitutional democracy

- BD (CE,82;NE,49)
  Knows personal qualities necessary for political leadership, and understands ethical dilemmas that might confront political leaders

- BD (CE,82;NI,45)
  Knows opportunities for political leadership in the student's own school, community, state,

---

Codes (right side of page):   BD = Benchmark, Declarative; BP = Benchmark, Procedural; BC = Benchmark, Contextual

1st letter of each code in parentheses	*2nd letter of code*	*Number*
C = CCE: National Standards for Civics	E = Explicitly stated in document	Page number of cited document
A1 = LFS: Authority, I (elementary)	I = Implied in document	*or, for duplicates,*
B = National Standards for Business Education		Standard number & level of duplicate
J1 = LFS: Justice, I (elementary)		
N = NAEP: Civics Consensus Project	R1 = LFS: Responsibility, I (elementary)	
P1, P2 = LFS: Privacy, I & II (elementary)	D = Duplicated in another standard	
Q = Quigley: Civitas		

McREL

and the nation; and understands the importance of individuals working cooperatively with their elected leaders

BD (CE,83;NE,49;QE,16-17)
- Understands the importance of public service in a constitutional democracy

BD (CE,83)
- Knows opportunities for public service in the student's own school, community, state, and nation; and knows career opportunities in public service

BD (CE,83)
- Understands the role of "the loyal opposition" in a constitutional democracy

BD (CE,83;DE,28.3.6,29.4.2;NI,47;QE,43)
- Understands why becoming knowledgeable about public affairs and the values and principles of American constitutional democracy and communicating that knowledge to others is an important form of participation, and understands the argument that constitutional democracy requires the participation of an attentive, knowledgeable, and competent citizenry

BD (CE,83;DE,29.4.3;NI,45)
- Understands how awareness of the nature of American constitutional change gives citizens the ability to reaffirm or change fundamental constitutional values

Level IV (Grades 9-12)

BD (CE,136;NI,48)
- Knows various ways students can exercise leadership in public affairs, and knows opportunities for citizens to engage in careers in public service

BD (CE,137;DE,28.3.6,29.3.7;NI,48;QE,43)
- Understands why becoming knowledgeable about public affairs and the values and principles of American constitutional democracy, and communicating that knowledge to others are important forms of participation, and understands the argument that constitutional democracy requires the participation of an attentive, knowledgeable, and competent citizenry

BD (CE,137;DE,29.3.8;NI,48)
- Understands how awareness of the nature of American constitutional change gives citizens the ability to reaffirm or change fundamental constitutional values

---

Codes (right side of page):	BD = Benchmark, Declarative; BP = Benchmark, Procedural; BC = Benchmark, Contextual	
1st letter of each code in parentheses	*2nd letter of code*	*Number*
C = CCE: National Standards for Civics	E = Explicitly stated in document	Page number of cited document
A1 = LFS: Authority, I (elementary)	I = Implied in document	*or, for duplicates,*
B = National Standards for Business Education		Standard number & level of duplicate
J1 = LFS: Justice, I (elementary)		
N = NAEP: Civics Consensus Project	R1 = LFS: Responsibility, I (elementary)	
P1, P2 = LFS: Privacy, I & II (elementary)	D = Duplicated in another standard	
Q = Quigley: Civitas		

470   MREL

13. Economics

The following process was used to identify standards and benchmarks for economics:

Identification of Significant Reports

Six reports were selected to assist in the identification of standards and benchmarks in economics. Two reports were published by the EconomicsAmerica: National Council on Economic Education (NCEE): *Voluntary National Content Standards* (1997), and *A Framework for Teaching Basic Economic Concepts with Scope and Sequence Guidelines, K–12* (Saunders & Gilliard, 1995). The Joint Council on Economic Education produced *Economics, What and When: Scope and Sequence Guidelines, K–12* (Gilliard et al., 1989), One report was authored by the Colorado Council on Economic Education, *Conceptual Content Standards: Grades K–12* (1994); another by the National Council for the Social Studies, *Expectations of Excellence: Curriculum Standards for Social Studies* (1994). Finally, supporting citations were developed from the International Baccalaureate Organisation's *Economics* (1996e).

Selection of the Reference Document

The NCEE's recently issued *Voluntary National Content Standards* was selected as the reference document. This work has content similar to *A Framework for Teaching Basic Economic Concepts*, the work that was used as the reference document in the previous edition of this report.

Identification of Standards and Benchmarks

The *Voluntary National Content Standards* work was useful for identifying benchmarks. The NCEE document identifies what students should know about economics at the end of 4th, 8th, and 12th grades. The source material is written such that the smallest organizational unit, which is termed a benchmark, is at the level of generality that is equivalent to what we term a benchmark. Thus, it was not difficult to determine what information was appropriate for identifying content at this level.

In some respects the reference document was not entirely compatible with our model for standards identification. The reference document arranges content statements under 21 topic areas, which we found somewhat too narrow in scope to be useful as standards for organizing benchmark information articulated across grades K–12. Inasmuch as we consider the benchmark (as well as the grade sequence of benchmarks) to provide critical subject information, but view the organization of benchmarks into standards as arbitrary to some degree (see Section 3), we elected to consolidate some material under slightly larger ideas in order to provide a more even distribution of benchmarks across standards. This reorganization was done through consulting the supplementary documents (see below). Finally, there were differences between the reference document and our model in the grade ranges provided. The reference document provides content information at three levels of schooling, K–4, 5–8, and 9–12; we prefer four: primary, upper elementary, middle, and high school. We were able to provide benchmarks at all four levels through the use of the supplementary material discussed below.

Integration of Information from Other Documents

Material from JCEE, *Economics, What and When: Scope and Sequence Guidelines, K–12*, was useful for constructing benchmarks at the four levels our model adopts (primary, elementary, middle, and high school), since the document presents content material at two-grade increments from K–1 through grades 11–12. The document also was found useful for the examples it provided to help clarify content statements. Additionally, each statement of content in *Scope and Sequence* is accompanied by "student language" — a version of the concept or generalization written in terms more accessible to students at the targeted grade levels. This language provided us with the means for composing benchmarks that were still accurate if somewhat less technical. Draft material from the Colorado Council for Economic Education (CCE) also provided guidance in writing benchmark statements. The CCE draft was found useful for the organization of benchmark statements into standards as well; some seven of our ten standards are closely modeled on that document. As is the case with all our supplementary documents, benchmarks include page number citations to the CCE document wherever similar content material has been identified.

Finally, the original reference work, *A Framework for Teaching Basic Economic Concepts,* has been cited at each benchmark wherever appropriate, so that users of the economics standards will be able to find supporting teaching materials. Similarly, the National Council for the Social Studies' *Expectations of Excellence: Curriculum Standards for Social Studies* has also been cited at the benchmark level so that users of the NCSS document are provided with a link to related economics content. Additionally, the citations just described, along with those from the CCE draft and the International Baccalaureate's work *Economics* might prove useful to those who desire additional criteria for selecting a subset of benchmarks from the economics standards.

Summary of Standards for Economics

1. Understands that scarcity of productive resources requires choices that generate opportunity costs
2. Understands characteristics of different economic systems, economic institutions, and economic incentives
3. Understands the concept of prices and the interaction of supply and demand in a market economy
4. Understands basic features of market structures and exchanges
5. Understands unemployment, income, and income distribution in a market economy
6. Understands the roles government plays in the United States economy
7. Understands savings, investment, and interest rates
8. Understands basic concepts of United States fiscal policy and monetary policy
9. Understands how Gross Domestic Product and inflation and deflation provide indications of the state of the economy
10. Understands basic concepts about international economics

(NE,2,5;EE,9-12)

1. Understands that scarcity of productive resources requires choices that generate opportunity costs

Level I (Grades K-2)

BD (NE,2;CE,3;EE,78;JE,15;SI,41)
- Knows that goods are objects that can satisfy people's wants, and services are activities that can satisfy people's wants

BD (NE,2;BE,12;CE,3;EE,78;JE,15;SE,41)
- Understands that since people cannot have everything they want, they must make choices about using goods and services to satisfy wants

BD (NE,5)
- Knows that a cost is what you give up when you decide to do something, and a benefit is something that satisfies your wants

BD (NE,3,16;CE,4;EE,78;JE,15;SI,41)
- Knows that people who use goods and services are called consumers, and people who make goods or provide services are called producers, and that most people both produce and consume

BD (NE,3;BI,12;CE,3;EE,78;JE,15;SI,41)
- Knows that natural resources are "gifts of nature" because they are present without human intervention

BD (NE,3;BE,12;CE,3;EE,78;JE,15;SI,41)
- Knows that capital resources are things made by people that are used to make other goods or to provide services

BD (NE,3,29;BE,12;CE,3;EE,78;JE,15;SI,41)
- Knows that human resources (i.e., labor or human capital) are the efforts of people who work to produce goods and to provide services

BD (NE,2;CE,3;EE,78;JE,18;SE,41)
- Knows that choices about what goods and services to buy and consume determine how resources will be used.

Level II (Grades 3-5)

BD (NE,3;CI,3;EE,78;JE,15;SI,41)
- Knows that productive resources are all natural resources, human resources, and capital resources used to produce goods and to provide services

BD (NE,3;CI,3;EE,92;JE,16;SE,41)
- Understands that goods and services are scarce because there are not enough productive

---

Codes (right side of page):   BD = Benchmark, Declarative; BP = Benchmark, Procedural; BC = Benchmark, Contextual
1st letter of each code in parentheses   *2nd letter of code*   *Number*
N = EconomicsAmerica: NCEE: Voluntary National   E = Explicitly stated in document   Page number of cited document
    Content Standards in Economics   I = Implied in document
B = International Baccalaureate: Economics
C = Colorado Council on Economic Education
E = NCEE: Framework for Economics
J = JCEE: Economics, What and When
S = NCSS: Curriculum Standards for Social Studies

474   M*REL*

resources to satisfy all of the wants of individuals, governments, and societies

- BD (NE,3;CI,3,4;EE,92;JE,16;SI,41)
  Understands that federal, state, and local governments have problems of scarcity also; because they have limited budgets, they must compare their revenues to the costs of public projects their citizens want

- BD (NE,31)
  Knows that innovation is the introduction of an invention into a use that has economic value

- BD (NE,31,32;CE,3;EE,92;JE,16;SI,41)
  Knows that entrepreneurs are people who use resources to produce innovative goods and services they hope people will buy

- BD (NE,31,32;CE,3;EE,92;JE,16;SI,41)
  Understands that entrepreneurs take the risk that people won't buy their products or won't pay enough for them to cover the entrepreneurs' costs

- BD (NE,2,4;BE,12;CE,3;EE,78;JE,17;SI,41)
  Understands that when productive resources are used to produce one good or service, the opportunity cost (i.e., what is given up) is other goods and services that would have been made with the same resources if the chosen good or service had not been made

- BD (NE,5;CE,3;EE,92;JE,17;SI,41)
  Understands that choices usually involve trade-offs; people can give up buying or doing a little of one thing in order to buy or do a little of something else

- BD (NE,13;EE,78;JE,18;SI,41)
  Knows that economic specialization occurs when people produce a narrower range of goods and services than they consume

- BD (NE,13,34;CE,4;EE,92;JE,18;SI,41)
  Understands how labor productivity can be increased as a result of specialization, division of labor, and more capital goods such as tools and machines

- BD (NE,3,33;CE,4;EE,92;JE,16;SI,41)
  Understands that the quality of labor resources (i.e., human capital) can be improved through investments in education, training, and health care

Level III (Grades 6-8)

- BD (NE,8;BE,12;CE,3;EE,92;JE,16;SE,41)
  Understands that scarcity of resources necessitates choice at both the personal and the societal levels

- BD (NE,6;BE,12;CE,4;EE,92;JE,17;SI,41)
  Knows that all decisions involve opportunity costs and that effective economic decision

Codes (right side of page):	BD = Benchmark, Declarative; BP = Benchmark, Procedural; BC = Benchmark, Contextual	
1st letter of each code in parentheses	*2nd letter of code*	*Number*
N = EconomicsAmerica: NCEE: Voluntary National Content Standards in Economics	E = Explicitly stated in document I = Implied in document	Page number of cited document
B = International Baccalaureate: Economics		
C = Colorado Council on Economic Education		
E = NCEE: Framework for Economics		
J = JCEE: Economics, What and When		
S = NCSS: Curriculum Standards for Social Studies		

making involves weighing the costs and benefits associated with alternative choices

- Understands that the evaluation of choices and opportunity costs is subjective and differs across individuals and societies
  BD (NE,4;SE,41)

- Knows that productivity can be measured as output per worker, per hour, per machine, or per unit of land
  BD (NE,14,34;CE,4;EE,92;JE,18;SI,41)

- Understands that increasing labor productivity is the major way in which a nation can improve the standard of living of its people
  BD (NE,34;CI,4;EE,121;JE,19;SI,41)

Level IV (Grades 9-12)

- Understands that marginal benefit is the change in total benefit resulting from an action, and marginal cost is the change in total cost resulting from an action
  BD (NE,6)

- Understands that optimal levels of output (e.g., production output, output of services provided by a public program) can be determined by comparing the marginal benefits and costs of producing a little more against the marginal benefits and costs of producing a little less
  BD (NE,6;SE,41)

- Understands that increases in productivity are affected by incentives that reward successful innovation and investments (e.g., in research and development, and in physical and human capital)
  BD (NE,35;EE,121;JE,19;SI,41)

- Understands that investing in new physical or human capital involves a trade-off of lower current consumption in anticipation of greater future production and consumption
  BD (NE,35;CI,4;EE,92;JE,18;SI,41)

- Understands that technological change and investments in capital goods and human capital may increase labor productivity but have significant opportunity costs and economic risks
  BD (NE,34,35;CE,4;EE,92,121;JE,19;SI,41)

Codes (right side of page):	BD = Benchmark, Declarative; BP = Benchmark, Procedural; BC = Benchmark, Contextual	
1st letter of each code in parentheses	*2nd letter of code*	*Number*
N = EconomicsAmerica: NCEE: Voluntary National	E = Explicitly stated in document	Page number of cited document
Content Standards in Economics	I = Implied in document	
B = International Baccalaureate: Economics		
C = Colorado Council on Economic Education		
E = NCEE: Framework for Economics		
J = JCEE: Economics, What and When		
S = NCSS: Curriculum Standards for Social Studies		

(NE,7,9,23;EE,14-17)

2. Understands characteristics of different economic systems, economic institutions, and economic incentives

Level I (Grades K-2)

BD (EE,62)

● Not appropriate for this level

Level II (Grades 3-5)

BD (NE,9;SI,41)

● Knows that people's choices and behavior are influenced by positive incentives (i.e., rewards that make people better off) and negative incentives (i.e., penalties that make people worse off)

BD (NE,9;SI,41)

● Knows that because people's views of rewards and penalties are different, the influence of an incentive can vary with the individual

BD (NE,10;CI,6;EE,79,93;JE,21;SI,41)

● Understands that the hope of earning profit (i.e., the difference between revenues and the costs of producing or selling a good or service) is the incentive that persuades entrepreneurs and business firms to take the risks of producing goods and services to sell

BD (NE,16;CE,5;EE,79,93;JE,21;SI,41)

● Knows that households (i.e., individuals or family units), as consumers, buy goods and services from business firms

BD (NE,29;CE,5;EE,79,93;JE,21;SI,41)

● Knows that households, as resource owners, sell productive resources (e.g., labor, natural resources, capital resources, entrepreneurial resources) to firms in order to earn income

BD (NE,7;CE,5;EE,92;JE,19;SE,41)

● Understands that all societies have developed various economic systems in order to allocate their resources to produce and distribute goods and services and there are advantages and disadvantages to each type of system

Level III (Grades 6-8)

BD (NE,29)

● Understands that employers are willing to pay wages and salaries to workers because they expect to sell the goods and services those workers produce at prices high enough to cover the wages and salaries and all other costs of production

---

Codes (right side of page):   BD = Benchmark, Declarative; BP = Benchmark, Procedural; BC = Benchmark, Contextual

1st letter of each code in parentheses	*2nd letter of code*	*Number*
N = EconomicsAmerica: NCEE: Voluntary National Content Standards in Economics	E = Explicitly stated in document	Page number of cited document
	I = Implied in document	

B = International Baccalaureate: Economics
C = Colorado Council on Economic Education
E = NCEE: Framework for Economics
J = JCEE: Economics, What and When
S = NCSS: Curriculum Standards for Social Studies

- Knows that in a command economic system a central authority, usually the government, makes the major decisions about production and distribution $\quad$ BD (NE,8;BE,13,16;CI,5;EE,93;JE,20;SI,41)

- Knows that in a market economic system individual households and business firms make the major decisions about production and distribution in a decentralized manner following their own self-interests $\quad$ BD (NE,8;BE,13;CI,5;EE,93;JE,20;SE,41)

- Understands that national economies vary in the extent to which they rely on government directives (central planning) and signals from private markets $\quad$ BD (NE,8;BE,13;CE,5;EE,93;JE,20;SI,41)

- Understands the types of specialized economic institutions found in market economies (e.g., corporations, partnerships, cooperatives, labor unions, banks, nonprofit organizations) $\quad$ BD (NE,24;CI,6;EE,93;JE,22;SE,41)

- Understands that economic incentives such as wanting to acquire money or goods and services and wanting to avoid loss are powerful forces affecting the way people behave $\quad$ BD (NE,10;CI,6;EE,93;JE,22;SE,41)

- Understands that entrepreneurs respond to incentives such as profits, the opportunity to be their own boss, the chance to achieve recognition, the satisfaction of creating new products, and disincentives such as losses and the responsibility, long hours, and stress of running a business $\quad$ BD (NE,32)

- Understands that in a market economy the pursuit of economic self-interest directs people and businesses in most of their economic decisions (e.g., to work, to save, to invest) $\quad$ BD (NE,10,22;CE,5;EE,93;JE,22;SI,41)

- Understands that many non-economic factors (e.g., cultural traditions and customs, values, interests, abilities) influence patterns of economic behavior and decision making $\quad$ BD (NE,10;CI,5;EE,93;JE,22;SE,41)

Level IV (Grades 9-12)

- Understands that the effectiveness of allocation methods can be evaluated by comparing costs and benefits $\quad$ BD (NE,8;SI,41)

- Understands that economic institutions (e.g., small and large firms, labor unions, not-for-profit organizations) have different goals, rules, and constraints, and thus respond differently to changing economic conditions and incentives $\quad$ BD (NE,10;CI,6;EE,121;JE,22-23;SE,41)

Codes (right side of page): $\quad$ BD = Benchmark, Declarative; BP = Benchmark, Procedural; BC = Benchmark, Contextual

1st letter of each code in parentheses	*2nd letter of code*	*Number*
N = EconomicsAmerica: NCEE: Voluntary National Content Standards in Economics	E = Explicitly stated in document I = Implied in document	Page number of cited document
B = International Baccalaureate: Economics		
C = Colorado Council on Economic Education		
E = NCEE: Framework for Economics		
J = JCEE: Economics, What and When		
S = NCSS: Curriculum Standards for Social Studies		

McREL

BD (NE,24;SI,41)
- Understands that incorporation encourages investment by allowing firms to accumulate capital for large-scale investment and reducing risk to individual investors

BD (NE,24;CE,5;EE,121;JE,23;SI,41)
- Knows that property rights, contract enforcement, standards for weights and measures, and liability rules affect incentives for people to produce and exchange goods and services

BD (NE,10;EE,121;JE,23)
- Understands that in every economic system consumers, producers, workers, savers, and investors respond to incentives in order to allocate their scarce resources to obtain the highest possible return, subject to the institutional constraints of their society

(NE,17,19;EE,18-22)
3. Understands the concept of prices and the interaction of supply and demand in a market economy

Level I (Grades K-2)

BD (NE,16;CE,5;EE,79;JE,25,SI,41-42)
- Knows that a price is the amount of money that people pay when they buy a good or service

BD (NE,16;CE,5;EE,79;JE,2;SI,41-42)
- Knows that a market exists whenever buyers and sellers exchange goods and services

Level II (Grades 3-5)

BD (NE,17;BE,14;CI,6;EE,94;JE,26;SI,41-42)
- Knows that in any market there is one price (i.e., the equilibrium or market clearing price) that makes the amount buyers want to buy equal to the amount sellers want to sell

BD (NE,17,19;CI,6;EE,94;JE,27;SE,41)
- Understands that people buy less of a product when its price goes up and more when its price goes down

BD (NE,17,19;CI,6;EE,94;JE,27;SE,41)
- Understands that businesses are willing and able to sell more of a product when its price goes up and less when its price goes down

BD (NE,42;BE,23;CE,6-7;EE,94;JE,26)
- Understands that when consumers make purchases, goods and services are transferred from businesses to households in exchange for money payments, which are used in turn by businesses to pay for productive resources and to pay taxes

---

Codes (right side of page): BD = Benchmark, Declarative; BP = Benchmark, Procedural; BC = Benchmark, Contextual

1st letter of each code in parentheses	*2nd letter of code*	*Number*
N = EconomicsAmerica: NCEE: Voluntary National Content Standards in Economics	E = Explicitly stated in document	Page number of cited document
	I = Implied in document	
B = International Baccalaureate: Economics		
C = Colorado Council on Economic Education		
E = NCEE: Framework for Economics		
J = JCEE: Economics, What and When		
S = NCSS: Curriculum Standards for Social Studies		

Level III (Grades 6-8)

- BD (NE,17;EE,94;JE,26;SI,41)
  Knows that relative prices refer to the price of one good or service compared to the prices of others goods and services

- BD (NE,8;CE,6;EE,94;JE,26;SE,41)
  Understands that relative prices and how they affect people's decisions are the means by which a market system provides answers to the basic economic questions: What goods and services will be produced? How will they be produced? Who will buy them?

- BD (NE,19;EE,94;JE,28;SI,41)
  Understands that the price of any one product is influenced by and also influences the prices of many other products

- BD (NE,20;CI,6;EE,122;JE,27;SI,41)
  Understands that scarce goods and services are allocated in a market economy through the influence of prices on production and consumption decisions

- BD (NE,19;BE,13;EE,122;JE,28;SI,41)
  Understands the "law of demand" (i.e., an increase in the price of a good or service encourages people to look for substitutes, causing the quantity demanded to decrease, and vice versa)

- BD (NE,19;BI,13,14;EE,122;JE,29;SI,41)
  Understands that an increase in the price of a good or service enables producers to cover higher costs and earn profits, causing the quantity supplied to increase (and vice versa), but that this relationship is true only as long as other factors influencing costs of product and supply do not change

Level IV (Grades 9-12)

- BD (NE,20;BE,13;CE,6;EE,122;JE,28;SI,41)
  Understands that the demand for a product will normally change (i.e., the demand curve will shift) if there is a change in consumers' incomes, tastes, and preferences, or a change in the prices of related (i.e., complementary or substitute) products

- BD (NE,20;BE,14;CE,6;EE,122;JE,29;SI,41)
  Understands that the supply of a product will normally change (i.e., the supply curve will shift) if there is a change in technology, in prices of inputs, or in the prices of other products that could be made and sold by producers

- BD (NE,20;SE,41)
  Understands that changes in supply or demand cause relative prices to change; in turn, buyers and sellers adjust their purchase and sales decisions

---

Codes (right side of page):	BD = Benchmark, Declarative; BP = Benchmark, Procedural; BC = Benchmark, Contextual

1st letter of each code in parentheses
N = EconomicsAmerica: NCEE: Voluntary National
    Content Standards in Economics
B = International Baccalaureate: Economics
C = Colorado Council on Economic Education
E = NCEE: Framework for Economics
J = JCEE: Economics, What and When
S = NCSS: Curriculum Standards for Social Studies

2nd letter of code
E = Explicitly stated in document
I = Implied in document

Number
Page number of cited document

McREL

BD (NE,17;SI,41)

- Understands that a shortage occurs when buyers want to purchase more than producers want to sell at the prevailing price, and a surplus occurs when producers want to sell more than buyers want to purchase at the prevailing price

BD (NE,17;BE,14;EE,122;JE,30;SI,41)

- Understands that shortages or surpluses usually result in price changes for products in a market economy

BD (NE,20;BE,14;EE,122;JE,30;SI,41)

- Understands that when price controls are enforced, shortages and surpluses occur and create long-run allocation problems in the economy

(NE,11,16,21,25;EE,22-23,24-26)

4. Understands basic features of market structures and exchanges

Level I (Grades K-2)

BD (NE,11;CI,6;EE,79;JE,23;SI,41)

- Understands that in an exchange people trade goods and services for other goods and services or for money

BD (NE,25;CE,6;EE,79;JE,23;SE,41)

- Knows that money is a good that can be used to buy all other goods and services

BD (NE,11;CE,6;EE,79;JE,24;SI,42)

- Understands that when two people trade because they want to, they expect to be better off after the exchange

BD (NE,11;CE,6;EE,79;JE,24;SI,42)

- Knows that barter is trading goods and services for other goods and services without using money

Level II (Grades 3-5)

BD (NE,21,22;CI,5,6;EE,94;JE,31;SI,41-42)

- Knows that competitive markets are those with many buyers and sellers, where no one person or firm controls prices or the number of products for sale

BD (NE,25;CI,6;EE,79;JE,24;SE,41)

- Understands that money reduces the problems barter faces because money is easy to divide, carry, and store

BD (NE,24;CE,6;EE,79;JE,25;SE,41)

- Knows that banks play a key role in providing currency and other forms of money to

---

Codes (right side of page):   BD = Benchmark, Declarative;   BP = Benchmark, Procedural;   BC = Benchmark, Contextual

1st letter of each code in parentheses   *2nd letter of code*   *Number*

N = EconomicsAmerica: NCEE: Voluntary National   E = Explicitly stated in document   Page number of cited document
    Content Standards in Economics   I = Implied in document

B = International Baccalaureate: Economics

C = Colorado Council on Economic Education

E = NCEE: Framework for Economics

J = JCEE: Economics, What and When

S = NCSS: Curriculum Standards for Social Studies

481

MᴄREL

consumers, and that banks serve as intermediaries between savers and borrowers

- Understands that when people and nations specialize, they become more interdependent (i.e., less self-sufficient and more dependent on exchange)

  BD (NE,13;CE,9;EE,79;JE,25;SE,41)

- Understands that money makes it easier to compare the value of different kinds of goods and services and allows people to save purchasing power for a later time because it can easily be traded for goods and services at any time

  BD (NE,26;CI,6;EE,93;JE,24;SE,41)

- Understands how active competition among sellers results in lower prices and costs, higher product quality, and better customer service

  BD (NE,21;BI,21;CI,6;EE,94;JE,31;SI,41)

Level III (Grades 6-8)

- Understands that not all competition is on the basis of price for identical products and that non-price competition includes style and quality differences, advertising, customer services, and credit policies

  BD (NE,21;CI,6;EE,94;JE,32;SI,41)

- Understands how competition among buyers of a product results in higher prices for the product

  BD (NE,21;CI,6;EE,94;JE,31;SI,41)

- Understands that the United States government uses laws and regulations to maintain competition, but sometimes the government reduces competition unintentionally or in response to special interest groups

  BD (NE,37;BE,22;CE,8;EE,123;JE,32;SE,41)

- Understands that money encourages people to specialize because they can operate more efficiently in an exchange (i.e., sell what they produce to anyone, not just to someone who has something they want)

  BD (NE,26;CE,6;EE,93;JE,25;SE,41)

Level IV (Grades 9-12)

- Knows that the basic money supply is usually measured as the total value of coins, currency, and checking account deposits held by the public

  BD (NE,26;CE,6;EE,93;JE,24;SI,41)

- Knows that collusion among buyers or sellers reduces the level of competition in a market

  BD (NE,22;CI,6;EE,123;JE,32;SI,41)

Codes (right side of page):   BD = Benchmark, Declarative; BP = Benchmark, Procedural; BC = Benchmark, Contextual

1st letter of each code in parentheses   *2nd letter of code*   *Number*

N = EconomicsAmerica: NCEE: Voluntary National   E = Explicitly stated in document   Page number of cited document
    Content Standards in Economics   I = Implied in document

B = International Baccalaureate: Economics

C = Colorado Council on Economic Education

E = NCEE: Framework for Economics

J = JCEE: Economics, What and When

S = NCSS: Curriculum Standards for Social Studies

and is more difficult in markets with large numbers of buyers and sellers

- Understands that in the long run the level of competition in an industry is determined largely by how difficult and expensive it is for new firms to enter the market and by consumers' information about the availability, price, and quantity of substitute goods and services
  BD (NE,22;EE,123;JE,32;SI,41)

- Understands that the introduction of new products and production methods by entrepreneurs is an important form of competition and source of technological progress and economic growth
  BD (NE,22;SI,41)

- Understands that externalities are unintended positive or negative side effects that result when the production or consumption of a good or service affects the welfare of people who are not the parties directly involved in the market exchange (e.g., a negative externality in consumption occurs when cigarette smoking by one individual has harmful or undesirable effects on nonsmokers, a positive externality in production occurs when a neighbor's home improvements increase the value of nearby properties)
  BD (NE,38;BE,15;EE,95;JE,35;SI,41)

- Understands that a natural monopoly exists when it is cheaper for one supplier to produce all of the output in a market than for two or more producers to share the output (e.g., electric companies)
  BD (NE,38;CI,6;EE,95;JE,36;SI,41)

- Understands that public service commissions typically regulate natural monopolies because people cannot rely on competition to control price and service levels in these cases
  BD (NE,38;CI,6;EE,95;JE,37;SE,41)

- Understands that when transaction costs (e.g., tariffs, costs of gathering or disseminating information on products, transportation costs paid by the consumer) decrease, more specialization and trading will occur
  BD (NE,37;CI,6;EE,122;JE,25;SE,41)

5. Understands unemployment, income, and income distribution in a market economy
(NE,29,42,44;EE,23,31-32)

Level I (Grades K-2)

- Not appropriate for this level
  BD (EE,62)

Level II (Grades 3-5)

- BD (NE,44;CI,5;EE,95;JE,45)
  Knows that unemployed people are those who are willing and able to work at current wage rates, but do not have jobs

Level III (Grades 6-8)

- BD (NE,29;BI,23;EE,94;JE,33)
  Knows the four basic categories of earned income: wages and salaries, rent, interest, and profit

- BD (NE,30;SI,41)
  Understands that wages and salary are influenced by forces of supply and demand for labor, as well as an individual's productivity, education, training and skills

- BD (NE,45;CI,5;EE,96;JE,45)
  Knows that the government defines "the labor force" as people at least 16 years old who either have a job or are actively looking for work

- BD (NE,44,45;BI,26;EE,96;JE,45)
  Understands that the unemployment rate (i.e., the percentage of the labor force considered to be unemployed) rises during a recession, and the economy's production is less than its potential level

Level IV (Grades 9-12)

- BD (NE,30)
  Understands that personal income is influenced by changes in the structure of the economy, the level of gross domestic product, technology, government policies, production costs and demand for specific goods and services, and discrimination

- BD (NE,30)
  Understands the concept of supply and demand in the labor market (e.g., if wage or salary payments increase, workers will increase the quantity of labor they supply and firms will decrease the quantity of labor they demand)

- BD (NE,30;EE,123;JE,33)
  Understands that for the functional distribution of income economists analyze what percentage of national income is paid out as wages and salaries, proprietors' income, rental income, and interest payments and trace that pattern of income distribution over time

- BD (NE,30;EE,123;JE,34)
  Understands that the personal distribution of income classifies the population according to the amount of income they receive, including transfer payments

---

Codes (right side of page):   BD = Benchmark, Declarative; BP = Benchmark, Procedural; BC = Benchmark, Contextual

1st letter of each code in parentheses   *2nd letter of code*   *Number*

N = EconomicsAmerica: NCEE: Voluntary National   E = Explicitly stated in document   Page number of cited document
    Content Standards in Economics   I = Implied in document

B = International Baccalaureate: Economics

C = Colorado Council on Economic Education

E = NCEE: Framework for Economics

J = JCEE: Economics, What and When

S = NCSS: Curriculum Standards for Social Studies

McREL

- BD (NE,38;SI,41)
  Understands that governments often redistribute income directly when individuals or interest groups are not satisfied with the income distribution resulting from markets, and that governments may also redistribute income indirectly as side-effects of other government actions that affect prices or output levels for various goods and services

- BD (NE,45;BE,26;EE,125;JE,45)
  Understands that the standard measure of the unemployment rate is flawed (e.g., it does not include discouraged workers, it does not weigh part-time and full-time employment differently, it does not account for differences in the intensity with which people look for jobs)

- BD (NE,45;BE,26;EE,125-126;JE,45-46)
  Understands that many factors contribute to differing unemployment rates for various regions and groups (e.g., regional economic differences; differences in labor force immobility; differences in ages, races, sexes, work experiences, training and skills; discrimination)

- BD (NE,46;BE,26;EE,126;JE,46)
  Knows that economists do not define full employment as 100 percent employment of the labor force because there is always some unavoidable unemployment due to people changing jobs (i.e., frictional employment) or entering the labor force for the first time

- BD (NE,45;BE,26;CE,5;EE,126;JE,46)
  Understands frictional, seasonal, structural, and cyclical unemployment and that different policies may be required to reduce each

(NE,36,40;EE,26-27)
6. Understands the roles government plays in the United States economy

Level I (Grades K-2)

- BD (NE,36;CE,7;EE,79;JE,37;SE,41)
  Knows that some of the goods and services we use are provided by the government (e.g., schools, parks, police and fire protection)

Level II (Grades 3-5)

- BD (NE,36;CE,7;EE,95;JE,37;SI,41)
  Knows that the government pays for the goods and services it provides through taxing and borrowing

---

Codes (right side of page):   BD = Benchmark, Declarative; BP = Benchmark, Procedural; BC = Benchmark, Contextual

1st letter of each code in parentheses	*2nd letter of code*	*Number*
N = EconomicsAmerica: NCEE: Voluntary National Content Standards in Economics	E = Explicitly stated in document	Page number of cited document
	I = Implied in document	

B = International Baccalaureate: Economics
C = Colorado Council on Economic Education
E = NCEE: Framework for Economics
J = JCEE: Economics, What and When
S = NCSS: Curriculum Standards for Social Studies

MREL

Level III (Grades 6-8)

- Knows that in a market economy the government helps markets to operate efficiently by protecting property rights (i.e. the right to exclude others from using a good or service and the right to transfer ownership) and by providing a system of weights and measures and a standard and stable currency

  BD (NE,37;BE,15;CE,7;EE,95;JE,37;SE,41)

- Understands that governments provide public goods because of the properties of shared consumption (i.e., non-rival products that can be used simultaneously by more than one person without reducing the amount of the product available for others to consume) and non-exclusion (i.e., public goods and service provide benefits to more than one person at the same time, and their use cannot be restricted only to those people who have paid to use them)

  BD (NE,36;BE,15;EE,95;JE,35;SE,41)

Level IV (Grades 9-12)

- Understands that because citizens, government employees, and elected officials do not always directly bear the costs of their political decisions, sometimes policies have costs that outweigh their benefits for society

  BD (NE,40)

- Understands that most federal tax revenue comes from personal income and payroll taxes, and these taxes are used to fund social security payments, the costs of national defense, medical expenditures, and interest payments on the national debt

  BD (NE,38;SI,41)

- Understands that most state and local government revenues come from sales taxes, grants from the federal government, personal income taxes, and property taxes, and are used to fund education, public welfare, road constructions and repair, and public safety

  BD (NE,38;SI,41)

- Understands that government can use subsidies to help correct for insufficient output, use taxes to help correct for excessive output, or can regulate output directly to correct for over- or under-production or consumption of a product

  BD (NE,38;BE,15;SI,41)

- Understands that governments provide an alternative method to markets for supplying goods and services when it appears that the benefits to society of doing so outweigh the costs to society but that not all individuals will bear the same costs or share the same benefits of these policies

  BD (NE,38;BI,15;SI,41)

Codes (right side of page):   BD = Benchmark, Declarative; BP = Benchmark, Procedural; BC = Benchmark, Contextual

1st letter of each code in parentheses   *2nd letter of code*   *Number*

N = EconomicsAmerica: NCEE: Voluntary National   E = Explicitly stated in document   Page number of cited document
     Content Standards in Economics   I = Implied in document

B = International Baccalaureate: Economics

C = Colorado Council on Economic Education

E = NCEE: Framework for Economics

J = JCEE: Economics, What and When

S = NCSS: Curriculum Standards for Social Studies

- Understands that incentives exist for political leaders to implement policies (e.g., price controls, barriers to trade) that disperse costs widely over large groups of people and benefit relatively small, politically powerful groups of people. BD (NE,40-41)

- Understands that few incentives exist for political leaders to implement policies that entail immediate costs and deferred benefits, even though these types of programs may be more economically effective BD (NE,41)

7. Understands savings, investment, and interest rates
(NE,27)

Level I (Grades K-2)

- Not appropriate for this level BD (EE,62)

Level II (Grades 3-5)

- Understands that savings is the part of income not spent on taxes or consumption BD (NE,23;SI,41)

Level III (Grades 6-8)

- Understands that funds are channeled from savers to borrowers through banks. BD (NE,24)

Level IV (Grades 9-12)

- Knows that an interest rate is a price of money that is borrowed or saved and that interest rates are determined by the forces of supply and demand BD (NE,27;SI,41)

- Knows that the real interest rate is the nominal or current interest rate minus the expected rate of inflation BD (NE,27;SI,41)

- Understands that higher interest rates provide incentives for people to save more and to borrow less, and vice versa BD (NE,27;SI,41)

Codes (right side of page):   BD = Benchmark, Declarative; BP = Benchmark, Procedural; BC = Benchmark, Contextual
1st letter of each code in parentheses   *2nd letter of code*   *Number*
N = EconomicsAmerica: NCEE: Voluntary National   E = Explicitly stated in document   Page number of cited document
    Content Standards in Economics   I = Implied in document
B = International Baccalaureate: Economics
C = Colorado Council on Economic Education
E = NCEE: Framework for Economics
J = JCEE: Economics, What and When
S = NCSS: Curriculum Standards for Social Studies

- BD (NE,28;SI,41)
  Understands that real interest rates are normally positive because people must be compensated for deferring the use of resources from the present into the future

- BD (NE,28;SI,41)
  Understands that riskier loans command higher interest rates than safer loans because of the greater chance of default on the repayment of risky loans

- BD (NE,28,35;SI,41)
  Understands that higher interest rates reduce business investment spending and consumer spending; thus, policies that raise and lower interest rates can affect spending

- BD (NE,46)
  Understands that expectations of increased inflation may lead to higher interest rates

(NE,47;EE,34-35)
8. Understands basic concepts of United States fiscal policy and monetary policy

Level I (Grades K-2)

BD (EE,62)
- Not appropriate for this level

Level II (Grades 3-5)

BD (EE,62)
- Not appropriate for this level

Level III (Grades 6-8)

BD (EE,62)
- Not appropriate for this level

Level IV (Grades 9-12)

BD (NE,47;CI,8;EE,96;JE,53)
- Knows that fiscal policy involves the use of national government spending and taxation programs to affect the level of economic activity in order to promote price stability, maximum employment, and reasonable economic growth

BD (NE,48;CI,8;EE,127;JE,53)
- Understands the concepts of balanced budget, budget deficit, and budget surplus

---

Codes (right side of page):   BD = Benchmark, Declarative; BP = Benchmark, Procedural; BC = Benchmark, Contextual
1st letter of each code in parentheses   *2nd letter of code*   *Number*
N = EconomicsAmerica: NCEE: Voluntary National   E = Explicitly stated in document   Page number of cited document
    Content Standards in Economics   I = Implied in document
B = International Baccalaureate: Economics
C = Colorado Council on Economic Education
E = NCEE: Framework for Economics
J = JCEE: Economics, What and When
S = NCSS: Curriculum Standards for Social Studies

- Understands that when the government runs a budget deficit, it must borrow from individuals, corporations, or financial institutions to finance the excess of expenditures over tax revenues
  BD (NE,48;EE,127;JE,53)

- Knows that the national debt is the total amount of money that the government has borrowed over all the years it ran deficits that have not been repaid
  BD (NE,48;EE,127;JE,54)

- Knows that monetary policy refers to actions by the Federal Reserve System that lead to changes in the amount of money in circulation and the availability of credit in the financial system
  BD (NE,48;CE,7;EE,127;JE,50)

- Understands that fiscal policies take time to affect the economy and that they may be reinforced or offset by monetary policies and changes in private investment spending by businesses and individuals
  BD (NE,47;EE,127;JE,54)

- Knows that the major monetary policy tools that the Federal Reserve System uses are open market purchases or sales of government securities, increasing the discount rate charged on loans it makes to commercial banks, and raising or lowering reserve requirements for commercial banks
  BD (NE,48)

- Understands that when banks make loans, the money supply increases, and when loans are paid back, the country's money supply shrinks
  BD (NE,26;CE,7;EE,126;JE,50)

- Understands that changes in the money supply lead to changes in interest rates and in individual and corporate spending which may influence the levels of spending, employment, prices, and economic growth in the economy
  BD (NE,48;CE,7;EE,126;JE,51)

(NE,42,44;EE,29,32-33)

9. **Understands how Gross Domestic Product and inflation and deflation provide indications of the state of the economy**

Level I (Grades K-2)

BD (EE,62)

- Not appropriate for this level

Codes (right side of page):	BD = Benchmark, Declarative; BP = Benchmark, Procedural; BC = Benchmark, Contextual	
1st letter of each code in parentheses	*2nd letter of code*	*Number*
N = EconomicsAmerica: NCEE: Voluntary National Content Standards in Economics	E = Explicitly stated in document I = Implied in document	Page number of cited document
B = International Baccalaureate: Economics		
C = Colorado Council on Economic Education		
E = NCEE: Framework for Economics		
J = JCEE: Economics, What and When		
S = NCSS: Curriculum Standards for Social Studies		

McREL

Level II (Grades 3-5)

- Not appropriate for this level

BD (EE,62)

Level III (Grades 6-8)

- Knows that inflation refers to a sustained increase in the average price level of the entire economy

BD (NE,44;BE,26;CE,7;EE,96;JE,47)

- Knows that deflation refers to a sustained decrease in the average price level of the entire economy

BD (NE,44;CE,7;EE,96;JE,47)

- Understands that inflation reduces the value of money and that people's purchasing power declines if their incomes increase more slowly than the inflation rate

BD (NE,45;BE,26)

- Knows that Gross Domestic Product (GDP) is the total market value, expressed in dollars, of all final goods and services produced in the economy in a given year and is used as an indicator of the state of the economy

BD (NE,42;CE,4;EE,124;JE,39)

Level IV (Grades 9-12)

- Knows that inflation is usually measured by the Consumer Price Index (CPI) which shows the increases or decreases in price level from one year to another

BD (NE,46;BE,26;CE,7;EE,96;JE,47)

- Knows the difference between "nominal" GDP (i.e., GDP stated in current dollars where an increase in GDP may reflect not only increases in the production of goods and services, but also increases in general prices) and "real" GDP (i.e., GDP which has been adjusted for price level changes)

BD (NE,43;EE,124;JE,40)

- Knows the factors upon which a country's GDP depends (e.g., quantity and quality of natural resources, size and skills of labor force, size and quality of capital stock)

BD (NE,43;EE,124;JE,40)

- Understands the economic growth is a sustained rise in GDP, which results from investments in human and physical capital, research and development, technological change, and improved institutional arrangements and incentives

BD (NE,34;SI,42)

Codes (right side of page):   BD = Benchmark, Declarative;   BP = Benchmark, Procedural;   BC = Benchmark, Contextual

1st letter of each code in parentheses   *2nd letter of code*   *Number*

N = EconomicsAmerica: NCEE: Voluntary National   E = Explicitly stated in document   Page number of cited document
     Content Standards in Economics   I = Implied in document

B = International Baccalaureate: Economics

C = Colorado Council on Economic Education

E = NCEE: Framework for Economics

J = JCEE: Economics, What and When

S = NCSS: Curriculum Standards for Social Studies

McREL

BD (NE,35)

- Understands that economic growth can alleviate poverty, raise standards of living, create new employment and profit opportunities in some industries, but can also reduce opportunities in other industries

BD (NE,46;BE,26;CE,7;EE,126;JE,48)

- Understands that inflation creates uncertainty because it affects different groups differently (e.g., inflation hurts people on fixed incomes, but helps people who have borrowed money at a fixed rate of interest) and because it causes people to devote resources to protect themselves from inflation

BD (NE,43,48;BE,26)

- Knows that inflation occurs (and/or employment increases) when money supply or desired expenditures for consumption, investment, government spending, and net exports are greater than the value of a nation's output of final goods and services, and vice versa (i.e., inflation decreases when these expenditures are less than the value of output)

BD (NE,47;BE,27;EE,126;JE,49)

- Understands that government policies designed to reduce unemployment (e.g., increasing federal spending, reducing taxes) may increase inflation, and vice versa

(NE,11,13,16;EE,35-40)

10.   Understands basic concepts about international economics

Level I (Grades K-2)

BD (EE,62)

- Not appropriate for this level

Level II (Grades 3-5)

BD (NE,25;CE,9;EE,96,128;JE,57;SI,42)

- Knows that different currencies are used in different countries

Level III (Grades 6-8)

BD (NE,12;CE,9;EE,96;JE,55;SI,42)

- Knows that exports are goods and services produced in one nation but sold to buyers in another nation

BD (NE,12;CE,9;EE,96;JE,55;SI,42)

- Knows that imports are goods or services bought from sellers in another nation

---

Codes (right side of page):   BD = Benchmark, Declarative; BP = Benchmark, Procedural; BC = Benchmark, Contextual
1st letter of each code in parentheses   *2nd letter of code*   *Number*
N = EconomicsAmerica: NCEE: Voluntary National   E = Explicitly stated in document   Page number of cited document
    Content Standards in Economics   I = Implied in document
B = International Baccalaureate: Economics
C = Colorado Council on Economic Education
E = NCEE: Framework for Economics
J = JCEE: Economics, What and When
S = NCSS: Curriculum Standards for Social Studies

491   MREL

- BD (NE,12,14;CE,9;EE,96;JE,56;SI,42)
Understands that international trade promotes greater specialization, which increases total world output, and increases material standards of living

- BD (NE,17;BE,31;CE,9;EE,128;JE,57;SI,42)
Knows that an exchange rate is the price of one nation's currency in terms of another nation's currency, and that exchange rates are determined by the forces of supply and demand

- BD (NE,17;EE,128;JE,57;SI,42)
Understands that extensive international trade requires an organized system for exchanging money between nations (i.e., a foreign exchange market)

- BD (NE,12;BE,28,29;CE,9;EE,128;JE,56,57;SI,42)
Knows that despite the advantages of international trade (e.g., broader range of choices in buying goods and services), many nations restrict the free flow of goods and services through a variety of devices known as "barriers to trade" (e.g., tariffs, quotas) for national defense reasons or because some companies and workers are hurt by free trade

- BD (NE,14;EE,129;JE,60;SI,42)
Understands that increasing international interdependence causes economic conditions and policies in one nation to affect economic conditions in many other nations

- BD (NE,42;EE,129;JE,60)
Knows how the level of real GDP per capita is used to compare the level of economic development in different nations

Level IV (Grades 9-12)

- BD (NE,14;CE,9;EE,128;JE,56;SI,42)
Understands that trade between nations would not occur if nations had the same kinds of productive resources and could produce all goods and services at the same real costs

- BD (NE,14;BE,28;CI,9;EE,128;JE,56;SI,42)
Knows that a nation has an absolute advantage if it can produce more of a product with the same amount of resources than another nation, and it has a comparative advantage when it can produce a product at a lower opportunity cost than another nation

- BD (NE,15)
Knows that comparative advantages change over time because of changes in resource prices and events that occur in other nations

- BD (NE,18;BE,31;CE,9;EE,128;JE,57;SI,42)
Understands that a change in exchange rates changes the relative price of goods and services traded by the two countries and can have a significant effect on the flow of trade between nations and on a nation's domestic economy

---

Codes (right side of page):	BD = Benchmark, Declarative; BP = Benchmark, Procedural; BC = Benchmark, Contextual	
1st letter of each code in parentheses	*2nd letter of code*	*Number*
N = EconomicsAmerica: NCEE: Voluntary National Content Standards in Economics	E = Explicitly stated in document I = Implied in document	Page number of cited document
B = International Baccalaureate: Economics		
C = Colorado Council on Economic Education		
E = NCEE: Framework for Economics		
J = JCEE: Economics, What and When		
S = NCSS: Curriculum Standards for Social Studies		

McREL

BD (NE,12;EE,128;JE,58)

- Knows that a nation pays for its imports with its exports

BD (NE,12,41;BE,29;CI,8;EE,129;JE,60;SI,42)

- Understands that public policies affecting foreign trade impose costs and benefits on different groups of people (e.g., consumers may pay higher prices, profits in exporting firms may decrease), and that decisions on these policies reflect economic and political interests and forces

---

Codes (right side of page):   BD = Benchmark, Declarative; BP = Benchmark, Procedural; BC = Benchmark, Contextual

1st letter of each code in parentheses   *2nd letter of code*   *Number*

N = EconomicsAmerica: NCEE: Voluntary National   E = Explicitly stated in document   Page number of cited document

    Content Standards in Economics   I = Implied in document

B = International Baccalaureate: Economics

C = Colorado Council on Economic Education

E = NCEE: Framework for Economics

J = JCEE: Economics, What and When

S = NCSS: Curriculum Standards for Social Studies

14. Foreign Language

The following process was used to identify standards and benchmarks in foreign language:

Identification of Significant Reports

Three reports were selected for identifying standards in foreign language: *Standards for Foreign Language Learning: Preparing for the 21st Century* (1996) from the National Standards in Foreign Language Education Project, the April 1995 draft of that work, and the second draft of *Content Standards for Foreign Language* (1996, June) from the Colorado department of education.

Selection of the Reference Document

The April 1995 draft of *Standards for Foreign Language Learning* was selected as the reference report. It was selected over the final, published version because in the opinion of the authors it provided greater specificity in regards to what students should know and be able to do. Both documents represent the collaborative work of the American Council on the Teaching of Foreign Languages, the American Association of Teachers of French, the American Association of Teachers of German, and the American Association of Teachers of Spanish and Portuguese.

Identification of Standards and Benchmarks

There are a number of similarities between the *Standards* draft and the model used to identify standards and benchmarks for this report. First, the draft's sample benchmarks, in a number of cases, provide descriptions of declarative, procedural or contextual knowledge, which accords with our requirements for a benchmark. Second, the standards statements are stated broadly enough to organize material across grades K–12.

In some ways, however, the *Standards* material differs from our approach. First, some of the draft benchmarks are broadly stated activities. For example, one benchmark states "students can work in groups to develop and propose solutions to problems that are of contemporary and historical interest in the target culture and in their own" (p. 19). From such descriptions as this it was not possible to extract specific knowledge and skills appropriate for a benchmark. In other cases, this tendency toward vagueness accompanies an emphasis on what we would describe as curriculum rather than content standards. For example, one standard, "Students reinforce and further their knowledge of other disciplines through the foreign language," contains benchmarks such as "students acquire information from authentic documents about a topic being studied in another class to integrate into activities in the foreign language classroom," and its correlate "students acquire information from authentic documents about a topic being studied in the foreign language classroom to integrate with other school subjects" (p. 32-33). As the rationale statement that accompanies the *Standards* material makes clear, this standard and its benchmarks are designed to foster the integration of foreign language into the broader curriculum. However worthwhile the goal, the effect of attempting such integration through content standards places new demands on students and teachers that might be unrealistic. For example, it requires that students be responsible for seeing to it that the content in one class is successfully integrated with the content in another. Furthermore, such a standard places special demands on the design of school programs if teachers of a foreign language are to assess whether students have appropriately integrated material from another discipline, or if teachers in a non-foreign language class are to determine whether students have appropriately interpreted and applied material from a foreign language. Since the model we apply defines content standards and benchmarks as descriptions of the specific knowledge and skills students should acquire, such standards and benchmarks as the foregoing were not included in the analysis.

Finally, our model and the reference document differ concerning the range and number of benchmark levels. The standards document specifies three benchmark levels: K–4, 5–8 and 9–12. Our model recommends four, corresponding to primary, upper elementary, middle, and high school. Unfortunately, no supplementary material was available to remedy this problem. Consequently the material is presented at three levels, K–4, 5–8, and 9–12.

Integration of Information from Other Documents

As indicated above, the final publication of the Foreign Language standards was not found to be useful for identifying specific content. Material from that work was cited at the benchmark level wherever possible, however, for those readers who use the 1996 document for curriculum planning. As to supplementary material that might provide examples or elaboration of the national standards, no material from states was available that appeared to be especially useful. However, in order to provide the user with a sense of the material in the Standards document that is frequently selected for use at the state level, we chose the Colorado draft document, which, albeit a draft, represents this selection fairly well.

Summary of Standards for Foreign Language

1. Uses the target language to engage in conversations, express feelings and emotions, and exchange opinions and information

2. Comprehends and interprets written and spoken language on diverse topics from diverse media

3. Presents information, concepts, and ideas to an audience of listeners or readers on a variety of topics

4. Demonstrates knowledge and understanding of traditional ideas and perspectives, institutions, professions, literary and artistic expressions, and other components of target culture

5. Recognizes that different languages use different patterns to communicate and applies this knowledge to the native language

(NDE,38)

1. Uses the target language to engage in conversations, express feelings and emotions, and exchange opinions and information

Level II (Grades K-4)

- Knows how to express likes, dislikes, and simple preferences in everyday situations (e.g., objects, categories, people, events) ^BP (NDE,18;CI,7;NE,38)

- Uses basic vocabulary to describe assorted objects (e.g., toys, dress, types of dwellings, foods) in everyday environments ^BP (CE,7;NE,38)

- Knows how to give and follow simple instructions in the target language (e.g., in games, with partners or groups, giving commands suggested by a picture) ^BP (NDE,18;CI,7;NE,38)

- Knows how to exchange information with peers about preferences (e.g., favorite activities) ^BP (NDE,18;CI,7;NI,38,62)

- Knows how to use non-verbal language (e.g., gestures) to clarify a verbal message when vocabulary is limited ^BP (NDE,18;NI,46,56)

- Knows how to exchange information about general events (e.g., classes, meetings, concerts, meals) and transportation (e.g., place, date, time) ^BP (NDE,18;CI,7;NI,38)

- Uses appropriate vocabulary, gestures, and oral expressions for greetings, introductions, leave takings, and other common or familiar interactions (e.g., name, address, phone number, place of origin, general health/state of being) ^BC (NDE,18,27;CE,11;NE,38,46,55,56)

Level III (Grades 5-8)

- Uses verbal and written exchanges to gather and share personal data, information, and opinions (e.g., events in one's life, past experiences, significant details related to topics that are of common interest, opinions about topics of personal or community interest) ^BP (NDE,18,19;CE,7;NI,38,62;)

- Uses the target language to plan events and activities with others (e.g., using authentic schedules, budgets) ^BC (NDE,18;NI,38)

- Uses vocabulary and cultural expressions to express the failure to understand the message or to request additional information (e.g., request that the speaker restate the message, ask appropriate questions for clarification) ^BC (NDE,18,19;CI,11;NI,38)

Codes (right side of page):	BD = Benchmark, Declarative; BP = Benchmark, Procedural; BC = Benchmark, Contextual
1st letter of each code in parentheses	*2nd letter of code* — *Number*
ND = NSFLE: Stan. for Foreign Lang. Learning	E = Explicitly stated in document — Page number of cited document
C = Colorado Foreign Language Standards	I = Implied in document
N = NSFLEP: Stan. for Foreign Lang. Learning	

- Uses non-verbal and verbal cues (e.g., rephrasing, circumlocution, repetition, gestures) to assist in communicating spoken messages and maintain listening comprehension **BP (NDE,18,21;CI,11;NI,46,56)**

- Uses appropriate vocabulary to give or follow directions for travel and other tasks **BC (NDE,19;CI,7;NI,38)**

- Uses appropriate vocabulary to acquire goods and services through basic negotiation of procedures and exchange of monies **BC (NDE,19;NI,39)**

- Knows how to express preferences concerning leisure activities and current events, in written form or orally, with peers who speak the language **BP (CI,7;NE,61)**

Level IV (Grades 9-12)

- Knows how to adequately express one's point of view through the exchange of personal feelings and ideas with members of the target culture **BP (NDE,19;CE,7;NI,39)**

- Uses appropriate vocabulary to exchange information about national and international topics (e.g., information from newspaper or magazine articles; programs on television, radio, or video) **BP (NDE,19;CI,7;NI,39)**

- Uses appropriate vocabulary to express personal reactions and feelings about and authentic literary texts (e.g., poems, plays, short stories, novels) **BP (NDE,19;CE,7;NE,39)**

- Uses appropriate vocabulary to exchange opinions and perspectives on issues of contemporary and historical interest in the target and native cultures **BP (CI,7;NE,39)**

- Uses rephrasing and circumlocution to communicate a message in the target language **BP (NDE,19)**

- Uses adequate vocabulary and non-verbal skills to acquire goods and services in the target language for personal needs and leisure (e.g., locating items in a pharmacy, finding a hotel or train station, repairing a tape recorder, asking for information) **BP (NDE,19)**

- Uses appropriate cultural responses in diverse exchanges (e.g., expressing gratefulness, extending and receiving invitations, apologizing, communicating preferences) **BP (NDE,19;CI,12)**

- Knows how to exchange information about current or past events and aspirations in one's personal life and in those of family, friends, and community **BP (NDE,19;CI,7;NI,39)**

Codes (right side of page):   BD = Benchmark, Declarative; BP = Benchmark, Procedural; BC = Benchmark, Contextual

1st letter of each code in parentheses	2nd letter of code	Number
ND = NSFLE: Stan. for Foreign Lang. Learning	E = Explicitly stated in document	Page number of cited document
C = Colorado Foreign Language Standards	I = Implied in document	
N = NSFLEP: Stan. for Foreign Lang. Learning		

(NDE,20;NE,39)

2. Comprehends and interprets written and spoken language on diverse topics from diverse media

Level II (Grades K-4)

BD (NDE,20;CE,5;NE,39)

- Understands the basic ideas of oral messages and short conversations based on simple or familiar topics appropriate at this developmental level (e.g., favorite activities, personal anecdotes, fairy tales)

BD (CI,8;NE,40)

- Understands the principle message in ability-appropriate, highly illustrated texts that use many words that are similar to those in one's native language (e.g., stories, newspaper articles, advertisements)

BD (NDE,20)

- Understands the main ideas of ability-appropriate video or television programs on familiar topics

BD (CI,8;NE,40)

- Understands the main ideas and/or the principal characters in written poems, short folk tales, or illustrated stories that are appropriate at this developmental level

BD (CI,8;NE,40)

- Understands brief written messages and personal notes on familiar topics (e.g., everyday school and home activities)

BD (NDE,20;NI,40)

- Recognizes common phrase groupings and voice inflection in simple spoken sentences

BC (NE,39)

- Identifies people and objects in the environment based on oral and written descriptions

Level III (Grades 5-8)

BD (CE,5;NE,40)

- Understands the main idea and themes, as well as some details, from diverse, authentic, ability-appropriate spoken media (e.g., radio, television, live presentation) on topics of personal interest or interest to peers in the target culture

BD (NDE,21;CI,8;NI,40)

- Understands the content of ability-appropriate primary sources on familiar topics (e.g., personal letters, pamphlets, illustrated newspaper and magazine articles, advertisements)

BD (NDE,21;CE,5;NI,40)

- Understands spoken announcements and messages from peers and familiar adults on familiar topics or topics of personal interest (e.g., favorite activities, popular events)

BC (NDE,21;NI,46,56)

- Recognizes and understands non-verbal and verbal cues when listening to or observing a user

---

Codes (right side of page): BD = Benchmark, Declarative; BP = Benchmark, Procedural; BC = Benchmark, Contextual
1st letter of each code in parentheses *2nd letter of code* *Number*
ND = NSFLE: Stan. for Foreign Lang. Learning E = Explicitly stated in document Page number of cited document
C = Colorado Foreign Language Standards I = Implied in document
N = NSFLEP: Stan. for Foreign Lang. Learning

of the target language

- Recognizes and understands various phrase groupings and structures in spoken forms of the target language

  BD (NDE,21;CI,5)

- Uses known language to make informed guesses about the meaning of longer, more complicated messages delivered orally and in writing (e.g., guesses at the meaning of unknown words based on the context in which they are used)

  BP (NDE,21;NI,40)

- Understands the main ideas, themes, principal characters, and significant details of ability-appropriate authentic literature

  BD (NDE,40;CI,5)

Level IV (Grades 9-12)

- Understands the main ideas and significant relevant details of extended discussions, lectures, formal presentations, and various forms of media (e.g., radio or television programs, movies) that are appropriate at this developmental level

  BD (NDE,21,22;CE,6;NE,40)

- Understands the main ideas and significant details of expository text forms (e.g., full length feature articles in newspapers and magazines) on topics of current and historical importance to members of the target culture

  BD (NDE,40;CI,9)

- Understands main plot and relevant sub-plots in authentic, ability-appropriate written literature, as well as the descriptions, roles, and significance of individual characters

  BD (NDE,40;CI,9)

- Recognizes characteristic features of an author's style in target-language literature that is appropriate at this developmental level

  BD (NDE,22;CI,9;NI,41)

- Understands the main ideas and significant relevant details of culturally significant songs, folk tales, comedy, and anecdotes in the target culture

  BD (NDE,22;CI,6;NI,41)

3. Presents information, concepts, and ideas to an audience of listeners or readers on a variety of topics

(NDE,22;NE,41)

Level II (Grades K-4)

- Presents simple oral reports or presentations about family members and friends, objects present in the everyday environment, and common school and home activities

  BP (NDE,22;NI,41)

Codes (right side of page):   BD = Benchmark, Declarative;   BP = Benchmark, Procedural;   BC = Benchmark, Contextual
1st letter of each code in parentheses   *2nd letter of code*   *Number*
ND = NSFLE: Stan. for Foreign Lang. Learning   E = Explicitly stated in document   Page number of cited document
C = Colorado Foreign Language Standards   I = Implied in document
N = NSFLEP: Stan. for Foreign Lang. Learning

501   MREL

- Recites poetry, songs, proverbs, or short anecdotes or narratives that are commonly known by same-age members of the target culture

  BP (NDE,41,62)

- Writes short, informal notes or messages that describe or provide information about oneself, friends and family, or school activities

  BP (NDE,23;CI,10;NI,41)

- Presents information about family, school events and celebrations via letters, E-mail, or in audio and video tapes

  BP (NDE,40;CI,10;NI,41,60)

Level III (Grades 5-8)

- Presents information in the target language on topics of shared personal interest in one's daily life at home or school (e.g., brief reports to the class, tape or video recorded messages)

  BP (NDE,23;NE,41)

- Presents cultural and literary works in the target language that are appropriate at this developmental level (e.g., presents short plays and skits, recites selected poems and anecdotes, performs songs)

  BP (NDE,41)

- Writes notes or short letters to peers in the target culture on topics of shared personal interest including everyday events and activities at home or in school

  BP (NDE,23;CI,10;NI,41)

- Summarizes the plot and provides brief descriptions of characters in selected poems, short stories, folk tales, and anecdotes

  BP (NDE,23;CI,8;NI,42)

- Uses repetition, rephrasing, and gestures effectively to assist in presenting oral reports or presentations

  BC (NDE,23)

Level IV (Grades 9-12)

- Writes letters to peers in the target cultures describing and analyzing current events of mutual interest

  BP (NDE,23;CI,10;NI,42,61)

- Summarizes orally or in writing the content of various expository texts appropriate at this developmental level (e.g., feature magazine or newspaper articles) on topics of current or historical interest to members of the target culture

  BP (NDE,23;CI,7,10;NI,42)

- Presents cultural and literary works in the target language that are appropriate at this developmental level (e.g., performs scenes from plays, recites poems or excerpts from short

  BP (NDE,42)

Codes (right side of page):	BD = Benchmark, Declarative; BP = Benchmark, Procedural; BC = Benchmark, Contextual	
1st letter of each code in parentheses	*2nd letter of code*	*Number*
ND = NSFLE: Stan. for Foreign Lang. Learning	E = Explicitly stated in document	Page number of cited document
C = Colorado Foreign Language Standards	I = Implied in document	
N = NSFLEP: Stan. for Foreign Lang. Learning		

McREL

stories)

BP (NDI,23;CI,7,10;NI,42)

- Presents information orally or in writing on literary and cultural topics that are appropriate at this developmental level (e.g., presents the plot, character descriptions and development, and themes found in authentic literary works; expresses opinions and appreciation for various forms of literature, radio programs, songs, films, visual works)

(NDE,27;NI,46,47)

4. Demonstrates knowledge and understanding of traditional ideas and perspectives, institutions, professions, literary and artistic expressions, and other components of target culture

Level II (Grades K-4)

BD (NDE,46;CI,11)

- Knows various age-appropriate cultural activities practiced in the target culture (e.g., games, songs, birthday celebrations, story telling, dramatizations, role playing)

BD (NDE,27,37;CI,11;NE,42,56)

- Knows simple patterns of behavior and interaction in various settings in the target culture (e.g., school, family, community) and how these patterns compare to those in one's native culture

BD (NE,47,56)

- Knows familiar utilitarian forms of the culture (e.g., toys, dress, types of dwellings, typical foods) and how they compare to those in one's native culture

BD (CE,11;NE,47,56)

- Knows some basic expressive forms of the target culture (e.g., children's songs, simple selections from authentic children's literature, types of artwork or graphic representations enjoyed or produced by the peer group in the culture studied)

BD (NDE,28,37;NI,47)

- Knows basic cultural beliefs and perspectives of people in both native and target cultures relating to family, school, work, and play

BP (NE,61)

- Identifies professions that require proficiency in the target language

Level III (Grades 5-8)

BD (NDE,28;CI,11;NI,46)

- Knows various age-appropriate cultural activities practiced in the target culture (e.g., adolescents' games such as card games, board games, and outdoor games; sports-related activities; music; television)

Codes (right side of page):   BD = Benchmark, Declarative;   BP = Benchmark, Procedural;   BC = Benchmark, Contextual
1st letter of each code in parentheses   *2nd letter of code*   *Number*
ND = NSFLE: Stan. for Foreign Lang. Learning   E = Explicitly stated in document   Page number of cited document
C = Colorado Foreign Language Standards   I = Implied in document
N = NSFLEP: Stan. for Foreign Lang. Learning

- Knows cultural traditions and celebrations that exist in the target culture and how these traditions and celebrations compare with those of the native culture (e.g., holidays, birthdays, "coming of age" celebrations, seasonal festivals, religious ceremonies, recreational gatherings) BD (NDE,37;CI,11;NI,56)

- Knows and recognizes patterns of behavior or interaction typical of one's age group in various settings in the target culture (e.g., dating, telephone usage, etiquette) BD (NDE,28;CI,11;NE,46)

- Knows a variety of age-appropriate utilitarian forms of the target culture (e.g., educational institutions or systems, means of transportation, various rules as they apply to the peer group in the culture being studied), their significance, and how these forms have influenced the larger community BD (NDE,28;NI,48,56)

- Knows a variety of age-appropriate expressive forms of the culture (e.g., popular music and dance; appropriate authentic texts, such as children's magazines, comic books, children's literature; the use of color; common or everyday artwork such as designs typical of the culture's clothing, pottery, ceramics, paintings, architectural structures) and how these expressive forms compare with those of the native culture BD (NDE,28,37;CE,14;NE,48,56)

- Knows how "local" opinions of various aspects of the native culture compare with the views of peers from the target culture BD (NDE,37;NI,48,56)

- Knows how various community members use the target language in their work BC (NE,61)

Level IV (Grades 9-12)

- Understands various patterns of behavior or interaction that are typical of one's age group (e.g., extra-curricular activities, social engagements) BD (CI,12;NE,47)

- Knows age-appropriate utilitarian forms of the target culture (e.g., social, economic, and political institutions; laws), how they are reflected in American culture, and their significance BD (NDE,28,37;CE,11;NI,48)

- Understands age-appropriate expressive forms of the target culture (e.g., literature; popular books; periodicals; videos; commercials; fine arts such as music, dance, design, painting) and their significance in the wider community BD (NDE,28-29;NE,48)

- Understands contrasting ways in which information about national and international events is reported in the target culture and the native culture BD (NDE,19)

Codes (right side of page):   BD = Benchmark, Declarative; BP = Benchmark, Procedural; BC = Benchmark, Contextual
1st letter of each code in parentheses   *2nd letter of code*   *Number*
ND = NSFLE: Stan. for Foreign Lang. Learning   E = Explicitly stated in document   Page number of cited document
C = Colorado Foreign Language Standards   I = Implied in document
N = NSFLEP: Stan. for Foreign Lang. Learning

504

McREL

BD (NDE,37;CI,11;NI,57)

- Understands contrasting ways in which familial, economic, environmental, and political issues are reflected through oral, written, and artistic expression in the native and target cultures

BP (NDI,37)

- Understands how other cultures view the role of the native culture in the world arena

BC (NDI,40;NI,61)

- Identifies career options that require knowledge of the target culture and proficiency in the target language

(NDE,36;NI,54)
5. Recognizes that different languages use different patterns to communicate and applies this knowledge to the native language

Level II (Grades K-4)

BD (NDE,36;NI,54)

- Knows words that have been borrowed from one language to another and how these word borrowings may have developed

BD (NE,55)

- Knows basic elements of the sound and writing systems of the target language and how these elements differ from the same elements of one's native language

BD (NE,54)

- Understands that an idea may be expressed in multiple ways in the target language

Level III (Grades 5-8)

BD (NDE,36;NI,55,57)

- Understands how idiomatic expressions have an impact on communication and reflect culture (e.g., anticipates larger units of meaning rather than individual word equivalencies)

BP (NE,52,62)

- Uses a variety of sources in the target language to obtain information on topics of personal interest

BP (NE,62)

- Uses various media from the target language and culture for entertainment

Level IV (Grades 9-12)

BD (NDE,36;NE,55)

- Knows various linguistic elements of the target language (e.g., time, tense) and how these elements compare to linguistic elements in one's native language

---

Codes (right side of page):   BD = Benchmark, Declarative; BP = Benchmark, Procedural; BC = Benchmark, Contextual
1st letter of each code in parentheses   *2nd letter of code*   *Number*
ND = NSFLE: Stan. for Foreign Lang. Learning   E = Explicitly stated in document   Page number of cited document
C = Colorado Foreign Language Standards   I = Implied in document
N = NSFLEP: Stan. for Foreign Lang. Learning

- Understands that the ability to comprehend language surpasses the ability to produce language ^{BD (NDE,19)}

- Uses a dictionary or thesaurus written entirely in the target language to select appropriate words for use in preparing written and oral reports ^{BP (NDE,23)}

Codes (right side of page):   BD = Benchmark, Declarative;   BP = Benchmark, Procedural;   BC = Benchmark, Contextual
1st letter of each code in parentheses   *2nd letter of code*   *Number*
ND = NSFLE: Stan. for Foreign Lang. Learning   E = Explicitly stated in document   Page number of cited document
C = Colorado Foreign Language Standards   I = Implied in document
N = NSFLEP: Stan. for Foreign Lang. Learning

506

MREL

GEOGRAPHY

15. Geography

The following process was used to identify standards and benchmarks for geography:

Identification of Significant Reports

Six reports were identified as important documents representing current thinking on standards in geography: *National Geography Standards* (1994) from the Geography Education Standards Project; *Item Specifications: 1994 National Assessment of Educational Progress in Geography* (1992) from the NAEP Geography Consensus Project; *Guidelines for Geographic Education* (1984) from the Joint Committee on Geographic Education; and *K–6 Geography: Themes, Key Ideas, and Learning Opportunities* (1987) from the Geographic Education National. Implementation Project. In addition, two documents from International Baccalaureate, *Geography* (1996g) and *Environmental Systems* (1996f).

Selection of the Reference Document

The Geography Education Standards Project's *National Geography Standards* (1994) was selected as the central document. The project has broad-based representation and was brought together for the express purpose of composing standards for geography. The project also makes use of the other important documents in the field (for further details, see the geography discussion under Section 2).

Identification of Standards and Benchmarks

The *Standards* work shares several aspects with our model for standards development. First, the standards statements in the document are expressed at a level of generality that fits our model for articulated standards. In addition, beneath each standard are provided descriptions of the knowledge and skills students should acquire in geography and in a range of closely related subjects.

There are a number of areas, however, in which the document is not directly compatible with our approach. For example, under each standard, student knowledge and skill are couched in terms of activities or tasks rather than in statements of declarative or procedural knowledge. For the most part it was possible, from a close analysis of the task, to discern what the authors considered to be the essential geographic knowledge or skill. Each activity, then, was studied to determine the knowledge or skill that might be presumed from a successful completion of the task. This analysis allowed us to generate benchmarks that describe declarative, procedural, and contextual content knowledge.

Another area of divergence between our model and the reference document concerns the range and number of benchmark levels. The standards document specifies three benchmark levels: K–4, 5–8, and 9–12. Our model recommends four, roughly corresponding to primary, upper elementary, middle, and high school. In this case, then, completion of our benchmark levels depended upon an analysis of supplementary materials that could provide us with further benchmark information, especially at the primary grades (discussed below).

Integration of Information from Other Documents

During the next stage of the process, the supplementary documents were reviewed, both to integrate information into the main document and to confirm our analysis of the reference document. That analysis, as described above, required us to deduce, from descriptions of tasks and activities, the knowledge and skills the authors believed the student should have. *Item Specifications: 1994 National Assessment of Educational Progress in Geography* provided us with an independent means to check the accuracy of our analysis. This document provides detailed descriptions as to the basic, proficient, and advanced levels of achievement in geography. For example, "Eighth grade basic" means that students should be able to, among other things, "...solve fundamental locational questions using latitude and longitude; interpret simple map scales; identify continents, oceans, and selected countries and cities..."(p. 54).

Another document used to support benchmark statements was *K–6 Geography: Themes, Key Ideas, and Learning Opportunities*. This guide for curriculum development also provided useful information for the elaboration of benchmarks at the primary level. This information was important because the reference document, as noted above, does not identify the knowledge and skills that might be especially suitable for the early (K–2) grades. Additionally, *Guidelines for Geographic Education*, which provides an instructional framework for teaching and learning geography by structuring content around five themes (Location, Place, Human-Environmental Interaction, Movement, and Regions), was analyzed and cited wherever appropriate at the benchmark level. Since page citations are provided for both these documents wherever appropriate, users are afforded easy reference to supporting material.

Finally, citations were added, where appropriate, to the course materials of the International Baccalaureate (IB) Program, which offers a Diploma Program for students in the final two years of secondary school and a Middle Years Program for students in the 11-16 age range. The programs, which are known for their intellectual rigor and high academic standards, are in place in 735 member schools in 92 countries.

Summary of Standards for Geography

The World in Spatial Terms
1. Understands the characteristics and uses of maps, globes, and other geographic tools and technologies
2. Knows the location of places, geographic features, and patterns of the environment
3. Understands the characteristics and uses of spatial organization of Earth's surface

Places and Regions
4. Understands the physical and human characteristics of place
5. Understands the concept of regions
6. Understands that culture and experience influence people's perceptions of places and regions

Physical Systems
7. Knows the physical processes that shape patterns on Earth's surface
8. Understands the characteristics of ecosystems on Earth's surface

Human Systems
9. Understands the nature, distribution, and migration of human populations on Earth's surface
10. Understands the nature and complexity of Earth's cultural mosaics
11. Understands the patterns and networks of economic interdependence on Earth's surface
12. Understands the patterns of human settlement and their causes
13. Understands the forces of cooperation and conflict that shape the divisions of Earth's surface

Environment and Society
14. Understands how human actions modify the physical environment
15. Understands how physical systems affect human systems
16. Understands the changes that occur in the meaning, use, distribution, and importance of resources

Uses of Geography
17. Understands how geography is used to interpret the past
18. Understands global development and environmental issues

1. **Understands the characteristics and uses of maps, globes, and other geographic tools and technologies** (GE,106)

Level I (Grades K-2)

- Not appropriate at this level

  BD (GE,106)

Level II (Grades 3-5)

- Knows the basic elements of maps and globes (e.g., title, legend, cardinal and intermediate directions, scale, grid, principal parallels, meridians, projection)

  BD (GE,106;EE,12;NE,35;TE,35)

- Interprets topography using aerial photos and maps

  BP (GE,106;EI,14;NI,34;TE,28)

- Uses map grids (e.g., latitude and longitude or alphanumeric system) to plot absolute location

  BP (GE,107;EI,13;NE,36;TE,27)

Level III (Grades 6-8)

- Knows the purposes and distinguishing characteristics of different map projections, including distortion on flat-map projections

  BC (GE,144,145;NE,52-53)

- Uses thematic maps (e.g., patterns of population, disease, economic features, rainfall, vegetation)

  BP (GE,144;NE,52-53)

- Understands concepts such as axis, major parallels, seasons, rotation, revolution, and principal lines of latitude and longitude (Earth-Sun relations)

  BD (GE,145;NE,37)

- Knows the advantages and disadvantages of maps, globes, and other geographic tools to illustrate a data set (e.g., data on population distribution, language-use patterns, energy consumption at different times of the year)

  BC (GE,145;NE,53)

- Knows the characteristics and uses of cartograms

  BD (GE,145;NE,52-53)

- Knows how maps help to find patterns of movement in space and time (e.g., mapping hurricane tracks over several seasons, mapping the spread of influenza throughout the world)

  BD (GE,145;NI,53)

  BD (GE,144;NI,53)

Codes (right side of page): BD = Benchmark, Declarative; BP = Benchmark, Procedural; BC = Benchmark, Contextual
1st letter of each code in parentheses *2nd letter of code* *Number*
G = GESP: National Geography Standards E = Explicitly stated in document Page number of cited document
E = JCGE: Guidelines for Geographic Education I = Implied in document *or, for duplicates,*
IE, IG = Int'l Bacc.:Environmental Systems, Geography Standard number & level of duplicate
N = NAEP: Item Specifications in Geography
T = GENIP: K-6 Geography: Themes, Key Ideas
D = Duplicated in another standard

MREL

- Knows the characteristics and purposes of geographic databases (e.g., databases containing census data, land-use data, topographic information)

Level IV (Grades 9-12)

BC (GE,185;NI,71-72)
- Understands the advantages and disadvantages of using maps from different sources and different points of view (e.g., maps developed by the media, business, government, industry and military to show how a recently closed military installation can be utilized for civilian purposes)

BD (GE,185;NE,71-72)
- Knows the characteristics and uses of geographic technologies (e.g., geographic information systems (GIS) and satellite-produced imagery)

BP (GE,184)
- Transforms primary data into maps, graphs, and charts (e.g., charts developed from recent census data ranking selected information on various topics, cartograms depicting the relative sizes of Latin American countries based on their urban populations)

(GI,108)
2. Knows the location of places, geographic features, and patterns of the environment

Level I (Grades K-2)

BD (GI,108;EE,11,12;NI,36;TE,11,15,21)
- Knows the location of school, home, neighborhood, community, state, and country

Level II (Grades 3-5)

BD (GE,108,109;EE,14;NE,34-36;TE,27)
- Knows major physical and human features of places as they are represented on maps and globes (e.g., shopping areas, fast food restaurants, fire stations, largest cities, rivers, lakes, wetlands, recreation areas, historic sites, landforms, locations of places discussed in history, language arts, science, and other school subjects)

BD (GI,109;EI,15;NE,34;TE,27)
- Knows the location of major cities in North America

BD (GE,109;EE,16;NE,34;TI,28)
- Knows the approximate location of major continents, mountain ranges, and bodies of water on Earth

---

Codes (right side of page):   BD = Benchmark, Declarative; BP = Benchmark, Procedural; BC = Benchmark, Contextual
1st letter of each code in parentheses   *2nd letter of code*   *Number*
G = GESP: National Geography Standards   E = Explicitly stated in document   Page number of cited document
E = JCGE: Guidelines for Geographic Education   I = Implied in document   *or, for duplicates,*
IE, IG = Int'l Bacc.:Environmental Systems, Geography   Standard number & level of duplicate
N = NAEP: Item Specifications in Geography
T = GENIP: K-6 Geography: Themes, Key Ideas
D – Duplicated in another standard

Level III (Grades 6-8)

- Knows the location of physical and human features on maps and globes (e.g., culture hearths such as Mesopotamia, Huang Ho, the Yucatan Peninsula, the Nile Valley; major ocean currents; wind patterns; land forms; climate regions) BD (GE,146;NI,52)

- Knows how mental maps can reflect attitudes and perceptions of places (e.g., how personal interests emphasize some details at the expense of others) BD (GE,147;NI,52)

- Knows the relative location of, size of, and distances between places (e.g., major urban centers in the United States) BD (GE,147;NI,52)

- Knows the factors that influence spatial perception (e.g., culture, education, age, gender, occupation, experience) BD (GE,147;NI,52)

Level IV (Grades 9-12)

- Knows the approximate locations of major political and economic cultures BD (GE,186;NE,71)

- Knows the spatial dynamics of various contemporary and historical events (e.g., the spread of radiation from the Chernobyl nuclear accident, how physical features have deterred migrations and invasions, trade and transportation in the contemporary world, the diffusion of contagious diseases such as the bubonic plague in 14th-century Europe or AIDS in the present-day world) BD (GE,186;NI,71)

- Knows the ways in which mental maps influence human decisions about location, settlement and public policy (e.g., locating houses in areas with scenic views; decisions to migrate based on newspaper and magazine advertisements, or television programs and movies) BD (GE,186-187;NI,71)

- Knows common factors that affect mental maps (e.g., how differences in life experiences, age, and gender influence people's housing preferences or their view of public transportation in a city; Eurocentric, Americentric, or Sinocentric mental maps of the world) BD (GE,187)

3. Understands the characteristics and uses of spatial organization of Earth's surface (GE,110)

Level I (Grades K-2)

- Identifies physical and human features in terms of the four spatial elements (e.g., locations BC (GE,110;EI,11,12;NI,36,38)

Codes (right side of page):   BD = Benchmark, Declarative; BP = Benchmark, Procedural; BC = Benchmark, Contextual
1st letter of each code in parentheses   *2nd letter of code*   *Number*
G = GESP: National Geography Standards   E = Explicitly stated in document   Page number of cited document
E = JCGE: Guidelines for Geographic Education   I = Implied in document   *or, for duplicates,*
IE, IG = Int'l Bacc.:Environmental Systems, Geography   Standard number & level of duplicate
N = NAEP: Item Specifications in Geography
T = GENIP: K-6 Geography: Themes, Key Ideas
D = Duplicated in another standard   512   McREL

[point], transportation and communication routes [line], regions [area], lakes filled with water [volume])

BD (GI,110-111;EI,11-12;NI,35;TE,15)
- Knows the absolute and relative location of a community and places within it (e.g., parks, stores, landmarks)

Level II (Grades 3-5)

BD (GE,112;EI,13-14;NE,34;TI,32;DI,7.3.1)
- Knows patterns on the landscape produced by physical processes (e.g., the drainage basin of a river system, the ridge-and-valley pattern of the Appalachians, vegetation on the windward and leeward sides of a mountain range)

BD (GE,110-111;EI,14;NE,45;TI,35)
- Understands the spatial organization of places through such concepts as location, distance, direction, scale, movement, and region

BD (GI,112;EI,14;NE,45-48;TE,38-39;DI,11.2.3)
- Understands how changing transportation and communication technology have affected relationships between locations

BD (GE,111;EI,13;NE,36;TE,25)
- Knows different methods used to measure distance (e.g., miles, kilometers, time, cost, perception)

Level III (Grades 6-8)

BD (GE,148;NE,54-57)
- Understands distributions of physical and human occurrences with respect to spatial patterns, arrangements, and associations (why some areas are more densely settled than others, relationships and patterns in the kind and number of links between settlements)

BD (GE,148-149;NE,66)
- Understands patterns of land use in urban, suburban, and rural areas (land uses that are frequently nearby and others not frequently adjacent to one another, dominant land-use patterns in city centers and peripheral areas)

BD (GE,149;NI,45)
- Understands how places are connected and how these connections demonstrate interdependence and accessibility (e.g., the role of changing transportation and communication technology, regions and countries Americans depend on for imported resources and manufactured goods)

BD (GE,149;NE,68)
- Understands the patterns and processes of migration and diffusion (spread of language,

---

Codes (right side of page): BD = Benchmark, Declarative; BP = Benchmark, Procedural; BC = Benchmark, Contextual
1st letter of each code in parentheses *2nd letter of code* *Number*
G = GESP: National Geography Standards E = Explicitly stated in document Page number of cited document
E = JCGE: Guidelines for Geographic Education I = Implied in document *or, for duplicates,*
IE, IG = Int'l Bacc.:Environmental Systems, Geography Standard number & level of duplicate
N = NAEP: Item Specifications in Geography
T = GENIP: K-6 Geography: Themes, Key Ideas
D = Duplicated in another standard

MREL

religion, and customs from one culture to another; spread of a contagious disease through a population; global migration patterns of plants and animals)

Level IV (Grades 9-12)

- Understands how concepts of spatial interaction (e.g., complementarity, intervening opportunity, distance decay, connections) account for patterns of movement in space (e.g., transportation routes, trade and migration patterns, commodity flows) _{BD (GE,188;NE,82)}

- Understands relationships in and between places (e.g., differences in threshold population or demand needed to support retail activities in a place, why there are many small central places and few large central places, law of retail gravitation) _{BD (GE,188-189;NE,82)}

- Understands how characteristics such as age, sex, employment, and income level affect the way people perceive and use space (e.g., school-age children traveling to and from school, employed people commuting by public transit, high-income people traveling long distances for vacations) _{BD (GE,189)}

- Understands principles of location (e.g., optimum plant-location decisions based on labor costs, transportation costs, market locations, climate; advantages for retailers to locate in malls rather than in dispersed locations) _{BD (GE,189;NE,83)}

4. Understands the physical and human characteristics of place (GE,113)

Level I (Grades K-2)

- Knows the physical and human characteristics of the local community (e.g., neighborhoods, schools, parks, creeks, shopping areas, airports, museums, sports stadiums, hospitals) _{BD (GE,113;EE,13;NE,45;TE,22)}

- Knows that places can be defined in terms of their predominant human and physical characteristics (e.g., rural, urban, forest, desert; or by types of landforms, vegetation, water bodies, climate) _{BD (GI,114;EI,14;NE,42;TE,22;DI,5.1.1)}

Level II (Grades 3-5)

- Knows how the characteristics of places are shaped by physical and human processes (e.g., _{BD (GE,114;NE,37,38;TE,28,29)}

Codes (right side of page):   BD = Benchmark, Declarative; BP = Benchmark, Procedural; BC = Benchmark, Contextual
1st letter of each code in parentheses   *2nd letter of code*   *Number*
G = GESP: National Geography Standards   E = Explicitly stated in document   Page number of cited document
E = JCGE: Guidelines for Geographic Education   I = Implied in document   *or, for duplicates,*
IE, IG = Int'l Bacc.:Environmental Systems, Geography   Standard number & level of duplicate
N = NAEP: Item Specifications in Geography
T = GENIP: K-6 Geography: Themes, Key Ideas
D = Duplicated in another standard   514

MREL

‌

effects of agriculture on changing land use and vegetation; effects of settlement on the building of roads; relationship of population distribution to landforms, climate, vegetation, or resources)

Level III (Grades 6-8)

- Knows the human characteristics of places (e.g., cultural characteristics such as religion, language, politics, technology, family structure, gender; population characteristics; land uses; levels of development)

  BD (GE,150;NE,56-57)

- Knows the physical characteristics of places (e.g., soils, landforms, vegetation, wildlife, climate, natural hazards)

  BD (GE,150;NE,61)

- Knows how technology shapes the human and physical characteristics of places (e.g., satellite dishes, computers, road construction)

  BD (GE,151;NI,61-62)

- Knows the causes and effects of changes in a place over time (e.g., physical changes such as forest cover, water distribution, temperature fluctuations; human changes such as urban growth, the clearing of forests, development of transportation systems)

  BD (GE,150-151;NI,56,57)

Level IV (Grades 9-12)

- Knows how social, cultural, and economic processes shape the features of places (e.g., resource use, belief systems, modes of transportation and communication; major technological changes such as the agricultural and industrial revolutions; population growth and urbanization)

  BD (GE,191;NI,75)

- Understands why places have specific physical and human characteristics in different parts of the world (e.g., the effects of climatic and tectonic processes, settlement and migration patterns, site and situation components)

  BD (GE,190;NI,72,75)

- Knows the locational advantages and disadvantages of using places for different activities based on their physical characteristics (e.g., flood plain, forest, tundra, earthquake zone, river crossing, coastal flood zone)

  BD (GE,191;NI,83)

Codes (right side of page):	BD = Benchmark, Declarative; BP = Benchmark, Procedural; BC = Benchmark, Contextual	
1st letter of each code in parentheses	*2nd letter of code*	*Number*
G = GESP: National Geography Standards	E = Explicitly stated in document	Page number of cited document
E = JCGE: Guidelines for Geographic Education	I = Implied in document	*or, for duplicates,*
IE, IG = Int'l Bacc.:Environmental Systems, Geography		Standard number & level of duplicate
N = NAEP: Item Specifications in Geography		
T = GENIP: K-6 Geography: Themes, Key Ideas		
D = Duplicated in another standard	515	

MREL

5.   Understands the concept of regions

(GE,115)

Level I (Grades K-2)

BD (GE,115;EI,13;NI,35;TI,10;DI,4.1.2)
- Knows areas that can be classified as regions according to physical criteria (e.g., landform regions, soil regions, vegetation regions, climate regions, water basins) and human criteria (e.g., political regions, population regions, economic regions, language regions)

Level II (Grades 3-5)

BD (GI,115;EE,13;NE,38;TE,32)
- Knows the characteristics of a variety of regions (landform, climate, vegetation, shopping, housing, manufacturing, religion, language)

BD (GE,116;EE,14;NI,38;TE,26)
- Understands how regions change over time and the consequences of these changes (e.g., changes in population size or ethnic composition; construction of a new shopping center, a regional hospital, or a new manufacturing plant; changes in transportation; changes in environmental conditions)

BD (GE,115;EE,13;NI,35;TE,20)
- Knows how regions are similar and different in form and function (e.g., local neighborhoods versus Central Business District)

Level III (Grades 6-8)

BD (GE,152;NI,45)
- Knows regions at various spatial scales (e.g., hemispheres, regions within continents, countries, cities)

BD (GE,152;NI,56-57)
- Understands criteria that give a region identity (e.g., its central focus, such as Amsterdam as a transportation center; relationships between physical and cultural characteristics, such as the Sunbelt's warm climate and popularity with retired people)

BD (GE,152)
- Knows types of regions such as formal regions (e.g., school districts, circuit-court districts, states of the United States), functional regions (e.g., the marketing area of a local newspaper, the "fanshed" of a professional sports team), and perceptual regions (e.g., the Bible Belt in the United States, the Riviera in southern France, the Great American Desert)

BD (GE,153;NE,64-65)
- Knows factors that contribute to changing regional characteristics (e.g., economic development, accessibility, migration, media image)

Codes (right side of page):   BD = Benchmark, Declarative; BP = Benchmark, Procedural; BC = Benchmark, Contextual
1st letter of each code in parentheses   *2nd letter of code*   *Number*
G = GESP: National Geography Standards   E = Explicitly stated in document   Page number of cited document
E = JCGE: Guidelines for Geographic Education   I = Implied in document   *or, for duplicates,*
IE, IG = Int'l Bacc.:Environmental Systems, Geography   Standard number & level of duplicate
N = NAEP: Item Specifications in Geography
T = GENIP: K-6 Geography: Themes, Key Ideas
D = Duplicated in another standard

McREL

BD (GE,153;NI,56-57)

- Understands the influences and effects of particular regional labels and images (e.g., Twin Peaks in San Francisco, Capitol Hill in Washington, D.C., the South, the rust belt, "developed" vs. "less-developed" regions)

BD (GE,153;NI,56-57)

- Understands ways regional systems are interconnected (e.g., watersheds and river systems, regional connections through trade, cultural ties between regions)

Level IV (Grades 9-12)

BD (GE,193;NE,64)

- Understands how regional boundaries change (e.g., changes resulting from shifts in population, environmental degradation, shifts in production and market patterns, wars)

BD (GE,193;NI,82)

- Knows factors that contribute to the dynamic nature of regions (e.g., human influences such as migration, technology, and capital investment; physical influences such as long-term climate shifts and seismic activity)

BD (GE,194;NI,82)

- Understands connections within and among the parts of a regional system (e.g., links involving neighborhoods within a city, municipalities within a metropolitan area, or power blocs within a defense or economic alliance)

BD (GE,192;NI,82)

- Understands how changing conditions can result in the redefinition of a region (e.g., the reshaping of South Africa resulting from the economic and political realignments that followed the end of European colonialism, the Caribbean Basin's transition from a major sugarcane and hemp producer to a center for tourism)

BD (GE,193)

- Knows ways in which the concept of a region can be used to simplify the complexity of Earth's space (e.g., by arranging an area into sections to help understand a particular topic or problem)

BD (GE,194;NI,82)

- Understands the different ways in which regional systems are structured (e.g., precinct, ward, county, state, and national levels of a political party hierarchy; hub-and-spoke airline operations; postal-service zip codes; assignment of Social Security numbers by region)

Codes (right side of page):   BD = Benchmark, Declarative;   BP = Benchmark, Procedural;   BC = Benchmark, Contextual

1st letter of each code in parentheses	*2nd letter of code*	*Number*
G = GESP: National Geography Standards	E = Explicitly stated in document	Page number of cited document
E = JCGE: Guidelines for Geographic Education	I = Implied in document	*or, for duplicates,*
IE, IG = Int'l Bacc.:Environmental Systems, Geography		Standard number & level of duplicate
N = NAEP: Item Specifications in Geography		
T = GENIP: K-6 Geography: Themes, Key Ideas		
D = Duplicated in another standard		

517

McREL

(GE,117)

6. Understands that culture and experience influence people's perceptions of places and regions

Level I (Grades K-2)

BD (GE,117)

- Not appropriate at this level

Level II (Grades 3-5)

BD (GE,117;EI,14;NE,44;TE,29)

- Understands ways in which people view and relate to places and regions differently (e.g., how children, mothers, joggers, and city park workers view a park)

Level III (Grades 6-8)

BD (GE,155;NI,56-57)

- Knows how places and regions serve as cultural symbols (e.g. Golden Gate Bridge in San Francisco; Opera House in Sydney, Australia; the Gateway Arch in St. Louis; Tower Bridge in London)

BD (GE,154;NI,56-57)

- Knows how technology affects the ways in which culture groups perceive and use places and regions (e.g., impact of technology such as air conditioning and irrigation on the human use of arid lands; changes in perception of environment by culture groups, such as the snowmobile's impact on the lives of Inuit people or the swamp buggy's impact on tourist travel in the Everglades)

BD (GE,154-155;NI,56-57)

- Knows the ways in which culture influences the perception of places and regions (e.g., religion and other belief systems, language and tradition; perceptions of "beautiful" or "valuable")

Level IV (Grades 9-12)

BD (GE,195;NI,79-80)

- Understands why places and regions are important to individual human identity and as symbols for unifying or fragmenting society (e.g., sense of belonging, attachment, or rootedness; symbolic meaning of places such as Jerusalem as a holy city for Muslims, Christians, and Jews)

BD (GE,195-196;NI,79-80)

- Understands how individuals view places and regions on the basis of their stage of life, sex,

---

Codes (right side of page):   BD = Benchmark, Declarative; BP = Benchmark, Procedural; BC = Benchmark, Contextual

1st letter of each code in parentheses   *2nd letter of code*   *Number*

G = GESP: National Geography Standards   E = Explicitly stated in document   Page number of cited document

E = JCGE: Guidelines for Geographic Education   I = Implied in document   *or, for duplicates,*

IE, IG = Int'l Bacc.:Environmental Systems, Geography   Standard number & level of duplicate

N = NAEP: Item Specifications in Geography

T = GENIP: K-6 Geography: Themes, Key Ideas

D = Duplicated in another standard

McREL

social class, ethnicity, values, and belief systems (e.g., perceptions of distance, impressions about what makes a place secure, views of public housing or wealthy urban neighborhoods)

BD (GE,196)

- Knows ways in which people's changing views of places and regions reflect cultural change (e.g., rural settings becoming attractive as recreation areas to people living in densely populated cities, old mining ghost towns becoming tourist and gambling centers)

(GE,118)

7.   Knows the physical processes that shape patterns on Earth's surface

Level I (Grades K-2)

BD (GE,118)

- Not appropriate at this level

Level II (Grades 3-5)

BD (GE,118,EI,16;NE,37;TI,28)

- Knows the physical components of Earth's atmosphere (e.g., weather and climate), lithosphere (e.g., landforms such as mountains, hills, plateaus, plains), hydrosphere (e.g., oceans, lakes, rivers), and biosphere (e.g., vegetation and biomes)

BD (GE,118;EI,16;NE,37;TI,28)

- Understands how physical processes help to shape features and patterns on Earth's surface (e.g., the effects of climate and weather on vegetation, erosion and deposition on landforms, mud slides on hills)

BD (GE,119;EI,11-12;NI,37;TI,16)

- Knows how Earth's position relative to the Sun affects events and conditions on Earth (e.g., how the tilt of the Earth in relation to the Sun explains seasons in different locations on Earth, how the length of day influences human activity in different regions of the world)

Level III (Grades 6-8)

BD (GE,156,190;NE,55-56;DI,3.2.1)

- Knows the major processes that shape patterns in the physical environment (e.g., the erosional agents such as water and ice, earthquake zones and volcanic activity, the ocean circulation system)

BD (GE,157;NI,55-56)

- Knows the processes that produce renewable and nonrenewable resources (e.g., fossil fuels, hydroelectric power, soil fertility)

Codes (right side of page):	BD = Benchmark, Declarative; BP = Benchmark, Procedural; BC = Benchmark, Contextual

1st letter of each code in parentheses — *2nd letter of code* — *Number*

G = GESP: National Geography Standards — E = Explicitly stated in document — Page number of cited document

E = JCGE: Guidelines for Geographic Education — I = Implied in document — *or, for duplicates,*

IE, IG = Int'l Bacc.:Environmental Systems, Geography — Standard number & level of duplicate

N = NAEP: Item Specifications in Geography

T = GENIP: K-6 Geography: Themes, Key Ideas

D = Duplicated in another standard

519

- Knows the consequences of a specific physical process operating on Earth's surface (e.g., effects of an extreme weather phenomenon such as a hurricane's impact on a coastal ecosystem, effects of heavy rainfall on hillslopes, effects of the continued movement of Earth's tectonic plates)

BD (GE,157;NI,55-56)

Level IV (Grades 9-12)

- Understands the distribution of different types of climate (e.g., marine climate or continental climate) that are produced by such processes as air-mass circulation, temperature, and moisture

BD (GE,197;IEE,24,26,27;NE,73-74)

- Understands the effects of different physical cycles (e.g., world atmospheric circulation, ocean circulation) on the physical environment of Earth

BD (GE,198;IEE,23,24,27;NE,73-74)

- Understands how physical systems are dynamic and interactive (e.g., the relationships between changes in landforms and the effects of climate such as the erosion of hill slopes by precipitation, deposition of sediments by floods, and shaping of land surfaces by wind)

BD (GE,198;IEE,23;NI,73-74)

- Understands how physical processes affect different regions of the United States and the world (e.g., effects of hurricanes in the Caribbean Basin and the eastern United States or of earthquakes in Turkey, Japan, and Nicaragua; effects of desertification and soil degradation, flash floods, dust storms, sand movement, soil erosion and salt accumulation in dry environments)

BD (GE,197;IEI,24,25,26,27;IGE,13;NE,73-74)

8.   Understands the characteristics of ecosystems on Earth's surface

(GE,120)

Level I (Grades K-2)

- Not appropriate at this level

BD (GE,120)

Level II (Grades 3-5)

- Knows the components of ecosystems at a variety of scales (e.g., fungi, insects, plants, and animals in a food chain or food web; fish and marine vegetation in coastal zones; grasses, birds, and insects in grassland areas)

BD (GE,120;EI,13;NI,37;TI,41)

Codes (right side of page):	BD = Benchmark, Declarative; BP = Benchmark, Procedural; BC = Benchmark, Contextual
1st letter of each code in parentheses	*2nd letter of code*	*Number*
G = GESP: National Geography Standards	E = Explicitly stated in document	Page number of cited document
E = JCGE: Guidelines for Geographic Education	I = Implied in document	*or, for duplicates,*
IE, IG = Int'l Bacc.:Environmental Systems, Geography		Standard number & level of duplicate
N = NAEP: Item Specifications in Geography		
T = GENIP: K-6 Geography: Themes, Key Ideas		
D = Duplicated in another standard	520	

- Knows ways in which humans can change ecosystems (e.g., clearing forests, widening channels of waterways, draining wetlands, wetting or suppressing fires)

  BD (GE,121;EI,14;NI,60;TE,42;DI,14.2.1)

- Knows plants and animals associated with various vegetation and climatic regions on Earth (e.g., the plant and animal life supported in a midlatitude forest in North America, the kinds of plants and animals found in a tropical rain forest in Africa, animals and trees that thrive in cities)

  BD (GE,120;NI,37;TE,33)

Level III (Grades 6-8)

- Understands the distribution of ecosystems from local to global scales (e.g., the consequences of differences in soils, climates, and human and natural disturbances)

  BD (GE,158;NI,54,55)

- Understands the functions and dynamics of ecosystems (e.g., interdependence of flora and fauna, the flow of energy and the cycling of energy, feeding levels and location of elements in the food chain)

  BD (GE,158;NI,59,60)

- Understands ecosystems in terms of their characteristics and ability to withstand stress caused by physical events (e.g., a river system adjusting to the arrival of introduced plant species such as hydrilla; regrowth of a forest after a forest fire; effects of disease on specific populations)

  BD (GE,159;NI,56)

- Knows changes that have occurred over time in ecosystems in the local region (e.g., natural wetlands on a floodplain being replaced by farms, farmlands on a floodplain being replaced by housing developments)

  BD (GE,159;NI,54-55)

- Knows the potential impact of human activities within a given ecosystem on the carbon, nitrogen, and oxygen cycles (e.g., the role of air pollution in atmospheric warming or the growing of peas and other legumes, which supply their own nitrogen and do not deplete the soil)

  BD (GE,159;NI,54-55)

- Understands the life cycle of a lake ecosystem from birth to death (including the process of eutrophication)

  BD (GE,159;NI,54-55)

Level IV (Grades 9-12)

- Understands how relationships between soil, climate, and plant and animal life affect the

  BD (GE,199;IEE,19,20;NE,73)

Codes (right side of page):	BD = Benchmark, Declarative; BP = Benchmark, Procedural; BC = Benchmark, Contextual	
1st letter of each code in parentheses	*2nd letter of code*	*Number*
G = GESP: National Geography Standards	E = Explicitly stated in document	Page number of cited document
E = JCGE: Guidelines for Geographic Education	I = Implied in document	*or, for duplicates,*
IE, IG = Int'l Bacc.:Environmental Systems, Geography		Standard number & level of duplicate
N = NAEP: Item Specifications in Geography		
T = GENIP: K-6 Geography: Themes, Key Ideas		
D = Duplicated in another standard		

MREL

distribution of ecosystems (e.g., effects of solar energy and water supply on the nature of plant communities)

BD (GE,200;IEE,19;NI,72-73)

- Knows ecosystems in terms of their biodiversity and productivity (e.g., the low productivity of deserts and the high productivity of midlatitude forests and tropical forests) and their potential value to all living things (e.g., as a source of oxygen for life forms, as a source of food for indigenous peoples, as a source of raw materials for international trade)

BD (GE,200;IEE,19;NI,72-73)

- Knows the effects of biological magnification in ecosystems (e.g., the increase in contaminants in succeeding levels of the food chain and the consequences for different life forms)

BD (GE,200;IEE,23,24,25,26,27;NI,78-79)

- Knows the effects of both physical and human changes in ecosystems (e.g., the disruption of energy flows and chemical cycles and the reduction of species diversity, how acid rain resulting from air pollution affects water bodies and forests and how depletion of the atmosphere's ozone layer through the use of chemicals may affect the health of humans)

(GE,122)

9. Understands the nature, distribution and migration of human populations on Earth's surface

Level I (Grades K-2)

BD (GE,122)

- Not appropriate at this level

Level II (Grades 3-5)

BD (GE,122-123;EE,13-14;NI,38;TE,22)

- Understands the characteristics of populations at a variety of scales (e.g., ethnicity, age distribution, number of families and single households, number of employed and unemployed, males and females, life expectancy, infant mortality)

BD (GE,122;EI,17;NI,34-45;TI,28-29)

- Knows the spatial distribution of population (e.g., that population density is higher east of the Mississippi River than west of it, population density is higher on the East Coast and West Coast than in the mountains and deserts of the western part of the country, few people live where it is very dry or very cold)

BD (GE,123;EI,16;NE,49-50;TI,43)

- Understands voluntary and involuntary migration

Codes (right side of page):   BD = Benchmark, Declarative;   BP = Benchmark, Procedural;   BC = Benchmark, Contextual

1st letter of each code in parentheses   *2nd letter of code*   *Number*

G = GESP: National Geography Standards   E = Explicitly stated in document   Page number of cited document

E = JCGE: Guidelines for Geographic Education   I = Implied in document   *or, for duplicates,*

IE, IG = Int'l Bacc.:Environmental Systems, Geography   Standard number & level of duplicate

N = NAEP: Item Specifications in Geography

T = GENIP: K-6 Geography: Themes, Key Ideas

D = Duplicated in another standard   522

MREL

BD (GE,123;EI,16;NI,49-50;TI,43)
- Knows the causes and effects of human migration (e.g., European colonists and African slaves to America, movement of people from drought areas in Africa, movement of people from East Asia to North America, effects of physical geography on national and international migration, cultural factors)

Level III (Grades 6-8)

BD (GE,160;NE,74-75)
- Understands demographic concepts and how they are used to describe population characteristics of a country or region (e.g., rates of natural increase, crude birth and death rates, infant mortality, population growth rates, doubling time, life expectancy, average family size)

BD (GE,161;NE,68-69)
- Knows the factors that influence patterns of rural-urban migration (e.g., urban commuting, effects of technology on transportation, communication and people's mobility, barriers that impede the flow of people, goods, and ideas)

BD (GE,161;EI,15-16;NI,68-69;TE,32)
- Knows the ways in which human movement and migration influence the character of a place (e.g., New Delhi before and after the partition of the Indian subcontinent in the 1940s and the massive realignment of the Hindu and Muslim populations; Boston before and after the large-scale influx of Irish immigrants in the mid-nineteenth century; the impact of Indians settling in South Africa, Algerians settling in France, Vietnamese settling in the United States)

Level IV (Grades 9-12)

BD (GE,201;IEE,28;IGE,9,10;NI,74-75)
- Understands population issues (e.g., the ongoing policies to limit population growth, the policy in the former Soviet Union to encourage ethnic Russians to have large families, economic considerations such as a country's need for more or fewer workers)

BD (GE,202;IGE,15,16;NE,68-69)
- Knows how human mobility and city/region interdependence can be increased and regional integration can be facilitated by improved transportation systems (e.g., the national interstate highway system in the United States, the network of global air routes)

BD (GE,202;IGE,9,10;NE,68-69)
- Knows how international migrations are shaped by push and pull factors (e.g., political conditions, economic incentives, religious values, family ties)

BD (GE,202;IGE,9,10;NI,87)
- Understands the impact of human migration on physical and human systems (e.g., the impact

---

Codes (right side of page):   BD = Benchmark, Declarative; BP = Benchmark, Procedural; BC = Benchmark, Contextual

1st letter of each code in parentheses   *2nd letter of code*   *Number*

G = GESP: National Geography Standards   E = Explicitly stated in document   Page number of cited document

E = JCGE: Guidelines for Geographic Education   I = Implied in document   *or, for duplicates,*

IE, IG = Int'l Bacc.:Environmental Systems, Geography   Standard number & level of duplicate

N = NAEP: Item Specifications in Geography

T = GENIP: K-6 Geography: Themes, Key Ideas

D = Duplicated in another standard

McREL

of European settlers on the High Plains of North America in the nineteenth century, impact of rural-to-urban migration on suburban development and the resulting lack of adequate housing and stress on infrastructure, effects of population gains or losses on socioeconomic conditions)

(GE,124)

10. Understands the nature and complexity of Earth's cultural mosaics

Level I (Grades K-2)

BD (GE,124;EI,12;NI,46;TI,22)
- Knows the basic components of culture (e.g., language, social organization, beliefs and customs, forms of shelter, economic activities, education systems)

Level II (Grades 3-5)

BD (GE,124;EI,14;NI,38-39;TI,29)
- Knows the similarities and differences in characteristics of culture in different regions (e.g., in terms of environment and resources, technology, food, shelter, social organization, beliefs and customs, schooling, what girls and boys are allowed to do)

BD (GE,124,172;EI,14;NE,44;TI,13)
- Understands how different people living in the same region maintain different ways of life (e.g., the cultural differences between Native Americans and Europeans living along the eastern seaboard in the 17th century; differences among Sikhs, Hindus, and Muslims living in India today)

BD (GE,125;EI,14;NI,61;TE,30)
- Understands how cultures differ in their use of similar environments and resources (e.g., comparing how people live in Phoenix, Arizona with how people live in Riyadh, Saudi Arabia)

BD (GE,125;EI,16;NI,46)
- Understands cultural change (in terms of, e.g., the role of women in society, the role of children in society, clothing styles, modes of transportation, food preferences, types of housing, attitudes toward the environment and resources)

Level III (Grades 6-8)

BD (GE,162;NI,56-57)
- Knows the distinctive cultural landscapes associated with migrant populations (e.g., Chinatowns in the Western world, European enclaves in Japan and China in the 19th century, Little Italy sections of American cities from the beginning of the 19th century to the present)

Codes (right side of page):   BD = Benchmark, Declarative;   BP = Benchmark, Procedural;   BC = Benchmark, Contextual
1st letter of each code in parentheses   *2nd letter of code*   *Number*
G = GESP: National Geography Standards   E = Explicitly stated in document   Page number of cited document
E = JCGE: Guidelines for Geographic Education   I = Implied in document   *or, for duplicates,*
IE, IG = Int'l Bacc.:Environmental Systems, Geography   Standard number & level of duplicate
N = NAEP: Item Specifications in Geography
T = GENIP: K-6 Geography: Themes, Key Ideas
D = Duplicated in another standard

BD (GE,162;NI,56,57)

- Knows ways in which communities reflect the cultural background of their inhabitants (e.g., distinctive building styles, billboards in Spanish, foreign-language advertisements in newspapers)

BD (GE,162-163;NI,57)

- Understands the significance of patterns of cultural diffusion (e.g., the use of terraced rice fields in China, Japan, Indonesia, and the Philippines; the use of satellite television dishes in the United States, England, Canada, and Saudi Arabia)

Level IV (Grades 9-12)

BD (GE,203;IGI,9,10;NI,56-57)

- Knows how cultures influence the characteristics of regions (e.g., level of technological achievement, cultural traditions, social institutions)

BD (GE,204;IGI,9,10)

- Understands how human characteristics make specific regions of the world distinctive (e.g., the effects of early Spanish settlement in the southwestern United States, the impact of Buddhism in shaping social attitudes in Southeast Asia, the specific qualities of Canada's culture regions resulting from the patterns of migration and settlement over four centuries)

BD (GE,205;IGI,11,12;NI,75)

- Understands how evolving political and economic alliances may affect the traditional cohesiveness of world culture regions (e.g., post-reunification Germany and its economic effect on the European Union, NAFTA's effect on trade relations among the United States, Canada, and Mexico)

BD (GE,203;IGI,9,10;NI,67)

- Knows the role culture plays in incidents of cooperation and conflict in the present-day world (e.g., conflicts in sub-Saharan Africa in the 1960s, Central Europe in the 1980s and 1990s, states within the former Soviet Union in the 1990s; cooperation such as the religious and linguistic ties between Spain and parts of Latin America; ethnic ties among the Kurds living in Iran, Iraq, and Turkey)

BD (GE,205;IGI,9,10;NI,75)

- Understands how communication and transportation technologies contribute to cultural convergence or divergence (e.g., convergence created by electronic media, computers, and jet aircraft; divergence created by technologies used to reinforce nationalistic or ethnic elitism or cultural separateness and independence)

Codes (right side of page):   BD = Benchmark, Declarative; BP = Benchmark, Procedural; BC = Benchmark, Contextual
1st letter of each code in parentheses   *2nd letter of code*   *Number*
G = GESP: National Geography Standards   E = Explicitly stated in document   Page number of cited document
E = JCGE: Guidelines for Geographic Education   I = Implied in document   *or, for duplicates,*
IE, IG = Int'l Bacc.:Environmental Systems, Geography   Standard number & level of duplicate
N = NAEP: Item Specifications in Geography
T = GENIP: K-6 Geography: Themes, Key Ideas
D = Duplicated in another standard   525   McREL

(GE,126)

11. Understands the patterns and networks of economic interdependence on Earth's surface

Level I (Grades K-2)

BD (GE,127;EI,12;NI,43;TI,10,18)
- Knows the modes of transportation used to move people, products and ideas from place to place (e.g., barges, airplanes, automobiles, pipelines, ships, railroads), their importance and their advantages and disadvantages

Level II (Grades 3-5)

BD (GE,127;EI,15;NE,46;TE,28)
- Knows the factors that are important in the location of economic activities (e.g., warehouses and industries near major transportation routes, fast-food restaurants in highly accessible locations close to population concentrations, production sites near the sources of their raw materials or close to the consumers who buy their products)

BD (GE,127;EI,15;NI,39;TI,29,33)
- Knows economic activities that use natural resources in the local region, state, and nation (e.g., agriculture, mining, fishing, forestry) and the importance of the activities to these areas

BD (GE,127;EI,14;NI,47-48;TE,31,32;DI,3.2.3)
- Knows how transportation and communication have changed and how they have affected trade and economic activities (e.g., regions can specialize economically; with improved roads and refrigerated trucking, more fresh fruits and vegetables are available out of season; regional, national, and global markets expand as transportation and communication systems improve)

BD (GE,126;NI,50-51)
- Knows the various ways in which people satisfy their basic needs and wants through the production of goods and services in different regions of the world (e.g., growing food and shopping for food in a developing vs. a developed society, economic activities in a rural region vs. those in an urban region in the same U.S. state)

BD (GE,126;NI,50)
- Knows how regions are linked economically and how trade affects the way people earn their living in each region (e.g., the flow of fuels from Southwest Asia to industrialized, energy-poor regions of the world; the flow of electronic goods from Pacific Rim nations to the United States)

Codes (right side of page):   BD = Benchmark, Declarative; BP = Benchmark, Procedural; BC = Benchmark, Contextual
1st letter of each code in parentheses   *2nd letter of code*   *Number*
G = GESP: National Geography Standards   E = Explicitly stated in document   Page number of cited document
E = JCGE: Guidelines for Geographic Education   I = Implied in document   *or, for duplicates,*
IE, IG = Int'l Bacc.:Environmental Systems, Geography   Standard number & level of duplicate
N = NAEP: Item Specifications in Geography
T = GENIP: K-6 Geography: Themes, Key Ideas
D = Duplicated in another standard   526

MREL

Level III (Grades 6-8)

- Understands the spatial aspects of systems designed to deliver goods and services (e.g., the movement of a product from point of manufacture to point of use; imports, exports, and trading patterns of various countries; interruptions in world trade such as war, crop failures, and labor strikes)

  BD (GE,164;EI,15;NI,38,40,46;TI,31)

- Understands issues related to the spatial distribution of economic activities (e.g., the impact of economic activities in a community on the surrounding areas, the effects of the gradual disappearance of small-scale retail facilities such as corner general stores and gas stations, the economic and social impacts on a community when a large factory or other economic activity leaves and moves to another place)

  BD (GE,165;EI,15;NI,38,41,46,48;TI,37)

- Understands factors that influence the location of industries in the United States (e.g., geographical factors, factors of production, spatial patterns)

  BD (GE,166;NI,66-67,70)

- Understands the primary geographic causes for world trade (e.g., the theory of comparative advantage that explains trade advantages associated with Hong Kong-made consumer goods, Chinese textiles, or Jamaican sugar; countries that export mostly raw materials and import mostly fuels and manufactured goods)

  BD (GE,165)

- Understands historic and contemporary economic trade networks (e.g., the triangular trade routes of the 16th and 17th centuries; national and global patterns of migrant workers; economic relationships under imperialism such as American colonies and England in the 18th and 19th centuries, or Belgium and the Congo in the 20th century)

  BD (GE,166;NI,57)

- Understands historic and contemporary systems of transportation and communication in the development of economic activities (e.g., the effect of refrigerated railroad cars, air-freight services, pipelines, telephone services, facsimile transmission services, satellite-based communications systems)

  BD (GE,166;NI,66)

- Knows primary, secondary, and tertiary activities in a geographic context (e.g., primary economic activities such as coal mining and salmon fishing; secondary economic activities such as the manufacture of shoes and the associated worldwide trade in raw materials; tertiary economic activity such as restaurants, theaters, and hotels)

  BD (GE,164)

Codes (right side of page):   BD = Benchmark, Declarative; BP = Benchmark, Procedural; BC = Benchmark, Contextual
1st letter of each code in parentheses   *2nd letter of code*   *Number*
G = GESP: National Geography Standards   E = Explicitly stated in document   Page number of cited document
E = JCGE: Guidelines for Geographic Education   I = Implied in document   *or, for duplicates,*
IE, IG = Int'l Bacc.:Environmental Systems, Geography   Standard number & level of duplicate
N = NAEP: Item Specifications in Geography
T = GENIP: K-6 Geography: Themes, Key Ideas
D = Duplicated in another standard

Level IV (Grades 9-12)

- Knows the spatial distribution of major economic systems and their relative merits in terms of productivity and the social welfare of workers (e.g., North Korea as a command economy, Burkina Faso as a traditional economy in the hinterlands beyond its cities, Singapore as a market economy)

  BD (GE,206;IGE,11;NI,74)

- Understands the historical movement patterns of people and goods and their relationships to economic activity (e.g., spatial patterns of early trade routes in the era of sailing ships, land-use patterns that resulted in a system of monoculture)

  BD (GE,207;IGE,9,10;NI,75)

- Understands the relationships between various settlement patterns, their associated economic activities, and the relative land values (e.g., land values and prominent urban features, the zoned uses of land and the value of that land, economic factors and location of particular types of industries and businesses)

  BD (GE,207;IGE,11,12;NI,75)

- Understands the advantages and disadvantages of international economic patterns (e.g., how land values in an area may change due to the investment of foreign capital; the causes and geographic consequences of an international debt crisis; the advantages and disadvantages of allowing foreign-owned businesses to purchase land, open factories, or conduct other kinds of business in a country)

  BD (GE,207;IGE,11,12;NI,83)

12. Understands the patterns of human settlement and their causes

(GE,128)

Level I (Grades K-2)

- Understands why people choose to settle in different places (e.g., job opportunities, available land, climate)

  BD (GE,129;EI,13;NI,38-39;TE,21)

- Knows the similarities and differences in housing and land use in urban and suburban areas (e.g., where people live, where services are provided, where products are made, types of housing, yard size, population density, transportation facilities, presence of infrastructure elements such as sidewalks and street lights)

  BD (GE,128;EI,12;NI,46;TI,18)

Level II (Grades 3-5)

- Knows areas of dense human settlement and why they are densely populated (e.g., fertile soil,

  BD (GE,128;EI,14;NI,38,48;TI,29)

Codes (right side of page):   BD = Benchmark, Declarative; BP = Benchmark, Procedural; BC = Benchmark, Contextual
1st letter of each code in parentheses   *2nd letter of code*   *Number*
G = GESP: National Geography Standards   E = Explicitly stated in document   Page number of cited document
E = JCGE: Guidelines for Geographic Education   I = Implied in document   *or, for duplicates,*
IE, IG = Int'l Bacc.:Environmental Systems, Geography   Standard number & level of duplicate
N = NAEP: Item Specifications in Geography
T = GENIP: K-6 Geography: Themes, Key Ideas
D = Duplicated in another standard

528

MREL

good transportation, and availability of water in the Ganges River Valley; availability of coal, iron, and other natural resources and river transportation in the Ruhr)

- Knows reasons for similarities and differences in the population size and density of different regions (e.g., length of settlement, environment and resources, cultural traditions, historic events, accessibility)

  BD (GE,129;EI,14;NI,38,48;TI,29,32)

- Knows the settlement patterns that characterize the development of a community or state (e.g., from the movement of people into an area previously unoccupied to the competition among villages for economic dominance and growth; from a small number of dispersed settlers with few services to the modern pattern of suburbanization and decentralization)

  BD (GE,129;NI,39)

- Knows reasons for the growth and decline of settlements (e.g., boomtowns to ghost towns in mining areas, the rise or decline of towns linked or not linked by highways or railroads, the history of company or single-industry towns in periods of prosperity or recession)

  BD (GE,129;NI,39;TE,28,29)

- Knows the characteristics and locations of cities (e.g., location along transportation routes, availability of resources, continued access to other cities and resources) and how cities have changed over time (e.g., the movement of industry from downtown to the edge of cities, suburban growth, changes in the shapes of urban areas)

  BD (GE,129;TE,37)

- Knows similarities and differences among the world's culture hearths (culture groups' places of origin), why humans settled in those places and why these settlements persist today (e.g., as centers of innovation and cultural, social, economic, and political development that attract people from other places)

  BD (GE,129;NI,38)

Level III (Grades 6-8)

- Knows the causes and consequences of urbanization (e.g., industrial development; cultural activities such as entertainment, religious facilities, higher education; economic attractions such as business and entrepreneurial opportunities; access to information and other resources)

  BD (GE,168;NI,57)

- Knows the similarities and differences in various settlement patterns of the world (e.g., agricultural settlement types such as plantations, subsistence farming, truck-farming communities; urban settlement types such as port cities, governmental centers, single-industry cities, planned cities)

  BD (GE,167;NI,52,57,65)

Codes (right side of page):	BD = Benchmark, Declarative; BP = Benchmark, Procedural; BC = Benchmark, Contextual
1st letter of each code in parentheses	*2nd letter of code*	*Number*

1st letter of each code in parentheses   *2nd letter of code*   *Number*
G = GESP: National Geography Standards   E = Explicitly stated in document   Page number of cited document
E = JCGE: Guidelines for Geographic Education   I = Implied in document   *or, for duplicates,*
IE, IG = Int'l Bacc.:Environmental Systems, Geography   Standard number & level of duplicate
N = NAEP: Item Specifications in Geography
T = GENIP: K-6 Geography: Themes, Key Ideas
D = Duplicated in another standard

McREL

- Knows ways in which both the landscape and society change as a consequence of shifting from a dispersed to a concentrated settlement form (e.g., a larger marketplace, the need for an agricultural surplus to provide for the urban population, the loss of some rural workers as people decide to move into the city, changes in the transportation system)

  BD (GE,167-168;NI,64)

- Knows the factors involved in the development of cities (e.g., geographic factors for location such as transportation and food supply; the need for a marketplace, religious needs, or for military protection)

  BD (GE,167;NE,56,57)

- Knows the internal spatial structures of cities (e.g., the concentric zone model and the sector model of cities; the impact of different transportation systems on the spatial arrangement of business, industry, and residence in a city)

  BD (GE,168;NI,66-67)

Level IV (Grades 9-12)

- Understands how the functions of cities today differ from those of towns and villages and cities in earlier times (e.g., more specialized economic and social activities, greater concentration of services, greater availability of the same services)

  BD (GE,208;IGE,15;NI,66)

- Knows the shape of cities in the United States and factors that influence urban morphology (e.g., transportation routes, physical barriers, zoning regulations)

  BD (GE,208;IGE,16;NI,75)

- Knows the similarities and differences in settlement characteristics of economically developing and developed nations (characteristics of cities; residential and transportation patterns; travel distance to schools, shopping areas, and health care facilities)

  BD (GE,209;IGE,11,12,15,16;NI,75)

- Knows the consequences of factors such as population changes or the arrival/departure of a major industry or business on the settlement patterns of an area (e.g., stress on infrastructure, problems of public safety and fire protection, crisis in delivering school and medical services)

  BD (GE,209;IGE,15,16;NI,75)

- Understands the physical and human impact of emerging urban forms in the present-day world (e.g., the rise of megalopoli, edge cities, and metropolitan corridors; increasing numbers of ethnic enclaves in urban areas and the development of legislation to protect the rights of ethnic and racial minorities; improved light-rail systems within cities providing ease of access to ex-urban areas)

  BD (GE,209;IGE,15,16)

Codes (right side of page):	BD = Benchmark, Declarative; BP = Benchmark, Procedural; BC = Benchmark, Contextual	
1st letter of each code in parentheses	*2nd letter of code*	*Number*
G = GESP: National Geography Standards	E = Explicitly stated in document	Page number of cited document
E = JCGE: Guidelines for Geographic Education	I = Implied in document	*or, for duplicates,*
IE, IG = Int'l Bacc.:Environmental Systems, Geography		Standard number & level of duplicate
N = NAEP: Item Specifications in Geography		
T = GENIP: K-6 Geography: Themes, Key Ideas		
D = Duplicated in another standard	530	

MREL

(GE,130)

13. Understands the forces of cooperation and conflict that shape the divisions of Earth's surface

Level I (Grades K-2)

BD (GE,131;EI,13;NI,48-49;TI,18)

- Knows ways that people solve common problems by cooperating (e.g., working in groups to pick up trash along a road, participating in a neighborhood crime-watch group, participating in community house-building projects)

BD (GE,131;EI,14;NI,48-49;TI,31)

- Knows examples of world conflict or cooperation (e.g., countries in trade pacts, areas of the world with refugee problems)

Level II (Grades 3-5)

BD (GE,130,131;EI,14;NI,48;TI,27)

- Knows the functions of political units (e.g., law-making, law enforcement, provision of services, powers of taxation) and how they differ on the basis of scale (e.g., precinct, census district, school attendance zone, township, metropolitan area, county, state, nation)

BD (GE,130;EI,13;NI,38;TI,27)

- Knows how and why people divide Earth's surface into political and/or economic units (e.g., states in the United States and Mexico; provinces in Canada; countries in North and South America; countries linked in cooperative relationships, such as the European Union)

BD (GE,131;NI,48)

- Knows how and why people compete for control of Earth's surface (e.g., ethnic or national differences, desire for political control, economic inequalities)

Level III (Grades 6-8)

BD (GE,169;NE,67)

- Understands factors that contribute to cooperation (e.g., similarities in religion, language, political beliefs) or conflict (e.g., economic competition for scarce resources, boundary disputes, cultural differences, control of strategic locations) within and between regions and countries

BD (GE,170;NI,52,67)

- Knows the social, political and economic divisions on Earth's surface at the local, state, national, and international levels (e.g., transnational corporations, political alliances, economic groupings, world religions)

BD (GE,170)

- Understands the various factors involved in the development of nation-states (e.g.,

---

Codes (right side of page):   BD = Benchmark, Declarative; BP = Benchmark, Procedural; BC = Benchmark, Contextual

1st letter of each code in parentheses   *2nd letter of code*   *Number*

G = GESP: National Geography Standards   E = Explicitly stated in document   Page number of cited document

E = JCGE: Guidelines for Geographic Education   I = Implied in document   *or, for duplicates,*

IE, IG = Int'l Bacc.:Environmental Systems, Geography   Standard number & level of duplicate

N = NAEP: Item Specifications in Geography

T = GENIP: K-6 Geography: Themes, Key Ideas

D = Duplicated in another standard   531

MREL

competition for territory and resources, desire for self-rule, nationalism, history of domination by powerful countries)

- Understands the reasons for multiple and overlapping spatial divisions in society (e.g., postal zones, school districts, telephone area codes, voting wards) BD (GE,169)

- Understands the factors that affect the cohesiveness and integration of countries (e.g., language and religion in Belgium, the religious differences between Hindus and Moslems in India, the ethnic differences in some African countries that have been independent for only a few decades, the elongated shapes of Italy and Chile) BD (GE,170;NE,67)

- Understands the symbolic importance of capital cities (e.g., Canberra, a planned city, as the capital of Australia; The Hague as both a national capital of the Netherlands and a center for such global agencies as the World Court) BD (GE,170)

Level IV (Grades 9-12)

- Understands how cooperation and/or conflict can lead to the allocation of control of Earth's surface (e.g., formation and delineation of regional planning districts, regional school districts, countries, free-trade zones) BD (GE,210;IGI,11,12;NI,85-86)

- Knows the causes of boundary conflicts and internal disputes between culture groups (e.g., the conflict between North Korea and South Korea, friction between the Spanish majority and Basque minority in Spain, the civil war between the Hutus and the Tutsis in Rwanda) BD (GE,210;IGI,10;NE,86)

- Understands why the boundaries of congressional districts change in the United States (e.g., the effects of statutory requirements, population shifts, ethnic and racial considerations, shifts in political power) BD (GE,210;IGI,10;NI,85-86)

- Understands the changes that occur in the extent and organization of social, political, and economic entities on Earth's surface (e.g., imperial powers such as the Roman Empire, Han Dynasty, Carolingian Empire, British Empire) BD (GE,210;NI,85-86)

- Understands why some countries are land-locked (e.g., wars between rival countries, isolation due to the size of landmasses and due to racial and cultural divisions) BD (GE,211;NI,85-86)

- Understands how external forces can conflict economically and politically with internal interests in a region (e.g., how the Pampas in Argentina underwent a significant BD (GE,211;IGI,11,12)

Codes (right side of page): BD = Benchmark, Declarative; BP = Benchmark, Procedural; BC = Benchmark, Contextual
1st letter of each code in parentheses *2nd letter of code* *Number*
G = GESP: National Geography Standards E = Explicitly stated in document Page number of cited document
E = JCGE: Guidelines for Geographic Education I = Implied in document *or, for duplicates,*
IE, IG = Int'l Bacc.:Environmental Systems, Geography Standard number & level of duplicate
N = NAEP: Item Specifications in Geography
T = GENIP: K-6 Geography: Themes, Key Ideas
D = Duplicated in another standard 532 MCREL

socioeconomic transformation in the 19th and early 20th centuries as a consequence of European demands for grain and beef; the consequences of the French colonization of IndoChina in the 19th century to procure tin, tungsten, and rubber; the friction between Hindus and Moslems in the Indian subcontinent in the 1940s which led to the formation of India and Pakistan)

(GE,132)

14. Understands how human actions modify the physical environment

Level I (Grades K-2)

BD (GE,132;TE,17)
- Knows ways in which people depend on the physical environment (e.g., food, clean air, water, mineral resources)

Level II (Grades 3-5)

BD (GE,132-133;EE,14;NI,42-43,TE,29-30;DI,8.2.2)
- Knows the ways people alter the physical environment (e.g., by creating irrigation projects; clearing the land to make room for houses and shopping centers; planting crops; building roads)

BD (GE,133;NI,42-43;TE,31)
- Knows the ways in which the physical environment is stressed by human activities (e.g., changes in climate, air pollution, water pollution, expanding human settlement)

BD (GE,133;NE,43;TI,42)
- Knows how human activities have increased the ability of the physical environment to support human life in the local community, state, United States, and other countries (e.g., use of irrigation and dry-land farming techniques to improve crop yields, reforestation to prevent erosion, flood-control projects to make land habitable)

Level III (Grades 6-8)

BD (GE,171;NE,61)
- Understands the environmental consequences of people changing the physical environment (e.g., the effects of ozone depletion, climate change, deforestation, land degradation, soil salinization and acidification, ocean pollution, groundwater-quality decline, using natural wetlands for recreational and housing development)

BD (GE,171)
- Understands the ways in which human-induced changes in the physical environment in one

---

Codes (right side of page):	BD = Benchmark, Declarative; BP = Benchmark, Procedural; BC = Benchmark, Contextual
1st letter of each code in parentheses	*2nd letter of code* *Number*

Codes (right side of page):   BD = Benchmark, Declarative; BP = Benchmark, Procedural; BC = Benchmark, Contextual
1st letter of each code in parentheses   *2nd letter of code*   *Number*
G = GESP: National Geography Standards   E = Explicitly stated in document   Page number of cited document
E = JCGE: Guidelines for Geographic Education   I = Implied in document   *or, for duplicates,*
IE, IG = Int'l Bacc.:Environmental Systems, Geography   Standard number & level of duplicate
N = NAEP: Item Specifications in Geography
T = GENIP: K-6 Geography: Themes, Key Ideas
D = Duplicated in another standard   533   MREL

place can cause changes in other places (e.g., the effect of a factory's airborne emissions on air quality in communities located downwind and, because of acid rain, on ecosystems located downwind; the effects of pesticides washed into river systems on water quality in communities located downstream; the effects of the construction of dams and levees on river systems in one region on places downstream)

- BD (GE,172)
  Understands the ways in which technology influences the human capacity to modify the physical environment (e.g., effects of the introduction of fire, steam power, diesel machinery, electricity, work animals, explosives, chemical fertilizers and pesticides, hybridization of crops)

- BD (GE,172;NI,61-62)
  Understands the environmental consequences of both the unintended and intended outcomes of major technological changes in human history (e.g., the effects of automobiles using fossil fuels, nuclear power plants creating the problem of nuclear-waste storage, the use of steel-tipped plows or the expansion of the amount of land brought into agriculture)

Level IV (Grades 9-12)

- BD (GE,212,214;IEE,18;NI,77)
  Understands how the concepts of synergy, feedback loops, carrying capacity and thresholds relate to the limitations of the physical environment to absorb the impacts of human activity (e.g., levee construction on a flood plain, logging in an old-growth forest, construction of golf courses in arid areas)

- BD (GE,212;IGE,14;NE,77)
  Understands the role of humans in decreasing the diversity of flora and fauna in a region (e.g., the impact of acid rain on rivers and forests in southern Ontario, the effects of toxic dumping on ocean ecosystems, the effects of overfishing along the coast of northeastern North America or the Philippine archipelago)

- BD (GE,212-213;IGE,14;NI,77-78)
  Understands the global impacts of human changes in the physical environment (e.g., increases in runoff and sediment, tropical soil degradation, habitat destruction, air pollution; alterations in the hydrologic cycle; increases in world temperatures; groundwater reduction)

- BD (GE,213;NI,80)
  Knows how people's changing attitudes toward the environment have led to landscape changes (e.g., pressure to replace farmlands with wetlands in flood plain areas, interest in preserving wilderness areas, support for the concept of historic preservation)

Codes (right side of page):	BD = Benchmark, Declarative; BP = Benchmark, Procedural; BC = Benchmark, Contextual

1st letter of each code in parentheses   *2nd letter of code*   *Number*
G = GESP: National Geography Standards   E = Explicitly stated in document   Page number of cited document
E = JCGE: Guidelines for Geographic Education   I = Implied in document   *or, for duplicates,*
IE, IG = Int'l Bacc.:Environmental Systems, Geography   Standard number & level of duplicate
N = NAEP: Item Specifications in Geography
T = GENIP: K-6 Geography: Themes, Key Ideas
D = Duplicated in another standard   534   *McREL*

(GE,134)

15. Understands how physical systems affect human systems

Level I (Grades K-2)

BD (GE,134)

- Not appropriate at this level

Level II (Grades 3-5)

BD (GE,134;EE,14;NE,42;TE,30)

- Knows how humans adapt to variations in the physical environment (e.g., choices of clothing, housing styles, agricultural practices, recreational activities, food, daily and seasonal patterns of life)

BD (GE,134-135;TE,23)

- Knows how communities benefit from the physical environment (e.g., people make their living by farming on fertile land, fishing in local water, working in mines; the community is a port located on a natural harbor, a tourist center located in a scenic or historic area, an industrial center with good access to natural resources)

BD (GE,135;NI,41-42;TE,23,30)

- Knows the ways in which human activities are constrained by the physical environment (e.g., effects of weather, climate and landforms on agriculture, recreational activities, availability of water, expansion of settlement)

BD (GE,135;NE,43)

- Knows natural hazards that occur in the physical environment (e.g., floods, wind storms, tornadoes, earthquakes)

Level III (Grades 6-8)

BD (GE,173)

- Knows the ways in which human systems develop in response to conditions in the physical environment (e.g., patterns of land use, economic livelihoods, architectural styles of buildings, building materials, flows of traffic, recreation activities)

BD (GE,173;NE,61)

- Knows how the physical environment affects life in different regions (e.g., how people in Siberia, Alaska, and other high-latitude places deal with the characteristics of tundra environments; limitations to coastline settlements as a result of tidal, storm, and erosional processes)

BD (GE,174)

- Knows the ways people take aspects of the environment into account when deciding on locations for human activities (e.g., early American industrial development along streams and

---

Codes (right side of page):	BD = Benchmark, Declarative; BP = Benchmark, Procedural; BC = Benchmark, Contextual	
1st letter of each code in parentheses	*2nd letter of code*	*Number*
G = GESP: National Geography Standards	E = Explicitly stated in document	Page number of cited document
E = JCGE: Guidelines for Geographic Education	I = Implied in document	*or, for duplicates,*
IE, IG = Int'l Bacc.:Environmental Systems, Geography		Standard number & level of duplicate
N = NAEP: Item Specifications in Geography		
T = GENIP: K-6 Geography: Themes, Key Ideas		
D = Duplicated in another standard	535	MREL

rivers at the fall line to take advantage of water-generated power)

- Understands relationships between population density and environmental quality (e.g., resource distribution, rainfall, temperature, soil fertility, landform relief, carrying capacity) BD (GE,174;NI,60)

- Knows the effects of natural hazards on human systems in different regions of the United States and the world (e.g., the effect of drought on populations in Ethiopia compared with populations in Australia or the southern part of the United States) BD (GE,174-175)

- Knows the ways in which humans prepare for natural hazards (e.g., earthquake preparedness, constructing houses on stilts in flood-prone areas, designation of hurricane shelters and evacuation routes in hurricane-prone areas) BD (GE,175)

Level IV (Grades 9-12)

- Knows changes in the physical environment that have reduced the capacity of the environment to support human activity (e.g., the drought-plagued Sahel, the depleted rain forests of central Africa, the Great Plains Dust Bowl, the impact of the economic exploitation of Siberia's resources on a fragile sub-Arctic environment) BD (GE,214;IGE,14)

- Knows how humans overcome "limits to growth" imposed by physical systems (e.g., technology, human adaptation) BD (GE,214;IEE,30,31;IGI,13)

- Knows conditions and locations that place limits on plant growth and therefore on the expansion of human settlement (e.g., soils with limited nutrients, high salt content, shallow depth; extremely cold, arid or humid tropical climates; mountainous and coastal environments) BD (GE,214-215;IEI,30,31;IGE,13;NI,78)

- Understands how people who live in naturally hazardous regions adapt to their environments (e.g., the use of sea walls to protect coastal areas subject to severe storms, the use of earthquake-resistant construction techniques in different regions within the Ring of Fire) BD (GE,215;IGE,13;NE,78)

- Knows factors that affect people's attitudes, perceptions, and responses toward natural hazards (e.g., religious beliefs, socioeconomic status, previous experiences) BD (GE,215;IGE,13;NI,79-80)

Codes (right side of page):   BD = Benchmark, Declarative; BP = Benchmark, Procedural; BC = Benchmark, Contextual
1st letter of each code in parentheses   *2nd letter of code*   *Number*
G = GESP: National Geography Standards   E = Explicitly stated in document   Page number of cited document
E = JCGE: Guidelines for Geographic Education   I = Implied in document   *or, for duplicates,*
IE, IG = Int'l Bacc.:Environmental Systems, Geography   Standard number & level of duplicate
N = NAEP: Item Specifications in Geography
T = GENIP: K-6 Geography: Themes, Key Ideas
D = Duplicated in another standard   536   *McREL*

(GE,136)

16. Understands the changes that occur in the meaning, use, distribution and importance of resources

Level I (Grades K-2)

BD (GE,137;EI,15;NI,51;TI,13)
- Knows the role that resources play in our daily lives (resources used to generate electricity; resources used to produce automobiles, medicines, clothing, and food)

Level II (Grades 3-5)

BD (GE,136;EI,15;NE,50;TI,23,37)
- Knows the characteristics, location, and use of renewable resources (e.g., timber), flow resources (e.g., running water or wind), and nonrenewable resources (e.g., fossil fuels, minerals)

BD (GE,136;EI,17;TI,42)
- Knows how settlement patterns are influenced by the discovery and use of resources (e.g., Colorado mining towns as centers of settlement in the late 19th century, the growth of industry and cities along the fall line of the Appalachians starting in the 18th century)

BD (GE,136;EE,17;NE,50;TE,37)
- Knows the relationships between economic activities and resources (e.g., the relationship of major industrial districts to the location of iron ore, coal, and other resources)

BD (GE,136;NI,39;TI,31)
- Knows the major transportation routes that link resources with consumers and the transportation modes used (e.g., ships, pipelines, barges, railroads)

BD (GE,137;EI,14;NE,43;TI,37)
- Knows advantages and disadvantages of recycling and reusing different types of materials

BD (GE,137;NI,44;TI,29-30)
- Knows the different ways in which resources are used and valued in different regions of the world (e.g., the use of wood in the United States for construction compared to the use of wood in the Dominican Republic for fuel)

Level III (Grades 6-8)

BD (GE,177-178;NE,67)
- Understands the reasons for conflicting viewpoints regarding how resources should be used (e.g., attitudes toward electric cars, water-rationing, urban public transportation, use of fossil fuels, excessive timber cutting in old growth forests, buffalo in the western United States, soil conservation in semiarid areas)

Codes (right side of page):	BD = Benchmark, Declarative; BP = Benchmark, Procedural; BC = Benchmark, Contextual

1st letter of each code in parentheses   *2nd letter of code*   *Number*

G = GESP: National Geography Standards   E = Explicitly stated in document   Page number of cited document

E = JCGE: Guidelines for Geographic Education   I = Implied in document   *or, for duplicates,*

IE, IG = Int'l Bacc.:Environmental Systems, Geography   Standard number & level of duplicate

N = NAEP: Item Specifications in Geography

T = GENIP: K-6 Geography: Themes, Key Ideas

D = Duplicated in another standard   537   *MREL*

- BD (GE,178;NI,61;DI,18.2.2)

  Knows strategies for wise management and use of renewable, flow, and nonrenewable resources (e.g., wise management of agricultural soils, fossil fuels, and alternative energy sources; community programs for recycling or reusing materials)

- BD (GE,176;NE,69)

  Knows world patterns of resource distribution and utilization (e.g., petroleum, coal, iron ore, diamonds, silver, gold, molybdenum)

- BD (GE,176-177;NI,67,70)

  Understands the consequences of the use of resources in the contemporary world (e.g., the relationship between a country's standard of living and its accessibility to resources, the competition for resources demonstrated by events such as the Japanese occupation of Manchuria in the 1930s or the Iraqi invasion of Kuwait in 1991)

- BD (GE,178;NI,62)

  Understands the role of technology in resource acquisition and use, and its impact on the environment (e.g., the use of giant earth-moving machinery in strip-mining, the use of satellite imagery technology in the search for petroleum, rates of resource consumption among countries of high or low levels of technological development)

- BD (GE,178;NI,59)

  Understands how energy resources contribute to the development and functioning of human societies (e.g., by providing power for transportation, manufacturing, the heating and cooling of buildings)

- BD (GE,178)

  Understands how the development and widespread use of alternative energy sources (e.g., solar, wind, thermal) might have an impact on societies (in terms of, e.g., air and water quality, existing energy industries, and current manufacturing practices)

Level IV (Grades 9-12)

- BD (GE,216-217;IGI,11;NI,75)

  Understands the relationships between resources and exploration, colonization, and settlement of different regions of the world (e.g., the development of mercantilism and imperialism and the consequent settlement of Latin America and other regions of the world by the Spanish and Portuguese; the abundance of fur, fish, timber, and gold in Siberia, Alaska, and California and the settlement of these areas by the Russians)

- BD (GE,218;IEI,29;IGE,11,12;NI,80)

  Understands programs and positions related to the use of resources on a local to global scale (e.g., community regulations for water usage during drought periods; local recycling programs for glass, metal, plastic, and paper products; different points of view regarding uses of the Malaysian rain forests)

Codes (right side of page):   BD = Benchmark, Declarative;   BP = Benchmark, Procedural;   BC = Benchmark, Contextual
1st letter of each code in parentheses   *2nd letter of code*   *Number*
G = GESP: National Geography Standards   E = Explicitly stated in document   Page number of cited document
E = JCGE: Guidelines for Geographic Education   I = Implied in document   *or, for duplicates,*
IE, IG = Int'l Bacc.:Environmental Systems, Geography   Standard number & level of duplicate
N = NAEP: Item Specifications in Geography
T = GENIP: K-6 Geography: Themes, Key Ideas
D = Duplicated in another standard   538   MREL

BD (GE,217;IEI,29,30;IGE,11,12;NI,88)

- Understands the impact of policy decisions regarding the use of resources in different regions of the world (e.g., the long-term impact on the economy of Nauru when its phosphate reserves are exhausted, the economic and social problems related to the overcutting of pine forests in Nova Scotia, the impact of petroleum consumption in the United States and Japan)

BD (GE,218;IEE,31;IGE,12;NI,80,88)

- Knows issues related to the reuse and recycling of resources (e.g., changing relocation strategies of industries seeking access to recyclable material, such as paper factories, container and can companies, glass, plastic, and bottle manufacturers; issues involved with the movement, handling, processing, and storing of toxic and hazardous waste materials; fully enforced vs. consistently neglected approaches to resource management)

(GE,138)

17. Understands how geography is used to interpret the past

Level I (Grades K-2)

BD (GE,138;EE,14;NE,38;TE,16,20)

- Knows how areas of a community have changed over time (in terms of, e.g., size and style of homes; how people earn their living; changes in the plant and animal population)

Level II (Grades 3-5)

BD (GE,138;TI,23-24)

- Knows the factors that have contributed to changing land use in a community (e.g., street and road development, population shifts, regulations governing land use)

BD (GE,139)

- Knows the ways in which changes in people's perceptions of environments have influenced human migration and settlement over time (e.g., the history of oil discovery and its effect on migration in different United States regions such as Pennsylvania, Louisiana, or Texas)

BD (GE,139)

- Knows the geographic factors that have influenced people and events in the past (e.g., the effects of the site of a Civil War battle on the course of the conflict, how trade routes followed by early European colonists were linked to the trade winds, how Muslim trading vessels used monsoon winds to cross the Indian Ocean in the 8th century)

Level III (Grades 6-8)

BD (GE,180;NI,68-69)

- Knows how physical and human geographic factors have influenced major historic events

---

Codes (right side of page):   BD = Benchmark, Declarative;   BP = Benchmark, Procedural;   BC = Benchmark, Contextual

1st letter of each code in parentheses	*2nd letter of code*	*Number*
G = GESP: National Geography Standards	E = Explicitly stated in document	Page number of cited document
E = JCGE: Guidelines for Geographic Education	I = Implied in document	*or, for duplicates,*
IE, IG = Int'l Bacc.:Environmental Systems, Geography		Standard number & level of duplicate
N = NAEP: Item Specifications in Geography		
T = GENIP: K-6 Geography: Themes, Key Ideas		
D = Duplicated in another standard	539	*MREL*

and movements (e.g., the course and outcome of battles and wars, the forced transport of Africans to North and South America because of the need for cheap labor, the profitability of the triangle trade and the locations of prevailing wind and ocean currents, the effects of different land-survey systems used in the U.S.)

- Knows historic and current conflicts and competition regarding the use and allocation of resources (e.g., the conflicts between Native Americans and colonists; conflicts between the Inuit and migrants to Alaska since 1950) BD (GE,179;NI,67)

- Knows the ways in which the spatial organization of society changes over time (e.g., process of urban growth in the United States; changes in the internal structure, form, and function of urban areas in different regions of the world at different times) BD (GE,179;NI,56-57)

- Knows significant physical features that have influenced historical events (e.g., mountain passes that have affected military campaigns such as the Khyber Pass, Burma Pass, or Brenner Pass; major water crossings that have affected U.S. history such as the Tacoma Strait in Washington or the Delaware River near Trenton, New Jersey; major water gaps, springs, and other hydrologic features that have affected settlement in the U.S. such as the Cumberland Gap, the Ogallala Aquifer, or the artesian wells of the Great Plains) BD (GE,180)

Level IV (Grades 9-12)

- Understands how the processes of spatial change have affected history (e.g., the diffusion of a phenomenon through regions of contact, such as the spread of bubonic plague, or the diffusion of tobacco smoking from North America to Europe, Africa, and Asia; the development of the national transportation systems in the U.S.; effects of migration streams and counterstreams) BD (GE,219)

- Understands how people's changing perceptions of geographic features have led to changes in human societies (e.g., the effects of religion on world economic development patterns, cultural conflict, social integration, resource use; the effects of technology on human control over nature, such as large-scale agriculture in Ukraine and northern China, strip-mining in Russia, and center-pivot irrigation in the southwestern United States) BD (GE,219-220;NI,79-80)

- Understands the ways in which physical and human features have influenced the evolution of significant historic events and movements (e.g., the effects of imperialism, colonization, and decolonization on the economic and political developments of the 19th and 20th BD (GE,220)

Codes (right side of page):   BD = Benchmark, Declarative; BP = Benchmark, Procedural; BC = Benchmark, Contextual

1st letter of each code in parentheses   *2nd letter of code*   *Number*

G = GESP: National Geography Standards   E = Explicitly stated in document   Page number of cited document

E = JCGE: Guidelines for Geographic Education   I = Implied in document   *or, for duplicates,*

IE, IG = Int'l Bacc.:Environmental Systems, Geography   Standard number & level of duplicate

N = NAEP: Item Specifications in Geography

T = GENIP: K-6 Geography: Themes, Key Ideas

D = Duplicated in another standard   540

McREL

centuries; the geographical forces responsible for the industrial revolution in England in the late 18th and early 19th centuries; physical and human factors that have led to famines and large-scale refugee movements)

(GI,140)

18. Understands global development and environmental issues

Level I (Grades K-2)

BD (GE,140)

● Not appropriate at this level

Level II (Grades 3-5)

BD (GE,140;EI,17)

● Knows the relationship between population growth and resource use

BD (GE,140;NI,43;TI,30;DI,16.3.2)

● Knows the ways in which resources can be managed and why it is important to do so (e.g., soil conservation practices, recycling nonrenewable resources)

BD (GE,140;NE,44)

● Knows how differences in perception affect people's interpretations of the world (e.g., how different groups of people perceive the same place, environment, or event; how children raised in different societies have different views regarding personal life, education, and aspirations)

BD (GE,141;NI,44)

● Knows human-induced changes that are taking place in different regions and the possible future impacts of these changes (e.g., development and conservation issues in terms of the wetland of coastal New Jersey)

Level III (Grades 6-8)

BD (GE,181;NI,60)

● Understands how the interaction between physical and human systems affects current conditions on Earth (e.g., relationships involved in economic, political, social, and environmental changes; geographic impact of using petroleum, coal, nuclear power, and solar power as major energy sources)

BD (GE,182;NI,60)

● Understands the possible impact that present conditions and patterns of consumption, production and population growth might have on the future spatial organization of Earth

---

Codes (right side of page):   BD = Benchmark, Declarative; BP = Benchmark, Procedural; BC = Benchmark, Contextual
1st letter of each code in parentheses   *2nd letter of code*   *Number*
G = GESP: National Geography Standards   E = Explicitly stated in document   Page number of cited document
E = JCGE: Guidelines for Geographic Education   I = Implied in document   *or, for duplicates,*
IE, IG = Int'l Bacc.:Environmental Systems, Geography   Standard number & level of duplicate
N = NAEP: Item Specifications in Geography
T = GENIP: K-6 Geography: Themes, Key Ideas
D = Duplicated in another standard

- Knows how the quality of environments in large cities can be improved (e.g., greenways, transportation corridors, pedestrian walkways, bicycle lanes) BD (GE,182)

- Understands why different points of view exist regarding contemporary geographic issues (e.g., a forester and a conservationist debating the use of a national forest, a man and a woman discussing gender-based divisions of labor in a developing nation) BD (GE,181-182;NI,62-63)

Level IV (Grades 9-12)

- Understands the concept of sustainable development and its effects in a variety of situations (e.g., toward cutting the rain forests in Indonesia in response to a demand for lumber in foreign markets, or mining the rutile sands along the coast of eastern Australia near the Great Barrier Reef) BD (GE,221;IEE,29;IGE,11,12;NI,79-80)

- Understands why policies should be designed to guide the use and management of Earth's resources and to reflect multiple points of view (e.g., the inequities of access to resources, political and economic power in developing countries, the impact of a natural disaster on a developed country vs. a developing country) BD (GE,221;IEE,29,30;IGE,11,12;NI,79)

- Understands contemporary issues in terms of Earth's physical and human systems (e.g., the processes of land degradation and desertification, the consequences of population growth or decline in a developed economy, the consequences of a world temperature increase) BD (GE,222;IEE,26,29,30,31;IGE,9,10,11,12;NI,76)

Codes (right side of page):   BD = Benchmark, Declarative; BP = Benchmark, Procedural; BC = Benchmark, Contextual
1st letter of each code in parentheses   *2nd letter of code*   *Number*
G = GESP: National Geography Standards   E = Explicitly stated in document   Page number of cited document
E = JCGE: Guidelines for Geographic Education   I = Implied in document   *or, for duplicates,*
IE, IG = Int'l Bacc.:Environmental Systems, Geography   Standard number & level of duplicate
N = NAEP: Item Specifications in Geography
T = GENIP: K-6 Geography: Themes, Key Ideas
D = Duplicated in another standard   542   McREL

16. Health

The following process was used to identify standards and benchmarks for health:

Identification of National Reports

Six reports were identified as providing useful information on health education standards in the schools: *National Health Education Standards: Achieving Health Literacy* (1995) from the Joint Committee on National Health Education Standards; *Benchmarks for Science Literacy* (1993) from Project 2061, American Association for the Advancement of Science; *Health Framework for California Public Schools* from the California Department of Education (1994); the *Report of the 1990 Joint Committee on Health Education Terminology*, from JCHET (1990); the *Michigan Essential Goals/Objectives for Health Education* (1988) from the Michigan State Board of Education; and the *National Science Education Standards* (1996) from the National Research Council.

Selection of the Reference Document

National Health Education Standards: Achieving Health Literacy was used as the reference document. However, some basic content information was also drawn from the Michigan and California documents identified above, and supporting material (as well as some primary material) came from the two science documents, *National Science Education Standards* and Project 2061's *Benchmarks*.

Identification of Standards and Benchmarks

At the benchmark level, information was derived from *National Health Education Standards* and from all other reports cited above. These reports, except for the California framework, which was more curricular in scope, provided relatively straightforward descriptions of knowledge and skills recommended for health education. Consequently, most of the effort in the identification of benchmarks for health education centered on the synthesis and citation of information from multiple sources.

After the content review, those benchmark items that arose in all the reports were analyzed and grouped. Thus, the standards were developed working up from the benchmark level. However, for the most part, it was found that the resulting standards were similar to the topic level recommendations found in the *Report of the 1990 Joint Committee on Health Education Terminology*. In addition to these topic areas, a standard on Growth and Development was added, derived largely from information in the two science documents, *Science Standards* and Project 2061's *Benchmarks for Science Literacy*.

Integration of Information from Other Documents

As mentioned above, material from the other documents was not only integrated with the reference material, but new material was added from them as well. This was done when information was found to be present in more than one of the selected reports. It should be noted, however, that all benchmark information from the reference document, the *National Health Education Standards*, will be found in this report.

Summary of Standards for Health

1. Knows the availability and effective use of health services, products, and information
2. Knows environmental and external factors that affect individual and community health
3. Understands the relationship of family health to individual health
4. Knows how to maintain mental and emotional health
5. Knows essential concepts and practices concerning injury prevention and safety
6. Understands essential concepts about nutrition and diet
7. Knows how to maintain and promote personal health
8. Knows essential concepts about the prevention and control of disease
9. Understands aspects of substance use and abuse
10. Understands the fundamental concepts of growth and development

(JE,106)
1. Knows the availability and effective use of health services, products, and information

Level I (Grades K-2)

- BP (HE,18;CE,71,89;ME,29)
  Knows community health service providers and their roles (e.g., paramedics, dentists, nurses, physicians, sanitarians, dietitians)

Level II (Grades 3-5)

- BD (HE,18,23;CI,71,89-90;ME,25)
  Knows general characteristics of valid health information and health-promoting products and services (e.g., provided by qualified health-care workers; supported by research)

- BD (HE,18,23;CE,85,89;ME,25,29)
  Knows various community agencies that provide health services to individuals and families (e.g., HMOs, public health clinics, mental health clinics, substance abuse treatment centers)

- BD (HE,18,4;CE,71,89;ME,25)
  Knows a variety of consumer influences and how those influences affect decisions regarding health resources, products, and services (e.g., media, information from school and family, peer pressure)

Level III (Grades 6-8)

- BD (HE,18;CE,148-149)
  Knows the costs and validity of common health products, services, and information

- BD (HE,18;CI,111)
  Knows how to locate and use community health information, products, and services that provide valid health information

- BD (CI,116-117;ME,25)
  Knows ways to influence the consumer health service system (e.g., assertive consumerism, selecting providers, communicating complaints)

- BD (CI,110;ME,25)
  Knows community health consumer organizations and the advocacy services they provide (e.g., American Heart Association, American Lung Association, Diabetes Association)

- BC (HE,18;CE,89,117)
  Knows situations that require professional health services (e.g., management of health conditions such as asthma, diabetes)

Codes (right side of page):	BD = Benchmark, Declarative; BP = Benchmark, Procedural; BC = Benchmark, Contextual

1st letter of each code in parentheses — *2nd letter of code* — *Number*
H = JHESC: National Health Education Standards — E = Explicitly stated in document — Page number of cited document
2 = Project 2061: Benchmarks for Science Literacy — I = Implied in document — *or, for duplicates:*
C = CDE: Health Framework for Calif. Public Schools — — Standard number & level of duplicate
J = Joint Committee on Health Ed. Terminology
M = MSBE: Michigan Essential Goals/Obj. for Health
S = NRC: National Science Education Standards
D = Duplicated in another standard

545

MREL

Level IV (Grades 9-12)

- Knows factors that influence personal selection of health care resources, products, and services (e.g., cost, benefits)
BD (HE,18;CE,149)

- Knows how to determine whether various resources from home, school, and the community present valid health information, products, and services
BD (HE,18;CI,148-149;ME,26)

- Knows local, state, federal, and private agencies that protect and/or inform the consumer (e.g., FDA, EPA, OSHA, local prosecutor's office)
BD (HI,18;CI,148-149;ME,25)

- Understands the cost and accessibility of a variety of health-care services (e.g., health insurance coverage)
BD (HE,18;CE,148-149)

- Knows situations that require professional health services in the areas of prevention, treatment, and rehabilitation (e.g., persistent depression, prenatal and perinatal care, treatment or management of disease, alcohol- or drug-related problems, neglect and child abuse)
BD (HE,18;CI,125-127,131;ME,11)

2.	**Knows environmental and external factors that affect individual and community health**
(JE,106)

Level I (Grades K-2)

- Knows sources and causes of pollution (e.g., air, ground, noise, water, food) in the community
BD (CI,68;ME,29)

Level II (Grades 3-5)

- Knows how the physical environment can impact personal health (e.g., the effects of exposure to pollutants)
BD (HE,17;ME,29)

- Knows how individuals, communities, and states cooperate to control environmental problems and maintain a healthy environment
BD (CI,85;ME,29)

- Knows how personal health can be influenced by society (e.g., culture) and science (e.g., technology)
BD (HI,20;CI,78;ME,29)

Codes (right side of page):	BD = Benchmark, Declarative; BP = Benchmark, Procedural; BC = Benchmark, Contextual
1st letter of each code in parentheses	*2nd letter of code*	*Number*
H = JHESC: National Health Education Standards	E = Explicitly stated in document	Page number of cited document
2 = Project 2061: Benchmarks for Science Literacy	I = Implied in document	*or, for duplicates:*
C = CDE: Health Framework for Calif. Public Schools		Standard number & level of duplicate
J = Joint Committee on Health Ed. Terminology
M = MSBE: Michigan Essential Goals/Obj. for Health
S = NRC: National Science Education Standards
D = Duplicated in another standard

Level III (Grades 6-8)

- BD (HE,17,20;CE,117;ME,29)

  Knows cultural beliefs, socioeconomic considerations, and other environmental factors within a community that influence the health of its members (e.g., relationship of values, socioeconomic status, and cultural experiences to the selection of health-care services)

- BD (HE,20;CE,89-90,116-117)

  Understands how various messages from the media, technology, and other sources impact health practices (e.g., health fads, advertising, misconceptions about treatment and prevention options)

- BD (CE,110-111;ME,30;SI,168)

  Knows local, state, federal, and international efforts to contain an environmental crisis and prevent a recurrence (e.g., acid rain, oil spills, solid waste contamination, nuclear leaks, ozone depletion)

- BD (HE,17,20;CE,108-109)

  Understands how peer relationships affect health (e.g., name calling, prejudice, exclusiveness, discrimination, risk-taking behaviors)

Level IV (Grades 9-12)

- BD (HE,17,20;CE,138)

  Knows how the health of individuals can be influenced by the community (e.g., information offered through community organizations; volunteer work at hospitals, food banks, child care centers)

- BD (HE,19;CE,138-139)

  Knows how individuals can improve or maintain community health (e.g., becoming active in environmental and economic issues that affect health, assisting in the development of public health policies and laws, exercising voting privileges)

- BD (HE,17;CE,139)

  Understands how the environment influences the health of the community (e.g., environmental issues that affect the food supply and the nutritional quality of food)

- BD (HE,17,20;CI,138-139)

  Understands how the prevention and control of health problems are influenced by research and medical advances

- BD (HE,17;CE,138;ME,25,30)

  Knows how public health policies and government regulations (e.g., OSHA regulations, Right to Know laws, DSS regulations, licensing laws) impact health-related issues (e.g., safe food handling, food production controls, household waste disposal controls, clean air, disposal of nuclear waste)

- Understands how cultural diversity enriches and challenges health behaviors (e.g., various food sources of nutrients available in different cultural and ethnic cuisines, influence of cultural factors on the treatment of diseases) BD (HE,20;CI,122-123,127)

3. Understands the relationship of family health to individual health (JE,106)

Level I (Grades K-2)

- Knows the roles of parents and the extended family in supporting a strong family and promoting the health of children (e.g., the limits parents set for children, the values or religious beliefs taught, behaviors and values modeled) BD (CE,65;ME,18)

- Knows effective strategies to cope with change that may occur in families (e.g., pregnancy, birth, marriage, divorce, relocation, unemployment) BD (CE,66;ME,18)

Level II (Grades 3-5)

- Knows how the family influences personal health (e.g., physical, psychological, social) BD (HE,17;CI,82;ME,18)

- Knows characteristics needed to be a responsible friend and family member (e.g., participating in family activities, assuming more responsibility for household tasks) BD (HE,21;CE,82,83)

- Knows how health-related problems impact the whole family BD (CE,83;ME,18)

Level III (Grades 6-8)

- Knows strategies that improve or maintain family health (e.g., how one's personal behavior can affect the behavior and feelings of other family members) BD (HE,19;CE,105;ME,18)

- Understands the development of adolescent independence BD (CE,106;ME,18)

- Knows how communication techniques can improve family life (e.g., talking openly and honestly with parents when problems arise) BD (HE,23;CE,105;DI,4.4.1)

Codes (right side of page):   BD = Benchmark, Declarative; BP = Benchmark, Procedural; BC = Benchmark, Contextual
1st letter of each code in parentheses   *2nd letter of code*   *Number*
H = JHESC: National Health Education Standards   E = Explicitly stated in document   Page number of cited document
2 = Project 2061: Benchmarks for Science Literacy   I = Implied in document   *or, for duplicates:*
C = CDE: Health Framework for Calif. Public Schools   Standard number & level of duplicate
J = Joint Committee on Health Ed. Terminology
M = MSBE: Michigan Essential Goals/Obj. for Health
S = NRC: National Science Education Standards
D = Duplicated in another standard   548   McREL

Level IV (Grades 9-12)

- Understands methods to facilitate the transition from the role of a child to the role of an independent adult in the family

  BD (CE,135;MI,18)

- Knows the effects of teenage pregnancy on teenagers, their children, their parents, and society

  BD (CE,146;ME,17,18)

- Understands the responsibilities inherent in dating relationships, marriage, and parenthood

  BD (CE,137-138;ME,18)

4.   Knows how to maintain mental and emotional health

(JE,106)

Level I (Grades K-2)

- Identifies and shares feelings in appropriate ways

  BP (2E,148;CE,59,67;ME,19)

Level II (Grades 3-5)

- Knows the relationships between physical health and mental health

  BD (2E,148;CE,75;ME,19)

- Knows common sources of stress for children and ways to manage stress

  BD (HE,19;CE,76;ME,19)

- Knows how mood changes and strong feelings affect thoughts and behavior, and how they can be managed successfully

  BD (HI,21;2E,148;CE,86;ME,19,20)

- Knows behaviors that communicate care, consideration, and respect of self and others (including those with disabilities or handicapping conditions)

  BP (HE,21;CE,59,84;ME,20)

- Understands how one responds to the behavior of others and how one's behavior may evoke responses in others

  BD (2I,148;CI,84;ME,20)

- Knows strategies for resisting negative peer pressure

  BD (CE,76,84;ME,20)

- Knows how attentive listening skills can be used to build and maintain healthy relationships

  BD (HE,21;CE,67)

Codes (right side of page):   BD = Benchmark, Declarative; BP = Benchmark, Procedural; BC = Benchmark, Contextual
1st letter of each code in parentheses   *2nd letter of code*   *Number*
H = JHESC: National Health Education Standards   E = Explicitly stated in document   Page number of cited document
2 = Project 2061: Benchmarks for Science Literacy   I = Implied in document   *or, for duplicates:*
C = CDE: Health Framework for Calif. Public Schools   Standard number & level of duplicate
J = Joint Committee on Health Ed. Terminology
M = MSBE: Michigan Essential Goals/Obj. for Health
S = NRC: National Science Education Standards
D = Duplicated in another standard   549   *McREL*

Level III (Grades 6-8)

- BD (HE,19,21;2E,149;CE,96,112)
  Knows strategies to manage stress and feelings caused by disappointment, separation, or loss (e.g., talking over problems with others, understanding that feelings of isolation and depression will pass, examining the situation leading to the feelings)

- BD (CE,95;ME,19)
  Knows characteristics and conditions associated with positive self-esteem

- BD (HE,21;CE,96,108;MI,20)
  Knows appropriate ways to build and maintain positive relationships with peers, parents, and other adults (e.g., interpersonal communication)

- BD (HE,19;CE,108-109;MI,20)
  Understands the difference between safe and risky or harmful behaviors in relationships

- BD (2I,149;CE,96;ME,21)
  Knows techniques for seeking help and support through appropriate resources

Level IV (Grades 9-12)

- BD (HE,21;CE,125;DI,3.3.3)
  Knows skills used to communicate effectively with family, friends, and others, and the effects of open and honest communication

- BD (HE,19,21;CE,124-125;MI,20-21)
  Knows strategies for coping with and overcoming feelings of rejection, social isolation, and other forms of stress

- BD (CE,125;MI,20-21)
  Understands the role of denial as a negative influence on mental and emotional health, and ways to overcome denial and seek assistance when needed

(JE,106)
5. Knows essential concepts and practices concerning injury prevention and safety

Level I (Grades K-2)

- BD (CE,62;ME,27)
  Knows basic fire, traffic, water, and recreation safety practices

- BD (CE,62;ME,27)
  Knows precautions that should be taken in special conditions (e.g., bad weather, Halloween, darkness, staying home alone, being approached by strangers, avoiding conflicts)

- BP (CE,62,64;ME,28)
  Knows how to recognize emergencies and respond appropriately (e.g., uses a telephone appropriately to obtain help; identifies and obtains help from police officers, fire fighters,

---

Codes (right side of page):   BD = Benchmark, Declarative; BP = Benchmark, Procedural; BC = Benchmark, Contextual
1st letter of each code in parentheses   *2nd letter of code*   *Number*
H = JHESC: National Health Education Standards   E = Explicitly stated in document   Page number of cited document
2 = Project 2061: Benchmarks for Science Literacy   I = Implied in document   *or, for duplicates:*
C = CDE: Health Framework for Calif. Public Schools   Standard number & level of duplicate
J = Joint Committee on Health Ed. Terminology
M = MSBE: Michigan Essential Goals/Obj. for Health
S = NRC: National Science Education Standards
D = Duplicated in another standard   550   MREL

and medical personnel; treats simple injuries such as scratches, cuts, bruises, and first-degree burns)

BD (CE,63;ME,27;SE,139)

- Knows ways to seek assistance if worried, abused, or threatened (e.g., physically, emotionally, sexually)

Level II (Grades 3-5)

BD (HI,19;CE,57;ME,27;SE,139)

- Knows safety rules and practices to be used in home, school, and community settings (e.g., using a seat belt or helmet, protecting ears from exposure to excessive noise, wearing appropriate clothing and protective equipment for sports, using sunscreen or a hat in bright sunlight)

BD (HE,19;CE,79,81)

- Knows methods used to recognize and avoid threatening situations (e.g., not leaning into a car when giving directions to a stranger) and ways to get assistance

BD (HI,21;CE,81;ME,28)

- Knows basic first aid procedures appropriate to common emergencies in home, school, and community (e.g., proper responses to breathing and choking problems, bleeding, shock, poisonings, minor burns; universal precautions to be taken when dealing with other people's blood)

BD (HE,21;CI,79;MI,19,20)

- Knows the difference between positive and negative behaviors used in conflict situations

BD (HE,21;CE,79;MI,19,20)

- Knows some non-violent strategies to resolve conflicts

Level III (Grades 6-8)

BD (HE,19;CE,104;SI,168)

- Knows injury prevention strategies for family health (e.g., having a personal and family emergency plan, including maintaining supplies in readiness for emergencies; identifying and removing safety hazards in the home)

BP (HE,19;CE,104;ME,28)

- Knows strategies for managing a range of situations involving injury (e.g., first aid procedures, abdominal thrust maneuver, cardiopulmonary resuscitation)

BD (HI,19;ME,20)

- Knows potential signs of self- and other-directed violence

BD (HE,21;CE,109)

- Knows the various possible causes of conflict among youth in schools and communities, and

---

Codes (right side of page):   BD = Benchmark, Declarative; BP = Benchmark, Procedural; BC = Benchmark, Contextual

1st letter of each code in parentheses   *2nd letter of code*   *Number*

II – JHESC: National Health Education Standards   E = Explicitly stated in document   Page number of cited document

2 = Project 2061: Benchmarks for Science Literacy   I = Implied in document   *or, for duplicates:*

C = CDE: Health Framework for Calif. Public Schools   Standard number & level of duplicate

J = Joint Committee on Health Ed. Terminology

M = MSBE: Michigan Essential Goals/Obj. for Health

S = NRC: National Science Education Standards

D = Duplicated in another standard   551   MREL

strategies to manage conflict

- Knows how refusal and negotiation skills can be used to enhance health

  BD (HE,21;CE,96;ME,17,20)

Level IV (Grades 9-12)

- Knows injury prevention strategies for community health (e.g., neighborhood safety, traffic safety, safe driving)

  BD (HE,19;SI,197)

- Knows possible causes of conflicts in schools, families, and communities, and strategies to prevent conflict in these situations

  BD (HE,21)

- Knows strategies for solving interpersonal conflicts without harming self or others

  BD (HE,21;CE,129)

- Knows how refusal, negotiation, and collaboration skills can be used to avoid potentially harmful situations

  BD (HE,21;CE,129)

6. Understands essential concepts about nutrition and diet

(JE,106)

Level I (Grades K-2)

- Classifies foods and food combinations according to the food groups

  BP (CE,58;ME,14)

Level II (Grades 3-5)

- Knows the nutritional value of different foods

  BD (CE,75,90;ME,14;SI,140)

- Knows healthy eating practices (e.g., eating a nutritious breakfast, eating a variety of foods, eating nutritious meals and snacks at regular intervals to satisfy individual energy and growth needs)

  BD (CE,75;ME,14;SE,140)

- Knows factors that influence food choices (e.g., activity level, peers, culture, religion, advertising, time, age, health, money/economics, convenience, environment, status, personal experience)

  BD (CE,75;ME,14)

Codes (right side of page):   BD = Benchmark, Declarative; BP = Benchmark, Procedural; BC = Benchmark, Contextual
1st letter of each code in parentheses   *2nd letter of code*   *Number*
H = JHESC: National Health Education Standards   E = Explicitly stated in document   Page number of cited document
2 = Project 2061: Benchmarks for Science Literacy   I = Implied in document   *or, for duplicates:*
C = CDE: Health Framework for Calif. Public Schools   Standard number & level of duplicate
J = Joint Committee on Health Ed. Terminology
M = MSBE: Michigan Essential Goals/Obj. for Health
S = NRC: National Science Education Standards
D = Duplicated in another standard   552

MREL

- Knows how food-preparation methods and food-handling practices affect the safety and nutrient quality of foods $\quad$ BD (CE,75;MI,15)

Level III (Grades 6-8)

- Understands how eating properly can help to reduce health risks (in terms of anemia, dental health, osteoporosis, heart disease, cancer, malnutrition) $\quad$ BD (CE,94;ME,14,15)

- Knows appropriate methods to maintain, lose, or gain weight according to individual needs and scientific research $\quad$ BD (CE,94,119;MI,15;SI,168)

- Knows eating disorders that affect health adversely (e.g., anorexia, overeating, bulimia) $\quad$ BD (CI,118;ME,15)

- Knows the principles of food safety involved with food storage and preparation (e.g., proper refrigeration, hand washing, proper cooking and storage temperatures) $\quad$ BD (CE,94;ME,15)

Level IV (Grades 9-12)

- Understands how nutrient and energy needs vary in relation to gender, activity level, and stage of life cycle $\quad$ BD (CE,122;ME,14;SI,197)

- Understands the reliability and validity of various sources of food and nutrition information (e.g., dietary supplements, diet aids, fad diets, food labels) $\quad$ BP (CE,149-150;ME,15;SI,197)

- Understands the role of food additives and their relationship to health $\quad$ BD (CI,150;ME,15)

(JE,106)

7. Knows how to maintain and promote personal health

Level I (Grades K-2)

- Knows basic personal hygiene habits required to maintain health (e.g., caring for teeth, gums, eyes, ears, nose, skin, hair, nails) $\quad$ BD (HI,19;CE,57;ME,13;SE,140)

Codes (right side of page): $\quad$ BD = Benchmark, Declarative; BP = Benchmark, Procedural; BC = Benchmark, Contextual
1st letter of each code in parentheses $\quad$ *2nd letter of code* $\quad$ *Number*
H = JHESC: National Health Education Standards $\quad$ E = Explicitly stated in document $\quad$ Page number of cited document
2 = Project 2061: Benchmarks for Science Literacy $\quad$ I = Implied in document $\quad$ *or, for duplicates:*
C = CDE: Health Framework for Calif. Public Schools $\quad$ Standard number & level of duplicate
J = Joint Committee on Health Ed. Terminology
M = MSBE: Michigan Essential Goals/Obj. for Health
S = NRC: National Science Education Standards
D = Duplicated in another standard $\quad$ 553 $\quad$ MREL

Level II (Grades 3-5)

- Understands the influence of rest, food choices, exercise, sleep, and recreation on a person's well-being
  BD (HE,17;CE,75,86;ME,13;SI,140)

- Knows common health problems that should be detected and treated early
  BD (HE,17;CE,78;MI,11)

- Knows behaviors that are safe, risky, or harmful to self and others
  BD (HE,19;MI,13)

- Sets a personal health goal and makes progress toward its achievement
  BP (HE,22)

- Knows that making health-related decisions and setting health goals sometimes requires asking for assistance
  BD (HE,22)

- Knows the basic structure and functions of the human body systems (e.g., how they are interrelated; how they function to fight disease)
  BD (HE,17;CE,74;ME,16)

Level III (Grades 6-8)

- Knows personal health strengths and risks (e.g., results of a personal health assessment)
  BD (HE,17;MI,13)

- Knows how positive health practices and appropriate health care can help to reduce health risks (e.g., good personal hygiene, health screenings, self-examinations)
  BD (HE,17,19;CE,93,97,98;ME,13)

- Knows strategies and skills that are used to attain personal health goals (e.g., maintaining an exercise program, making healthy food choices)
  BD (HE,22;CE,94,95;MI,13;SE,168)

- Understands how changing information, abilities, priorities, and responsibilities influence personal health goals
  BD (HE,22)

- Knows how health is influenced by the interaction of body systems
  BD (HE,17;CI,93)

Level IV (Grades 9-12)

- Knows how personal behaviors relate to health and well-being and how these behaviors can be modified if necessary to promote achievement of health goals throughout life (e.g., following a personal nutrition plan to reduce the risk of disease, periodically self-assessing
  BP (HE,17,19,22;CE,122-123;MI,13;SI,197)

Codes (right side of page):	BD = Benchmark, Declarative; BP = Benchmark, Procedural; BC = Benchmark, Contextual	
1st letter of each code in parentheses	*2nd letter of code*	*Number*
H = JHESC: National Health Education Standards	E = Explicitly stated in document	Page number of cited document
2 = Project 2061: Benchmarks for Science Literacy	I = Implied in document	*or, for duplicates:*
C = CDE: Health Framework for Calif. Public Schools		Standard number & level of duplicate
J = Joint Committee on Health Ed. Terminology		
M = MSBE: Michigan Essential Goals/Obj. for Health		
S = NRC: National Science Education Standards		
D = Duplicated in another standard		

physical fitness)

BD (HE,3;CI,128-129)

- Understands the short- and long-term consequences of safe, risky, and harmful behaviors

BD (HI,1;CE,121)

- Understands how personal health needs change during the life cycle

BD (HE,17)

- Understands the impact of personal health behaviors on the functioning of body systems

(JE,106)

8. Knows essential concepts about the prevention and control of disease

Level I (Grades K-2)

BD (CE,61;ME,11;SI,140)

- Knows the signs and symptoms of common illnesses (e.g., fever, rashes, coughs, congestion, wheezing)

Level II (Grades 3-5)

BD (HE,17;2E,144;CE,60,77;ME,11,12;SE,140)

- Knows ways in which a person can prevent or reduce the risk of disease and disability (e.g., practicing good personal hygiene, making healthy food choices, acknowledging the importance of immunizations, cooperating in regular health screenings)

BD (CI,77;ME,11)

- Knows the benefits of early detection and treatment of disease

BD (CE,78,89;ME,12)

- Knows ways to maintain a functional level of health in the presence of disease or disability (e.g., cooperating with parents and health care providers, taking prescription or over-the-counter medicines properly, correctly interpreting instructions for taking medicine)

Level III (Grades 6-8)

BD (HE,17;CE,97;ME,11)

- Understands how lifestyle, pathogens, family history, and other risk factors are related to the cause or prevention of disease and other health problems

BD (CE,97-98;ME,11;SI,168)

- Knows communicable, chronic, and degenerative disease processes and the differences between them

---

Codes (right side of page):   BD = Benchmark, Declarative; BP = Benchmark, Procedural; BC = Benchmark, Contextual
1st letter of each code in parentheses   *2nd letter of code*   *Number*
H = JHESC: National Health Education Standards   E = Explicitly stated in document   Page number of cited document
2 = Project 2061: Benchmarks for Science Literacy   I = Implied in document   *or, for duplicates:*
C = CDE: Health Framework for Calif. Public Schools   Standard number & level of duplicate
J = Joint Committee on Health Ed. Terminology
M = MSBE: Michigan Essential Goals/Obj. for Health
S = NRC: National Science Education Standards
D = Duplicated in another standard   555   M*REL

BD (HI,17;CE,99)

- Understands personal rights and responsibilities involved in the treatment of disease (e.g., proper use of medication; the influence of family and culture on the treatment of disease)

Level IV (Grades 9-12)

BD (2E,145;CE,125-126;MI,11;SI,197)

- Understands how the immune system functions to prevent or combat disease

BD (HE,17;CE,126;MI,12)

- Understands the importance of regular examinations (including self-examination of the breasts or testicles) in detecting and treating diseases early

BD (CE,126;ME,17;DI,10.4.3)

- Understands the importance of prenatal and perinatal care to both the mother and the child

BD (CE,125;ME,11)

- Understands the social, economic, and political effects of disease on individuals, families, and communities

(JE,106)

9.   Understands aspects of substance use and abuse

Level I (Grades K-2)

BD (CE,63;MI,22;SI,140)

- Knows how to distinguish between helpful and harmful substances

Level II (Grades 3-5)

BP (CE,80;MI,22;SI,140)

- Differentiates between the use and misuse of prescription and nonprescription drugs

BD (CE,80;ME,23)

- Knows influences that promote alcohol, tobacco, and other drug use (e.g., peer pressure, peer and adult modeling, advertising, overall availability, cost)

BP (CE,80;ME,23)

- Recognizes high-risk substance abuse situations that pose an immediate threat to oneself or one's friends or family (e.g., drunk and drugged driving, violent arguments) as well as how and where to obtain help

BD (HE,21;CE,80;ME,24)

- Knows ways to avoid, recognize, and respond to negative social influences and pressure to use alcohol, tobacco, or other drugs (e.g., refusal skills, self-control)

Codes (right side of page):   BD = Benchmark, Declarative; BP = Benchmark, Procedural; BC = Benchmark, Contextual
1st letter of each code in parentheses   *2nd letter of code*   *Number*
H = JHESC: National Health Education Standards   E = Explicitly stated in document   Page number of cited document
2 = Project 2061: Benchmarks for Science Literacy   I = Implied in document   *or, for duplicates:*
C = CDE: Health Framework for Calif. Public Schools   Standard number & level of duplicate
J = Joint Committee on Health Ed. Terminology
M = MSBE: Michigan Essential Goals/Obj. for Health
S = NRC: National Science Education Standards
D = Duplicated in another standard   556   M*REL*

Level III (Grades 6-8)

- Knows conditions that may put people at higher risk for substance abuse problems (e.g., genetic inheritability, substance abuse in family, low frustration tolerance)

  BD (CE,102;ME,22;SI,168)

- Knows factors involved in the development of a drug dependency and the early, observable signs and symptoms (e.g., tolerance level, drug-seeking behavior, loss of control, denial)

  BD (CI,102;ME,23;SI,168)

- Knows the short- and long-term consequences of the use of alcohol, tobacco, and other drugs (e.g., physical consequences such as shortness of breath, cirrhosis, lung cancer, emphysema; psychological consequences such as low self-esteem, paranoia, depression, apathy; social consequences such as crime, domestic violence, loss of friends)

  BD (CE,101-102;ME,22,23;SE,168)

- Knows public policy approaches to substance abuse control and prevention (e.g., pricing and taxation, warning labels, regulation of advertising, restriction of alcohol consumption at sporting events)

  BD (CE,102;ME,24)

- Knows community resources that are available to assist people with alcohol, tobacco, and other drug problems

  BD (CE,102,ME,24)

Level IV (Grades 9-12)

- Knows the short- and long-term effects associated with the use of alcohol, tobacco, and other drugs on reproduction, pregnancy, and the health of children

  BD (CE,129-130;MI,23;SI,197)

- Knows how the abuse of alcohol, tobacco, and other drugs often plays a role in dangerous behavior and can have adverse consequences on the community (e.g., house fires, motor vehicle crashes, domestic violence, date rape, transmission of diseases through needle sharing or sexual activity)

  BD (CE,130;ME,22;SE,197)

- Understands that alcohol, tobacco, and other drug dependencies are treatable diseases/conditions

  BD (CE,131;ME,24)

Codes (right side of page): BD = Benchmark, Declarative; BP = Benchmark, Procedural; BC = Benchmark, Contextual
1st letter of each code in parentheses   *2nd letter of code*   *Number*
H = JHESC: National Health Education Standards   E = Explicitly stated in document   Page number of cited document
2 = Project 2061: Benchmarks for Science Literacy   I = Implied in document   *or, for duplicates:*
C = CDE: Health Framework for Calif. Public Schools   Standard number & level of duplicate
J = Joint Committee on Health Ed. Terminology
M = MSBE: Michigan Essential Goals/Obj. for Health
S = NRC: National Science Education Standards
D = Duplicated in another standard

McREL

10.   Understands the fundamental concepts of growth and development   (JE,106)

Level I (Grades K-2)

- Understands individual differences (in terms of appearance, behavior)   BD (CE,70;MI,16)

- Knows the cycle of growth and development in humans from infancy to old age   BD (2E,132;CE,69;ME,16)

Level II (Grades 3-5)

- Knows the changes that occur during puberty (e.g., physical changes such as sexual maturation, changes in voice, acne; emotional and social changes such as a growing sensitivity to peer influence, family tensions, mood swings; cognitive and intellectual development)   BD (2E,132;CE,86-87;ME,17)

- Knows that the rate of change during puberty varies with each individual and that people vary widely in size, height, shape, and rate of maturation   BD (2I,132;CE,87-88;ME,16)

Level III (Grades 6-8)

- Understands how the human body changes as people age (e.g., muscles and joints become less flexible, bones and muscles lose mass, energy levels diminish, senses become less acute)   BD (2E,133;CI,140)

- Knows the similarities and differences between male and female sexuality   BD (CE,114;MI,16,17)

- Understands the processes of conception, prenatal development, and birth   BD (2E,133;CE,141;ME,17)

- Knows strategies for coping with concerns and stress related to the changes that occur during adolescence   BD (CE,112;MI,16)

Level IV (Grades 9-12)

- Understands a variety of physical, mental, emotional, and social changes that occur throughout life, and how these changes differ among individuals (e.g., young adulthood, pregnancy, middle age, old age)   BD (CE,140-141;MI,16-17)

Codes (right side of page):   BD = Benchmark, Declarative; BP = Benchmark, Procedural; BC = Benchmark, Contextual
1st letter of each code in parentheses   2nd letter of code   *Number*
H = JHESC: National Health Education Standards   E = Explicitly stated in document   Page number of cited document
2 = Project 2061: Benchmarks for Science Literacy   I = Implied in document   *or, for duplicates:*
C = CDE: Health Framework for Calif. Public Schools   Standard number & level of duplicate
J = Joint Committee on Health Ed. Terminology
M = MSBE: Michigan Essential Goals/Obj. for Health
S = NRC: National Science Education Standards
D = Duplicated in another standard

McREL

- Understands how physical, mental, social, and cultural factors influence attitudes and behaviors regarding sexuality

  BD (2I,134;CE,147;MI,16-17;SE,197)

- Knows sound health practices in the prenatal period that are important to the health of the fetus and young child (e.g., diet, refraining from cigarette smoking or use of alcohol or other drugs)

  BD (2I,133;CE,141-142;ME,17;DI,8.4.3)

Codes (right side of page):   BD = Benchmark, Declarative; BP = Benchmark, Procedural; BC = Benchmark, Contextual
1st letter of each code in parentheses   *2nd letter of code*   *Number*
H = JHESC: National Health Education Standards   E = Explicitly stated in document   Page number of cited document
2 = Project 2061: Benchmarks for Science Literacy   I = Implied in document   *or, for duplicates:*
C = CDE: Health Framework for Calif. Public Schools   Standard number & level of duplicate
J = Joint Committee on Health Ed. Terminology
M = MSBE: Michigan Essential Goals/Obj. for Health
S = NRC: National Science Education Standards
D = Duplicated in another standard   559   McREL

17. Physical Education

The following process was used to identify standards and benchmarks for physical education:

Identification of Significant Reports

Three reports were identified as useful documents for identifying physical education standards: *Moving into the Future: National Standards for Physical Education: A Guide to Content and Assessment* (1995) and *Outcomes of Quality Physical Education Programs* (1992), both from the National Association for Sport and Physical Education (NASPE); and a draft of the Michigan Department of Education's *Physical Education: Content Standards and Benchmarks* (1996).

Selection of the Reference Document

The NASPE's *Moving into the Future: National Standards for Physical Education: A Guide to Content and Assessment* (1995) was selected as the reference document for identifying standards and benchmarks. The *Standards* were developed with the input of physical education professionals across the country. The work was also based on the *Outcomes of Quality Physical Education Programs* (1992) from NASPE.

Identification of Standards and Benchmarks

NASPE's *Standards* work shares a number of features with our model for the identification of benchmarks and standards. First, the standards statements in the document are expressed at an appropriate level of generality, since they are stated broadly enough to allow for benchmark statements to be articulated across K–12. In addition, beneath each standard, the document provides various descriptions of the knowledge and skills that students should acquire from K–12, stated for selected developmental levels.

There were a few areas, however, in which the document was not directly compatible with our approach. Beneath each standard, student knowledge and skill is described in several sections: a paragraph summarizing the knowledge and abilities expected for the grade range under discussion; a more specific list of those skills that should receive particular emphasis; and sample "performance benchmarks," assessment examples, and criteria for assessment. Frequently, it was necessary to take information from several of these sections in order to construct each benchmark. This was done, for example, when the assessment criteria section could provide additional information on the knowledge or skills identified, or when material from still another section helped to make a benchmark less narrow in scope, or when specific examples of the kind of knowledge and skills required was found to be useful. In addition to this modification in the content, some changes for the grade range of the material were necessary. The reference work has seven levels: kindergarten, and grades 2, 4, 6, 8, 10, and 12. Because our benchmarks are at primary, upper elementary, middle, and high school, we adopted the following method for aligning the grade levels between the two documents in order to maintain as much grade-specific information as possible. For the primary grades (level I), the information from grade 2 of the reference material was our primary source, but it was supplemented with information from kindergarten for any descriptions of knowledge or skill that weren't encompassed by the material at grade 2. Similarly, for our level II, we identified grade

6 as the primary source of information, using grade 4 material from the reference document wherever material was found that was not presented at grade 6. Middle school (level III) was defined as grades 7–8 and was taken solely from grades 7–8 in the reference work; high school (level IV) was identified from the material at grades 10 and 12, again using the material from the earlier grade to supplement information taken primarily from the later grade.

Integration of Information from Other Documents

Additional material from NASPE was also used and cited in many benchmarks. Their 1992 *Outcomes* document provided us numerous examples or elaborations on material found in their *Standards* document. Also helpful was a draft of physical education standards from Michigan's department of education. This draft occassionally provided some explanatory material that was useful for completing benchmark ideas developed from the NASPE documents. The Michigan document was cited not only in those instances where additional material was used, but also wherever similar ideas were found both in the Michigan draft and in the standards and benchmarks that were developed for this report.

Summary of Standards for Physical Education

1. Uses a variety of basic and advanced movement forms
2. Uses movement concepts and principles in the development of motor skills
3. Understands the benefits and costs associated with participation in physical activity
4. Understands how to monitor and maintain a health-enhancing level of physical fitness
5. Understands the social and personal responsibility associated with participation in physical activity

1. Uses a variety of basic and advanced movement forms

(PE,6;MI,4-7;OE,7)

Level I (Grades K-2)

- Uses a variety of basic locomotor movements (e.g., running, skipping, hopping, galloping, sliding) ^{BP (PE,18;ME,4;OE,7,11)}

- Uses a variety of basic non-locomotor skills (e.g., bending, twisting, stretching, turning, lifting) ^{BP (PE,6;ME,4;OE,7)}

- Uses a variety of basic object control skills (e.g., underhand and overhand throw, catch, hand dribble, foot dribble, kick and strike) ^{BP (PI,18;ME,4;OE,10,11)}

- Uses simple combinations of fundamental movement skills (e.g., locomotor, non-locomotor, object control, body control, and rhythmical skills) ^{BP (PE,18;ME,6;OI,11)}

- Uses control in weight-bearing activities on a variety of body parts (e.g., jumping and landing using combinations of one and two foot take-offs and landings) ^{BP (PE,18;OI,11)}

- Uses control in balance activities on a variety of body parts (e.g., one foot, one hand and one foot, hands and knees, headstands) ^{BP (PE,18,19;ME,5;OE,10,11)}

- Uses control in travel activities on a variety of body parts (e.g., travels in backward direction and changes direction quickly and safely, without falling; changes speeds and directions in response to various rhythms; combines traveling patterns to music) ^{BP (PE,18;ME,6;OE,11)}

- Uses smooth transitions between sequential motor skills (e.g., running into a jump) ^{BP (PE,18;ME,6;OI,11)}

- Uses locomotor skills in rhythmical patterns (e.g., even, uneven, fast, and slow) ^{BP (PE,18;ME,4;OI,11)}

Level II (Grades 3-6)

- Uses mature form in object control skills (e.g., underhand and overhand throw, catch, hand dribble, foot dribble, kick and strike, batting, punt, pass) ^{BP (PE,46;ME,4;OE,12,13)}

- Uses basic sport-specific skills for a variety of physical activities (e.g., basketball chest pass, soccer dribble, fielding a softball with a glove) ^{BP (PE,32,46;ME,7;OI,13)}

- Uses mature form and appropriate sequence in combinations of fundamental locomotor, ^{BP (PI,46;ME,6;OI,13)}

Codes (right side of page):   BD = Benchmark, Declarative; BP = Benchmark, Procedural; BC = Benchmark, Contextual
1st letter of each code in parentheses   *2nd letter of code*   *Number*
P = NASPE: Standards for Physical Education   E = Explicitly stated in document   Page number of cited document
M = MDOE: Physical Education Standards Draft   I = Implied in document
O = NASPE: Outcomes of Physical Education

McREL

object control, and rhythmical skills that are components of selected modified games, sports, and dances (e.g., combining steps to perform certain dances; combining running, stopping, throwing, shooting, kicking for sideline soccer)

- BP (PE,32;MI,5;OE,12)

  Uses mature form in balance activities on a variety of apparatuses (e.g., balance board, large apparatus, skates)

- BP (PE,46;MI,11;OE,13)

  Uses beginning strategies for net and invasion games (e.g., keeping object going with partner using striking pattern, placing ball away from opponent in a racket sport, hand and foot dribble while preventing an opponent from stealing the ball in basketball)

Level III (Grades 7-8)

- BP (PI,63-64;ME,7;OE,14)

  Uses intermediate sport-specific skills for individual, dual, and team sports

- BP (PI,63-63;ME,7;OE,14)

  Uses intermediate sport-specific skills for dance and rhythmical activities

- BP (PI,63-64;ME,7;OE,14)

  Uses intermediate sport-specific skills for outdoor activities

Level IV (Grades 9-12)

- BP (PI,90;MI,7;OE,16)

  Uses advanced sport-specific skills in selected physical activities (e.g., aquatics, dance, outdoor pursuits, individual, dual, and team sports and activities)

- BP (PE,2,76,90)

  Uses skills in complex rather than modified versions of physical activities (e.g., more players or participants, rules and strategies)

(PE,7;MI,10;OE,7)

2. Uses movement concepts and principles in the development of motor skills

Level I (Grades K-2)

- BD (PE,8;MI,9-10;OI,10)

  Understands a vocabulary of basic movement concepts (e.g., personal space, high/low levels, fast/slow speeds, light/heavy weights, balance, twist)

- BD (PE,8;ME,10;OE,10)

  Understands terms that describe a variety of relationships with objects (e.g., over/under, behind, alongside, through)

Codes (right side of page):   BD = Benchmark, Declarative; BP = Benchmark, Procedural; BC = Benchmark, Contextual
1st letter of each code in parentheses   *2nd letter of code*   *Number*
P = NASPE: Standards for Physical Education   E = Explicitly stated in document   Page number of cited document
M = MDOE: Physical Education Standards Draft   I = Implied in document
O = NASPE: Outcomes of Physical Education

- Uses concepts of space awareness and movement control with a variety of basic skills (e.g., running, hopping, skipping) while interacting with others   BC (PE,20;MI,9;OI,10,11)

- Understands the critical elements of a variety of basic movement patterns such as throwing (e.g., the ready position, arm preparation, step with leg opposite the throwing arm, follow-through, accuracy of throw)   BC (PE,20;ME,10;OI,11)

- Uses feedback to improve performance (e.g., peer/coach review)   BC (PE,20-21;ME,11)

- Understands the importance of practice in learning skills   BC (OE,10;ME,11)

Level II (Grades 3-6)

- Uses information from a variety of internal and external sources to improve performance (e.g., group projects, student journal, self-assessment, peer and coach review)   BC (PE,48;ME,11;OE,13)

- Understands principles of practice and conditioning that improve performance   BC (PE,48;OI,13)

- Understands proper warm-up and cool-down techniques and reasons for using them   BC (PE,48;OE,13)

- Uses basic offensive and defensive strategies in unstructured game environments (e.g., limited rules, modified equipment, small numbers of participants)   BC (PE,48;MI,11;OI,13)

Level III (Grades 7-8)

- Understands principles of training and conditioning for specific physical activities   BC (PE,64;MI,11;OE,14)

- Understands the critical elements of advanced movement skills (e.g., such as a racing start in freestyle swimming)   BD (PE,63-64;MI,11)

- Uses basic offensive and defensive strategies in a modified version of a team and individual sport   BC (PE,62;MI,11;OE,14)

- Understands movement forms associated with highly skilled physical activities (e.g., moves that lead to successful serves, passes, and spikes in an elite volleyball game)   BD (PE,63-64;MI,11)

Codes (right side of page):   BD = Benchmark, Declarative; BP = Benchmark, Procedural; BC = Benchmark, Contextual
1st letter of each code in parentheses   *2nd letter of code*   *Number*
P = NASPE: Standards for Physical Education   E = Explicitly stated in document   Page number of cited document
M = MDOE: Physical Education Standards Draft   I = Implied in document
O = NASPE: Outcomes of Physical Education

566   MREL

Level IV (Grades 9-12)

- Understands biomechanical concepts that govern different types of movement (e.g., gymnastics skills)
  BD (PE,77,92;OE,15)

- Understands how sport psychology affects the performance of physical activities (e.g., the effect of anxiety on performance)
  BD (PE,2,92;OI,14)

- Understands the physiological principles governing fitness maintenance and improvement (e.g., overload principle, law of specificity)
  BD (PE,92;OI,14)

- Uses offensive and defensive strategies and appropriate rules for sports and other physical activities
  BC (PI,2,76,90;MI,11;OI,15)

3. Understands the benefits and costs associated with participation in physical activity
(OE,7)

Level I (Grades K-2)

- Understands the health benefits of physical activity (e.g., good health, physical endurance)
  BD (PE,22-23;OI,10)

Level II (Grades 3-6)

- Knows about opportunities for participation in physical activities both in and out of school (e.g., recreational leagues, intramural sports, clubs)
  BD (PE,50,59;MI,15;OE,13)

- Chooses physical activities based on a variety of factors (e.g., personal interests and capabilities, perceived social and physical benefits, challenge and enjoyment)
  BP (PE,50;MI,15;OE,13)

- Knows factors that inhibit physical activity (e.g., substance abuse)
  BD (PE,51;MI,13;OE,14)

- Knows how to modify activities to be more health-enhancing (e.g.,walking instead of riding, taking the stairs rather than the elevator)
  BC (PE,51;MI,13)

- Understands detrimental effects of physical activity (e.g., muscle soreness, overuse injuries, over-training, temporary tiredness, and discovering inability)
  BD (OE,12;ME,12)

- Understands activities that provide personal challenge (e.g., risk-taking, adventure, and competitive activities)
  BD (PE,57)

Codes (right side of page):   BD = Benchmark, Declarative; BP = Benchmark, Procedural; BC = Benchmark, Contextual
1st letter of each code in parentheses   *2nd letter of code*   *Number*
P = NASPE: Standards for Physical Education   E = Explicitly stated in document   Page number of cited document
M = MDOE: Physical Education Standards Draft   I = Implied in document
O = NASPE: Outcomes of Physical Education

Level III (Grades 7-8)

- BD (PE,66,67;OE,14)
Understands long-term physiological benefits of regular participation in physical activity (e.g., improved cardiovascular and muscular strength, improved flexibility and body composition)

- BD (PE,66;ME,12;OE,14)
Understands long-term psychological benefits of regular participation in physical activity (e.g., healthy self-image, stress reduction, strong mental and emotional health)

Level IV (Grades 9-12)

- BD (PE,80;OI,15)
Understands factors that impact the ability to participate in physical activity (e.g., type of activity, cost, available facilities, equipment required, personnel involved)

- BD (PE,93;OE,16)
Understands how various factors (e.g., age, gender, race, ethnicity, socioeconomic status, and culture) affect physical activity preferences and participation

- BD (PE,97;ME,12;OE,16)
Understands the potentially dangerous consequences and outcomes of participation in physical activity (e.g., physical injury, potential conflicts with others)

(PE,10;MI,8,9,12,15;OE,7)
4.   Understands how to monitor and maintain a health-enhancing level of physical fitness

Level I (Grades K-2)

- BP (PE,23;ME,8)
Engages in basic activities that cause cardiorespiratory exertion (e.g., running, galloping, skipping, hopping)

- BD (PI,24;MI,8)
Knows how to measure cardiorespiratory fitness (e.g., listening to heartbeat, counting pulse rate)

- BD (PE,23;ME,8;OE,11)
Knows the physiological indicators (e.g., perspiration, increased heart and breathing rate) that accompany moderate to vigorous physical activity

- BP (PI,23;ME,8)
Engages in activities that develop muscular strength and endurance (e.g., climbing, hanging, taking weight on hands)

- BP (PI,23,25;ME,9;OE,11)
Engages in activities that require flexibility (e.g., stretching toward the toes while in the sit-and-reach position, moving each joint through its full range of motion)

Codes (right side of page):   BD = Benchmark, Declarative; BP = Benchmark, Procedural; BC = Benchmark, Contextual
1st letter of each code in parentheses   *2nd letter of code*   *Number*
P = NASPE: Standards for Physical Education   E = Explicitly stated in document   Page number of cited document
M = MDOE: Physical Education Standards Draft   I = Implied in document
O = NASPE: Outcomes of Physical Education

- Knows how body composition influences physical fitness levels (e.g., proportion of lean body mass to fat body mass) BD (PI,23;ME,9;OI,11)

- Knows similarities and differences in body height, weight, and shape BD (PI,23;ME,9;OI,10)

Level II (Grades 3-6)

- Engages in activities that develop and maintain cardiorespiratory endurance (e.g., timed or distance walk/run and other endurance activities at a specified heart rate) BP (PE,52;ME,8;OE,13)

- Engages in activities that develop and maintain muscular strength (e.g., push-ups, pull-ups, curl-ups, isometric strength activities, jump rope) BP (PE,52;ME,8;OE,13)

- Engages in activities that develop and maintain flexibility of the major joints (e.g., sit and reach, trunk twists, and arm-shoulder stretches) BP (PE,52;ME,9;OE,13)

- Knows the effects of physical activity and nutrition on body composition BD (PI,52;ME,9)

- Knows how to monitor intensity of exercise (e.g., heart rate, breathing rate, perceived exertion, and recovery rate) BD (PE,52;MI,8;OE,13)

- Meets health-related fitness standards for appropriate level of a standardized physical fitness test (e.g., aerobic capacity, body composition, muscle strength, endurance, and flexibility) BP (PE,52-53;ME,8-9)

- Knows the characteristics of a healthy lifestyle (e.g., daily health-enhancing physical activity, proper nutrition) BD (PE,50;MI,12-13;OI,13)

- Uses information from fitness assessments to improve selected fitness components (e.g., cardiorespiratory endurance, muscular strength and endurance, flexibility, and body composition) BC (PE,52;MI,8-9)

- Participates in moderate to vigorous physical activity in a variety of settings (e.g., gymnastics clubs, community sponsored youth sports) BP (PE,52;OE,13)

Level III (Grades 7-8)

- Engages in more advanced activities that develop and maintain cardiorespiratory endurance (e.g., timed or distance walk/run and other endurance activities at specified heart rate/heart BP (PE,67;ME,8;OI,14)

Codes (right side of page):	BD = Benchmark, Declarative; BP = Benchmark, Procedural; BC = Benchmark, Contextual	
1st letter of each code in parentheses	*2nd letter of code*	*Number*
P = NASPE: Standards for Physical Education	E = Explicitly stated in document	Page number of cited document
M = MDOE: Physical Education Standards Draft	I = Implied in document	
O = NASPE: Outcomes of Physical Education		

569

MCREL

rate recovery)

- Engages in more advanced activities that develop and maintain muscular strength and endurance (e.g., calisthenics activities, resistance, and weight training) ^{BP (PE,67;ME,8;OI,14)}

- Engages in more advanced levels of activity that develop and maintain flexibility ^{BP (PE,67;ME,9)}

- Understands the role of exercise and other factors in weight control and body composition ^{BD (PI,67;OE,14)}

- Understands basic principles of training that improve physical fitness (e.g., threshold, overload, specificity, frequency, intensity, duration, and mode of exercise) ^{BD (PE,67;MI,11;OE,14)}

- Meets health-related fitness standards for appropriate level of a standardized physical fitness test (e.g., aerobic capacity, body composition, muscle strength, endurance, and flexibility) ^{BP (PE,68;ME,8-9;OI,14)}

- Knows how to interpret the results of physical fitness assessments and use the information to develop individual fitness goals ^{BC (PE,67;OI,14)}

- Knows how to differentiate the body's response to physical activities of various exercise intensities (e.g., measurement of heart rate, resting heart rate, heart rate reserve; taking pulse at rest and during exercise) ^{BD (PE,69;MI,8)}

Level IV (Grades 9-12)

- Knows personal status of cardiorespiratory endurance ^{BD (PI,95;ME,8;OE,15)}

- Knows personal status of muscular strength and endurance of the arms, shoulders, abdomen, back, and legs ^{BD (PI,95;ME,8;OE,15)}

- Knows personal status of flexibility of the joints of the arms, legs, and trunk ^{BD (PI,95;ME,9;OE,15)}

- Knows personal status of body composition ^{BD (PI,95;ME,9;OE,15)}

- Meets health-related fitness standards for appropriate level of a physical fitness test (e.g., aerobic capacity, body composition, muscle strength, endurance, and flexibility) ^{BP (PE,95;ME,8-9;OI,16)}

- Knows how to monitor and adjust activity levels to meet personal fitness needs ^{BC (PE,95;OI,16)}

- Understands how to maintain an active lifestyle throughout life (e.g., participate regularly in ^{BD (PE,93;ME,15;OI,16)}

Codes (right side of page): BD = Benchmark, Declarative; BP = Benchmark, Procedural; BC = Benchmark, Contextual
1st letter of each code in parentheses 2nd letter of code Number
P = NASPE: Standards for Physical Education E = Explicitly stated in document Page number of cited document
M = MDOE: Physical Education Standards Draft I = Implied in document
O = NASPE: Outcomes of Physical Education

physical activities that reflect personal interests)

- Designs a personal fitness program that is based on the basic principles of training and encompasses all components of fitness (e.g., cardiovascular and respiratory efficiency, muscular strength and endurance, flexibility, and body composition)

  BP (PE,95;MI,8-9;OI,16)

5. Understands the social and personal responsibility associated with participation in physical activity

(PI,11,13,14;ME,14;OI,7)

Level I (Grades K-2)

- Follows rules and procedures (e.g., playground, classroom, and gymnasium rules) with little reinforcement

  BP (PE,12-13,25;ME,11;OI,11)

- Uses equipment and space safely and properly (e.g., takes turns using equipment, puts equipment away when not in use)

  BP (PE,12,25;ME,11;OE,10)

- Understands the purpose of rules in games

  BD (PE,25;ME,11;OI,11)

- Understands the social contributions of physical activity (e.g., learning to cooperate and interact with others, having a role in team sports)

  BP (PE,21,23;ME,15;OI,11)

- Works cooperatively (e.g., takes turns, is supportive, assists partner) with another to complete an assigned task

  BP (PE,25;ME,15;OI,11)

- Understands the elements of socially acceptable conflict resolution in physical activity settings (e.g., cooperation, sharing, consideration)

  BD (PE,27;MI,15;OI,11)

- Understands the importance of playing, cooperating, and respecting others regardless of personal differences (e.g., gender, ethnicity, disability) during physical activity

  BD (PE,27;MI,15;OI,11)

Level II (Grades 3-6)

- Knows how to develop rules, procedures, and etiquette that are safe and effective for specific activity situations

  BC (PE,54;MI,11)

- Works in a group to accomplish a set goal in both cooperative and competitive activities

  BP (PE,54;MI,15;OI,13)

Codes (right side of page):   BD = Benchmark, Declarative; BP = Benchmark, Procedural; BC = Benchmark, Contextual
1st letter of each code in parentheses   *2nd letter of code*   *Number*
P = NASPE: Standards for Physical Education   E = Explicitly stated in document   Page number of cited document
M = MDOE: Physical Education Standards Draft   I = Implied in document
O = NASPE: Outcomes of Physical Education

571

MᴄREL

- Understands the role of physical activities in learning more about others of like and different $^{\text{BD (PI,56;ME,15;OE,13)}}$ backgrounds (e.g., gender, culture, ethnicity, and disability)

- Understands the physical challenges faced by people with disabilities (e.g., wheelchair $^{\text{BD (PE,57;MI,15;OI,13)}}$ basketball, dancing with a hearing disability)

- Understands the origins of different sports and how they have evolved $^{\text{BD (PE,56)}}$

Level III (Grades 7-8)

- Understands the importance of rules, procedures, and safe practice in physical activity $^{\text{BD (PE,69;MI,11;OE,14)}}$ settings

- Understands proper attitudes toward both winning and losing $^{\text{BD (PE,70;ME,15)}}$

- Knows the difference between inclusive (e.g., changing rules of activity to include less $^{\text{BD (PE,71;MI,15;OI,14)}}$ skilled players) and exclusionary (e.g., failing to pass ball to less skilled players) behaviors in physical activity settings

- Understands physical activity as a vehicle for self-expression (e.g., dance, gymnastics, and $^{\text{BD (PE,73;MI,15;OE,14)}}$ various sport activities)

- Understands the concept that physical activity (e.g., sport, games, dance) is a microcosm of $^{\text{BD (PE,71-72)}}$ modern culture and society

Level IV (Grades 9-12)

- Uses leadership and follower roles, when appropriate, in accomplishing group goals in $^{\text{BP (PI,97;MI,14)}}$ physical activities

- Works with others in a sport activity to achieve a common goal (e.g., winning a team $^{\text{BP (PE,87;MI,14,15)}}$ championship)

- Understands how participation in physical activity fosters awareness of diversity (e.g., $^{\text{BD (PE,99;ME,12;OI,16)}}$ cultural, ethnic, gender, physical)

- Includes persons of diverse backgrounds and abilities in physical activity $^{\text{BP (PE,99;MI,12;OI,16)}}$

Codes (right side of page):   BD = Benchmark, Declarative; BP = Benchmark, Procedural; BC = Benchmark, Contextual
1st letter of each code in parentheses   *2nd letter of code*   *Number*
P = NASPE: Standards for Physical Education   E = Explicitly stated in document   Page number of cited document
M = MDOE: Physical Education Standards Draft   I = Implied in document
O = NASPE: Outcomes of Physical Education

- Understands the history and purpose of international competitions (e.g., Olympics, Special Olympics, Pan American Games, World Cup Soccer) $^{BD\ (PE,85;MI,15;OE,15)}$

- Understands the role of sport in a diverse world (e.g., the influence of professional sport in society, the usefulness of dance as an expression of multiculturalism, the effect of age and gender on sport participation patterns) $^{BD\ (PE,85;MI,15;OI,16)}$

- Understands the concept of "sportsmanship" and the importance of responsible behavior while participating in physical activities $^{BD\ (PI,97-98;ME,15)}$

Codes (right side of page):   BD = Benchmark, Declarative; BP = Benchmark, Procedural; BC = Benchmark, Contextual
1st letter of each code in parentheses   *2nd letter of code*   *Number*
P = NASPE: Standards for Physical Education   E = Explicitly stated in document   Page number of cited document
M = MDOE: Physical Education Standards Draft   I = Implied in document
O = NASPE: Outcomes of Physical Education

TECHNOLOGY

18. Technology

The following process was used to identify standards and benchmarks for technology:

Identification of Significant Reports

Fourteen documents were identified as useful for developing content standards for technology. They include *Technology for All Americans: A Rationale and Structure for the Study of Technology* (1996) from the International Technology Education Association (ITEA), *Benchmarks for Science Literacy* (1993) from Project 2061 of the American Association for the Advancement of Science, *Technology - A Curriculum Profile for Australian Schools* (1994) from the Australian Education Council, *National Standards for Business Education: What America's Students Should Know and Be Able to Do in Business* (1995) from the National Business Education Association, *Science Framework for the 1996 National Assessment of Educational Progress* (1996) from the National Assessment of Educational Progress Science Consensus Project, and the *National Science Education Standards* (1996) from the National Research Council. The National Center for Improving Science Education has published two useful works addressing technology, *Science and Technology Education for the Elementary Years: Frameworks for Curriculum and Instruction* (Bybee, et al., 1989) and *Science and Technology Education for the Middle Years: Frameworks for Curriculum and Instruction* (Bybee et al., 1990). Additionally, useful curriculum material on technology was available from a number of State Departments of Education (California, North Carolina, and Texas). Finally, material from International Baccalaureate was consulted, specifically, *Design Technology* (1996d), *Environmental Systems* (1996f), and *Information Technology in a Global Society* (1995b).

Selection of the Reference Documents

As noted in section 2, the Technology for All Americans Project, the most likely source of standards for technology, has indicated that content standards will not be available until 1999. No single reference document was available for the identification of standards and benchmarks in technology for this report, because no single document treated all topics comprehensively or at a level of specificity required by our model for standards identification. Thus, for the two standards that address the computer skills that students should acquire, two documents from state departments of education served as reference documents, the *Teacher Handbook Component: Computer skills* (1992) from North Carolina, and the *Texas Essential Knowledge and Skills for Technology Applications* (draft, 1996). On the topic of technology as it impacts and is affected by society and the individual, *Benchmarks for Science Literacy* was selected as the reference document. For the standard treating the nature of technology design, the *National Science Education Standards* was used as the primary document. The standard on the nature and operation of systems was developed using two documents, *Benchmarks for Science Literacy* and *Technology - A Curriculum Profile for Australian Schools*.

Identification of Standards and Benchmarks

A review of the fifteen documents selected for technology showed that most documents consistently addressed five topics. These topics, mentioned above, eventually formed the five standards in this section, once the identification of benchmarks confirmed that there was sufficient material to warrant their construction.

Of these standards, the standard on the nature and operation of systems might benefit from some explanation. The idea of systems is often presented in education materials as a useful theme for instruction (see *National Science Standards*, p. 116-117, *California Science Framework*, p.33ff.). According to the model adopted in this report, such a use would suggest that the material is more suited for the development of a curriculum or program standard, which provides suggestions or guidelines for instruction, rather than a content standard, which identifies the knowledge and skills students should acquire. However, our analysis showed that the topic of systems, unlike other themes, such as change and constancy, models, and scale and structure, is associated with a substantial and consistent vocabulary (e.g., input, output, boundary) across a range of source materials. In addition to consistent language and the coherency of concept that such usage suggests, the material on systems provided a sufficient level of detail for the identification of benchmarks, and most important for our purposes, an indication as to the appropriate grade level for the introduction of content material. As to the placement of systems within the section on technology, rather than science, this was done principally because the National Science Standards treated systems as a theme, while works exclusively addressing technology consistently addressed it as important content for students studying technology. As the authors of *Technology for All Americans* (p. 12) state, "the basic building block of technology is the system."

Once all five standards were identified, information for benchmark development was drawn from the reference report(s) selected for each standard, as described earlier. The method of benchmark identification varied by document because each document varied in its presentation of content. In keeping with our model, for example, when a document provided model activities rather than description of content, the activities were examined to determine what could be inferred about the knowledge and skills required of a student who successfully engaged in those activities; the knowledge and skills identified were then formed into benchmarks.

Integration of Information from Other Documents
Owing to the somewhat inchoate nature of technology standards currently, material was necessarily taken from a wide range of documents for each of the standards. This means that the approach taken was somewhat different from the standard model. Usually, a reference document provides the scope of the standard and the material for a majority of benchmarks that support it. Support documents are then examined and cited to verify the content analysis and to provide some sense of how broadly the content identified is supported in similar documents. In the case of the Technology section, however, not only were different reference documents selected according to the topic addressed by the standards (noted above) but many more documents were consulted in the event related ideas might contribute to the development of the standard, rather than just to support the ideas identified in the reference document.

Supplementary material for the first two standards, which deal with the understanding and use of computer hardware and software, was developed in part from *National Standards for Business*

Education and the International Baccalaureate's *Information Technology*. Standard three, which addresses issues related to technology, the individual, and society, was supplemented with material from all fifteen documents. Benchmarks on the nature of technology design, the subject of standard four, were primarily supplemented with material from the International Baccalaureates' *Design Technology*. The fifth standard, on systems, was supplemented with citations from science and technology frameworks for elementary and middle school from the National Center for Improving Science Education.

Summary of Standards for Technology

1. Knows the characteristics and uses of computer hardware and operating systems
2. Knows the characteristics and uses of computer software programs
3. Understands relationships among science, technology, society, and the individual
4. Understands the nature of technological design
5. Understands the nature and operation of systems

(BI,92;NC,155;TE,2)

1. Knows the characteristics and uses of computer hardware and operating systems

Level I (Grades K-2)

BP (BE,92;ITI,15;NCE,152;TI,2)
- Identifies basic computer hardware (e.g., keyboard and mouse, printer, monitor, output, hard and floppy disk, case for the cpu [central processing unit])

BP (TI,3)
- Powers-up computer, monitor, and starts a computer program (e.g., checks that printer is switched on and on-line; reboots the computer when necessary)

BD (BI,94;NCE,152;TI,3)
- Knows the alphanumeric keys and special keys (e.g., function keys, escape key, space bar, delete/backspace, return/enter)

BD (BI,94 TI,3;NCE,157)
- Knows proper finger placement on the home row keys

BP (BI,92;NCE,152;TI,2)
- Handles diskettes and other computer equipment with care

Level II (Grades 3-5)

BD (BI,92;ITI,15;NCE,160;TI,56)
- Knows the basic functions of hardware (e.g., keyboard and mouse provide input; printer and monitor provide output; hard and floppy disk provide storage; the cpu processes information)

BP (BI,94;NCI,160;TE,6)
- Uses proper fingering for all keys, beginning from the homerow, maintaining proper posture while using the keyboard

BD (BI,92;NCI,161)
- Knows potential hazards to computer media (e.g., the damage caused to floppies by magnetic fields, dirt, and dust; caused to computers by excessive heat, smoke, and moisture)

BD (AI,50;BI,94;ITI,15;NCI,167)
- Knows basic facts about networked computers (e.g., computers can connect to each other via modem and telephone line, or through local network systems, or internet and intranet)

Level III (Grades 6-8)

BD (BI,93;TI,11)
- Knows the differing capacities and trade-offs for computer storage media, such as CD-

---

Codes (right side of page):	BD = Benchmark, Declarative; BP = Benchmark, Procedural; BC = Benchmark, Contextual	
1st letter(s) of each code in parentheses	*2nd letter of code*	*Number*
2 = Project 2061: Benchmarks for Science Literacy	E = Explicitly stated in document	Page number of cited document
A = AEC: Australian Technology Standards	I = Implied in document	
B = NBEA: Nat'l Standards for Business Education		
C = CDE: Science Framework for CA Public Schools	NC = North Carolina Computer Standards	
F = NAEP: 1996 Science Framework	R = ITEA: Technology for All Americans	
ID,IE,IT = Int'l Bacc.: Design Tech., Environmental	S = NRC: National Science Education Standards	
Systems, Information Technology	T= Texas Technology Application Standards	
N1,N2 = NCISE: Science and Technology Education Elementary, Middle		

McREL

ROMs, floppy disks, hard disks, and tape drives

- Types with some facility, demonstrating some memorization of keys

  BP (BI,94-95;TI,10)

- Connects via modem to other computer users via the internet, an on-line service, or bulletin board system

  BP (BE,94,ITE,19;NCE,173;TI,10)

- Knows basic characteristics and functions of an operating system

  BD (ITE,17;TE,9)

Level IV (Grades 9-12)

- Knows of significant advances in computers and peripherals (e.g., data scanners, digital cameras)

  BD (BI,92;ITI,17;NCI,18)

- Uses a variety of input devices (e.g., keyboard, scanner, voice/sound recorders, mouse, touch screen)

  BP (ITI,17;TE,15)

- Knows limitations and trade-offs of various types of hardware (e.g., laptops, notebooks, modems)

  BD (BE,92;ITE,18)

- Identifies malfunctions and problems in hardware (e.g., hard drive crash, monitor burn-out)

  BP (BE,92;ITI,16;RI,22)

- Knows features and uses of current and emerging technology related to computing (e.g., optical character recognition, sound processing, cable TV, cellular phones, ABS brakes)

  BD (ITE,17,24)

2.   Knows the characteristics and uses of computer software programs

(BI,92;ITI,15;NC,155;TE,2)

Level I (Grades K-2)

- Types on a computer keyboard, using correct hand and body positions

  BP (AI,20;BI,95;ITE,17;NCI,158;TI,3)

- Knows basic distinctions among computer software programs, such as word processors, special purpose programs, and games

  BD (BI,92;ITI,17;TI,2)

Codes (right side of page):	BD = Benchmark, Declarative; BP = Benchmark, Procedural; BC = Benchmark, Contextual	
1st letter(s) of each code in parentheses	*2nd letter of code*	*Number*
2 = Project 2061: Benchmarks for Science Literacy	E = Explicitly stated in document	Page number of cited document
A = AEC: Australian Technology Standards	I = Implied in document	
B = NBEA: Nat'l Standards for Business Education		
C = CDE: Science Framework for CA Public Schools	NC = North Carolina Computer Standards	
F = NAEP: 1996 Science Framework	R = ITEA: Technology for All Americans	
ID,IE,IT = Int'l Bacc.: Design Tech., Environmental	S = NRC: National Science Education Standards	
Systems, Information Technology	T= Texas Technology Application Standards	
N1,N2 = NCISE: Science and Technology Education		
Elementary, Middle		

MREL

BP (AI,18;TI,6)

- Uses menu options and commands

Level II (Grades 3-5)

BP (BE,95;ITI,17;NCE,161)

- Uses a word processor to edit, copy, move, save, and print text with some formatting (e.g., centering lines, using tabs, forming paragraphs)

BP (AI,50;ITI,16;NCI,166;TI,6)

- Makes back-up copies of stored data, such as text, programs, and databases

BC (ITI,16;BI,92)

- Trouble-shoots simple problems in software (e.g., re-boots, uses help systems)

BD (BI,93;ITE,17;NCE,163)

- Knows the common features and uses of data bases (e.g., data bases contain records of similar data, which is sorted or organized for ease of use; data bases are used in both print form, such as telephone books, and electronic form, such as computerized card catalogs)

BP (AI,66;BE,93;ITE,19;NCE,166;TI,7)

- Uses data base software to add, edit, and delete records, and to find information through simple sort or search techniques

BD (BI,92;TI,6)

- Knows how formats differ among software applications (e.g., word processing files, database files) and hardware platforms (e.g., Macintosh, Windows)

Level III (Grades 6-8)

BP (BI,95;ITE,17;NCI,171;TI,11)

- Uses advanced features and utilities of word processors (e.g., uses clip art, a spell-checker, grammar checker, thesaurus, outliner)

BD (BE,95;ITE,17;TI,12)

- Knows the common features and uses of desktop publishing software (e.g., documents are created, designed, and formatted for publication; data, graphics, and scanned images can be imported into a document using desktop software)

BD (BE,95;NCI,171)

- Knows the common features and uses of spread sheets (e.g., data is entered in cells identified by row and column; formulas can be used to update solutions automatically; spreadsheets are used in print form, such as look-up tables, and electronic form, such as to track business profit and loss)

Codes (right side of page):	BD = Benchmark, Declarative; BP = Benchmark, Procedural; BC = Benchmark, Contextual

1st letter(s) of each code in parentheses   *2nd letter of code*   *Number*

2 = Project 2061: Benchmarks for Science Literacy   E = Explicitly stated in document   Page number of cited document

A = AEC: Australian Technology Standards   I = Implied in document

B = NBEA: Nat'l Standards for Business Education

C = CDE: Science Framework for CA Public Schools   NC = North Carolina Computer Standards

F = NAEP: 1996 Science Framework   R = ITEA: Technology for All Americans

ID,IE,IT = Int'l Bacc.: Design Tech., Environmental   S = NRC: National Science Education Standards

   Systems, Information Technology   T= Texas Technology Application Standards

N1,N2 = NCISE: Science and Technology Education

   Elementary, Middle

McREL

- Uses a spread sheet to update, add, and delete data, and to write and execute valid formulas on data ^BP (AI,84;BE,95;ITE,19;NCE,176;TI,11-12)

- Uses boolean searches to execute complex searches on a data base ^BP (BI,93;NCE,172;TE,11)

Level IV (Grades 9-12)

- Understands the uses of listservs, usenet newsreaders, and bulletin board systems ^BD (BI,94;ITI,15;NCI,167)

- Knows how to import, export, and merge data stored in different formats (e.g., text, graphics) ^BP (BE,92;ITI,19;TI,48)

- Knows how to import and export text, data, and graphics between software programs ^BP (BE,92;ITI,19)

- Identifies some advanced features of software products (e.g., galleries, templates, macros, mail merge) ^BP (BE,92;ITI,19)

- Uses desktop publishing software to create a variety of publications ^BP (BE,95;ITE,17;NCE,187;TE,25)

3. Understands relationships among science, technology, society, and the individual ^(2E,43;RE,22)

Level I (Grades K-2)

- Knows ways that technology is used at home and school (e.g., paging systems, telephones, VCRs) ^BD (N1I,35;NCE,153)

- Knows that new tools and ways of doing things affect all aspects of life, and may have positive or negative effects on other people ^BD (2E,54;AI,32;ITI,21;N1I,16;SI,138;RI,25)

- Understands that when an individual creates something on a computer, the created work is that person's property, and only that person has the right to change it ^BD (NCE,156;TI,3)

Codes (right side of page):   BD = Benchmark, Declarative;   BP = Benchmark, Procedural;   BC = Benchmark, Contextual

1st letter(s) of each code in parentheses	*2nd letter of code*	*Number*
2 = Project 2061: Benchmarks for Science Literacy	E = Explicitly stated in document	Page number of cited document
A = AEC: Australian Technology Standards	I = Implied in document	
B = NBEA: Nat'l Standards for Business Education		
C = CDE: Science Framework for CA Public Schools	NC = North Carolina Computer Standards	
F = NAEP: 1996 Science Framework	R = ITEA: Technology for All Americans	
ID,IE,IT = Int'l Bacc.: Design Tech., Environmental	S = NRC: National Science Education Standards	
Systems, Information Technology	T= Texas Technology Application Standards	
N1,N2 = NCISE: Science and Technology Education		
Elementary, Middle		

Level II (Grades 3-5)

BD (2I,55;ITI,21;N1I,16;NCI,159;SE,140;RI,36)

- Knows that technologies often have costs as well as benefits and can have an enormous effect on people and other living things

BD(2E,45;ITI,21;SE,141;N1E,23;RI,26)

- Knows areas in which technology has improved human lives (e.g., transportation, communication, nutrition, sanitation, health care, entertainment)

BD (2E,54;SI,148;RI,25)

- Knows that new inventions often lead to other new inventions and ways of doing things

BD (NCI,159;TI,6)

- Understands the concept of software piracy (i.e., illegally copying software), and that piracy is a violation of copyright laws

Level III (Grades 6-8)

BD (2E,51;FI,27;IDI,30;N2E,30;SE,166;RI,38)

- Knows that scientific inquiry and technological design have similarities and differences (e.g., scientists propose explanations for questions about the natural world that are always tentative and evolving, and engineers propose solutions relating to human problems, needs, and aspirations; both science and technology depend on accurate scientific information and they cannot contravene scientific laws)

BD (2E,55;SE,169)

- Knows that science cannot answer all questions and technology cannot solve all human problems or meet all human needs

BD (2E,17;N2E,37,38;SE,166;RI,22)

- Knows ways in which technology has influenced the course of history (e.g., revolutions in agriculture, manufacturing, sanitation, medicine, warfare, transportation, information processing, communication)

BD (2E,46;FI,27;N2E,30;SE,148;RI,28)

- Knows that technology and science are reciprocal (e.g., technology drives science, as it provides the means to access outer space and remote locations, collect and treat samples, collect, measure, store, and compute data, and communicate information; science drives technology, as it provides principles for better instrumentation and techniques, and the means to address questions that demand more sophisticated instruments)

BD (2E,46;AI,64;N2I,31;SE,165;RE,38)

- Knows ways in which technology and society influence one another (e.g., new products and

---

Codes (right side of page):	BD = Benchmark, Declarative; BP = Benchmark, Procedural; BC = Benchmark, Contextual

1st letter(s) of each code in parentheses   *2nd letter of code*   *Number*

2 = Project 2061: Benchmarks for Science Literacy   E = Explicitly stated in document   Page number of cited document

A = AEC: Australian Technology Standards   I = Implied in document

B = NBEA: Nat'l Standards for Business Education

C = CDE: Science Framework for CA Public Schools   NC = North Carolina Computer Standards

F = NAEP: 1996 Science Framework   R = ITEA: Technology for All Americans

ID,IE,IT = Int'l Bacc.: Design Tech., Environmental   S = NRC: National Science Education Standards

     Systems, Information Technology   T= Texas Technology Application Standards

N1,N2 = NCISE: Science and Technology Education

     Elementary, Middle

processes for society are developed through technology; technological changes are often accompanied by social, political, and economic changes; technology is influenced by social needs, attitudes, values, and limitations, and cultural backgrounds and beliefs)

BD (AI,84;NCE,170;TE,10)

- Knows examples of copyright violations and computer fraud (e.g., computer hacking, computer piracy, intentional virus setting, invasion of privacy) and possible penalties (e.g., large fines, jail sentences)

Level IV (Grades 9-12)

BD (2E,47;SE,192-193;RI,26)

- Knows that science and technology are pursued for different purposes (scientific inquiry is driven by the desire to understand the natural world and seeks to answer questions that may or may not directly influence humans; technology is driven by the need to meet human needs and solve human problems)

BD (2E,57;AE,102;IDI,29;SI,199;RI,40)

- Knows ways in which social and economic forces influence which technologies will be developed and used (e.g., personal values, consumer acceptance, patent laws, availability of risk capital, the federal budget, local and national regulations, media attention, economic competition, tax incentives)

BD (2E,57;AI,102;FI,27-28;IDI,30;N2I,29;SI,199;RI,40)

- Knows that alternatives, risks, costs, and benefits must be considered when deciding on proposals to introduce new technologies or to curtail existing ones (e.g., Are there alternative ways to achieve the same ends? Who benefits and who suffers? What are the financial and social costs and who bears them? How serious are the risks and who is in jeopardy? What resources will be needed and where will they come from?)

BD (2E,57;N2E,28;SE,193)

- Knows that technological knowledge is often not made public because of patents and the financial potential of the idea or invention; scientific knowledge is made public through presentations at professional meetings and publications in scientific journals

BD (ITE,24;NCE,183;RI,22)

- Knows examples of advanced and emerging technologies (e.g., virtual environment, personal digital assistants, voice recognition software) and how they could impact society

BP (ITI,21;TE,16)

- Observes common courtesies and acceptable use policies while telecomputing

---

Codes (right side of page):	BD = Benchmark, Declarative; BP = Benchmark, Procedural; BC = Benchmark, Contextual

1st letter(s) of each code in parentheses	*2nd letter of code*	*Number*
2 = Project 2061: Benchmarks for Science Literacy	E = Explicitly stated in document	Page number of cited document
A = AEC: Australian Technology Standards	I = Implied in document	
B = NBEA: Nat'l Standards for Business Education		
C = CDE: Science Framework for CA Public Schools	NC = North Carolina Computer Standards	
F = NAEP: 1996 Science Framework	R = ITEA: Technology for All Americans	
ID,IE,IT = Int'l Bacc.: Design Tech., Environmental	S = NRC: National Science Education Standards	
Systems, Information Technology	T= Texas Technology Application Standards	
N1,N2 = NCISE: Science and Technology Education		
Elementary, Middle		

BD (2E,47;SE,176;RI,29)

- Knows that mathematics, creativity, logic, and originality are all needed to improve technology

BP (BI,99;ITI,22;NCE,174;TI,11;RI,30)

- Identifies the role of technology in a variety of careers

(2E,48;RE,18)

4. Understands the nature of technological design

Level I (Grades K-2)

BD (2E,49;SE,138;RI,25)

- Knows that objects occur in nature; but people can also design and make objects (e.g., to solve a problem, to improve the quality of life)

BD (2E,44;AI,33;SE,138;RI,28)

- Knows that tools can be used to observe, measure, make things, and do things better or more easily

BD (2E,54;NCE,151;RE,25)

- Knows that people are always inventing new ways to solve problems and get work done (e.g., computer is a machine that helps people work and play)

Level II (Grades 3-5)

BC (SE,138)

- Categorizes items into groups of natural objects and designed objects

BP (AI,48;SE,137;RI,36)

- Identifies a simple problem that can be solved using technology

BD (2E,49,55;AI,48;FE,27;N1I,39;SE,137)

- Knows constraints that must be considered when designing a solution to a problem (e.g., cost, materials, time, space, safety, scientific laws, engineering principles, construction techniques, appearance, environmental impact, what will happen if the solution fails)

BP (AI,49;SE,137)

- Implements proposed solutions using appropriate tools, techniques, and quantitative measurements

BP (AE,49;SE,137-138;RI,36)

- Evaluates a product or design (e.g., considers how well the product or design met the challenge to solve a problem; considers the ability of the product or design to meet

---

Codes (right side of page):   BD = Benchmark, Declarative;   BP = Benchmark, Procedural;   BC = Benchmark, Contextual

1st letter(s) of each code in parentheses	*2nd letter of code*	*Number*
2 = Project 2061: Benchmarks for Science Literacy	E = Explicitly stated in document	Page number of cited document
A = AEC: Australian Technology Standards	I = Implied in document	
B = NBEA: Nat'l Standards for Business Education		
C = CDE: Science Framework for CA Public Schools	NC = North Carolina Computer Standards	
F = NAEP: 1996 Science Framework	R = ITEA: Technology for All Americans	
ID,IE,IT = Int'l Bacc.: Design Tech., Environmental	S = NRC: National Science Education Standards	
Systems, Information Technology	T= Texas Technology Application Standards	
N1,N2 = NCISE: Science and Technology Education		
Elementary, Middle		

M◖REL

constraints), and makes modifications based on results

BD (2E,54;SE,138;RI,22)
- Knows that people have invented and used tools throughout history to solve problems and improve ways of doing things

Level III (Grades 6-8)

BP (AI,64;IDE,21;N2I,36;SE,165;2I,51;RI,38)
- Identifies appropriate problems for technological design (e.g., identifies a specific need, considers its various aspects, considers criteria for a suitable product)

BP (AI,64;2E,51;ITI,16;IDE,21;N2E,29;SE,165)
- Designs a solution or product, taking into account needs and constraints (e.g., cost, time, trade-offs, properties of materials, safety, aesthetics)

BP (AI,65;ITI,16;IDE,21;SE,165)
- Implements a proposed design (e.g., organizes materials and other resources, plans one's work, makes use of group collaboration when appropriate, chooses suitable tools and techniques, works with appropriate measurement methods to ensure accuracy)

BP (2I,51;AE,65;IDE,22;SE,165)
- Evaluates the ability of a technological design to meet criteria established in the original purpose (e.g., considers factors that might affect acceptability and suitability for intended users or beneficiaries; develop measures of quality with respect to these factors), suggests improvements, and tries proposed modifications

Level IV (Grades 9-12)

BP (AI,102;IDI,21;SE,192;RI,40)
- Proposes designs and chooses between alternative solutions (e.g., models, simulations)

BP (AI,103;IDI,21;ITI,16;SE,192)
- Implements a proposed solution (e.g., constructs artifacts for intended users or beneficiaries)

BP (AE,103;2E,52;IDE,22;SE,192;RI,22)
- Evaluates a designed solution and its consequences based on the needs or criteria the solution was designed to meet

---

Codes (right side of page):	BD = Benchmark, Declarative; BP = Benchmark, Procedural; BC = Benchmark, Contextual	
1st letter(s) of each code in parentheses	*2nd letter of code*	*Number*
2 = Project 2061: Benchmarks for Science Literacy	E = Explicitly stated in document	Page number of cited document
A = AEC: Australian Technology Standards	I = Implied in document	
B = NBEA: Nat'l Standards for Business Education		
C = CDE: Science Framework for CA Public Schools	NC = North Carolina Computer Standards	
F = NAEP: 1996 Science Framework	R = ITEA: Technology for All Americans	
ID,IE,IT = Int'l Bacc.: Design Tech., Environmental	S = NRC: National Science Education Standards	
Systems, Information Technology	T= Texas Technology Application Standards	
N1,N2 = NCISE: Science and Technology Education		
Elementary, Middle		

5. Understands the nature and operation of systems

Level I (Grades K-2)

BD (2E,264;AI,36;FI,73)

- Knows that most things are made of parts and they may not work if some parts are missing

BD (2E,264;FI,73;N1I,45)

- Knows that when parts are put together, they can do things that they couldn't do by themselves

BD (2I,264;AE,36;N1I,37;RI,30)

- Understands how some elements or components of simple systems work together (e.g., parts of a bicycle)

BP (2I,264;AE,19;N1I,37;RI,36)

- Creates and tests a simple linear system (e.g., a production line process for making sandwiches)

Level II (Grades 3-5)

BD (2E,264;AI,52;FI,73;N1I,35)

- Knows that when things are made up of many parts, the parts usually affect one another

BD (2E,264;AI,52;FI,73;N1I,37)

- Knows that things that are made of parts may not work well if a part is missing, broken, worn out, mismatched, or misconnected

BP (AE,68;FI,73;N1I,35;RI,30)

- Identifies the relationships between elements (i.e., components, such as people or parts) in systems

BP (2I,264;AE,52;N1I,33;RI,36)

- Assembles, disassembles, and tests systems (e.g., in logo programming, using paper and pencil designs)

Level III (Grades 6-8)

BD (2E,265;AI,86;N2I,47;RI,20)

- Knows that a system can include processes as well as components

BD (2E,265;AI,86;CE,33;FI,73;N2I,47;RE,20)

- Knows how part of a system can provide feedback when its output (in the form of material, energy, or information) becomes input for another part of the system

---

Codes (right side of page):   BD = Benchmark, Declarative;   BP = Benchmark, Procedural;   BC = Benchmark, Contextual

1st letter(s) of each code in parentheses	*2nd letter of code*	*Number*
2 = Project 2061: Benchmarks for Science Literacy	E = Explicitly stated in document	Page number of cited document
A = AEC: Australian Technology Standards	I = Implied in document	
B = NBEA: Nat'l Standards for Business Education		
C = CDE: Science Framework for CA Public Schools	NC = North Carolina Computer Standards	
F = NAEP: 1996 Science Framework	R = ITEA: Technology for All Americans	
ID,IE,IT = Int'l Bacc.: Design Tech., Environmental	S = NRC: National Science Education Standards	
Systems, Information Technology	T= Texas Technology Application Standards	
N1,N2 = NCISE: Science and Technology Education		
Elementary, Middle		

- Identifies the elements, structure, sequence, operation, and control of systems

  BD (2I,265;AE,86;FI,73;N2I,47;RI,38)

- Assembles and disassembles systems to manage, control, and improve their performance (e.g., a computer program, a simple machine based on a pulley mechanism)

  BP (AE,86;RI,38)

- Knows that systems are usually linked to other systems, both internally and externally, and can contain subsystems as well as operate as subsystems

  BD (2E,265;AI,86;CI,32;FI,73;N2I,47;RI,19)

Level IV (Grades 9-12)

- Knows that a system usually has some properties that are different from those of its parts, but appear because of the interaction of those parts

  BD (2E,266;AI,106;FI,74;IEI,18)

- Knows that understanding how things work and designing solutions to problems of almost any kind can be facilitated by systems analysis

  BD (2E,266;AI,106;IDI,43)

- Knows that in defining a system, it is important to specify its boundaries and subsystems, indicate its relation to other systems, and identify what its input and its output are expected to be

  BD (2E,266;AI,106;CI,33;FI,74;IDI,4;IEI,18;RI,40)

- Knows how feedback can be used to help monitor, control, and stabilize the operation of a system

  BD (2E,266;AI,106;IDI,44;IEE,18;RI,20)

- Knows that even in simple systems, accurate prediction of the effect of changing some part of the system is not always possible

  BD (2E,266;AI,106;IEI,18)

- Constructs and operates systems (e.g., organizes and adjusts subsystems)

  BD (AE,106)

- Knows that complex systems are subject to failure and are designed with various elements and procedures (e.g., performance testing, overdesign, redundancy, more controls) that help reduce system failure

  BD (2E,51;AI,106;FI,28;IEI,18;N2I,38)

Codes (right side of page):   BD = Benchmark, Declarative; BP = Benchmark, Procedural; BC = Benchmark, Contextual
1st letter(s) of each code in parentheses   *2nd letter of code*   *Number*
2 = Project 2061: Benchmarks for Science Literacy   E = Explicitly stated in document   Page number of cited document
A = AEC: Australian Technology Standards   I = Implied in document
B = NBEA: Nat'l Standards for Business Education
C = CDE: Science Framework for CA Public Schools   NC = North Carolina Computer Standards
F = NAEP: 1996 Science Framework   R = ITEA: Technology for All Americans
ID,IE,IT = Int'l Bacc.: Design Tech., Environmental   S = NRC: National Science Education Standards
    Systems, Information Technology   T= Texas Technology Application Standards
N1,N2 = NCISE: Science and Technology Education
    Elementary, Middle

MREL

19. Behavioral Studies

The following process was used to identify standards and benchmarks for behavioral studies:

Identification of Significant Reports
Four reports were found useful for the identification of standards in behavioral studies, by which we mean content related to sociology, psychology, and social anthropology. These reports are *Benchmarks for Science Literacy* (AAAS, 1993), *Expectations of Excellence: Curriculum Standards for Social Studies* (National Council for the Social Studies, 1994), and *Psychology* (1996j) and. *Social Anthropology* (1996k) from the International Baccalaureate Organization.

Selection of the Reference Document
Project 2061's *Benchmarks* document was selected as the reference document. This report provides content information in the behavioral sciences that is articulated across four grade ranges. The NCSS social studies book, by contrast, is more oriented to the development of curriculum; that is, the content is more generally stated and geared toward the organization rather than the description of specific knowledge and skills.

Identification of Standards and Benchmarks
Benchmarks for Science Literacy shares a number of features with our model for the identification of standards. Statements labeled "Literacy Goals" are pitched at a level of generality that accords with our level for standards, which means that material beneath each "Goal" is articulated across K–12. In addition, *Benchmarks* provides developmentally appropriate content at grade levels K–2, 3–5, 6–8, and 9–12, a range that corresponds with our preference for benchmarks at primary, upper elementary, middle, and high school.

Much material in *Benchmarks* focuses on earth and space, physical, and life science. But the work also contains useful material in other areas, including the behavioral sciences; hence, this section on behavioral studies. Material from the *Benchmarks* document was altered primarily when the original statements carried more than one basic idea, or when stylistic changes helped the sense of the statement.

Integration of Information from Other Documents
Once the benchmarks and standards were identified from the *Benchmarks* document, the material was compared with NCSS's *Curriculum Standards*. Though somewhat more generally stated, the information from the NCSS standards was found to support many of the same ideas. Citations to that document are provided for those who use the *Curriculum Standards* but would like more specifically stated content. Finally, the International Baccalaureate Organization's curriculum materials on psychology and social anthropology were cited wherever benchmark topics were addressed. This was done to provide readers with another view on what topics are considered important for coverage in a curriculum.

Summary of Standards for Behavioral Studies

1. Understands that group and cultural influences contribute to human development, identity, and behavior
2. Understands various meanings of social group, general implications of group membership, and different ways that groups function
3. Understands that interactions among learning, inheritance, and physical development affect human behavior
4. Understands conflict, cooperation, and interdependence among individuals, groups, and institutions

(2E,153;SE,37)

1. Understands that group and cultural influences contribute to human development, identity, and behavior

Level I (Grades K-2)

BD (2E,154;SI,37)
- Understands that people are alike in many ways and different in many ways

BD (2E,154;IPI,13;SI,37)
- Understands that different families and classrooms have different rules and patterns of behavior, but there are some behaviors that are not accepted in most families or schools

BD (2E,154;SI,37)
- Understands that people often choose to do the same kinds of things that their friends do (e.g., dress, talk, act), but that people also often choose to do certain things their own ways

BD (2E,158;IPI,32;ISI,11;SE,33,37)
- Understands that the groups to which a person belongs (e.g., family, friends, team, community) influence in varying degrees how she or he thinks and acts

Level II (Grades 3-5)

BD (2E,154;SI,37)
- Understands that people can learn about others in many different ways (e.g., direct experience, mass communications media, conversations with others about their work and lives)

BD (2E,154;SI,37)
- Understands that people sometimes imitate people or characters they see presented in the media

BD (2E,154;SI,37)
- Understands that people might feel uncomfortable around other people who dress, talk, or act very differently from themselves

BD (2E,154;IPI,13,23;SI,37)
- Understands that "acceptable" human behavior varies from culture to culture and from one time period to another, but there are some behaviors that are "unacceptable" in almost all cultures, past and present

BD (2E,153;IPI,15,21,22,28,30,33;ISI,11,12;SE,37)
- Understands that various factors (e.g., interests, capabilities, values) contribute to the shaping of a person's identity

BD (2I,154;IPI,32;SE,37,59)
- Understands that the way a person views an incident reflects personal beliefs, experiences, and attitudes

---

Codes (right side of page):   BD = Benchmark, Declarative;   BP = Benchmark, Procedural;   BC = Benchmark, Contextual
1st letter of each code in parentheses   *2nd letter of code*   *Number*
2 = Project 2061: Benchmarks for Science Literacy   E = Explicitly stated in document   Page number of cited document
S = NCSS: Curriculum Standards for Social Studies   I = Implied in document
IP, IS = Int'l Bacc.: Psychology, Social Anthropology

McREL

Level III (Grades 6-8)

- Understands that each culture has distinctive patterns of behavior that are usually practiced by most of the people who grow up in it

  BD (2E,155;IPI,13,22,25;ISI,10;SI,37)

- Understands that usually within any society there is broad general agreement on what behavior is "unacceptable," but that the standards used to judge behavior vary for different settings and different subgroups and may change with time and in response to different political and economic conditions

  BD (2E,155;IPI,13,21;ISI,11;SI,37)

- Understands that punishments vary widely among, and even within, different societies

  BD (2E,155;IPI,21;SI,37)

- Understands that technology, especially in transportation and communication, is increasingly important in spreading ideas, values, and behavior patterns within a society and among different societies

  BD (2E,155;IPI,13,29,30;ISI,11;SI,37)

- Understands that various factors (e.g., wants and needs, talents, interests, influence of family and peers and media) affect decisions that individuals make

  BD (2I,155;IPI,15;SE,37,89)

Level IV (Grades 9-12)

- Understands that cultural beliefs strongly influence the values and behavior of the people who grow up in the culture, often without their being fully aware of it, and that people have different responses to these influences

  BD (2E,156;IPI,13,21,22,25;ISI,10;SI,37)

- Understands that punishment for "unacceptable" social behavior depends partly on beliefs about the purposes of punishment and about its effectiveness (which is difficult to test scientifically because circumstances vary greatly and because legal and ethical barriers interfere)

  BD (2E,156;IPI,13,21;SI,37)

- Understands that social distinctions are a part of every culture, but they take many different forms (e.g., rigid classes based solely on parentage, gradations based on the acquisition of skill, wealth, and/or education)

  BD (2E,156;IPI,24;ISI,10,11;SI,37)

- Understands that people often take differences (e.g., in speech, dress, behavior, physical features) to be signs of social class

  BD (2E,156;SI,37)

- Understands that the difficulty of moving from one social class to another varies greatly with time, place, and economic circumstances

  BD (2E,156;IPI,21;SI,37)

Codes (right side of page):   BD = Benchmark, Declarative; BP = Benchmark, Procedural; BC = Benchmark, Contextual
1st letter of each code in parentheses   *2nd letter of code*   *Number*
2 = Project 2061: Benchmarks for Science Literacy   E = Explicitly stated in document   Page number of cited document
S = NCSS: Curriculum Standards for Social Studies   I = Implied in document
IP, IS = Int'l Bacc.: Psychology, Social Anthropology

- Understands that heredity, culture, and personal experience interact in shaping human behavior, and that the relative importance of these influences is not clear in most circumstances
  BD (2E,156;IPI,13,22,24,25,26,27;SI,37)

- Understands that family, gender, ethnicity, nationality, institutional affiliations, socioeconomic status, and other group and cultural influences contribute to the shaping of a person's identity
  BD (2I,156;IPI,15,21,22,24,28,30,33;ISI,10,11,12;SE,37)

2. Understands various meanings of social group, general implications of group membership, and different ways that groups function
(2E,157;SE,33)

Level I (Grades K-2)

- Knows that people belong to some groups because they are born into them and to some groups because they join them
  BD (2E,158;ISI,11;SI,33)

- Knows unique features of different groups to which she or he belongs (e.g., family, team, class), and also features of these groups that overlap with other groups
  BD (2E,158;SE,37)

- Understands that different groups, societies, and cultures have some similar wants and needs
  BD (2I,154,158;ISI,10;SE,33,49)

- Knows that people tend to live in families and communities in which individuals have different roles
  BD (2E,128;SI,33)

Level II (Grades 3-5)

- Understands that people often like or dislike other people because of membership in or exclusion from a particular social group
  BD (2E,158;IPI,32;ISI,11;SI,33)

- Understands that individuals tend to support members of their own groups and may think of them as being like themselves
  BD (2E,158;IPI,32;ISI,11;SI,33)

- Understands that different groups have different expectations for how their members should act
  BD (2E,158;ISI,11;SI,33)

- Understands that the "rules" for group behaviors and expectations sometimes are written down and strictly enforced or are just understood from example
  BD (2E,158;IPI,13,32;ISI,11;SI,33)

Codes (right side of page):   BD = Benchmark, Declarative; BP = Benchmark, Procedural; BC = Benchmark, Contextual
1st letter of each code in parentheses   *2nd letter of code*   *Number*
2 = Project 2061: Benchmarks for Science Literacy   E = Explicitly stated in document   Page number of cited document
S = NCSS: Curriculum Standards for Social Studies   I = Implied in document
IP, IS = Int'l Bacc.: Psychology, Social Anthropology

MREL

- Understands that members of a group and even people in a crowd sometimes do and say things, good or bad, that they would not do or say on their own
  BD (2E,158;IPI,32;ISI,11;SI,33)

- Understands that different groups, societies, and cultures may have different ways of meeting similar wants and needs
  BD (2I,158;IPI,22;ISI,10;SE,33,49)

- Knows that language, stories, folktales, music, and artistic creations are expressions of culture
  BD (ISI,10;SE,33)

- Understands that "social group" has many meanings (e.g., any set of people who regularly spend time together for any reason; groups classified according to region or occupation such as Southerners or blue-collar workers; groups that people formally and deliberately join or are assigned to such as sororities, military units, scouts, street gangs, or the Shriners)
  BD (2I,157-158;ISI,11;SI,33)

- Understands that although rules at home, school, church, and in the community usually remain the same, sometimes they change for various reasons (e.g., some rules do not work, new people are involved, outside circumstances change)
  BD (2E,162;SE,33)

Level III (Grades 6-8)

- Understands that affiliation with a group can increase the power of members through pooled resources and concerted action
  BD (2E,159;IPI,32;ISI,11;SI,33)

- Understands that joining a group often has personal advantages (e.g., companionship, sense of identity, recognition by others inside and outside the group)
  BD (2E,159;IPI,15,22,32;ISI,11,12;SI,33)

- Understands that group identity may create a feeling of superiority, which increases group cohesion, but may also occasion hostility toward and/or from other groups
  BD (2E,159;IPI,15,22,32,33;ISI,11,12;SI,33)

- Understands that people sometimes react to all members of a group as though they were the same and perceive in their behavior only those qualities that fit preconceptions of the group (i.e., stereotyping) which leads to uncritical judgments (e.g., showing blind respect for members of some groups and equally blind disrespect for members of other groups)
  BD (2E,159;IPI,32;ISI,11;SI,33)

- Understands that a variety of factors (e.g., belief systems, learned behavior patterns) contribute to the ways in which groups respond differently to their physical and social environments and to the wants and needs of their members
  BD (2I,155;IPI,26,32;ISI,11;SE,33,80)

Codes (right side of page):   BD = Benchmark, Declarative;   BP = Benchmark, Procedural;   BC = Benchmark, Contextual

1st letter of each code in parentheses   *2nd letter of code*   *Number*

2 = Project 2061: Benchmarks for Science Literacy   E = Explicitly stated in document   Page number of cited document

S = NCSS: Curriculum Standards for Social Studies   I = Implied in document

IP, IS = Int'l Bacc.: Psychology, Social Anthropology

594

McREL

- BD (IPI,22;30;ISI,10;SE,33,79)
  Understands how language, literature, the arts, architecture, other artifacts, traditions, beliefs, values, and behaviors contribute to the development and transmission of culture

- BD (2I,159;IPI,32;ISI,11;SE,33)
  Understands that there are similarities and differences within groups as well as among groups

- BD (2E,155;IPI,21;SI,37)
  Understands that a large society may be made up of many groups, and these groups may contain many distinctly different subcultures (e.g., associated with region, ethnic origin, social class, interests, values)

Level IV (Grades 9-12)

- BD (2E,160;IPI,13,32;ISI,11;SI,33)
  Understands that while a group may act, hold beliefs, and/or present itself as a cohesive whole, individual members may hold widely varying beliefs, so the behavior of a group may not be predictable from an understanding of each of its members

- BD (2E,160;IPI,30;ISI,11;SI,33)
  Understands that social organizations may serve business, political, or social purposes beyond those for which they officially exist, including unstated ones such as excluding certain categories of people from activities

- BD (IPI,22,30;ISI,10;SE,33)
  Understands how the diverse elements that contribute to the development and transmission of culture (e.g., language, literature, the arts, traditions, beliefs, values, behavior patterns) function as an integrated whole

- BD (2I,163;IPI,22,30,32;ISI,10,11,12;SE,33)
  Understands that groups have patterns for preserving and transmitting culture even as they adapt to environmental and/or social change

- BD (2I,160;IPI,30,32;ISI,10;SE,33)
  Understands that social groups may have patterns of behavior, values, beliefs, and attitudes that can help or hinder cross-cultural understanding

(2E,139;SE,37)
3. Understands that interactions among learning, inheritance, and physical development affect human behavior

Level I (Grades K-2)

- BD (2E,140;SI,37)
  Knows that people use their senses to find out about their surroundings and themselves and that different senses provide different information

---

Codes (right side of page):   BD = Benchmark, Declarative;   BP = Benchmark, Procedural;   BC = Benchmark, Contextual
1st letter of each code in parentheses   *2nd letter of code*   *Number*
2 = Project 2061: Benchmarks for Science Literacy   E = Explicitly stated in document   Page number of cited document
S = NCSS: Curriculum Standards for Social Studies   I = Implied in document
IP, IS = Int'l Bacc.: Psychology, Social Anthropology

595

MREL

- Understands that sometimes a person can get different information about the same thing by moving closer to it or further away from it
  BD (2E,140;SI,37)

- Understands that some of the things people do (e.g., playing soccer, reading, writing) must be deliberately learned
  BD (2E,140;SI,37)

- Understands that practice helps people to improve, and that how well a person learns sometimes depends on how she or he does it as well as how often and how hard she or he tries to learn
  BD (2E,140;IPI,22;SI,37)

- Knows that people can learn from each other in many ways (e.g., telling and listening, showing and watching, imitating)
  BD (2E,140;IPI,22;SI,37)

Level II (Grades 3-5)

- Knows that human beings have different interests, motivations, skills, and talents
  BD (2E,140;IPI,31;SE,37)

- Understands that human beings can use the memory of their past experiences to make judgments about new situations
  BD (2E,140;IPI,14;SI,37)

- Understands that many skills can be practiced until they become automatic, and that if the right skills are practiced, performance may improve
  BD (2E,140;SI,37)

- Understands that human beings tend to repeat behaviors that feel good or have pleasant consequences and to avoid behaviors that feel bad or have unpleasant consequences
  BD (2E,140;IPI,13;SI,37)

- Knows that learning means using what one already knows to make sense out of new experiences or information, not just storing the new information in one's head
  BD (2E,140;SI,37)

- Understands roles as learned behavior patterns in group situations (e.g., student, family member, team member)
  BD (2I,140;IPI,13,21,22;ISI,11;SE,38)

- Understands that as roles vary depending on expectations and changing conditions (e.g., worker, parent, volunteer, student), behavior, attitudes, and goals change
  BD (2I,140;IPI,13,21,32;SE,38,61)

Level III (Grades 6-8)

- Understands that all behavior is affected by both inheritance and experience
  BD (2E,141;IPI,13;SI,37)

Codes (right side of page):	BD = Benchmark, Declarative; BP = Benchmark, Procedural; BC = Benchmark, Contextual
1st letter of each code in parentheses	*2nd letter of code* ⸱ *Number*
2 = Project 2061: Benchmarks for Science Literacy	E = Explicitly stated in document ⸱ Page number of cited document
S = NCSS: Curriculum Standards for Social Studies	I = Implied in document
IP, IS = Int'l Bacc.: Psychology, Social Anthropology	

- Knows that some animal species are limited to a repertoire of genetically determined behaviors and others have more complex brains and can learn a wide variety of behaviors
  BD (2E,141;IPI,13,19;SI,37)

- Understands that the level of skill a person can reach in any particular activity depends on a variety of factors (e.g., innate abilities, amount of practice, the use of appropriate learning technologies)
  BD (2E,141;ISI,11;SI,37)

- Knows that human beings can detect a tremendous range of visual and olfactory stimuli and that the strongest stimulus they can tolerate may be more than a trillion times as intense as the weakest they can detect, but there are many kinds of signals in the world that people cannot detect directly
  BD (2E,141;SI,37)

- Understands that paying attention to any one input of information usually reduces the ability to attend to others at the same time
  BD (2E,141;IPI,14;SI,37)

- Understands that learning often results from two perceptions or actions occurring at about the same time, and the more often the same combination occurs, the stronger the mental connection between them is likely to be
  BD (2E,142;IPI,14,22;SI,37)

- Understands that occasionally a single vivid experience will connect two things permanently in people's minds
  BD (2E,142;SI,37)

- Understands that language and tools enable human beings to learn complicated and varied things from others
  BD (2E,142;SI,37)

Level IV (Grades 9-12)

- Understands that differences in the behavior of individuals arise from the interaction of heredity and experience
  BD (2E,142;IPI,13,24,26;SI,37)

- Understands that even instinctive behavior may not develop well if a person is exposed to abnormal conditions
  BD (2E,142;IPI,13;SI,37)

- Understands that expectations, moods, and prior experiences of human beings can affect how they interpret new perceptions or ideas
  BD (2E,142;IPI,14;SI,37)

- Understands that people might ignore evidence that challenges their beliefs and more readily accept evidence that supports them
  BD (2E,142;SI,37)

Codes (right side of page):   BD = Benchmark, Declarative; BP = Benchmark, Procedural; BC = Benchmark, Contextual
1st letter of each code in parentheses   *2nd letter of code*   *Number*
2 = Project 2061: Benchmarks for Science Literacy   E = Explicitly stated in document   Page number of cited document
S = NCSS: Curriculum Standards for Social Studies   I = Implied in document
IP, IS = Int'l Bacc.: Psychology, Social Anthropology

McREL

- Understands that the context in which something is learned may limit the contexts in which the learning can be used BD (2E,142;IPI,14,22;SI,37)

- Knows that human thinking involves the interaction of ideas, and ideas about ideas BD (2E,142;SI,37)

- Knows that people can produce many associations internally without receiving information from their senses BD (2E,142;SI,37)

4. Understands conflict, cooperation, and interdependence among individuals, groups, and institutions (2E,171;SE,38)

Level I (Grades K-2)

- Knows that disagreements are common, even between family members or friends BD (2E,172;SI,38,44)

- Understands that some ways of dealing with disagreements work better than others, and that people who are not involved in an argument may be helpful in solving it BD (2E,172;IPI,31;SI,38,44)

- Understands that rules at home, at school, and in the community let individuals know what to expect and so can reduce the number of disputes BD (2E,172;SI,38)

Level II (Grades 3-5)

- Knows that communicating different points of view in a dispute can often help people to find a satisfactory compromise BD (2E,172;IPI,31;SI,38,44)

- Understands that resolving a conflict by force rather than compromise can lead to more problems BD (2E,172;IPI,31;SI,38,44)

- Understands that one person's exercise of freedom may conflict with the freedom of others and that rules can help to resolve conflicting freedoms BD (2E,172;SI,38)

- Understands that if a conflict cannot be settled by compromise, it may be decided by a vote if everyone agrees to accept the results BD (2E,172;IPI,31;SI,38)

- Understands that beliefs and customs held by certain groups can help or hinder people as they strive to use their talents and that sometimes individuals can change those beliefs and BD (2I,172;IPI,14;ISI,11,12;SE,38,61-62)

Codes (right side of page):	BD = Benchmark, Declarative; BP = Benchmark, Procedural; BC = Benchmark, Contextual	
1st letter of each code in parentheses	*2nd letter of code*	*Number*
2 = Project 2061: Benchmarks for Science Literacy	E = Explicitly stated in document	Page number of cited document
S = NCSS: Curriculum Standards for Social Studies	I = Implied in document	
IP, IS = Int'l Bacc.: Psychology, Social Anthropology		

customs in ways that will help people to succeed more easily in the future

- Knows various forms that institutions take (e.g., religious, social, political)

BD (IPI,22;ISI,10,11;SE,38)

Level III (Grades 6-8)

- Understands that being a member of a group can increase an individual's social power and also can increase hostile actions toward or from other groups or individuals

BD (2E,159,173;IPI,32;ISI,11;SI,38)

- Understands that most groups have formal or informal procedures for arbitrating disputes among their members

BD (2E,173;IPI,31;SI,38,44)

- Understands how various institutions (e.g., banks, schools, hospitals, the military) influence people, events, and elements of culture and how people interact with different institutions

BD (2I,173;IPI,22;ISI,10;SE,38)

- Understands how role, status, and social class may affect interactions of individuals and social groups

BD (2I,173;IPI,21,32;ISI,11;SE,38)

- Understands how tensions might arise between expressions of individuality and group or institutional efforts to promote social conformity

BD (2I,173;IPI,22,32;ISI,10,11;SE,38)

Level IV (Grades 9-12)

- Understands that conflict between people or groups may arise from competition over ideas, resources, power, and/or status

BD (2E,173;IPI,31;ISI,11,12;SI,38,44)

- Understands that social change, or the prospect of it, promotes conflict because social, economic, and political changes usually benefit some groups more than others (which is also true of the status quo)

BD (2E,173;IPI,21,31;ISI,11,12;SI,38)

- Understands that conflicts are especially difficult to resolve in situations in which there are few choices and little room for compromise

BD (2E,173;IPI,31;SI,38)

- Understands that some informal ways of responding to conflict (e.g., pamphlets, demonstrations, cartoons) may reduce tensions and lead to compromise but may be inflammatory and make agreement more difficult to reach

BD (2E,173;IPI,31;SI,38)

- Understands that conflict within a group may be reduced by conflict between it and other

BD (2E,174;IPI,31,32;ISI,12;SE,38)

Codes (right side of page):   BD = Benchmark, Declarative; BP = Benchmark, Procedural; BC = Benchmark, Contextual
1st letter of each code in parentheses   *2nd letter of code*   *Number*
2 = Project 2061: Benchmarks for Science Literacy   E = Explicitly stated in document   Page number of cited document
S = NCSS: Curriculum Standards for Social Studies   I = Implied in document
IP, IS = Int'l Bacc.: Psychology, Social Anthropology

MREL

groups

- BD (2E,174;IPI,31;SI,38,44)
Understands that intergroup conflict does not necessarily end when one segment of society gets a decision in its favor because the "losers" then may work even harder to reverse, modify, or circumvent the change

- BD (2E,174;SI,38)
Understands that even when the majority of people in a society agree on a social decision, the minority who disagree must be protected from oppression, just as the majority may need protection against unfair retaliation from the minority

- BD (2E,163;IPI,13,22;ISI,10,11,12;SE,38)
Understands how various institutions (e.g., social, religious, political) develop and change over time (i.e., what is taught in school and school policies toward student behavior have changed over the years in response to family and community pressures), and how they further both continuity and change in societies

- BD (2I,163;IPI,21,22,30;ISI,10,11,12;SE,38,124)
Understands how changes in social and political institutions (e.g., church, school, political party) both reflect and affect individuals' career choices, values, and significant actions

- BD (2E,163;SI,38)
Understands that the decisions of one generation both provide and limit the range of possibilities open to the next generation

- BD (2E,163;IPI,30;ISI,12;SI,38)
Understands that mass media, migrations, and conquest affect social change by exposing one culture to another, and that extensive borrowing among cultures has led to the virtual disappearance of some cultures but only modest change in others

---

Codes (right side of page):   BD = Benchmark, Declarative; BP = Benchmark, Procedural; BC = Benchmark, Contextual
1st letter of each code in parentheses   *2nd letter of code*   *Number*
2 = Project 2061: Benchmarks for Science Literacy   E = Explicitly stated in document   Page number of cited document
S = NCSS: Curriculum Standards for Social Studies   I = Implied in document
IP, IS = Int'l Bacc.: Psychology, Social Anthropology

600

20. Life Skills

Life skills describes a category of knowledge that is useful across the content areas as well as important for the world of work. This category is comprised of four areas: Thinking and Reasoning, Working with Others, Self-Regulation, and Life Work.

Thinking and Reasoning

The following process was used to identify standards and benchmarks in the category of thinking and reasoning:

Identification of Target Reports

No single document was used as the reference report for standards and benchmarks in the thinking and reasoning category. Rather, those statements that were judged to articulate thinking and reasoning processes that can be applied across content areas were extracted from the various documents reviewed. The following documents have been used to construct standards and benchmarks in the thinking and reasoning category:

* *Benchmarks for Science Literacy* (Project 2061, 1993).
* *Curriculum and Evaluation Standards for School Mathematics* (NCTM, 1989).
* *Expectations of Excellence: Curriculum Standards for Social Studies* (NCSS, 1994).
* *Geography for Life: National Geography Standards* (Geography Education Standards Project, 1994).
* *Moving Into the Future, National Standards for Physical Education: A Guide to Content and Assessment* (NASPE, 1995).
* *National Health Education Standards: Achieving Health Literacy* (JHESC, 1995).
* *National Science Education Standards* (NRC, 1996).
* *National Standards for Arts Education: What Every Young American Should Know and Be Able to Do in the Arts* (CNAEA, 1994).
* *National Standards for Civics and Government* (CCE, 1994).
* *National Standards for History: Basic Edition* (NCHS, 1996).
* *Standards for Foreign Language Learning: Preparing for the 21st Century* (NSFLEP, 1996).
* *Standards in Practice*: *Grades K-2* (Crafton, 1996).
* *Standards in Practice*: *Grades 3-5* (Sierra-Perry, 1996).
* *Standards in Practice*: *Grades 6-8* (Wilhelm, 1996).
* *Standards in Practice*: *Grades 9-12* (Smagorinsky, 1996).
* *What Work Requires of Schools: A SCANS Report for America 2000* (The Secretary's Commission on Achieving Necessary Skills, 1991).
* *Workplace Basics: The Essential Skills Employers Want* (Carnevale, Gainer & Meltzer, 1990).

Identification of Standards and Benchmarks from Target Reports

Explicit statements of thinking and reasoning were identified in all target reports. To illustrate, consider the following statements from NCTM's *Curriculum and Evaluation Standards for School Mathematics* (1989):

- make and test conjectures
- formulate counter examples
- follow logical arguments
- judge the validity of arguments
- construct simple valid arguments

Each of these statements represents a reasoning process or subprocess that could be used in a variety of subject areas. For example, one could judge the validity of arguments or construct simple valid arguments in mathematics, in science, or in history. Statements such as these found in any document were extracted and used as the statement base from which the thinking and reasoning standards were constructed.

In addition to explicit statements of general reasoning processes like those above, implicit statements of general thinking and reasoning processes were also identified. For example, the NCTM document contains the following statement:

- formulate problems from everyday and mathematical situations (p.23)

In this case, the thinking and reasoning process was made explicit:

- formulate problems within a variety of situations

In summary, both implicit and explicit statements of general thinking and reasoning processes were used to construct the standards and benchmarks in the thinking and reasoning category. It is again important to emphasize that our listing of these processes is not meant to imply that thinking and reasoning can or should be addressed in isolation of domain-specific content. However, providing a listing of generalized processes allows a school or district to distribute thinking and reasoning processes systematically throughout the various content domains. Additionally, it is our hope that a listing such as ours will help schools and districts break the perceptual set regarding many thinking and reasoning processes. For example, it is usually assumed that problem solving should be assigned exclusively to the domain of mathematics and hypothesis testing exclusively to the domain of science. However, careful examination of the standard in this section entitled "applies basic trouble-shooting and problem-solving techniques" will show that it is applicable to many domains, as is the standard "understands and applies basic principles of hypothesis testing and scientific inquiry."

Working with Others

The following process was used to identify standards and benchmarks in the category of working with others:

Identification of National Reports and Reference Documents
The category of standards entitled "working with others" deals with skills and abilities that are associated within groups and with those skills and abilities associated with effective interpersonal communications. Even though many of the national reports mentioned the need for students to work in cooperative environments and use interpersonal communication skills, it was primarily those reports from the domain of workplace literacy that identified specific skills and abilities that should be demonstrated by students. Two documents from this domain were selected as the reference reports for this category: *What Work Requires of Schools: A SCANS Report for America 2000* (The Secretary's Commission on Achieving Necessary Skills, 1991) and *Workplace Basics: The Essential Skills Employers Want* (Carnevale, Gainer, & Meltzer, 1990). These documents were selected as co-reference documents because of their similar purpose and format. *Workplace Basics* places heavy emphasis on this category of standards, although it does not explicitly identify a category referred to as "working with others." Rather, it articulates related categories such as interpersonal skills, negotiation skills, teamwork, and listening and oral communication skills. The SCANS report identifies working with others as one of the five general competencies important in the workplace. Within this category it lists such areas as: participates as a team member, teaches others new skills, and exercises leadership.

Additionally, one content-area document contained explicit statements of what students should know and be able to do while working with others: *Expectations of Excellence: Curriculum Standards for Social Studies* (NCSS, 1994). Also, the document from NCTE entitled *Democracy through Language* (1989) contained general references to the skills students should exhibit while working with others.

Identification of Standards and Benchmarks and the Integration of Information from Other Documents
Both the *SCANS* report and *Workplace Basics* articulate skills and abilities at a level of generality highly compatible with the specific declarative, procedural, and contextualized structures that serve as the foundation for the standards and benchmarks identified in this report. However, one convention adopted by both reports was not compatible with this study. Specifically, neither report identifies the levels at which articulated skills and abilities should be emphasized. The SCANS report simply notes that all identified skills and abilities should be reinforced at kindergarten through 12th-grade levels; *Workplace Basics* lists the skills and abilities it identifies as important for graduation. Rather than arbitrarily identify the levels at which the various skills and abilities should be emphasized, we adopted the convention of placing them all at level IV (Grades K–12). Thus, a school or district wishing to adopt the skills and abilities in this section would need to devise a system to determine appropriate benchmark levels.

Self-Regulation
The following process was used to identify standards and benchmarks in the category of self-regulation:

Identification of Significant Reports and Reference Documents

Self-regulation standards include skills and abilities that address executive and metacognitive functions such as setting and monitoring goals and maintaining a healthy sense of self. Because of their similar purpose and format, two documents were identified as co-reference reports for this category of standards: *What Work Requires of Schools: A SCANS Report of America 2000* (The Secretary's Commission on Achieving Necessary Skills, 1991) and *Workplace Basics: The Essential Skills Employers Want* (Carnevale, Gainer & Meltzer, 1990). Although neither document contains a category referred to as self-regulation per se, both contain categories that are strongly related. For example, the SCANS report lists skills and abilities in the general areas of setting goals, managing resources, self-esteem, and self-management. *Workplace Basics* describes skills and abilities in categories such as self-esteem, goal setting, motivation, and learning to learn.

Identification of Standards and Benchmarks

Both documents report their skills and abilities at levels highly compatible with the format for benchmarks adopted in this study. That is, both documents present statements that are easily translated into specific elements of declarative, procedural, and contextual knowledge. Neither document, however, describes the levels at which their identified skills and abilities should be emphasized. Rather, both allude to the fact that all skills and abilities should be acquired by students by the time they graduate. The declarative, procedural, and contextual elements in this category were assigned to level IV (Grades K–12). The knowledge and skills were identified as important across all grade levels. For a discussion of grades and the levels to which they are assigned, see Section 6.

Life Work

The following process was used to identify standards and benchmarks in the category of life work:

Identification of Significant Reports and Reference Documents

Standards in the life work category encompass those skills and abilities commonly considered necessary to secure and maintain employment. Two co-reference documents were selected for this category of standards because of their similar purpose and format: *What Work Requires of Schools: A SCANS Report for America 2000* (The Secretary's Commission on Achieving Necessary Skills, 1991) and *Workplace Basics: The Essential Skills Employers Want* (Carnevale, Gainer, & Meltzer, 1990). As their titles indicate, both documents are explicitly designed to provide students with guidance in terms of those skills that are valued and expected in the marketplace. In fact, *Workplace Basics* lists as one of its sixteen categories of skills, Employability — Career Development. Additionally, *Benchmarks for Science Literacy* (Project 2061, 1993) was identified as relevant to this category.

Identification of Standards and Benchmarks and Integration of Information from Other Documents

Although both reference documents list skills and abilities at a high level of specificity that renders them quite compatible with the structure of standards used in this study, neither identifies the level at which these skills and abilities should be addressed. Consequently, with one exception, the elements listed under the standards in this section are all assigned to level IV (grades 9–12). The one exception is the standard entitled "Makes effective use of basic tools." All components for this standard were drawn from the document *Benchmarks for Science Literacy* (1993), which lists skills and abilities by grade level.

Summary of Standards for Life Skills

Thinking and Reasoning
1. Understands and applies the basic principles of presenting an argument
2. Understands and applies basic principles of logic and reasoning
3. Effectively uses mental processes that are based on identifying similarities and differences (compares, contrasts, classifies)
4. Understands and applies basic principles of hypothesis testing and scientific inquiry
5. Applies basic trouble-shooting and problem-solving techniques
6. Applies decision-making techniques

Working with Others
1. Contributes to the overall effort of a group
2. Uses conflict-resolution techniques
3. Works well with diverse individuals and in diverse situations
4. Displays effective interpersonal communication skills
5. Demonstrates leadership skills

Self-Regulation
1. Sets and manages goals
2. Performs self-appraisal
3. Considers risks
4. Demonstrates perseverance
5. Maintains a healthy self-concept
6. Restrains impulsivity

Life Work
1. Makes effective use of basic tools
2. Uses various information sources, including those of a technical nature, to accomplish specific tasks
3. Manages money effectively
4. Pursues specific jobs
5. Makes general preparation for entering the work force
6. Makes effective use of basic life skills
7. Displays reliability and a basic work ethic
8. Operates effectively within organizations

Thinking and Reasoning

(CI,93;GE,55;HI,23;NSI,176;WI,64)

1. Understands and applies the basic principles of presenting an argument

Level I (Grades K-2)

- Understands that people are more likely to believe a person's ideas if that person can give good reasons for them
  BD (2E,232)

- Provides coherent (though not necessarily valid or convincing) answers when asked why one believes something to be true or how one knows something
  BP (2I,298;WI,64)

- Asks "how do you know" in appropriate situations
  BP (2I,298;NHE,21)

Level II (Grades 3-5)

- Uses facts from books, articles, and databases to support an argument
  BC (2I,299)

- Identifies basic informal fallacies, including appeals to authority, the use of statements such as "everybody knows," and vague references such as "leading doctors say"
  BP (2I,299;WI,64)

- Understands that reasoning can be distorted by strong feelings
  BD (2E,232)

- Analyzes arguments to determine if they are supported by facts from books, articles, and databases
  BP (2I,299)

- Raises questions about arguments that are based on the assertion that "everybody knows" or "I just know"
  BP (2E,299)

- Seeks reasons for believing things other than the assertion that "everybody agrees"
  BP (2I,299)

- Recognizes when a comparison is not fair because important characteristics are not the same
  BP (2I,299)

Codes (right side of page):   BD = Benchmark, Declarative; BP = Benchmark, Procedural; BC = Benchmark, Contextual

1st letter(s) of each code in parentheses   *2nd letter of code*   *Number*

2 = Project 2061: Benchmarks for Science Literacy   E = Explicitly stated in document   Page number of cited document

A = CNAEA: National Standards for Arts Education   I = Implied in document

C = CCE: National Standards for Civics and Govt.

F = ACTFL: Standards for Foreign Lang. Learning

G = GESP: National Geography Standards   P = NASPE: National Standards for Physical Education

H = JHESC: National Health Education Standards   S = SCANS: Report for America 2000

M = NCTM: Curric. & Eval. Stan. for School Math   SP 1,2,3,4 = NCTE: Standards in Practice

NH = NCHS: Nat'l Standards for History: Basic Ed   SS = NCSS: Curriculum Standards for Social Studies

NS = NRC: National Science Education Standards   W = Carnevale: Workplace Basics

Level III (Grades 6-8)

- Evaluates arguments that are based on quantitative data and mathematical concepts
  BP (MI,78;ME,105)

- Questions claims that use vague references such as "leading experts say..." or are based on the statements of people speaking outside of their expertise (e.g., celebrities)
  BP (2E,299;SSE,148)

- Questions conclusions based on very small samples of data, biased samples, or samples for which there is no central sample
  BP (2E,299)

- Makes basic distinctions between information that is based on fact and information that is based on opinion
  BP (2E,299;HI,18;NHE,66;SSE,148)

- Identifies and questions false analogies
  BP (2E,299;SSE,148)

- Identifies and questions arguments in which all members of a group are implied to possess nearly identical characteristics that are considered to be different from those of another group
  BP (2E,299;SSE,148)

- Compares and contrasts the credibility of differing accounts of the same event
  BC (NHI,68;SSE,148)

Level IV (Grades 9-12)

- Understands that when people try to prove a point, they may at times select only the information that supports it and ignore the information that contradicts it
  BD (2I,300;NHI,68;SSE,148;WI,64)

- Identifies techniques used to slant information in subtle ways
  BP (NHI,68;SSE,148;WI,64)

- Identifies the logic of arguments that are based on quantitative data
  BC (MI,143)

- Identifies or seeks out the critical assumptions behind a line of reasoning and uses that to judge the validity of an argument
  BP (2I,300;AI,71;SSE,148)

- Understands that to be convincing, an argument must have both true statements and valid connections among them
  BD (2E,234;NSE,176)

Codes (right side of page):   BD = Benchmark, Declarative; BP = Benchmark, Procedural; BC = Benchmark, Contextual
1st letter(s) of each code in parentheses   *2nd letter of code*   *Number*
2 = Project 2061: Benchmarks for Science Literacy   E = Explicitly stated in document   Page number of cited document
A = CNAEA: National Standards for Arts Education   I = Implied in document
C = CCE: National Standards for Civics and Govt.
F = ACTFL: Standards for Foreign Lang. Learning   _____
G = GESP: National Geography Standards
H = JHESC: National Health Education Standards   P = NASPE: National Standards for Physical Education
M = NCTM: Curric. & Eval. Stan. for School Math   S = SCANS: Report for America 2000
NH = NCHS: Nat'l Standards for History: Basic Ed   SP 1,2,3,4 = NCTE: Standards in Practice
NS = NRC: National Science Education Standards   SS = NCSS: Curriculum Standards for Social Studies
                                                     W = Carnevale: Workplace Basics

McREL

BP (2E,297)
- Uses tables, charts, and graphs in constructing arguments

BP (2E,299;AI,71;CI,113;FLI,39;NHI,66;SSE,148)
- Evaluates the overall effectiveness of complex arguments

(SI,xviii;WI,64)

2. Understands and applies basic principles of logic and reasoning

Level III (Grades 6-8)

BP (MI,81)
- Uses formal deductive connectors ("if...then," "not," "and," "or") in the construction of deductive arguments

BD (2E,233)
- Understands that some aspects of reasoning have very rigid rules but other aspects do not

BD (2E,233;SP3I,33)
- Understands that when people have rules that always hold for a given situation and good information about the situation, then logic can help them figure out what is true about the situation

BD (2E,233;SP3I,33)
- Understands that reasoning by similarities can suggest ideas but cannot be used to prove things

BD (2E,233)
- Understands that people are using incorrect logic when they make a statement such as "if x is true, then y is true; but x isn't true, therefore y isn't true"

BD (2E,233)
- Understands that a single example can never prove that something is true, but a single example can prove that something is not true

BD (2E,233)
- Understands that some people invent a general rule to explain how something works by summarizing observations

BD (2E,233)
- Understands that people overgeneralize by making up rules on the basis of only a few observations

BD (SSI,149)
- Understands that personal values influence the types of conclusions people make

---

- Recognizes situations in which a variety of conclusions can be drawn from the same information ^{BP (SSE,149)}

Level IV (Grades 9-12)

- Understands the differences between the formal and informal uses (e.g., in everyday situations) of the logical connectors: "if...then," "not," "and," "or" ^{BD (2I,297)}

- Analyzes the deductive validity of arguments based on implicit or explicit assumptions ^{BP (2I,300)}

- Understands the difference between formal and informal uses (e.g., in everyday situations) of the terms "sufficient" and "necessary" ^{BD (2I,297)}

- Understands the formal meaning of the logical quantifiers: "some," "none," and "all" ^{BD (2I,297)}

- Understands that formal logic is mostly about connections between statements and that these connections can be considered without attention to whether the statements themselves are true or not ^{BD (2E,234;NSI,175)}

- Understands that people sometimes reach false conclusions either by applying faulty logic to true statements or by applying valid logic to false statements ^{BD (2E,234)}

- Understands that a reason may be *sufficient* to get a result but may not be the only way to get the result (i.e., may not be *necessary*), or a reason may be *necessary* to obtain a result but not *sufficient* (i.e., other things are also required; some reasons may be both *necessary* and *sufficient*) ^{BD (2E,234,297)}

- Understands that logic can be used to test how well any general rule works ^{BD (2E,234)}

- Understands that proving a general rule to be false can be done by finding just one exception; this is much easier than proving a general rule to be true for all possible cases ^{BD (2E,234)}

- Understands that logic may be of limited help in finding solutions to problems if the general rules upon which conclusions are based do not always hold true; most often, we have to deal ^{BD (2E,234)}

Codes (right side of page):   BD = Benchmark, Declarative; BP = Benchmark, Procedural; BC = Benchmark, Contextual
1st letter(s) of each code in parentheses   *2nd letter of code*   *Number*
2 = Project 2061: Benchmarks for Science Literacy   E = Explicitly stated in document   Page number of cited document
A = CNAEA: National Standards for Arts Education   I = Implied in document
C = CCE: National Standards for Civics and Govt.
F = ACTFL: Standards for Foreign Lang. Learning
G = GESP: National Geography Standards   P = NASPE: National Standards for Physical Education
H = JHESC: National Health Education Standards   S = SCANS: Report for America 2000
M = NCTM: Curric. & Eval. Stan. for School Math   SP 1,2,3,4 = NCTE: Standards in Practice
NH = NCHS: Nat'l Standards for History: Basic Ed   SS = NCSS: Curriculum Standards for Social Studies
NS = NRC: National Science Education Standards   W = Carnevale: Workplace Basics

610

McREL

with probabilities rather than certainties

BD (2E,234)
- Understands that once a person believes a general rule, he or she may be more likely to notice things that agree with that rule and not notice things that do not; to avoid this "confirmatory bias," scientific studies sometimes use observers who do not know what the results are supposed to be

BD (2E,234)
- Understands that very complex logical arguments can be formulated from a number of simpler logical arguments

BP (ME,143)
- Identifies counter examples to conclusions that have been developed

(CE,16;FE,54,56;NHI,77;NSI,135;PE,48;WI,90,202)
3. Effectively uses mental processes that are based on identifying similarities and differences (compares, contrasts, classifies)

Level I (Grades K-2)
BC (NHI,18;WE,90)
- Classifies objects by size, color, or other significant characteristics

BC (AE,24;FE,54;HI,21;MI,32,60;NHE 21,26;SP1E,11)
- Identifies the similarities and differences between persons, places, things, and events using concrete criteria

BC (2E,296;FI,38;SP1I,11;AE,23;CE,15;HE,19;NHI,21)
- Describes and compares things in terms of number, shape, texture, size, weight, color, motion, sound, and behavior

BC (2I,217;AI,24;FE,46,56;PI,6)
- Recognizes simple patterns in the surrounding events and objects

Level II (Grades 3-5)
BD (2E,232;FI,56;PI,40;SP2I,24)
- Understands that one way to make sense of something is to think how it is like something more familiar

BP (2E,299)
- Recognizes when comparisons might not be fair because some characteristics are not the

---

Codes (right side of page):   BD = Benchmark, Declarative;   BP = Benchmark, Procedural;   BC = Benchmark, Contextual

1st letter(s) of each code in parentheses   *2nd letter of code*   *Number*
2 = Project 2061: Benchmarks for Science Literacy   E = Explicitly stated in document   Page number of cited document
A = CNAEA: National Standards for Arts Education   I = Implied in document
C = CCE: National Standards for Civics and Govt.
F = ACTFL: Standards for Foreign Lang. Learning
G = GESP: National Geography Standards   P = NASPE: National Standards for Physical Education
H = JHESC: National Health Education Standards   S = SCANS: Report for America 2000
M = NCTM: Curric. & Eval. Stan. for School Math   SP 1,2,3,4 = NCTE: Standards in Practice
NH = NCHS: Nat'l Standards for History: Basic Ed   SS = NCSS: Curriculum Standards for Social Studies
NS = NRC: National Science Education Standards   W = Carnevale: Workplace Basics

same

- Compares people in terms of important ethnic, religious, and cultural characteristics

  BC (FE,56;HE,23;MI,32,60;NHE,27,83;PI,40)

- Makes comparisons between countries in terms of relatively concrete characteristics (e.g., size, population, products,) and abstract characteristics (e.g. the arts)

  BC (AI,41;FE,56;GI,48;MI,32,60)

Level III (Grades 6-8)

- Compares consumer products on the basis of features, performance, durability, and cost, and considers personal tradeoffs

  BC (2E,299;HE,18)

- Understands that an analogy not only contains some likenesses but also some differences

  BD (2E,233)

- Selects criteria or rules for category membership that are relevant and important

  BP (AI,40,44;SP3E,93,113;SSI,149)

- Orders information and events chronologically or based on frequency of occurrence

  BC (NHE,62;SSI,149)

- Orders information based on importance to a given criterion

  BC (AE,45;CE,48;NHI,62;SSE,149)

- Articulates abstract relationships between existing categories of information

  BD (AE,45;FE,56;HE,17;NHI,64;NSI,145;PI,66;SP3E,114;SSE,149)

- Creates a table to compare specific abstract and concrete features of two items

  BP (GE,50)

- Compares different sources of information for the same topic in terms of basic similarities and differences

  BC (AI,45;CI,64;FI,38;NHI,63;SSI,149)

- Identifies the abstract relationships that form the basis for analogies

  BP (NHI,63,64;SSI,149)

Level IV (Grades 9-12)

- Uses a comparison table to compare multiple items on multiple abstract characteristics

  BP (GI,54)

- Identifies abstract patterns of similarities and differences between information on the same

  BC (AI,58,62;CI,114;FI,52;GE,55;NHI,66;SSI,149)

Codes (right side of page):	BD = Benchmark, Declarative; BP = Benchmark, Procedural; BC = Benchmark, Contextual

1st letter(s) of each code in parentheses   *2nd letter of code*   *Number*

2 = Project 2061: Benchmarks for Science Literacy   E = Explicitly stated in document   Page number of cited document

A = CNAEA: National Standards for Arts Education   I = Implied in document

C = CCE: National Standards for Civics and Govt.

F = ACTFL: Standards for Foreign Lang. Learning

G = GESP: National Geography Standards   P = NASPE: National Standards for Physical Education

H = JHESC: National Health Education Standards   S = SCANS: Report for America 2000

M = NCTM: Curric. & Eval. Stan. for School Math   SP 1,2,3,4 = NCTE: Standards in Practice

NH = NCHS: Nat'l Standards for History: Basic Ed   SS = NCSS: Curriculum Standards for Social Studies

NS = NRC: National Science Education Standards   W = Carnevale: Workplace Basics

topic but from different sources

BP (AE,62;CI,93;FE,48;HI,17;ME,146;NHI,66;SSI,149)

- Identifies abstract relationships between seemingly unrelated items

BP (AE,63;NHI,62;SSE,149)

- Identifies the qualitative and quantitative traits (other than frequency and obvious importance) that can be used to order and classify items

(NSE,121;WI,64)

4. Understands and applies basic principles of hypothesis testing and scientific inquiry

Level I (Grades K-2)

BP (2E,298;NHE,21;NSE,122,123)

- Asks "how do you know" in appropriate situations and attempts to provide reasonable answers when others ask the same question

BD (2I,217)

- Understands that changing one thing sometimes causes changes in something else and that changing the same thing in the same way usually has the same result

Level II (Grades 3-5)

BP (2I,293;NSE,122)

- Keeps a notebook that describes observations made

BP (MI,23,36,75;NSI,123)

- Attempts to verify the results of experiments done by others

BP (2E,293;NSE,122,123)

- Distinguishes between actual observations and ideas or conclusions about what was observed

BC (GE,46;NHI,21;NSE,122)

- Makes records of observations regarding time and place to formulate hypotheses

BC (GE,47;NSE,122)

- Keeps systematic records of temperature, precipitation, cloud cover, and other weather information to formulate hypotheses

Level III (Grades 6-8)

BD (2I,233;NHI,66;NSI,145)

- Understands that there are a variety of ways people can form hypotheses, including basing

---

Codes (right side of page):   BD = Benchmark, Declarative; BP = Benchmark, Procedural; BC = Benchmark, Contextual

1st letter(s) of each code in parentheses	*2nd letter of code*	*Number*
2 = Project 2061: Benchmarks for Science Literacy	E = Explicitly stated in document	Page number of cited document
A = CNAEA: National Standards for Arts Education	I = Implied in document	
C = CCE: National Standards for Civics and Govt.		

F = ACTFL: Standards for Foreign Lang. Learning
G = GESP: National Geography Standards   P = NASPE: National Standards for Physical Education
H = JHESC: National Health Education Standards   S = SCANS: Report for America 2000
M = NCTM: Curric. & Eval. Stan. for School Math   SP 1,2,3,4 = NCTE: Standards in Practice
NH = NCHS: Nat'l Standards for History: Basic Ed   SS = NCSS: Curriculum Standards for Social Studies
NS = NRC: National Science Education Standards   W = Carnevale: Workplace Basics

613   MREL

them on many observations, basing them on very few observations, and constructing them on only one or two observations

- Verifies results of experiments

  BP (MI,75;NSI,148,171)

- Understands that there may be more than one valid way to interpret a set of findings

  BD (2E,299;NHI,66;NSI,145)

- Questions findings in which no mention is made of whether the control group is very similar to the experimental group

  BP (2E,299;NSI,171)

- Reformulates a new hypothesis for study after an old hypothesis has been eliminated

  BP (SSE,149;NSE,145;NSI,171)

- Makes and validates conjectures about outcomes of specific alternatives or events regarding an experiment

  BP (MI,78,81,143;NSI,145,171)

Level IV (Grades 9-12)

- Identifies and critiques studies in which data, explanations, or conclusions are presented as the only ones worth considering

  BP (2E,300;NSI,200)

- Tests hypotheses statistically

  BP (ME,167;NSI,145,175)

- Presents alternative explanations and conclusions to one's own experiments and those of others

  BP (2E,300;NSE,175;SP4I,37-38)

- Critiques procedures, explanations, and conclusions in one's own experiments and those of others

  BP (NSE,145;AI,71;SP4I,37-38)

- Gathers and analyzes field data using spatial sampling (e.g., place a transparent grid of squares on maps to count whether two characteristics—such as corn production and hogs—that are hypothesized to be spatially related coexist within the grid cells)

  BP (GE,53)

Codes (right side of page):   BD = Benchmark, Declarative; BP = Benchmark, Procedural; BC = Benchmark, Contextual
1st letter(s) of each code in parentheses   *2nd letter of code*   *Number*
2 = Project 2061: Benchmarks for Science Literacy   E = Explicitly stated in document   Page number of cited document
A = CNAEA: National Standards for Arts Education   I = Implied in document
C = CCE: National Standards for Civics and Govt.
F = ACTFL: Standards for Foreign Lang. Learning
G = GESP: National Geography Standards   P = NASPE: National Standards for Physical Education
H = JHESC: National Health Education Standards   S = SCANS: Report for America 2000
M = NCTM: Curric. & Eval. Stan. for School Math   SP 1,2,3,4 = NCTE: Standards in Practice
NH = NCHS: Nat'l Standards for History: Basic Ed   SS = NCSS: Curriculum Standards for Social Studies
NS = NRC: National Science Education Standards   W = Carnevale: Workplace Basics

(CE,26;SI,xviii;WE,182;WI,64)

5. Applies basic trouble-shooting and problem-solving techniques

Level I (Grades K-2)

BP (AI,24;NSE,137)
- Identifies simple problems and possible solutions (e.g., ways to make something work better)

Level II (Grades 3-5)

BP (AI,40;CI,26,27;NHI,23;NSE,137)
- Identifies issues and problems in the school or community that one might help solve

BP (CI,60;NHE,23,27;NSE,138)
- Studies problems in the community and how they were solved

BP (CI,60;NHE,23,27;NSE,138)
- Analyzes the problems that have confronted people in the past in terms of the major goals and obstacles to those goals

Level III (Grades 6-8)

BP (AE,40;CI,48;NHE,70;PI,69;SSI,148)
- Identifies alternative courses of action and predicts likely consequences of each

BP (AE,40;NHE,70;NSI,137;PI,69;SSE,148)
- Selects the most appropriate strategy or alternative for solving a problem

BC (CE,56,68;NHE,23,70)
- Examines different alternatives for resolving local problems and compares the possible consequences of each alternative

Level IV (Grades 9-12)

BP (AE,70;HI,21,37;NSI,192;SI,xvii)
- Applies trouble-shooting strategies to complex real-world situations

BD (2E,233)
- Understands that trouble-shooting almost anything may require many-step branching logic

BP (2E,234)
- Trouble-shoots common mechanical and electrical systems, checking for possible causes of malfunction, and decides on that basis whether to make a change or get advice from an expert before proceeding

---

Codes (right side of page):   BD = Benchmark, Declarative; BP = Benchmark, Procedural; BC = Benchmark, Contextual

1st letter(s) of each code in parentheses	*2nd letter of code*	*Number*
2 = Project 2061: Benchmarks for Science Literacy	E = Explicitly stated in document	Page number of cited document
A = CNAEA: National Standards for Arts Education	I = Implied in document	
C = CCE: National Standards for Civics and Govt.		
F = ACTFL: Standards for Foreign Lang. Learning		
G = GESP: National Geography Standards	P = NASPE: National Standards for Physical Education	
H = JHESC: National Health Education Standards	S = SCANS: Report for America 2000	
M = NCTM: Curric. & Eval. Stan. for School Math	SP 1,2,3,4 = NCTE: Standards in Practice	
NH = NCHS: Nat'l Standards for History: Basic Ed	SS = NCSS: Curriculum Standards for Social Studies	
NS = NRC: National Science Education Standards	W = Carnevale: Workplace Basics	

*M*REL

- Isolates a problem component in a schematic diagram and traces it to the cause of the problem
  BP (WE,90-91)

- Engages in problem finding and framing for personal situations and situations in the community
  BP (AE,70;NSE,192;SI,xviii;WI,64)

- Represents a problem accurately in terms of resources, constraints, and objectives
  BP (AI,70;MI,23;NHE,70;WE,182,329)

- Provides summation of the effectiveness of problem-solving techniques
  BP (AI,70;CI,106;NSE,192;WE,182)

- Reframes problems when alternative solutions are exhausted
  BP (WE,182,202)

- Examines different options for solving problems of historical importance and determines why specific courses of action were taken
  BC (CI,103;NHE,70)

- Evaluates the feasibility of various solutions to problems; recommends and defends a solution
  BP (AI,70;CI,106;GE,55;NHE,70;NSI,192)

6.   Applies decision-making techniques
(HI,22;SSE,149)

Level I (Grades K-2)

- Makes and defends decisions about daily activities (e.g., what books to read)
  BC (SP1E,10)

Level II (Grades 3-5)

- Studies decisions that were made in the community in terms of the alternatives that were considered
  BP (NHE,23,24)

- Analyzes important decisions made by people in the past in terms of possible alternatives that were considered
  BP (NHE,23,24)

Codes (right side of page):   BD = Benchmark, Declarative; BP = Benchmark, Procedural; BC = Benchmark, Contextual
1st letter(s) of each code in parentheses   *2nd letter of code*   *Number*
2 = Project 2061: Benchmarks for Science Literacy   E = Explicitly stated in document   Page number of cited document
A = CNAEA: National Standards for Arts Education   I = Implied in document
C = CCE: National Standards for Civics and Govt.
F = ACTFL: Standards for Foreign Lang. Learning
G = GESP: National Geography Standards   P = NASPE: National Standards for Physical Education
H = JHESC: National Health Education Standards   S = SCANS: Report for America 2000
M = NCTM: Curric. & Eval. Stan. for School Math   SP 1,2,3,4 = NCTE: Standards in Practice
NH = NCHS: Nat'l Standards for History: Basic Ed   SS = NCSS: Curriculum Standards for Social Studies
NS = NRC: National Science Education Standards   W = Carnevale: Workplace Basics

Level III (Grades 6-8)

- BP (NSI,169;PI,54,70;SSE,149)
  Identifies situations in the community and in one's personal life in which a decision is required

- BP (AI,44;CE,46,77;SSE,149)
  Secures factual information needed to evaluate alternatives

- BP (AI,62;CI,75,77;SSI,149)
  Identifies the values underlying the alternatives that are considered and the criteria that will be used to make a selection among the alternatives

- BP (CI,48;HE,22;PE,70;SSI,148)
  Predicts the consequences of selecting each alternative

- BP (AI,62;CI,69;PI,54;SSE,148)
  Makes decisions based on the data obtained and the criteria identified

- BC (NSE,192;SSE,148)
  When appropriate, takes action to implement the decision

- BP (2E,299;HI,18)
  Makes effective decisions about consumer products based on important criteria, including external features, performance, durability, cost, and personal tradeoffs

- BP (HI,22)
  Analyzes personal decisions in terms of the options that were considered

- BP (GI,51;SSI,149)
  Uses a decision-making grid or matrix to make or study decisions involving a relatively limited number of alternatives and criteria

- BC (GE,52)
  Selects appropriate locations for specific service industries within the community

Level IV (Grades 9-12)

- BP (NHE,70)
  Analyzes decisions that were major turning points in history and describes how things would have been different if other alternatives had been selected

- BP (CI,76;NHI,70)
  Analyzes current or pending decisions that can affect national or international policy and identifies the consequences of each alternative

- BP (GI,54;SSI,149)
  Uses a decision-making grid or matrix to make or study decisions involving a relatively large

---

Codes (right side of page):   BD = Benchmark, Declarative; BP = Benchmark, Procedural; BC = Benchmark, Contextual

1st letter(s) of each code in parentheses	*2nd letter of code*	*Number*
2 = Project 2061: Benchmarks for Science Literacy	E = Explicitly stated in document	Page number of cited document
A = CNAEA: National Standards for Arts Education	I = Implied in document	
C = CCE: National Standards for Civics and Govt.		
F = ACTFL: Standards for Foreign Lang. Learning		
G = GESP: National Geography Standards	P = NASPE: National Standards for Physical Education	
H = JHESC: National Health Education Standards	S = SCANS: Report for America 2000	
M = NCTM: Curric. & Eval. Stan. for School Math	SP 1,2,3,4 = NCTE: Standards in Practice	
NH = NCHS: Nat'l Standards for History: Basic Ed	SS = NCSS: Curriculum Standards for Social Studies	
NS = NRC: National Science Education Standards	W = Carnevale: Workplace Basics	

MREL

number of alternatives and criteria advocate

- Uses a balance sheet to evaluate the costs and benefits of various alternatives within a decision

  BP (CI,97;GE,55)

- Evaluates major factors that influence personal decisions

  BP (AI,67;HI,22)

Codes (right side of page):   BD = Benchmark, Declarative; BP = Benchmark, Procedural; BC = Benchmark, Contextual
1st letter(s) of each code in parentheses   *2nd letter of code*   *Number*
2 = Project 2061: Benchmarks for Science Literacy   E = Explicitly stated in document   Page number of cited document
A = CNAEA: National Standards for Arts Education   I = Implied in document
C = CCE: National Standards for Civics and Govt.
F = ACTFL: Standards for Foreign Lang. Learning
G = GESP: National Geography Standards   P = NASPE: National Standards for Physical Education
H = JHESC: National Health Education Standards   S = SCANS: Report for America 2000
M = NCTM: Curric. & Eval. Stan. for School Math   SP 1,2,3,4 = NCTE: Standards in Practice
NH = NCHS: Nat'l Standards for History: Basic Ed   SS = NCSS: Curriculum Standards for Social Studies
NS = NRC: National Science Education Standards   W = Carnevale: Workplace Basics

Working with Others

1. Contributes to the overall effort of a group

(EI,3;WI,64;WE,307)

Level IV (Grades K-12)

- Challenges practices in a group that are not working

  BP (SE,xvii)

- Demonstrates respect for others in the group

  BP (SI,xviii)

- Identifies and uses the strengths of others

  BP (WE,307)

- Takes initiative when needed

  BP (WE,307)

- Identifies and deals with causes of conflict in a group

  BP (WE,307)

- Helps the group establish goals

  BP (WE,397)

- Engages in active listening

  BP (WE,307-308)

- Takes the initiative in interacting with others

  BP (WE,307-308)

- Evaluates the overall progress of a group toward a goal

  BP (WE,329)

- Keeps requests simple

  BP (WE,231)

- Contributes to the development of a supportive climate in groups

  BP (SSE,149)

2. Uses conflict-resolution techniques

(WI,349)

Level IV (Grades K-12)

- Communicates ideas in a manner that does not irritate others

  BP (SE,xvii)

- Resolves conflicts of interest

  BP (SE,xvii)

- Identifies goals and values important to opponents

  BD (WE,349)

Codes (right side of page):   BD = Benchmark, Declarative; BP = Benchmark, Procedural; BC = Benchmark, Contextual
1st letter of each code in parentheses   *2nd letter of code*   *Number*
S = SCANS: Report for America 2000   E = Explicitly stated in document   Page number of cited document
W = Carnevale: Workplace Basics   I = Implied in document
E = NCTE: Democracy Through Language
SS = NCSS: Curriculum Standards for Social Studies

- Understands the impact of criticism on psychological state, emotional state, habitual behavior, and beliefs BD (WE,231)

- Understands that three ineffective responses to criticism are (1) being aggressive, (2) being passive, and (3) being both BD (WE,231)

- Understands that three effective responses to criticism are (1) acknowledgement, (2) token agreement with a critic, and (3) probing clarifications BD (WE,231)

- Determines the causes of conflicts BP (WE,329)

- Does not blame BP (WE,231)

- Identifies an explicit strategy to deal with conflict BP (WE,329)

- Determines the seriousness of conflicts BP (WE,349)

- Identifies mutually agreeable times for important conversations with opponents BP (WE,231)

- Identifies individual vs. group or organizational interests in conflicts BP (WE,349)

- Establishes guidelines and rules for negotiating BP (WE,349)

- Determines the mini-max position of those in a conflict BP (WE,349)

3. **Works well with diverse individuals and in diverse situations** (EI,3)

Level IV (Grades K-12)

- Works well with the opposite gender BP (SE,xvii)

- Works well with different ethnic groups BP (SI,xvii)

- Works well with those of different religious orientations BP (SI,xvii)

- Works to satisfy needs of customers BP (SE,xvii)

Codes (right side of page): BD = Benchmark, Declarative; BP = Benchmark, Procedural; BC = Benchmark, Contextual
1st letter of each code in parentheses *2nd letter of code* *Number*
S = SCANS: Report for America 2000 E = Explicitly stated in document Page number of cited document
W = Carnevale: Workplace Basics I = Implied in document
E = NCTE: Democracy Through Language
SS = NCSS: Curriculum Standards for Social Studies

620

MREL

(WI,134-136,307-308)

4.   Displays effective interpersonal communication skills

Level IV (Grades K-12)

BP (SI,xviii;WE,307-308)

- Displays empathy with others

BP (SI,xviii)

- Displays friendliness with others

BC (SI,xviii)

- Displays politeness with others

BP (WI,64,151-154)

- Seeks information nondefensively

BP (WE,64;151-154)

- Provides feedback in a constructive manner

BP (WI,151)

- Uses nonverbal communication such as eye contact, body position, voice tone effectively

BP (WI,151)

- Does not react to a speaker's inflammatory deliverance

BP (WE,151)

- Identifies with speaker while maintaining objectivity

BP (WE,307)

- Uses emotions appropriately in personal dialogues

BP (WE,307)

- Makes use of confrontation when appropriate

BP (WE,134-136)

- Makes eye contact when speaking

BP (WE,151-154)

- Reacts to ideas rather than to the person presenting the ideas

BP (WE,134-136)

- Adjusts tone and content of information to accommodate the likes of others

BP (WI,307-308)

- Communicates in a clear manner during conversations

BP (WE,307-308)

- Acknowledges the strengths of others

Codes (right side of page):   BD = Benchmark, Declarative; BP = Benchmark, Procedural; BC = Benchmark, Contextual
1st letter of each code in parentheses   *2nd letter of code*   *Number*
S = SCANS: Report for America 2000   E = Explicitly stated in document   Page number of cited document
W = Carnevale: Workplace Basics   I = Implied in document
E = NCTE: Democracy Through Language
SS = NCSS: Curriculum Standards for Social Studies

MREL

5. Demonstrates leadership skills

(SSE,149)

Level IV (Grades K-12)

- Occasionally serves as a leader in groups

  BP (SSE,149)

- Occasionally serves as a follower in groups

  BP (SSE,149)

- Enlists others in working toward a shared vision

  BP (WE,397)

- Plans small wins

  BP (WE,397)

- Celebrates accomplishments

  BP (WE,397)

- Recognizes the contributions of others

  BP (WE,397)

- Passes on authority when appropriate

  BP (WE,397)

Codes (right side of page):   BD = Benchmark, Declarative;   BP = Benchmark, Procedural;   BC = Benchmark, Contextual
1st letter of each code in parentheses   *2nd letter of code*   *Number*
S = SCANS: Report for America 2000   E = Explicitly stated in document   Page number of cited document
W = Carnevale: Workplace Basics   I = Implied in document
E = NCTE: Democracy Through Language
SS = NCSS: Curriculum Standards for Social Studies

622

MREL

Self-Regulation

(WE,284-285)

1.　Sets and manages goals

Level IV (Grades K-12)

BP (SI,xviii)
- Sets explicit long-term goals

BP (SE,xvii;WI,284-285)
- Identifies and ranks relevant options in terms of accomplishing a goal

BP (SE,xvii;WI,284-285)
- Prepares and follows a schedule for carrying out options

BD (WE,231)
- Understands personal wants versus needs

BP (WI,231)
- Establishes personal milestones

BP (WI,231,241)
- Identifies resources necessary to complete a goal

BP (WI,64)
- Displays a sense of personal direction and purpose

BP (WI,241;WE,64)
- Maintains an awareness of proximity to goal

BP (WE,182-184)
- Makes a cumulative evaluation of goal

BD (WE,241)
- Understands the differences between various types of goals

BP (WE,241)
- Sets routine goals for improving daily life

BP (WE,241)
- Identifies explicit criteria for evaluating goals

BP (WE,284-285)
- Makes contingency plans

(WI,231;SE,xviii)

2.　Performs self-appraisal

Level IV (Grades K-12)

BP (SE,xvii)
- Distributes work according to perceived strengths

BD (WI,64)
- Identifies personal styles

Codes (right side of page):　　　　　　　　BD = Benchmark, Declarative;　BP = Benchmark, Procedural;　BC = Benchmark, Contextual
1st letter of each code in parentheses　　　*2nd letter of code*　　　　　　*Number*
S = SCANS: Report for America 2000　　　　E = Explicitly stated in document　　　Page number of cited document
W = Carnevale: Workplace Basics　　　　　I = Implied in document

MREL

- Identifies personal strengths and weaknesses   BD (WE,231)

- Utilizes techniques for overcoming weaknesses   BP (WE,231)

- Identifies basic values   BD (WE,231)

- Performs analysis of employability   BP (WE,284-285)

- Understands preferred working environments   BD (WE,284)

- Understands career goals   BD (WE,284)

- Identifies a compensating strength for each weakness   BP (WE,231)

- Develops an inventory of wants versus needs   BP (WI,231)

- Determines explicit behaviors that are used and should be adopted to obtain wants and/or needs   BD (WE,231)

- Identifies personal motivational patterns   BD (WE,284-285)

- Keeps a log documenting personal improvement   BP (WE,231)

- Summarizes personal educational background   BP (WE,284-285)

- Summarizes personal work experience   BP (WE,284-285)

- Identifies key accomplishments and successes in life   BD (WE,284-285)

- Identifies peak experiences and significant life experiences   BD (WE,284-285)

- Identifies desired future accomplishments   BD (WE,284-285)

- Identifies preferred lifestyle   BD (WE,284-285)

Codes (right side of page): BD = Benchmark, Declarative; BP = Benchmark, Procedural; BC = Benchmark, Contextual
1st letter of each code in parentheses   2nd letter of code   Number
S = SCANS: Report for America 2000   E = Explicitly stated in document   Page number of cited document
W = Carnevale: Workplace Basics   I = Implied in document

624

McREL

(SI,xviii;WI,90-91)

3. Considers risks

Level IV (Grades K-12)

BP (SI,xviii)
- Weighs risks in making decisions and solving problems

BP (WE,90-91)
- Uses common knowledge to avoid hazard or injury

BP (WE,90-91)
- Applies preventative measures prior to a task to minimize security or safety problems

BP (WE,90-91)
- Selects an appropriate course of action in an emergency

BP (WE,281-283)
- Identifies emergency and safety procedures before undertaking hazardous procedures

BP (WE,349)
- Thinks clearly under stress

(SE,xviii;WE,202)

4. Demonstrates perseverance

Level IV (Grades K-12)

BP (SE,xviii)
- Demonstrates perseverance relative to personal goals

BP (WI,64)
- Demonstrates a sense of purpose

BP (WE,202)
- Maintains a high level of energy over a prolonged period of time when engaged in tasks

BP (WE,202)
- Persists in the face of difficulty

BP (WE,151-154)
- Concentrates mental and physical energies

(WE,231)

5. Maintains a healthy self-concept

Level IV (Grades K-12)

BD (SI,xviii)
- Has basic belief in ability to succeed

BP (WE,231)
- Uses techniques to remind self of strengths

Codes (right side of page): | BD = Benchmark, Declarative; BP = Benchmark, Procedural; BC = Benchmark, Contextual
1st letter of each code in parentheses | *2nd letter of code* | *Number*
S = SCANS: Report for America 2000 | E = Explicitly stated in document | Page number of cited document
W = Carnevale: Workplace Basics | I = Implied in document

- Uses techniques to offset the negative effects of mistakes BP (WE,231)

- Avoids overreacting to criticism BP (WE,231)

- Uses affirmations to improve sense of self BP (WE,231)

- Analyzes self-statements for their positive and negative effects BP (WE,231)

- Examines "shoulds" to determine their negative and positive effects BP (WE,231)

- Revises "shoulds" to reflect the reality of personal needs BP (WE,231)

- Understands that everyone makes mistakes BD (WE,231)

- Understands that mistakes are a natural consequence of living and of limited resources BD (WE,231)

- Takes criticism in a dispassionate manner BP (WE,231)

- Analyzes criticisms to determine their accuracy and identifies useful lessons learned BP (WE,231)

- Uses high self-esteem body language BP (WE,231)

6. Restrains impulsivity (WI,202)

Level IV (Grades K-12)

- Keeps responses open as long as possible BP (WE,202)

- Remains passive while assessing situation BP (WE,151-154)

- Suspends judgment BP (WE,202)

Codes (right side of page):   BD = Benchmark, Declarative; BP = Benchmark, Procedural; BC = Benchmark, Contextual
1st letter of each code in parentheses   *2nd letter of code*   *Number*
S = SCANS: Report for America 2000   E = Explicitly stated in document   Page number of cited document
W = Carnevale: Workplace Basics   I = Implied in document

626

McREL

Life Work

(2I,292)

1. Makes effective use of basic tools

Level I (Grades K-2)

- Uses hammers, screwdrivers, clamps, rulers, scissors, and hard lenses; operates ordinary audio equipment ^BP (2E,293)

- Assembles, describes, takes apart, and reassembles constructions using interlocking blocks, erector sets and the like ^BP (2E,293)

- Makes something out of paper, cardboard, wood, plastic, metal, or existing objects that can be used to perform a task ^BP (2E,293)

Level II (Grades 3-5)

- Chooses appropriate common materials for making simple mechanical constructions and controlling things ^BP (2E,293)

- Measures and mixes dry and liquid materials in prescribed amounts, exercising reasonable safety ^BP (2E,293)

Level III (Grades 6-8)

- Uses hand and power tools to shape, fasten, and unfasten such materials as wood, plastic, and soft metal, exercising reasonable safety ^BP (SI,xvii)

- Inspects, disassembles, and reassembles simple mechanical devices and describes the various parts ^BP (2E,294)

Codes (right side of page):   BD = Benchmark, Declarative; BP = Benchmark, Procedural; BC = Benchmark, Contextual
1st letter of each code in parentheses   *2nd letter of code*   *Number*
S = SCANS: Report for America 2000   E = Explicitly stated in document   Page number of cited document
W = Carnevale: Workplace Basics   I = Implied in document
2 = Project 2061: Benchmarks for Science Literacy

627

MREL

Level IV (Grades 9-12)

- Uses work space effectively   BP (SE,xvii)

- Learns the proper use of new instruments by following instructions in a manual or by taking instructions from an experienced user   BP (2E,294)

- Uses power tools safely to shape, smooth, and join wood, plastic, and soft metal   BP (2E,294)

(SI,xviii;WI,90)
2.   Uses various information sources, including those of a technical nature, to accomplish specific tasks

Level IV (Grades 9-12)

- Interprets information from and detects inconsistencies in a data matrix   BP (WE,90)

- Follows basic linear paths in organizational charts   BP (WE,90-91)

- Identifies major sections in schematic diagrams   BP (WE,90)

- Uses the linear path of a flowchart to provide visual and textual directions to a procedure   BP (WE,90-91)

- Interprets symbols in a flowchart to indicate flow of direction, test points, components, and diagrammatic decision points   BP (WE,90-91)

- Obtains factor specification information from various sources (e.g., two-column chart, intersection of row by column in a table or chart)   BP (WE,90-91)

- Uses a table or chart to identify a malfunction in a mechanism   BP (WE,90-91)

- Interprets drawings (e.g., cross sections) for assembly or disassembly   BP (WE,90-91)

Codes (right side of page):	BD = Benchmark, Declarative; BP = Benchmark, Procedural; BC = Benchmark, Contextual
1st letter of each code in parentheses	*2nd letter of code* *Number*
S = SCANS: Report for America 2000	E = Explicitly stated in document Page number of cited document
W = Carnevale: Workplace Basics	I = Implied in document
2 = Project 2061: Benchmarks for Science Literacy	

McREL

(SI,xvii;WE,281)

3. Manages money effectively

Level IV (Grades 9-12)

BP (SE,xvii;WE,281-283)

- Prepares and follows a budget

BP (SE,xvii)

- Makes forecasts regarding future income and expenses

BP (WE,281-283)

- Uses sound buying principles for purchasing goods and services

BP (WE,281-283)

- Understands credit and uses it effectively

(WI,281)

4. Pursues specific jobs

Level IV (Grades 9-12)

BP (WE,281)

- Determines key contacts within a prospective employer's organization

BP (WE,281)

- Determines specific procedures for applying for a specific job

BD (WE,281)

- Identifies important benefits and procedures of prospective employers (salary, deductions, vacation)

BD (WE,281-283)

- Identifies a prospective employer's products and services

BD (WE,281-283)

- Identifies the procedures involved in applying for a job at a company's personnel office

BP (WE,281-283)

- Fills out a job application

BP (WE,281-283)

- Prepares letters of inquiry or application

BP (WE,281-283)

- Identifies and engages in necessary steps to prepare for a job interview

---

Codes (right side of page):   BD = Benchmark, Declarative; BP = Benchmark, Procedural; BC = Benchmark, Contextual
1st letter of each code in parentheses   *2nd letter of code*   *Number*
S = SCANS: Report for America 2000   E = Explicitly stated in document   Page number of cited document
W = Carnevale: Workplace Basics   I = Implied in document
2 = Project 2061: Benchmarks for Science Literacy

McREL

(WI,281)

5.   Makes general preparation for entering the work force

Level IV (Grades 9-12)

- Understands basic market trends
  BD (WE,281)

- Determines the types of preparation and training needed for entry-level jobs
  BP (WE,281)

- Understands occupational apprenticeships and other training opportunities
  BD (WE,281)

- Understands available educational opportunities (e.g., college, junior college)
  BD (WE,281)

- Understands availability of child care
  BD (WE,281)

- Understands significant life decisions and their effect on the present
  BD (WE,284)

- Analyzes a current job and its future possibilities
  BP (WE,284)

- Develops an employment profile
  BP (WE,284)

- Uses multiple resources to obtain information about prospective jobs (e.g., classified, word of mouth, free services provided by state)
  BP (WE,281)

- Determines how private employment agencies operate on a fee basis to help people find jobs
  BP (WE,281-283)

- Prepares for common types of employment tests
  BP (WE,281-283)

- Applies for a social security card, work permit, and license
  BP (WE,281-283)

- Prepares a resume summarizing experience, education, and job training
  BP (WE,281-283)

- Establishes an explicit career action plan
  BP (WE,284-285)

- Makes an accurate appraisal of prior work experience, career goals, personal character, job references, and personal aptitudes
  BP (WE,281-283)

- Understands the nature and function of worker's compensation and unemployment insurance
  BD (WE,281-283)

Codes (right side of page):   BD = Benchmark, Declarative; BP = Benchmark, Procedural; BC = Benchmark, Contextual
1st letter of each code in parentheses   *2nd letter of code*   *Number*
S = SCANS: Report for America 2000   E = Explicitly stated in document   Page number of cited document
W = Carnevale: Workplace Basics   I = Implied in document
2 = Project 2061: Benchmarks for Science Literacy

MREL

BP (WE,281-283)

- Evaluates the chances of getting a job now and in the future in fields of work that are of interest

BP (WE,284-285)

- Makes an accurate appraisal of available work options

BP (WE,281-283)

- Makes an accurate appraisal of basic insurance needs

(WE,281)

6.   Makes effective use of basic life skills

Level IV (Grades 9-12)

BP (WE,281)

- Uses a telephone effectively

BP (WE,281)

- Uses public transportation effectively

BD (WE,281)

- Understands the rules and regulations of the Internal Revenue Service

BD (WE,281)

- Understands the availability of health care and child care services

BD (WE,281)

- Understands the basic nature of contracts

BD (WE,281)

- Understands the basic process of renting an apartment

BD (WE,281)

- Understands basic banking services (e.g., checking accounts, savings accounts)

BD (WE,281-283)

- Understands the basic process of buying and maintaining a car

BP (WE,90)

- Knows how to correctly enter information into basic forms

Codes (right side of page):   BD = Benchmark, Declarative; BP = Benchmark, Procedural; BC = Benchmark, Contextual
1st letter of each code in parentheses   *2nd letter of code*   *Number*
S = SCANS: Report for America 2000   E = Explicitly stated in document   Page number of cited document
W = Carnevale: Workplace Basics   I = Implied in document
2 = Project 2061: Benchmarks for Science Literacy

631

McREL

(WI,281)

7. Displays reliability and a basic work ethic

Level IV (Grades 9-12)

- Completes tasks on time

  BP (WE,281)

- Chooses ethical courses of action

  BP (SI,xviii)

- Establishes an acceptable attendance record

  BP (WE,281)

- Uses appropriate language in work situations

  BP (WE,281)

- Maintains a sense of congeniality at work

  BP (WE,281)

- Maintains an effective work station

  BP (WE,281)

- Is attentive to requests and preferences of supervisors

  BP (WE,281)

- Requests clarification when needed

  BP (WE,281)

- Accurately identifies important goals and priorities of employer

  BP (WE,375)

- Practices appropriate hygiene and dress at work

  BP (WE,281-283)

- Carries out assigned tasks

  BP (WE,281-283)

- Does not bring personal problems into work

  BP (WE,281-283)

- Prepares, plans, and organizes job responsibilities

  BP (WE,281-283)

- Recognizes and respects authority

  BP (WE,281-283)

- Accepts guidance and constructive criticism

  BP (WE,281-283)

- Demonstrates loyalty to the organization

  BP (WE,281-283)

Codes (right side of page): BD = Benchmark, Declarative; BP = Benchmark, Procedural; BC = Benchmark, Contextual
1st letter of each code in parentheses   *2nd letter of code*   *Number*
S = SCANS: Report for America 2000   E = Explicitly stated in document   Page number of cited document
W = Carnevale: Workplace Basics   I = Implied in document
2 = Project 2061: Benchmarks for Science Literacy

McREL

(WE,375)

8. Operates effectively within organizations

Level IV (Grades 9-12)

BD (WE,375)
- Understands the organization's basic goals and values

BD (WE,375)
- Understands the extent to which organizational values are compatible with personal values

BP (WE,375)
- Develops an action plan that identifies how personal skills can be used to increase organizational effectiveness

BP (WE,375)
- Develops and carries out strategies to make personal skills and abilities more visible to an organization

Codes (right side of page):   BD = Benchmark, Declarative; BP = Benchmark, Procedural; BC = Benchmark, Contextual
1st letter of each code in parentheses   *2nd letter of code*   *Number*
S = SCANS: Report for America 2000   E = Explicitly stated in document   Page number of cited document
W = Carnevale: Workplace Basics   I = Implied in document
2 = Project 2061: Benchmarks for Science Literacy

McREL

Appendix A
Documents Used in This Report

Australian Education Council. (1994). *English: A curriculum profile for Australian schools.* Commonwealth of Australia: Curriculum Corporation.

Australian Education Council. (1994). *Technology: a curriculum profile for Australian schools.* Carlton, Victoria, Australia: Curriculum Corporation.

Board of Education, Commonwealth of Virginia. (1995, June). *Standards of Learning for Virginia Public Schools.* Richmond, VA: Author.

Bybee, R. W., Buchwald, C. E., Crissman, S., Heil, D. R., Kuerbis, P. J., Matsumoto, C., & McIreney, J. D. (1989). *Science and technology education for the elementary years: Frameworks for curriculum and instruction.* Andover, MA: National Center for Improving Science Education.

Bybee, R. W., Buchwald, C. E., Crissman, S., Heil, D. R., Kuerbis, P. J., Matsumoto, C., & McIreney, J. D. (1990). *Science and technology education for the middle years: Frameworks for curriculum and instruction.* Andover, MA: National Center for Improving Science Education.

California Department of Education. (1989). *Recommended literature, grades nine through twelve.* Sacramento, CA: Author.

California Department of Education. (1989). *Visual and performing arts framework for California public schools: Kindergarten through grade twelve.* Sacramento, CA: Author.

California Department of Education. (1990). *Recommended readings in literature, kindergarten through grade eight.* Sacramento, CA: Author.

California Department of Education. (1990). *Science framework for California public schools: Kindergarten through grade 12.* Sacramento, CA: Author.

California Department of Education. (1994). *Health framework for California public schools: Kindergarten through grade twelve.* Sacramento, CA: Author.

Carnevale, A. P., Gainer, L. J., & Meltzer, A. S. (1990). *Workplace basics: The essential skills employers want.* San Francisco: Jossey-Bass.

Center for Civic Education. (1994). *National standards for civics and government.* Calabasas, CA: Author.

Colorado Department of Education (1996, June). *Content standards for foreign language.* (Second Draft). Denver, CO: Author

Colorado Council on Economic Education. (1994). *Economics: Conceptual content standards, grades K-12.* (Draft). Denver: Colorado Council on Economic Education.

Consortium of National Arts Education Associations. (1994). *National standards for arts education: What every young American should know and be able to do in the arts.* Reston, VA: Music Educators National Conference.

Crabtree, C., Nash, G. B., Gagnon, P., & Waugh, S. (Eds.). (1992). *Lessons from history: Essential understandings and historical perspectives students should acquire.* Los Angeles: National Center for History in the Schools.

Crafton, Linda K. (1996). *Standards in Practice: Grades K-2.* Urbana, IL: National Council of Teachers of English.

EconomicsAmerica: National Council on Economic Education. (1997). *Voluntary National Content Standards*. In Virtual Economics Version 2.0 [CD-ROM]. New York, NY: Author.

Edison Project. (1994a). *Student standards for the elementary academy*. New York: Author.

Edison Project. (1994b). *Student standards for the junior academy*. New York: Author.

Edison Project. (1994c). *Student standards for the primary academy*. New York: Author.

Gagnon, P., & Bradley Commission on History in the Schools (Eds.). (1989). *Historical literacy: The case for history in American education*. Boston: Houghton Mifflin Company.

Geographic Education National Implementations Project. (1987). *K-6 geography: Themes, key ideas, and learning opportunities*. Washington, DC: Author.

Geography Education Standards Project. (1994). *Geography for life: National geography standards*. Washington, DC: National Geographic Research and Exploration.

Gillespie, John T. (Ed.) (1991a). *Best books for junior high readers*. New Providence, NJ: Bowker.

Gillespie, John T. (Ed.) (1991b). *Best books for senior high readers*. New Providence, NJ: Bowker.

Gilliard, J. V., Caldwell, J., Dalgaard, B. R., Highsmith, R. J., Reinke, R., & Watts, M. (with Leet, D. R., Malone, M. G., & Ellington, L.). (1989). *Economics, what and when: Scope and sequence guidelines, K-12*. New York: Joint Council on Economic Education.

Hirsch, E. D., Jr. (1987). *Cultural literacy: What every American needs to know*. Boston: Houghton Mifflin Company.

Hirsch, E.D., Jr. (Ed.). (1993a). *What your 1st grader needs to know: Fundamentals of a good first-grade education. The core knowledge series: Resource books for grades one through six, book I*. New York: Delta.

Hirsch, E.D., Jr. (Ed.). (1993b). *What your 2nd grader needs to know: Fundamentals of a good second-grade education. The core knowledge series: Resource books for grades one through six, book II*. New York: Delta.

Hirsch, E.D., Jr. (Ed.). (1993c). *What your 3rd grader needs to know: Fundamentals of a good third-grade education. The core knowledge series: Resource books for grades one through six, book III*. New York: Delta.

Hirsch, E.D., Jr. (Ed.). (1993d). *What your 4th grader needs to know: Fundamentals of a good fourth-grade education. The core knowledge series: Resource books for grades one through six, book IV*. New York: Delta.

Hirsch, E.D., Jr. (Ed.). (1993e). *What your 5th grader needs to know: Fundamentals of a good fifth-grade education. The core knowledge series: Resource books for grades one through six, book V*. New York: Delta.

Hirsch, E.D., Jr. (Ed.). (1993f). What your 6th grader needs to know: Fundamentals of a good sixth-grade education. *The core knowledge series: Resource books for grades one through six, book VI*. New York: Delta.

International Baccalaureate. (1992). *Language A1 guide*. Geneva, Switzerland: Author.

International Baccalaureate. (1993). *Group 5 mathematics guide* (Edition 1.2). Geneva, Switzerland: Author.

International Baccalaureate. (1995a). *Middle years programme: Arts*. Geneva, Switzerland: Author.

International Baccalaureate (1995b). *Information technology in a global society*. Geneva, Switzerland: Author.

International Baccalaureate. (1995c). *Middle Years programme: Humanities* (Edition 1.1). Geneva, Switzerland: Author.

International Baccalaureate. (1995d). *Middle years programme: Language A.* Geneva, Switzerland: Author.

International Baccalaureate. (1995e). *Middle Years programme: Mathematics* (Edition 1.1).Geneva, Switzerland: Author.

International Baccalaureate. (1995f). *Middle Years programme: Sciences* (Edition 1.1). Geneva, Switzerland: Author.

International Baccalaureate. (1996a, May). *Language A1: World Literature List.* Geneva, Switzerland: Author.

International Baccalaureate. (1996b, May). *Prescribed Booklist: English A1.* Geneva, Switzerland: Author.

International Baccalaureate. (1996a). *Art/Design.* Geneva, Switzerland: Author.

International Baccalaureate. (1996b). *Biology.* Geneva, Switzerland: Author.

International Baccalaureate. (1996c). *Chemistry.* Geneva, Switzerland: Author.

International Baccalaureate. (1996d). *Design technology.* Geneva, Switzerland: Author.

International Baccalaureate. (1996e). *Economics.* Geneva, Switzerland: Author.

International Baccalaureate. (1996f). *Environmental systems.* Geneva, Switzerland: Author.

International Baccalaureate. (1996g). *Geography.* Geneva, Switzerland: Author.

International Baccalaureate. (1996h). *History.* Geneva, Switzerland: Author.

International Baccalaureate. (1996i). *Physics.* Geneva, Switzerland: Author.

International Baccalaureate. (1996j). *Psychology.* Geneva, Switzerland: Author.

International Baccalaureate. (1996k). *Social anthropology.* Geneva, Switzerland: Author.

International Technology Education Association. (1996). *Technology for all Americans: A rationale and structure for the study of technology.* Reston, VA: Author.

Joint Committee on Geographic Education. (1984). *Guidelines for geographic education: Elementary and secondary schools.* Washington, DC: Association of American Geographers.

Joint Committee on Health Education Terminology. (1991). Report of the 1990 Joint Committee on Health Education Terminology. *Journal of Health Education, 22,* (2), 97-107.

Joint Committee on National Health Education Standards. (1995). *National health education standards: Achieving health literacy.* Reston, VA: Association for the Advancement of Health Education.

Law in a Free Society. (1983). *Responsibility I (elementary): a civic education unit* (Teacher's ed.). Calabasas, CA: Author.

Law in a Free Society. (1977a). *Authority I (elementary): a civic education unit* (Teacher's ed.). Calabasas, CA: Author.

Law in a Free Society. (1977b). *Privacy I (elementary): a civic education unit* (Teacher's ed.). Calabasas, CA: Author.

Law in a Free Society. (1977c). *Privacy II (elementary): a civic education unit* (Teacher's ed.). Calabasas, CA: Author.

Law in a Free Society. (1979d). *Justice I (elementary): a civic education unit* (Teacher's ed.). Calabasas, CA: Author.

Myers, Miles, & Spalding, Elizabeth (Eds.). (1997). *Exemplar series: Grades 6-8.* Urbana, IL: National Council of Teachers of English.

Myers, Miles, & Spalding, Elizabeth (Eds.). (1997). *Standards exemplar series: Assessing student performance grades 9-12.* Urbana, IL: National Council of Teachers of English.

Michigan State Board of Education. (1988). *Michigan essential goals and objectives for health education*. Lansing, MI: Author.

Michigan Department of Education. (1996, September). *Physical education: Content standards and benchmarks*. (Draft). Lansing: Author.

Mississippi State Department of Education. (1994). *Mississippi curriculum structure: English language arts*. Jackson, MS: Author.

Music Educators National Conference. (1986). *The school music program: Description and standards*. Reston, VA: Author.

National Assessment of Educational Progress. (n.d.). *Framework for the 1994 National Assessment of Educational Progress U.S. history assessment*. Washington, DC: Author.

National Assessment of Educational Progress. (n.d.) *Mathematics framework for the 1996 National Assessment of Educational Progress*. Washington, DC: Author

National Assessment of Educational Progress. (1989). *Science objectives: 1990 assessment*. Princeton, NJ: Educational Testing Service.

National Assessment of Educational Progress. (1992a). *Description of writing achievement levels-setting process and proposed achievement level definitions*. Iowa City, IA: American College Testing Program.

National Assessment of Educational Progress. (1992b). *Framework for the 1994 National Assessment of Educational Progress mathematics assessment*. Washington, DC: Author.

National Assessment of Educational Progress. (1992c). *Item specifications: 1994 national assessment of educational progress in geography*. Washington, DC: National Assessment Governing Board.

National Assessment of Educational Progress. (1992d). *Provisional item specifications: 1994 national assessment of educational progress in U.S. history*. Washington, DC: National Assessment Governing Board.

National Assessment of Educational Progress Arts Education Consensus Project. (1994). *Arts education assessment framework*. Washington, DC: National Assessment Governing Board.

National Assessment of Educational Progress Civics Consensus Project. (n.d.). *Civics Framework for the 1998 National Assessment of Educational Progress*. Washington, DC: National Assessment Governing Board.

National Assessment of Educational Progress Geography Consensus Project. (1992). *Geography assessment framework for the 1994 National Assessment of Educational Progress*. (Draft). Washington, DC: National Assessment Governing Board.

National Assessment of Educational Progress Reading Consensus Project. (1990a). *Assessment and exercise specifications: 1992 NAEP reading assessment*. Washington, DC: National Assessment Governing Board.

National Assessment of Educational Progress Reading Consensus Project. (1990b). *Reading assessment framework for the 1992 National Assessment of Educational Progress*. Washington, DC: National Assessment Governing Board.

National Assessment of Educational Progress Science Consensus Project. (n.d.). *Science framework for the 1996 National Assessment of Educational Progress*. Washington, DC: National Assessment Governing Board.

National Assessment of Educational Progress Science Consensus Project. (1993). *Science assessment and exercise specifications for the 1994 National Assessment of Educational*

Progress. Washington, DC: National Assessment Governing Board.

National Assessment of Educational Progress in U.S. History. (1994). *Provisional item specifications*. Washington, DC: Council of Chief State School Officers.

National Association for Sport and Physical Education. (1995). *Moving into the future, national standards for physical education: A guide to content and assessment.* St. Louis: Mosby.

National Association for Sport and Physical Education. (1992). *Outcomes of quality physical education programs*. Reston, VA: Author.

National Business Education Association (1995). *National standards for business education: What America's students should know and be able to do in business*. Reston, VA: Author.

National Center for History in the Schools. (1994a). *National standards for history for Grades K-4: Expanding children's world in time and space*. (Expanded ed.). Los Angeles: Author.

National Center for History in the Schools. (1994b). *National standards for United States history: Exploring the American experience*. (Expanded ed.). Los Angeles: Author.

National Center for History in the Schools. (1994c). *National standards for world history: Exploring paths to the present*. (Expanded ed.). Los Angeles: Author.

National Center for History in the Schools. (1996). *National standards for history*. (Basic ed.). Los Angeles: Author

National Council for the Social Studies. (1994). *Expectations of excellence: Curriculum standards for social studies*. Washington, DC: Author.

National Council of Teachers of English. (1989). *The English coalition conference: Democracy through language*. Urbana, IL: Author.

National Council of Teachers of English and the International Reading Association (October, 1995). *Standards for the English Language Arts*. (Draft). Urbana, IL: National Council of Teachers of English.

National Council of Teachers of Mathematics. (1989). *Curriculum and evaluation standards for school mathematics*. Reston, VA: Author.

National Research Council. (1996). *National science education standards*. Washington, DC: National Academy Press.

National Standards in Foreign Language Education. (1995, April). *Standards for foreign language learning: Preparing for the 21st century*. (Draft). Yonkers, NY: Author.

National Standards in Foreign Language Education Project (1996). *Standards for foreign language learning: Preparing for the 21st century*. Lawrence, KS: Author.

New Standards. (1997a). *Performance standards: English language arts, mathematics, science, applied learning, volume 1, elementary school*. Washington, DC: National Center on Education and the Economy.

New Standards. (1997b). *Performance standards: English language arts, mathematics, science, applied learning, volume 2, middle school*. Washington, DC: National Center on Education and the Economy.

New Standards. (1997c). *Performance standards: English language arts, mathematics, science, applied learning, volume 3, high school*. Washington, DC: National Center on Education and the Economy.

North Carolina Department of Public Instruction (1992). *Teacher handbook component: Computer skills*. Raleigh, NC: Author.

Pearsall, M. K. (Ed). (1993). *Scope, sequence, and coordination of secondary school science. Vol.*

1. The content core: A guide for curriculum designers. Washington, DC: National Science Teachers Association..

Project 2061, American Association for the Advancement of Science. (1993). *Benchmarks for science literacy.* New York: Oxford University Press.

Quigley, C. N., & Bahmmeller, C. F. (Eds.). (1991). *Civitas: A framework for civic education.* (National council for social studies, bulletin no. 86). Calabasas, CA: Center for Civic Education.

Ravitch, D. and Finn, C. E., Jr. (1987). *What do our 17-year-olds know?* New York: Harper & Row.

Saunders, P., & Gilliard, J. (Eds.). (1995). *A framework for teaching basic economic concepts with scope and sequence guidelines, K-12.* New York: National Council on Economic Education.

Secretary's Commission on Achieving Necessary Skills. (1991). *What work requires of schools: A SCANS report for America 2000.* Washington, DC: U.S. Department of Labor.

Sierra-Perry, Martha. (1996). *Standards in Practice: Grades 3-5.* Urbana, IL: National Council of Teachers of English.

Smagorinsky, Peter. (1996). *Standards in Practice: Grades 9-12.* Urbana, IL: National Council of Teachers of English.

Speech Communication Association. (1996). *Speaking, Listening, and Media Literacy Standards for K through 12 Education.* Annandale, VA: Author.

Stotsky, S., Anderson, P., & Beierl, D. (1989). *Variety and individualism in the English class: Teacher-recommended lists of reading for grades 7 - 12.* Boston, MA: New England Association of Teachers of English.

Texas Education Agency. (1996, February) *English Language Arts and Reading: Texas Essential Knowledge and Skills.* (Draft) Austin, TX: Author

Texas Education Agency. (1996). *Texas essential knowledge and skills for technology applications.* (draft) [online]. Available: http://www.tea.state.tx.us:70/sboe/schedule/ 9702/ch126.htm [1997, March 6]

Utah State Office of Education. (1993, August). *Core Curriculum: Language Arts.* (Online). Author. http://www.uen.org/utahlink/UtahCore/LangArts.html (1996, July 3).

Wilhelm, Jeffrey D. (1996). *Standards in Practice: Grades 6-8.* Urbana, IL: National Council of Teachers of English

Appendix B
Professional Subject-Area Organizations

THE ARTS
Music Educators National Conference
1902 Association Drive
Reston, VA 22091
703-860-4000

CIVICS AND GOVERNMENT
The Center for Civic Education
5146 Douglas Fir Road
Calabasas, CA 91203
818-591-9321

ECONOMICS
The National Council on Economic
  Education
1140 Avenue of the Americas
New York, NY 10036
212-730-7007

FOREIGN LANGUAGE
American Council on the Teaching of
  Foreign Languages
Six Executive Plaza
Yonkers, NY 10801-6801
914-963-8830

GEOGRAPHY
National Council for Geographic Education
1600 M Street, NW
Suite 2500
Washington, DC 20036
202-775-7832

HEALTH EDUCATION
Association for the Advancement of Health
  Education
1900 Association Drive
Reston, VA 22091
703-476-3437

HISTORY
National Center for History in the Schools
UCLA, 231 Noore Hall
Los Angeles, CA 90024
310-825-4702

LANGUAGE ARTS
National Standards for the English Language
  Arts Project
The International Reading Association
  Division of Research
800 Barksdale Road
P.O. Box 8139
Newark, DE 19714-8139
302-731-1600, ext. 226

MATHEMATICS
National Council of Teachers of Mathematics
1906 Association Drive
Reston, VA 22091
703-620-9840

PHYSICAL EDUCATION
National Association for Sport and Physical
  Education
1900 Association Drive
Reston, VA 22091
703-476-3410

SCIENCE
National Science Education Standards
2101 Constitution Ave., NW
HA 486
Washington, DC 20418
202-334-1399

SOCIAL STUDIES
National Council for the Social Studies
3501 Newark St., NW
Washington, DC 20016
202-966-7840

TECHNOLOGY EDUCATION
International Technology Education
  Association
1914 Association Drive
Reston, Virginia 20191-1539
703-860-2100

VOCATIONAL EDUCATION
National Center for Research in Vocational
  Education
University of California, Berkeley
2150 Shattuck Avenue, Suite 1250
Berkeley, CA 94704
510-642-4004

References

Aldridge, B. G. (Ed). (1995). *Scope, sequence, and coordination of secondary school science: Vol. 3. A high school framework for national science education standards.* Arlington, VA: National Science Teachers Association.

Aldridge, B. G., & Strassenburg, A. A. (Eds.). (1995). *Scope, sequence, and coordination of national science education content standards: An addendum to the content core based on the 1994 draft national science education standards.* Arlington, VA: National Science Teachers Association.

American Federation of Teachers. (1985, September). Critical thinking: It's a basic. *American Teacher,* p. 21.

Anderson, J. R. (1990). *Cognitive Psychology and Its Implications.* New York: W. H. Freeman and Company.

Australian Education Council. (1994). *English: A curriculum profile for Australian schools.* Commonwealth of Australia: Curriculum Corporation.

Australian Education Council. (1994). *Technology: a curriculum profile for Australian schools.* Carlton, Victoria, Australia: Curriculum Corporation.

Board of Education, Commonwealth of Virginia. (1995, June). *Standards of Learning for Virginia Public Schools.* Richmond, VA: Author.

Bradley Commission on History in the Schools. (1988). *Building a history curriculum: Guidelines for teaching history in the schools.* Washington, DC: Educational Excellence Network.

Bybee, R. W., Buchwald, C. E., Crissman, S., Heil, D. R., Kuerbis, P. J., Matsumoto, C., & McIreney, J. D. (1989). *Science and technology education for the elementary years: Frameworks for curriculum and instruction.* Andover, MA: National Center for Improving Science Education.

Bybee, R. W., Buchwald, C. E., Crissman, S., Heil, D. R., Kuerbis, P. J., Matsumoto, C., & McIreney, J. D. (1990). *Science and technology education for the middle years: Frameworks for curriculum and instruction.* Andover, MA: National Center for Improving Science Education.

California Department of Education. (1989). *Recommended literature, grades nine through twelve.* Sacramento, CA: Author.

California Department of Education. (1989). *Visual and performing arts framework for California public schools: Kindergarten through grade twelve.* Sacramento, CA: Author.

California Department of Education. (1990). *Recommended readings in literature, kindergarten through grade eight.* Sacramento, CA: Author.

California Department of Education. (1990). *Science framework for California public schools: Kindergarten through grade 12.* Sacramento, CA: Author.

California Department of Education. (1991). *Model curriculum standards: Grades nine through twelve.* Sacramento, CA: Author.

California Department of Education (1993). *The writing assessment handbook: High School.* Sacramento, CA Author.

California Department of Education. (1994a). *Health framework for California public schools: Kindergarten through grade twelve.* Sacramento, CA: Author.

California Department of Education. (1994b). *1994 elementary performance assessments: Integrated English-language arts illustrative material, grade 4.* Sacramento, CA: Author.

California Department of Education. (1994c). *1994 middle grades performance assessments: Integrated English-language arts illustrative material, grade 8.* Sacramento, CA: Author.

Carnevale, A. P., Gainer, L. J., & Meltzer, A. S. (1990). *Workplace basics: The essential skills employers want.* San Francisco: Jossey-Bass.

Center for Civic Education. (1994). *National standards for civics and government.* Calabasas, CA: Author.

College Board. (1983). *Academic preparation for college: What students need to know and be able to do.* New York: College Entrance Examination Board.

Colorado Department of Education (1996, June). *Content standards for foreign language.* (Second Draft). Denver, CO: Author

Colorado Council on Economic Education. (1994). *Economics: Conceptual content standards, grades K-12.* (Draft). Denver: Colorado Council on Economic Education.

Committee on the Junior High and Middle School Booklist of the National Council of Teachers of English & Nilsen, A.P. (Ed.). (1991). *Your reading: A booklist for junior high and middle school students* (8th ed.). Urbana, IL: National Council of Teachers of English.

Committee on the Senior High School Booklist of the National Council of Teachers of English & Wurth, S. (Ed.). (1992). *Books for you: A booklist for senior high students* (11thed.). Urbana, IL: National Council of Teachers of English.

Consortium of National Arts Education Associations. (1994). *National standards for arts education: What every young American should know and be able to do in the arts.* Reston, VA: Music Educators National Conference.

Council for Basic Education. (1995, October 11). Review panels find history standards worth revising. News release submitted for publication.

Crabtree, C., Nash, G. B., Gagnon, P., & Waugh, S. (Eds.). (1992). *Lessons from history: Essential understandings and historical perspectives students should acquire.* Los Angeles: National Center for History in the Schools.

Crafton, Linda K. (1996). *Standards in Practice: Grades K-2.* Urbana, IL: National Council of Teachers of English.

Dewey, J. (1916). *Democracy and education.* New York: Macmillan.

Draft standards tackle slippery subject: English (1995, October 25). *Education Daily,* pp. 1,3.

EconomicsAmerica: National Council on Economic Education. (1997). *Voluntary National Content Standards.* In Virtual Economics Version 2.0 [CD-ROM]. New York, NY: Author.

Edison Project. (1994a). *Student standards for the elementary academy.* New York: Author.

Edison Project. (1994b). *Student standards for the junior academy.* New York: Author.

Edison Project. (1994c). *Student standards for the primary academy.* New York: Author.

Educational Policies Commission. (1961). *The central purpose of American education.* Washington, DC: National Education Association.

Farkas, F., Friedman, W., Boese, J., & Shaw, G. (1994). *First Things First: What Americans Expect From Public Schools.* New York: Public Agenda.

Friedman, W. & Duffett, A. (1997). *Getting By: What American Teenagers Really think about their Schools.* New York: Public Agenda.

Futrell, M. H. (1987, December 9). A message long overdue. *Education Week,* p. 9.

Gagnon, P., & Bradley Commission on History in the Schools (Eds.). (1989). *Historical literacy: The case for history in American education.* Boston: Houghton Mifflin Company.

Gandal, M. (1996). *Making Standards Matter, 1996: An Annual Fifty-State Report on Efforts to Raise Academic Standards.* Washington, DC: American Federation of Teachers.

Geographic Education National Implementations Project. (1987). *K-6 geography: Themes, key ideas, and learning opportunities.* Washington, DC: Author.

Geography Education Standards Project. (1994). *Geography for life: National geography standards.* Washington, DC: National Geographic Research and Exploration.

Gillespie, John T. (Ed.) (1991a). *Best books for junior high readers.* New Providence, NJ. Bowker.

Gillespie, John T. (Ed.) (1991b). *Best books for senior high readers.* New Providence, NJ:Bowker.

Gilliard, J. V., Caldwell, J., Dalgaard, B. R., Highsmith, R. J., Reinke, R., & Watts, M. (with Leet, D. R., Malone, M. G., & Ellington, L.). (1989). *Economics, what and when: Scope and sequence guidelines, K-12.* New York: Joint Council on Economic Education.

Glaser, R. (1984). Education and thinking: The role of knowledge. *American Psychologist, 39,* 93-104.

Hazen, R. M., & Trefil, J. (1991). *Science matters: Achieving scientific literacy.* New York: Doubleday.

Hirsch, E. D., Jr. (1987). *Cultural literacy: What every American needs to know.* Boston: Houghton Mifflin Company.

Hirsch, E.D., Jr. (Ed.). (1993a). *What your 1st grader needs to know: Fundamentals of a good first-grade education. The core knowledge series: Resource books for grades one through six, book I.* New York: Delta.

Hirsch, E.D., Jr. (Ed.). (1993b). *What your 2nd grader needs to know: Fundamentals of a good second-grade education. The core knowledge series: Resource books for grades one through six, book II.* New York: Delta.

Hirsch, E.D., Jr. (Ed.). (1993c). *What your 3rd grader needs to know: Fundamentals of a good third-grade education. The core knowledge series: Resource books for grades one through six, book III.* New York: Delta.

Hirsch, E.D., Jr. (Ed.). (1993d). *What your 4th grader needs to know: Fundamentals of a good fourth-grade education. The core knowledge series: Resource books for grades one through six, book IV.* New York: Delta.

Hirsch, E.D., Jr. (Ed.). (1993e). *What your 5th grader needs to know: Fundamentals of a good fifth-grade education. The core knowledge series: Resource books for grades one through six, book V.* New York: Delta.

Hirsch, E.D., Jr. (Ed.). (1993f). What your 6th grader needs to know: Fundamentals of a good sixth-grade education. *The core knowledge series: Resource books for grades one through six, book VI.* New York: Delta.

History standards project opens door to revisions. (1995, January 17). *Education Daily, 28,* 1-2.

International Baccalaureate. (1992). *Language A1 guide.* Geneva, Switzerland: Author.

International Baccalaureate. (1993). *Group 5 mathematics guide* (Edition 1.2).Geneva, Switzerland: Author.

International Baccalaureate. (1995a). *Middle years programme: Arts.* Geneva, Switzerland: Author.

International Baccalaureate (1995b). *Information technology in a global society.* Geneva, Switzerland: Author.

International Baccalaureate. (1995c). *Middle Years programme: Humanities* (Edition 1.1). Geneva, Switzerland: Author.

International Baccalaureate. (1995d). *Middle years programme: Language A.* Geneva, Switzerland: Author.

International Baccalaureate. (1995e). *Middle Years programme: Mathematics* (Edition 1.1).Geneva, Switzerland: Author.

International Baccalaureate. (1995f). *Middle Years programme: Sciences* (Edition 1.1). Geneva, Switzerland: Author.

International Baccalaureate. (1996a, May). *Language A1: World Literature List.* Geneva, Switzerland: Author.

International Baccalaureate. (1996b, May). *Prescribed Booklist: English A1.* Geneva, Switzerland: Author.

International Baccalaureate. (1996a). *Art/Design.* Geneva, Switzerland: Author.

International Baccalaureate. (1996b). *Biology.* Geneva, Switzerland: Author.

International Baccalaureate. (1996c). *Chemistry.* Geneva, Switzerland: Author.

International Baccalaureate. (1996d). *Design technology.* Geneva, Switzerland: Author.

International Baccalaureate. (1996e). *Economics.* Geneva, Switzerland: Author.

International Baccalaureate. (1996f). *Environmental systems.* Geneva, Switzerland: Author.

International Baccalaureate. (1996g). *Geography.* Geneva, Switzerland: Author.

International Baccalaureate. (1996h). *History.* Geneva, Switzerland: Author.

International Baccalaureate. (1996i). *Physics.* Geneva, Switzerland: Author.

International Baccalaureate. (1996j). *Psychology.* Geneva, Switzerland: Author.

International Baccalaureate. (1996k). *Social anthropology.* Geneva, Switzerland: Author.

International Technology Education Association. (1996). *Technology for all Americans: A rationale and structure for the study of technology.* Reston, VA: Author.

Johnson, J. & Farkas, S. (1996). *Given the Circumstances: Teachers Talk about Public Education Today.* New York: Public Agenda.

Joint Committee on Geographic Education. (1984). *Guidelines for geographic education: Elementary and secondary schools.* Washington, DC: Association of American Geographers.

Joint Committee on Health Education Terminology. (1991). Report of the 1990 Joint Committee on Health Education Terminology. *Journal of Health Education, 22,* (2), 97-107.

Joint Committee on National Health Education Standards. (1995). *National health education standards: Achieving health literacy.* Reston, VA: Association for the Advancement of Health Education.

Kendall, J. S., & Marzano, R. J. (1996). *Content knowledge: A compendium of standards and benchmarks for K-12 education.* Aurora, CO: Mid-continent Regional Education Laboratory

Kendall, J. S., & Marzano, R. J. (1994). *The systematic identification and articulation of content standards and benchmarks: Update, January 1994.* Aurora, CO: Mid-continent Regional Education Laboratory.

Kendall, J. S., & Marzano, R. J. (1995). *The systematic identification and articulation of content standards and benchmarks: Update, March 1995.* Aurora, CO: Mid-continent Regional Education Laboratory.

Law in a Free Society. (1983). *Responsibility I (elementary): a civic education unit* (Teacher's ed.). Calabasas, CA: Author.

Law in a Free Society. (1977a). *Authority I (elementary): a civic education unit* (Teacher's ed.). Calabasas, CA: Author.

Law in a Free Society. (1977b). *Privacy I (elementary): a civic education unit* (Teacher's ed.). Calabasas, CA: Author.

Law in a Free Society. (1977c). *Privacy II (elementary): a civic education unit* (Teacher's ed.). Calabasas, CA: Author.

Law in a Free Society. (1979d). *Justice I (elementary): a civic education unit* (Teacher's ed.). Calabasas, CA: Author.

Levine, D.V., & Associates. (1985). *Improving student achievement through mastery learning programs.* San Francisco: Jossey-Bass.

Linn, Robert L. (1995). *Assessment-Based Reform: Challenges to Educational Measurement.* (William H. Angoff Memorial Lecture Series). Princeton, NJ: Educational Testing Service

Mager, Robert F. (1962). *Preparing instructional objectives.* Palo Alto, CA: Fearon Publishers.

Marzano, R. J., & Kendall, J. S. (1993). *The systematic identification and articulation of content standards and benchmarks: An illustration using mathematics.* Aurora, CO: Mid-continent Regional Educational Laboratory.

Marzano, R.J., & Kendall, J.S. (1996). *A comprehensive guide to designing standards-based schools, districts, and classrooms.* Aurora, CO: Mid-continent Regional Educational Laboratory

Myers, Miles, & Spalding, Elizabeth (Eds.). (1997). *Exemplar series: Grades 6-8.* Urbana, IL: National Council of Teachers of English.

Myers, Miles, & Spalding, Elizabeth (Eds.). (1997). *Standards exemplar series: Assessing student performance grades 9-12.* Urbana, IL: National Council of Teachers of English.

Michigan State Board of Education. (1988). *Michigan essential goals and objectives for health education.* Lansing, MI: Author.

Michigan Department of Education. (1996, September). *Physical education: Content standards and benchmarks.* (Draft). Lansing: Author.

Mississippi State Department of Education. (1994). *Mississippi curriculum structure: English language arts.* Jackson, MS: Author.

Music Educators National Conference. (1986). *The school music program: Description and standards.* Reston, VA: Author.

National Assessment of Educational Progress. (n.d.). *Framework for the 1994 National Assessment of Educational Progress U.S. history assessment.* Washington, DC: Author.

National Assessment of Educational Progress. (n.d.) *Mathematics framework for the 1996 National Assessment of Educational Progress.* Washington, DC: Author

National Assessment of Educational Progress. (1989). *Science objectives: 1990 assessment.* Princeton, NJ: Educational Testing Service.

National Assessment of Educational Progress. (1992a). *Description of writing achievement levels-setting process and proposed achievement level definitions.* Iowa City, IA: American College Testing Program.

National Assessment of Educational Progress. (1992b). *Framework for the 1994 National Assessment of Educational Progress mathematics assessment.* Washington, DC: Author.

National Assessment of Educational Progress. (1992c). *Item specifications: 1994 national assessment of educational progress in geography.* Washington, DC: National Assessment

Governing Board.

National Assessment of Educational Progress. (1992d). *Provisional item specifications: 1994 national assessment of educational progress in U.S. history.* Washington, DC: National Assessment Governing Board.

National Assessment of Educational Progress Arts Education Consensus Project. (1994). *Arts education assessment framework.* Washington, DC: National Assessment Governing Board.

National Assessment of Educational Progress Civics Consensus Project. (n.d.). *Civics Framework for the 1998 National Assessment of Educational Progress.* Washington, DC: National Assessment Governing Board.

National Assessment of Educational Progress Geography Consensus Project. (1992). *Geography assessment framework for the 1994 National Assessment of Educational Progress.* (Draft). Washington, DC: National Assessment Governing Board.

National Assessment of Educational Progress Reading Consensus Project. (1990a). *Assessment and exercise specifications: 1992 NAEP reading assessment.* Washington, DC: National Assessment Governing Board.

National Assessment of Educational Progress Reading Consensus Project. (1990b). *Reading assessment framework for the 1992 National Assessment of Educational Progress.* Washington, DC: National Assessment Governing Board.

National Assessment of Educational Progress Science Consensus Project. (n.d.). *Science framework for the 1996 National Assessment of Educational Progress.* Washington, DC: National Assessment Governing Board.

National Assessment of Educational Progress Science Consensus Project. (1993). *Science assessment and exercise specifications for the 1994 National Assessment of Educational Progress.* Washington, DC: National Assessment Governing Board.

National Assessment of Educational Progress in U.S. History. (1994). *Provisional item specifications.* Washington, DC: Council of Chief State School Officers.

National Association for Sport and Physical Education. (1995). *Moving into the future, national standards for physical education: A guide to content and assessment.* St. Louis: Mosby.

National Association for Sport and Physical Education. (1992). *Outcomes of quality physical education programs.* Reston, VA: Author.

National Business Education Association (1995). *National standards for business education: What America's students should know and be able to do in business.* Reston, VA: Author.

National Center for History in the Schools. (1994a). *National standards for history for Grades K-4: Expanding children's world in time and space.* (Expanded ed.). Los Angeles: Author.

National Center for History in the Schools. (1994b). *National standards for United States history: Exploring the American experience.* (Expanded ed.). Los Angeles: Author.

National Center for History in the Schools. (1994c). *National standards for world history: Exploring paths to the present.* (Expanded ed.). Los Angeles: Author.

National Center for History in the Schools. (1996). *National standards for history.* (Basic ed.). Los Angeles: Author

National Commission on Excellence in Education. (1983). *A nation at risk: The imperative for educational reform.* Washington, DC: Government Printing Office.

National Council for the Social Studies. (1994). *Expectations of excellence: Curriculum standards for social studies.* Washington, DC: Author.

National Council of Teachers of English. (1982). *Essentials of English: A document for reflection and dialogue.* Urbana, IL: Author.

National Council of Teachers of English. (1989). *The English coalition conference: Democracy through language.* Urbana, IL: Author.

National Council of Teachers of English and the International Reading Association (October, 1995). *Standards for the English Language Arts.* (Draft). Urbana, IL: National Council of Teachers of English.

National Council of Teachers of Mathematics. (1989). *Curriculum and evaluation standards for school mathematics.* Reston, VA: Author.

National Council on Education Standards and Testing. (1992). *Raising standards for American education: A report to Congress, the Secretary of Education, the National Education Goals Panel, and the American people.* Washington, DC: Government Printing Office.

National Education Goals Panel. (1991). *The National Education Goals Report: Building a Nation of Learners.* Washington, DC: Author.

National Education Standards and Improvement Council. (1993). *Promises to keep: Creating high standards for American students. Report on the review of educational standards from the Goals 3 and 4 Technical Planning Group to the National Education Goals Panel.* Washington, DC: National Goals Panel.

National Governors Association. (1996, March). *1996 National Education Summit Policy Statement.* Washington, DC: Author.

National Research Council. (1996). *National science education standards.* Washington, DC: National Academy Press.

National Science Board Commission on Precollege Education in Mathematics, Science and Technology. (1983). *Educating Americans for the 21st century.* Washington, DC: National Science Board Commission.

National Standards in Foreign Language Education. (1995, April). *Standards for foreign language learning: Preparing for the 21st century.* (Draft). Yonkers, NY: Author.

National Standards in Foreign Language Education Project (1996). *Standards for foreign language learning: Preparing for the 21st century.* Lawrence, KS: Author.

NCTE/IRA say standards effort will continue. (1994, June). *The Council Chronicle, 3,* 1,4.

New Standards. (1997a). *Performance standards: English language arts, mathematics, science, applied learning, volume 1, elementary school.* Washington, DC: National Center on Education and the Economy.

New Standards. (1997b). *Performance standards: English language arts, mathematics, science, applied learning, volume 2, middle school.* Washington, DC: National Center on Education and the Economy.

New Standards. (1997c). *Performance standards: English language arts, mathematics, science, applied learning, volume 3, high school.* Washington, DC: National Center on Education and the Economy.

North Carolina Department of Public Instruction (1992). *Teacher handbook component: Computer skills.* Raleigh, NC: Author.

Pearsall, M. K. (Ed). (1993). *Scope, sequence, and coordination of secondary school science. Vol. 1. The content core: A guide for curriculum designers.* Washington, DC: National Science Teachers Association..

Project 2061, American Association for the Advancement of Science. (1992). *Science for all Americans*. Washington, DC: Author.

Project 2061, American Association for the Advancement of Science. (1993). *Benchmarks for science literacy*. New York: Oxford University Press.

Quigley, C. N., & Bahmmeller, C. F. (Eds.). (1991). *Civitas: A framework for civic education*. (National council for social studies, bulletin no. 86). Calabasas, CA: Center for Civic Education.

Ravitch, D. (1992, January 27). National Educational Standards. *Roll call: Education policy briefing*. pp. 24-25.

Ravitch, D. (1995). *National Standards in American Education: A Citizen's Guide*. Washington, DC: Brookings Institution.

Ravitch, D. and Finn, C. E., Jr. (1987). *What do our 17-year-olds know?* New York: Harper & Row.

Resnick, L. B. (1987). *Education and learning to think*. Washington, DC: National Academy Press.

Saunders, P., & Gilliard, J. (Eds.). (1995). *A framework for teaching basic economic concepts with scope and sequence guidelines, K-12*. New York: National Council on Economic Education.

Secretary's Commission on Achieving Necessary Skills. (1991). *What work requires of schools: A SCANS report for America 2000*. Washington, DC: U.S. Department of Labor.

Shanker, A. (1992, June 17). Coming to terms on world-class standards. *Education Week: Special Report*. p. S11.

Shavelson, R., Baxter, G., & Pine, J. (1992). Performance assessment: Political rhetoric and measurement reality. *Educational Researcher, 21*, (4), 22-27.

Shepard, L. (1993). *Setting performance standards for student achievement: A report of the National Academy of Education Panel on the evaluation of the NAEP trial state assessment: An evaluation of the 1992 achievement levels*. Stanford, CA: The National Academy of Education, Stanford University.

Sierra-Perry, Martha. (1996). *Standards in Practice: Grades 3-5*. Urbana, IL: National Council of Teachers of English.

Smagorinsky, Peter. (1996). *Standards in Practice: Grades 9-12*. Urbana, IL: National Council of Teachers of English.

Spady, W. G. (1988). Organizing for results: The basis of authentic restructuring and reform. *Education Leadership, 46*, (2), 4-8.

Speech Communication Association. (1996). *Speaking, Listening, and Media Literacy Standards for K through 12 Education*. Annandale, VA: Author.

Standards Project for English Language Arts. (1994, February). *Incomplete work of the task forces of the standards project for English language arts*. (Draft). Urbana, IL: National Council of Teachers of English.

Stotsky, S., Anderson, P., & Beierl, D. (1989). *Variety and individualism in the English class: Teacher-recommended lists of reading for grades 7 - 12*. Boston, MA: New England Association of Teachers of English.

Texas Education Agency. (1996, February) *English Language Arts and Reading: Texas Essential Knowledge and Skills*. (Draft) Austin, TX: Author

Texas Education Agency. (1996). *Texas essential knowledge and skills for technology applications*. (draft) [online]. Available: http://www.tea.state.tx.us:70/sboe/schedule/ 9702/ch126.htm [1997, March 6]

Tucker, M. (1992, June 17). A new social compact for mastery in education. *Education Week: Special Report*. p. S3.

Uchida, D., Cetron, M., & McKenzie, F. (1996). *Preparing Students For the 21st Century*. Reston, VA: American Association of School Administrators.

Utah State Office of Education. (1993, August). *Core Curriculum: Language Arts*. (Online). Author. http://www.uen.org/utahlink/UtahCore/LangArts.html (1996, July 3).

Viadero, D. (1993, June 16). Standards deviation: Benchmark-setting is marked by diversity. *Education Week*, pp. 1, 14-17.

Wilhelm, Jeffrey D. (1996). *Standards in Practice: Grades 6-8*. Urbana, IL: National Council of Teachers of English

Yoon, B., Burstein, L., & Gold, K. (n.d.). *Assessing the content validity of teacher's reports of content coverage and its relationship to student achievement*. (CSE Report No. 328). Los Angeles: Center for Research on Evaluation, Standards and Student Testing, University of California, Los Angeles.

Wiggins, G. (1989). Teaching to the (authentic) test. *Educational Leadership, 46*, (7), 41-47.

Wiggins, G. (1993, November). Assessment: authenticity, context, and validity. *Phi Delta Kappan*, 200-214.